Social Media Marketing

ALL-IN-ONE

FOR DUMMIES®

**by Jan Zimmerman
and
Doug Sahlin**

WILEY

Wiley Publishing, Inc.

Social Media Marketing All-in-One For Dummies®

Published by
Wiley Publishing, Inc.
111 River Street
Hoboken, NJ 07030-5774

www.wiley.com

Copyright © 2010 by Wiley Publishing, Inc., Indianapolis, Indiana

Published by Wiley Publishing, Inc., Indianapolis, Indiana

Published simultaneously in Canada

For general information on our other products and services, please contact our Customer Care Department within the U.S. at 877-762-2974, outside the U.S. at 317-572-3993, or fax 317-572-4002.

For technical support, please visit www.wiley.com/techsupport.

Wiley also publishes its books in a variety of electronic formats. Some content that appears in print may not be available in electronic books.

Library of Congress Control Number: 2010933470

ISBN: 978-0-470-58468-2

Manufactured in the United States of America

10 9 8 7 6 5 4 3 2 1

WILEY

About the Authors

Jan Zimmerman has found marketing to be the most creative challenge of owning a business for the more than 30 years she has spent as an entrepreneur. Since 1994, she has owned Sandia Consulting Group and Watermelon Mountain Web Marketing (www.watermelonweb.com) in Albuquerque, New Mexico. (*Sandia* is Spanish for *watermelon.*) Her previous companies provided a range of services including video production, grant writing, and linguistic engineering R&D.

Jan's Web marketing clients at Watermelon Mountain are a living laboratory for experimenting with the best social media, search engine optimization, and other online marketing techniques for Web success. Ranging from hospitality and tourism to retail stores, B2B suppliers, trade associations, and service companies, her clients have unique marketing needs but share similar business concerns and online challenges. Her consulting practice, which keeps Jan aware of the real-world issues facing business owners and marketers, provides the basis for her pragmatic marketing advice.

Throughout her business career, Jan has been a prolific writer. She has written two editions of *Web Marketing For Dummies*, four editions of another book about marketing on the Internet, as well as the books *Doing Business with Government Using EDI* and *Mainstreaming Sustainable Architecture.* Her concern about the impact of technological development on women's needs led to her book *Once Upon the Future* and the anthology *The Technological Woman.*

The writer of numerous articles and a frequent speaker on Web marketing and social media, Jan has long been fascinated by the intersection of business, technology, and human beings. In her spare time, she crews for the hot air balloon named *Levity* to get her feet off the ground and her head in the clouds.

Jan can be reached at books@watermelonweb.com or 505-344-4230. Your comments, corrections, and suggestions are welcome.

Doug Sahlin is an author and a photographer living in Venice, Florida. He has written 22 books on computer applications such as Adobe Flash and Adobe Acrobat. He has written books on digital photography and co-authored 13 books on applications such as Adobe Photoshop and Photoshop Elements. Recent titles include *Flash Web Sites For Dummies*, *Digital Photography Workbook For Dummies,* and *Digital Portrait Photography For Dummies*. Many of his books have been bestsellers at Amazon.com.

Doug is president of Superb Images, Inc., a wedding-and-event photography company. Doug teaches Adobe Acrobat to local businesses and government institutions and uses social media to promote his books and photography business.

Dedications

Jan Zimmerman:

In Memoriam

Sam Hutchison, 9

Milton Feinberg, 91

In the game, every moment — they rocked!

Doug Sahlin:

For Roxanne: my soulmate and the love of my life.

Authors' Acknowledgments

Jan Zimmerman:

No nonfiction writer works alone, and this book is no exception. It couldn't have been written without a cast of dozens, especially with my experienced researcher Diane Duncan Martin, who did her usual fine job of finding and organizing information and locating copyright holders.

She and Web marketing assistant Esmeralda Sanchez both provided background research, compiled sites for the numerous tables in this book, created graphics, and rooted out arcane online facts. Working on my truly crazy schedule, they checked thousands of links and reviewed hundreds of sites for screen shots. (Not many people are asked to search for a good marketing tweet!) Finding exemplary companies for case studies — and clearing hundreds of copyrights — required endless calls and e-mails, for which these two people deserve all the credit.

Shawna Araiza, senior Web marketing associate at Watermelon Mountain Web Marketing, supplemented their efforts, drawing on her extensive knowledge of the Internet to suggest sites, experiment with new techniques, and help with Photoshop. I owe my staff a great debt for giving me the time to write by working overtime with our clients — not to mention their patience and computer support.

As always, my family, friends, and cats earn extra hugs for their constant encouragement. I'm lucky to have friends who accept that I could not always be there for them as much as they are there for me. The garden, the house, the car, and the cats, alas, are not so forgiving. Special thanks to my clients, who teach me so much and give me the opportunity to practice what I preach.

I'd also like to thank Rebecca Senninger, project editor at Wiley, for her flexibility and patience with a challenging book, copy editor Rebecca Whitney, and technical editor Michelle Oxman. Together, they have made this book much better than it started out. My thanks to all the other staff at Wiley — from the art department to legal — who have provided support. If errors remain, I am absolutely certain they are mine.

My appreciation also to my coauthor, Doug Sahlin, for sharing this journey; acquisitions editor Amy Fandrei, for this opportunity; and my agent, Margot Hutchison of Waterside Productions. I don't know how this superwoman worked through the past few years as her young son struggled with cancer. Margot and her extraordinary family continue to teach us, at `http://teamsam.com`, lessons about what's truly important in life. If you profit from reading this book, please join me in donating to The Magic Water Project in memory of Sam Hutchison at `www.magicwater.org`. Thank you in advance, dear readers, for making a contribution "because of Sam."

Doug Sahlin:

Although only two names are on the front of this book, this project would not have been possible without a large support team. Thanks to my coauthor, Jan Zimmerman; it has been a pleasure to work with her on this project. Many thanks to the team at Wiley Publishing for fine-tuning our text and producing the book you hold in your hands. Thanks to Margot Hutchison and Amy Fandrei for making this project possible.

I'd also like to thank my friends for their continued support. Special thanks to my author friends, for being a constant source of inspiration, and to my wonderful family, especially Ted and Karen. Kudos and hugs to Roxanne, for supplying the missing pieces to the puzzle that is my life. And special thanks to the furry kids: Niki and Micah.

Publisher's Acknowledgments

We're proud of this book; please send us your comments at http://dummies.custhelp.com. For other comments, please contact our Customer Care Department within the U.S. at 877-762-2974, outside the U.S. at 317-572-3993, or fax 317-572-4002.

Some of the people who helped bring this book to market include the following:

Acquisitions, Editorial, and Media Development

Project Editor: Rebecca Senninger

Acquisitions Editor: Amy Fandrei

Copy Editor: Rebecca Whitney

Technical Editor: Michelle Oxman

Editorial Manager: Leah Cameron

Media Development Project Manager: Laura Moss-Hollister

Media Development Assistant Project Manager: Jenny Swisher

Editorial Assistant: Amanda Graham

Sr. Editorial Assistant: Cherie Case

Cartoons: Rich Tennant (www.the5thwave.com)

Composition Services

Project Coordinator: Sheree Montgomery

Layout and Graphics: Ashley Chamberlain

Proofreaders: Lauren Mandelbaum, Christine Sabooni

Indexer: BIM Indexing & Proofreading Services

Publishing and Editorial for Technology Dummies

    Richard Swadley, Vice President and Executive Group Publisher

    Andy Cummings, Vice President and Publisher

    Mary Bednarek, Executive Acquisitions Director

    Mary C. Corder, Editorial Director

Publishing for Consumer Dummies

    Diane Graves Steele, Vice President and Publisher

Composition Services

    Debbie Stailey, Director of Composition Services

Contents at a Glance

Table of Contents

Introduction

You sit back, sighing with relief that your Web site is running faultlessly, optimized for search engines, and producing traffic, leads, and sales. Maybe you've ventured into e-mail marketing or pay-per-click advertising to generate new customers. Now, you think with satisfaction, "I'll just let the money roll in."

Instead, you're inundated with stories about Facebook and fan pages, Twitter and tweets, blogs and vlogs, and all other manner of social media buzz. The statistics are astounding: Facebook closing in on 500 million active users; 126 million blogs on the Internet; more than 10 billion tweets sent on Twitter since 2006; 2 billion videos streamed daily on YouTube. New company names and bewildering new vocabulary terms flood the online world: Gowalla, Groupon, SocialMention, CoTweet, engagement, community building, content posting, and comment monitoring, for example.

Should your business get involved in social media marketing? Is it all more trouble than it's worth? Will you be left hopelessly behind if you don't participate? If you jump in, how do you keep it all under control and who does the work? This book helps you answer both sets of questions: Should or shouldn't your business undertake social media marketing? If so, how? (Quick answer: If your customers use a social media service, you should consider it. If not, skip it.)

About This Book

The philosophy behind this book is simple: Social media marketing is a means, not an end in itself. Social media services are new tools, not new worlds. In the best of all worlds, you see results that improve customer acquisition, retention, and buying behavior — in other words, your bottom line. If this sounds familiar, that's because everything you already know about marketing is correct.

Having the most "likes" on Facebook or more retweets of your posts than your competitors doesn't mean much if these achievements don't have a positive impact on your business. Throughout this book, you'll find concrete suggestions for applying social media tactics to achieve those goals.

If you undertake a social marketing campaign, we urge you to keep your plans simple, take things slowly, and always stay focused on your customers. Most of all, we urge you to follow the precepts of guerrilla marketing: Target one niche market at a time; grow that market; reinvest your profits in the next niche.

What You Don't Have to Read

You don't have to read anything that seems overwhelming or insanely complicated, deals with a particular social marketing service that you dislike or disdain, or doesn't apply to your business. Content following a Technical Stuff icon is intended for developers or particularly tech-savvy readers.

Reading the case studies in sidebars isn't critical, though you might enjoy reading about honest-to-goodness business owners who successfully use the social marketing techniques we discuss. Often, they share a helpful tip that will make your social media life easier.

If you have a limited budget, focus your explorations on the free or low-cost tools and resources that appear in various tables, instead of enterprise-level options, which are designed for large companies with large marketing budgets. Sometimes, however, a tool with a moderate price tag can save you lots of time or expensive labor.

You can skip any of the Books III, IV, V, or VI on individual social media services (blogs, vlogs, podcasts, Twitter, Facebook, or LinkedIn) if you don't include them in your social media marketing plan. If you decide to add one or more of them later, simply return to that book for freestanding information. Of course, if you're looking for a thorough understanding of the social media whirl, read the book straight through, from cover to cover. You'll find out all about social media — at least until a totally new service launches tomorrow.

Foolish Assumptions

In our heads, we visualize our readers as savvy small-business owners, marketers in companies of any size, and people who work in any of the multiple services that support social media efforts, such as advertising agencies, Web developers, graphic design firms, copywriting, or public relations. We assume that you

+ Already have or will soon have a Web site or blog that can serve as the hub for your online marketing program

+ Are curious about social media because it seems to be everywhere

+ Are comfortable using keywords on search engines to find information online

+ Know the realities of your industry, though you may not have a clue whether your competitors use social media

+ Can describe your target markets, though you may not be sure whether your audience is using social media

✦ Are trying to decide whether using social media makes sense for your company (or your boss has asked you to find out)

✦ May already use social media personally and are interested in applying your knowledge and experience

✦ May already have tried using social media for your company but want to improve results or measure return on your investment

✦ Have a passion for your business, appreciate your customers, and enjoy finding new ways to improve your bottom line

If our assumptions are correct, this book will help you organize a social marketing presence without going crazy or spending all your waking hours online. It will help you figure out whether a particular technique makes sense, how to get the most out of it, and how to measure your results.

How This Book Is Organized

We've built this book like a sandwich: The first two and last two books are overviews of marketing or business issues, or of social media tools and techniques. The four books in the middle are how-to manuals for incorporating blogs, podcasts or vlogs, Twitter, Facebook, or LinkedIn into your social media marketing campaign.

Like most For Dummies books, this one enables you to get as much (or as little) information as you need at any particular moment on a specific topic. You can return to it as a reference guide at any time. However, unless you're certain that you're interested only in a specific social marketing service covered in Books III through VI, we recommend that you read Book I first to establish your goals, objectives, and schedule for social media marketing.

For information on a specific topic, check the headings in the table of contents or look at the index.

Book 1: The Social Media Mix

Book I gets you off on the right foot. Chapter 1 explains what social media services are, individually and collectively, categorizes the overwhelming number of social media options by type, and explores how social media are the same and different from other forms of online and offline marketing. In the next two chapters, you define your own marketing goals, objectives, and methods for social media and research where your target audiences "hang out." This book includes three key planning forms: the Social Media Marketing Goals form, to establish the purpose of your campaign; the Social Media Marketing Plan, to select and document your tactics; and the Social Media Activity Calendar, to assign and schedule tasks.

Book II: Cybersocial Tools

Implementing and tracking social media marketing campaigns across multiple services is a daunting task. In the first chapter of Book II, we offer a variety of productivity tools to help you post content in multiple locations, notify search engines, and monitor your growing social notoriety. The second chapter deals in depth with integrating social media into a coordinated search engine optimization strategy, and the third deals with social bookmarking, social news, and social sharing as new methods of viral marketing.

Book III: Blogs, Podcasts, and Vlogs

In Book III, we show you how to set up a blog and create posts, procure the necessary hardware and software to create your own podcast, and determine which software and hardware you need in order to create a video blog. We also give you information about picking the right Web server, or securing a third party to host your blog, podcast, or vlog, and we give you information on how to gauge your success.

Book IV: Twitter

Twitter is one of the hottest social media spots on the Web. You send your message out, 140 characters at a time, to the people you're following. We show you how to use Twitter to market your goods and services. In Book IV, we show you how to get started on Twitter and network with a group of people who may become clients. We also show you how to customize your Twitter page and how to tweet (Twitterspeak for "create a post") using mobile devices.

Book V: Facebook

At the happy online community Facebook, you can find schoolkids talking about the latest singing sensation, soccer moms talking about their kids, and major businesses marketing their products. Facebook is indeed a viable tool for marketing virtually any product or service. In Book V, we show you how to set up a Facebook page for your business and show you how to use the many Facebook features at your disposal. We also show you how to create custom tabs, add photos and videos to your page, show your blog posts on Facebook, and more.

Book VI: LinkedIn

At LinkedIn, professionals network with other professionals. You can use LinkedIn to find clients for your services, establish relationships with businesses that support your industry, and more. In Book VI, we show you how to establish an account and set up your LinkedIn page, and we even show you how to mine gold with LinkedIn.

Book VII: Other Social Media Marketing Sites

In addition to the "big guys" covered in the Books III through VI are hundreds of social media services with smaller audiences. Some of them compete for a general audience, and some focus on narrowly targeted vertical markets. Book VII, which analyzes the value of working with smaller services and surveys many options, also includes chapters on Ning platforms for building communities, MySpace for social networking, Squidoo for topical blogs, and Flickr for photosharing.

Book VIII: Measuring Your Results; Building on Your Success

Book VIII returns to business principles with several chapters on important measurement tools: analytics to assess the performance of your social media campaign in Web terms and return on investment to assess its performance in financial terms. We discuss the integration of social media into other forms of online marketing, and the last chapter in this book concludes with a survey of up-and-coming social media techniques you might consider using in the future.

Icons Used in This Book

To make your experience easier, we use various icons in the margins to identify special categories of information.

These hints help you save time, energy, or aggravation. Sharing them is our way of sharing what we've figured out the hard way — so that you don't have to. Of course, if you prefer to get your education through the school of hard knocks, be our guest.

This book has more details in it than any normal person can remember. This icon reminds you of points made elsewhere in the book or perhaps helps you recall business best practices that you know from your own experience.

Heed these warnings to avoid potential pitfalls. Nothing we suggest will crash your computer beyond repair or send your marketing campaign into oblivion. But we tell you about business and legal pitfalls to avoid, plus a few traps that catch the unprepared during the process of configuring social media services. Not all those services create perfect user interfaces with clear directions!

The geeky-looking Dummies Man marks information to share with your developer or programmer — unless you are one. In that case, have at it. On the other hand, you can skip any of the technical-oriented information without damaging your marketing plans or harming a living being.

Conventions Used in This Book

Doing something the same way over and over again may be boring, but consistency makes information easier to understand. In this book, those consistent elements are *conventions.* We use only a few:

✦ When URLs (Web addresses) appear within a paragraph or table, they look like this: www.dummies.com.

✦ New terms appear in *italics* the first time they're used, thanks to the copy editor.

✦ Navigation on Web sites appears as tab or option names in sequence, to indicate the order in which you should make selections, such as choose Tab Name⇨Choice One⇨Choice Two.

✦ Any text that you have to type is in **bold**.

Where to Go from Here

You can find helpful information on the companion Web site for this book at www.dummies.com/go/socialmediamarketingaio. From the site, you can download copies of the Social Media Goals and Social Media Marketing Plan forms, which you can use to develop your own marketing plans. You can also find an online Cheat Sheet to print and keep handy near your computer at www.dummies.com/cheatsheet/socialmediamarketingaio.

If you find errors in this book, or have suggestions for future editions, please e-mail us at books@watermelonweb.com. We wish you a fun and profitable experience going social!

Book I

The Social Media Mix

Contents at a Glance

Chapter 1: Making the Business Case for Social Media

In This Chapter

✔ Defining social media

✔ Accentuating the positives

✔ Eliminating the negatives

✔ Latching on to the affirmatives

✔ Integrating social media into your overall marketing plan

✔ Evaluating the worth of social media

In the best of all worlds, social media — a suite of online services that facilitates two-way communication and content sharing — can become a productive component of your overall marketing strategy. These services can enhance your company's online visibility, strengthen relationships with your clients, and expand word-of-mouth advertising, which is the best type.

Given its rapid rise in popularity and its hundreds of millions of worldwide users, social media marketing sounds quite tempting. These tools require minimal upfront cash and, theoretically, you'll find customers flooding through your cyberdoors, ready to buy. It sounds like a no-brainer — but it isn't.

Has someone finally invented a perfect marketing method that puts you directly in touch with your customers and prospects, costs nothing, and generates profits faster than a perpetual motion machine produces energy? The hype is yes; the real answer, unfortunately, is no. Marketing nirvana is not yet at hand.

This chapter provides an overview of the pros and cons of social media to help you decide whether to join the social whirl and gives a framework for approaching a strategic choice of which media to use.

Making Your Social Debut

Like any form of marketing, social media takes some thought. It can become an enormous siphon of your time, and short-term profits are rare. Social media is a long-term marketing commitment.

So, should you or shouldn't you invest time and effort in this new marketing avenue? If you answer in the affirmative, you immediately confront another decision: What form should that investment take? The number of options is overwhelming; you can never use every technique and certainly can't do them all at once.

Figure 1-1 shows how small businesses are using social media. True to form, many U.S. small businesses have taken a wait-and-see attitude, although more are trying it out. According to a recent survey (see www.penn-olson. com/2010/03/03/more-small-businesses-using-social-media-successfully) as of December 2009, about 24 percent of small businesses used some form of social media marketing, up from 12 percent the preceding year. Most businesses on the sidelines give the best reason in the world for not participating — their customers aren't there yet.

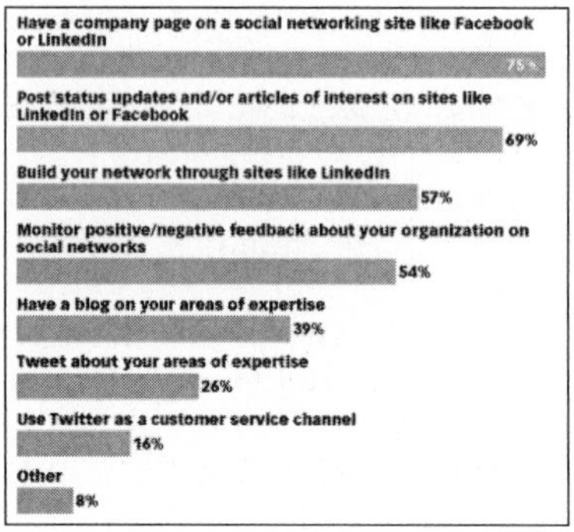

Figure 1-1:
Of the 24 percent of small businesses using social media, the greatest number created profile pages on social networking sites as part of their strategy.

Have a company page on a social networking site like Facebook or LinkedIn
75%

Post status updates and/or articles of interest on sites like LinkedIn or Facebook
69%

Build your network through sites like LinkedIn
57%

Monitor positive/negative feedback about your organization on social networks
54%

Have a blog on your areas of expertise
39%

Tweet about your areas of expertise
26%

Use Twitter as a customer service channel
16%

Other
8%

Courtesy eMarketer

Defining Social Media Marketing

The bewildering array of social media (which seem to breed new services faster than rabbits) makes it hard to discern what they have in common: shared information, often on a peer-to-peer basis. Although many social media messages look like traditional "broadcasts" from one business to many consumers, their interactive component offers an enticing illusion of "one-to-one" communication that invites individual readers to respond.

The phrase *social media marketing* generally refers to using these online services for relationship selling — a subject you already know all about. *Social media services* or *channels* make innovative use of new online technologies to accomplish familiar communication and marketing goals.

TIP

Everything you already know about marketing is correct. Social media marketing is a new technique, not a new world.

This book covers a variety of *social media services* or *channels.* You may hear social media referred to as *Web 2.0* (interactive) techniques. At least one prominent marketing company distinguishes between the two, constraining the term *Web 2.0* to enabling technologies and reserving *social media* for relationship building activities.

For the purpose of this book, this distinction is somewhat academic. Instead, we group tools that improve the performance or effectiveness of social media into one category, regardless of the underlying technology. We use the phrase *social media site* to refer to a specific, named online service or product.

You can categorize social media services (or *channels*) into categories. The channels have fuzzy boundaries: They may overlap, and some sites fall into multiple channels. For instance, some social networks and communities allow participants to share photos and may include a blog.

Here are the different types of social media channels:

✦ **Blogs:** Web sites designed to let you easily update or change content and allow readers to post their own opinions or reactions. Figure 1-2 shows you an example of a business blog with verve, from Crafty Chica. Her blog, which is only part of a suite of her social media activities, exchanges messages with Facebook and Twitter.

   Examples of blogging software are

   • WordPress, TypePad, and Blogger (formerly Blogspot) (freestanding blog services)

   • Other blog software, freestanding sites or integrated into standard Web sites

Figure 1-2:
A Diary of a Crafty Chica is a blog on Blogspot.

✦ **Social networking services:** Originally developed to facilitate the exchange of personal information (messages, photos, video, audio) to groups of friends and family, these full-featured services offer multiple functions. From a business point of view, many of them support sub-groups that offer the potential for more targeted marketing.

- *Full networks* such as Facebook, MySpace, or myYearbook

  Figure 1-3 shows the Facebook site of ArtBizCoach.com, which teaches artists how to promote their art.

- *Microblogging (short message) networks* such as Twitter or Plurk

  Figure 1-4 shows how Scania Group, a B2B manufacturer of trucks and buses, uses its Twitter account to provide information and alert customers to new opportunities.

- *Professional networks* such as LinkedIn and Plaxo

- *Other specialty networks within vertical industry, demographic, or activity segments*

Figure 1-3:
Companies
use the
popular
social
networking
service
Facebook
to maintain
an ongoing
public
dialogue
with
colleagues,
customers,
and
prospects.

Alyson Stanfield's community page for ArtBiz /Stanfield Art Associates at facebook.com/artbizcoach

Figure 1-4:
Twitter, a
rapidly grow-
ing, micro-
blogging
social
network, is
excellent for
disseminat-
ing announ-
cements,
events,
sales
notices, and
promotions
and for
quickly
alerting
customers
of new
information.

✦ **Social-media sharing services:** These media channels facilitate posting and commenting on videos, photos, and podcasts (audio):

   • *Video:* Examples are YouTube, Vimeo, or Ustream. Figure 1-5 shows how the Roger Smith Hotel takes advantage of its YouTube channel. For more about the hotel's social media presence, see the nearby sidebar.

   • *Photos:* Flickr, Photobucket, or Picasa

   • *Audio:* Podcast Alley or BlogTalkRadio

Figure 1-5: The YouTube channel for the Roger Smith Hotel is an integral part of its social media strategy.

Courtesy Roger Smith Hotel

✦ **Social bookmarking services:** Similar to private bookmarks for your favorite sites on your computer, social bookmarks are publicly viewable lists of sites that others have recommended:

   • *Recommendation services* such as StumbleUpon, Delicious

   • *Social shopping services* such as Kaboodle or ThisNext

   • *Other bookmarking services organized by topic or application,* such as book recommendation sites

✦ **Social news services:** On these peer-based lists of recommended articles from news sites, blogs, or Web pages, users often "vote" on the value of the postings:

- Digg

- reddit

- Other news sites

✦ **Social geolocation and meeting services:** For a change, these services bring people together in real space rather than in cyberspace:

- Foursquare, Gowalla, Loopt

- Other GPS (global positioning system) applications, many of which operate on mobile phones

- Meet-ups and tweet-ups

✦ **Community building services:** Many comment- and content-sharing sites have been around for a long time, such as forums, message boards, and Yahoo! and Google groups. Other examples are

- *Community building sites* with multiple sharing features such as *Ning*

- *Wikis* such as Wikipedia for group-sourced content

- *Review sites* such as TripAdvisor and Epinions to solicit consumer views

Dozens, if not hundreds, of social tools, apps (freestanding online applications), and widgets (small applications placed on other sites, services, or desktops) monitor, distribute, search, analyze, and rank content. Many are specific to a particular social network, especially Twitter.

Others are designed to aggregate information across the social media landscape, including such monitoring tools as Google Alerts or Social Mention or distribution tools such as RSS or Ping.fm. Book II offers a survey of many more of these tools; service-specific tools are covered in their respective books.

Understanding the Benefits of Social Media

Social media marketing carries many benefits. One of the most of important is that you don't have to front any cash for most services. Of course, there's a downside: Most services require a significant investment of time to initiate and maintain a social media marketing campaign.

As you read the list of benefits, think about whether the benefit is one that applies to your needs. How important is it to your business? How much time are you willing to allocate to it? What kind of a payoff would you expect?

Figure 1-6 shows how small businesses rate the relative effectiveness of social media in meeting their goals.

Figure 1-6: eMarketer surveyed how small businesses rate the effective-ness of social media in meeting their goals.

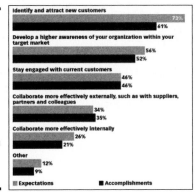

Courtesy eMarketer

Casting a wide net to catch your target market

The audience for social media is huge. In mid-2010, Facebook claimed almost 500 million users, many of whom use the service multiple times per week (and others who never use it after the first time). By mid-March 2010, weekly traffic on Facebook had exceeded weekly traffic on Google, which had worn the traffic crown for years. Twitter claims more than 100 million users and insists that millions of *tweets* (short messages) are posted daily. Even narrowly focused networking sites claim hundreds of thousands of visitors.

A relatively small number of power users — those who post ten or more times per day — drive a huge number of tweets. The vast majority of users either read messages only, without posting, or post only one or two messages per week. It's probably the old 80/20 rule at play: 80 percent of the users produce 20 percent of the tweets, and 20 percent of the users produce 80 percent of the tweets!

Surely, some of the people using these sites must be your customers or prospects. In fact, one popular use of social media is to cast a wide net to capture more potential visitors to your Web site. The classic conversion funnel shown in Figure 1-7 shows the value of bringing new traffic to the top of the funnel.

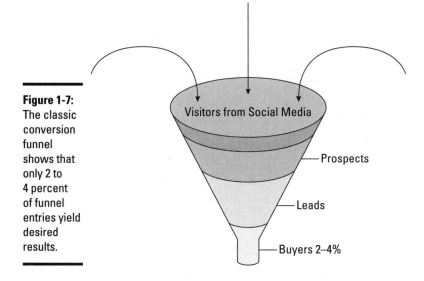

Figure 1-7:
The classic
conversion
funnel
shows that
only 2 to
4 percent
of funnel
entries yield
desired
results.

If more people arrive at the top of the funnel, theoretically more will prog-ress through the steps of prospect and qualified lead to become a customer. Only 2 to 4 percent, on average, make it through a funnel regardless of what the funnel decision is.

In Book I, Chapter 2, we discuss how you can assess traffic on social media sites using tools such as Quantcast or Alexa and match their visitors to the profiles of your customers.

Branding

Basic marketing focuses on the need for branding, name recognition, vis-ibility, presence, or top-of-mind awareness. Call it what you will — you want people to remember your company name when they're in need of your product or service. Social media services, of almost every type, are excellent ways to build your brand.

Social media works for branding as long as you get your name in front of the right people. Plan to segment the audience on the large social media services. You can look for more targeted groups within them or search for specialty services that may reach fewer people overall but more of the ones who are right for your business.

Building relationships

You will hear repeatedly that social media marketing requires the long view. To build effective relationships in social media, you're expected to

- ✦ Establish your expertise
- ✦ Participate regularly as a "good citizen" of whichever social media world you're inhabiting
- ✦ Avoid overt self-promotion
- ✦ Sell softly
- ✦ Provide value with links, resources, and unbiased information

Watch for steady growth in the number of your followers on a particular service; the number of people who recommend your site to others; increased downloads of white papers; or repeat visits to your site. All these signs indicate you're building relationships that may later lead, if not to a direct sale, then to a word-of-Web recommendation to someone who does buy.

In the world of social media, the term *engagement* refers to the length of time and quality of interaction between your company and your followers.

Social media is a long-term commitment. Other than little experiments or pilot projects, don't bother starting a social media commitment if you don't plan to keep it going. Any short-term benefits you see aren't worth the effort you have to make.

Improving business processes

Already, many clever businesses have found ways to use social media to improve business processes. Though individual applications depend on the nature of your business, consider leveraging social media to

- ✦ Promptly detect and correct customer problems or complaints
- ✦ Obtain customer feedback and input on new product designs or changes
- ✦ Provide tech support to many people at one time; if one person has a question, changes are good that others do, too
- ✦ Improve service delivery, such as cafés that accept to-go orders on Twitter or Facebook or cupcake carts and food caravans that notify customers where and when their carts will arrive
- ✦ Locate qualified new vendors, service providers, and employees by using professional networks such as LinkedIn
- ✦ Collect critical market intelligence on your industry and competitors by watching content on appropriate social media
- ✦ Use new geolocation services to drive local traffic during slow times and acquire new customers

Marketing is only part of your company, but all of your company is marketing. Social media is a ripe environment for this hypothesis, where every part of a company, from human resources to tech support, and from engineering to sales, can be involved.

Improving search engine rankings

Just as you optimize your Web site, you should optimize your social media outlets for search engine ranking. Now that search engines are cataloging Twitter and Facebook and other appearances on social media, you can gain additional front page real estate for your company on Google, Yahoo!, and Bing.

Search engines recognize some, but not all, appearances on social media as inbound links, which also improve the page rank of your site.

Use a core set of search terms and keywords across as many sites as possible. Book II, Chapter 2 deals with search optimization in detail.

Optimization pays off in other ways: in results on real-time searches, which are now available on primary search engines; on external search engines that focus on blogs or other social media services; and on internal, site-specific search engines.

Selling when opportunity arises

Conventional thinking says that social media is designed for long-term engagement, for marketing and branding rather than for sales. However, a few obvious selling opportunities exist, particularly for business-to-consumer (B2C) companies, that won't offend followers:

✦ **Sell CDs and event tickets.** Services such as MySpace cater to music and entertainment and are considered appropriate places.

✦ **Include a link to your store on social shopping services.** Recommend products — particularly apparel, jewelry, beauty, and decor — as Stylehive does.

✦ **Offer promotional codes or special offers to followers.** Offering them on particular networks encourages your followers to visit your site to make a purchase. You can even announce sales or events.

✦ **Place links to online or third-party stores on your profile pages on various services.** You can rarely sell directly from a social media service, but some permit you to place widgets that visually showcase your products and links to your online store, PayPal, or the equivalent to conclude a transaction.

✦ **Include a sign-up option for your e-newsletter.** It offers a bridge to sales.

The chart in Figure 1-8 shows a 2010 HubSpot survey of the percentage of companies that succeeded in acquiring a customer by way of a specific social media channel. The survey encompassed both B2B companies on the left of each pairing and B2C companies on the right. It shows that many businesses that make the effort succeed in closing sales that were initiated in a social media channel.

Figure 1-8:
This survey indicates that you can, with a little effort, make a sale by way of social media.

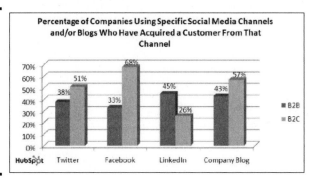

Courtesy HubSpot® www.hubspot.com

 Include sales offers within a stream of information and news to avoid turning your social media site into a series of never-ending advertisements. Throughout this book, you read about other businesses that have found unique ways to sell socially.

Saving money on advertising

The magic word is *free*. If you're a start-up company, "free" social media is likely the only advertising you can afford. If you decide to approach social media for this purpose, construct your master campaign just as carefully as you would a paid one:

✦ Create a plan that outlines target markets, ad offers, publishing venues, and scheduled "flights" for different ad campaigns.

✦ If necessary, conduct comparative testing of messages, graphics, and offers.

✦ Monitor results and focus on the outlets that work best at driving qualified visits that lead to conversions.

✦ Supplement your free advertising with search optimization and press releases and other forms of free promotion.

 Advertising is only one part of marketing!

As you see traffic and conversions building from your social media marketing campaigns, you may want to reduce existing paid advertising campaigns. Just don't stop your paid advertising until you're confident that you have an equally profitable stream of customers from social media. Of course, if your ad campaign isn't working, there's no point continuing it.

Understanding the Cons of Social Media

For all its upsides, social media has its downsides. As social media has gained in popularity, it has also become increasingly difficult to gain visibility among its hundreds of millions of users.

In fact, sometimes you have to craft a campaign just to build an audience on a particular social media site. It's quite similar to conducting optimization and inbound link campaigns so that your site is found in natural search results.

Don't participate in social media for its own sake, or just because "everyone else is."

By far, the biggest downside in social media is the amount of time you need to invest to see results. You need to make an ongoing commitment to review and respond to comments and to provide an ongoing stream of new material. An initial commitment to set up a profile is just the tip of the iceberg.

If you became addicted to news alerts during the 2008 presidential campaign or couldn't take your eyes off live coverage of the Mars landing, or if you play Farmville or other video games with a passion, continuously run instant messaging, or check e-mail every ten seconds, watch out for social media.

Individually and collectively, social media is the biggest-ever time sink. Without self-discipline and a strong time schedule, you can easily become so socially overbooked that other tasks go undone.

As you consider each of the social media options in this book, consider the level of human resources that are needed. Do you have the time and talents yourself? If not, do other people within your organization have the time and talent? Which other efforts will you need to give up to make room for social media? Will you have to hire new employees or contract out services, leading to hard costs for this supposedly "free" media?

Integrating Social Media into Your Overall Marketing Effort

Social media is only part of your online marketing. Online marketing is only part of your overall marketing. Don't mistake the part for the whole.

Consider each foray into social marketing as a strategic choice to supplement your other online marketing activities, which may include creating or managing a marketing-effective Web site, content updates, search engine optimization (SEO), inbound link campaigns, online press releases, event calendar postings, e-mail newsletters, testimonials and reviews, affiliate or loyalty programs, online events or promotions, not to mention pay-per-click ads, banners, or sponsorships.

Social media is neither necessary nor sufficient for all your online marketing.

Use social media strategically to

+ Meet an otherwise unmet marketing need

+ Increase access to your target market

+ Open the door to a new niche market

+ Move prospects through the conversion funnel

+ Improve the experience for existing customers

For example, Emerson Salon (http://emersonsalon.com; see Figure 1-9) developed a social media presence to attract a younger clientele already actively involved in social networking. For more information on overall online marketing, see Jan's book *Web Marketing For Dummies,* 2nd Edition.

You must have a hub site to which Web traffic will be directed, as shown in Figure 1-10. It can be a full-bore Web site or a blog, as long as the site has its own domain name. It doesn't matter where the site is hosted — only that you own its name, which appears as yourcompany.com, or blog. yourcompany.com. Though you can link to yourcompany.wordpress. com, you cannot effectively optimize or search for it. Besides, it doesn't look professional.

Figure 1-9:
The
Emerson
Salon
maintains
an active
presence on
Facebook,
Yelp, and
Twitter and
has multiple
RSS feeds.

Courtesy Emerson Salon

Blog drives many of the internal parts of
pinkcakebox.com keeping content fresh.

Internal

| Press | Photo Gallery | Video Gallery |

BLOG

RSS Syndication to external
sites/channels

External

| Other Blogs | Facebook | Newsletter | Mobile, etc |

Figure 1-10:
Pink
Cake Box
developed
a block
diagram
with its blog
as its hub,
connecting
to both
internal and
external
"spokes."

Courtesy Pink Cake Box www.pinkcakebox.com

Consider sketching for your own campaign a block diagram that shows the relationship between components, the flow of content between outlets, and perhaps even the criterion for success and how it will be measured.

Developing a Strategic Social Media Marketing Plan

Surely you wrote an overall marketing plan when you last updated your business plan and an online marketing plan when you first created your Web site. If not, it's never too late! For business planning resources, see the Small Business Planner page at www.sba.gov/smallbusinessplanner/plan/ writeabusinessplan/index.html or read *Business Plans For Dummies,* 2nd Edition, by Paul Tiffany and Steven D. Peterson.

You can further refine a marketing plan for social media marketing purposes. As with any other marketing plan, you start with strategy. A Social Media Marketing Strategic Goals Statement (Figure 1-11 shows an example) would incorporate sections on strategic goals, objectives, target markets, methods, costs, and return on investment (ROI). You can find this statement on this book's Web site (see the Introduction). Read more about ROI in Book VIII, Chapter 3.

Here are some points to keep in mind when putting together your own strategic marketing overview:

✦ The most important function of the form isn't for you to follow it slavishly, but rather to force you to consider the various facets of social media marketing before you invest too much effort or money.

✦ The form also helps you communicate decisions to your board of advisors or your boss, in case you need to make the business case for getting involved in social media.

✦ The form provides a coherent framework for explaining to everyone involved in your social media effort — employees, volunteers, or contractors — the task you're trying to accomplish and why.

Book II, Chapter 2 includes a separate Social Media Marketing Plan, which helps you develop a detailed tactical approach for specific services and sites, tools, and timelines.

Social Media Marketing Strategic Goals

Related to Hub Site (URL): _____

Prepared by: _____ **Date:** _____

Business Profile

Is the social media plan for a new or established company?
- ○ New company
- ○ Existing company, in business _____ years.

Does the company have an existing brick-and-mortar operation?
- ○ Yes
- ○ No

Does the company have an existing Web site or Web presence?
- ○ Yes
- ○ No

Does the company have an existing blog or social media presence?
- ○ Yes   If yes, list all current URLs for social media.
- ○ No

Will your site serve:
- ○ Businesses
- ○ Consumers

What type of business is the Web site for?
- ❑ Manufacturer
- ❑ Distributor
- ❑ Retailer
- ❑ Service provider
- ❑ Professional

What does the company sell?
- ❑ Goods
- ❑ Services

Describe your goods or services:

What geographical range does the social media campaign address?
- ○ Local (specify)
- ○ Regional (specify)
- ○ National (specify if not US)
- ○ International (specify)

Social Media Campaign Goals

Rank the applicable goals of your social media campaign from 1–7 with 1 your top goal

Figure 1-11:
Establish
your own
strategic
social
marketing
goals,
objectives,
and target
market
definition on
this form.

_____ Increasing traffic/visits to hub site

_____ Branding

_____ Building relationships

_____ Improving business process (e.g. customer service, tech support)

_____ Improving visibility in natural search

_____ Increasing sales revenue

_____ Saving money on paid advertising

Financial Profile

Social Media Campaign Budget for First Year

Outside development, contractors, includes writing, design, technical $ _____

Special content production (e.g. video, podcasts, photography): $ _____

Marketing/paid ads on social media $ _____

Inhouse labor (burdened rate) $ _____

Other costs, e.g. tools, equipment $ _____

TOTAL: $ _____

Break-even point: $ _____   Within: _____ mo/yr

Return on investment: _____ %   Within: _____ mo/yr

Sample Objectives

Repeat for appropriate objectives for each goal within timeframe specified (for instance, 1 year).

Traffic objective (# visitors per month):   _____   Within: _____

Conversion objective: _____ %   Within: _____

Sales objectives (# sales per month): $ _____   Within: _____

Average $ per sale: $ _____   Within: _____

$ revenue per month: $ _____   Within: _____

Other objectives specific to your site, e.g. for branding, relationships, search ranking   _____   Within: _____

   _____   Within: _____

   _____   Within: _____

Marketing Profile

Describe your target markets. Give specific demographic or other segmentation information. For B2B, segment by industry and/or job title.

_____

_____

_____

_____

_____

_____

_____

What is your marketing tag?

_____

Value proposition: Why should someone buy from your company rather than another?

_____

Name at least six competitors and list their Web sites, blogs, and social media pages

_____   _____

_____   _____

_____   _____

_____   _____

_____   _____

In the following sections, we talk about the information you should include on your form.

Establishing goals

The Goals section prioritizes the overall reasons you're implementing a social media campaign. You can prioritize your goals from the list of seven benefits of social media, described in the earlier section "Understanding the Benefits of Social Media," or add your own. Most businesses have multiple goals, which you can specify on the form.

Setting quantifiable objectives

For each goal, set at least one quantifiable, measurable objective. "More customers" isn't a quantifiable objective. A quantifiable objective is "Increase number of visits to Web site by 10 percent," or "add 30 new customers within three months," or "obtain 100 new followers for Twitter account within one month of launch." Enter this information on the form.

Identifying your target markets

Specify one or more target markets on the form, not by what they consume, but rather by who they are. "Everyone who eats dinner out" isn't a submarket you can identify online. However, you can find "high-income couples within 20 miles of your destination who visit wine and classical music sites."

You may want to reach more than one target market by way of social media or other methods. Specify each of them. Then, as you read about different methods in this book, write down next to each one which social media services or sites appear best suited to reach that market. Prioritize the order in which you plan to reach them.

Book II, Chapter 2 suggests online market research techniques to help you define your markets, match them to social media services, and find them online.

Think niche!

Estimating costs

Estimating costs from the bottom up is rather tricky, and this approach rarely includes a cap. Consequently, costs often wildly exceed your budget. Instead, establish first how much money you're willing to invest in the overall effort, including in-house labor, outside contractors, and miscellaneous hard costs such as purchasing software or equipment. Enter those amounts in the Cost section.

Then prioritize your social marketing efforts based on what you can afford, allocating or reallocating funds within your budget as needed. This approach not only keeps your total social marketing costs under control but also lets you assess the results against expenses.

To make cost-tracking easier, ask your bookkeeper or CPA to set up an "activity" or a "job" within your accounting system for social media marketing. Then you can easily track and report all related costs and labor.

Valuing social media ROI

Return on investment (ROI) is your single most important measure of success for social media marketing. In simple terms, *ROI* is the ratio of revenue divided by costs for your business or, in this case, for your social media marketing effort.

You also need to set a realistic term in which you will recover your investment. Are you willing to wait ten weeks? Ten months? Ten years? Some forms of social media are unlikely to produce a fast fix for drooping sales, so consider what you're trying to accomplish.

Figure 1-12 presents a brief glimpse of how others assess the average cost of lead acquisition for B2B companies for social marketing compared to other forms of marketing. It's just a guide. Keep in mind that the only ROI or cost of acquisition that truly matters is your own.

Figure 1-12:
This HubSpot chart compares the cost of B2B lead generation for social media and blogs compared to PPC and natural search.

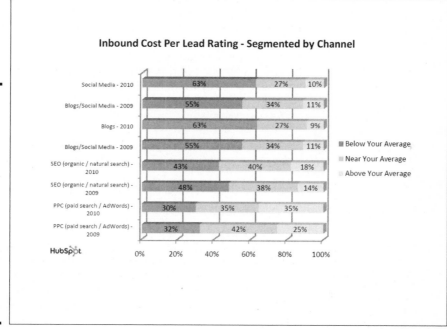

Costs usually turn out to be simpler to track than revenues that are traceable explicitly to social media. Book VIII, Chapter 3 discusses techniques for figuring out ROI and other financial metrics in detail.

Whatever you plan online will cost twice as much and take twice as long as anticipated.

A social media service is likely to produce results only when your customers or prospects are already using it or are willing to try. Pushing people toward a service they don't want is quite difficult. If in doubt, first expand other online and offline efforts to drive traffic toward your hub site.

Staying with social media at the Roger Smith Hotel

The Roger Smith Hotel, a family run, boutique, art hotel located in the heart of midtown Manhattan, is promoted regionally, nationally, and internationally. The public spaces of the hotel are filled with colorful murals and beautiful bronze sculptures by artist-in-residence James Knowles, and its rooms are designed in a comfortable New England bed-and-breakfast style.

The DeLima family has owned the hotel since they founded it in the 1930s. Knowles (husband of Suzanne De Lima Knowles), who is also the current president and CEO, has run the hotel since the late 1980s. He initiated the social media program with the Roger Smith team in 2006 with the video-based site *Roger Smith News*, which told stores about the interesting community around the hotel. This effort has since evolved into the hotel's video-based blog, www.RogerSmithLife.com.

In the fall of 2008, Brian Simpson, now director of social hospitality, joined the hotel staff to run the restaurant, Lily's. Simpson, who already had personal experience with Twitter, quickly realized that he could use Twitter, as well as Facebook, to interact with guests, build community, and share even more stories created around the hotel.

The social media campaign grew rapidly and organically from there, says Adam Wallace, director of digital marketing. In 2008 the hotel added www.12seconds.tv to promote lunch specials in Lily's with a 12-second video of the plating of the dishes. It also started posting images taken all around the hotel on Flickr. In the years following, the team at the Roger Smith experimented with other platforms and started separate blogs for different areas. For instance, they added a blog and Facebook page dedicated to the LAB Gallery, for those interested specifically in the art initiative. There are now accounts for the Roger Smith Hotel on each major social media platform.

CEO James Knowles encourages individual managers to create their own blogs and Twitter accounts to tell their own stories and build their own networks because they reach different people. "It all encourages word-of-mouth."

The hotel Web site, at www.rogersmith.com (see the nearby figure), is the booking site, with all the basic information about the hotel, events, and Lily's Restaurant. However, their first blog, RogerSmithLife.com, remains the true hub for the hotel's online presence. It presents videos from YouTube, images from Flickr, live broadcasts from Ustream.com, an events schedule from Google Calendar, and blog posts about everything happening around the hotel.

Over time, the media channels have become more strategically focused. "We use Twitter and Facebook to build relationships and community, and to share the content that goes on the blog and other media channels. Each site has a different role and each site has been important to our online presence," Wallace explains.

The combination of media and direct personal communication has helped the hotel build an active, supportive, and somewhat unexpected following. Although it began using social media to distribute artistic and narrative content, the hotel's expanded social media program has actually increased revenue from room bookings, private events, and restaurant usage.

The hotel's extensive social media program itself has become a form of promotion. It hosts many public events related to social media that, in turn, help build its reputation. "We have gained exposure nationally largely through word-of-mouth in our social channels, but also from attending and speaking at conferences around the country," notes Wallace. Speaking with other thought leaders, he adds, is a great way to share ideas.

Content for social media comes from many sources: employees; guests and visitors who post videos, photos, and blog entries and casually produced videos shot with Flip Video cameras, for example. Professional video comes from Panman Productions, an in-house production company. The production company handles live broadcasts, films events, and produces featured video content and stories.

"We have a great team of people involved with our online activity at the hotel," says Wallace. His full-time position managing digital marketing includes work on the Web site, blog, and various social media channels. Simpson manages Twitter outreach and is active on all the hotel's social media initiatives. John Knowles and the Panman Productions team contribute video and live stream content, while Matt Semler runs the LAB Gallery for Installation and Performance Art, and manages the LAB's online presence. Add to that, many other managers who interact with the public via Twitter, blogs, Facebook, and other channels.

"It is a lot of channels to manage," Wallace acknowledges, but it "is great to have an enthusiastic team across the board. We do not generally schedule content, but rather produce content as things come up...When there are big events, we will announce the event, cover the events with a live broadcast, and then document the event." The hotel maintains an extensive archive of stories about the various personalities at the hotel and content related to the arts.

In spite of the complexity of multiple channels, Wallace tries to keep things simple. He doesn't actively use syndication tools for all postings, but has done some syndication with Tumblr.com for blogs, uses TweetDeck as a Twitter dashboard, and is experimenting with Postling to post content on multiple services. The team also created a list of all of the hotel's accounts on www.RogerSmithnews.com, which helps

them jump to anyone's personal accounts to see what is being said.

"For us, it is not about sophisticated tools, it is about connecting with people and telling stories. There are tools that can help with this, but for the most part, you can do a lot and generally be more human with the basic posting tools," Wallace contends.

For metrics, the Roger Smith relies primarily on Google Analytics, but has installed Omniture on the hotel site. "We see a lot of incoming traffic to our blog from Twitter and some from Facebook. We track room bookings through a promo code and also word-of-mouth mentions on calls." The 10% discount offered on Twitter, Facebook, and the blog helps with tracking, while benefiting those who tie into the social media network.

The hotel generally eschews sophisticated monitoring tools, relying on the staff's own constant online presence, plus Google Alerts, to see new blog posts and social web mentions. They have just added Revinate, a new tool specifically for hotels, to monitor social media.

The hotel doesn't invest much in traditional advertising campaigns but incorporates some additional online marketing. It runs a limited PPC campaign, basic SEO on the booking site, and two e-mail marketing campaigns — one with monthly room specials and packages and another with event announcements and arts programming.

Other than that, the company does a lot of cross-promotion, with Twitter and Facebook logos on the Web sites and in its e-mail signatures. It even places logos for its social media sites in elevators, and includes all the links on the hotel's Wi-Fi login page.

Wallace is unabashedly enthusiastic about social media. "We are learning new things and experimenting every day...We are not afraid if one initiative does not work as well as others."

(continued)

(continued)

He advises other companies to follow the hotel's lead. "Don't be scared to try things... Focus on people and stories and [try] not to get caught up on complicated plans and sophisticated tools."

URLs for Roger Smith Hotel's Web Presence

```
http://rogersmith.com
```
(primary Web site)

```
http://rogersmithlife.com
```
(primary blog and six other blogs)

```
http://twitter.com/rshotel
```
(and 16 other personal Twitter accounts)

```
www.facebook.com/rogersmith
hotel
```

```
www.facebook.com/pages/New-
York-NY/Roger-Smith-News-
20/38572720863?ref=ts
```

```
www.facebook.com/thelab
gallery
```

```
www.flickr.com/photos/roger
smithhotel
```

```
http://12seconds.tv/channel/
rogersmithhotelwww.youtube.
com/user/rogersmithnews
```

```
www.youtube.com/user/panman
productions
```

```
www.ustream.tv/discovery/
live/all?q=roger+smith+hotel
```

```
http://vimeo.com/groups/
rogersmithshorts
```

```
www.yelp.com/biz/lilys-
restaurant-and-bar-new-york
```

```
www.tripadvisor.com/
Hotel_Review-g60763-d80107-
Reviews-Roger_Smith_Hotel-New_
York_City_New_York.html
```

Courtesy Roger Smith Hotel

Chapter 2: Plotting Your Social Media Marketing Strategy

In This Chapter

✔ Finding your audience online

✔ Segmenting B2C markets

✔ Conducting B2B research online

✔ Planning your strategy

*I*n Book I, Chapter 1, we talk about making the business case for social media marketing, looking at the question of whether you should or shouldn't get involved. This chapter helps you decide which forms of social media fit your target market. If the previous chapter was about strategy, goals, and objectives, this one is about tactics.

Let your customers and prospects drive your selection of social media alternatives. To see the best return on your investment in social media, you need to try to use the same social media as they do. This principle is exactly the same one you apply to all your other marketing and advertising efforts. Social media is a new tactic, not a new world.

Fish where your fish are. If your potential customers aren't on a particular social media outlet, don't start a campaign on that media.

In this chapter, we show how to use online market research to assess the match between your target markets and various social media outlets. After you do that, you're ready to start filling out your own tactical Social Media Marketing Plan, which appears at the end of this chapter.

Locating Your Target Market Online

Nothing is more important in marketing than identifying and understanding your target audience (or audiences). After you can describe your customers' and prospects' demographic characteristics, where they live, and what they do online, you're in a position to focus your social marketing efforts on those people most likely to buy your products or services. (Be sure to include the description of your target market on your Social Media Marketing Strategic Goals Statement in Book I, Chapter 1.)

Because social media techniques focus on inexpensive ways to reach niche markets with specific messages, they're tailor-made for a guerrilla marketing approach. As with all guerrilla marketing activities, target one market at a time.

Don't dilute your marketing budget or labor by trying to reach too many audiences at a time. People still need to see your message or brand name at least seven times to remember it. Trying to boost yourself to the forefront of everyone's mind all at once is expensive.

Focus your resources on one niche at a time. After you succeed, invest your profits in the next niche. It may seem counterintuitive, but it works.

Don't let setting priorities among niches paralyze you. Your choice of niches usually doesn't matter. If you aren't sure, go for what seems to be the biggest market first, or the easiest one to reach.

Segmenting Your B2C Market

If you have a business-to-consumer company, you can adapt the standard tools of *market segmentation* to define various niche audiences by where they live and how they spend their time and money. The most common types of segmentation are

- ✦ Demographics
- ✦ Geographics
- ✦ Life stages
- ✦ Psychographics or lifestyle
- ✦ Affinity or interest groups

These categories affect not only your social media tactics but also your graphics, message, content, offers, and every other aspect of your marketing.

Your messages need to be specific enough to satisfy the needs and wants of the distinct subgroups you're trying to reach.

Suppose that you want to sell a line of organic, herbal hair care products using social media. If you described your target market as "everyone who uses shampoo" on your Social Media Marketing Goals form (see Book I, Chapter 1), segment that market into different subgroups before you select appropriate social marketing techniques.

When you're creating subgroups, keep these concepts in mind:

- ✦ **Simple demographics affect your market definition.** The use of fragrances, descriptive terms, and even packaging may vary by gender.

How many shampoo commercials for men talk about silky hair? For that matter, what's the ratio of shampoo commercials addressed to women versus men?

✦ **Consider geography.** Geography may not seem obvious, but people who live in dry climates may be more receptive to a message about moisturizers than people who live in humid climates. Or, perhaps your production capacity constrains your initial product launch to a local or regional area.

✦ **Think about life stages.** For instance, people who dye their hair look for different hair care products than those who don't, but the reason they color their hair affects your selling message. (Teenagers and young adults may dye their hair unusual colors in an effort to belong to a group of their peers; older men may hide the gray with Grecian Formula; women with kids may be interested in fashion or color their hair as a pick-me-up.)

✦ **Even lifestyles (psychographics) affect decisions.** People with limited resources who are unlikely to try new products may respond to messages about value and satisfaction guarantees; people with more resources or a higher status may be affected by messages related to social grouping and self-esteem.

✦ **Affinity or interest groups are an obvious segmentation parameter.** People who participate in environmental organizations or who recycle goods may be more likely to be swayed by a "green shampoo" appeal or shop in specific online venues.

Different niche markets are drawn to different social media activities in general and to specific social media service providers in particular. In the following several sections, we look in detail at different online tools you can use to explore the parameters that seem the most appropriate for segmenting your audience and selecting specific social media sites.

For more information on market segmentation and research, see *Small Business Marketing For Dummies,* by Barbara Findlay Schenck.

The most successful marketing campaigns are driven by your target markets, not by techniques.

Demographics

Demographic segmentation, the most common type of market differentiation, covers such standard categories as gender, age, ethnicity, marital status, family size, household income, occupation, social class, and education.

Sites such as Quantcast (www.quantcast.com) and Alexa (www.alexa.com) provide basic demographic information compared to the overall Internet population, as shown in Figure 2-1. Quantcast also displays the distribution by subcategory within the site. As you can see, the sites don't always share the same subcategory breakdowns or completely agree on the data. However, either is close enough for your social marketing purposes.

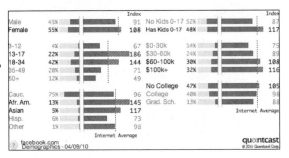

Figure 2-1: Both Quantcast (top) and Alexa (bottom) provide demographic profiles comparing the users of a particular site against the general Internet population.

(Top) Courtesy Quantcast.com (Bottom) "Alexa the Web Information Company," "Alexa Top Sites," "Alexa Site Thumbnail," the Alexa® logo and name are trademarks of Amazon.com, Inc. or its affiliates in the United States and/or other countries."

Use these tools to check out the demographic profile of users on various social media services, as well as your own users and those of your competitors. For instance, we've seen some discussion of MySpace appealing to a more ethnically diverse, younger audience than Facebook does.

Look for a general match between your target audience and that of the social media service you're considering.

Figure 2-2 from Flowtown (www.flowtown.com) shows the correlation between the demographics of Internet users and their use of social media. Of course, these profiles may change over time — sometimes quickly — as a wave of interest washes through a particular demographic segment and then recedes.

Always check for current information before launching your social media campaign.

Figure 2-2:
A comparison of demographic profiles (by gender, age, income, and educational level) using eight different social marketing services.

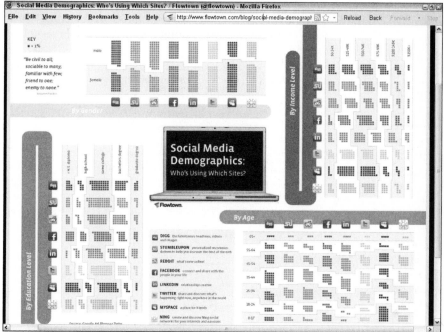

Flowtown: Know your customers? We do.

Geographics

Marketing by country, region, state, city, zip code, or even neighborhood is obviously the key for location-based social media outlets such as foursquare or Gowalla, mobile marketing with GPS, or any other form of online marketing that involves local search.

Geographic segmentation also makes sense if your business draws its primary target audience from within a certain distance from your brick-and-mortar storefront — for example, grocery stores, barber shops, gas stations, restaurants, movie theaters, and many other service providers, whether or not your social media service itself is location-based.

Many social media services offer a location search function to assess the number of users within your geographical target area:

✦ **Twitter users within a certain radius:** Enter the city, state, and radius at `http://search.twitter.com/advanced`.

✦ **LinkedIn users within a certain radius:** Enter the zip code or city, state, and radius at `www.linkedin.com/search`.

✦ **Facebook users near a certain location:** Enter a search term, for example, consultants, in the search box and click the magnifying glass icon.

Select People in the left navigation. In the Filter By Location box, type a city name, state, region, or zip code. Click the Refine Search button to view results for those people who permit their profiles to appear in search results.

If you can't determine the number of potential users of a service within your specific geographic location, use the Help function, check the blog, or contact the company.

Several companies combine geographical information with demographics and behavioral characteristics to segment the market more finely. For example, the Nielsen Claritas PRIZM, available from Tetrad (`www.tetrad.com/demographics/usa/claritas/prizmneappend.html`), offers demo-geographic data organized into 66 distinct segments, some of which are described in Table 2-1. You can download the entire list at `www.tetrad.com/pub/prices/PRIZMNE_Clusters.pdf`.

Again, you're looking for a fit between the profile of your target audience and that of the social media service.

Table 2-1	Top-Level Demo-Geographic Social Groups from Nielsen PRIZM
Name	*Description*
Urban Uptown	Wealthiest urban (highest-density) consumers (5 segments)
Midtown Mix	Midscale, ethnically diverse, urban population (3 segments)
Urban Cores	Modest income, affordable housing, urban living (4 segments)
Elite Suburbs	Affluent, suburban elite (4 segments)
The Affluentials	Comfortable suburban lifestyle (6 segments)
Middleburbs	Middle-class suburbs (5 segments)
Inner Suburbs	Downscale inner suburbs of metropolitan areas (4 segments)
Second City Society	Wealthy families in smaller cities on fringes of metro areas (3 segments)
City Centers	Middle-class, satellite cities with mixed demographics (5 segments)
Micro-City Blues	Downscale residents in second cities (5 segments)
Landed Gentry	Wealthy Americans in small towns (5 segments)

Name	*Description*
Country Comfort	Upper–middle-class homeowners in bedroom communities (5 segments)
Middle America	Middle-class homeowners in small towns and exurbs (6 segments)
Rustic Living	Most isolated towns and rural areas (6 segments)

Courtesy The Nielsen Company Source: Nielsen Claritas

Life stages

Rather than look at a target market solely in terms of demographics, *life stage analysis* considers what people are doing with their lives, recognizing that it may affect media behavior and spending patterns.

Figure 2-3 shows the percentage of Internet users who access social media frequently sorted by life stage. The eight life stages shown in the figure differ from the more traditional set shown in Table 2-2. However, the set described in the table may not accurately reflect the wider range of today's lifestyles.

Table 2-2	**Life Stage Segmentation**
Life Stage	*Products They Buy*
Single, no children	Fashion items, vacations, recreation
Married, no children	Vacations, cars, clothing, entertainment
New nesters, children under 6	Baby food and toys; furniture and new homes
Full nest, youngest over 6	Children's items, activities, and education
Full nest, children over 16	College; possibly travel and furniture
Empty nest, children gone	Travel, cruises, vacations
Retired couples	Moves to warmer climates, housing downsizing
Solitary working retiree	Travel, vacations, medical expenses
Retired solitary survivor	Medical expenses

Source: adapted from http://academic.brooklyn.cuny.edu/economic/friedman/mmmarket segmentation.htm#C1

Figure 2-3:
Recent research indicates that the use of social media varies by stage of life.

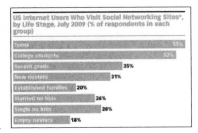

US Internet Users Who Visit Social Networking Sites*, by Life Stage, July 2009 (% of respondents in each group)

Teens	55%
College students	52%
Recent grads	35%
New nesters	31%
Established families	20%
Married no kids	26%
Single no kids	28%
Empty nesters	18%

Courtesy eMarketer

With more flexible timing for going through life passages, demographic analysis isn't enough for many types of products and services. Women may have children later in life; many older, nontraditional students go back to college; some retirees re-enter the workforce to supplement social security earnings. What your prospective customers do each day may influence what they buy and which media outlets they use more than their age or location.

Recent research has, in fact, documented that life stages are more likely to predict word-of-mouth and social media behavior than demographics alone. One report found that "new nesters" are the most satisfied (33 percent are very satisfied) with social networking, using it to stay in touch with friends and family. In contrast, the "married, no children cohort," of whom only 20 percent are very satisfied, use social networking primarily to "maintain/ expand [their] professional network."

Psychographics or lifestyle

Psychographic segmentation divides a market by social class or lifestyle or by the shared activities, interests, and opinions of prospective customers. It helps identify groups within a social networking service or other, smaller, social networks that attract users meeting your desired profile.

Behavioral segmentation, which is closely related, divides potential buyers based on their uses, responses, or attitudes toward a product or service. To obtain this information about your own customers, consider taking a quick poll as part of your e-newsletter, Web site, or blog. Although the results from those who reply may not be exactly representative of your total customer base — or that of prospective customers — a survey gives you some starter data.

Don't confuse the psychographic profile of a group with personality traits specific to an individual.

Psychographic segmentation helps you not only identify where to promote your company but also craft your message. For instance, understanding social class might help you determine how to appeal to customers (such as the Innovators or Experiencers shown in Figure 2-4), who might be interested in your high-end line of fashion, home decor, cosmetics, restaurants, or vacation destinations. Or, your ads might show people enjoying a natural, outdoor lifestyle using a product such as organic shampoo.

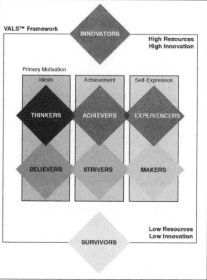

Figure 2-4: Psychographic segmentation is shown on the values, attitudes, and life styles (VALS) chart.

Courtesy Strategic Business Insights (SBI)
www.strategicbusinessinsights.com/VALS

To develop a better understanding of psychographic profiling, take the quick values, attitudes, and life styles (VALS) survey yourself at `www.strategic businessinsights.com/vals/presurvey.htm`.

Affinity, or interest, groups

Segmenting by affinity, or interest, group fills in the blank at the end of the statement "People who like this also like. . . ." Because activity is a subsection of psychographic segmentation, the approach is somewhat similar.

Figure 2-5 shows other interests of Facebook users under the Lifestyle option at the Quantcast site. The Related tab and Clickstream tab at the Alexa site provide lists of other Web sites that visitors to a particular site also visit. For more on *clickstream analysis* (where visitors come from and where they go), see Book VIII, Chapter 2.

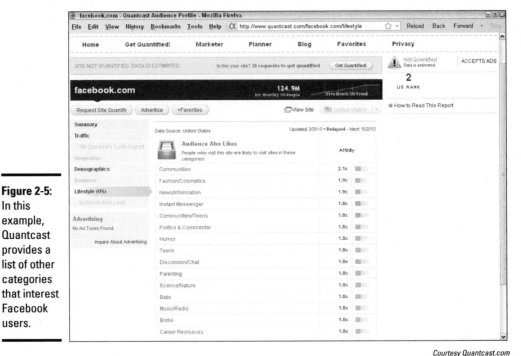

Figure 2-5: In this example, Quantcast provides a list of other categories that interest Facebook users.

Using Quantcast and Alexa, you can obtain public information on interest areas for specific social media services or your competitors or other related businesses. You can also use these services to profile your own business, although your Web site might be too small to provide more than rough estimates. If your business is too small, estimate the interest profile for your target market by running Alexa for a large corporation that offers a similar product or service.

Request a free profile of your site at www.quantcast.com/user/signup.

Interest categories for your own site, based on the types of other Web sites your visitors frequent, are also available from a Yahoo! Web Analytics account under Visitor Behavioral Reports (http://web.analytics.yahoo.com/features). Yahoo! Web Analytics free enterprise-level solution is Yahoo's answer to Google Analytics. Otherwise, consider polling your own customers to find out more about their specific interests.

Google Analytics doesn't offer a similar capability, but you can use Google Insights (www.google.com/insights/search/#), which sorts Google searches by interest category, as shown in Table 2-3. Because searches are organized by search term trend, not by source site, you gain a different form of market intelligence.

Table 2-3	Main Categories Available on Google Insights	
Arts and Humanities	Automotive	Beauty and Personal Care
Business	Computers and Electronics	Entertainment
Finance and Insurance	Food and Drink	Games
Health	Home and Garden	Industries
Internet	Lifestyles	Local
News and Current Events	Photo and Video	Real Estate
Recreation	Reference	Science
Shopping	Social Networks and Online Communities	Society
Sports	Telecommunications	Travel

Researching B2B Markets

Market research and social media choices for business-to-business markets are somewhat different from business-to-consumer markets because the sales cycle is different. Usually, B2B companies have a longer sales cycle and high-ticket purchases and multiple people who play a role in closing a sale; consequently, B2B marketing requires a different social media presence.

In terms of social media, more B2B marketing efforts focus on branding, top-of-mind visibility, customer support, and problem-solving compared to more sales-focused messages from B2C companies.

You can treat the interest groups in the earlier section "Affinity, or interest, groups" as vertical market segments and take advantage of Google Insights to discern trends over time. You might also want to assess competitor presence on different forms of social media.

One key step in B2B marketing is to identify people who make the buying decision. Professional social networks such as LinkedIn and Plaxo may help you research people on your B2B customer or prospect lists.

The value of various forms of social media appears to differ by company size, according to research by Marketing Sherpa, shown in Figure 2-6. Marketing Sherpa also found differences in efficacy by industry type. Their findings may reflect available budget and human resources as well as techniques. For more information, visit www.sherpastore.com/Social MediaMkt2010.html or www.sherpastore.com/B2BMarketing BenchmarkGuide.html to download excerpts. HubSpot, at www.hubspot. com, also offers a range of B2B market research tools and webinars.

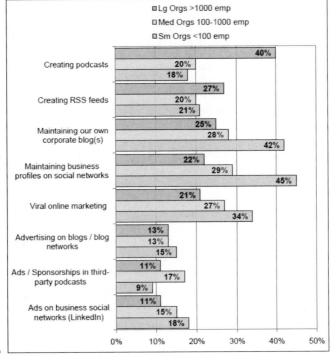

Figure 2-6: B2B companies of different sizes find different forms of social media effective for reaching their target audiences.

Source: MarketingSherpa.com

As always, the key is ensuring that your customers are using the type of social media you're considering. Use the search feature and group options on major social networking sites to test your list of existing customers. Chances are good that if a large number of your existing customers are using that service, it will be a good source for future customers as well.

In addition to participating in general market research, you might want to try Compete.com, which offers a free basic tool (https://my.compete.com/login/?origin=https://my.compete.com/%3F) that compares as many as five competitors at a time. (More extensive paid versions are also available.) You can use Compete.com to assess audience profiles and export data for your own analysis.

Check competing sites for inbound links from other sites, as well as their own outbound links, to see how they reach their customers.

Conducting Other Types of Market Research Online

The amount of research available online can be paralyzing. A well-crafted search yields most, if not all, the social marketing research you need. You aren't writing an academic paper; you're running a business with limited time and resources. Set aside a week or two for research and then start laying out your approach.

Don't be afraid to experiment on a small scale. In the end, what matters is what happens with your business as you integrate social media into your marketing plan, not what happens to businesses on the average.

Despite these statements, you might want to touch on two other research points:

✦ **The most influential sites, posters, or pages on your preferred social media:** You can learn from them.

✦ **Understanding what motivates people to use certain types of social media:** Make the content you provide meet their expectations and desires.

Identifying influencers

Whether you have a B2B or B2C company, you gain valuable insight by seeing which companies or individuals are driving the conversation within your industry sector. To see the most popular posters on Twitter, use services such as Klout, at `http://klout.com` (by topic), or Twitaholic, at `http://twitaholic.com` (by followers or number of posts), shown in Figure 2-7, to identify people you might want to follow for research purposes. You can find more information about tools for each of the major services in their respective books.

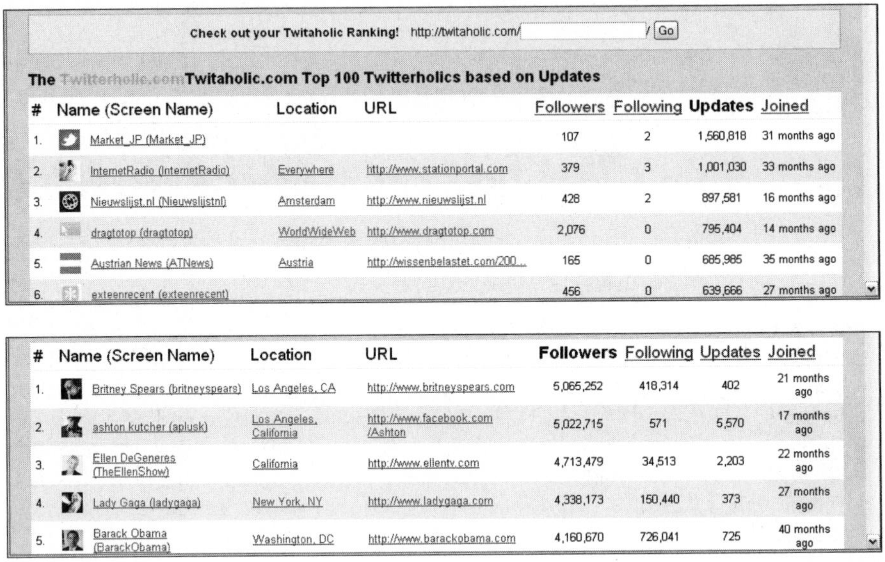

Check out your Twitaholic Ranking! http://twitaholic.com/ / Go

The Twitterholic.com Twitaholic.com Top 100 Twitterholics based on Updates

#	Name (Screen Name)	Location	URL	Followers	Following	Updates	Joined
1.	Market_JP (Market_JP)			107	2	1,560,818	31 months ago
2.	InternetRadio (InternetRadio)	Everywhere	http://www.stationportal.com	379	3	1,001,030	33 months ago
3.	Nieuwslijst.nl (Nieuwslijstnl)	Amsterdam	http://www.nieuwslijst.nl	428	2	897,581	16 months ago
4.	dragtotop (dragtotop)	WorldWideWeb	http://www.dragtotop.com	2,076	0	795,404	14 months ago
5.	Austrian News (ATNews)	Austria	http://wissenbelastet.com/200...	165	0	685,985	35 months ago
6.	exteenrecent (exteenrecent)			456	0	639,666	27 months ago

#	Name (Screen Name)	Location	URL	Followers	Following	Updates	Joined
1.	Britney Spears (britneyspears)	Los Angeles, CA	http://www.britneyspears.com	5,065,252	418,314	402	21 months ago
2.	ashton kutcher (aplusk)	Los Angeles, California	http://www.facebook.com/Ashton	5,022,715	571	5,570	17 months ago
3.	Ellen DeGeneres (TheEllenShow)	California	http://www.ellentv.com	4,713,479	34,513	2,203	22 months ago
4.	Lady Gaga (ladygaga)	New York, NY	http://www.ladygaga.com	4,338,173	150,440	373	27 months ago
5.	Barack Obama (BarackObama)	Washington, DC	http://www.barackobama.com	4,160,670	726,041	725	40 months ago

Courtesy Twitaholic.com

Figure 2-7: Twitaholic ranks the most influential tweeters by either number of updates (top) or number of followers (bottom). The most frequent posters aren't the ones with the most followers and vice versa.

Understanding why people use social media services

The expectation that people gravitate toward different types of social media to meet different needs seems reasonable. The challenge, of course, is to match what people seek with particular social sites. The advertising network Chitika compiled the results (`http://chitika.com/research/2010/twitter-and-facebook-are-for-news-myspace-is-for-leisure`), shown in Figure 2-8, by reviewing downstream visits from social networks and sorting them by type. Ask yourself whether these patterns match your expectations and whether they match what you see on these sites.

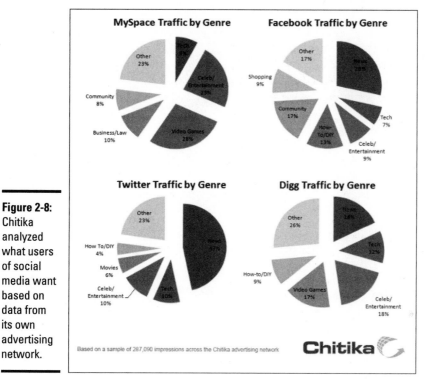

Figure 2-8:
Chitika
analyzed
what users
of social
media want
based on
data from
its own
advertising
network.

Courtesy Chitika, Inc.

A review of successful social media models may spark creative ideas for
your own campaign. Take a look at the Web site featured in Figure 2-9 and
the nearby sidebar "Social media wears well for iwearyourshirt.com." This
advertising and promotion company, which uses multiple social media outlets to reach the widest possible range of viewers, wouldn't even exist if not
for social media.

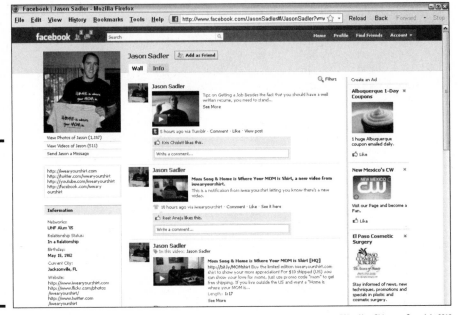

Figure 2-9:
iwear
yourshirt.
com
publishes
on two
Facebook
sites,
including
this one.

Social media wears well for iwearyourshirt.com

You have to see the site at http://iwear yourshirt.com to believe it —late one night in September 2008, founder Jason Sadler, who has a background in graphics, advertising, and Web design, had an "aha" moment. He realized that he could develop social media content as a promotional method. iweary-ourshirt.com operates as an online, interactive version of a walking billboard, somewhat akin to people who paint their heads or wrap their cars.

"I saw all the social media channels as a way to promote a brand," Sadler says. All he needed was an easy way to create a message he could port easily to multiple outlets — the T-shirt. By January 2009, Sadler had his plan in place and the first customers willing to pay him to wear their branded T-shirts on his blog (see the nearby figure), on Facebook, Flickr, and Twitter and on video channels.

Sadler, in Florida, and his partner, Evan White, in Los Angeles, develop all creative content. Each one writes his own blog posts and tweets, takes photos, and makes videos. Every day, both men chat with a group of people online, using Ustream for live video. They may receive a list of key selling points from clients, but they create their own new stories daily. "Scripts would get a poor response," Sadler observes wryly.

With their lighthearted, quirky personalities, Sadler and White have developed a bit of an international cult following. At this point, their traffic is 65 to 70 percent from the United States, with the rest from Canada and Europe. Usually, Sadler notes, "We have 30 to 50 people waiting for our videocasts and receive an average of 600 views per day on the videos alone."

Running online promotional campaigns may sound easy and fun, but Sadler spends 10 to 12 hours every day getting everything done. The site's advertising rates are affordable enough that Sadler doesn't worry about promising clients a certain number of page views or sales. Neither does he provide analytic reports, because clients can see the number of viewers themselves on each service. He has also added creative giveaways and sponsorships.

Promoting the site has been fairly simple, involving a few paid ads and paying a reporter from `http://helpareporter.com` for assistance with public relations. Sadler also e-mails contacts in the public relations industry to advertise his services.

Between word-of-mouth and some cascading press coverage, traffic at various iwearyourshirt sites took off. Sadler sold out all 2009 dates and by mid-June 2010 had only eight days left to sell in the year. Prices start at $2 per day on January 1 and increase $2 every day, to $730 on December 31. After booking a date online, a customer e-mails a logo to Sadler and ships two T-shirts. Though the content is designed for its daily impact, it lives on in cyberspace for clients to link to.

Sadler hopes to go mainstream: Nissan, Pizza Hut, and 1800flowers have already paid him to wear their shirts. He advises other businesses to be patient with social media. "Success doesn't happen overnight." (He figures it took him 11 months.) "Be focused, and consistent in the channels you use. You have to put out good content. Social media is all about interaction with people. [They] want to share with others." He just gives them a reason.

URLs for iwearyourshirt.com

`http://iwearyourshirt.com`

`http://iwearyourshirt.com/blogs`

`http://twitter.com/yourfriendevan`

`http://twitter.com/iwearyourshirt`

`www.facebook.com/jasonsadler`

`www.facebook.com/yourfriendevan`

`www.ustream.tv/iwearyourshirt`

`www.youtube.com/iwearyourshirt`

`http://flickr.com/photos/iwearyourshirt`

`http://feeds.feedburner.com/iwearyourshirt`

(continued)

(continued)

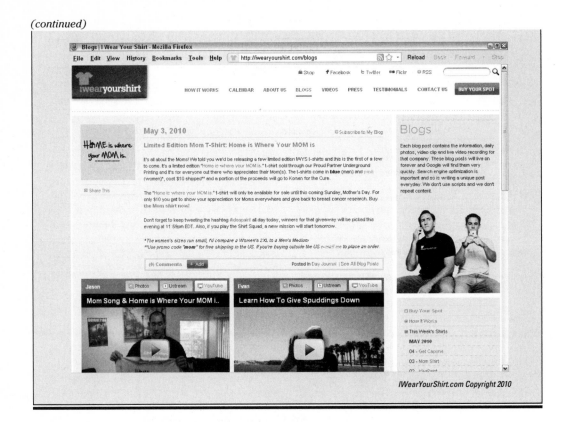

IWearYourShirt.com Copyright 2010

Setting Up Your Social Marketing Worksheet

You can dive into social media marketing headfirst and see what happens. Or, you can take the time to research, plan, execute, and evaluate your approach. The Social Media Marketing Plan, shown in Figure 2-10, is for people taking the latter approach. (You can download the form from this book's Web site; see the Introduction for more details.)

Social Media Marketing Form
Tactical Options

Company Name _____ Date _____

Hub Site(s)   (URL of Web site or blog with domain name to which traffic will be driven)
_____

Standard Social Media Identification Name/Handle _____

Social Media Project Director _____

Social Media Team Members & Tasks _____   _____
                                   _____   _____
                                   _____   _____
Programming/Technical Team   _____   _____
Social Media Policy URL   _____

Check boxes for all applications used. Shadow categories are strongly recommended.

SOCIAL MEDIA PLANNING

- ❑ **Dashboard (Select One: Enter URL & Log In Info)**
  - ❑ NetVibes
  - ❑ Hootsuite
  - ❑ Other - Name
  - ❑ Custom
- ❑ **Calendar (Select One: Enter URL & Log In Info)**
  - ❑ Google Calendar
  - ❑ Yahoo! Calendar
  - ❑ Windows Calendar
  - ❑ Other
- ❑ **Social Sharing Service (Select One: Enter URL & Log In Info)**
  - ❑ AddThis
  - ❑ ShareThis
  - ❑ AddToAny
  - ❑ Other
- ❑ **Social Media Resources (Insert One Resource Site or Blog to Follow**
  - ❑

SOCIAL MEDIA TOOL KIT

- ❑ **Monitoring (Select at least one; Enter Name, URL, Log In Info for all used)**
  - ❑ Brand Reputation/Sentiment Tool, e.g. BrandsEye, MyReputation
  - ❑ Topic Monitoring Tool, e.g. Addict-o-Matic, Google Trends
  - ❑ How Sociable
  - ❑ Monitor This
  - ❑ Social Mention
  - ❑ Trackur
  - ❑ WhosTalkin
  - ❑ Blog Monitoring Tool
  - ❑ Twitter Monitoring Tool
  - ❑ Social News, Forums, RSS Monitoring Tool
  - ❑ Google Alerts

Figure 2-10:
Build a tactical social media marketing plan for your company.

- ❏ Other
- ❏ **Distribution Tools (Select at least one; Enter Name, URL, & Log In Info for all used)**
  - ❏ RSS/Atom Feeds
  - ❏ ping.fm
  - ❏ Hellotxt
  - ❏ Hootsuite
  - ❏ Only Wire
  - ❏ TweetDeck
  - ❏ Other
- ❏ **Update Notification Tools (Select at least one; Enter Name, URL, Log In Info for all)**
  - ❏ FeedPing
  - ❏ Feed Shark
  - ❏ Google Ping
  - ❏ King Ping
  - ❏ Other
- ❏ **URL Clipping Tool (Select One; Enter URL & Log In Info)**
  - ❏ Bit.ly
  - ❏ SnipURL
  - ❏ TinyURL
  - ❏ Other
- ❏ **Ecommerce Tool or Widget (Select One: Enter URL & Log In Info)**
  - ❏ Netcarnation
  - ❏ CartFly
  - ❏ SELLit
  - ❏ ShopIt
  - ❏ ProductCart
  - ❏ Etsy Widget
  - ❏ Amazon Widget
  - ❏ Paypal Widget
  - ❏ Custom Widget
  - ❏ Other
- ❏ **Search Engine Tools (If needed, enter URL & Log In Info; include submission dates)**
  - ❏ Search Engine Ranking Tool (Select One)
  - ❏ Google Search Engine Submission
  - ❏ Yahoo! Search Engine Submission
  - ❏ Bing Search Engine Submission
  - ❏ Automated XML Feed
  - ❏ Specialty Search Submission Sites
  - ❏ Other

- ❏   **STANDARD SET PRIMARY KEYWORDS/TAGS**
  - ❏ Enter at least 8
  - ❏
  - ❏
  - ❏
  - ❏
  - ❏
  - ❏
  - ❏
- ❏   **STANDARD PAGE DESCRIPTION TAG**
  Enter 150-character description, preferably including at least 4 of the keywords above

SOCIAL MEDIA SERVICES

❑   **Social Bookmarking Sites (Select at least one; Enter Name, URL, Log In Info for all)**
- ❑ Delicious
- ❑ StumbleUpon
- ❑ Twine
- ❑ Other

❑   **Social News Sites (Select at least one; Enter Name, URL, Log In Info for all)**
- ❑ Digg
- ❑ Reddit
- ❑ Propeller
- ❑ Y! Buzz
- ❑ Other

❑   **Social Shopping & Specialty Bookmark Sites (Enter Name, URL, Log In Info for all)**
- ❑ Kaboodle
- ❑ This Next
- ❑ StyleHive
- ❑ Other

❑   **Blogging Site (Enter Name, URL, Log In Info for all)**
- ❑ Primary blog
- ❑ Blog directory submission site
- ❑ Blog monitoring site
- ❑ Blog measuring tool sites
- ❑ Other

❑   **Social Networking Sites (Select at least one; Enter Name, URL, Log In Info for all; expand rows as needed)**
- ❑ Facebook
  - ❑ Groups
  - ❑ Tools
  - ❑ Metrics
  - ❑ Follow Us On
- ❑ Twitter
  - ❑ Groups
  - ❑ Tools
  - ❑ Metrics
  - ❑ Follow Us On
- ❑ LinkedIn
  - ❑ Groups
  - ❑ Tools
  - ❑ Metrics
  - ❑ Follow Us On
- ❑ MySpace
  - ❑ Groups
  - ❑ Tools
  - ❑ Metrics
  - ❑ Follow Us On
- ❑ Google Buzz
- ❑ Squidoo
- ❑ Specialty Networks
- ❑ Other Professional Networking, e.g. Plaxo
- ❑ Other Vertical Industry Networks, e.g. DeviantArt
- ❑ Other Demographic Networks, e.g. myYearbook

❑   **Social Media Sharing Sites (Enter Name, URL, Log In Info for all)**
- ❑ YouTube
- ❑ UStream

- ❏ Vimeo
- ❏ FlickR
- ❏ Picasa
- ❏ Podcasts
- ❏ Other
- ❏ **Social Community Sites (Enter Name, URL, Log In Info for all)**
  - ❏ Ning
  - ❏ Forums
  - ❏ Message Boards
  - ❏ Other
- ❏ **Other Social Media Services (Enter Name, URL, Log In Info for all)**
  - ❏ Geolocation, e.g. Foursquare, Loopt, Gowalla
  - ❏ Collective Shopping, e.g. Groupon
  - ❏ Social Gaming
  - ❏ Virtual Social
  - ❏ Social Mobile
  - ❏ Other

SOCIAL MEDIA METRICS

- ❏ **Key Performance Indicators**
  - ❏ Enter at least 8 (e.g. Traffic, CPM, CPC, Conversion Rate, ROI)
  - ❏
  - ❏
  - ❏
  - ❏
  - ❏
  - ❏
  - ❏
- ❏ **Analytical/Statistical Tool (Select at least One: Enter Name, URL, Log In Info for all)**
  - ❏ Google Analytics
  - ❏ Yahoo! Analytics
  - ❏ AWstats
  - ❏ SociafyQ
  - ❏ Xinu
  - ❏ Other
- ❏ Advertising Metrics (Enter Name, URL, Log In Info for Each Publication)
  - ❏ Other
  - ❏ Other

Depending on its complexity and availability of support, think in terms of a timeline of 3 to 12 months, to allow time to complete the following steps. Estimate spending half your time in the planning phase, one-quarter in execution, and one-quarter in evaluation and modification:

1. Market research and online observation

2. Draft marketing goals, objectives, and plan

3. In-house preparation
   - Hiring, outsourcing, or selecting in-house staff
   - Training
   - Team-building
   - Writing social media policy document
4. Preparatory development tasks
   - Design
   - Content
   - Measurement plan and metric implementation
   - Social media tool selection and dashboard development
   - Set up your social media activity calendar (see Book I, Chapter 3)
   - Programming and content modifications to existing Web site(s) as needed
5. Create accounts and pilot social media program
6. Evaluate pilot program, de-bug, and modify as needed
7. Launch and promote your social media campaign one service at a time
8. Measure and modify social media in a process of constant feedback and reiteration

Don't be afraid to build a pilot program — or several — into your plan to see what works.

Plan your work; work your plan.

The remaining chapters in this book cover additional ways to prepare your social media campaign for success. Book II reviews useful tools and resources to make your plan easier to execute. Before you start, you may also want to read Chapters 1 through 3 in Book VIII — they focus on measurement tools for traffic, costs, and return on investment.

Chapter 3: Managing Your Cybersocial Campaign

In This Chapter

✔ Scheduling social media activities

✔ Building a team

✔ Writing a social media policy

✔ Keeping it legal

✔ Protecting your brand reputation

*A*fter you have a social media marketing plan, one major task you face is managing the effort. If you're the only one doing the work, the simplest — and likely the hardest — task is making time for it. Though social media need not carry a lot of up-front development costs, it carries a significant cost in labor.

In this chapter, we discuss how to set up a schedule to keep your social media from draining all your available time. If you have employees, both you and your company may benefit by delegating some of the social media tasking to them, and supplementing your in-house staff with limited time from outside professionals.

For small businesses, it's always your money or your life. If you can't afford to hire help to work on social media, you carve it out of the time you've allocated to other marketing activities — unless, of course, you want to stretch your workday from 10 to 12 hours to 12 to 14 hours.

Finally, this chapter carries a word of precaution. Make sure that everyone posting to a social media outlet knows your policy about what is and isn't acceptable, and how to protect the company's reputation and confidential material. As you launch your marketing boat onto the churning waters of social media, you should ensure that everyone is wearing a legal life preserver.

Managing Your Social Media Schedule

As you know from the rest of your business experience, if something isn't important enough to schedule, it never gets done. Social media, like the rest of your marketing efforts, can easily be swallowed up by day-to-day demands. You must set aside time for it and assign tasks to specific people.

Allocate a minimum of two hours per week if you're going to participate in social media, rather than set up pages and abandon them. Otherwise, you simply don't see a return from your initial investment in setup. If you don't have much time, stick with the marketing you're already doing.

Bounding the time commitment

Social media can become addictive. If you truly like what you're doing, the time problem might reverse. Rather than spend too little time, you spend too much. You might find it difficult to avoid the temptation of continually reading what others have to say about your business or spending all your time tweeting, streaming, and posting.

Just as you stick to your initial dollar budget, keep to your initial time budget, at least for the first month until you see what works. After you determine which techniques have the greatest promise, you can rearrange your own efforts, and your team's.

As you can see from the sidebar about artist Natasha Wescoat, "Social media as an art form," one way to reduce the time you spend on social media is to turn social media into part of your art, or a product in and of itself. Of course, that strategy may not work for everyone's business.

Social media marketing is only part of your online marketing effort, and online marketing is only part of your overall marketing.

Selecting "activity" days

One way to control the time you spend on social media is to select specific days and times for it. Many businesspeople set aside regularly recurring blocks of time, such as on a quiet Friday afternoon, for marketing-related tasks, whether they're conducting competitor research, writing press releases or newsletters for release the following week, obtaining inbound links, or handling their social marketing tasks.

Other people prefer to allocate their time early in the morning, at lunchtime, or just before leaving work each evening. The time slot you choose usually doesn't matter, unless you're offering a time-dependent service, such as accepting to-go orders for breakfast burritos via Twitter.

Whatever the case, allot time for every task on your social media activity calendar, followed by the initials of the person responsible for executing the task.

Allowing for ramp-up time

Even if you're the only person involved, allow time for learning before your official social media launch date. Everyone needs time to observe, master new tools, practice posting and responding, experiment, and decide what works before you can roll out your plan.

Bring your new social media venues online one at a time. This strategy not only helps you evaluate which social media venue works but also reduces stress on you and your staff.

Developing your social date book

There are as many ways to schedule social media activities as there are companies. Whatever you decide, don't leave your schedule to chance.

Larger companies may use elaborate project management software, either proprietary solutions or open source programs such as Endeavour Software Project Management (`http://endeavour-mgmt.sourceforge.net`), GanttProject (`www.ganttproject.biz`), or OpenProj (`www.serena.com/products/openproj`). Alternatively, you can schedule tasks using spreadsheet software.

However, the simplest solution may be the best: Calendaring software, much of which is free, may be all you need. Paid options may merge schedules for more people and allow customized report formats. Several options are listed in Table 3-1. Look for a solution that lets you

✦ Choose a display by day, week, or month or longer

✦ Lists events or tasks in chronological format

✦ Select different timeframes easily

✦ Easily schedule repeat activities without requiring duplicate data entry

Table 3-1	Calendaring Software	
Name	*URL*	*Free or Paid*
Calendar & Time Management Software Reviews	`http://download.cnet.com/windows/calendar-and-time-management-software`	Free, shareware, and paid
Connect Daily	`www.mhsoftware.com/connectdaily.htm`	Paid, free trial
EventsLink Network	`www.eventslink.net`	Paid, free trial
Google Calendar	`www.google.com/intl/en/googlecalendar/about.html`	Free

(continued)

Table 3-1 *(continued)*

Name	URL	Free or Paid
Trumba	`www.trumba.com/connect/default.aspx`	Paid, free trial
Yahoo! Calendar	`http://calendar.yahoo.com`	Free

If several people are involved in a substantial social media effort, select calendaring software that lets you synchronize individual calendars, such as Google, Yahoo!, Mozilla Sunbird, and others. Figure 3-1 shows a sample of a simple social marketing calendar using Yahoo! The calendar shows the initials of the person responsible. Clicking an event or a task reveals item details, including the time allotted to the task, the sharing level, and whether a reminder is sent and to whom. Figure 3-2 offers an example of an event detail listing in Mozilla Sunbird.

Throughout this book, we refer to this calendar as your *Social Media Activity Calendar,* and we add frequent recommendations of tasks to include on your schedule.

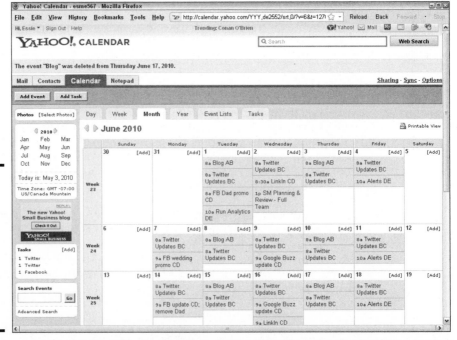

Figure 3-1: Using Yahoo! Calendar, you can easily schedule your social media activities.

Figure 3-2:
On the
Sunbird
event detail
screen, you
configure
each social
media task
as needed.

New Event: New Event	✕

File   Edit   View   Options   Help

Save and Close   Invite Attendees   Privacy   Attach

Title: Facebook Promo Ad by BC
Location: Wall
Category: [   ]   Calendar: [   ]

☐ All day Event
Start: 06/11/2010   8:00 AM
End: 06/11/2010   8:30 AM

Repeat: [   ]

Reminder: [   ]

Description:
Father's Day Promo
runs through 6/15

Attachments: [   ]

🔒 Private Event   Priority: ▫▫▪

Set your calendar to private, but give access to everyone who needs to be aware of your social media schedule. Depending on the design of your social media program, some outside subcontractors may need access to your calendar to schedule their own production deadlines.

Creating a social media dashboard

Your social media marketing efforts may ultimately involve many tasks: Post to multiple venues; use tools to distribute content to multiple locations; monitor visibility for your company on social media outlets; and measure results by using several different analytical tools. Rather than jump back and forth among all these different sources, a graphical dashboard or control panel can be a convenient timesaver.

Like the dashboard of a car, a social media dashboard puts the various required functions at your fingertips, in (you hope) an easy-to-understand and easy-to-use visual layout. When you use this approach, the customized dashboard provides easy access in one location to all your social media accounts, tools, and metrics. Figures 3-3 and 3-4 show several tabs of a customized Netvibes dashboard — one for social media postings and another for tools.

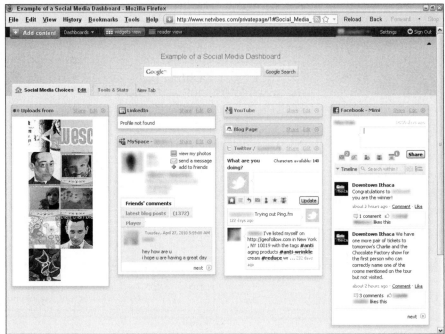

Figure 3-3:
This mock-up of a social media dashboard from Netvibes gathers various social media services on the first tab for a user who manages multiple accounts.

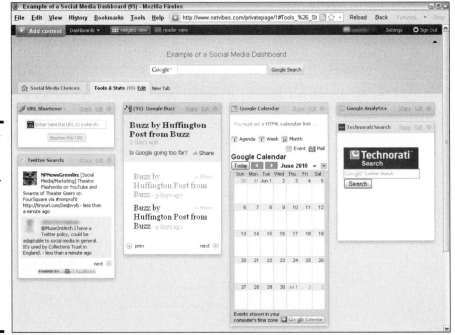

Figure 3-4:
The second tab of this mock-up for a Netvibes dashboard gathers tools for distributing, monitoring, searching, and analyzing.

The items on your primary dashboard may link to other, application-specific dashboards, especially for analytical tools and high-end enterprise solutions; those application dashboards are designed primarily to compare the results of multiple social media campaigns.

Table 3-2 provides a list of dashboard resources, some of which are generic (such as iGoogle and MyYahoo!) and others of which, such as Netvibes and HootSuite (see Figure 3-5), are specific to social media.

Table 3-2	Social Media Dashboard Resources	
Name	**URL**	**Description**
Goojet	www.goojet.com	Free mobile short-message dashboard client
HootSuite	www.hootsuite.com	Free short-message dashboard that focuses on Twitter
iGoogle	www.google.com/ig	Free, customizable Google home page
MarketingProfs	www.marketingprofs.com/articles/2010/3454/how-to-create-your-marketing-dashboard-in-five-easy-steps	Instructions for customizing a dashboard (sign up for the free trial to view)
MyYahoo!	http://my.yahoo.com	Free, customizable Yahoo! home page
Netvibes	http://netvibes.com	Free, customizable dashboard for social media
Pageflakes	www.pageflakes.com/Default.aspx	Free, customizable dashboard
Search Engine Land	http://searchengineland.com/b2b-social-media-dashboard-a-powerful-tool-to-uncover-key-customer-insights-17839	Tips on how to use a social media dashboard for B2B
uberVU	www.ubervu.com	Paid social media dashboard client
Unilyzer	http://unilyzer.com	Paid social media dashboard client

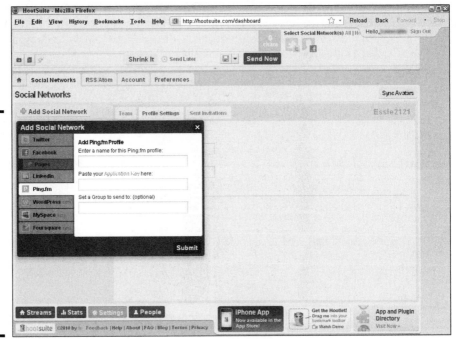

Courtesy HootSuite. The HootSuite wordmark is ™ of HootSuite Media, Inc.

Figure 3-5:
The social media dashboard from HootSuite lets you easily add social network services to your list of monitored sites.

Before you try to build a dashboard, list all the social media sources, services, and reports you want to display, along with their associated URLs, usernames, and passwords. It will help if you indicate whether services are interconnected (for example, note if you're using a syndication service to update multiple social media at once) and how often statistical reports should be updated for each service (hourly, daily, weekly, or monthly).

The more complex the social media campaign, the more functionality the dashboard needs. For example, Natasha Wescoat's home page (www.natashawescoat.com), shown in Figure 3-6, indicates that her dashboard might include controls and analytics for a Facebook fan page, her blog, and other components of the social Web. Read more in the nearby sidebar about Ms. Wescoat's social presence.

Dashboards sound simple to use, but they can be a bit of a challenge to set up. In some cases, your programmer needs to create or customize *widgets* (mini applications). Plan to create and test several versions of the dashboard until everyone is satisfied with the results.

Consider implementing password access for approved users to various functions within the dashboard. Some users might be constrained to viewing reports whereas others might be allowed to change the dashboard configuration.

**Book I
Chapter 3**

Managing Your
Cybersocial
Campaign

Figure 3-6:
The number of social media options, shown here in the lower right navigation area, affects the complexity of a dashboard.

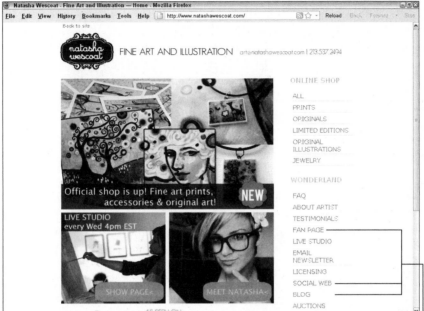

Social media

Courtesy Natasha Wescoat

Social media as an art form

Artist Natasha Wescoat is a one-woman band, selling her exuberant art (refer to Figure 3-6) online directly to consumers in the United States, United Kingdom, and Australia. Wescoat learned how to use the social media tools herself. "I'm naturally inclined towards technology and studied graphic design in school, so I did all of my design and site work, as well as putting up my own profiles and Web sites."

For Wescoat, social media was a match between technology and personality. "I've always loved using the Internet, so it was natural to incorporate it. I started in 2004 with blogging on LiveJournal. I felt that it could possibly be good to fill in my new collectors on what I was doing and what I was interested

in, as well as what I was offering." Over the next three years, she added video blogging and Facebook, MySpace, and Twitter accounts. In each case, she was an early adopter, experimenting with the capability of each medium and its potential profitability. "I never had a master plan. I just did what I wanted to do," says Wescoat, in true artistic form.

As she explains, "The centerpiece of my Web presence is definitely my blog (see the nearby figure). I keep it going and update it a lot, so I have people going there first to find out anything. I'm on these sites all the time, and it can be exhausting. I spend probably 30 hours per week on my social networks, answering e-mails [reviewing] comments, commenting back, sharing content and new work, adding

(continued)

(continued)

people, posting on walls, reading, and exploring their content."

Wescoat spends five hours or more creating each video. "I try not to spend a lot of money on anything I use, because I don't have the money to. A lot of what is available to use online is free." She does now use sites such as HootSuite or TweetDeck to post her content to multiple social networks, "so it's not such a hassle any more to update."

In any case, Wescoat has made a serious time commitment to social media. "Sometimes I use press releases, but my marketing is strictly social media. I haven't found the need for traditional marketing for anything, and that's the great thing about it all." Wescoat also incorporates Follow and Share icons on her site and places links in posts and throughout her social networks to other sites in her suite of outlets.

Wescoat is unconventional in her approach, treating social media almost as an artistic medium. "I don't even think about it as marketing. I think about it as sharing and offering. I love to talk to others and connect with people [with whom] I could possibly have a personal or business relationship. The relationships really matter. People who use social media or live on these things can tell when someone is not honest or is just out there to sell something. You have to really enjoy the Web, and really enjoy the tools and the people that use them."

"I'm not trying to target a specific market. I try to focus on the audience that is drawn to me. Every artist [who] uses social media has a different audience, and [he or she] will use different tools or not use the Internet at all. It really depends greatly on your product and you. Newsletters however, are still very important and really matter in my marketing scheme, because the majority, if not all, of my true collectors are not even interested in social media sites or use them."

As for assessing effectiveness, "I try to manage it by instinct," Wescoat adds, "I know by the results of my efforts. I have enjoyed, however, sites such as Social Mention, Alexa, and Google Analytics for traffic, keywords, backlinks, references, and rates of visits."

"Social media isn't the end-all to success," reminds Wescoat. "It's the icing on the cake. It's the communicator. It goes great in combination with other efforts. I see those who do traditional marketing as well, and they are much more successful than I. When using social media, learn to enjoy the tools and get to know people. It takes a *long* time to build a reputation and trust with others. If you want to sell, you have to put that on the shelf and build the relationships first."

Natasha Wescoat's URLs

www.natashawescoat.com	www.natashawescoat.com/blog
www.natashasartcandy.com	http://artcandy.tv
www.twitter.com/natasha	www.facebook.com/natashawescoat
www.vimeo.com/natashawescoat	www.youtube.com/user/postmodern artist
www.linkedin.com/in/ natashawescoat	www.flickr.com/photos/ natashawescoat
www.myspace.com/ natashawescoatart	

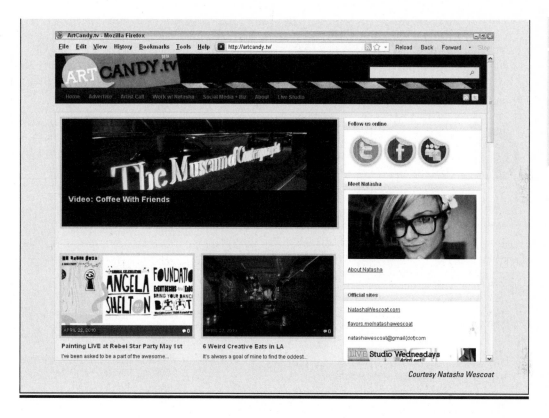

Courtesy Natasha Wescoat

Building Your Social Media Marketing Dream Team

Just for the moment, assume that you have employees who can — and are willing to — share the burden of social media. If you live a rich fantasy life, assume that you might even hire someone to take the lead.

In a larger company, the nexus for control of social media varies: In some cases, it's the marketing department; in others, corporate communications, public relations, sales, or customer support takes the lead.

Some companies disperse responsibilities throughout the company and have tens to dozens of people blogging and tweeting.

If your plan requires multiple employees to leverage LinkedIn profiles for B2B reasons, as well as post on multiple blogs in their individual areas of expertise and tweet current events in their departments, your need for coordination will increase.

Be cautious about asking employees to coordinate links and comments with their personal social media accounts. This task should be voluntary.

Alternatively, on company time and on an account that "belongs" to your company (using a business e-mail address), ask employees to develop a hybrid personal-and-business account where their personalities can shine. Now, individual privacy and First Amendment rights are respected on their separate personal accounts, and you have no liability for the content they post there.

No matter who does the bulk of the work — your staff members or contractors or a combination — always monitor your program randomly but regularly. In addition to getting routine reports on the results, log in to your accounts for a few minutes at various times of the day and week to see what's going on.

Seeking a skilled social director

A good social media director should have an extroverted personality. This person should truly enjoy interacting with others and take intrinsic pleasure in conversation and communication. You might want to look, based on your chosen tactics, for someone who can

✦ Write quickly and well, with the right tone for your market

✦ Listen well, with an "ear" for your target audiences and their concerns

✦ Post without using defamatory language or making libelous statements about competitors

✦ Communicate knowledgeably about your company and products or services

✦ Recognize opportunities and develop creative responses or campaigns

✦ Work tactfully with others, alerting them when problems or complaints surface

✦ Articulate the goals of social media well enough to take a leadership role in encouraging others to explore its potential

✦ Analyze situations to draw conclusions from data

✦ Adapt to new social media and mobile technologies as they arise

✦ Learn quickly (because this field is extremely fluid)

This combination of skills, experience, and personality may be hard to find. Add to it the need to reach different submarkets for different reasons. Now you have several reasons to build a team with a leader, rather than rely on a single individual to handle all your social media needs.

You usually can't just "add" social media to someone's task list; be prepared to reassign some tasks to other people.

Depending on the size and nature of your social media effort, your dream team may also need someone with production skills for podcasting or videocasting, or at least for producing and directing the development of those components. Though this person may not need extensive graphical, photographic, presentation, or data crunching skills, having some skills in each of those areas is helpful.

Hiring twentysomethings (or younger) because they're "familiar" with social media may sound like a good idea, but people in this age group aren't as likely to be familiar with business protocol or sensitive to business relationships, as someone older and more experienced might be. You might need to allow extra time for training, review, and revision.

Looking inside

Before implementing a social media plan, speak with your employees to invite their input, assess their level of interest in this effort, evaluate existing skill sets, and ascertain social media experience. Consider all these factors before you move forward; by rearranging task assignments or priorities, you may be able to select in-house personnel to handle this new project.

Leave time for communication, education, and training, not only at the beginning but also on an ongoing basis.

Hiring experts

Think about using professionals for the tech-heavy pieces, such as podcasts, videocasts, or design, unless you're going for the just-us-folks tone. Professionals can get you started by establishing a model for your staff to follow, or you may want to hire them for long-term tasks such as writing or editing your blogs for consistency.

Many advertising agencies, PR firms, search engine optimizers, marketing companies, and copywriters now take on social media contracts. If you've already worked with someone you like, you can start there. If not, select social media professionals the same way you would select any other professional service provider:

✦ Ask your local business colleagues for referrals.

✦ Check sources such as LinkedIn and Plaxo. If appropriate, post your search criteria on your site, blog, social media outlets, and topic-related sites. In Book VI, Chapter 3, we show you how to post job opportunities on LinkedIn.

✦ Request several price quotes. If your job is large enough, write and distribute a formal Request for Proposal (RFP).

✦ Review previous work completed by the contractors.

✦ Check references.

Creating a Social Media Marketing Policy

Even if you're the only person involved in social media marketing at the beginning, write up a few general guidelines for yourself that you can expand later. In Figure 3-7, the ITBusinessEdge site (www.itbusinessedge.com) shows a simple social media policy.

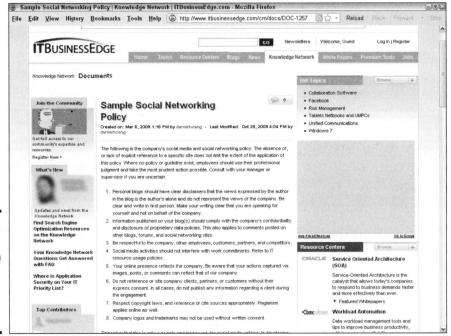

Figure 3-7:
A simple social media policy may be enough to get you started.

Courtesy NarrowCast Group/IT Business

Most policies address the social media issue both in terms of what employees are allowed to do on behalf of the company and on what they aren't allowed to do. For example:

✦ Employees may not be allowed to use personal social accounts on company time.

✦ Some trained employees may be allowed to post customer support replies on behalf of the company, while others are responsible for new product information.

For additional information, see the resources listed in Table 3-3.

Table 3-3	Social Media Policy Resource Sites	
Name	*URL*	*Description*
Daniel Hoang	`www.danielhoang.com/2009/02/21/social-media-policies-and-procedures`	Social media policy article
Digital Brand Expressions	`www.digitalbrandexpressions.com/services/company-social-media-policy.asp`	Free checklist
emTrain	`www.emtrain.com/site/page.php?p=whitepapers`	Free articles and guidelines
Inc.com	`www.inc.com/articles/2010/01/need-a-social-media-policy.html`	Article titled "Do You Need a Social Media Policy?"
Mashable	`http://mashable.com/2009/04/27/social-media-policy`	Article titled "Should Your Company Have a Social Media Policy?"
Mashable	`http://mashable.com/2009/06/02/social-media-policy-musts`	"10 Must-Haves for Your Social Media Policy"
Policy Tool for Social Media	`http://socialmedia.policytool.net`	Free social media policy generator
Social Media Governance	`http://socialmediagovernance.com/policies.php`	Free database of policies for review
Toolkit Café	`http://toolkitcafe.com/social_media_policies.php`	Policies toolkit ($149)

To increase compliance, keep your policy short and easy to read. Try to focus on what people *can do* rather than on what they cannot do.

A typical policy addresses risk management, intellectual property protection, individual privacy protection, and the respect of your audience, company, and fellow employees. Try to incorporate the following suggested concepts, adapted from Mashable (`http://mashable.com/2009/06/02/social-media-policy-musts`):

+ Hold individuals responsible for what they write.

+ Disclose who you are, including your company name and title.

+ Recognize that clients, prospects, competitors, and potential future employees are part of your audience.

+ Be respectful of everyone.

+ Understand the tenor of each social media community and follow its precepts.

+ Respect copyright and trademarks.

+ Protect your company's confidential trade secret and proprietary information in addition to client data, especially trade secret information under nondisclosure agreements.

+ Do *not* allow personal social media activity to interfere with work.

 The complexity of your social media policy depends on the extent of your social media marketing effort and the number of people and departments involved. Generally, the larger the company, the longer the policy.

Staying on the Right Side of the Law

Just about everything in social media pushes the limits of existing intellectual property law. So much information is now repeated online that ownership lines are becoming blurred, much to some people's dismay and damage.

When in doubt, don't copy. Instead, use citations, quote marks, and links to the original source. Always go back to the original to ensure that the information is accurate.

 Watch blogs such as Mashable and TechCrunch for information about legal wrangling. New case law, regulations, and conflicts bubble up continually.

Obtaining permission to avoid infringement

 You can't (legally) use extended content from someone else's Web site, blog, or social media page on your own site, even if you can save it or download it. Nope, not even if you include a credit line saying where it came from. Not even if you use only a portion of the content and link to the rest. Not text, not graphics, not compiled data, not photos. Nothing. Nada. Nil. Zilch.

Though small text extracts with attribution are permitted under fair use doctrine, the copyright concept is intended for individuals and educational institutions, not for profit-making companies. If you don't obtain permission, you and your company can be sued for copyright infringement. In the best-case scenario, you can be asked to cease and desist. In the worst case, your site can be shut down, and you might face other damages.

The way around this situation is simple: Send a permission request such as the one in the nearby sidebar "Sample copyright permission."

Sample copyright permission

Dear _____:

Watermelon Mountain Web Marketing wants permission to use your *(information, article, screen shot, art, data, photograph)* on our (*Web site/blog/social media page*) at *[this URL: WatermelonWeb. com]* and in other media not yet specified. We have attached a copy of the information we want to use. If it meets with your approval, please sign the following release and indicate the credit line you want. You can return the signed form as an e-mail message, a PDF file, a digitally signed document, a fax, or a first class mail message. Thank you for your prompt response.

The undersigned authorizes Watermelon Mountain Web Marketing to use the attached material without limit for no charge.

Signature:

Printed name:

Title:

Company name:

Company address:

Telephone/fax/e-mail:

Company domain name:

Credit line:

Be especially careful with photographs, which are usually copyrighted. Here are a few places to find free or low-cost images legally:

+ Select from the wealth of material offered under a Creative Commons license (`http://creativecommons.org`) or copyright-free images from the federal government.

+ Flickr Commons (`www.flickr.com/commons`) has thousands of free photographs.

+ Search `http://images.google.com` and read the copyright information at the top of each image.

+ Look for stock images from inexpensive sources such as iStockphoto (`wwwistockphoto.com`), Stock Exchange (`http://www.sxc.hu`), or freerangestock.com.

Trademarks and logos also usually require permission to use, though the logos (icons) that social media companies provide for Share This or Follow Us On functionality are fine to use without permission. If you find an image in the Press or Media section of a company's Web site, you can assume that you have permission to reproduce it without further permission. Generally, a disclaimer that "all other logos and trademarks are the property of their respective owners" will suffice.

If it's illegal offline, it's illegal online.

Respecting privacy

Providing a disclaimer about keeping user information private is even more critical now that people sign up willy-nilly online. Individual privacy, already under threat, has become quite slippery with the newly released plans for making a Facebook Connect sign-in available on all sorts of third-party sites. Facebook Connect may make sign-ins simpler for a user, but it gives Facebook access to user behavior on the Web while giving third parties access to users' Facebook profiles for demographic analysis.

Photographs of identifiable individuals, not taken in a public space, historically have required a waiver to use for commercial purposes. When individuals post their images on Facebook, LinkedIn, MySpace, or elsewhere, they may not intend to give permission for that image to appear elsewhere.

Respect a person's space; do not post publicly viewable images of people's faces on any of your social media pages unless you have permission. For a simple photo waiver, see `www.nyip.com/ezine/techtips/model-release.html`.

Revealing product endorsement relationships

Taking aim at companies that were arranging paid recommendations from bloggers (think about the deejay payola scandal of the 1950s), the Federal Trade Commission (FTC) issued new regulations in October 2009 that gave the blogosphere conniptions. The new rule requires bloggers to disclose whether they've received any type of payment or free products in exchange for a positive review.

The rule doesn't appear to apply to individuals who post a review on public review sites such as Epinions.com or TripAdvisor or Yelp, but it applies if you review other companies' products on your blog or send products to other bloggers to request a review. (In 2010, Yelp ran into other legal problems for allegedly requiring companies to buy advertising to balance the appearance of positive and negative reviews on a results page — but that's a topic for another book.)

You can find out more about this requirement from the disclosure resources listed in Table 3-4. Many bloggers, offended by the rules, have found humorous or sarcastic ways to comply; others, such as the blogger shown in Figure 3-8, are more matter-of-fact about it.

**Book I
Chapter 3**

Managing Your Cybersocial Campaign

Figure 3-8:
The blogger sets out a clear acknowledgment policy on product endorsement.

Courtesy 15 Minute Beauty Fanatic

Table 3-4	**Legal Resource Sites**	
Name	*URL*	*Description*
American Bar Association	`www.abanet.org/intelprop/home.html`	Intellectual property resource lists
Cases Blog	`http://casesblog.blogspot.com/2010/04/guidance-on-blogger-disclosure-and-ftc.html`	Blog disclosure summary
U.S. Copyright Office	`www.copyright.gov`	Copyright information and submission
Edelman Digital	`http://edelmandigital.com/2010/03/18/sxsw-essentials-practical-guidance-on-blogger-disclosure-and-ftc-guidelines`	Blog disclosure article
Electronic Frontier Foundation	`www.eff.org`	Not-for-profit focused on free speech, privacy, and consumer rights
FindLaw	`http://smallbusiness.findlaw.com/business-operations/small-business-internet/`	Online legal issues
International Technology Law Association	`www.itechlaw.org`	Online legal issues
Internet Legal Research Group	`www.ilrg.com`	Index of legal sites, free forms, and documents
Nolo	`http://www.nolo.com/legal-encyclopedia/ecommerce-website-development`	Online legal issues
United States Patent and Trademark Office	`www.uspto.gov`	Patent and trademark information, databases, and submission
Word of Mouth Marketing Association	`http://womma.org/ethics/disclosure`	Blog disclosure article

Regardless of what you think of the policy, reveal any payments or free promotional products you've received. You can, of course, be as clever, funny, cynical, or straightforward as you want.

Protecting Your Brand

The three important aspects to protecting your brand online are copyright protection, trademark protection, and brand reputation.

Copyrighting your material

Copyright protects creative work in any medium — text, photos, graphics, audio, video, multimedia, software — from being used by others without permission or payment. Your work becomes your intellectual property as soon as you've created it in a fixed form. The rules for copyright are simple: Protect your own work and don't use other people's work without permission.

Whenever you sign an agreement with a subcontractor, especially a photographer, to create original work for your Web site, social media pages, or other advertising venue, read the contract to determine who will own the copyright on the work they create. In most cases, you can stipulate that their efforts constitute a work-for-hire arrangement, so the copyright belongs to you. (Photographers may give you only a limited license to use their creative work in one application.)

Your employee agreement should clearly state that your company retains ownership of any intellectual property that employees create for you. This area gets interesting if employees post things about your company on their personal social media accounts. It's another reason, if you needed one, for creating a hybrid personal/business account.

Put a copyright notice on your Web site. The standard format includes the word *copyright* or *copr* or the symbol © followed by the year, name of copyright holder, and, usually, the term *All Rights Reserved.* The easiest way to do this is in the footer so that it appears on every page. Here's an example you can incorporate into your Web site or blog, or other uniquely created material:

© 2010 Watermelon Mountain Web Marketing All rights reserved.

This common law copyright notice informs other people that the material is copyrighted and gives you basic protections. For more protection, file officially at `www.copyright.gov`. Basic online submissions start at only $35. Copyright is usually easy enough to file yourself, but call the copyright office or your attorney if you have questions.

You cannot copyright ideas or titles.

Trademarking your brand names

Trademarks (for goods) or *service marks* (for services) give you the exclusive right to use a particular name or logotype within specific commercial categories. You can trademark your own name, if you want, and you must acknowledge the trademarks and service marks of others. The first time you use a trademarked name (including your own) in text on your site, follow it with the superscript ® for a registered mark or ™ for a pending mark that hasn't yet been issued. Provide a notice of trademark ownership somewhere on your sites.

Trademark rights apply online. For instance, only the trademark owner has the legal right to register domain name with that trademark. The same constraint applies to celebrity names. If you think a competitor is infringing one of your trademarks, see your intellectual property (IP) or business attorney.

Fees for online filing start at $275 but depend on which form you must file. Filing a trademark is a bit more complicated than filing a copyright application. For directions, see the trademark section of the United States Patent and Trademark Office site (`www.uspto.gov/trademarks/index.jsp`). Check the trademark database (`http://tess2.uspto.gov`) for availability of the trademark within your class of goods or services, and then follow the prompts. Though you can legally submit a trademark application yourself, you might want to call an IP attorney for help.

Filing a patent is much more difficult, and much more expensive, than filing a trademark. Be sure to consult an IP attorney for patent filings.

Protecting your brand reputation

Start protecting your brand now by registering your name for social media accounts. To avoid "brandjacking," try to choose the most popular, available "handle" that will work across multiple sites. Use your company or product name and keep it short.

Even if you don't plan to do anything else in social media for a year or more, register your name now on Facebook, Twitter, LinkedIn, and Google Buzz and on any other sites you might want in the future, such as Flickr, MySpace, or YouTube. You can do this on every site as you read this book or reserve them all now.

A number of companies now offer tools that claim to assess the "quality" of what people are saying about your company, products, or staff. In addition to counting how many times your name appears, they try to assess the "sentiment" of postings — whether statements are negative or positive. Some also offer an assessment of the degree of engagement — how enthusiastic or hostile a statement might be.

Some people then take this information, along with frequency of posting, and use their own, proprietary formulas to assign a quantitative value to your online reputation, as shown in the example in Figure 3-9.

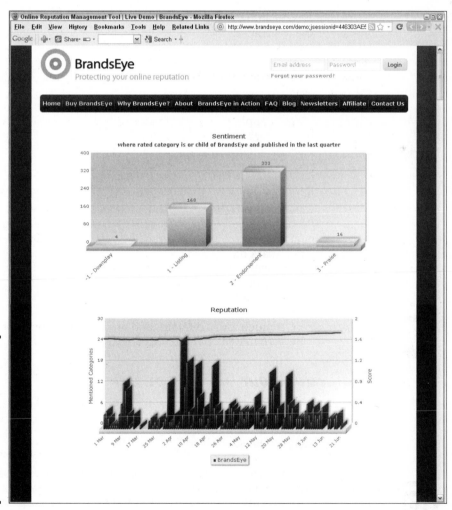

Figure 3-9: BrandsEye offers an inexpensive "reputation" management tool that scales up for larger users.

Courtesy BrandsEye

Be cautious about assigning too much weight to these brand reputation tools, some of which are described in Table 3-5. They may produce widely varying results, and most rely on software that cannot understand complex sentences or shortened phrases with words omitted. If you think your dense sibling doesn't understand irony, don't try sarcasm with a computer!

Table 3-5	Brand Sentiment Resources	
Name	*URL*	*Description*
Alterian	`www.alterian-social-media.com`	Social media sentiment tool; paid, free trial
Biz360	`www.biz360.com/products/community insights.aspx`	Blog and message board sentiment analysis; paid
BlogPulse (from Nielsen)	`www.blogpulse.com`	Automated trend discovery tool for blogs
BrandsEye	`www.brandseye.com`	Online reputation tool that starts at $1 per month
Collective Intellect	`www.collective intellect.com`	Consumer perception tool based on semantic analysis
Jodange	`http://jodange.com/index.html`	Sentiment tool for social and traditional media
Naymz	`www.naymz.com`	Personal reputation on social media
The Net-Savvy Executive	`http://net-savvy.com/executive/tools/monitoring-social-media-before-you-have-a-bud.html`	List of sentiment tools
ReputationDefender	`www.reputation defender.com/my reputation`	Online personal reputation tool
Scout Labs	`www.scoutlabs.com`	Social media sentiment tool; paid, free trial

Name	URL	Description
SitePoint	`www.sitepoint.com/blogs/2009/05/21/tools-manage-online-reputation`	List of 16 free reputation tools
TopRank Online Marketing	`www.toprankblog.com/2008/05/top-10-reasons-for-monitoring-brands-in-social-media`	Article about monitoring your brand online to protect your corporate reputation
Trackur	`www.trackur.com`	Reputation protection tool; free trial
Trendpedia	`http://trendpedia.com`	Blog trend tool; free
Trendrr	`www.trendrr.com`	Qualitative, influence, sentiment, and other trends across multiple social media; paid
TweetFeel	`www.tweetfeel.com`	Twitter sentiment tool; free
Twitrratr	`http://twitrratr.com`	Twitter sentiment tool; free
Twitter Sentiment	`http://twittersentiment.appspot.com`	Twitter sentiment tool; free
WE twendz pro	`http://twendz.waggeneredstrom.com`	Twitter sentiment tool; paid, free trial

Notwithstanding the warnings, experiment with one of the free or freemium sentiment-measuring tools in Table 3-5 to see what, if anything, people are saying. (*Freemium* tools offer a free version with limited features; more extensive feature sets carry a charge.) Those results, such as they are, will become one of many baselines for your social media effort. Unless you already have a significant Web presence, you may not find much.

Of course, many of these tools are designed for use by multinational corporations worried about their reputations after negative events, such as the Toyota auto recall or the British Petroleum oil spill in the Gulf of Mexico.

For you, the sentiment results might be good for a laugh or make excellent party chatter at your next tweet-up.

Chapter 4: Joining the Conversation

In This Chapter

✔ **Lurking and listening**

✔ **Minding your online manners**

✔ **Keeping your audience engaged**

✔ **Creating content that draws and applauds**

*I*t takes some practice to discern relevant information when you first skim the flow of a stream of comments on Facebook or Twitter. Even when you join a threaded discussion in a group or reply to a blog, you're stepping into an already running river of information and relationships.

It seems obvious that the first step is to "get your bearings," just as you would at a conference or party. You can, almost intuitively, assess how many people are present, who they are, how they behave, the emotional tone of the event, and who or what is the center of attention.

Yet many people start gabbing online before they truly grasp what's going on in that particular little corner of cyberspace. Whichever social networking methods you've chosen, start by watching and learning for at least a few days before you contribute. Unless you have unlimited time, select only a few groups, people, or companies to observe in each venue.

Each form of social media has its own search tools, described in Book II, Chapter 2 or in their corresponding books. Search for competitors, keywords, topics, and groups that are relevant to your business. Google Search now also incorporates social media. To sort for those results, click Show Options in the upper-left corner of any search results page; then select Updates in the left navigation area. Results from recent posts on social media feeds are displayed.

After you decide whom to follow or which groups to join, you can incorporate the principles in this chapter to gain invaluable market intelligence and become a valued participant in an ongoing conversation.

Lurking and Listening

You don't have to make detailed charts, but you should pay attention to several factors as you decide whether a specific account is worth following or a particular group is worth your time:

✦ The frequency and quantity of comments on a particular topic

✦ The length of a typical post

✦ Who posts and who receives the most responses

✦ The content of the posts and their relevance to your needs

✦ The quality of the posts and the value of the information they provide

✦ The tone of the communication

✦ The ratio of wheat (relevant to you) to chaff (nonrelevant to you)

Recognize that your goal isn't to become the center of attention, but rather to understand the concerns and interests of your target market, to build relationships, and to establish a reputation for your business. Social media conversations are much more about marketing than about sales.

Recall the old aphorism "You have two ears and one mouth because you should listen twice as much as you talk." That's a good rule to follow for your participation on social media. If in doubt, listen more.

Listening actively

The most important part of any offline conversation isn't the talking; it's the listening. The same concept is true online. You can easily apply active listening techniques to social media. If you're good at sales, you may already use this approach intuitively to understand the underlying problem that a prospective customer is trying to solve.

When you're online, you don't have the luxury of nonverbal cues, such as tone of voice and body language, but you can still pay careful attention to the words on the page and any unstated concerns that may underlie them. The steps for your reply are simple:

1. Thank people for their interest or for bringing up their concern.

2. Repeat the key element of their post in their own words.

3. Ask nonjudgmental questions for clarification, paraphrasing their point or concern. Try to detect an underlying emotional quality to which you can relate or respond.

4. When you're ready to answer with your own point of view, give an example or tell a story. Try to incorporate their point, restated in your own words.

5. Invite further response.

In some cases, you're better off extending a conversation with multiple back-and-forth posts than trying to accomplish all these goals in one message.

Active listening works best when you're sincerely interested in what someone else has to say.

Hearing an opportunity and taking it

The social media world is replete with examples of someone who was truly listening and took an action that made a difference. In many cases, that action resulted in invaluable word-of-mouth recommendations and, in some cases, publicity worth more than any paid advertising.

For instance, FreshBooks, a Canadian-based online billing and bookkeeping service (www.freshbooks.com) with more than a million clients, is a committed user of Twitter (http://twitter.com/freshbooks). One evening in May 2008, an alert employee noticed a stream of tweets from a FreshBooks customer describing how she had been stood up for a date. FreshBooks not only tweeted a message, shown at the top of Figure 4-1, but also sent the client a bouquet of flowers.

The surprised client blogged and tweeted her delight, resulting in hundreds of devoted followers for FreshBooks. The company now gathers from its Twitter feed remarkable insight into problems and requested product features. The gesture by FreshBooks earned it the loyalty of hundreds of volunteer product evangelists who now help with online tech support, reducing the cost of calls to the FreshBooks customer support center. All this was a result of empathizing with a customer's feelings.

Others have followed in the footsteps of FreshBooks. Targus, Inc., an international manufacturer of computer cases and accessories, uses its Twitter account (http://twitter.com/targus_inc) as an inexpensive way to build brand loyalty and increase its number of fans. It frequently offers special giveaways and promotions to its Twitter followers and monitors conversations to discover prospects who are close to a purchase.

Careful attention to the Twitter stream identified a conversation involving someone who had purchased a bag from a competitor and wasn't happy with it. Targus sent him a coupon code for 25 percent off, as shown at the bottom of Figure 4-1. Again, the happy customer wrote others about his experience, became a long-term loyal client, and yielded valuable word-of-mouth recommendations.

The secret to success in each case is being alert, attentive, and responsive.

Figure 4-1:
FreshBooks followed up this famous tweet to a client with a bouquet of flowers (top). Targus tweeted an online promo code to a prospective customer (bottom).

(Top) Courtesy FreshBooks; (Bottom) Courtesy Targus Inc.

A curious and media-savvy operations manager was already using Twitter in October 2008 to build up the clientele for the Houston coffee shop The Coffee Groundz (`http://coffeegroundz.net`). When he received what is now recognized as the first "to-go" order on Twitter, he responded as though it were the most natural thing in the world (see Figure 4-2). Now that the Library of Congress is archiving the entire repertoire of Twitter messages, these two will probably end up on display!

Figure 4-2:
When The Coffee Groundz in Houston received the world's first tweeted to-go order, on the left, it responded immediately, as shown on the right.

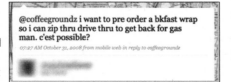

Soon, The Coffee Groundz was accepting Twitter preorders from all its clientele, which has since doubled from all the attention. Continuing its love affair with social media, the business hosts numerous Houston tweet-ups and foursquare events — proof, perhaps, that good things come to those who listen.

Minding Your Social Media P's & Q's

The more the technology changes, the more technology stays the same. Common courtesy and common sense will get you far. The old rules of netiquette apply to social media, whether you're blogging, tweeting, commenting in a LinkedIn group, or posting to your Facebook stream.

Keeping these points in mind keeps your social capital high:

✦ **Be subtle, not self-promotional in your posts.** Avoid blatant advertising.

✦ **Content is king.** Whatever the venue, freely contribute real information. Share resources, connections, and links with other members of the community.

✦ **Avoid using ALL CAPITAL letters in any post.** It's considered "shouting."

✦ **Avoid e-mailing individuals directly.** This advice applies unless they have requested a personal response.

✦ **Respect your audience.** Avoid negative comments, name-calling, and expletives. "If you can't say something nice, don't say anything at all."

If your powers of observation aren't enough to detect the unwritten rules or customs for each of the various networking options, the social media etiquette resources listed in Table 4-1 can help.

Table 4-1	Some Social Media Etiquette Resources	
Name	*URL*	*Article Title*
Forbes magazine	`www.forbes.com/2009/10/09/social-networking-etiquette-entrepreneurs-management-wharton.html`	Are You Practicing Proper Social Networking Etiquette?
DaniWeb.com	`www.daniweb.com/news/story220189.html#`	@Miss Manners — Social Media Etiquette

(continued)

Table 4-1 *(continued)*

Name	URL	Article Title
Community Organizer 2.0	www.communityorganizer20.com/2009/01/12/social-media-etiquette-roundup-understanding-cultural-norms	Social Media Etiquette Roundup: Understanding Cultural Norms
Techipedia	www.techipedia.com/2008/social-media-etiquette-handbook	The Ultimate Social Media Etiquette Handbook

Sticking to business

Though some social media-istas encourage writing from a personal frame-work, that strategy may get you into trouble. The line between being personable and being personal is so faint that it's often hard to follow. You can generally talk safely about your personal evaluation of a product or event or share work-related information about business contacts you met at a trade show, but keep intimate information about your personal friends and children on your personal, friends-only blog.

It's fine to include a brief notice that no one will be tweeting for a week. But don't post that picture of you sipping a drink with a little paper umbrella or riding a surfboard on your social media pages (unless, of course, you're in the business of drinks with paper umbrellas, or surfboards, or travel).

When you become too chatty, you may inadvertently disclose private information about someone else or information that truly is company-confidential. If you feel you must disclose this type of information to a particular prospect, for goodness' sake, use a direct e-mail or, better, the phone. Request a signed nondisclosure agreement before discussing any proprietary or trade secret information!

Do not disclose confidential, proprietary, personnel, or trade secret information. Duh! If you aren't certain what to disclose, just review or revise your company policy. See Book I, Chapter 3 to brush up on your social media policy, if needed.

Selling them softly with your song

Some businesses experiment with hard-core sales promotions, making their feeds nothing more than a continuous stream of ads. Though this strategy might make sense for a coupon distribution site such as http://twitter.com/mommysavers, it doesn't make sense for most B2B businesses or service companies.

There are many ways to reduce the promotional density with other content, especially on Facebook and Twitter:

✦ Include industry news in your feeds.

✦ Increase the frequency of your responses to posts from followers.

✦ Include news and teasers about new products and about appearances at trade shows or craft fairs, or describe how you find new lines to carry or manufacture.

✦ Cultivate a circle of friends in related businesses whose news you can retweet; celebrate achievements, share business suggestions; and encourage each other, as Rotem Gear does with its Twitter feed at http://twitter.com/jrotem, shown in Figure 4-3.

✦ If your company donates to a nonprofit organization, talk about the cause that you believe in and fundraisers related to the organization, whether it's animal welfare, breast cancer, hunger, planned parenthood, or saving the rain forest.

Figure 4-3:
Rotem Gear balances a tweet about its own product line with messages to business colleagues.

Courtesy R. Jean Roth / Rotem Design Studio

Engaging Your Audience

Whether you're blogging or tweeting or posting on Facebook, grabbing — and holding — readers' attention is extremely difficult. The competition is fierce. Nothing succeeds like originality, humor, and meaningful content. Of course, it's an extremely difficult order to fulfill.

Look at the "most popular" writers and posts on different social media. Try to discern the factor that's attracting readers. Use the internal search function for each social media to find people who post in topic area; focus on those with the high numbers of readers or fans.

Keeping it short and sweet

Except for followers of news and educational sites, most readers are looking for short, quick snippets of information. The snippets don't have to be as short as a tweet, but try to avoid long posts, even on your blog. Instead, use multiple short posts on multiple days and link to your hub Web site for more information.

For instance, break the content of a white paper into multiple blog posts of no more than several screens (about 500 words maximum). After each one, provide a link to obtain your complete white paper, for which you can request registration.

Keeping your posts short and sweet is likely to improve your search engine ranking as well as traffic. Find out more about optimizing for search engines using social media in Book II, Chapter 2.

Finding your voice

When you read something by Hemingway or Austen, you know immediately who wrote it. (If only we all had that gift.) Writers may spend years searching for their unique "voices." Every once in a while, you run across someone with a truly creative and original voice — and you know it when you see it.

Heather Gorringe, the founder and creative force behind Wiggly Wigglers (www.wigglywigglers.co.uk), has just that kind of voice. Take a look at her blog at www.wigglywigglers.blogspot.com, shown in Figure 4-4, or listen to the podcasts on her Web site at www.wigglywigglers.co.uk/podcasts/index.html. The story of Wiggly Wigglers appears in the nearby sidebar "Wiggly Wigglers squirms to social success."

Figure 4-4:
The founder
of Wiggly
Wigglers
has an
earthy,
humorous,
accessible,
and
appealing
"voice" on
her blog.

Courtesy Heather Gorringe, Wiggly Wigglers

Wiggly Wigglers squirms to social success

Wiggly Wigglers sells squirming worms for composting, along with seeds and tools and other gardening accessories, to consumers in the United Kingdom and Europe through its online store at www.wigglywigglers.co.uk/shop. Founded in 1991, the company now employs 15 people and was named the 2008 global winner of the Dell Small Business Excellence Award. Unique from its origins, the company envisions itself as "environmentally sustainable and passionate about helping people bring a positive and measurable impact to their surroundings."

According to founder and chief podcaster Heather Gorringe, "We had to go to the market rather than waiting for it to come to us. We are based in a village with a population of 63 with no passing trade and no large towns nearby." She and her husband, "Farmer Phil," who farms their land at Lower Blakemere in England, built their first Internet site in 1996 and starting selling online as soon as possible.

For promotion, "I really wanted a radio show," she explains, "but because we were a commercial organization, that was a real challenge. In June 2005, I found a new section on iTunes called Podcasts and had a real "Eureka" moment. If I could make my own radio show, reach people globally, and talk with them directly, then surely this would build my brand."

(continued)

(continued)

A true podcasting pioneer, she went to the first podcast conference in the United Kingdom in September 2005, with Wiggly Wigglers holding its own against huge companies such as the BBC and Virgin. "We went home, made the podcast on Wednesday, and put it out the Monday after! My plan was simply to reduce my advertising budget and form a direct relationship with potential customers and advocates worldwide. There was no strategy. I just thought that if fans could recommend our company at a click, it did not much matter where they were physically or whether we could actually sell to them."

"We soon realized the power of repurposing content. For example, we have made Wiggly podcasts for gardening magazines at the same moment the Wiggly podcast goes out on our local hospital radio. Our videocasts are now part of our Web site; our blog is used as extra content for our Facebook group and to point folks from Twitter." The site's "Web guy" assists with creating podcasts, but Gorringe and her staff handle the blog, Facebook stream, and Twitter themselves, with a little help from several knowledgeable volunteer customers who assist with the Facebook group.

"It all comes under general marketing and customer service," Gorringe says. "I have enthused about social media, and gradually folks inside the company picked it up and used it or at least respected the power. It doesn't take too much explaining to the customer services manager that someone on Twitter is complaining that their order is late and they have 2,000 followers."

Gorringe, who has a unique and authentic "voice" on her blog (refer to the nearby figure) and podcasts, does most of the writing. "I feel an obligation to communicate with folks. We do what we do. If you like it, follow us. If you don't, find another company. We are not set up to be sophisticated and do not want to appear too clever. This way, we can be controversial

if we want to; we can challenge. And we therefore enjoy our jobs. We are not here to please a certain demographic." (Her podcasts draw several thousand listeners, so it seems that plenty of people like the Wigglers just the way they are.)

Gorringe believes that "small companies can just be themselves and succeed. Honesty and integrity are essential. I think this transparency is beneficial for small companies like ours and allows us to compete against the corporations that are frightened of it."

As for analytics, Gorringe uses the bottom line. "I can see if a particular offer works on Facebook by using a specific [promo] code... Twitter is more difficult to measure. You don't measure the phone; you measure the conversation. Same goes for social media — if it isn't working, you aren't saying the right things!"

She acknowledges that there have been issues, "Like someone saying our service was rubbish. But because I was tracking our company name, I was able to contact them and sort out the problem really well. This turned the customer 'round from fed-up to a fan – brilliant!"

The added benefits are huge, Gorringe notes. "We get TV appearances because of the brand building. We record famous people for our podcast because of the listeners we have." In addition, Wigglers sends out a regular e-newsletter, which she gauges as successful, and attends several shows, like the Malvern Spring Show and the Hay Festival. Occasionally Wiggly Wigglers will advertise on Facebook, post Goggle AdWords, or — rarely — run a print ad. Its other major marketing effort is a print catalogue produced several times a year.

Wiggly Wigglers promotes their social media venues with icons on the Web site and on each other. "We tell folks to follow us on Twitter on the podcast, refer to the podcast on Facebook, etc. And we print details of all these things in our catalogue," Gorringe explains.

"I absolutely love social media. It has enabled us to have the water cooler effect without a busy office or living in a city. We are able to create interest and conversations around our business and contribute easily without physically traveling everywhere."

Wiggly Wigglers URLs

`www.wigglywigglers.co.uk`

`www.wigglywigglers.co.uk/podcasts/index.html?session=shopper:DCFF07C6160c50D94FNkLL4EA719`

`http://twitter.com/wiggled www.wigglywigglers.co.uk/podcasts/index.html` (on-site podcasts)

`www.wigglywigglers.co.uk/cinema/index.html` (on-site podcasts)

`http://wigglywigglers.blogspot.com`

`www.facebook.com/group.php?gid=3120520301`

`www.youtube.com/user/michael`

You can also check out Heather Gorringe's thesis, Nuffield Farming Scholarship, "Web 2.0 & Social Media. Identifying the Opportunities That New Media Can Bring to Farmers and Rural Business" at `www.nuffieldinternational.org/rep_pdf/1253750899Gorringe_Heather_nuffield_report.pdf`

Courtesy Heather Gorringe, Wiggly Wigglers

Staying Engaged

Sometimes the trick to keeping customers engaged is simply to luck into (or plan for) a topic on which people have plenty of opinions. Then let 'er rip. Sometimes you don't have to comment often; just watch and observe.

You're engaged in social media conversations for the long haul. Try not to drop a thread that has had lots of comments.

For example, people debated for more than a year on the blog My Starbucks Idea (`http://mystarbucksidea.force.com`) about the benefits and downsides of Starbucks using compact fluorescent lights. A franchise operator, not Starbucks, initiated the topic, but it caught on. The posting public maintained the thread with little input from Starbucks for about 17 months.

If you're interested in the complete transcript, see `http://mystarbucks idea.force.com/ideaView?id=087500000004CnkAAE`.

This list describes what Starbucks did so well. Try to emulate its work in your social media channels:

✦ **Praise commenters.** In the entry on 8/12/2009 (which concludes the chain), Sue from the Starbucks Global Responsibility department explains which actions the company has decided to take on store lighting and credits blog commenters by saying "with an update to this great idea." She adds other phrases that reflect to readers both the advantages and disadvantages they raised in their postings.

✦ **Show commenters that they're important to you.** The last displayed entry in the sidebar is from Jim Hanna, the head of environmental affairs. First, Hanna introduces himself. Having a department head respond gives greater credibility to the answer and implies, "This comment is important enough that someone with authority is responding." He is answering for the company, not in his personal role.

✦ **Give follow-up explanations with no defensiveness or derision.** Hanna thanks everyone for their posts and the good points they made, validating their input. He simply ignores the crankier posts. Carefully responding to each issue in turn, Hanna explains how Starbucks is addressing it. He makes every point positively, but not defensively. When providing explanatory material, Hanna avoids a patronizing tone. He concludes by describing the Starbucks decision-making process, leaving the floor open to additional comments ("Stay tuned").

You might want to set up your blog to review all posts before publishing so that you can remove any highly objectionable material. However, don't set the filter so high that you remove any negative or critical comments, which would quickly shut off the conversation.

Asking questions . . .

If you don't happen to have readers who are as engaged as the ones at Starbucks (see the preceding section), you can easily encourage responses. At the end of each primary post, ask readers for their opinions by posing open-ended questions. Avoid questions that prompt a simple yes-or-no answer. Here are some examples of helpful ways to ask these questions:

✦ What do you think about this topic, or how do you feel about this topic?

✦ How would you handle a certain situation?

✦ What's your opinion about this topic?

✦ What's your experience with this widget? or How would you rate this widget? Why?

✦ Will you share your story about a certain topic?

✦ What are you doing or working on now in this area?

✦ How would you improve it?

✦ What ideas do you have to solve this problem?

. . . and answering questions

Some topics truly lend themselves to a question-and-answer format. You can repurpose questions submitted by readers and customers, and present them in your blog, Twitter, and Facebook entries. For example, the blog for K9 Cuisine, an online retailer of dog food, has a panel of experts handle the enormous range of questions that bedevil dog owners at `http://blog.k9cuisine.com`, shown in Figure 4-5. It's a helpful way to distribute content from multiple points of view while sharing the workload involved in maintaining a blog.

Being helpful

Sometimes the simplest posts are best. Readers may often need only straightforward information. The best thing to do is supply it, as Milwaukee Electric Tool does on its Facebook page (`www.facebook.com/MilwaukeeElectricTool`), shown in Figure 4-6.

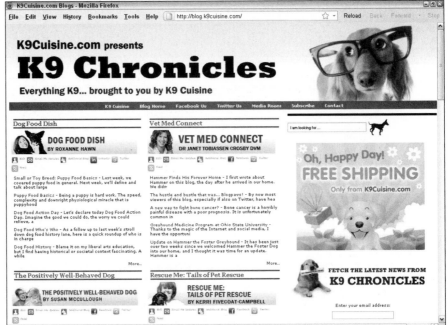

Figure 4-5:
K9Cuisine.com has eight different contributors on its blog, which is set up as a topic index.

Figure 4-6:
Milwaukee Electric Tool responds to customer inquiries that simply require information.

Finding content

Every once in a while, the creative well simply runs dry. Try as you might, you can't figure out what in the world to write about. Try some of the sources listed in Table 4-2 for ideas. If you're truly stuck, look around for a guest contributor to take over for a couple weeks until your juices start flowing again. Or, consider hiring a professional copywriter to help you, perhaps on a long-term basis.

Table 4-2	Blog Writing Resources	
Name	*URL*	*What You Can Find*
BLOGBloke	`www.blogbloke.com/ blogging-by-osmosis`	Blog-writing resources and tips
Copyblogger	`www.copyblogger.com`	Copywriting tips for online marketing success
ProBlogger	`www.problogger.net`	Blogging tips for bloggers
Direct Creative Blog	`www.directcreative. com/blog/writing- resources`	Quick online writing resources
Smashing magazine	`www.smashingmagazine. com/2009/06/28/50- free-resources-that- will-improve-your- writing-skills`	Free online writing resources
Vivid Image	`www.vimm.com/wp- content/uploads/2009/ 07/50-Sources-of- Inspiration-for-Blog- Content.pdf`	Fifty sources of inspiration for blog content
Writers Write	`www.writerswrite.com/ blogging`	Blogging news, resources, tools, and articles

If you decide to use contributors or contractors to write your blog, monitor their postings randomly for accuracy and tone.

Goofing with grace

Stay positive, even when you make a mistake. Graciously thanking a follower for correcting your error and moving on is more gracious than getting involved in defense of your position. If a reader's facts are incorrect, of course, gently call attention to the discrepancy, perhaps with a link to a third-party source.

Some mistakes are minor enough that you should simply ignore them. You don't want your readers to feel that they will be criticized or corrected for every post they make. That's a total turnoff!

Handling critics

One of the trickiest problems for any writer is handling conflicts and critics. For an example, see the e-mail exchange at www.huffingtonpost. com/2010/03/08/personal-responsibilty-v_n_489822.html between Arthur Delaney, a blogger for The Huffington Post, and a reader who took issue with an article about foreclosures, evictions, and bailouts, topics sure to stir emotional embers. The exchange, which took multiple responses to reach a conclusion, took place as a series of direct, private e-mails. This discussion illustrates several good points about how to handle criticism:

✦ Try not to be defensive, and acknowledge the value of another party's point of view.

✦ If the criticism is correct, thank the writer for their input and make the correction public.

✦ If you need clarification, ask the critic to explain himself or herself further.

✦ Use facts, not emotions in your response.

✦ Persist until a point of clarity is reached, even if it's nothing more than agreeing to disagree.

✦ Sometimes it's better to resolve an issue via e-mail, which remains between two parties, instead of conducting a public disagreement. Use your judgment and discretion.

Book II

Cybersocial Tools

The 5th Wave   By Rich Tennant

"How long has he been programming our META tags?"

Contents at a Glance

Chapter 1: Discovering Helpful Tech Tools

In This Chapter

✔ **Learning more about social media**

✔ **Distributing content efficiently**

✔ **Keeping search engines in the loop**

✔ **Giving long URLs a haircut**

✔ **Selecting shopping tools that work with social media**

✔ **Monitoring the buzz**

In Book I, you discover that the key to social media success is planning. As you select tools and schedule tasks, enter your choices on your Social Media Marketing Plan and Social Media Activity Calendar.

Try to select one or more tools from each of these categories:

✦ Resource, news, and blog sites that cover online marketing and social media

✦ Content distribution tools

✦ Tools for notifying search engines and directories of updates

✦ URL clipping tools

✦ Shopping widgets for social media

✦ Buzz-tracking tools to monitor mentions of your business

Fortunately, all these tools are online, so you don't have to lug them around!

You can always jump right into the social media scene and figure out these things later, but your efforts will be more productive if you build the right framework first.

Keeping Track of the Social Media Scene

Unless you take advantage of online resources, you'll never be able to stay current with the changes in social media. Within the space of several weeks in early 2010, for instance, Google deployed its new social networking site, Google Buzz (www.google.com/buzz), companies acquired each other, and NBC, together with Stamen Design, launched the NBC Olympics Twitter Tracker (http://bits.blogs.nytimes.com/2010/02/19/a-visual-tool-to-track-olympic-tweets/?scp=2&sq=Twitter%20Tracker&st=cse), a visual representation of the popularity of events based on the overall number of tweets submitted by individual users, shown in Figure 1-1. You can view the video at www.youtube.com/watch?v=1Rl92Q1IJ0w&feature=player_embedded.

Figure 1-1:
The NBC Olympics Twitter Tracker ran in real time, with video images updated continually as the frequency of tweets varied on different tags.

Courtesy NBC Universal

You might want to subscribe to feeds about social marketing from one or more social marketing blogs or news services or make a habit of checking at least one of them weekly. You might also want to review traffic trends on various social media services weekly; they're amazingly volatile. Table 1-1 lists some helpful resource sites.

Table 1-1	Social Media Marketing Resources	
Name	*URL*	*Description*
AddThis	`http://addthis.com/services`	Traffic trends on social media
BIG Marketing for Small Business	`www.bigmarketingsmallbusiness.com`	Social media, online, and offline marketing tips
HubSpot	`http://blog.hubspot.com`	Inbound marketing blog
MarketingProfs	`www.marketingprofs.com/marketing/library/100/social-media`	Social media marketing tips, including B2B
MarketingSherpa	`www.marketingsherpa.com/social-networking-evangelism-community-category.html`	Social networking research with B2B focus
Mashable	`http://mashable.com`	Well-known social media guide
Museum Marketing	`www.museummarketing.co.uk`	Blog with social media marketing tips for museums but applicable elsewhere
Online Marketing Blog	`www.toprankblog.com`	Blog about online and social marketing
Practical eCommerce	`www.practicalecommerce.com/blogs/5-The-Social-Retailer`	Blog about social marketing for retailers
Slashdot	`http://slashdot.org`	Social news service about technology
Social Media Marketing Blog	`www.scottmonty.com`	Perspectives on social media data from the head of social media for Ford
Social Media Marketing Group on LinkedIn	`www.linkedin.com/groups?gid=66325`	Professional, nonpromotional discussion group; approval required
Social Media Today Blog	`www.socialmediatoday.com/SMC/blog`	Social media blog
Social Networking Business Blog	`http://social-networking-business.blogspot.com`	Social networking blog for business

(continued)

Table 1-1 *(continued)*

Name	URL	Description
Sphinn	http://sphinn.com	Internet marketing news and forums
TechCrunch	http://techcrunch.com	Technology industry blog
Techmeme	http://techmeme.com	Top technology news site

Include the names of resource sites on your Social Media Marketing Plan and schedule weekly research as a task on your Social Media Activity Calendar.

Saving Time with Content Distribution Tools

Social media marketing obviously can quickly consume all your waking hours and then some. Just the thought of needing to post information quickly to Facebook, Twitter, LinkedIn, social bookmarks, blogs, Flickr, or social news services might make any social marketer cringe.

Fortunately, some tools enable you to post your content to all these places at once. You can choose from many good applications for a distribution tool:

✦ **Routine maintenance:** Use a content distribution tool whenever you make updates according to your Social Media Activity Calendar. What a timesaver!

✦ **Quick event postings:** If you want to share information from a conference, trade show, meeting, or training session, you can use most of these distribution tools from your phone to send short text updates to Twitter and LinkedIn. Or, take a picture with your cellphone and send it to Flickr and Facebook. If you want to send something longer, simply use a distribution tool to e-mail your post to your blog and Facebook.

✦ **Daily updates:** Group all social media services that you might want to update with rapidly changing information, such as a daily sale or the location of your traveling cupcake cart by the hour.

In addition to Ping.fm, OnlyWire, and other tools described in the next few sections, you can use Real Simple Syndication (RSS) to feed content to users and to your various social media profiles.

If you have more than three social media outlets or frequently update your content, choosing at least one distribution tool is a "must-have" way to save time.

Reconfigure your settings on Ping.fm or other content distribution tools whenever you decide to add or drop a social media service, or create a new, special purpose group for marketing purposes.

Ping.fm by Seesmic

Ping.fm, shown in Figure 1-2, lets you update some or all your social media sites at one time, for free, and without needing technical help. What's more, you don't have to be at your office computer to do it. You can send text and images from various devices, including your cellphone, e-mail program, instant messaging program, or Skype.

Book II
Chapter 1

Discovering Helpful
Tech Tools

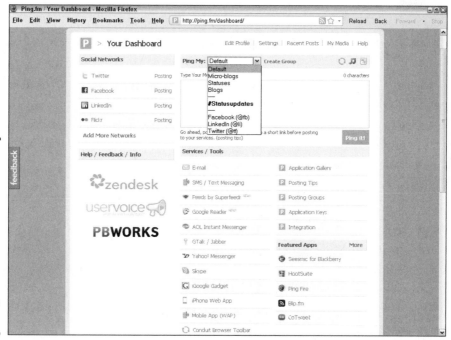

Figure 1-2:
The
Dashboard
page for
Ping.fm
distributes
a posting of
a particular
type to your
selected
social media
services.

Courtesy Ping.fm by Seesmic

Ping.fm posts your updates to whichever social media services you have preselected. You can specify which types of messages go to which services (for example, photos to Flickr and short messages to Twitter).

In the Ping.fm Dashboard (`http://ping.fm/dashboard`), you select the destination services you want. If you don't want everything to go everywhere, you simply create groups to determine who gets what. Other tools operate in a similar manner.

Here's how to use Ping.fm:

1. **Start up at `Ping.fm`.**

2. **Click Add More Networks on the left side of the dashboard (refer to Figure 1-2) to see the full list of dozens of possible destination services at `http://ping.fm/networks`.**

3. **Click Add Network next to each destination service you want.**

   As you select each service, you may be prompted to establish an account or to permit connections in a dialog box. If you don't return to the dashboard or network pages automatically, just click the Dashboard tab at the top of `http://ping.fm/networks`.

4. **Keep clicking Add More Networks, toggling between the dashboard and network pages until you finish.**

5. **Click the Dashboard tab at the top.**

   At this point, you're ready to start submitting content, with each post distributed to your preselected destinations.

6. **To be more selective about which content goes to which service, click Create Group above the message field on the dashboard (refer to Figure 1-2).**

   This step takes you to `http://ping.fm/groups`, where a dialog box appears.

7. **Select the content type (Status Updates, Blogging, Microblogging, or Photo Posting) from the drop-down list in the dialog box and name your group. Click Add Posting Group.**

   Your list of chosen destination services appears.

8. **Select all the services you want to associate with that content group. Then click Add Posting Group.**

   For example, you might want to post photos to your accounts on both Flickr and Photobucket.

9. **Repeat Steps 6 through 8 until you're done setting up various groups. Click the Dashboard tab at the top of the page.**

10. **If you're using a particular tool, such as e-mail, text messaging, cellphone, or another application to deliver your update, get directions by selecting that tool from the list that appears on the dashboard below the message field.**

11. **On the dashboard, select a group or service type from the drop-down list next to the phrase "Ping My." Then enter some appropriate content in the message field and click the Ping It button.**

   All done!

Ping.fm posts to many social media services, but it may not include some of your desired specialty destinations. Try selecting Custom URL from the Ping. fm network page. If this URL points to a script that can accept Ping.fm messages, you're all set. Otherwise, you might need a secondary service or RSS feed to accommodate everything on your list.

Although you can see a history of your postings, Ping.fm doesn't let you track results on these services. For that task, use either the monitoring tools described later in this chapter or some of the measurement tools discussed in Book VIII.

Alternative content distribution services

You have other choices for content distribution to social media services. They all work roughly the same as Ping.fm, but each has its own peculiarities. Choose the one that's the best fit for you.

HelloTxt

According to the HelloTxt dashboard (http://hellotxt.com/dashboard), HelloTxt updates 50 services but doesn't allow you to create groups for different types of content. However, you can add hash tags (# tag) to help your postings end up in the right categories on the destination services. As with Ping.fm, you can update by instant message, e-mail, and text message.

HootSuite

Self-described as "the professional Twitter client," HootSuite (http://hootsuite.com) functions primarily as a way to manage your entire Twitter experience — from scheduling to stats — from one location. However, it now integrates Twitter, Facebook, LinkedIn, and Ping.fm accounts for multiservice postings with one submission.

OnlyWire

OnlyWire (http://onlywire.com) updates as many as 33 services simultaneously, and it's the only tool listed in this section that passes updates to your own Web site or blog via a content management system. You'll need to implement the OnlyWire API (Application Programming Interface) or ask your programmer to do it for you.

OnlyWire also offers two handy bookmarklets:

✦ A toolbar add-in to submit to OnlyWire with one click from your own browser.

✦ A customizable Bookmark & Share button that lets users share your site with all their own accounts at one time. OnlyWire offers the choice of an ad-supported free version or a paid service for $3 per month or $25 per year.

**Book II
Chapter 1**

Discovering Helpful
Tech Tools

Posterous

Posterous (`http://posterous.com`) has a unique approach: You e-mail your text, photo, video, or audio files to `Post@Posterous.com` and it automatically creates a blog page or appends your material. Then it autoposts your content to as many as 26 social media and video services. You can specify posting to only a subset by e-mailing to a different address (`http://posterous.com/manage/#autopost`) or specify an e-mail address for a service that it doesn't ordinarily support. Posterous also handles RSS subscriptions and integrates with Google Analytics for statistical tracking.

TweetDeck

If you love Twitter, this content distribution tool might be the one for you. TweetDeck allows you to control much of your social media campaign through Twitter. Among its many capabilities, TweetDeck lets you update Facebook, MySpace, LinkedIn, Google Buzz, foursquare, and other social networks directly from Twitter (`www.tweetdeck.com/features/update-in-a-click/index.htmltweetdeck.com`). You can update your status, post comments, upload photos or videos, and follow friends' activities on these other sites from the TweetDeck control panel. We talk more about TweetDeck in Book IV.

Putting Real Simple Syndication (RSS) to work

It almost sounds quaint, but RSS technology, which has been around for a decade, is still a viable way to distribute (syndicate) information for publication in multiple locations. The familiar orange-and-white icon shown in Figure 1-3 gained prominence about five years ago as a way to notify others automatically about often-updated content such as headlines, blogs, news, or music. The RSS icon indicates that a site offers a Real Simple Syndication feed.

Figure 1-3:
The RSS
icon.

The published content, or *feed*, is provided for free in a standardized format that can be viewed in many different programs. RSS feeds are read on the receiving end in an RSS reader, a feed reader, or an aggregator. Readers come in three species: standalone, like FeedDemon; add-ons that are compatible with specific applications; or Web-based, like Mozilla Firefox's Live Bookmarks, which adds RSS feeds to a user's Favorites folder.

Feeds may be delivered to an individual subscriber's desktop, e-mail program, or browser favorites folder, or they can be reproduced on another Web site, blog page, or social media page.

You can offer an RSS feed from your site, blog, or social media pages (or display your own or others' RSS feeds on your pages). This feature requires some technical skills; if you're not technically inclined, ask your programmer to handle the implementation.

Subscribing is easy: Users simply click the RSS icon and follow directions. After that, the RSS reader regularly checks the list of subscribed feeds and downloads any updates. Users can receive automatic alerts or view their updates on demand. The provided material is usually a linkable abstract or headline, along with the publisher's name and date of publication. The link opens the full article or media clip.

Subscribers not only receive timely updates from their favorite sites but also can use RSS to collect feeds from many sites in one convenient place. Rather than check multiple Web sites every day, for instance, political junkies can have RSS feeds about Congress delivered automatically from The Huffington Post, *The Nation, The Washington Post,* and *The New York Times.*

Unless you're targeting a market that's highly proficient technically, be cautious about using RSS as your only option for sharing content. Recent studies have found that more than 12 times the number of people will subscribe to an e-mail newsletter than to an RSS feed, except in technology fields. The general public sees RSS as too technical or complicated.

Be sure to enter your choices for content distribution on your Social Media Marketing Plan, and create a schedule for distributing updates (daily? weekly? monthly?) on your Social Media Activity Calendar.

If you're interested in RSS, you'll find the resources in Table 1-2 helpful.

Table 1-2	RSS Resources	
Name	*URL*	*Function*
Atom	`www.xml.com/lpt/a/1619`	Atom feed details
Feedage. com	`www.feedage.com`	Directory of RSS feeds
FeedDemon	`www.newsgator.com/ Individuals/FeedDemon`	Free-standing RSS reader for Windows
FeedForAll	`www.feedforall.com`	RSS feed creation tool

(continued)

Table 1-2 *(continued)*

Name	URL	Function
FeedBurner	`https://feedburner.google.com`	Create, manage, and monitor RSS feeds
Netvibes	`www.netvibes.com/#General`	Combination personal aggregator and social network
NewsFire	`www.newsfirerss.com`	RSS reader for Macs
NewsGator	`www.newsgator.com/individuals/default.aspx`	Offers RSS readers for multiple applications
RSS: News You Choose	`http://reviews.cnet.com/4520-10088_7-5143460-1.html`	About RSS feeds
RSS Toolbox	`http://mashable.com/2007/06/11/rss-toolbox`	Annotated list of more than 120 RSS tools

RSS offers a distinct advantage for sharing site content with readers: one-time-and-forget-about-it installation. After RSS is installed on your site or blog, you don't have to do anything except update your master site. You don't even have to type an entry as you do with the other content distribution tools. Everyone who subscribes gets your feed automatically; you know that they're prequalified prospects because they've opted in.

From a user's point of view, RSS means that after requesting a feed, the user doesn't have to go anywhere or do anything to receive updates — updates arrive at their fingertips.

Unfortunately, RSS coordinates with social media distribution services only if you (or your programmer) enable your other social media pages to accept and display your RSS feed. Alternatively, that person might be able to use a tool such as the OnlyWire API to program your RSS feed to accept updates for distribution to social media.

You may see an icon or a link for an Atom feed. A newer format for syndication, an Atom operates similarly to RSS but uses different technical parameters. While many blogs use Atom feeds, the older RSS format remains more popular overall. Some sites offer or accept only one or the other, so your choice of source and destination services partly drives your selection of syndication format. For more information, see www.atomenabled.org or www. intertwingly.net/wiki/pie/Rss20AndAtom10Compared.

Notifying Search Engines about Updates

Some people think that search engines, especially Google, know everything about everybody's Web sites all the time. Not so. Even the Google grandmaster needs a tip now and again. Though all search engines routinely crawl or spider (visit and scan) Web sites to keep their own results current and relevant, your cycle for updates won't necessarily match their cycles for crawling.

Keeping search engines updated is valuable: Your site is not only more likely to appear in relevant search results but its ranking will also improve from frequent updates.

The solution, *pinging*, is a simple way to get the attention of search engines and directories whenever you update your blog or Web site. Pinging has several other uses online: to confirm that a site or server is operating; as a diagnostic tool for connectivity problems; or to confirm that a particular IP address exists.

Don't confuse the type of pinging that notifies search engines of changes to your site or blog with Ping.fm, the tool for distributing content to multiple social media services.

Pinging can be done on demand with a third-party service, or you can configure your blog, Squidoo lens, RSS feed, and some other sites to do it automatically. Generally, you simply enter the name of your blog or post, your URL, select your destination(s), and click the Submit button, as shown in Figure 1-4. The service then broadcasts a message that your site contains a new post or other content.

Select only one service. Search engines don't take kindly to "double pinging."

WordPress, TypePad, Blogger, and most other blog services offer built-in, automatic pinging every time you post. On some smaller blog hosts, you may have to set up pinging (or submit to search engines) in a control panel. Table 1-3 summarizes some of the most popular pinging options.

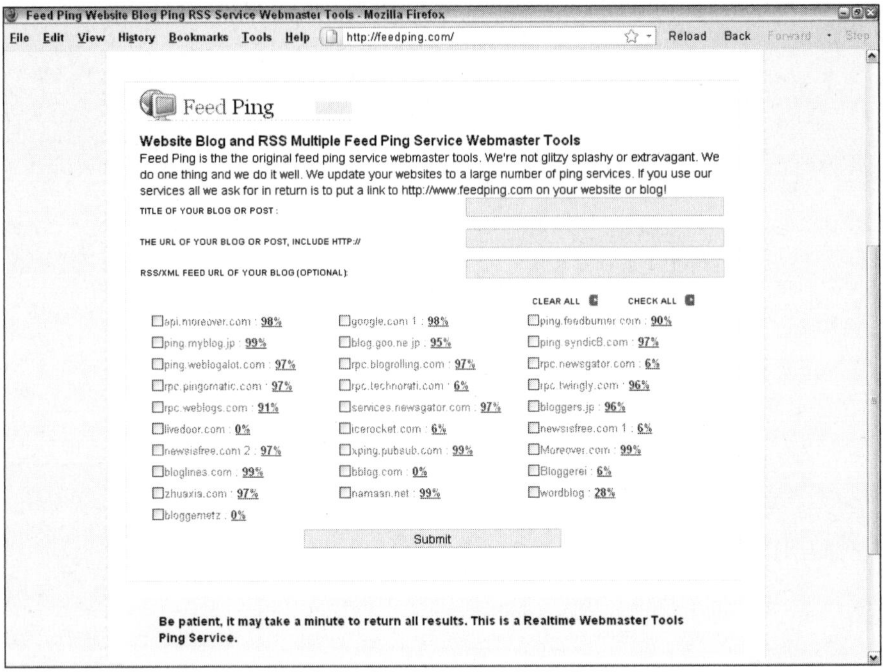

Figure 1-4:
FeedPing
offers
pinging
services for
blogs and
RSS feeds
with an
easy user
interface.

Courtesy Rentex™

Table 1-3	Pinging Resources	
Name	*URL*	*Description*
Feed Ping	www.feedping.com	Free ping service for blogs, RSS, Web sites, international
Feed Shark	http://feedshark.brainbliss.com	Free ping service for blogs, RSS feeds, and podcasts; offers tracking
Google Ping	www.google.com/support/faqs/bin/static.py?page=faq_blog_search_pinging.html	Ping Google blog search
King Ping	www.kping.com	Paid, automated pinging for blogs, tweets, online publishers; free manual version
Pingdom	www.pingdom.com/about	Uptime monitoring service, free for one site; paid service for multiple sites

Name	URL	Description
Pingates	www.pingates.com	Ping service for blog search engines and directories
Pingler	www.pingler.com	Free and paid services for pinging multiple sites on a regular schedule; useful for developers and hosts
Ping-O-Matic!	http://pingomatic.com	Ping service for blogs, RSS, and podcasts
Ping Tool for Squidoo	www.squidutils.com/ping-lens.php	Third-party tool that pings blog search engines when you update your Squidoo lens
Weblogs	http://weblogs.com	Original, free pinging service on the Web for blogs, news, and other sources
What is Pinging	http://ezinearticles.com/?What-is-Pinging-and-Why-Do-You-Need-to-Ping-Your-Blog?&id=1584692	Pinging information
WordPress Pinging	http://en.blog.wordpress.com/2010/02/11/reach-out-and-ping-someone	WordPress pinging service (owns Ping-O-Matic!)

Be sure to enter your choices for a pinging service on your Social Media Marketing Plan. If pinging isn't automatic, enter a task item for pinging below each update on your Social Media Activity Calendar.

Snipping Ugly URLs

The last thing you need when microblogging on sites such as Twitter is a URL that takes up half your 140-character limit! Long, descriptive URLs that are useful for search engines are also messy in e-mail, text messages, text versions of e-newsletters, and blogs, not to mention making it difficult to re-tweet within the limit. The solution is to snip, clip, nip, trim, shave, or otherwise shorten ungainly URLs with a URL truncating service. Take your choice of those in Table 1-4 or search for others.

Table 1-4	URL Snipping Services	
Service Name	**URL**	**Notes**
10 Short URL Services Face Off	`http://www.makeuseof.com/tag/short-url-truncators`	Comparison review article
bit.ly	`http://bit.ly/pages/about`	Popular for Twitter, free and paid versions with history, stats, and preferences
is.gd	`www.is.gd`	Users can find out where a short URL points
Ow.ly	`http://ow.ly/url/shorten-url`	HootSuite's URL shortener
Snipurl	`http://snipurl.com`	Stores, manages, and tracks traffic on short URLs
TinyURL	`http://tinyurl.com`	One of the oldest and best-known truncators

The downside is that the true owner of shortened URLs may be a mystery, so it doesn't do much for your branding. Figure 1-5 shows a typical URL truncating service and the result.

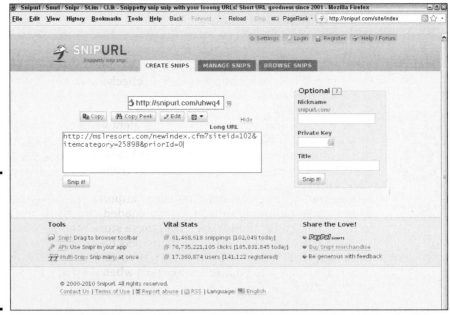

Figure 1-5:
Enter a long URL at SnipURL and receive a short URL in exchange.

Courtesy SnipURL and Mountain Springs Lake Resort (MSLresort.com)

As always, enter the name of your URL snipping service on your Social Media Marketing Plan. To make it easier to track URLs and their snipped versions, select just one service.

Using E-Commerce Tools for Social Sites

If money makes the world go round, e-commerce takes the cybersocial world for a dizzying spin. You have many different options for promoting or linking to your online store from blogs and social networks, but in most cases you can't sell directly. Either the platforms don't support transactions or selling would violate the terms of service.

Always check the terms of service on social media sites to be sure you aren't violating their rules.

Instead, most e-commerce tools display items on your blog or social profile and then link to a third-party application or an existing Web store to complete the transaction.

Indeed, the easiest way to sell from social networks and blogs is simply to post a banner or text link to your own Web site or to other sites that sell your products. Composer and intuitive counselor Max Highstein does this successfully on the Meditations tab of his Facebook site (www.facebook. com/pages/The-Healing-Waterfall/111483778861659), shown in Figure 1-6. Each meditation links to the primary Web site store (www.guided imagerydownloads.com) for downloads and payment. Omelle does something similar in Figure 1-7, using shortened links in its Twitter stream to take visitors directly to its on-site store.

E-commerce widgets are mini-displays of products in your store; these changeable badges link to a real cyberstore. If you already have an online store, check your own shopping cart or check-stand provider to see if it offers a widget for social media, too.

Many vendors offer customers the equivalent widget functionality for use on some compatible social media services. For instance, Zazzle.com offers a Merch Store application for Facebook and Merchbook widget for MySpace; PayPal offers one for TypePad blogs and MySpace.

By comparison, a *virtual storefront* either imports products from an existing online store or allows products to be uploaded directly to a freestanding, online store. At the add-to-cart stage, these storefronts link to your regular Web store or to a third-party site to process the transactions. Though virtual storefront strategies may be a useful way to cast a wider net for customers, they may complicate your recordkeeping when used in addition to an existing Web store.

**Book II
Chapter 1**

Discovering Helpful
Tech Tools

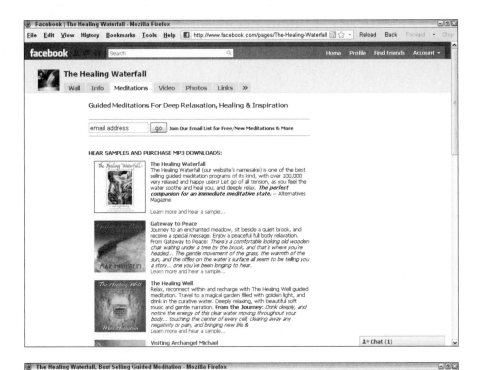

Figure 1-6:
A product offering for The Healing Waterfall guided meditation begins on Facebook and links to the corresponding page on the primary Web site to continue the process.

Courtesy www.GuidedImageryDownloads.com

Figure 1-7:
Omelle,
a luxury
footwear
site, links
visitors from
its Twitter
feed to its
online store.

Book II
Chapter 1

Discovering Helpful
Tech Tools

You can find a list of e-commerce widgets, storefronts, and resources in
Table 1-5.

Table 1-5	Social E-Commerce Widgets, Storefronts, and Resources	
Name	*URL*	*Notes*
Amazon	`https://affiliate-program.amazon.com/gp/associates/network/store/widget/main.html`	E-commerce widget for your Amazon store
Cartfly	`https://www.cartfly.com/stores/new`	E-commerce widget for blogs, social networks (MySpace, Facebook), elsewhere
eBay	`http://blog.widgetbox.com/2009/01/ebay-sellers-build-ebay-widgets-to-drive-bids`	E-commerce widget for your eBay store

(continued)

Table 1-5 *(continued)*

Name	URL	Notes
E-junkie	`www.e-junkie.com`	Cart or buy now buttons for MySpace; fee based on size and volume; handles downloads
Etsy	`www.etsy.com/storque/ etsy-news/tech-updates- etsy-mini-679`	Directions for using e-commerce widget for your Etsy store
Mercantec	`www.mercantec.com/google/ index.html`	Snippet Generator adds shopping cart to sites, blogs, MySpace, or Facebook; has analytics
Netcarnation	`www.netcarnation.com`	Free e-commerce store-front for Facebook, MySpace, Hi5, Orkut, Ning, and Friendster
PayPal	`http://storefront. paypallabs.com/ authenticate/ review`	E-commerce widget for TypePad blogs, MySpace
Practical eCommerce	`www.practicalecommerce. com/search?q=social+ media+ecommerce+widgets`	Articles about using e-commerce widgets with social media
ProductCart	`www.widgetbox.com/widget/ ProductCartEcommerce`	Offers its own e-commerce widget for blogs, social net-work, or elsewhere
Sellit	`www.sellit.com`	Integrates existing hosted shops with social media sites
Shopit	`http://shopit.com/tour#4`	E-commerce on multiple forms of social media and Web sites
Social Sell	`www.provencommerce.com/ social-sell`	Customizable app that integrates with Facebook to share products, coupons; one-time fee
ToldYa	`www.toldya.com`	Sell on Facebook, MySpace, other social networks and blogs; transaction-based fees
Zazzle	`www.zazzle.com/sell/ promotion/promotionbasic# flashPanelWidget`	E-commerce Facebook app and MySpace widget

E-commerce tools, which let you promote and sell only your own products, are quite different from social shopping services, which aggregate products from multiple sources often suggested by consumers themselves and link viewers back to your Web site. We discuss social shopping services, which essentially are social bookmarks for products, in Book II, Chapter 3.

Freestanding e-commerce tools that link to PayPal or other third-party services generally don't integrate with inventory and accounting packages as might a full-featured, on-site shopping cart. If you don't link to your existing cart, you may need to adjust those records manually.

If you use a virtual storefront in addition to an existing on-site store, but don't track inventory automatically, there's another way to track the source of sales. You could create separate SKUs for products that will be listed on different online store locations or at a different price for tracking purposes; for example, items specifically discounted for your audience on Twitter. This approach wouldn't work with automated inventory controls. Some virtual storefront options are listed in the following sections.

Cartfly

Cartfly operates in a manner similar to Netcarnation (see the next section) but doesn't take data from an existing store. You create an independent online store that you can then replicate elsewhere, as long as the site accepts HTML. You can install your store display on MySpace, Friendster, Hi5, Perfspot, Blogger, Xanga, TypePad, Tagworld, Facebook (which has a separate installation procedure), and other sites.

Cartfly (cartfly.com) is unique in offering to let your friends and followers "share" your store, almost as though the store were a YouTube video. By copying and pasting your "share" code on their own Web sites, social media pages, or blogs, your friends can generate dozens of online points of sale. It's like having push carts all over town.

Free to set up and use, Cartfly charges a 3 percent transaction fee on all sales. It defaults to Amazon for payment processing, so you need to set up an Amazon merchant account as well; PayPal is available as an alternative. This option is reasonable if you have no existing online store but want to start selling on the Web.

Netcarnation

Netcarnation Marketplace (netcarnation.com), a virtual storefront tool, supports customizable displays on Facebook, MySpace, Hi5, Orkut, Ning, and Friendster. A mini-storefront can appear on your profile page as well. It imports product information from many platforms, including Zen Cart, Etsy, Amazon, and eBay.

If you have no existing Web store, you can upload individual products and integrate Netcarnation with a PayPal shopping cart.

Netcarnation comes in free or premium versions. The free version, which is ad-supported, displays as many as 10 products. It's perfect if you're just dipping a toe into e-commerce or if you want to feature a subset of your products for a particular audience. The premium version, for $1 per month, accepts as many as 1,000 products and includes multiple-site displays, integration, and promotion.

Premium Netcarnation storefronts can be managed from any of the sites on which they appear. For instance, when you add, delete, or edit products on Facebook, the changes automatically appear on your other selected sites, such as MySpace or Ning.

ProductCart

The ProductCart "ECommerce Widget for Blogs" is designed for its own customers to use. It's an easy way for ProductCart (`www.earlyimpact.com`) store owners to redisplay products taken from their Web site store on a blog (as shown in Figure 1-8) or on a social networking page or on another site. Free with the purchase of the shopping cart, the widget is generated in one click from the user Control Panel. Figure 1-8 shows how aHa! Modern Living uses its blog at `www.ahamodernliving.com/blog` to drive traffic to its online store at `www.ahamodernliving.com/store/pc/viewCategories.asp`.

Operation is straightforward. First, the Web store manager designates specific items in the store catalog as "portable." The widget dynamically loads the selected product information from the store database and displays it on the page where the widget is placed. Simply copy and paste the generated code into any blogging platform or another site that supports JavaScript. For some sites, such as Facebook and MySpace, you must place the widget by using Widgetbox.

When viewers click on items in the ProductCart widget, they link to the existing ProductCart store on your site. The advantages of this approach lie in already centralized inventory and reporting functions.

The ProductCart widget is also an easy way to help affiliates, if you have them. Because they can attach their IDs to the product links, they can also easily use the widget on their own blogs or Web sites, reducing the amount of support you may need to provide. By treating different social media sites as affiliates, you can identify sales generated by each source.

You might want to offer a special sale price or discount just for members of a particular social network. If your shopping cart doesn't provide a linkable widget but supports promotion codes you can always advertise a promotion code, in text or as a graphic, on your social profile pages.

Display products through an e-commerce widget.

Figure 1-8:
The aHa!
Modern
Living blog
uses the
e-commerce
widget from
ProductCart.

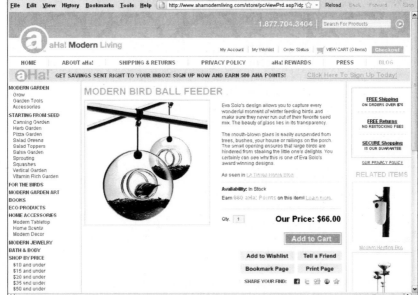

Screenshots courtesy of aHa! Modern Living ™

Sellit

Sellit (www.sellit.com) works like Netcarnation, importing products from Yahoo!, CafePress, Etsy, or Cartfly stores and reproducing product offerings in a Flash-based widget on a blog or elsewhere. Developed by the same team as Cartfly, it works in a similar manner but accepts material from elsewhere. You simply register and paste in your existing shop URL. Sellit does the rest.

Like Cartfly, Sellit offers a Shout icon so that you can post your store on multiple sites and others can distribute it, as long as the destination site accepts an embedded Web application. The Shout function is compatible with Twitter, Facebook, social bookmarking sites, and most blogs.

Basic services are free, with a $12 per month solution for Sellit Pro, which accepts up to 150 products, offers advanced features, and additional advertising impressions.

Shopit

Shopit (www.shopit.com) takes a distinctly different approach. Billing itself as "empowering every Internet user to be a merchant," Shopit is an ad-supported social network itself, but it contains a built-in store for selling products or services.

You can quickly upload items for sale and build a custom widget that's distributed to other social networks, blogs, and e-mails. The widget drives visitors from those sites (for example, from MySpace, Facebook, LinkedIn, Plaxo, Bebo, Friendster, eBay, Craigslist, or blogs) back to a Shopit-hosted storefront.

Though listings are free, Shopit charges a transaction fee and runs through PayPal.

Keeping Your Ear to the Social Ground

The onslaught of data from social media sites can be overwhelming. To garner some value from all the noise, you can take advantage of certain tools to monitor what's being said about your company.

Social media monitoring is about who's saying what. It's about your brand, your products, and your reputation. It's not the same as *social media measurement,* which deals with traffic statistics, conversion rates, and return on investment. Measurement is covered in Book VIII; some measurement tools specific to particular social networks are covered in their individual books (for example, Facebook tools are covered in Book V).

Bring user feedback directly to you. Place a free feedback widget on your site from `http://feedback.widget.me`, `http://crowdsound.com` or `www.makeuseof.com/dir/snapabug-visual-feedback`. More elaborate versions are available for a fee from GetSatisfaction.com. This feature takes some programming knowledge; if you're not up to the task, ask your programmer.

You can find some monitoring tools for specific types of services in the sections that follow.

Deciding what to monitor and why

If you didn't have anything else to do, you could monitor everything. That situation isn't realistic, so you need to set some constraints. Start with your goal and ask yourself what you want to accomplish. For example, you may want to

**Book II
Chapter 1**

**Discovering Helpful
Tech Tools**

✦ Track what's being said about your company and products, both positive and negative

✦ Conduct competitor or market research

✦ Stay up-to-date on what's happening in your industry

✦ Watch trends over time in terms of mentions, topics of interest, or volume of comments

✦ Gain a competitive advantage

✦ Monitor the success of a specific press release, media campaign, or product promotion

✦ Monitor for infringement of trademark or other intellectual property

✦ Obtain customer feedback so you can improve your products and services

After you've decided your goal, it should be obvious what search terms or keywords to monitor. Your list might include:

✦ Your company name

✦ Your domain name

✦ Names of executives and staff who speak with the public

✦ Product names and URLs

✦ Competitors' names

✦ Keywords

✦ Topic tags

Deciding which tools to use

The number of monitoring tools is almost as great as the amount of data they sift through. Research your options and choose at least one tool that monitors across multiple types of social media. Depending on the social media services you're using, you might want to select one from each appropriate service category as well.

The frequency with which you check results from these tools will depend on the overall visibility of your company, the schedule for your submissions to different services, and the overall intensity of your social media presence. For some companies, it might be a daily task. For others, once a week or even once a month will be enough.

If you're not sure where to start, begin with weekly Google Alerts to monitor the Web and daily Social Mention alerts to monitor social media. Add one tool each for blogs and Twitter, if you use them actively or think people may be talking about your business on their own. Adjust as needed.

Using free or cheap social monitoring tools

Pick one or more of the tools in this section to monitor across multiple types of social media.

Mark your choices on your Social Media Marketing Plan. If the tool doesn't offer automated reporting, you'll need to enter the submission task, as well as the review task, on your Social Media Activity Calendar.

Addictomatic: Inhale the Web

Addictomatic (`http://addictomatic.com/about`) lets you "instantly create a custom page with the current buzz on any topic." It searches hundreds of live sites including news, blog posts, videos, and images, and offers a personalized dashboard that you can bookmark and return to for updates.

Alterian SM2

Alterian (`http://alterianSM2.com`), formerly Techrigy, monitors and measures social media, stores the results, and allows in-depth analysis. The free version allows you to store up to five profiles and 1,000 search results per query. You can customize reports and view multiple characteristics of social mentions, as shown in Figure 1-9.

BrandsEye

BrandsEye (`www.brandseye.com`) claims to comprehensively track every online mention of your brand to protect your reputation. The basic package for $1/month offers twice-daily updates on five phrases.

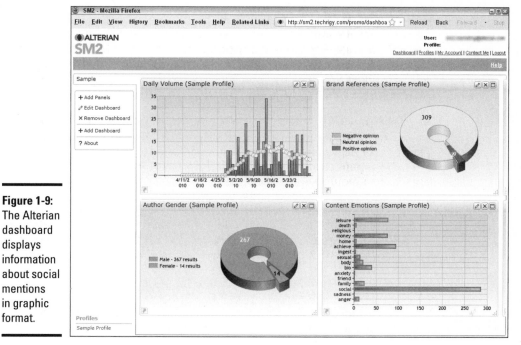

Figure 1-9:
The Alterian dashboard displays information about social mentions in graphic format.

Google Alerts

One of the easiest and most popular of free monitoring services, Google Alerts (www.google.com/alerts) are notifications of new results on up to 1,000 search terms. Alerts can be delivered via e-mail, your iGoogle page, or RSS feed.

You can receive results for news articles, Web sites, blogs, video, Google groups, or a comprehensive version, which comprises news, Web, and blog results.

You set the frequency with which Google checks for results and other features on a "Manage Your Alerts" page. Think of Alerts as an online version of a "clipping" service. Yahoo! (http://alerts.yahoo.com) offers something similar.

Google Trends

Google Trends (www.google.com/trends) compares how frequently searches have been made on up to five topics over time, how frequently those terms have appeared in Google News, and the geographic location that generated the searches.

HowSociable?

Type any brand name at www.howsociable.com to see how visible it is in social media. It's great for monitoring competitors, as shown in Figure 1-10.

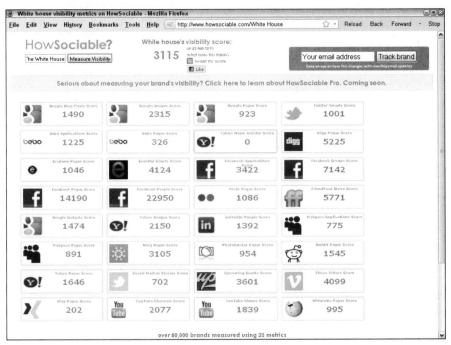

Figure 1-10: How Sociable displays the social media visibility for the White House.

Courtesy Inuda Innovations Ltd. All third-party trademarks and icon designs shown on the Web page are the property of their respective owners.

monitorThis

A free aggregator for up to 26 search engine feeds covering Web sites, blogs, microblogs, articles, news, photos, video, and tags, monitorThis (http://monitorthis.info) is a manual search on a single term. Results can be sorted by publication date or search engine.

Moreover Technologies

Moreover (http://w.moreover.com/public/free-rss/free-feeds.html) offers free RSS feeds from thousands of news and social media sources, enabling you to track your company, your competitors, and a nearly endless list of keywords and topics. For in-depth business intelligence, their Social Media Metabase (http://w.moreover.com/public/products/social-media-metabase.html) searches and monitors hundreds of thousands of blogs, podcasts, video-sharing sites, photo-sharing sites, microblogs, wikis, reviews, and forums on a paid basis.

PostRank Analytics

PostRank (`https://analytics.postrank.com`) monitors something it calls "engagement" on a variety of social media services. It quantifies how often individuals take action after reviewing a particular piece of content (for example, a blog post), which it calls an engagement event. For instance, tweeting, posting a comment, or voting one digg would constitute an event. PostRank integrates with Google Analytics. It costs $9 per month or $99 per year to track five sites, with a 30-day free trial.

Social Mention

Social Mention (`http://socialmention.com`) tracks and measures what is being said about a specific topic in real time across more than 100 social media services. It provides a social ranking score based on "popularity" for every search. Figure 1-11 shows the results for the term "Twitter."

Figure 1-11:
Social Mention provides a social ranking score based on its definition of strength, sentiment, passion, and reach.

Courtesy of Social Mention

You can select to monitor only specific services and choose among service categories of bookmarks, blogs, microblogs, comments, news, networks, video, audio, images, Q&A, or all. While you can input only one term at a time, if you set up social alerts (`http://socialmention.com/alerts`), you can receive daily reports — much like Google Alerts — for multiple terms compiled into a spreadsheet.

In addition, Social Mention aggregates trends (`www.socialmention.com/trends`) in near real time about social media discourse. This feature is handy for market research.

Social Mention also offers real-time widgets (`http://socialmention.com/tools`) to place on your site or in your browser bar. The browser is a simple plug-in, but your programmer will need to copy and paste the widget code onto your site.

Well-heeled social success for Omelle luxury shoes

Luxury footwear company Omelle.com officially launched its Web site with its spring/summer 2009 shoe collection. Founded two years before by Cherise Angelle (president) and Nicole LaFave (creative director), Omelle targets lovers of high-end fashion, particularly those who adore shoes.

LaFave describes Omelle's consumers as "confident, expressive, well-educated, fashion-savvy women living in metropolitan areas." Members of their target market are daily computer users who appreciate the convenience of shopping online, sign up for electronic newsletters from their favorite brands, and read fashion blogs.

Acknowledging that profile, Omelle manages its B2C marketing strictly through social networking and online e-mail campaigns. It reached out specifically to blogs and Web sites already accessed by its target market to increase brand momentum in the fashion industry. Both LaFave and Angelle directly contact bloggers through e-mail to make the experience more personal.

In addition to its Web site, Omelle uses Twitter (`http://twitter.com/omelle` (refer to Figure 1-7), Facebook (`www.facebook.com/pages/omelle/19617863068`) (see the following figure), and their own *Shoetales* blog (`http://omelle.com/shoetales`) to connect directly with customers. They also both use their own Facebook and Twitter pages (`twitter.com/nicolelafave` and `twitter.com/cheriseangelle`) to give customers a more personal connection to the brand, while linking back to the primary Omelle site.

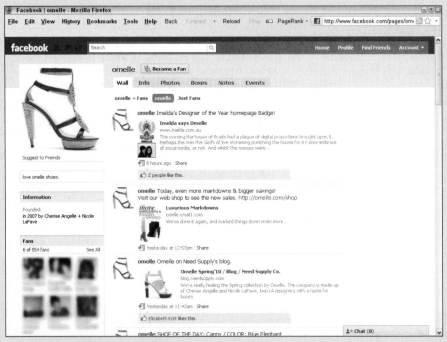

Courtesy Angelle & LaFave, LLC dba Omelle

"Places like Facebook and Twitter allow us to interact with a broad, captive audience with little or no marketing costs associated," LaFave says. "As a start-up, in these current economic conditions, you would be a fool not to." However, she segments the social media marketplace carefully. Core customers willing to buy at regular price points may not be on Twitter, she explains, but Twitter has a secondary market that watches for designer merchandise on sale.

Social bookmarks on sites like Kaboodle, StumbleUpon, and Delicious followed organically afterwards.

On average, LaFave and Angelle each spend about an hour per day researching what is being said about the Omelle brand online, implementing social networking, tweeting about sales or news, and maintaining the Omelle.com Web store. They rely primarily on Google Alerts to follow the "buzz" and Google Analytics to track results of their efforts.

Trackur

Trackur (www.trackur.com) tracks all forms of social media including blogs, news, networks, RSS feeds, Tweets, images, and video. In addition to displaying conversational content, it presents trends over time and analyzes any Web site mentioning a term being monitored. You can get a free account with one saved search and unlimited results. Monthly plans with updates twice/hour start at $18/month.

WhosTalkin.com

WhosTalkin.com (www.whostalkin.com) is another free, real-time search tool. It surveys 60 social media services for current conversations in the categories of blogs, news, networks, videos, images, forums, and tags. It lacks the reporting capabilities of Social Mention, but it does include actual comments. WhosTalkin.com provides results for only one term at a time, but offers a browser search plug-in and an iGoogle gadget.

Measuring the Buzz by Type of Service

The number of monitoring tools competing for market share is astonishing. The following tables are not intended to be comprehensive lists but simply to provide some idea of what's out there. You can always search for free tools in each category to get more options.

Table 1-6 lists tools for monitoring blogs and forums; Table 1-7 tools for news, RSS, and geo-location sites; Table 1-8 tools for Twitter; and Table 1-9, some high-end tools at the enterprise level.

To ensure that your own blog appears in a timely fashion in blog monitoring tools, submit your blog to each one and set up pinging.

Table 1-6 **Blog and Forum Monitoring Tools**

Name	URL	Description
BackType	`www.backtype.com`	Monitors conversations on blogs and Twitter
BoardTracker	`www.boardtracker.com`	Searches forums and message boards, free and premium accounts
Blogdigger	`www.blogdigger.com`	Delivers blog search content in an RSS feed
Bloglines	`www.bloglines.com`	Delivers blog search content in an RSS feed
BlogPulse	`www.blogpulse.com`	Automated keyword or URL search of blogosphere with RSS feed; profile, tracking, and trend tools available
coComment	`www.cocomment.com`	Track comments on any Web page; compiles trends and top commentators
Google Blog Search	`http://blogsearch.google.com`	Master search engine for all blogs with an RSS or Atom feed, not just Google's own blogger.com; can segment by topic; displays by popularity
Lijit	`www.lijit.com`	Customizable search tool with statistics for your own blog to monitor what topics readers are searching for; can add sites you have bookmarked, your blogroll, posts by your social networking contacts, and other feeds
Technorati	`http://technorati.com`	The first real-time blog search engine; ranks authority and influence of blogs and has more comprehensive index of blog popularity
Trendpedia	`http://www.trendpedia.com/`	Free blog search tool

Table 1-7   Social News, RSS, and Geo Monitoring Tools

Name	URL	Description
Find Articles	`www.findarticles.com`	Monitor traditional media channels for keyword mentions
foursquare	`http://foursquare.com`	A geo-location tool for mobile phone or Web that displays where users are located; good for local marketing
Google News	`http://news.google.com`	Keyword search of Google News saved into RSS for automated updates
Google Reader	`http://reader.google.com`	Aggregates your news services and blogs in one place
IceRocket	`www.icerocket.com`	RSS feed for results of your keyword search
Loopt	`www.loopt.com`	Shows where users are located when they access social media via mobile phone; good for local marketing
PubSub	`www.pubsub.com`	Keyword searches saved to RSS feed; allows alerts for posts constrained to specific areas such as press releases, SEC/EDGAR filings, news groups, or blogs
Yahoo! News	`http://news.yahoo.com`	Keyword search of Yahoo!News saved into RSS for automated updates

Table 1-8   Twitter Monitoring Tools

Name	URL	Description
BackTweets	`www.backtweets.com`	searches for links mentioned on Twitter; from BackType
CoTweet	`www.cotweet.com`	Allows multiple people to communicate, in sync, through corporate Twitter accounts

(continued)

Table 1-8 *(continued)*

Name	URL	Description
SocialOomph	`www.socialoomph.com`	Formerly TweetLater.com, one-stop shop to monitor and manage Twitter
twalala	`http://twalala.com`	Twitter client that filters your twitter stream by keywords; has a mute button
TweetBeep	`http://tweetbeep.com`	Like Google Alerts for Twitter
TweetDeck	`www.tweetdeck.com/features/follow-topics-in-real-time-with-saved-searches/index.html`	Auto-update search results from Twitter on multiple search terms; one of many tools available
TweetMeme	`http://tweetmeme.com`	Aggregates popular links on Twitter for popularity reporting
Twellow	`http://twellow.com`	Analyzes public tweets by categories to narrow search and identify influential tweeters in your categories
Twitter Search	`http://search.twitter.com`	Twitter's own search filter with advanced queries

Figure 1-12 shows the results of a typical Twitter search.

Figure 1-12:
Results
page from
search.
twitter.
com for *san
+ francisco
+ hotels.*

Table 1-9   Fee-Based, Enterprise-Level Monitoring Tools

Name	*URL*	*What It Does*
Cymfony	www.cymfony.com	Identifies people, issues, and trends in social and traditional media; for marketing and PR pros
eCairn Conversation	www.ecairn.com	Integrates and analyzes multiple social media sources for marketing and PR pros; starts at $99/ month
Gigya	www.gigya.com/public/ platform/Analyze.aspx	Social optimization tools for online businesses, including monitoring and analysis
FiltrBox	www.filtrbox.com	Tracks across multiple sources online for master list of mentions

(continued)

Table 1-9 *(continued)*

Name	URL	What It Does
Klout	http://klout.com	Measures influence and impact of your content across social media
Nielsen's BuzzMetrics	http://en-us.nielsen. com/tab/product_ families/nielsen_buzz metrics	Deep Web analysis of consumer-generated content in online communities, message boards, groups, blogs, opinion sites, and social networks.
Radian6	www.radian6.com	Monitors real-time conversations in all forms of social media, including boards, forums, networks, blogs, video, images, opinion sites, and mainstream media; designed for marketing and PR pros
Scout Labs	www.scoutlabs.com	Web-based application to monitor customer response
Spiral16's Spark	www.spiral16.com/ spark	Advanced software tools for monitoring social media and sentiment with sophisticated reporting
Sysomos' Heartbeat	www.sysomos.com/ products/overview/ heartbeat	Real-time monitoring and measurement tool for buzz and sentiment

Chapter 2: Leveraging Search Engine Optimization (SEO) for Social Media

In This Chapter

✔ Focusing on the right search engines

✔ Choosing keywords

✔ Writing metatags

✔ Optimizing content and sites for search engines

✔ Conducting inbound link campaigns

✔ Implementing SEO on social media

✔ Gaining visibility in real-time search

*N*o matter how popular social media may be, search engine optimization (SEO) must still be a part of your toolkit for a successful, broad spectrum Web presence. The goal of SEO is to get your Web pages to appear near the top of search results — preferably in the top ten — on general search engines or in search results for specific social media services. You accomplish this by selecting appropriate search terms or keywords and then optimizing content, navigation, and structure to create a Web page or profile that's "search-friendly" for your selected terms.

You can optimize social media, from blogs to Facebook, very much the same way that you optimize a Web site. Some people call this Social Media Optimization (SMO), referring to the application of SEO techniques to social media.

If you do a good job optimizing multiple components of your Web presence — your Web site, blog, Facebook page, Twitter profile, and more — they will all appear near the top of Search Engine Result Pages (SERP) on selected terms, increasing your company's share of that premium screen real estate. As mentioned in Book I, Chapter 1, improving search engine ranking is one strategic justification for implementing a social media campaign in the first place.

Making the Statistical Case for SEO

News of the growth of social media usage sometimes overshadows the actual numbers. For instance, The Nielsen Company shows that by April 2010, Facebook — with its exponential growth in the second half of 2009 — rose to third place in unique U.S. monthly visitors (122.3 million), but Google (150.1 million) and Yahoo! (128.5 million) still topped the charts.

And just because more than 400 million people worldwide (70 percent outside the U.S.) are called active Facebook users doesn't mean they're all using it to search for information that might lead them to your company.

In fact, Nielsen research showed that though a committed segment of Internet users dubbed the *socializers* — about 18 percent across multiple social sites — prefer peer-reviewed social media to find new information, the vast majority of users still opt for portals, search engines, or other information-heavy sites, as shown in Figure 2-1. To reach that majority, SEO remains the technique of choice.

Figure 2-1:
In October 2009, The Nielsen Company surveyed Internet users to see how they look for new information online.

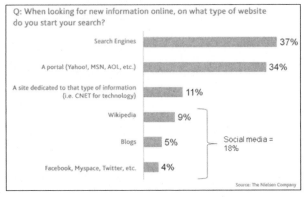

Courtesy The Nielsen Company

Though U.S. Internet users spent more than five times as many hours per month on Facebook as they did on Google in April 2010, this disparity reflects the difference in the nature of the task and purpose of each site. The data is interesting for many other reasons, but isn't relevant when you decide whether to include SEO in your online marketing efforts.

At the moment, no social media alternative covers as wide a base of Web pages or as commanding an algorithm for assessing relevance as search engines. What will happen in the future? Get out your crystal ball, or watch Nielsen and other sites for more data. One thing about the Web is for sure — like the world, it always turns.

Given these statistics, do you still need to bother with search engine optimization techniques for your Web hub? Absolutely. Here's why:

✦ Not all members of your target audience are active users of social media, especially if you have a business-to-business (B2B) company.

✦ The techniques and tools used to find good search terms and to optimize pages transfer quickly to social media, especially to blogs and tweets.

✦ You can optimize social media pages all you want, but they are always of secondary importance except in real-time search. You must first optimize your hub Web site or blog, registered under your own domain name, to get good results.

✦ Social media services still aren't well equipped to handle e-commerce, database applications, forms, or many of the other myriad features that a full-fledged Web site can deliver. For your Web site or blog to be found other than by links from social media, it must perform well on search engines.

✦ SEO remains an essential, though not sufficient, method of ensuring site visibility based on a method other than the number of friends, fans, or followers you have. You're chasing profits, not popularity.

Book II
Chapter 2

Leveraging
Search Engine
Optimization (SEO)

SEO isn't an end in itself. The goal is to draw qualified visitors to your Web site so that you can turn them into customers and clients. A strong SEO foundation helps direct traffic to your full-featured hub from your social media presence.

For more information about search engine optimization, see *Search Engine Optimization All-in-One For Dummies,* by Bruce Clay.

Thinking Tactically and Practically

The best results for SEO sprout from the best content — and so does the largest stream of qualified prospects. Though we talk about many SEO techniques in this chapter, none of them will work unless you offer appealing content that draws and holds the attention of your audience.

Two schools of thought drive SEO tactics for social media:

✦ Optimize your Web site and all your social media for the same search terms, occupying many slots on page one of results with one or more of your Web sites.

✦ Use your social media pages to grab a good position for some relatively rare search terms that your Web site doesn't use.

Search engine jargon

Help yourself by mastering the terminology you see on search engine resource sites or in articles:

- **Spiders, crawlers, or robots (bots)** are automated programs used by search engines to visit Web sites and index their content.

- **Search engine optimization (SEO)** is the process of adjusting Web sites and pages to gain higher placement in search engine results.

- **Natural or organic search** refers to the type of search results produced by a search engine's algorithm (set of rules) when indexing unpaid submissions.

- **Paid search** results are those for which a submission fee or bid has been paid to appear in sponsorship banners at the top of a page, in pay per click (PPC) ads in the right margin, or in some cases at the top of the list of search results.

- **Search engine marketing (SEM)** combines both natural and paid search activities.

 Get greedy. Go for the best of both worlds. Use your standard search terms on social media profiles and the more rarely used terms on individual posts, photo captions, or updates.

Use the free trial at WebPosition.com or the low-cost trial at ZoomRank.com to see how your site ranks on different search terms. Your tactical decisions about keyword selection may depend on those results, as well as on the goals and objectives of your social media campaign.

In the later section, "Selecting the Right Keywords," you discover how to select terms that people are likely to use and ones on which you have a chance of breaking through to the first page of search results.

Focusing on the Right Search Engines

Ignore all those e-mails about submitting your site to 3,000 search engines. You need to submit to the top three: Google, Yahoo!, and Bing. (Table 2-1 tells where to find where to submit your sites to those search engines.)

Table 2-1   Submission URLs for Three Key Search Engines

Name	URL	Search Percentage in January 2010	Feeds
Google	www.google.com/addurl	65.4	AOL, Ask, iWon, Netscape
Yahoo!	http://siteexplorer.search.yahoo.com/submit	17	AltaVista, AlltheWeb, Lycos
Bing	www.bing.com/docs/submit.aspx	11.3	Stand-alone

According to Comscore, these three accounted for 93.7 percent of all searches in January 2010, with Google executing almost four times as many searches as Yahoo!, its closest competitor. All remaining search engines together accounted for the remaining 6.3 percent of searches. Together, these primary search engines feed results to all the significant secondary search engines (refer to Table 2-1). You can also check out www.bruce clay.com/searchenginerelationshipchart.htm.

These primary search engines now spider the Web incessantly. You don't need to resubmit your site routinely. But you should resubmit to trigger a visit from the arachnids if you add new content or products, expand to a new location, or update your search terms.

Fortunately, you can ping search engines to notify them of changes automatically, as discussed in Book II, Chapter 1. After receiving a ping, search engines crawl your site again.

Different search engines use different *algorithms* (sets of rules) to display search results, which may vary rapidly over time. To complicate matters further, they tend to attract different audiences. Optimize your site for the search engine that best attracts your audience:

✦ Google has about a 77 percent market share for B2B purchasing.

✦ According to Quantcast,com, Google's 2010 audience tends to be users who are younger (13 to 34), but more affluent than the overall Internet population, and more have a graduate school education. Alexa data show more users who browse at work use Google than use Yahoo! or Bing, which is congruent with its B2B role.

✦ Yahoo! users skew older than Google's, and are more likely to be female and more ethnically diverse than the Internet population overall.

✦ Bing, while having a much smaller share of users, attracts those who are older than 45 and more likely to be male. It has a reputation for searchers who are more apt to convert to buyers, especially for shopping and travel searches. Like Yahoo!, its users are more affluent than the Internet population overall.

Selecting the Right Keywords

First, let's dispense with one major source of confusion. *Tags* are the social media equivalent of *keywords* or *search terms* (several keywords together, such as *New Mexico artists*). Users enter keywords, phrases, or tags into the query box on a search engine, Web site, or social media service to locate the information they seek.

For good visibility on a search term, your site or social media profile needs to appear within the top ten positions on page one of search results for that term. Only academic researchers and obsessive-compulsives are likely to search beyond the first page.

Fortunately or unfortunately, everyone's brain is wired a little differently, leading to different choices of words and different ways of organizing information. Some differences are simple matters of dialect: Someone in the southern United States may look for *bucket* while someone in the north looks for a *pail*. Someone in the U.K. may enter *cheap petrol* while someone in the United States types *cheap gas*.

Other differences have to do with industry-specific jargon. *Rag* has one meaning to someone looking for a job in the garment industry and another meaning to someone wanting to buy a chamois to polish their car.

Other variations have to do with spelling simplicity. Users invariably look for words spelled phonetically; they rarely type a phrase that's longer than four words.

The average length of a search query has been increasing. As of March 2009, it was about 3.1 words per search, but this number varies by search engine. Longer search queries are more likely to lead to conversions.

Try to come up with a list of at least 30 search terms that can be distributed among different pages of your Web site. You must juggle the terms people are likely to use to find your product or service with the likelihood that you can show up on the first page of search results.

Here are some tips to help you build a list of potential keywords to thread that needle:

✦ Brainstorm all possible terms that you think your target audience might use. Ask your customers, friends, and employees for ideas.

✦ Be sure your list includes the names of all your products and service packages and your company name. Someone who has heard of you must absolutely be able to find you online.

✦ Incorporate all the industry-specific search terms and jargon you can think of.

✦ If you sell to a local or regional territory, incorporate location into your terms: for example, *Lancaster bakery* or *Columbus OH chiropractor*. It's very difficult to appear on the first page of results for a single word like *bakery*, *chiropractor*, or *hotel*.

✦ Use one or more of the free search tools listed in Table 2-2 to get ideas for other keywords, how often they're used, and how many competing sites use the same term. Figure 2-2 displays results and synonyms from the Google Keyword Search tool for the phrase *portrait photographer*. (Intended to help buyers of Google AdWords, this tool is also useful when brainstorming search terms.)

Table 2-2	Keyword Selection Resources	
Name	*URL*	*Description*
Digital Point	`www.digitalpoint.com/tools/keywords`	Free keyword tracker and keyword ranking tool
EzineArticles.com	`http://ezinearticles.com/?Keyword-Selection-For-Your-Website-Marketing---Top-Tips-to-Think-About-For-Your-Website&id=3487516`	Keyword selection tips
Google Insights	`www.google.com/insights/search`	Research trends in search terms
Google Keyword Tool	`https://adwords.google.com/select/KeywordToolExternal`	Free keyword generator and statistics
Google Wonder Wheel	`www.googlewonderwheel.com/google-wonder-wheel-step-by-step`	Free visual display of related keywords for brainstorming
KGen	`https://addons.mozilla.org/en-US/firefox/addon/4788`	Shareware add-on for Firefox toolbar showing which keywords are strong on visited Web pages

(continued)

Table 2-2 *(continued)*

Name	URL	Description
SEMrush.com	http://semrush.com	Competitor keyword research for Google organic search and AdWords
Wordpot	www.wordpot.com	Keyword suggestion tool; free basic version
WordStream	www.wordstream.com/keyword-generator	Free basic keyword tools
Wordtracker	www.wordtracker.com	Keyword suggestion tool; free trial

Figure 2-2:
The Google Keyword Tool displays the frequency of requests for related search terms and the volume of competing advertisers for that term.

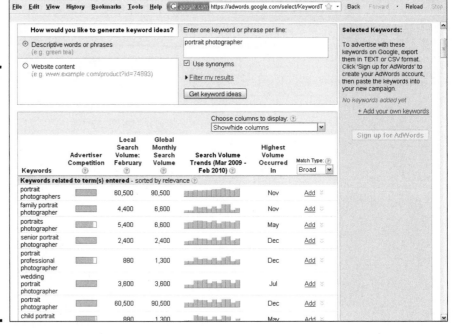

✦ Check your competitors' search terms for ideas. Visit your competitors' sites and, in Internet Explorer, choose View⇨Source. (Look for a similar command in other Internet browsers.) The keywords are usually listed near the top of the source code for a page. If you don't see them, try using the Find command CTRL-F to search for *keyword*.

✦ Not sure who your competitors are? Enter one of your search terms to identify similar companies appearing on the first page of search results. Then you can go look at their other keywords, too.

✦ Look at the *tag clouds* for topics on social news services or blog search engines such as Technorati (www.technorati.com) to assess the relative popularity of different search terms. Tag clouds visualize how often keywords appear in specific content or how often they're used by searchers, with the most popular terms usually appearing in larger type.

✦ Avoid using single words except in technical fields or where the word is a "term of art," such as *seismometer* or *angiogram*, with only hundreds of thousands, instead of millions, of competing pages. Not only will you have too much competition on generalized single words but results for single words also produce too wide a range of options. People simply give up.

Understanding tags and tag clouds

Tags, another term for keywords, are commonly used on blogs, social media, and content-heavy sites other than search engines to categorize content and help users find material. *Tag clouds* are simply a way to visualize either how often keywords appear in specific content or how often they are used by searchers.

Keywords in a tag cloud are usually arranged alphabetically or with common terms grouped and displayed as a paragraph. The more frequently used terms (minus common elements such as articles and prepositions) appear in the largest font, as shown in Figure 2-3.

Reproduced with permission of Yahoo! Inc. © 2010 Yahoo! Inc. YAHOO!, the YAHOO! logo, FLICKR, the FLICKR logo, DELICIOUS, and the DELICIOUS logo are registered trademarks of Yahoo! Inc.

Figure 2-3:
The large tag cloud shows the most popular tags given to photos uploaded to Flickr.

Tag clouds can help you quickly grasp the popularity of particular topics, the terms that people most often use to find a topic, or the relative size or frequency of something, such as city population or usage of different browser versions.

When you submit to social bookmarking or social news services, you're often asked to enter a list of helpful tags so that other people can search for your story. The first rule is to use tags that match your primary search terms and ensure that those terms appear within your text.

Often, people simply "guess" which terms to use, leading to a process of collaborative tagging known as a *folksonomy,* a kind of common-sense group classification of material. The tags that people actually use may diverge from your ideal set, particularly on social media.

You can quickly generate a tag cloud for content by using a tool like the Tag Cloud Builder at `http://tagcloud.oclc.org/tagcloud/TagCloudDemo`. Simply paste in text or enter a URL and select the number of terms to display. You can then enter the most frequently appearing words as the tags when you submit content to a social service.

Use the tag clouds on social media to help determine the popularity of various topics as you decide which content to post. You can also modify the tags you use to categorize your postings. Include or default to commonly used tags when you make your submission, to increase the likelihood that your posting shows up in search results.

Crafting a page, blog posting, or social media profile for more than four or five search terms is difficult. Break up your list of terms into sets that you think you can work into a single paragraph of text while still making sense.

Optimizing for search terms that real people rarely use doesn't make sense. Sure, you can be number one because you have no competition, but why bother? The exceptions are your company and product names and terms highly specific to your business.

Always test your selected search terms to be sure that sites like yours show up in the results for that term. For instance, entering *artificial trees* as a search term yields inexpensive artificial Christmas trees, especially at the holiday season, and perhaps some silk palm trees. However, that term doesn't produce appropriate results if your company offers $30,000 model trees used in zoos or museums.

Maximizing Metatag Muscle

Search engines, especially Yahoo! and Bing, use *metatags* to help rank the relevance of a Web site, blog, or social media page to a search query. Historically, engines needed many types of *metadata* (data that describes a Web page overall) to categorize a Web site, but now only the Page Title and Page Description tags are required; the Keyword tag remains helpful to human beings as well as engines. Search engines can automatically detect the rest of the information they need, and too many metatags just slow them down.

Don't confuse the term *metatags*, which appear in page source code, with the term *tags*, the label used to refer to keywords in social media.

To view metatags for any Web site, choose View⇨Source in Internet Explorer; look for a similar command in other browsers. (On a PC, you can also right-click a Web page and choose View Source.) You see a display like the one shown in Figure 2-4, which shows the primary metatags for the main weddings page on MSLresort.com, a resort that offers vacation cabins and destination weddings in the Pocono Mountains of Pennsylvania.

Meta tags in the page source...

Figure 2-4:
The page source (top) for the main weddings page on MSLresort. com (bottom) shows the keyword, description, and title metatags.

...become keywords on the Web site.

Courtesy Mountain Springs Lake Resort, MSLresort.com

The first paragraph of the weddings page shown in Figure 2-4 is optimized for some the same search terms that appear in the keyword list. Note the `<title>` tag above the browser toolbar, which also includes two of the keywords. We talk more about this tag in a later section of this chapter.

If you see no metatags in the page source for your own site, you may be in trouble. Certainly, that could account for poor results in search engines.

You can usually insert metatags and `<alt>` tags for photos quite easily if you use a content management system (CMS) to maintain your Web site or if you use blog software. If you don't, you may need to ask your programmer or Web developer for assistance.

Keeping up with keyword metatags

Though the `<keyword>` metatag, which lists your chosen search terms for a page, isn't absolutely essential for search engines, it helps you track keywords manually. This tag isn't visible to others while viewing pages; however, it's visible in the source code. Because different search engines truncate the `<keyword>` tag at different lengths, try to vary the position of search terms within the tag on different pages.

Book II
Chapter 2

Leveraging Search Engine Optimization (SEO)

You have as many different ways to list search terms as there are search engine optimizers. Try these helpful guidelines:

✦ Make an alphabetical list of all your search terms in lowercase.

✦ Search engines ignore prepositions, conjunctions, articles, and punctuation; you can include them, but engines see the terms without them.

✦ Because simple plurals include singulars (*comets/comet*), use only the plurals. However, if the spelling of a plural changes its root, include both versions in your list (for example, *scarf/scarves* or *salary/salaries*).

✦ If your list is too long, stick with root words; for example, *photograph* covers *photographs, photography, photographer, photographers, photographed,* and *photographing.*

✦ Separate phrases with commas; commas don't matter to search engines, but they make reading easier for you.

✦ If words within a term must be kept together, put them between quotes — for example, "north dakota." Otherwise, search engines index words in any order. The term *red sneakers* is indexed in results even if someone enters the search term *sneakers red.*

✦ Put your unique words, such as your company or product name, at the end of the list. It doesn't matter as much if they're trimmed off because search engines will find your unique term anyway. Those terms are likely to appear so often on your site that you don't have to optimize for them.

✦ Pull out the four or five terms that will comprise the primary "set" of keywords for a particular page and put them at the beginning of the list.

Refer to Figure 2-4 to see how MSLresort.com handles the `<keyword>` tag on one page of its Web site.

You can reuse the terms from the set assigned to your home page on multiple social media pages, so keep that set handy!

Tipping the scales with title tags

Perhaps the most important tag, `<title>` appears above the browser toolbar when users are on a Web site. A good `<title>` tag includes one or more keywords followed by your company name. Select one of more search terms from the "set" you've assigned to that particular page.

Because browsers may truncate the title tag display, place the search term first. Limit the title tag to seven to ten words and fewer than 70 characters. Once upon a long, long time ago, way back in the dinosaur age of the Internet, page names were used to index a Web site. That method is now unnecessary; it's an absolute waste of time to write a title tag with a phrase such as *home page* rather than a search term. It's almost as big a waste of time as having no title tag. The title tag that appears earlier, in Figure 2-4 (*Romantic Poconos Wedding Venue: Mountain Spring Lake Resort & Lodge*), is a good example.

Google and other search engines dislike multiple pages with identical metatags. Changing the title tag on each page is one of the easiest ways to handle this preference. Simply pull another relevant search term from your list of keywords and insert it in front of the company name in the title tag.

Pumping up page description tags

The page description tag appears as several sentences below the link to each site in natural search results, as shown in Figure 2-5. Search engines display the first line of text when a page description tag isn't available.

Depending on the search engine, search engines may truncate description tags after 150 to 250 characters. Just in case, front-load the description with all the search terms from the set you've assigned to that page.

Why pass up a marketing opportunity? Just because your site appears near the top of search results, you have no guarantee that someone will click through to your site. Write your page description tag as though it were ad copy, including a benefits statement and a call to action. Figure 2-5 displays natural search results on Yahoo! with the page description for several other internal wedding pages from MSLresort.com. Note the inclusion of search terms from the keyword tag in Figure 2-4 (*wedding planners, wedding packages, pocono weddings, wedding locations*), the benefits statement (*Our wedding planners will customize a wedding package just for you*), and the call to action (*Enjoy*).

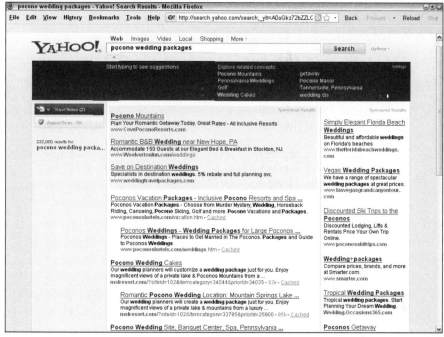

Reproduced with permission of Yahoo! Inc. © 2010 Yahoo! Inc. YAHOO!, the YAHOO! logo, FLICKR, the FLICKR logo, DELICIOUS, and the DELICIOUS logo are registered trademarks of Yahoo! Inc.

Figure 2-5:
The page description tag for several wedding pages on the Mountain Springs Lake resort site appears in the natural search results for *pocono wedding packages.*

Book II
Chapter 2

Leveraging
Search Engine
Optimization (SEO)

Working out with <alt> tags

An <alt> tag, which appears when a user hovers the mouse over an image, is not considered a metatag, because every image theoretically should have its own <alt> tag. Note the <alt> tag by the image of the couple shown earlier, in Figure 2-4.

Originally, the <alt> tag was designed to act as a picture caption read by speech synthesizers for visually impaired people. In addition, <alt> tags are another place to incorporate search terms. Although they aren't technically metatags, they offer similar benefits in terms of helping to improve your ranking in search results.

You can place an <alt> tag for every image. Because <alt> tags appear when someone hovers the mouse over an image (but only on PCs, not on Macintoshes), keep these tags fairly short so that they don't interfere with other content. Include one or two search terms per image from your set for each page (refer to Figure 2-3). The code for the <alt> tag (*A Poconos Mountain wedding resort*) that appears over the image of the bride looks like this:

```
<img width="200" src="http://beta.asoundstrategy.com/
    sitemaster/userUploads/site102/ms1_wed_h1.jpg" alt="A
Poconos Mountain wedding resort" border="0">
```

Optimizing Your Site and Content for Search Engines

Optimization is the process of adjusting your site, blog, or social media profiles to "play well" with search algorithms. It's done primarily by having plenty of relevant content, updating it often, and making sure that your Web presence is easy for general and on-site search engines to spider. I cover a few of the most important tricks of the trade in the following sections. For additional information on search engines and site optimization, check out some of the resources listed in Table 2-3.

Table 2-3   Search Engine and Optimization Resources

Name	*URL*	*Description*
Google Webmaster	`https://www.google.com/support/webmasters/bin/answer.py?answer=35769`	Guidelines and suggestions for site optimization
LinkVendor	`www.linkvendor.com`	Suite of SEO tools
MarketingSherpa	`www.marketingsherpa.com/Search2010Excerpt.pdf`	Search Marketing Benchmark Report 2009-2010 (free excerpt)
Pandia Search Central	`www.pandia.com`	Search engine news
Search Engine Guide	`www.searchengineguide.com/marketing.html`	Search engine articles, blog, marketing
Search Engine Journal	`www.searchenginejournal.com/seo-best-practices-for-url-structure/7215`	Best practices for URLs
SearchEngineWatch.com (ClickZ)	`www.searchenginewatch.com`	Articles, tutorials, forums, blogs, SEO articles, and tips

Name	URL	Description
SEOmoz	www.seomoz.org	SEO resources, toolbar, blog, spam detector, membership
UrlTrends	www.urltrends.com	Suite of SEO tools and reports

Writing an optimized first paragraph

First and foremost, use the four or five search terms from each assigned set in the first paragraph of text on a page or the first paragraph of a blog posting (refer to Figure 2-3). Basically, most search engines don't check entire Web sites or blogs, so the engines continue until they reach a hard return or 200 words. That's too many words for a paragraph on the Web, so get those search terms in early.

There's nothing like on-site social media, such as a blog or forum, to generate keyword-rich content for search engines to munch on. Best of all, other folks are helping you feed the beast!

Figure 2-6 shows a well-optimized posting and its source code from the Changing Aging blog. Ecumen, a nonprofit organization specializing in senior housing and services, owns the blog. This entry at www.changingaging blog.org/posts/view/1272-boston-college-analysis-projects-seniors%27-long-term-care-costs includes the phrase *long term care* in its URL, post title, tags, categories, and text. The source code uses the same term in the title and keyword tags, and indicates that the Ecumen Changing Aging blog has both an XML site map and an RSS feed.

Don't try to force more than that set of terms into the paragraph. If another phrase or two from the keyword tag fit naturally, that's fine. Trying to cram more words into your text may render it unintelligible or jargon-loaded to human readers.

No matter where the first paragraph of text appears on the page, place the text near the top of the source code. The text should appear above any tags for images, video, or Flash.

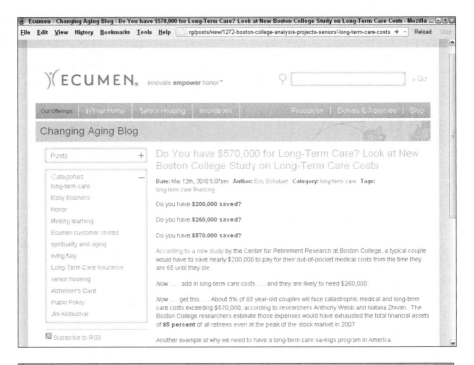

Figure 2-6: This blog post uses several keywords in its title, tags, categories, and text and includes an XML site map and RSS feed.

Updating often

Search engines, especially Google, love to see updated content. A sign that a Web site is loved and cared for, easily updated content is one of many reasons for having a blog or content management system on your site. If changing content is simple and free, you're more likely to do it.

At least once a month, change a paragraph of content on your site. Include this task on your Social Media Activity Calendar (see Book I, Chapter 3). If you can't commit to this task, at least ask your programmer to incorporate some kind of automatically updated material, whether it's a date-and-time stamp, a quote, or an RSS feed, for example.

If you follow no other search optimization tips in this chapter, make sure that you follow at least these two: Update often and optimize the first paragraph of text on every page.

Using search terms elsewhere on pages

Guess what? You score extra jelly beans in the relevance jar if your search terms appear in particular places on your Web site. Follow these tips to help optimize your Web page or blog for your selected set of search terms. If they don't work naturally, don't force them.

+ **Links:** Use the words from your priority set of search terms as *text links* or *anchor text* (words that form an active link to another internal page or external site). Don't waste valuable real estate on meaningless phrases such as *Learn more* or *Click here.* They don't do a darn thing for your search ranking.

If a clickable image opens another page, such as a product detail page, add a clickable caption that includes a search term or the product name. Score some points!

+ **Headings:** Headlines and subheads help organize text and assist readers who are skimming your copy for the information they want. Headings that include your search terms can also improve your search engine ranking.

Onscreen, these words usually appear in bold and in a larger font size or different color (or both) from the body copy.

Headings must carry the `<h1>` to `<h6>` tags that define HTML headings, rather than appear as graphics. Search engines can't "read" words embedded in a picture.

+ **Navigation:** Search terms that appear as navigational items, whether for main or secondary pages, also earn extra relevance "jelly beans." As with headings, navigation must be in text form, not in graphic form.

Sometimes you have to weigh the design considerations or limitations of your CMS or blog against search engine optimization needs. Some designers prefer the greater control and flexibility of font styles available in a graphic. Ultimately, only you can decide what matters more to you.

Under no circumstances should you implement *black hat* techniques, such as stuffing a page with keywords, hiding search terms in the same color as the background, installing "magic pixels," or using any other scam technique promoted as the search engine equivalent of a get-rich-quick scheme. These techniques might get you blacklisted from search engines.

Making your site search engine friendly

In addition to trying the techniques in the previous section, which apply at the page level, you can take specific actions to make your site, as a whole, friendly to search engines.

Avoiding elements that search engines hate

If you expect a search engine to rank your site or blog favorably, you have to give it something to work with. Computers may be getting smarter all the time, but they cannot yet "read" pictures, videos, or soundtracks, let alone minds. They need to be fed a rich diet of words. The list of search engine "detestables" is short, but they can all be avoided without harming your message.

✦ **Pictures:** As much as artists and photographers love pages without words, search engines hate them. Simple solutions can make your pictures search-engine friendly: provide an `<alt>` tag and/or caption; have text appear below the fold (as long as the text appears near the top of the code); or include a descriptive paragraph near the image. For an extra boost, include keywords in the filenames for photos.

✦ **Flash animations:** Whether developers provide Flash animation because it's lucrative or because their clients demand it, search engines detest it. A search engine has nothing to "grab on to" at an all-Flash site. Though you can now find some sneaky ways around this problem, your best bet is to incorporate Flash much as you would incorporate a video — as an element on a page, not as an entire page.

✦ **Frames:** This old-fashioned way (anything ten years old on the Internet is practically an antique) of controlling the appearance of pages lets you modify content within a box. Unfortunately, search engines cannot see anything inside a frame. Many alternatives now exist, from tables to cascading style sheets. If your developer insists on using frames, find a new developer.

✦ **Duplicate content:** Be sure to delete old versions of pages that have been replaced. Even if they sit in archives, search engines may try to index them and "ding" you for duplicate information.

✦ **Splash pages:** This misguided attempt to design a Web site as though it were a book with a cover does real harm to site traffic. Generally, a site loses half its audience every time a click is required. Why cut your prospect list in half before you even have a chance to explain your benefits? Splash pages often consist of beautiful images or animations that make a statement about a company but carry no content or navigation.

Often found on sites of companies specializing in entertainment, Web development, architecture, arts and crafts, or graphic design, splash pages usually offer viewers an option to skip the introduction and an arrow cuing them to click to enter the "real" site.

The simple solution is to not include a splash page on your site. If you must, have an entry page with a nice graphical element that includes one paragraph of text (preferably filled with benefits) and primary navigation.

If you insist on having a splash or entry page, at least don't annoy your visitors. Direct the navigational link for *Home* to the main page of real content, not to the splash page. With a bit of clever naming, you may be able to get search engines to spider the first page of content and ignore the splash page.

Configuring URLs

The best URLs are readable and might include one of your search terms or a descriptive title: `www.yourdomain.com/social-media-small-businesses`. Using a search term from your set of keywords for your Web or blog page earns you another relevance "jelly bean." At least try to keep the URLs as readable text, as in `www.yourdomain.com/pages/socialmedia/article1234.htm`.

Problems with page URLs tend to occur when they're automatically assigned by a content management system or when the pages are created dynamically. Those URLs tend to look like gobbledygook: `www.yourdomain.com/shop/AS-djfa-16734-QETR`. Though search engines can review these URLs, they do nothing for your search engine ranking and aren't helpful to users.

Even worse are database-generated URLs or pages created on the fly that include multiple nonalphanumeric characters: `www.yourdomain.com/cgi-bin/shop.pl?shop=view_category=ASDFJ%20&subcategory=XYZ%6734`. Search engines are becoming less fussy than they used to be, but many still have problems indexing URLs that have more than four nonalphanumeric characters. (Hyphens and underscores are okay.) Some still have problems with only three such characters.

Be careful when redesigning a blog or Web site, especially if you're changing developers or platforms. If the existing site is already doing well in search engines, try to preserve its URLs. Not all transitions to a new platform accommodate this strategy. Ask your programmer before you begin.

A badly configured URL is simply not indexed. This problem can become significant with product databases on e-commerce sites, especially when you want every individual product detail page to appear in search engines.

If your site is hosted on an Apache server, a technical fix exists. You (or your programmer) can implement the Apache Mod Rewrite Module, which converts URLs on the fly to a format that's search engine friendly. See `http://httpd.apache.org/docs/1.3/mod/mod_rewrite.html` for more information.

Indexing a site

You can easily create a virtual path to ensure that search engines crawl your entire site. This element is especially important in two cases:

✦ When the top and left navigational elements are graphics, making it impossible for search engines to know which pages are really on the site

✦ When you have a large, deep, database-driven site, without links to all pages easily available in the navigation

For a small site with graphical navigation, you have a simple fix: Create a parallel series of linkable main pages in the footer of your site, as shown in Figure 2-7. The linkable footer on each page of AirOnePhoto.com highlights key site pages and acts as a partial site index for search engines. Alternatively, create a navigational *breadcrumb trail* at the top of the page to help both search engines and human beings know where they are within your site structure.

A breadcrumb trail (think Hansel and Gretel) helps users track where they are on a complex Web site. It typically consists of a series of page links that extend horizontally across each page, just above the content. Breadcrumb trails, which may either display the site structure or the actual navigation path a user has followed, usually look something like this:

`Home page > Main section page > Internal page > Detail page`

Put these links in a server-side include (SSI) within the footer to ensure that links are displayed consistently on all pages. You then make future changes in only one place (other than in the site itself, of course).

For a site with a significant number of pages, especially on several tiers, the best solution is to include a linkable site map or site index, shown in Figure 2-8. It may look a lot like a junior high school outline, which is a perfectly fine solution for both search engine friendliness and site usability.

Figure 2-7:
The footer on this Web site highlights pages and acts as a partial site index.

Figure 2-8:
A linkable site index page provides easy access to all pages on the site.

Another solution exists for very large database-driven sites and large stores. Sitemap (XML) feeds directly to Google, Yahoo!, and Bing provide current content to all your pages. Direct your programmer to `www.xml-sitemaps.com`, `www.antezeta.com/yahoo/site-map-feed.html`, or `www.google.com/support/webmasters/bin/topic.py?topic=8476` for more information. If nothing changes often, these feeds can be updated manually every month. If you have continually changing inventory and other content, have your programmer upload these feeds automatically, at least once a day, using RSS.

If you want to index your site to see what pages you have, try one of these free tools:

✦ **Yahoo! Site Explorer,** `https://siteexplorer.search.yahoo.com`: Enter your domain name and then click Status and then the Explore button.

✦ **Xenu's Link Sleuth,** `http://home.snafu.de/tilman/xenulink.html`: Download and run this link verification program. In the results, click the Site Map of Valid HTML Pages with a Title link.

Minimizing download time

Google now includes download time in its methods for ranking Web sites in search results. Companies continue to post pages that take too long to download, testing viewers' patience and occasionally overloading their Internet service provider's (ISP's) facilities. Perhaps it's a case of content expanding to fit the bandwidth available.

Try to keep sites to less than 70KB to 80KB per page, even though many users now have high-speed connections such as DSL and cable. High-resolution photos are usually the main culprits when a page is too large. It isn't the number of photos, but rather the total size of files on a page that counts. A couple of tips can help reduce the size of your page:

✦ When saving photos to use online, choose the Save for Web menu option. Stick to JPEG or GIF files, which work well online, and avoid TIFF and BMP files that are intended for print.

✦ Post a thumbnail with a click-to-view action for the larger version in a pop-up window. Be sure to save the larger image for the Web (refer to the first bullet).

Check the download size and time for your home page for free at sites such as `www.websiteoptimization.com/services/analyze` or `www.gomez.com/instant-test-pro`. Call your developer if changes are needed.

Building Effective Inbound Links

An *inbound link* from another site to your Web site, blog, or social media page acts as a recommendation. Its presence implicitly suggests that visitors to the original site might find useful content on yours. Testimonial links are particularly important for social media, where they are measured in rating stars, number of views, retweets, "likes," and "favorites." These recommendations enhance credibility and build traffic, as they encourage other viewers to visit your original post.

Conversely, an *external link* goes from your page to someone else's, providing the same referral function. All these links form a web of connections in cyberspace. A site may require a *reciprocal link* back to its site before it will post one to yours.

It sounds simple. However, identifying places that will link to yours and getting them to post the link can be quite time-consuming.

Why bother? Although all search engines track the number of sites that link to yours, Google (and only Google) uses the number and quality of these inbound links to determine your position on search engine results pages. In essence, Google runs the world's largest popularity contest, putting to shame every high school's search for a prom king and queen.

TECHNICAL STUFF Sometimes companies link to `http://yourdomain.com` and sometimes to `http://www.yourdomain.com`. Search engines consider them separate pages and may not give full credit for your inbound links. Do a permanent 301 redirect from one to the other. (Google likes `www` domains better.) Alternatively, you can accomplish this task from Google Webmaster Central, but it applies to only Google.

Google PageRank

The popularity contest is truly an apt metaphor for Page Rank because not all inbound links are equal in the eyes of Google. Links from `.edu` and `.org` domains carry extra credit, as do links you receive from other sites that Google ranks as having good content and good traffic. Think of them as votes from the in crowd. Google factors these parameters, and others, into its proprietary PageRank algorithm. For more information, see `www.google.com/corporate/tech.html`.

The algorithm ranks pages on an earthquake-style scale from 0 to 10. (Google is 10; *The New York Times* is 9.) Empirically speaking, a Google PageRank of 5 is usually enough to place your site on the first page of search results — with no guarantees, of course. Figure 2-9 shows the Google PageRank tool in action. You can download the Google toolbar with the PageRank display from `www.google.com/toolbar`.

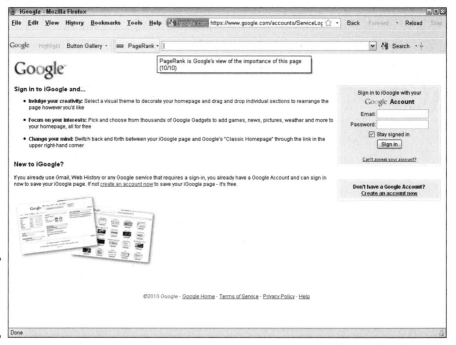

Figure 2-9:
Google has
a PageRank
of 10.

If you're serious about SEO, install the Google PageRank tool on your browser so that you can quickly check the PageRank of your own site or blog and that of your competitors. Follow these steps:

1. **Download the Google toolbar at `www.google.com/toolbar` and install it.**

The PageRank tool doesn't automatically appear on the toolbar, so you must enable it.

2. **Choose View⇨Toolbars⇨Google Toolbar. If that option is not already checked, do so.**

The Google toolbar should now be visible.

3. **Click the Wrench icon to open the Toolbar Options dialog box.**

If you don't see the Wrench icon in the Google Toolbar, right-click any option on the toolbar.

4. **From the Tools tab, select the PageRank check box and click Save.**

You now see the PageRank tool on the Google toolbar (refer to Figure 2-9). Its specific location and size depend on how you have personalized your toolbar.

To see the page rank for a Web site, enter its domain name into the address box on your browser and wait for the page to load. Hover your mouse over the page rank tool until the box with page rank results appears below the toolbar.

To check page rank for multiple competitors' sites at once, try the free tool at www.cascandra.com/web-tools/multiple-pagerank-checker.

Knowing what makes a good inbound link

In a nutshell, good inbound links (sometimes called backlinks) come from sites that have these characteristics:

**Book II
Chapter 2**

**Leveraging
Search Engine
Optimization (SEO)**

+ **Relevance:** The quickest way to determine relevance is to see whether the other site shares a search term or tag with your site.

+ **A decent amount of traffic:** Check www.alexa.com or www.quantcast.com to estimate traffic on other sites.

+ **Your target market:** Whether or not a link helps with PageRank, links from other appropriate sites help with branding and deliver qualified traffic to your site.

+ **A good Google PageRank:** Look for a score of 5 or higher in the PageRank tool. Higher-ranking sites, which often themselves have high traffic volume and good content value, are considered more credible references; they pass along *link juice* from their site to yours.

Links are search engine specific, so lists of inbound links differ on different search engines. Because Google "counts" only sites with a high PageRank, the list on Google is always the shortest.

To see your own or others' inbound links on a particular engine, enter link:http://yourdomainname.com (where yourdomainname.com is replaced by your own domain name) in the search term box for Yahoo! or Google.

Hunting for elusive links

No matter how hard you try, it's hard to find a good link to your Web site or blog. Use link-checking tools such as LinkPopularity.com or Alexa (www.alexa.com), shown in Figure 2-10, and the other tools listed in Table 2-4.

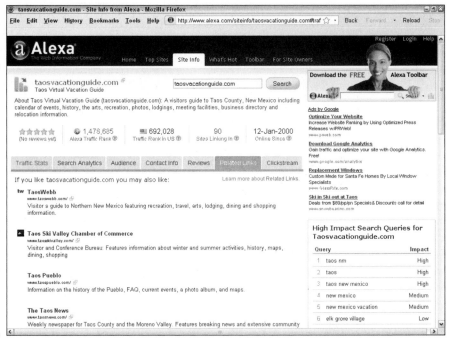

Figure 2-10: For each site it indexes, Alexa displays a list of not only inbound links but also "related links," such as these for the Taos Vacation Guide.

"Alexa the Web Information Company," "Alexa Top Sites", "Alexa Site Thumbnail", the Alexa® logo and name are trademarks of Amazon.com, Inc. or its affiliates in the United States and/or other countries.

Table 2-4	Free Inbound Link Resources	
Name	*URL*	*Description*
Alexa	`www.alexa.com`	Link checker, related links, clickstream, and more

Ezine Articles	`http://ezinearticles.`
	`com/?Top-5-Ways-`
	`to-Get-Inbound-`
	`Links&id=233380`
		Tips on link campaigns

Internet Public Library	`www.ipl2.org/IPL/Fin`
	`ding?Key=search+eng`
	`ine+directories&but`
	`ton.x=49&button.y=12`
		Directory of search engines

LinkPopularity.com	`http://linkpopular` `ity.com`	Link checker for Google, Bing, and Yahoo!
Majestic-SEO	`www.majesticseo.com`	Check backlinks and history on other sites in bulk

Name	URL	Description
Page Inlink Analyzer	`http://ericmiraglia.com/inlink/`	Check backlinks plus tags and bookmarks on Delicious
Search Engine Colossus	`www.searchenginecolossus.com`	Directory of international search engines
Search Engine Guide	`www.searchengineguide.com/searchengines.html`	Meta-index of topical search engines
Webmaster Toolkit	`http://webmaster-toolkit.com/link-popularity-checker.shtml`	Link checker for multiple engines
WhoLinksToMe	`http://wholinkstome.com`	Backlink analysis and link buidling tools

You can hunt for potential links in a few tried-and-true places:

✦ Inbound links to other sites that rank highly in Google on your search terms

Be sure that your company truly has something in common with the other. Shared terms may not be enough — there's a big difference between companies that run a fish restaurant and those that sell lead-free weights for catching fish.

✦ Inbound links to your competitors' sites

✦ "Related link" sites at `www.alexa.com` for your competitors or highly ranked sites that share your share terms

✦ The resource lists of outbound links found on competitors' sites or other highly ranked sites

✦ Industry-based business directories

✦ Yellow Pages and map sites

✦ Local business directories

✦ Blog-specific directories

✦ Trade associations and other organizations you belong to or sponsor

✦ Suppliers, including your Web development and hosting company

✦ Sites owned by distributors, clients, customers, or affiliates

✦ *Meta-indices* (sites with master lists of directories), some of which appear in Table 2-4

✦ Cross-links with all your social media sites, even though some of these do not help with PageRank.

✦ Exchange a link in your *blogroll* with other, well-ranked blogs

✦ Related but not directly competing businesses that your target audience might also visit

Prequalify every potential link. Visit every link site to ensure that it accepts links and is truly relevant and that it has a Google PageRank of 5 or higher and represents the quality and audience you want.

Stay away from *link farms* (sites that exist only to sell links); *Web rings* (a closed loop of companies that agree to link to each other); and *gray-market link sites* (sites that sell links at exorbitant prices and guarantee a certain result). Your site can be exiled from search engines for using them. Besides, they don't raise your PageRank!

Implementing your link campaign

Try for at least 50 links and hope that 30 of them come through. There's no upper limit — the more, the better.

You might want to create a spreadsheet to track link requests. Create columns for these elements:

✦ Domain name

✦ Appearance URL

✦ Submission URL or e-mail address

✦ Submission date

✦ URL of the landing page you asked others to link to

✦ Reciprocal link requirement

✦ Date you checked to see whether a link was posted

Don't be afraid to group spreadsheet rows by target market. For instance, if you sell products for toddlers, you might have a group of links for sites used by single parents and another group for sites used by daycare centers.

Break this task into bite-size pieces so that it doesn't become overwhelming. On your Social Marketing Activity Calendar (found in Book I, Chapter 3), limit the search-and-submission task to only five to ten links per week.

After you qualify prospective links and add them to your spreadsheet, follow the directions on each site to submit your URL or e-mail your request to the site owner.

Getting inbound links from social bookmarks and social news services

Leverage your social marketing activities to increase the number of inbound links to your site. If it's permissible, post your site to some of the social bookmarking, shopping, and news services described in Book II, Chapter 3. (Not all social bookmarks allow you to submit your own site, so you may need to ask a friend to help.) You're generally required to include either your domain name or a specific page URL with your submission.

These links encourage both inbound links and traffic. Some of these sites pass link juice, especially if you have multiple links from social news sites back to different news stories or content on your main site. For more information, see Book II, Chapter 3.

Just as with inbound link campaigns for search engines, don't link everything from social bookmarking, news, or shopping services to your home page. For example, multiple product recommendations on social shopping sites should link to the appropriate product detail pages in your store.

Cross-link by submitting especially good blog entries to several social news services or by linking from one product recommendation to another on social shopping sites or from one review site to another.

Reaping other links from social media

Another easy way to build inbound links is by distributing (syndicating) content as described in the previous chapter. By re-purposing content on multiple social media sites, you not only increase your audience but also increase the number of inbound links.

Taking advantage of the many places to post links on social media pages will not only drive traffic to multiple elements of your Web presence but also improve your search engine rankings in the process.

Somewhere on your Web site or blog — at least on the About Us or Contact page — display a list of links to all your profiles on social media services. Search engines can't see graphical links such as the Follow Us *chiclets* (those ubiquitous rectangular Facebook and Twitter icons, for example). They're useful for people, but not for search engines.

You can also repeat text links to your social media pages in your linkable footer.

✦ Every profile on a social network has a place to enter at least your Web address and blog address, if you have one. If possible, link to both. The links in profiles usually provide link juice, although the ones in status updates usually do not.

✦ Include your Web address when you make comments on other people's blogs, post reviews on recommendation sites, or submit someone else's news story. You may have to work it into the content. Use at least your company e-mail address@yourdomain.com for branding reasons!

✦ Include your company name for branding and your Web address for linking when you post to groups on any social networking site, as long as it's appropriate, relevant, and not too self-promotional.

Read the Terms of Service on each site to be sure that you comply with requirements for use of e-mail addresses, submissions, and links.

✦ Post events on LinkedIn, MySpace, Facebook, and elsewhere with a link to your site for more information.

✦ Include a Social Sharing button, described in Book II, Chapter 3, to encourage additional distribution. People who receive content they like often pass it along or link to it from their own pages or blogs.

✦ Be sure to post cross-links on all your social media profiles to all your other Web pages, including to your primary site and your blog.

Now that social media are included in ordinary search results, using search terms consistently can help you occupy more than one slot in search engine results pages. This strategy works well for The Brooklyn Kitchen, shown in Figure 2-11. The WordPress blog and Yelp review, as well as its Web site and store links, help The Brooklyn Kitchen occupy four of the top five results. Search results are shown at the top, and the Web site is shown at the bottom.

Creating a resource page for outbound links

One item to include when optimizing your site for search engines is a Link Resources page, by that name or any other, for external or outbound links.

You need this page in order to post reciprocal links to other sites but also to help viewers find useful, neutral information on .edu, .gov, and .org domains. Nestling reciprocal links within an annotated list of informational sites makes reciprocal links less noticeable and less self-serving. Good ideas for neutral links are described in this list:

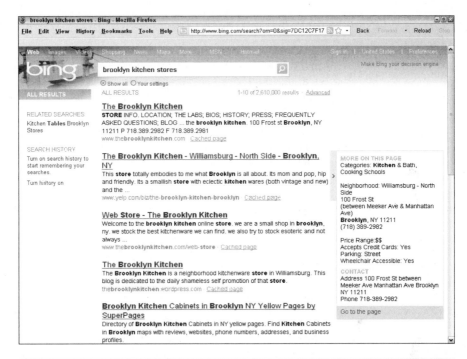

Book II
Chapter 2

Leveraging
Search Engine
Optimization (SEO)

Figure 2-11:
Social
media are
included in
Bing search
results for
*brooklyn
kitchen
store.*

Courtesy The Brooklyn Kitchen

✦ Sites with information about materials used in your products or how to care for them

✦ Educational sites discussing the services you provide, such as feng shui for offices, the benefits of massage, or tips on tax deductions

✦ Trade associations and other business organizations to which you belong

✦ Local, state, and federal government sites whose regulations or procedures may affect your business or customers

✦ Nonprofit sites that share your values; for example, sites talking about recycling electronics or supporting entrepreneurs in developing countries

✦ Sites that talk about the history of your business or industry or the local history of your brick-and-mortar storefront

✦ Other sites that may interest visitors to your site; for example, a hotel site that links to a local dining guide or events calendar

New Mexico Community Capital, for example, links to helpful sites at `www.nmccap.org/Learn_and_Engage/Industry_Links` (see Figure 2-12).

Figure 2-12: New Mexico Community Capital offers visitors helpful links to other sites.

Courtesy New Mexico Community Capital

Risking the personalized search

All bets are off with personalized search, one of Google's more problematical recent ideas. Google now defaults to a customized list of search results based on an individual's past searches and the results she clicked. In theory, these search results, derived either from a browser cookie or Web history, are continuously refined to become more relevant to users' needs.

In practice, that relevance is debatable; users tend to see results that are "more of the same," distorting the reality of what's out there and reducing the likelihood of receiving new information.

Users must take a distinct action to turn off personalized search by clicking the Web History link in the upper-right corner of any Google search results page and then toggling the Disable Customizations Based on Search Activity option. Most users don't even know that personalized search exists, let alone how to turn it off or how to delete repeatedly occurring, undesirable sites from results to make room for new ones. (The latter option requires logging into your Google account to personalize settings for your Web History.)

Unfortunately, the algorithm for personalized search tends to produce results reflecting a philosophy of "Them that has, gets." Your Web site may have more difficulty breaking through to new prospects or achieving a presence on the first page of some individuals' search results. Unfortunately, you can do nothing about it. Whether users who see your site are more qualified as prospects and more likely to buy remains to be seen.

 A good starting place for neutral outbound links is to see related links for a high-ranked competitor. Enter its domain name into the search field on Alexa; then click the Get Details button on the results. On the ensuing page, click the Related Links tab. Also look under Resources by Subject at the Internet Public Library (www.ipl2.org/div/subject).

Optimizing Social Media for Search Engines

Here's the good news: Everything we've covered in this chapter about using SEO for your Web site or blog applies to other social media too. Whew! You still have to implement the techniques, but you can save time by reusing search terms, metatags, inbound links, and optimized text.

 Every search engine has its own rules. You may need to tweak your terms for not only general search engines but also internal search engines on specific social media services.

Placing your search terms on social media

Start by reviewing your research for keywords and phrases. Decide on a primary set of four to six terms that best describe your company. Because your search terms must still relate to your content, you may want to reuse other sets for individual posts from your SEO research, mix them up, or include additional terms not optimized on your primary site.

You can place these terms in many locations:

✦ **Tags:** Tags are the social media equivalents of keywords. Because many social media services place a limit on the number of tags, pick a few from your primary set of search terms and select others (for example, brands, products, market, or competition) from your secondary list or elsewhere that are specific to your content.

If you're pulling tags out of thin air, remember to confirm which synonyms are most popular with the users of that service. For example, do people search for *Barack* or *Obama* or *president?* Use a keyword selection tool for Web sites listed earlier in this chapter (refer to Table 2-2) or check the tag cloud, discussed earlier in this chapter, on the service you're using for the latest trends in tag usage.

✦ **Profiles:** Just about every form of social media asks you to establish an account. Most profiles ask for a brief description of your company and location as well as the URLs for your Web site and blog. Work your primary set of keywords and brands into your profile and any other place you can comfortably integrate them, including featured products, department names, marketing tagline, and staff bios.

Occasionally, a service requests only your e-mail address. Of course, you use the one with your domain name in it.

If you haven't already set up e-mail to forward from `you@yourdomain.com` to whatever e-mail address you have from your ISP, do so now. Most hosting packages include at least five free e-mail addresses. E-mail from `@yourdomain.com` not only makes you look more professional but also adds to brand value.

✦ **Page content, status updates, and comments:** Obviously, you should include search terms in the first paragraph of text for each blog post. They don't need to be part of your primary set of terms, so you have some creative flexibility. Incorporate search terms in updates and comments, too, to increase the likelihood of being found in on-site search results.

✦ **Metatags, titles, and headlines:** Use search terms from your list in the title of your blog or page name; in the title of your post; in `<alt>` tags, captions, or descriptions for images; and within metatags. Each service handles these elements a little differently, as we discuss in the sections on individual services.

Duplicate content can reduce rankings on search engines. If you use a service such as Ping.fm to update everything at one time, you may pay a bit of a penalty. Because SEO is only one of the online marketing arrows in your quiver, you might not want to worry about duplicate content until your social media campaigns take off. Only you can weigh the pros and cons based on your available time, staffing levels, and campaign objectives.

Optimizing blogs

Because blogs (discussed in Book III, Chapter 2), are basically Web sites in a different format, the same principles of site optimization and configuration apply, including the need for inbound links and cross-promotion on social media services. Hard-learned lessons and best practices truly pay off because search engines crawl frequently updated blogs at least daily. Oh, frabjous day!

**Book II
Chapter 2**

Leveraging
Search Engine
Optimization (SEO)

Integrate your domain name with your blog URL or buy a separate, related domain name (`yourblog.yourdomain.com` or `yourcompanyblog.com`), even if a third-party server hosts your blogs. For SEO purposes, you must own your own blog domain name. A blog at `www.MyCompanyBlog.blogspot.com` or `www.TypePad.com/MyCompanyBlog` isn't acceptable.

Blogs are primo link bait. The casual sharing of relevant, text-based links within posts, the use of *blogrolls* (bloggers' linkable recommendations of other blogs), and related thematic material attract inbound links like black jackets attract white cat fur. With all that link juice, plus rapidly updated content, many blogs quickly zoom to page one in search engine results.

Review all requests for inclusion on your blog roll or reciprocal link offers. Make sure that the requesting site is relevant, has a decent page rank, and is one that you feel good about recommending.

Different blog platforms operate somewhat differently, leading to some confusion on the part of bloggers trying to optimize sites for search engines. Whatever your platform, the same methods you follow for Web sites still apply, with a multitude of additions:

+ Include keywords from your primary list in your blog name. such as `YourCompany.com/social_media_blog`. The blog name should appear with an HTML <h1> tag on only the front page. On other pages of your blog, the heading level can be as low as <h3>.

+ Include keywords in individual titles for each post. Use these keywords in the title metatag in the source code for that entry, as well as in the page URL. Put those titles at the HTML <h1> level.

+ Include primary keywords in the first sentence of content, which becomes the description metatag by default, unless you write one manually. Use your secondary keywords in the body of your post.

✦ Fill out the tag box with your keywords.

✦ Incorporate search terms in anchor text for links on your blog.

✦ Use `<alt>` tags, captions, and descriptions with search terms for any images or media you upload to your blog.

✦ Post rich, appealing content with search terms regularly and often.

✦ Make sure search engines can spider your blog easily by including a side navigation column on all pages, and offering access to archives and previous posts from all pages of your blog.

✦ Include a linkable, keyword-loaded, breadcrumb trail.

✦ Provide internal text links to your own related posts.

✦ Submit your blog to blog directories and RSS submission sites. An excellent list is at `www.masternewmedia.org/rss/top55`.

✦ Use your blogroll as a source to request a backlink or reciprocal appearance on other people's blogrolls; just having a blogroll is not enough.

✦ Get backlinks to your blog with *trackbacks* (automated way of notifying other bloggers that you've referenced their blog) or by posting comments on other blogs. Not all blogging hosts support trackbacks. See Book III, Chapter 2 for more information.

✦ Create an XML site map and submit it to search engines, just as you would for your Web site.

✦ Use *permalinks* (permanent links) to maintain blog URLs permanently.

✦ Use analytics tools to monitor traffic and user behavior.

If you need quick suggestions for good blog keywords, install the free tool at `http://labs.wordtracker.com/seo-blogger`. It sits next to your blog editor on the screen so that you can consider keyword suggestions as you write.

Long blog pages, with lots of responses, may end up with too many links. You can place an HTML `nofollow` attribute in the code just before links from comments.

Optimizing WordPress

Although WordPress automatically optimizes titles for search engines and generates metatags, you may want to tweak the automated SEO results for important posts. Autogeneration is fine for mundane posts or when you're short on time.

For more flexibility and additional optimization features, try the All in One SEO Pack at `http://wordpress.org/extend/plugins/all-in-one-seo-pack`.

Make your overall WordPress life easier by reviewing the entire list of plug-ins at `http://wordpress.org/extend/plugins`.

Here are a few things you can do to optimize your WordPress blog posts:

✦ **Swap elements of the blog post title.** Reverse the WordPress default arrangement by putting the post title first, which contains keywords, followed by the name of your blog.

✦ **Use a consistent format for keyword-rich page titles on all pages.** You can set up the format once in your template and apply it everywhere by using the All in One SEO Pack plug-in.

✦ **Insert a longer title description, with more search terms, into the image title field.** WordPress automatically uses the title you give an image as its `<alt>` tag. Insert a longer title description with more search terms into the image title field.

When you write a post and add tags, WordPress automatically adds your tags to its global tag system. The global system determines the WordPress list of hot topics in real time. Users can click any word in the real-time cloud tag to view the most recent posts for that tag.

WordPress, like other blogs, often duplicates content by showing the same posts on archive, author, category, index, and tag pages. To remove duplicate content, which can have a negative effect on SEO, create a `robots.txt` file. See `http://sixrevisions.com/wordpress/optimizing-wordpress-for-search-engines`.

Optimizing Blogger

Contrary to myth, Google doesn't necessarily give preference to blogs hosted on its own service, Blogger. However, Blogger poses some unique advantages and challenges:

✦ Blogger templates place `<h1>` through `<h6>` tags into the source code automatically, thereby helping with SEO. You can easily adjust page titles and blog names for the correct heading level in page templates.

✦ Blogger lacks theme-related categories, which makes it a little more difficult for you and for theme-based SEO. To overcome that problem, create permalinks that include your categories or directory names. We discuss permalinks in the next section.

✦ Because Blogger doesn't provide a related-links feature, create that list of related text links within or at the bottom of each post. These links should open your other postings on the same topic. Or, take advantage of unlimited sidebar space to create a separate section for related links above your blogroll.

✦ Blogger defaults to weekly archiving, but the timeframes for archiving are malleable. Adjust the timeframe based on your volume of posts and comments to maintain good keyword density. If you post only weekly, it might make more sense to archive monthly. For an extremely active blog, you might want to archive daily.

✦ Creating text links is easy, so use your keywords in links whenever possible.

Assigning permalinks

Because most blogs are created on dynamic, database-driven platforms, their posts don't have fixed Web addresses. Links to individual posts disappear after the posting is archived and no longer available on a page. Obviously, that's bad news for inbound links and SEO.

Permalinks (short for *perma*nent *links*) solve that problem by assigning a specific Web address to each post. Then individual posts can be bookmarked or linked to from elsewhere, forever.

Most blog software programs, like WordPress, already offer this option; you just have to use it. If your blog doesn't offer it, you can generate permalinks at `www.generateit.net/mod-rewrite`, though you may need help from your programmer to install them. Try to avoid links that look like this: `www.yourblog.com/?p=123`. Instead, choose an option to use one or more keywords, such as `www.yourblog.com/contests/summer-travel-sweepstakes`.

To generate WordPress permalinks, open the Settings option in the Admin panel. From there, select the Permalinks panel and choose a common option or enter your own. (For example, you might want to insert a category.) For new blogs, that's it; for existing blogs, you may need to use the Redirection Plug-in as well. For more information, see `http://codex.wordpress.org/Using_Permalinks`. Permalinks on Blogger.com are a little more complicated. Go to `www.google.com/support/blogger/bin/answer.py?hl=en&answer=41436` for directions.

Optimizing images, video, and podcasts

Because search engines can't directly parse the contents of multimedia, you must take advantage of all opportunities to use your relevant search terms in every metatag, descriptive field, or `<alt>` tag. You'll find more about podcasts in Book III, Chapter 3 and about video in Book III, Chapter 4.

Make these fields as keyword- and content-rich as you can. In these elements you can often use existing keyword research, metatags from your Web site or blog, or optimized text that you've already created:

✦ **Title and title metatag:** This catchy name includes a search term.

✦ **Filenames:** Using names such as `image1234.jpg` or `podcast1.mp3` doesn't help with SEO as much as `PlushBrownTeddyBear.jpg` or `tabbycats-sing-jingle-bells.mp3` do. Use terms also in category or directory names.

✦ **Tags:** Use relevant keywords, just as you would with other social media.

✦ **`<alt>` tags:** Use these tags for a short description with a search term; for example, *Used cat tree for sale*.

✦ **Long description metatags:** Follow this example: `longdesc=for sale-gently used, gray, carpeted 6 foot cat tree with 4 platforms`.

✦ **Content:** Surround multimedia elements with keyword-rich, descriptive content.

✦ **Transcriptions:** Transcribe and post a short excerpt from a keyword-loaded portion of your video or podcast.

✦ **Anchor text:** Use keywords in the text link that opens your multimedia file.

✦ **Large images:** Upload large versions as well as the thumbnails that are visible on your blog or Web site.

✦ **RSS and XML:** Expand your reach with media RSS and site maps.

For more information on indexing multimedia, see `www.google.com/support/webmasters/bin/answer.py?hl=en&answer=114016`.

Even though search engines can't read watermarks, you may want to mark both videos and large images with your domain name and logo to encourage visits and for branding purposes.

Optimizing Twitter

In addition to adhering to the standard admonishments about providing good content and using well-researched keywords, you can follow a few extra guidelines to improve your ranking in search results on both internal Twitter searches and on external searches:

✦ **Your name on Twitter acts like a title tag.** If you want to benefit from branding and to rank on your own or your company name, you have to use it! If you haven't already done this, log in to your Twitter account and click the Settings link. Then change your name.

✦ **Your username, or Twitter *handle*, should relate to your brand, company name, or campaign and be easy to remember.** It can include a keyword or topic area. Change it in the Settings area.

✦ **Pack your one-line bio with keywords.** Your Twitter bio serves as the description metatag and is limited to 160 characters. Use résumé-style language and include some of your primary search terms. Talk about yourself or your company in the third person. Click Settings on the top right of the page, then click the Profile tab in the navigation bar. Complete the Bio box.

✦ **On the same Profile page, use your business address as your location.** (Or click the Settings link and then the Profile tab to modify.) Doing so helps with local searches. Remember to save your changes.

✦ **Collect Twitter followers.** Essentially internal, inbound links on Twitter. They carry special value if your followers themselves have a large number of followers. As the Twitter variant of link popularity, a good follower count may improve your PageRank.

✦ **Include keywords in your tweets and retweets whenever possible.** With the 140-character limit, Twitter might be a good place to use those single-word terms.

Use keywords in your Twitter #hashtags, too.

✦ **Remember the importance of the initial 42 characters of a tweet.** They serve as the title tag for that post. Your account name will be part of that count. Search engines will index the full tweet, however.

✦ **Format your retweets.** Keep them under 120 characters so there's room for someone to add their retweet information at the front. When you re-tweet, avoid sending duplicate content by changing the message a bit.

✦ **Maximize retweets as a measure of popularity.** Write interesting content or share good articles, especially when the direct link to detailed content goes to your own site.

✦ **Increase your visibility.** Link to your Twitter profile from other sites using your name or company name as the link text, rather than your @ Twitter address or Twitter handle.

Because Twitter adds a `nofollow` attribute to links placed by users, linking to your site doesn't help with PageRank. Truncated URLs (such as the TinyURLs described in Book II, Chapter 1) behave just like their longer-version cousins because they're permanent redirects.

However, links from Twitter still boost branding and drive traffic to your site. More traffic to your site improves your ranking at Alexa (`www.alexa.com`), which in turn improves one of the quality factors Google uses for setting PageRank. It's all one giant loop.

For more information on Twitter, see Book IV.

Optimizing Facebook

Take advantage of myriad opportunities to gain traffic from your Facebook pages by applying optimization techniques. Next to blogs, Facebook pages offer the highest number of opportunities to use SEO on social media to reach people who don't already know you. Fortunately, Facebook search engines can index all shared content on Facebook.

Every social network has different rules for its account names and profiles. Though consistency is preferable for branding purposes, follow the rules carefully.

Book II Chapter 2

Leveraging Search Engine Optimization (SEO)

Try these techniques when you first create your business page:

✦ On the initial login page at www.facebook.com, click the Create a Page for a Celebrity, Band, or Business link. If you already have a personal account, scroll down any of your pages all the way to the bottom and click the Create a Page for My Business link. Either option takes you to www.facebook.com/pages/create.php. (If you create your business page from your personal page, you're automatically listed as the Administrator for the page.)

✦ Use an easy-to-remember version of your business name alone or combined with a search term as your Facebook business page name. If possible, use the same username on both Twitter and Facebook for branding reasons. Facebook doesn't like generic names.

Once you have at least 25 people connected to your page, you can claim a username as your own at www.facebook.com/username, instead of seeing a long string of numbers in your Facebook URL. After you select a name, you cannot change it.

✦ Once your business page has been created, click on the Info tab and then on the pencil icon to Edit Information. You will see two gray bars with triangle icons: Basic Information and Detailed Information. Click the triangle on Basic Information to enter the date of founding and Save. Then click the triangle to expand Detailed Information. You'll see four boxes: Website, Company Overview, Mission, and Products. All boxes expand so you can enter all essential information.

✦ Under Websites, list all your relevant domain names, including your blog and other social media pages. Later, you can also place links to your Web site or blog or another type of social media within your page stream. Generally, it's easier to use the actual URL.

✦ Place keyword-loaded content in the first paragraph of each of the remaining boxes, all of which help with on-site product searches. Include your address and contact information in the Company Overview box; address information also helps with local searches. Your page description metatag may work well in the Mission box since it is already optimized for search terms. Be sure to include all your brand names and all the products or services that you offer in the Products box.

✦ As with Twitter, popularity matters. The more Facebook fans you have, the more internal links you have to your own page. Even better, when fans comment on or recommend your content, Google sees reciprocal links between your page and your fans' pages, which may increase your PageRank.

✦ More search term opportunities abound in the Static FBML Box application offered by Facebook. You can create additional boxes or tabs to display text, images, and more links. Be sure to use a good search term in your box name (which is limited to ten characters) and include text links in your content. It's a bit of a pain, but you can do this on your own.

For more information on creating a Facebook account and business pages, see Book V.

Optimizing LinkedIn

LinkedIn (discussed in Book VI) doesn't offer quite as many options for SEO as other forms of social media do. Start by including search terms within your profile text, with descriptions of any groups you start, and within postings to a group. Just keep it gentle and unobtrusive. Follow these steps to optimize your profile and to pass along some SEO credibility:

✦ Use your name or company name in your LinkedIn URL (for example, `www.linkedin.com/in/watermelonweb` or `www.linkedin.com/in/socialmarketing`). Because search engines look at keywords in URLs, this technique makes your company easier to find.

✦ Use content similar to your page description metatag within the first paragraph of your LinkedIn profile. It should already contain some of your primary search terms.

✦ Unlike Twitter, links from LinkedIn to other sites carry link juice. You can have as many as three links on your profile. Set one to your Web site and another to your blog. Use keyword-based link text on a third link to drive traffic to another page on your site or to another of your social media pages. Nothing says that all links have to lead to different domains.

Gaining Visibility in Real-Time Search

Needless to say, all the emphasis on social media has forced search algorithms to adjust accordingly. Social media services not only are now included in natural search results (refer to Figure 2-9) but are also driving a demand for results displayed in near real time.

It remains to be seen how this integration will affect your overall standings in search engine results. Watch one of the search engine resource blogs for changing news.

Dedicated real-time search engines are available for different services, such as Facebook, Twitter, RSS feeds, and blogs. These engines, some of which are listed in Table 2-5, may also index comments and other elements found only on a particular social media service.

Table 2-5	Real-Time and Specialty Search Engines for Social Media	
Name	*URL*	*Description*
Aardvark	`http://vark.com`	Connects people with questions to people with answers; acquired by Google in February 2010
BackType	`www.backtype.com`	Real-time conversational search of blogs and social networks and other social media by topic
Collecta	`http://myspace.collecta.com`	Real-time search of MySpace by topic; from third-party developer
Facebook	`www.facebook.com/#!/home.php?sk=lf`	Real-time (most recent) search of Facebook for postings and public stories from friends
IceRocket	`www.icerocket.com`	Real-time search of Twitter, MySpace, other social media sites, images, and blogs
LinkedIn	`www.linkedin.com/search`	Real-time search built-in for people, jobs, answers, groups

(continued)

Table 2-5 *(continued)*

Name	URL	Description
OneRiot	www.oneriot.com	Real-time social media, Web, and video search engine ranked by currency, relevance, and popularity
PubSub	www.pubsub.com	Real-time search engine for RSS and Atom feeds
Scoopler	www.scoopler.com	Real-time search engine indexing Twitter, Flickr, Digg, Delicious, and more
Twitter Search	http://search.twitter.com	Real-time Twitter search

Naturally, where others have broken the trail, Google, Yahoo!, and Bing cannot be far behind. In December 2009, Google launched real-time search in partnership with Facebook, FriendFeed (since bought by Facebook), Twitter, MySpace, Jaiku, Identi.ca, and other services. Results from all these sites are incorporated, based on relevance, directly into regular search feeds for both Web sites and mobile phones, along with news items, blog posts, photos, videos, MySpace moods, and other content.

To view real-time results in Google, search for a term and then, on the search results page, follow these steps:

1. **Select Show Options, directly above the Sponsored Link section.**

2. **Click Latest from the navigation bar on the left.**

This step displays the most recent relevant postings first.

3. **To filter results for social media only, click Updates in the top section of the left navigation column.**

The results are filtered to show the most recently updated sites, including social media, in reverse chronological order, as shown in Figure 2-13. Results update automatically as new posts appear.

Note the word *relevant* in Step 2. Try to use at least one of your researched keywords in tweets and updates so that you have more to offer than a time stamp.

You can't benefit from real-time search unless you're active on Facebook, Twitter, and other services. Add your twist on the latest trends in your market sector on Twitter, Facebook, and your blog. For ideas on current topics, use Google Trends (http://google.com/trends), or the "hot topic" searches on most social media services.

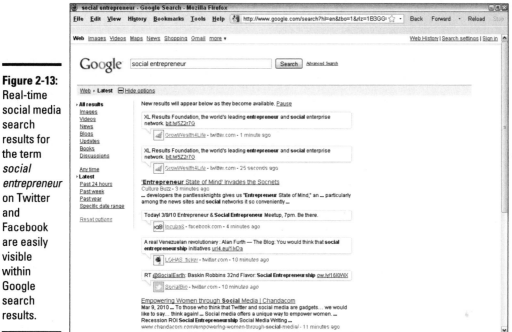

Figure 2-13:
Real-time social media search results for the term *social entrepreneur* on Twitter and Facebook are easily visible within Google search results.

Real-time search creates pressure to update frequently on social media so that you can stay near the top of the results stream. If this placement is critical for your business, schedule times on your Social Media Activity Calendar (found in Book I, Chapter 3) to post to your blog, add to your Facebook page stream, or send tweets at least twice a day.

Get some sleep! There's no point tweeting in the middle of the night when your customers are in bed (unless you're selling to insomniacs or international customers halfway around the world). Your tweets may be long buried by tweets from dozens — if not hundreds — of others by the time the sun rises.

Think about which messages are truly time-critical and save your real-time efforts for them. On your Social Media Activity Calendar, enter the times that you expect your target market might be searching, such as first thing in the morning or right before lunch. Make sure to ping all search engines with your updates.

Monitoring Your Search Engine Ranking

As always, if you're serious about SEO, you'll want to monitor how well you're doing. Table 2-6 lists some search engine ranking software that will show where your site appears on search engines by keyword or page. Most ranking software carries a charge, but some either offer a free trial or rank a limited number of pages, keywords, or engines for free.

Table 2-6	Search Engine Ranking Services	
Name	*URL*	*Starting Price*
Googlerankings.com	`www.googlerankings.com/index.php`	Free, need free API key
RankTracker	`www.link-assistant.com/rank-tracker/buy.html`	Free trial; then $99.75
Search Engine Rankings	`www.mikes-marketing-tools.com/ranking-reports`	Free
SERank	`www.ragesw.com/products/search-engine-rank.html`	Free trial; then $79.95
SiteReportCard	`www.sitereportcard.com/checkranking`	Free
WebPosition 4 Standard	`http://webposition.com`	Free trial; then $149
ZoomRank	`www.zoomrank.com`	Trial period $4.95; then $8.95 per month

SEO is a long-term strategy to deliver solid traffic over time to your hub Web site or blog. It takes time for your investment in SEO to pay off, and results can vary unpredictably from one week or month to the next. Generally, after you have everything set up and running smoothly, monitoring once per quarter should be enough except for exceptionally large and constantly growing sites.

Enter your preferred SEO tools in your Social Media Marketing Plan and insert the tasks into your Social Marketing Activity Calendar.

Chapter 3: Using Social Bookmarks and Social News

In This Chapter

✔ **Differentiating between social bookmarks and social news**

✔ **Gaining marketing benefits from bookmarks**

✔ **Submitting to social bookmarking sites**

✔ **Submitting to social news sites**

✔ **Motivating people to bookmark and rate your site or content**

✔ **Using Social Sharing buttons**

Social bookmarks and social news services are essentially peer-to-peer referral networks. Each one is an expansion of the former "tell-a-friend" call to action. Rather than e-mail to one or two people a link to a site or some content, users can notify many people at a time. Advocates of these recommendation services often argue that they filter the avalanche of Web sites that appear in standard search engines. Because social bookmarks and social news services rely on popular input from "real people" rather than from algorithms, some Internet users place a greater value on these search results.

Hundreds of these services exist, which you can see on the All Services tab at `http://addthis.com/services/all`.

Search engines recognize inbound links from many (but not all) of these services, so appearing on them can improve your search engine ranking. (See Book II, Chapter 2 for more information on search engine optimization.)

Bookmarking Your Way to Traffic

You most likely already know how to bookmark sites in a browser to make them easy to find again. Social bookmarking services work in much the same way, but you save bookmarks to a public Web site rather than to an individual computer. Users of bookmarking services can easily share links to their favorite sites or content with friends or colleagues (or with the world) while enjoying convenient access to their own bookmarks from any browser anywhere.

Social bookmarks act as testimonials from one amorphous group of Web users to many others. Bookmarking services such as StumbleUpon and Delicious (shown in Figure 3-1) recommend Web sites, blogs, videos, products, or content. At StumbleUpon, among other things, users can view bookmarks from their own list of favorites, from friends' favorites, or from everyone in the StumbleUpon database of submitters. Several subsets of bookmarking services are specific to certain applications (blogs only, for example) or activities (shopping only, for example).

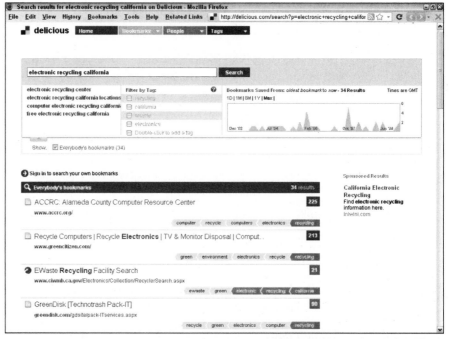

Figure 3-1:
These sites are recommended by "everyone" on Delicious for the search term *electronics recycling california.*

Reproduced with permission of Yahoo! Inc. © 2010 Yahoo! Inc. YAHOO!, the YAHOO! logo, DELICIOUS, and the DELICIOUS logo are registered trademarks of Yahoo! Inc.

Participating in social bookmarking is a no-brainer. Even if you do no other social media marketing, you should submit your site to several social bookmarking services, if they permit it, as part of your search engine optimization efforts. Some services may not permit direct submission, but allow you to include a badge on your site to encourage your viewers to submit the site (for example, `http://su.pr`).

Users generally search for listings by tag (keyword), category, most recent, most popular, or individual submitter. Bookmarking services rank items by the number of people who have cited them.

Table 3-1 lists some of the dozens of popular social bookmarking services and shows whether you're allowed to submit your own site. The Passes Link Juice column indicates whether search engines recognize a link from that service, as discussed in Book II, Chapter 2.

Table 3-1	Popular Social Bookmarking Services		
Name	*URL*	*Allows Self-Submission*	*Passes "Link Juice"*
BlinkList	`www.blinklist.com`	Yes	No
Delicious	`http://delicious.com`	No	No
Diigo	`www.diigo.com`	Yes	No
Faves	`http://faves.com`	Yes	No
Google Bookmarks	`www.google.com/book marks`	Yes	Yes
Linkroll	`www.linkroll.com`	Yes	No
Mister Wong	`www.mister-wong.com`	No	No
Spurl.net	`www.spurl.net`	No	Yes
StumbleUpon	`www.stumbleupon.com`	No	Yes
Y! Bookmarks	`http://bookmarks. yahoo.com`	No	Yes

Book II Chapter 3

Using Social Bookmarks and Social News

Sites that don't pass "link juice" contain a `NoFollow` attribute, which is visible by searching the source code.

You can find more on the Mashable list of social bookmarking sites at `http://mashable.com/2007/08/08/social-bookmarking-2`. The three largest search engines (Google, Yahoo!, and Bing) also have bookmarking services.

Later in this chapter, we discuss how to research bookmarking services, decide which ones to use, and submit a site.

Sharing the News

By comparison to social bookmarking services, social news services such as reddit and Digg (shown in Figure 3-2) point to time-sensitive individual postings and articles. Social news services focus on "what's news now," while bookmarking services look at sites without reference to timeliness.

Users can recommend dozens of different content pages on a particular Web site to a social news service, quickly driving significant amounts of traffic to the originating site. Many social news services rely on users to "vote" on submissions with more popular results appearing on the service's front page. Unlike bookmarks, social news services aren't designed to share a list of recommendations with friends.

Figure 3-2 shows recently posted popular articles in the World & Business category on Digg. Though most entries link to standard news sources, business press releases and even special offers may appear, as you can see in the third item in the list.

Figure 3-2: Digg shows links to individual articles submitted by hundreds of thousands of Internet readers.

Courtesy Digg.com

Peer-based recommendations aren't always golden. Because they reflect whoever randomly happens to have posted, these posts may be volatile, biased, and nonrepresentative. They certainly don't reflect scientific results.

Table 3-2 lists some most popular social news sites and shows whether you can submit your own site or press releases. The Passes Link Juice column indicates whether search engines recognize a link from that service.

Table 3-2	Popular Social News Services				
Name	*URL*	*Uses Popularity Voting*	*Allows Self-Submission*	*Allows Press Releases*	*Passes "Link Juice"*
Buzzup	`http://buzzup.com/us`	Yes	Yes	Yes	Yes
Digg	`http://digg.com`	Yes	Yes	Yes	No
Dropjack	`www.dropjack.com`	No	Yes	Yes	No
Fark	`www.fark.com`	No	Yes	Yes	No
Mixx	`www.mixx.com`	Yes	Yes, but not often	Yes	No
Newsvine	`www.newsvine.com`	Yes	No	Yes	Yes
reddit	`www.reddit.com`	Yes	Yes, but not often	Yes	No
Sphinn	`http://sphinn.com`	Yes	Yes	Yes	Yes
Slashdot	`http://slashdot.org`	No	Yes	Yes	No
Twingly	`www.twingly.com`	Yes	Yes	Yes	Yes
Y! Buzz	`http://buzz.yahoo.com`	Yes	Yes	Yes	No

Benefiting from Social Bookmarks and News Services

Social bookmarks and news services offer multiple benefits. To start with, they're free — always a positive factor for online guerrilla marketers. In addition, you may benefit in many other ways by using these services:

✦ **Improved search engine ranking:** By using your primary search terms in tags and other elements of your submissions, you may improve your overall Web presence in general search engines. The appearance of your content on these services supplements your own site in general search results.

✦ **Inbound links:** Inbound links from social bookmarking and news services may dramatically improve your position in search engine results and your Google PageRank as well as deliver visitors directly to your site.

✦ **Increased brand visibility and traffic:** The more people who see your Web site or content listed on one of these services, the more people will remember your name and visit your site. Like many other social marketing techniques, bookmarks and news services help fill the conversion funnel.

✦ **Increased readership and membership:** If you're a writer, pundit, professional speaker, or consultant, these services can be extraordinarily valuable. After you have established a reputation on a service, you may find that you have loyal followers as well as many new readers, subscribers, clients, and speaking gigs.

✦ **Increased earnings:** You can consider people who visit your URL from social bookmarking and news services as prequalified prospects, pushing them farther down the funnel toward "likely buyer" status. Be sure that your site validates the ratings it has earned. Monitor comments about your site to confirm that recommended pages, content, or products continue to appear and that links still work. Visitors shouldn't see "404 File Not Found" messages.

✦ **Triggering the influentials:** Many online "influentials" watch social bookmarking and news services to spot trends and decide whether to mention a site or an article in their own blogs or tweets. Of course, submissions by these influential people carry additional value in the eyes of their followers.

Your task is to ensure that your business is listed in the appropriate services and shows up near the top of results. Always review a potential social news service to make sure it's not just a spam aggregator; that postings are recent; what is permitted in its Terms of Use; and how it ranks on Google. Sounds a lot like the process of finding inbound links in the prior chapter, doesn't it?

In the following sections, we talk about researching social news services, selecting the right ones for your business, and submitting to them.

Check out `http://addthis.com/services/all?c=social_news` or `www.doshdosh.com/list-of-social-media-news-websites` for more social news sites.

Researching a Social Bookmark and Social News Campaign

Listing your Web site, blog, or content initially is easy. You, or others, can post your site on as many services as you want. It's a more difficult task, though, to be listed high in the rankings.

Check the Terms of Use on these services; in some cases, you cannot submit your own site or content. Many news services have more constraints on the voting process than on submissions.

Here's how to do it:

Book II
Chapter 3

Using Social
Bookmarks and
Social News

1. **Research appropriate social bookmarking and news services.**

   For an overview, try Quantcast or Alexa to review the user base, demographics, and traffic statistics for each prospective service. A handy chart on the Trends tab at `http://addthis.com/services` shows traffic trends on more than 200 social media services, or you can select only bookmarking or social news subsets. Generally, you're looking for services that

   - Receive a lot of traffic

   - Specialize in your market niche

   - Attract your target market

2. **Visit each site to confirm that it fits your needs and attracts your audience.**

   To understand more about the kinds of people who use a particular service, look at other top sites bookmarked in your category or at the content rated most favorably. Are the businesses and articles complementary to yours? To your competitors? Are the users of each service likely to try the products or services you offer?

   You can sometimes tell whether an audience might be receptive to your offerings by looking at who's paying for ads on particular pages.

3. **Sort by the names of those who have submitted postings to see which individuals or companies are responsible for most of the public listings.**

   Don't be surprised if the results follow the 80/20 rule: 80 percent of posts will come from 20 percent of users. The top ten submitters are likely to be the influentials on that service.

Executing your plan

Because a distinct effort is involved in recruiting other people to submit your site, select just a few services from your research to begin. Start with the popular ones listed in Tables 3-1 or 3-2 to see whether readers will vote for your content or repost your links on smaller services without making the effort yourself.

Some groupthink takes place on these services. If you have a popular post on Digg, for instance, someone may copy it to reddit or StumbleUpon for you. Some services, such as Dropjack, display a list of icons above every story for readers to share elsewhere.

Most users select only one social bookmarking service because they want only one place for their own favorites. That behavior complicates your task because you may need to submit to multiple services to obtain broad coverage. Strive for a realistic balance between coverage and the level of effort you can commit. If you're short of time, don't worry. Start small — you can always do another campaign later.

After you've selected your list of appropriate services, write them into your Social Media Marketing plan (found in Book I, Chapter 2) with a schedule for regular postings and review. Then create an account and a profile, if appropriate, for each selected service. Finally, submit the URLs for your site (or sites) or content as appropriate. Your schedule will probably reflect

✦ An initial mix of multiple one-time submissions to social bookmarking services

✦ Regular, repeat submissions to one or two social news services, within the constraints of their Terms of Use

✦ Occasional additions to your social bookmarks

✦ Regular monitoring of links to your site and mentions in the cybersocial whirl

Watch for scam services offering hundreds of automated social bookmark submissions. You don't need hundreds, any more than you need hundreds of search engines. Besides, you could end up blacklisted for using them.

Many services offer a toolbar add-in to help users easily submit sites or content whenever they find something they like. You might find it handy to install toolbar add-ins for the specific services you expect to use regularly. Better yet, install a Social Sharing button (see the section "Using Social Media Buttons" later in this chapter) on your site and use the button to access your suite of accounts.

Monitoring results

As we discuss in Book VIII, you always need to monitor the results of all your marketing techniques. Watch traffic statistics to identify which services produce the most referrals and when you see spikes in traffic. Stick with the services that become good referrers, of course, especially if they eventually lead to qualified prospects and sales. Replace the ones that don't work.

You might find it useful to try a tool specifically designed for monitoring appearances on social bookmarking and social news sites, including when others have recommended or rated you. You can use these monitoring tools to assess these elements:

Book II
Chapter 3

- ✦ The success of your social bookmarking and social news campaign

- ✦ The efficacy of one posting compared to another

- ✦ The unauthorized use of trademarks

- ✦ The effectiveness of a specific press release or sales promotion

- ✦ The appearances of your competitors on social bookmarks and news services

Book II, Chapter 1 discussed multiple tools for monitoring mentions of your business or Web site on social networks and blogs. Many of those tools also monitor bookmarking and news services.

You might also want to try:

- ✦ **Alltop.com:** Collects current headlines and lead paragraphs from Web sites and blogs and sorts by topic.

- ✦ **Backtype.com:** Graphs tweets and comments across social media by domain name.

- ✦ **BuzzFeed.com:** Monitors "hot" stuff online to share.

- ✦ **popurls.com:** Aggregates current headlines from the most popular sites on the Internet.

- ✦ **Social Media for Firefox:** Status bar add-on that displays how many votes content has at Digg, StumbleUpon, Twitter, Delicious, reddit, Mixx, Sphinn, Tip'd, Bit.ly, and other social sites (`www.97thfloor.com/social-media-for-firefox`).

- ✦ **Social Meter:** Scans Delicious, Digg, Furl, Google, Linkroll, Netscape, reddit, Spurl.net, Technorati, and Yahoo!. My Web offers bookmarklet add-on for toolbars.

- ✦ **Trackur:** A fee-based topic search.

- ✦ **WhosTalkin.com:** A free topic search for multiple social media sites.

Using Social
Bookmarks and
Social News

Submitting to Bookmarking Services

You might want to submit URLs to bookmarking services from a personal, rather than business, address or have friends or employees use their personal e-mail addresses as the submission source. Use neutral, nonpromotional language in any comment or review. Figure 3-3 shows how to submit a site to Delicious.com, a popular social bookmarking service.

Figure 3-3:
Submitting to social book-marking services is usually very simple: Create an account and submit a URL with a brief description.

Reproduced with permission of Yahoo! Inc. © 2010 Yahoo! Inc. YAHOO!, the YAHOO! logo, DELICIOUS, and the DELICIOUS logo are registered trademarks of Yahoo! Inc.

Try to use appropriate search terms in category names, tags, text, or titles when you submit your site. Select terms that searchers are particularly likely to use. Generally, you can find those terms in traffic statistics for your Web site or in tag clouds from the target service. (There's more on tag clouds in Book II, Chapter 2.) Enter your site in as many categories as possible.

If you have separate domain names or subdomains for your blog or community site, submit a few of them as bookmarks, along with your primary Web site, as long as the number is reasonable. You can also post social bookmarks to where links are permitted on Facebook or LinkedIn or other social networking pages to further enhance your visibility. Just don't personally submit too many of your own pages to one bookmarking site or else you might be marked as a spammer.

Be discrete. Do not spam social bookmarking or news services with multiple frequent submissions. Though you can organize a few submissions from others to get the ball rolling, don't set up multiple accounts per user on a social news service to vote for yourself or use automated submitters, which not only might have malware but also might be prohibited. Like regular search engines, these social services act aggressively to detect and blacklist spammers. Read the Terms of Use on every site if you have questions.

Submitting to Social News Services

Think of social news services as peer-reviewed indexes to short-term, contemporary articles, whereas social bookmarks are more useful for longer-term content. Submitting frequently to social news services is not only acceptable but also practically obligatory, particularly if your site generates news within a particular industry or geographical region or if your livelihood is content dependent. Figure 3-4 shows how to submit content to Digg.com. As with most social news service, you must create an account first and then submit content.

Because users are in and out of these services often, you always need new content to catch their attention. These users prefer peer-recommended stories versus ones selected by staff editors or that appear in an unfiltered RSS feed from other sources.

People who view your content are asked to "vote" stories up or down and are often given an opportunity to comment as well. You generally need to create an account to post, vote, or comment on stories, but anyone can read the listings.

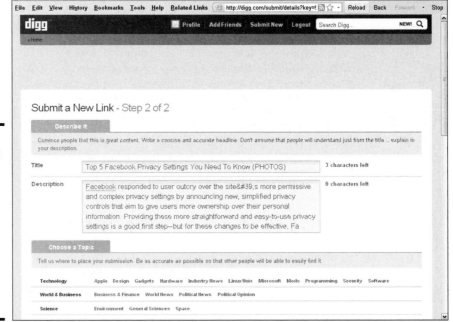

Figure 3-4:
Most social news services have a straight-forward submission process. Digg has two simple screens.

Always select appropriate categories for your material, such as Technology, World News, Politics, Business, Entertainment, Life Style, or Environment. Avoid vague categories such as General, Other, or Miscellaneous — they're deep, dark pits from which your content may never escape!

Selecting content for social news services

The choice of content is critical. Not every item on your blog or Web site will entice readers to submit or rate an article. Generally, the ones that drive the most traffic to your site will have timely content, such as breaking news, or entertainment, humor, or quality resource information not found elsewhere.

By their nature, these services are quite culturally dependent; you may need to submit in languages other than English. Other countries and languages may have their own localized social bookmarking and news services. Visit `http://addthis.com/services/compare-countries` or international search engines to identify them.

Avoid out-of-date material. If you must submit older stories, look for items such as features, interviews, how-to's, and essays that have longer-lasting interest. Those items are good for social bookmarking sites, too.

Be sure to match your content submissions to sites where readers like the types of stories you want to recommend. Look at the tag cloud for frequency of use on tags similar to yours over the past 6 to 12 months.

Some social news services allow links to images, video, and audio; others accept only links to text. Select the services that best match the information you have to offer and the audience you're trying to reach.

Think tactically: Initiate posts for specific pages, posts, or articles that have the potential to lead to traffic, prospects, or sales, not for your everyday internal "company news" update.

If you get a reputation for posting meaningless items or using the comment space for hard-sell language, you might find it hard to gain traction on these sites; you might even be banned for posting junk.

Preparing social news stories for success

Though you might be tempted to splatter social news services with your stories, just give them a little thought. Set up tags, titles, and lead lines carefully. Follow these online journalistic steps for improved results:

✦ **Write a catchy headline, not an academic title.** Keep headlines short and memorable. Try to use "vivid" verbs (not just nouns) and active voice.

✦ **Write a good lede.** The headline and first line of a story (the lede) are often the only elements that viewers see. Set a "hook" to catch readers and make them want to link back to your original content. Tell people what's in it for them or how they will benefit by reading the story.

✦ **Write a good description, comment, or summary.** Keep it short (20 to 25 words!) and focus on benefits.

✦ **Check your facts, your spelling, and your links.** If you make errors, someone is likely to post a negative comment. If your links don't work, you lose potential traffic, which is a primary reason you're using social bookmarking and news services in the first place.

✦ **Prepare your site for success.** Just in case, be sure you've structured your site to take advantage of new traffic. Links to related articles on your site or blog give interested readers more than one story to explore, thus increasing the number of page views per visit. To increase conversion rates, use calls to action and visual reminders to sign up for RSS feeds and newsletters, subscribe to a paid publication, or make a purchase.

✦ **Serving up your site.** Be sure that your hosting package allows for increased traffic. Traffic from social bookmarks tends to build slowly, but an appearance on the front page of a social news site can flood your server with more traffic than it's set up to handle. A quick call to your host or IT department should confirm your preparations.

These writing tactics not only help attract the kind of viewers who are more likely to click-through but also help increase the time users spend on your blog or Web site.

Using Application-Specific Bookmarks

Some bookmarking and social news services are constrained to specific types of content, such as blogs or video, and others are specific to topic, or activity, such as shopping or product reviews. Table 3-3 provides some examples.

Table 3-3	Bookmarks for Specific Applications
Name	*URL*
Blogs	
BlogCatalog	`www.blogcatalog.com`
Bloglines	`www.bloglines.com`
BlogPulse	`www.blogpulse.com`
Product, Software, and Travel Reviews	
Epinions	`www.epinions.com`
SnapFiles	`http://www.snapfiles.com/opinions/latestopinions.html`
TripAdvisor	`http://tripadvisor.com`
Shopping	
Kaboodle	`www.kaboodle.com`
Stylehive	`www.stylehive.com`
ThisNext	`www.thisnext.com`
Sports	
BallHype	`http://ballhype.com`
Video	
Kazivu	`www.kazivu.com/index.html`
myVidster	`www.myvidster.com`
Simfany	`www.simfany.com0`

You can find more shopping bookmark sites on the Mashable list at `http://mashable.com/2007/08/8/social-shopping-2` and more sports sites at `www.smmreport.com/top-social-bookmarking-sites-for-sport`. Search for *topic area + bookmarking site* on any search engine to find more specialty bookmarking services.

Receiving mentions in blogs and bookmarks placed by others on social shopping sites such as Kaboodle (shown in Figure 3-5) as well as on Faves, Delicious, and StumbleUpon, helped Barry's Farm laptop sleeves catch popular attention. See the nearby sidebar for more information about Barry's Farm social media story.

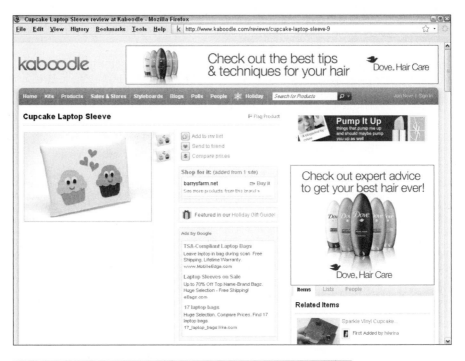

Figure 3-5:
Receiving
mentions in
blogs and
bookmarks
on sites
such as
Kaboodle
can help
your site
draw
popular
attention.

Timing Your Submissions

As with search engines, getting yourself on the first page of bookmarking
and social news services can be difficult. You generally have only a 24-hour
window on social news services to attract enough attention for either lasting

value or timeliness. Remember that you may need to coordinate submissions by others to get things started.

There's no point in posting in the middle of the night, when many people are asleep on one side of the country or both. Generally, posting between 10 a.m. and 4 p.m. U.S. Central Time works well, with an anecdotal peak of best results around 3 p.m. Workdays are generally better for generating traffic, although less competition exists on weekends. Of course, you need to adjust submission times if "getting a scoop" is critical or if you seek visibility on an international site.

On the other hand, if you're posting to specific bookmarking services, such as a social shopping or sports bookmarking site, that isn't time-dependent, weekends may find more of your audience available. It's a lot like scheduling an e-newsletter delivery or press release, both of which are audience dependent.

Your best bet is to experiment for yourself. Try submitting the same post to different services at different times of the day, or try submitting different posts to the same service at different times. Monitor traffic to your site by the hour and day, and adjust your plans accordingly.

Generally, social bookmarks drive traffic to your site slowly as people find your URL, but you can generate a spike in traffic by pushing your site on social news services (if they permit it). You can ask several people to submit your site, but leave it to others to vote it up-or-down.

Try to get 15 to 25 people to submit your posting within the first few hours of its publication. That's usually enough to get attention from others and build momentum for votes. Receiving 25 recommendations within a few hours means a lot more than receiving 25 recommendations within a week!

As your visibility on the service rises, so too does traffic to your site. Barry's Farm, a small business that makes and sells laptop sleeves, describes its experience in the nearby sidebar, "Blogs and social bookmarks spur growth at Barry's Farm."

For all the value these services may have as "recommendation" search engines, the traffic on them is nothing compared to traffic on major search engines such as Google, Yahoo!, and Bing. Optimization for general search engines is still absolutely necessary, as discussed in Book II, Chapter 2, and forms the basis for your success.

Blogs and social bookmarks spur growth at Barry's Farm

Known for its charming laptop and phone sleeves, Barry's Farm is a two-person business. Co-owners Katie Martin, who handles product design, and Barry Abrams, Web developer, started the company in 2004 to sell custom T-shirts. After Barry used one of Katie's monster-patterned, furry laptop sleeves on a business trip, the proverbial new star was born. In response to a flood of inquiries, they posted their first laptop sleeve on BarrysFarm.net that summer.

"We received a large quantity of orders that first weekend due to a mention on the popular blog BoingBoing.net," says Martin. "Many other blogs linked to it and the social bookmarks grew. Other people placed bookmarks on Kaboodle (refer to Figure 3-5), StumbleUpon, Delicious, and Faves almost immediately. We knew then there was a demand for laptop sleeves that were both fun and functional."

The site now targets college students and young professionals because both groups "appreciate carrying a unique and humorous product.... It's a way to make a statement in a world where everyone carries the same, boring black bag and has the same laptop."

Martin tracks how the bookmarks contribute to lead generation with Google Analytics, which shows that 55 percent of their traffic comes from referring sites. Usually, when a new bookmark pops up on StumbleUpon, she finds that the site experiences a spike in traffic, but not necessarily in sales. Still, Martin values the bookmarks for increased visibility. "Internet word-of-mouth (or word-of-blog!) has been a huge driving force behind our overall popularity. Without it, we feel that our small business may not have succeeded."

Barry's Farm also uses Facebook and Twitter to post upcoming sales and announce new products. "Facebook (`www.facebook.com/pages/Barrys-Farm/110378560770?ref=tsis`) is a great way to interact with people interested in your products because they can ask questions and offer product suggestions. Twitter (`http://twitter.com/barrysfarm`) works well for simple notices and secret sales," she explains. Follow Us On icons for both services appear on the home page of BarrysFarm.net, shown in the nearby figure.

Martin, who shoulders the day-to-day business responsibility full-time, is grateful for the marketing boost. "Because a lot of our traffic comes from referring sites such as StumbleUpon and Delicious, we don't have to spend as much time on marketing as other businesses do."

The power of blogs was her biggest surprise: "Getting a mention on just one blog that has a large readership can cause a spike in visits and skyrocket sales for a short period of time. If you have a product that you think would appeal to a certain sector, find a site that blogs about that sector and send them a link to it. For example, our laptop sleeves appeal to the techie world, so we have sent notices to blogs with large daily readerships, such as Gizmodo and BoingBoing, to announce new sleeves."

She advises using social media as much as possible. "By increasing overall visibility, you will increase sales over time. Social bookmarking sites like StumbleUpon can be utilized to promote your site, or allow your customers or fans to spread the word about your products.... It is important to make your product stand out in order to succeed, so find your niche and explore how other people in your sector are marketing and networking."

Courtesy BarrysFarm.net

Encouraging Others to Bookmark or Rate Your Site

Like most political campaigns, the "popularity" contest on services that rely on votes or frequency of submission can be managed to your advantage. It just takes a little preplanning. Though illegal vote-rigging and outright manipulation are forms of cyberfraud, these techniques are valid ways to encourage others to submit or rate your site.

✦ **We all get by with a little help from our friends.** Always have other people submit your material; on some services, submission by others is required. One easy way is to e-mail a circle of employees, colleagues, and friends to help when you post a new page or content, or help them set up RSS feeds from your selected services. Ask them to submit or comment on your posting within a few hours after being notified.

✦ **Scratch backs.** In addition to posting your own stories, it's good practice to recommend material on other sites that complement yours (as long as you don't drive traffic to your competition). If you help others increase the ratings on their stories through your repostings and votes, they're more likely to return the favor. These practices establish your reputation as a fair-minded individual who's interested in the topic, not just in sales.

✦ **Be a courteous responder.** You make friends and influence people by responding to comments on your stories and commenting on others. Again, one good turn deserves another. Consider it as building your cyberkarma.

✦ **Become known as the "go-to" poster.** If you frequently post interesting material on one service, you may develop a reputation and a following, with readers watching for new items from you. They will happily rate or rank items you suggest.

✦ **Ask.** People who visit your site might be willing to let others know about it, but you need to remind them. Put a call to action or Social Sharing button at the end of a story or post, reminding them to tell a friend or share your content publicly. If you've decided to focus on a particular service, display its icon with a link (see the later section "Using Social Media Buttons"). You might even include a call to action to install a toolbar.

Don't confuse *popularity* — a subjective and manipulated quantity — with the *quality* of leads that a bookmark or social news mention may generate. Popularity is a means, not an end. Ultimately, you're better off with fewer, but higher-quality, visitors arriving at your site.

Swapping bookmarks

Like exchanging reciprocal links to improve search engine ranking, exchanging bookmarks has become common practice. Like linking, bookmark swapping can be done honestly, but it has a darker side.

Follow the same principles as you do with links:

✦ Don't exchange bookmarks with spam-like junk sites, only with ones that offer value.

✦ Be suspicious of people who offer to sell bookmarks or votes.

✦ Look for relevance, including shared tags or search terms, as well as traffic rankings on the exchanging site.

Because submitting too many of your own pages to a bookmarking service can tag you as a spammer, you can participate in a service in which members bookmark each other. These are similar to some of the old link exchanges, banner exchanges, and Web rings. Be cautious. Avoid anything that looks illegitimate.

If you have no friends or colleagues to help you out, you might examine the options of piqqus (`www.piqqus.com`) for exchanges among Digg, StumbleUpon, and Propeller; `socialbookmarkexchange.com` or `www.lavalinx.com/social-bookmarking.lava` offer more comprehensive exchange services.

Avoid automated submission services or scripts. The safest way to participate in social bookmarking is the old-fashioned way: individually, by hand.

Using Social Media Buttons

Social media buttons have two functions: Follow Us On buttons crosslink visitors to multiple elements of your Web presence; Social Sharing buttons enable visitors easily to share your content or Web site with others. Place buttons consistently near the top of a page or article, where the key information is.

You can repeat smaller versions of the buttons at the end of each post on your blog, so users can share a specific item instead of the entire blog. Social media buttons can also be placed on e-newsletters and on multiple social media networks. Anecdotal evidence from some companies who have tried organized campaigns shows dramatic increases in traffic on their social media sites.

Follow Us buttons

Follow Us buttons, shown Figure 3-6, sometimes called *chiclets*, link visitors to other elements of your Web presence, such as to your Facebook profile, Twitter page, or blog. In Figure 3-6, the Follow Us On button links to Behind the Burner's social media pages, while the Socially Bookmark Us icons encourage users to share the site with their friends on their own accounts. Some services, such as Flickr and Ning, provide large, customizable graphical badges to promote a link to your alternative presence (see Book VII).

Almost all services offer free standard icons along with code to insert them. Alternatively, you can search for creative icons online at sites like www. evohosting.co.uk/blog/web-development/design/more-free-social-media-icons and create your own link or use a social bookmark links generator, such as Keotag (www.keotag.com/sociable.php).

Social Sharing buttons

Social Sharing buttons (such as those shown in Figure 3-7) let visitors easily share content by linking them to the sign-in page for their own accounts on other social sharing services. On SexyBookmarks.net (top), the buttons rise up as a user hovers over them; AddThis.com (bottom) shows a small drop-down option. Several sources for other social sharing buttons are listed in Table 3-4.

Follow Us buttons   Socially Bookmark Us buttons

Figure 3-6:
This blog
uses a
block of
social media
buttons for
following
and another
row for
sharing.

Courtesy Behind the Burner

Table 3-4	Sources for Social Sharing Buttons
Name	*URL*
AddThis	http://addthis.com
AddToAny	www.addtoany.com
FreeTellAFriend	www.freetellafriend.com
Open Share Icon Set	www.openshareicons.com
Shareaholic	www.shareaholic.com
ShareThis	http://sharethis.com
Social Notes Widget for Products	http://strongmail.com/technology/ socialnotes

These free, easy-to-install buttons allow users to transfer content quickly to their own profiles, blogs, preferred social bookmarking service, instant messages, e-mail, or text messages. You can even use a special Social Notes widget from www.strongmail.com/technology/socialnotes that facilitates sharing of products from your e-commerce site, as shown in Figure 3-8. This is viral marketing at an epidemic level!

Social Sharing buttons

Social Sharing buttons

Figure 3-7:
Social
sharing
buttons,
such as
the ones
shown here,
encourage
visitors to
pass along
your site
or content
through
their own
accounts.

Courtesy Pink Cake Box and Courtesy New Mexico SBDC

Figure 3-8:
Social
sharing
widgets
enable
users to
recommend
products
direct from
your online
store.

STRONGMAIL, SOCIALNOTES, SOCIAL NOTES, and the STRONGMAIL logo are the registered trademarks of StrongMail Systems, Inc. in the United States, other countries or both. All Rights Reserved

Register for free analytics on those sharing services that offer it; the analytics tell you how and where users elected to share your material or site. You can often find a toolbar add-on for each service on the site. You may want to install the ones you need in your browser and offer that option to your users in a call to action.

Always include Print, E-mail, and Favorites (for personal bookmarks) in your set of Social Sharing buttons. Some people like the convenience of the "old stuff."

If you aren't comfortable inserting code on your site, ask your Web developer or programmer to do it for you. Sometimes even your hosting company can help. Specify which Social Sharing or Follow Us buttons you want to have visible and ask to have the buttons appear on every page of your site.

If all these tasks seem overwhelming, plenty of providers are willing to help you for a fee. Most SEO firms, press and public relations firms, online marketing companies, specialized social marketing ad agencies, and copywriters who specialize in online content now offer assistance with social bookmarking, social news, and other forms of social media marketing. Try searching for *social media services, social media agencies,* or *social media marketing.*

Book III

Blogs, Podcasts, and Vlogs

Contents at a Glance

Chapter 1: Developing Your Strategic Mix

In This Chapter

✔ **Getting started with the media of your choice**

✔ **Setting goals**

✔ **Getting to know the community**

✔ **Maintaining your presence**

Many venues are available for marketing yourself or your company on the Internet. On social networking sites such as Twitter or Facebook, you're somewhat limited in the type of material you can publish. However, by using any social media, you can leave breadcrumbs to the tailor-made content for your business marketing material, such as a blog, podcast, or video blog (vlog). When you have a blog, podcast, or vlog, you have total control over its content. If you build it and pique the curiosity of potential clients, they will come.

You have many issues to consider when determining the type of multimedia platform to use. In this chapter, we introduce you to blogging, podcasting, and vlogging and help you determine which components to add to your social media marketing mix.

Welcome to the Wild World of Multimedia Social Media

So many options, so little time. As a businessperson, you must make wise time investments. Participating in social media can be a huge time drain. If you don't choose the right components for your social media mix, or if you choose too many, you create high levels of frustration and stress. You're also making a huge time investment with little or no return, and you may end up letting other tasks or projects go by the wayside. Therefore, whatever you choose to do is vital to your success. For many busy professionals, time management is robbing from Peter to pay Paul.

Determining whether you need a blog

A *weblog,* or *blog,* is an ideal format for you to use to get the word out about your company. Think of Speaker's Corner in London: A bunch of people who want to get something off their chests gather in a corner in Hyde Park and start babbling about whatever topic they want. Some speakers attract a huge audience, and others draw a miniscule but devoted audience. Blogs are a lot like that. They caught everybody's attention when Howard Dean used one to raise funds and keep in touch with his supporters in the 2004 presidential election. Since then, blogs have become mainstream. Many businesses now use blogs to keep customers informed, and performers use blogs to communicate with their fans. Photographers use blogs to show people their latest work, as shown in Figure 1-1.

Figure 1-1: Photographers use blogs to strut their stuff.

This list describes several advantages of blogging:

✦ **Search engines love them.** To do right by your blog, you must make the time to update it frequently. For that reason, search engines rank sites with blogs higher than sites without blogs. Every blog post is like a magazine article: It contains current and relevant information. As the needs and interests of your clients or your company change, your new blog posts reflect these changes. Search engines like blogs because the content is fresh and relevant — as long as you update it frequently, of course. The worst thing you can do is let a blog stagnate. Plan to post to your blog several times a week.

✦ **Your blog can grow with your business.** Because a blog is an ongoing work in progress, you can change your viewpoint or slant as time marches forward. When your marketing plans change, you can change your blog posts to reflect the new marketing schema.

✦ **Your blog can be optimized for search engines.** A blog can be optimized for specific keywords. You can also optimize each blog post for certain keywords. When your marketing changes, change the keywords to reflect the new content of your posts, and interested parties will be able to find your content by typing the applicable keyword or phrase into their favorite search engine.

✦ **Blogs are simple to set up and maintain.** You don't need to be a rocket scientist or a Web designer to create a blog post. In fact, creating one is almost as easy as writing an e-mail, a task you might perform several times per day. You simply log in to your blog, create a new blog post, and start typing. Figure 1-2 shows a post being created in WordPress. After you've had your say and publish the post, it's there for everybody and his little brother to see. Then you sit back and wait for the accolades about your brilliant post. Well, almost. You have to get people to come to visit your blog.

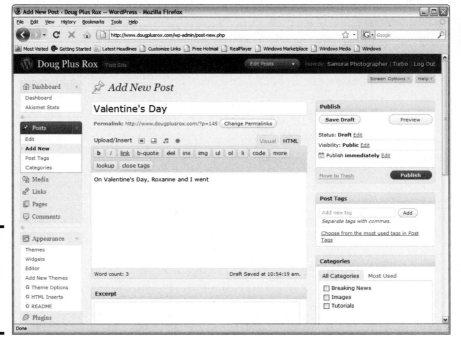

**Book III
Chapter 1**

**Developing Your
Strategic Mix**

Figure 1-2:
Authoring a
blog post is
as easy as
writing an
e-mail.

✦ **You can delegate some responsibilities.** Your blog can be a team effort. If you're the company marketing guru, you can start the ball rolling and then assign posting responsibilities to other members of your team. You simply add users to the blog and tell the blogging software which permissions they have.

✦ **Your blog can serve as the hub for your marketing efforts.** If regular blog posts are all you need to turn your target market into paying customers, create a catchy domain name, register it, find a hosting service, and upload your blogging software. As a matter of fact, many Web hosting services have built-in blogging software. All you need to do is tell a tech-support person to initialize it and you're ready to start blogging. After the blog is set up, you can optimize it so that search engines can find it.

We show you how to set up a blog in Book III, Chapter 2.

Podcasting to reach your audience

The written word and accompanying images are all well and good, but maybe your target customers have no time to read blog posts and prefer to listen to content while doing other things. Or, maybe your target market is highly mobile and prefers to receive their daily enlightenment from a portable device such an iPhone or iPod touch. Podcasting is a natural fit if you're a ham or if one of your team members has a pleasing voice and the gift of gab. A podcast is the equivalent of an Internet TV or radio broadcast. The podcast has a beginning, middle, and end. The middle and the end are the same for each podcast, just like the beginning and ending of your favorite TV shows. The middle is the meat of the podcast, the information you want to distribute about your company or product.

Here are some podcasting guidelines:

✦ **Remember that getting started is simple.** All you need is a good microphone and software program to record the podcast and you're in business. (Well, it's almost that simple.)

✦ **Take your podcast to the next level of quality.** To do this, create a video podcast. Doug records a weekly podcast about digital photography, where he can show techniques not easily conveyed with words (see Figure 1-3). The National Association of Photoshop Professionals, or NAPP, uses its video podcasts at Photoshop User TV (`http://kelbytv.com/photoshopusertv/`) to entertain viewers and show new Photoshop techniques.

Figure 1-3:
This podcast is about digital photography.

If you want to show viewers how to use a piece of software or manage a task, consider a video podcast.

✦ **Capture the excitement of live events.** The group Professional Photographers of America (PPA) creates video podcasts for its annual Imaging USA event, attended by thousands of photographers.

✦ **Podcast wherever you are.** A podcast can be recorded almost anywhere. If you're creating a podcast at a live event, you can use a small handheld recorder — a professional-quality recorder, of course — or a small video recorder. If you're recording a podcast at home, all you need is a laptop computer, a good microphone, and a quiet room.

We talk more about podcasting and what you need to do to start one in Book III, Chapter 3.

Vlogging: Marketing with video

Podcasting and blogging are fun and productive ways to promote your business. But what to do when you need to create a series of videos only to promote a product or, for that matter, yourself? In this case, video blogging, or *vlogging* — the process of creating a series of videos about a product, service, or concept. You can use a video hosting service such as YouTube to host your vlog posts and then embed the video in your blog or Web site.

You produce vlog posts as needed rather than on a schedule. Though a vlog is similar to a podcast production, the frequency at which content is delivered is their biggest difference.

Vlogging has many uses. Try these two types, for starters:

✦ **Educational videos for customers or employees:** You can use video to let existing customers or potential clients take a behind-the-scenes look at your business. For example, if your company manufactures a product, a series of videos of this type is a helpful way to show clients and potential customers the quality and craftsmanship that go into your product.

✦ **Slice-of-life videos, such as a wedding photographer working with a bride:** A few still images sprinkled in a video give a prospective bride an idea of how the photographer interacts with her clients as well as a sample of the finished product.

When you create videos to promote your company, you need to put your best foot forward — no garbled sound or pixilation allowed. Many digital cameras are capable of capturing stunning high-definition video and stereo sound. For much better results, use the best video and audio equipment you can afford. Turn to Book III, Chapter 4 to find equipment recommendations.

Before jumping into vlogging, consider the bandwidth available for your Web site. (Ask your Web host, if you aren't sure.) If lots of people access your videos, you can exceed the allowable bandwidth for your Web hosting package and incur extra charges that may be quite hefty.

To bypass these charges, look at free video-sharing services that can host your videos, such as YouTube (`www.youtube.com`). Doug posts instructional videos about digital photography there. His channel is shown in Figure 1-4.

We discuss video podcasting and other hosting alternatives in Book III, Chapter 4.

Figure 1-4:
Posting
videos on
YouTube.

**Book III
Chapter 1**

**Developing Your
Strategic Mix**

Determining Your Lofty — or Not So Lofty — Goals

Now that you have an idea about the type of media you can use to market
your company or products, you can figure out how to mix them in with your
current marketing strategies. To put your plan in motions, consider these
points:

✦ **Your marketing goals:** If your goal is to provide customers with timely
information about your product or industry, a blog is the logical choice.
If you want to entertain and inform customers, a podcast is a great way
to go. If you need to provide video information at irregular intervals,
consider setting up an account on a video sharing service such as
YouTube and then embed your vlog post in a blog or Web page.

A blog hosted on your own domain can serve as your Web site. The blog
can be optimized for specific keywords that help potential customers
easily find your online presence.

✦ **Any services or products you want to promote:** If you have company
videos, you can create a blog or podcast or use one of the video sharing
services to host them. Your ultimate choice depends on the technology
at your disposal. If you're just dipping your toe into the shallow end of
the pool, consider using a blog and reinforcing your marketing efforts
with other forms of social media.

✦ **Multimedia content that you want to include:** A blog handles photos with no problem, and you can embed video into a blog. However, if you're considering combining audio, video, and images, try creating a podcast.

✦ **Your schedule:** If feeding information to your customers regularly is your goal, a blog is the perfect choice. If you want to combine multimedia content such as slide shows or videos, host your multimedia content at one of the video sharing services and embed the content in your blog.

You should devote at least a couple of hours a week to either a blog or a podcast. If you don't have the time, are a solopreneur with too much on your plate, or don't have an available and capable employee who can create the content for you, consider using other forms of social media. The only thing worse than an irregular blog or podcast is a poorly done blog or podcast.

✦ **Software you need:** If you're technically adept at working on your own Web server or you have an IT department, you can easily upload blog software to your Web site and install it. After it's installed, you're ready to start blogging, or hosting a podcast in the blog.

If you've decided to add a blog to your Web site, determine whether your Web hosting service provides the latest version of MySQL and PHP. Blogs require a database into which blog posts and other pertinent information is written and stored. The blog application is PHP based. The Web server parses the PHP code and delivers it to the client's browser. The latest version of PHP as of this writing is 5.31; the latest version of MySQL is 5.144. When choosing a Web hosting service, make sure it has the proper versions of both application installed to support the blogging software you choose.

Putting the Wheels in Motion

After you've decided to invest your time in a blog, podcast, or vlog, you have to get your ducks in a row. Before you jump headlong into writing your first blog post, recording your first podcast, or creating the first installment of your vlog, you need to do your homework. Follow these guidelines:

✦ **Study your competition:** If your competitors blog or create a weekly podcast, determine what type of information they offer for potential clients. For example, your competitors might present offerings that are beneficial to potential clients or are just blatant advertisements. If their messages consists of the latter, you have a leg up on your competition. However, chances are good that at least some of them offer valuable content about a similar product or service that you offer. Study the best contributions offered by your competition and then figure out how you can do better by providing more timely or pertinent information. Or perhaps your offering can fill an unfilled niche.

✦ **Read the blogs of the leaders in your industry:** To determine what type of information is considered the norm for your industry, read the blogs of industry leaders. Find out what type of information they're dispensing, how frequently they post to their blogs, and whether they have guest contributors, for example. Popular blogs have large audiences that read every post. That's because the information is timely, pertinent, and relevant. Study the topics that industry leaders blog about, and you'll form a good idea of what you can write about on your blog to build a large and loyal following. After you study popular blogs, put on your thinking cap and come up with a way to put your own spin on similar topics.

✦ **Study the podcasts of leaders in your industry:** Industry podcasts generally have a similar format. After all, they're all vying for the same target audience. Develop a feel for the format, and then use your own creativity to create a podcast that's similar to others in your industry, but with your company's personality and flair.

✦ **Create an editorial calendar:** Many podcasts and blogs run out of steam after a few weeks because the authors have difficulty staying on track and thinking of good content. You can alleviate this problem if you create an editorial calendar. See Book I, Chapter 3 to create a social media calendar where you can schedule time and topics.

Be sure to keep your editorial calendar filled a few weeks ahead of your current post or episode. Also, schedule a weekly time for brainstorming and for adding new content to your editorial calendar.

Book III
Chapter 1

✦ **Practice:** Before you create your first podcast or blog post, pick a topic from your outline and write a blog post about it. Or, if your chosen media is podcasting, go ahead and create a podcast. After your practice session is complete, solicit some feedback: Contact friends or colleagues and tell them you want a critique of the session.

Developing Your Strategic Mix

Introducing Yourself to the Online World

After you decide which social media format to use, it's time to put the rubber to the road. You may think that creating content for social media is as simple as writing your first blog post, creating your first podcast, or recording your first vlog and then uploading it to the appropriate server. But there's more involved than you would think.

From the beginning, your blog post or podcast is a reflection on your company. Think of the old adage, "You never get a second chance to make a good first impression."

Creating your first blog post

Before you "go live" with your blog, follow these suggestions:

✦ **Limber up your writing "muscles."** Create several blog posts to get the feel of working with the software. Creativity is also involved.

✦ **Allocate enough time to complete the post from start to finish with no interruptions.** Inform your staff, or family members if you work at home, that you need an uninterrupted block of time. You don't need to specify why. Your goal is to work with no interruptions.

As with any task, when you're writing your first blog post, resist the temptation to check e-mail or voice mail.

✦ **If you're adding images to a blog post, resize them for the post and upload them to the server.** This process doesn't qualify as rocket science, but you have to know what you're doing. If you try to add an image from your digital camera to a blog post, you distort the blog template because the physical size of the image is much larger than the dimensions of the blog template.

✦ **Consider your first blog posts as a beta test.** The proof, as they say, is in the pudding. After you create your first blog post, you may be tempted to upload it to your Web server and publicize it by e-mail and on other social media you use. But before doing so, send a copy of the post to other industry professionals you trust. Ask for feedback on the content and value of the post. Remember that your goal is to make an impression with potential clients, not to bore them with a relentless advertisement. After receiving feedback from colleagues, make any necessary changes and upload your post. Upload remaining posts on the schedule you think is right for your target audience.

We show you a lot more about blogging in Book III, Chapter 2.

Creating your first podcast

Before starting your first podcast, follow these suggestions:

✦ **Make sure you have all the equipment you need.** If you're creating a video podcast, don't use a Webcam to record episodes. Use the best camcorder you can afford. If you're a photographer, your digital camera may be capable of capturing high-definition video. Refer to your owner's manual.

You also need good audio equipment to record your podcast. Don't use the microphone that's built in to your computer. You're likely to be too far away from the microphone to gain sufficient volume, and the sound quality won't be up to snuff. You need a good condensor microphone to get the job done. If you record podcasts in the field or add live interviews to your podcasts, you need a professional handheld recorder.

✦ **Find a place to record your podcast.** Many podcasts are created in the comfort of a home or work office space. You need peace and quiet to create a podcast, for not only you but also your intended audience. A podcast episode interrupted by a plane flying overhead has *Amateur* written all over it. Even if you live or work in a noisy area, you can do some things to soundproof your studio. We describe them and more in Book III, Chapter 3.

✦ **Find a place to practice your podcast.** If you're not a natural entertainer or a good presenter, your results can be disastrous. Have you ever attended a presentation and fallen asleep from sheer boredom? A bad podcast can do that to you, too. If creating a presentation or speaking in public isn't your specialty, consider having someone else in your organization create your podcast. Know your strengths as a presenter and use them in your podcast.

Your first podcasts will help make you comfortable with the equipment and the nuts-and-bolts involved in creating a podcast. Unless you're a professional performer or a competent public speaker, you won't be perfect. We show you techniques for editing your podcast in Book III, Chapter 3.

✦ **Create a stockpile of completed podcasts.** Have at least six podcasts recorded before you go live with your site. Your first podcast introduces the online world to you and gives listeners an idea of what your podcast is all about. It can serve as the introduction for new subscribers as well.

✦ **Treat your first podcasts as test episodes.** Show the episodes to trusted colleagues in your industry and ask them for feedback about the content, value, and quality of your podcast. Your goal is to deliver valuable information to prospective clients; information that entices them to subscribe to your podcast and perhaps become loyal customers. You may have to redo a couple of episodes after you get feedback, but that's much better than putting something out there with flaws you may not have noticed during your review.

After you create your first podcast episodes, it's time to upload Episode 1 to your Web hosting service. After you upload the content, you have to create a way for people to find your podcast. The easiest way to do that is to register your podcast with iTunes. You can then use other social media sites to publicize it. You also need to create some kind of physical presence on the Web where people who don't subscribe to iTunes can view and download your content.

Creating a video Web log

A vlog, which bears a striking resemblance to a podcast, is a podcast's little brother. The big difference between them is in the frequency of the vlog. A podcast is — or, at least, should be — recorded regularly, just like a TV show is. You can create a vlog, however, whenever you need to deliver new content to customers. Someone else can host your vlog. We show you a couple of popular services for hosting video in Book III, Chapter 4.

Here are a couple more vlogging suggestions:

✦ **Be sure to make the result as professional as possible.** As with podcasting, you should use the best video equipment you can afford. The content you create will be compressed by the video sharing service you upload it to. During the compression process, some data is lost, which leads to image degradation. If you work with a poor-quality video, it looks worse after you put it online. The same problem occurs with audio, which you know if you've ever watched a YouTube video in which the audio was garbled or the speakers sounded like they were underwater.

✦ **Practice using your equipment until you're comfortable with it.** Create a couple of test vlogs and show them to people in your industry whose opinions you value. Use their feedback to perfect the final result. You may have to rerecord your first attempts. When you're confident that you got it right, you're ready to upload your content to a video sharing service. At that point, you can embed the video in your blog or company Web site.

Getting noticed

Putting any content on the Web and expecting somebody to find it is like dropping the proverbial needle in the haystack and hoping someone sees it. You have to put in a little effort to make your cream rise to the top of your genre of social media.

Here are some things you can do to get noticed:

✦ **Use keywords in your posts.** This strategy helps with search engine optimization (see Book II, Chapter 2).

✦ **Allow people to add comments and trackbacks to your blog posts.** Add links so that people can rave about your content on other sites, such as Digg. Trackbacks, links, and raves on sites such as Digg act like breadcrumbs that lead people to your content. When you're considering using link backs and trackbacks, the more, the merrier — which means, of course, that your site is more visible on the Internet.

Mixing and matching your content with other social media

If you only create a blog or a podcast or occasionally upload a video to your favorite video hosting service, you'll never get the exposure you're looking for. Mix and match your content with other forms of social media.

You can set up a Facebook page relatively easily, and you can use Facebook tools to display blog posts and Twitter messages on your wall. You can also use Twitter to announce a new blog, podcast, or video.

Maintaining your enthusiasm

Setting up a blog or podcast takes a lot of work. You also spend more than just a bit of effort when you create vlog posts and upload them to your favorite video hosting service. In a perfect world, you get instant results from all your marketing efforts. But in a far-from-perfect world, your initial results may be somewhat disappointing. In fact, many people start using social media for marketing and stop when they don't see a reasonable return for the time they invest. The trick is to be persistent and continue creating posts, sending messages on Twitter, and adding content to your Facebook page. Use the other tricks of the social media marketing trade throughout this book to build a loyal base of fellow businesspeople and followers to build your brand and get your marketing message out there. It takes persistence on your part, but persistence pays.

Chapter 2: Building Your Blog

In This Chapter

✔ Securing a home for your blog

✔ Choosing a blog application

✔ Setting up your blog

✔ Tweaking your blog

✔ Engaging in the fine art of blogging

✔ Finding content for your blog

A blog is a wonderful platform for getting your message out there. Creating a blog post is as easy as writing e-mail, and you can include images and multimedia content in your posts. If you're also hosting video on sites such as YouTube or Vimeo, you can embed this content in a blog post as well. You can include specific keywords in your blog posts to help potential clients easily find your posts. You can host a blog on your own domain, add it to your existing Web site, or use a free blogging service.

When you decide to go blogging, you have choices. You can host a blog on your own domain, or use an existing blogging service like WordPress or Blogger. If you decide to host a blog on your own domain, you can choose the software with which you make your blog posts and manage your blog. You can personalize a blog to match your personal tastes or existing corporate material. You can also modify a blog by choosing a theme (changing the page that the outside world sees, adding plug-ins that handle tasks such as defeating spam or adding widgets to the blog sidebar).

In this chapter, we cover the fine points of blogging, including securing a Web host, choosing blogging software, using blog templates, and creating blog posts.

Choosing a Blogging Application and Web Host

Hosting a blog on your own Web domain has some distinct advantages. You're in total control of the situation. You can choose a reliable Web hosting service, optimize your blog for search engines, and so on. If you choose one of the free blogging services, you're limited to the version of blogging software the service uses and the plug-ins you can use to tweak your blog.

If you're going to host your own blog, you need blogging software. These three blogging applications are the most popular: b2evolution, MovableType, and WordPress.

These PHP applications serve up content on demand. In the case of a database, the PHP code plucks data from a MySQL database that's hosted on the server. The PHP software is hosted on the server as well.

The blogging software stores your published posts and drafts in its database. The software also creates the links, which are also stored in the database. Other blog features give visitors a chance to provide feedback about your blog post. Each software application handles common tasks a tad differently.

If you've already secured a Web hosting service for your Web site, you can host your blog there as well, as long as it meets the requirements for the blog software you use. If you have no Web hosting service, choose one that meets the requirements of the blog software you're using.

The following sections briefly describe these three blogging solutions.

Getting to know b2evolution

`http://b2evolution.net`

This free blogging software b2evolution has been around for a while and has all the features you need. However, you don't find as many plug-ins or templates for b2evolution as you do with WordPress (see the later section "Getting wordy with WordPress").

Many Web hosting companies offer b2evolution as an option for their customers. Check with your Web hosting company, or the company you're considering, and ask whether it offers this application and can help you set up the blog. If you're tackling the installation yourself, the b2evolution Web site includes detailed information that shows you how to install the application on your Web server.

You can find out more about b2evolution and see a sample blog at `http://b2evolution.net/index.php`. Click the Demo tab to see a live blog.

If you decide to use b2evolution as your blogging software, your Web hosting service must meet these requirements:

✦ **Web server:** b2evolution is typically run on the Apache Web server.

✦ **PHP:** b2Evolution requires PHP 4.32 or later.

✦ **MySQL:** b2Evolution requires MySQL 4.1 or later.

Moving in on MovableType

www.movabletype.com

MovableType is another potent blogging solution. It also offers two business packages — one for 5 authors and one for 20 authors. As of this writing, the first business package is available for $395; the second, for $995.

If you decide to use MovableType 5.0 as your blogging solution, your Web hosting service must meet these requirements:

✦ **Scripts:** Your Web server must be configured to run CGI scripts written in PERL.

✦ **Web server:** MovableType typically runs on the Apache Web server version 1.3x or 2.x. Ask your Web hosting service if it meets the requirements for hosting Movable Type

✦ **PERL:** MovableType requires PERL 5.81 or later.

✦ **PHP:** MovableType 5.0 requires PHP 5.0 or later.

✦ **MySQL:** MovableType requires MySQL 5.0 or later.

Getting wordy with WordPress

www.wordpress.org

The WordPress blogging application is extremely popular. The software is easy to install and easy to use. Writing a blog post couldn't be easier with WordPress, and it has lots of templates available for you to get the look you want. If you have an existing Web site, chances are good that you can find a template to match your site. Using a little bit of wizardry, you can customize the template to include the banner from your main Web site.

If you decide to use WordPress for your blogging needs, your Web hosting service must meet these requirements:

✦ **MySQL:** WordPress requires MySQL 4.1.2 or later.

✦ **PHP:** WordPress requires PHP 4.3 or later.

Hosting your own blog for nongeeks

If you don't have a huge amount of technical savvy, the thought of setting up a blog on your own server may petrify you. Alternatives are available. When you're shopping for a Web hosting service, ask whether someone can set up the blog for you. For a nominal fee, the tech-support crew at many Web hosting companies can set up the database and blog for you. Or, your Web hosting company may offer robust tech support that walks you through the process of setting up the database and blog. Many Web hosting companies also have an extensive library of help material.

Using a Blog Hosting Service

Some people would rather have their teeth cleaned before attempting a technical task such as setting up a blog. If you fall into this category, you can get someone to host your blog for you. You won't have your own domain, but you can still blog.

If you have an existing Web site, you can have a Web designer add a link to your Web site from your hosted blog.

Setting up a new blog with Blogger

Google is everywhere. It even has a slice of the blog pie, with Blogger. If the idea of creating a blog on your own Web domain doesn't strike your fancy, you can still get the word out with a blog from the free service Blogger (www.blogger.com).

Follow these steps to set up your blog on Blogger:

1. **Launch your favorite Web browser and navigate to www.blogger.com.**

The Blogger home page appears, and you can find information about the service and other delights, as shown in Figure 2-1.

2. **Click the Create a Blog button.**

The Create a Google account page appears. You must have a Google account in order to use this service. A Google account is free, so fill in the blanks if you want to blog. If you already have a Google account, click the Sign In link.

3. **Create a Google account or sign in.**

The Name Your Blog page appears.

Figure 2-1:
Get your
free blog —
right here,
right now.

4. Enter a name for your blog.

Choose the name wisely because you won't be able to change it later. The name you choose appears as a header in your blog, on your profile, and on your blog dashboard.

5. Enter a URL (or blog address) for your blog.

When you create a blog with Blogger, you're creating a subdomain. If you were to enter the URL *myblog,* the final URL for your site would be `myblog.blogspot.com`, as shown in Figure 2-2.

6. Enter the word verification and then click Continue.

The Name Blog page appears.

7. Enter a name and URL for your blog, and then click the Check Availability link.

Blogger checks to see whether the URL is available. If it isn't, you see an error message. Try another name in the URL field.

The Choose a Template page appears, as shown in Figure 2-3.

Figure 2-2:
Almost
signed,
sealed, and
delivered.

Figure 2-3:
Choosing a
template for
your blog.

8. **Choose a template for your blog and click Continue.**

The Your Blog Has Been Created page appears.

9. **Click Start Blogging.**

You're transported to the dashboard of your blog.

Creating a blog post with Blogger

After you create a Blogger blog, it's your job to create posts, and create them often. Creating a post is relatively easy. To create a blog post with Blogger, follow these steps:

1. **Launch your favorite Web browser and navigate to the URL of your blog.**

Your blog appears in live and living color.

2. **Click the Sign In link.**

The Blogger page appears.

3. **Enter your Google account username and password, and then click Sign In.**

You're transported to the dashboard of your blog. The dashboard is Mission Control for your blog. That's where you create posts, edit posts, and handle comments, for example. Notice that you have quite a few options. We describe the other options later.

4. **Click New Post.**

The New Post page appears. By default, the page appears with the Compose tab selected (see Figure 2-4). Notice that you have options here also. You can edit posts and pages and moderate comments.

5. **Enter a title for your new post.**

The title of any post is important. Use words that prospective clients may use to find your type of content at a search engine. Yep, you guessed it: You're *optimizing* the blog post for search engines, and Google just happens to be the granddaddy of them all. (It also happens to own Blogger. Talk about stacking the deck.) Turn to Book II, Chapter 2 for more about search engine optimization.

6. **Enter the content of your post.**

Use words that prospective clients will use to find content such as yours on the Web. When you're entering content, you can stylize the text using the buttons in the upper left corner of the dialog box in which you're composing the post.

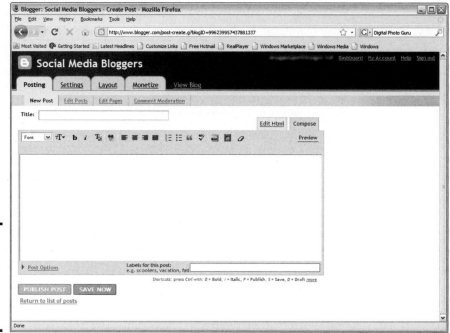

Figure 2-4:
I'm gonna sit right down and write a blog post.

7. **Perform other options as needed.**

   You can stylize the text, change the font, add bulleted and numbered lists, change the text color, and spell-check the document.

8. **Click Post Options.**

   A menu appears, giving you the option to allow comments on the post. You can also delay the day and time the post is published.

9. **(Optional) Enter labels for the post.**

   Search engines recognize labels. Enter labels applicable to the content of the post.

10. **Click Preview.**

    This option displays the post as it will be published. Even though you performed a spell check, you should check your grammar and make sure that the post is easy to understand.

11. **Click Publish Post.**

    If you're including video in the post, and the video is still being processed, your only alternative is to save the post.

Your blog has a profile. Use it to tell visitors a bit about yourself. You can also upload an attractive photo or your company logo. When people associate blog posts with a smiling face, it makes the connection more personal. Your blog profile can be a valuable asset in your social media marketing campaign. Make sure your blog profile is similar to other profiles you've sprinkled throughout the Web. You can edit your profile in the Blogger dashboard.

Adding links, images, and video

In the previous section, we showed you how to create a basic blog post. But you most likely want to add linkable URLs, or images and videos as well. Here's how you do those three things:

✦ **To create a link:** Creating a link to content outside your blog is helpful. Links are like breadcrumbs that draw visitors to your blog. Highlight the text you want to link and click the Link button. Type the URL to which the text will be linked and click OK.

Make sure to enter the correct URL including the `http`.

✦ **To add an image:** Place the cursor at the point where you want the image to appear and then click the Add Image button. (It looks like a small picture.) You can upload images from your desktop to Blogger or specify the URL to an image stashed on the Web (see Figure 2-5). Note that if you create a link to an image, you must include the image extension as well. Select the radio button to agree to the Blogger terms of service. Click Upload Image.

The maximum file size you can upload is 8MB. Blogger accepts images in the formats BMP, GIF, JPEG, and PNG.

**Book III
Chapter 2**

Building Your Blog

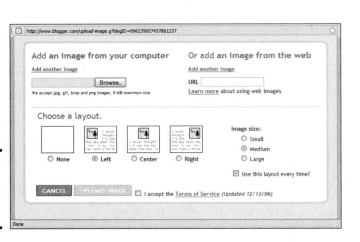

Figure 2-5:
Adding images to a post.

Here are the other options you have

- *Layout:* The left and right options are useful when you want to keep an image inline with text. For example, if you position the cursor at the beginning of a paragraph before inserting an image, you can position the image to the left or right of the paragraph. The text wraps around the image.

- *Image size:* Accept the default Medium image size or choose Small or Large.

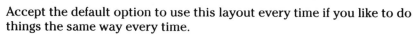

Accept the default option to use this layout every time if you like to do things the same way every time.

✦ **To add a video:** Position the cursor wherever you want the video to appear, and then click the Add Video button. Click the Browse button (see Figure 2-6) and navigate to the video you want to upload. Enter a title that contains a keyword applicable to the content of the post. (The title appears as alternative text, which can be read by search engines.) Agree to the terms and conditions and click the Upload Video button.

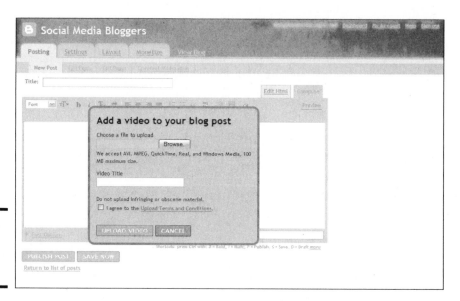

Figure 2-6:
Adding video to a blog post.

You can upload a video file whose size doesn't exceed 100MB. Blogger accepts the video formats AVI, MPEG (including the popular and Web-perfect MPEG-4), QuickTime (MOV), Real, and Windows WMV.

You can find more information about video in Book III, Chapter 4.

Managing your blog

The Blogger Dashboard is a wonderful thing. From there, you can create new posts, edit existing posts, change the layout, add pages to your blog, and perform other tasks. Here's a list of what you can accomplish after clicking the Dashboard link:

✦ **Edit posts:** Click the Edit Posts link to display the Posting tab and view all posts you've created, including drafts. You can then edit individual posts and delete or view selected posts. Click the Edit Pages button to add pages to your blog or to edit existing pages. You can add as many as ten pages to your blog.

Add at least one page with a detailed bio of yourself and your company. A mission statement is another nice touch.

✦ **Change settings:** Click the Settings link to change your blog settings. To prevent users from spamming your blog with comments, change the Comment Moderation default setting in the Comments tab to Always (which allows you to check all comments before they're posted to your blog). On the Permissions tab, you can invite other authors to post to your blog by clicking the Add Authors button.

✦ **Customize your blog:** Click the Layout link to change the look and feel of your blog. You can change its background colors, choose a different template, change the image banner to match your other online content, and more.

✦ **Monetize your blog:** If you're only in it for the money (as Frank Zappa might have said), you can click the Monetize link to monetize your blog with AdSense (a Google service you can use to post targeted non-competing ads on your blog). You can choose to display ads in the blog sidebar and posts, display ads only in the sidebar, display ads below the post, or choose not to add new ads.

A thing of beauty is a joy forever, and a blog can be beautiful if you customize it to your liking. Okay, maybe it can't be beautiful, but with a bit of work, you can certainly make it attractive.

Hosting your blog with WordPress

If you don't need the features of a Web hosting service, consider hosting your blog with WordPress. It's free and you still get all the features of the robust WordPress application. To host a blog with WordPress, follow these steps:

1. **Launch your favorite Web browser and navigate to www.wordpress.com.**

The site's home page appears, as shown in Figure 2-7.

**Book III
Chapter 2**

Building Your Blog

Figure 2-7:
Logging
on to the
WordPress.
com site.

2. **Click the Sign Up Now button.**

   The browser refreshes and displays the information required to set up a WordPress blog, as shown in Figure 2-8.

3. **Enter a username and password, confirm the password, and then enter your e-mail address.**

   Choose a username that reflects your business. If the name of your business is long, consider an acronym that users associate with your business. Remember that some people have to type this information on the Address bar of their browsers. Your username becomes part of the URL for your blog — for example, `myblog.wordpress.com`.

4. **Accept the legal flotsam and the option to create a blog, and then click Next.**

   Your browser refreshes, showing the URL of your blog and its title, as shown in Figure 2-9. You can make changes to the URL and the blog title, but you can't make those changes after you click the Signup button. Be sure to double-check them.

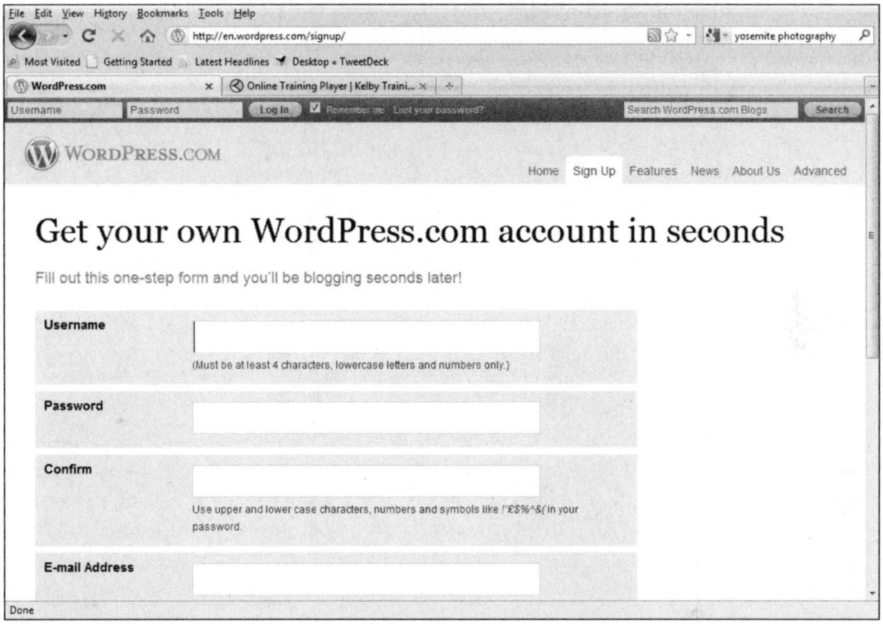

Figure 2-8:
Setting up a
WordPress
blog.

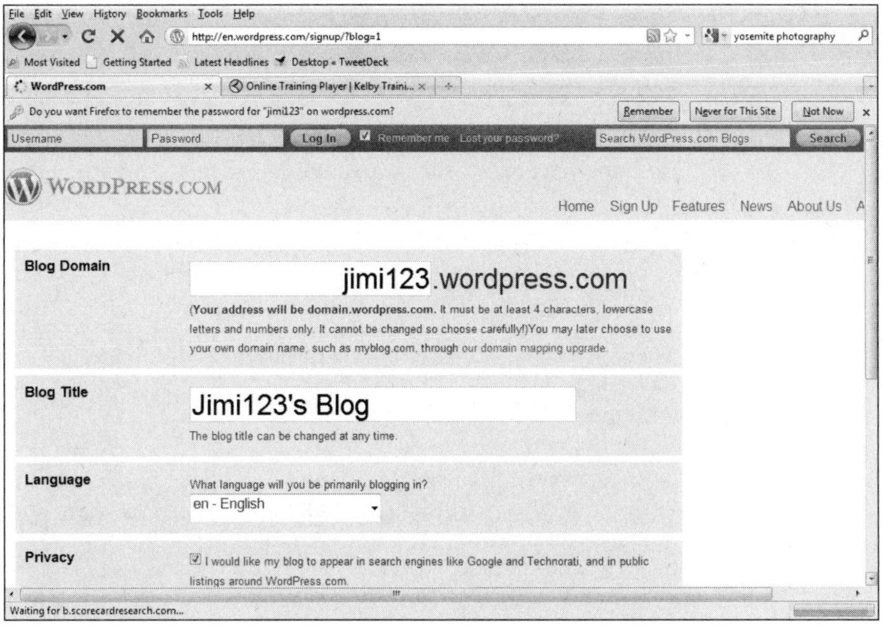

Figure 2-9:
Changing
the blog
particulars.

5. **Click Signup.**

   The Check Your Email to Complete Registration page appears. This page notifies you that a message has been sent to your e-mail address. You have to respond to it to complete the signup process. On this page, you can also update your profile. Add your first and last names and create a brief bio in the About Yourself section.

6. **Click Save Profile.**

   This option saves your profile to the blog database.

7. **Check your e-mail.**

   You should have a message from WordPress.com.

8. **Click the link to activate your blog.**

   A Web page appears, telling you that your account is active. At this point, you can log in to your blog. The Dashboard then opens — a place where you can manage your blog, add new users, create posts, and more. We introduce you to the fine art (or black art) of blogging in the later section "Discovering the Fine Art of Blogging."

Setting Up Your WordPress Blog

If you host your own blog with a Web hosting service, you have to upload a blog application to your server.

You set up a MySQL database into which each blog post is saved. Most blog applications use PHP code to parse a visitor's request and serve up a blog post. If this task is beyond your technical ability, you can ask your Web hosting service for assistance in setting up your blog.

We recommend using WordPress. This robust blogging application is well documented. In fact, your Web hosting service may offer WordPress.

Follow these steps to set up a blog on your own domain:

1. **Set up a MySQL database on your domain.**

   You usually complete this step on your Web site Control Panel. Check with your Web hosting service for more information on setting up a MySQL database. When you set up the database, write down the path to the database on your server, as well as your username and password. You need this information in order to configure the blog.

2. **Download the WordPress application from `wordpress.org/download`.**

3. **Extract the documents from the zipped file.**

4. **Rename the file wp-config.sample.php to** wp-config.php.

   This document is further modified to include the information to open the MySQL database.

5. **Modify the wp-config.php document.**

   Include the path to your MySQL database, database username, and database password. Installation instructions are on the Web page `http://codex.wordpress.org/Installing_WordPress`. The link named The Famous Five Minute Installation tells you everything you need to know to install WordPress on your Web site.

6. **Use your favorite FTP client to upload the files to your Web site.**

   If you're using WordPress as the basis for your Web site, upload the files to the root directory. If you have an existing Web site to which you're adding the blog, create on your Web site a folder named `blog` and upload WordPress to it.

7. **Run the installation program.**

   If you uploaded WordPress in the root directory of your Web site, the path to the installation program is `http://www.mysite.com/wp-admin/install.php`. If you uploaded WordPress to a folder named blog, the path is `http://www.mysite.com/blog/wp-install.php`.

   If you've done everything correctly, a page tells you that the install was successful. It also shows your blog username and password.

8. **Write down your username and password.**

   You may be tempted to change your password to one that's easier to remember. Don't do it. If the password is easy to decipher, your blog is prone to hackers.

You now have everything you need to begin blogging. We show you how to blog in the section "Discovering the Fine Art of Blogging," later in this chapter.

Using the WordPress one-click install

If you're technophobic, the thought of installing an application on your own domain probably scares you worse than a long-overdue visit to the dentist. Though the vast majority of Web hosting services are robust enough to support WordPress, you have to work with their tech support team and manually install the software. Wouldn't it be helpful if you could get your blog up and running in one click? You can do it: WordPress has partnered with a few Web hosting services that offer this powerful option. As of this writing, these Web hosting companies support one-click WordPress installation:

- **BlueHost:** www.bluehost.com
- **DreamHost:** www.dreamhost.com
- **Go Daddy:** https://www.godaddy.com
- **Laughing Squid:** http://laughingsquid.net
- **Media Temple:** http://mediatemple.net

Other Web hosting services may support a simplified installation of WordPress. Be sure to ask any Web hosting service you're looking at whether it offers one-click service.

Modifying your blog with themes

The standard WordPress blog template has been around since the invention of dirt. It isn't particularly eye-catching. You can, however, download a spiffy-looking blog theme and upload it to your blog site. A great-looking blog theme that looks similar to your other Web content unifies your online marketing strategy. You can find a wide variety of WordPress blog themes for download at http://wordpress.org/extend/themes, as shown in Figure 2-10.

You upload your theme to the Themes folder at your blog Web site and activate it from the WordPress Dashboard. At http://codex.wordpress.org/Using_Themes, you can find complete documentation for installing and working with WordPress blog themes.

After a WordPress update, your blog theme may not work. (WordPress is updated frequently.) Therefore, you should install a blog theme that has been around for a while and is updated for new versions of WordPress as they're released. You can decide, of course, not to upgrade to the latest version of WordPress. However, some updates are crucial and have security fixes for potential problems. Failing to update can put your site at risk.

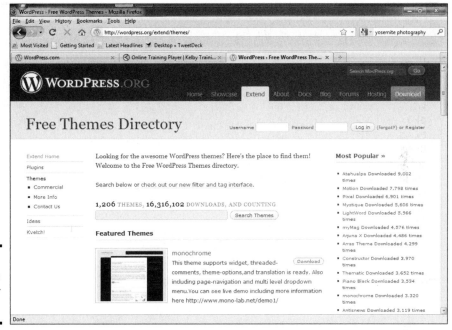

Figure 2-10:
The Themes
directory for
WordPress.

Modifying your blog with plug-ins

You can extend the usefulness of the standard WordPress application by
using plug-ins, which add multimedia support, spam control, widget additions,
and many other features to your site. A plethora of plug-ins is available for
the WordPress blog at `http://wordpress.org/extend/plugins`, as
shown in Figure 2-11.

Be sure to choose plug-ins that are compatible with the version of
WordPress you're using. (We hope that you're using the *latest* version.)
Otherwise, you may create undesirable results.

Plug-ins are loaded into the `Plugins` folder in your blog (`www.mysite/
blog/wp-content/plug-ins`). After you upload a plug-in, you activate it
from the WordPress Dashboard, shown in Figure 2-12. After installing a plug-
in, you may end up with additional tabs in your Dashboard. Detailed instructions for using a specific plug-in are usually at the developer's site.

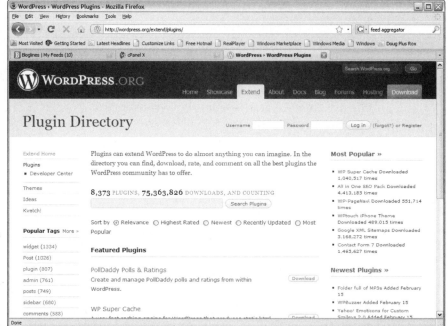

Figure 2-11:
Adding
functionality
with
plug-ins.

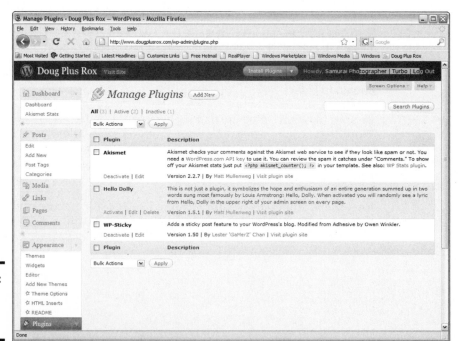

Figure 2-12:
Activate
plug-ins
here.

The Featured Plug-ins section in the `Plugin` directory is a good place to start your search.

Like themes, plug-ins are applicable to certain versions of WordPress. Make sure that the plug-ins you download have been tested for the version of WordPress you're using.

Check to see whether the plug-in has a history of updates. If you're downloading the first iteration of a plug-in and the developer decides not to keep it updated, you'll have issues when you update to new versions of WordPress.

Check the date of the last update for the plug-in. A plug-in with an old date stamp is almost as bad as tuna with an expiration date of last month.

In the following sections, we discuss three plug-ins that we think are essential to have on a blog.

Captcha

A *captcha* is a funky-looking string of letters you enter in order to gain access to a download or to submit a comment. The WordPress application has a useful plug-in named Captcha. You can find more information about it at `http://recaptcha.net`. You can also find one or more Captcha plug-ins on the WordPress plug-in page.

The Captcha plug-in creates a word verification similar to the one on the Blogger Web site shown in Figure 2-13. The word verification makes sure a human being is accessing the page and not a robot computer. A computer would not be able to recognize the gibberish as actual letters and therefore would not gain access to the site or form the plug-in is protecting.

RSS

You must have an RSS icon on your blog. Users click the orange icon to subscribe to the feed from your blog. If you're adept at using HTML, you can manually create the code to display the icon.

You can also find plug-ins that do the grunt work for you. Like Web sites, plug-ins come and go. To find a list of current RSS plug-ins, enter *RSS* in the Search box on the WordPress plug-ins page.

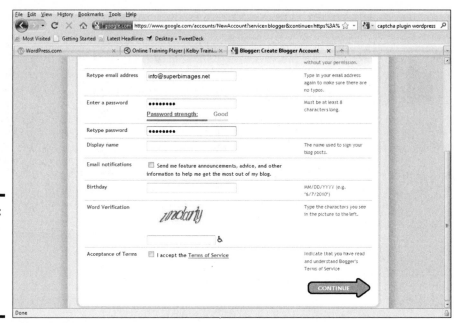

Figure 2-13:
Add a
captcha
plug-in on
your blog
similar to
this one.

ShareThis

Face it: You blog to get noticed and to get your message to potential customers. Whenever someone sees your blog and finds out how totally cool and informative it is, they want to share it with others. Enter the ShareThis plug-in, which you can find at `http://sharethis.com`. Click the button labeled Get the Button, in the upper-right corner of the page. When you register at the site, you receive the code to display the green ShareThis button on your blog (see Figure 2-14).

If the thought of manually adding code to your blog scares you, copy the code from the site to Notepad (in Windows) or TextEdit (on the Mac). Enable a text widget on your blog and paste the code into it. The result is the ShareThis icon in your blog. Whenever someone clicks it, it reveals every social media site and its little brother.

Using Google Analytics

Google has a wide variety of useful tools for social media marketers, and they're free for Google accountholders. You can use Google Analytics to track site visits, bouncebacks, page views, and other statistics, which of course tells you whether your blog is successful. Figure 2-15 shows Google Analytics for a podcast site. For more information on setting up Google Analytics, see Book VIII, Chapter 1.

Display a ShareThis button

Figure 2-14:
Adding a
ShareThis
icon to a
blog.

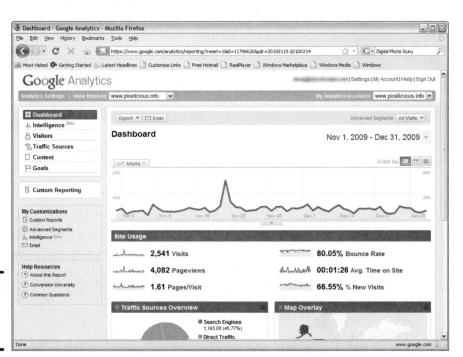

Figure 2-15:
Google
Analytics at
work.

Google FeedBurner

As a blogger, you can use Google FeedBurner (`www.feedburner.google.com`), which has been around for a while, to notify subscribers whenever you create a new blog post. (Podcasters use FeedBurner to burn feeds for iTunes.) It's a quick and easy way to deliver content to people who want to see your content immediately, without having to journey to your Web site.

The outstanding quality of FeedBurner is its huge syndicate. You can reach out to more people who may be potential clients by disseminating your feed to the Google network of syndicates. Figure 2-16 shows the information you get when you burn a feed with FeedBurner.

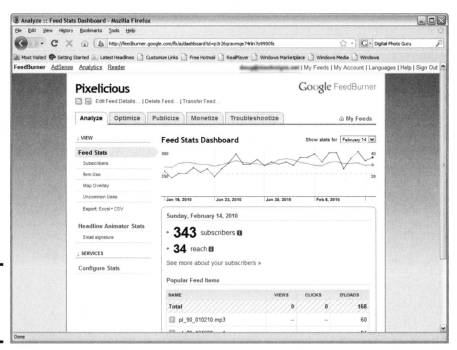

Figure 2-16: Just the facts, ma'am.

Burning a feed

Burning a feed with Google FeedBurner is easy. You need a Google account, which is free. After that, all you need to do is follow these steps:

1. **Open your favorite Web browser and navigate to `http://feedburner.google.com`.**

2. **Sign in with your e-mail address and Google password.**

   If you don't have a Google account, you can create one at this time by clicking the Create an Account button. If you have a Google account and have existing feeds, they're listed at the top of the page.

3. **Enter the URL for the feed you want to burn, as shown in Figure 2-17.**

4. **Click Next.**

   The page refreshes with the Google FeedBurner address filled in.

5. **Enter a title for your blog.**

   Subscribers see this information in their feed aggregators. If you set up a blog at WordPress.com, the title is already filled in, as shown in Figure 2-18. It doesn't hurt to use words that visitors would associate with your site, to provide — yep, you guessed it — more optimization for search engines.

**Book III
Chapter 2**

Building Your Blog

Figure 2-17:
What's your
URL, Duke?

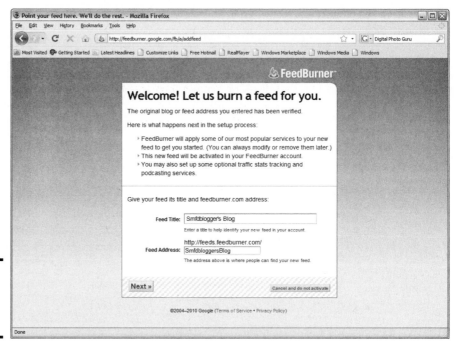

Figure 2-18:
Christening
your feed
with a title.

6. Click Next.

The page refreshes with a note congratulating you on burning your feed. FeedBurner makes your feed browser friendly by default and gives you basic FeedBurner stats to track circulation, readership, and uncommon uses. You now have the option to spiff it up with the optional FeedBurner Stats plug-in.

7. Click Next.

The page refreshes and you see other options for feed stats.

8. Choose the other statistics options you want to track.

You can add any of these:

- *Clickthroughs:* Monitor the number of people who click items back to your site. If someone creates a link to one of your blog posts from their Web site or blog, it shows up as a clickthrough.

- *Item Enclosure Downloads:* Monitor podcasts downloaded directly from your site.

- *I Want More:* Monitor individual item views and resyndication. This option tells you which posts are the most popular. You can also target the *reach* (the viewed or clicked content in your feed) of your blog or podcast.

9. **Click Next.**

The page refreshes and you have options for integrating the feed into your blog, as shown in Figure 2-19.

10. **Choose to integrate the FeedBurner Google feed with a blog hosted by Blogger, TypePad, or WordPress.com or a self-hosted WordPress blog. Choose whether to publish a chiclet (small icon) on your MySpace page or offer an e-mail subscription to your MySpace blog.**

Publicizing a feed with FeedBurner

After you burn a feed, it's time to tell the world all about it. You can do so with your other social media outlets, such as Facebook and Twitter. However, you can also tap in to the far-reaching Google network. To get your feed noticed in the Google network, follow these steps:

1. **Launch your favorite Web browser and navigate to `www.feedburner.google.com`.**

The Google Feedburner home page appears.

2. **Enter your e-mail address and Google password, and then click Sign In.**

You're redirected to a page that shows your current feeds. In addition, you see stats for every feed you've burned.

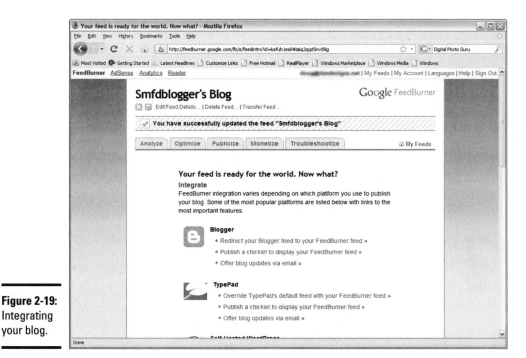

Figure 2-19:
Integrating your blog.

3. **Select the feed you want to publicize and then click the Publicize tab.**

   The page refreshes and shows your current content and the options available for publicizing your podcast or blog. The options are on the left side of the page. Click the desired link to use that service to publicize your blog.

Discovering the Fine Art of Blogging

Blogging began as a way for anybody to have a voice. By using a blog, you can publish your thoughts for a few hundred or several thousand people to see. Many blogs serve as ways for their authors to vent their feelings. Though you also want to express your opinions, your primary goal is to dispense information about your industry and product without creating an advertisement. When you do it right, you attract a throng of interested readers who subscribe to your blog and eventually become paying customers. But first, you must learn the fine art of blogging.

Doing your homework

When you use a blog to market your company, you may think it's as easy as typing some material and posting it in your blog. Do some homework before starting to post. Check out other blogs in your industry. Search the Internet for the name of your industry followed by the word *blogs* (as in *wedding photography blogs*).

Creating a post

Creating a blog post in most blogging applications is straightforward: After you enter the blog dashboard and click the button or icon to create a new post, you end up with a cross between an e-mail application and a word processing application. Figure 2-20 shows a post being created in a WordPress blog.

You edit a post from the dashboard in the blog application. The WordPress blog application has a Posts section under which you see the Edit option. Click the link and all your blog posts appear. Then just pause the cursor over the post you want to edit and click Edit, as shown in Figure 2-21.

Before publishing, double-check your grammar and spelling. Most software programs check spelling and grammar. Nothing turns off an educated buyer or a potential customer quicker than a Web site with typos and grammatical errors.

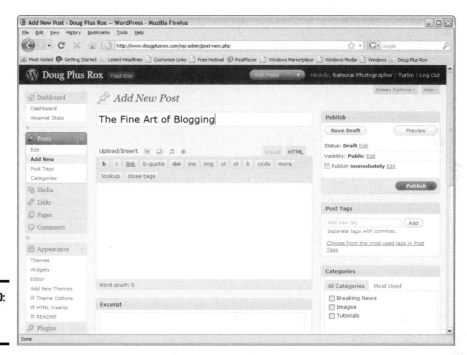

Figure 2-20:
Creating a post.

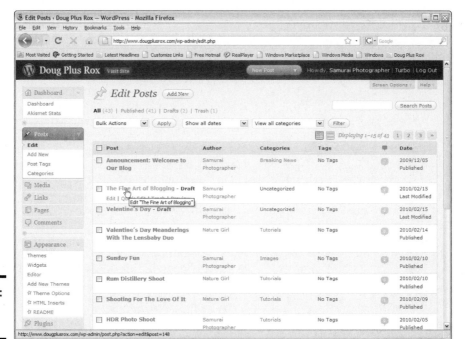

Figure 2-21:
Editing a post.

Adding keywords and tags

When you create a post, your goal is to persuade as many potential customers as possible to read it. But first they have to *find* your needle in the haystack. Unless they're already subscribed, this task may be next to impossible unless you optimize your post for search engines. You can optimize a post in two ways:

✦ Add keywords directly to the post text.

✦ Add tags to the post.

When you add keywords, make sure the text is readable. Some blog authors try to pepper their posts with so many keywords that the resulting post is grammatically incorrect or reads as though it were written by a chimpanzee. The trick is to pepper the post with *relevant* keywords and then mirror them as tags. In WordPress, you add tags in the Tags text field, as shown in Figure 2-22. Each tag must be separated by a comma, and you can use multiple words to create a tag. A tag is a word or phrase that people would use in a search engine to find the type of information in your blog post. For example, if we were creating a blog post about this book, we would add the tag *social media marketing*.

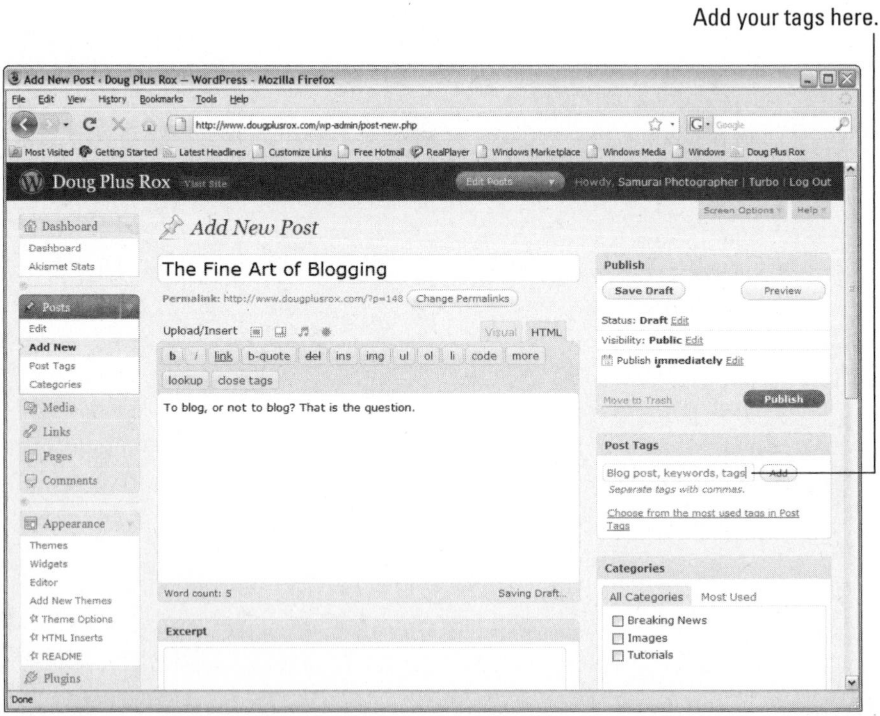

Add your tags here.

Figure 2-22: Adding tags to a post.

Book II, Chapter 2 talks more about search engine optimization. All the tricks in that chapter apply to blogs as well.

Making posts public, private, or sticky

When you create a post using the WordPress blog application, you have options for the visibility of your post. You can create one for all the world to see, keep it private for other authors on your blog, or password-protect it. However, if a post has instructions or information for a few select people, this option may be perfect.

Don't post sensitive information about your company even though you can designate a post as private. Hackers have a way of getting to see what they want to see.

Another useful option is to create a sticky post. When you create a *sticky* post, it's displayed as the top entry in your blog, no matter when you created it. A sticky post is useful for welcoming visitors to your blog. You can make a WordPress post public, private, password-protected, or sticky by choosing an option, as shown in Figure 2-23.

Choose a visibility level here.

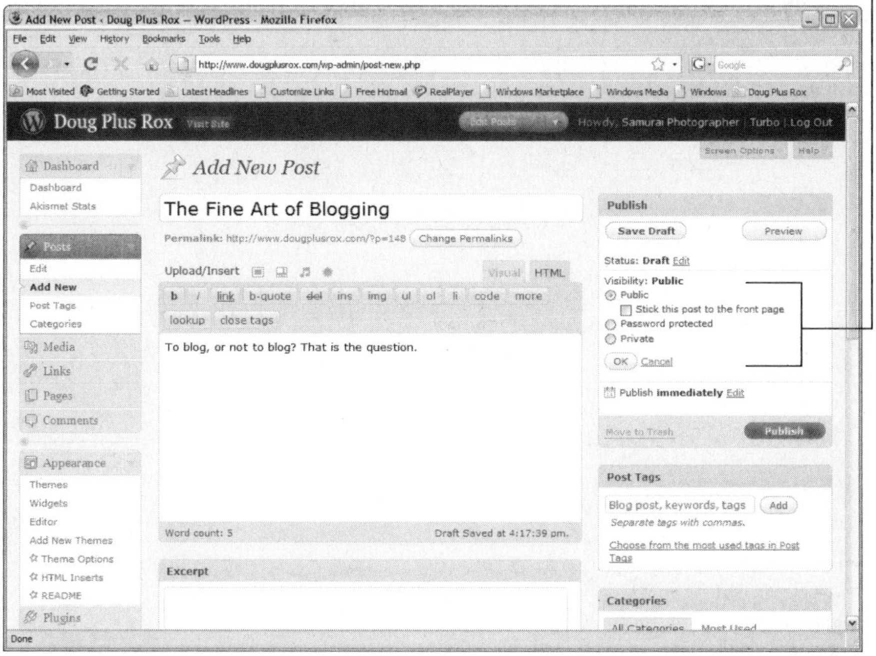

Book III
Chapter 2

Building Your Blog

Figure 2-23:
Is this post public, private, password-protected, or sticky?

Keeping posts timely

Readers of a blog look forward to receiving its posts at about the same time of whatever day or days you write your blog posts. It's like the morning paper: Readers get their regular dose of your blog on the same days and at the same time. Notice that we said *days.* That's right: You should create more than one blog post per week. What happens when you can't write a post on the day or time that your subscribers expect one to be published? You delay the post from the time it's written to the applicable day and time.

You can easily schedule a post in WordPress. After you write and proofread it, click the Edit link next to the Publish Immediately option. The current date and time are shown on drop-down menus, as shown in Figure 2-24. Choose the date and time you want to publish the post, and then click OK. Write enough posts to keep subscribers satisfied, and delay the post to the applicable days and times.

Choose a day and time here.

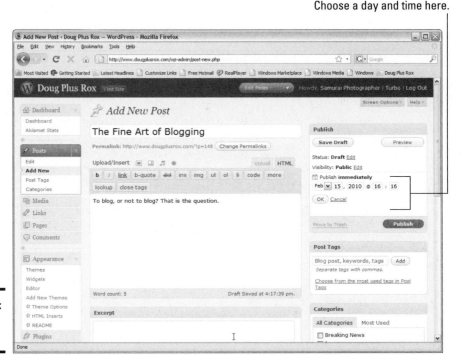

Figure 2-24: Delaying a post.

Handling comments and spam and other delights

Comments on your blog posts show that you have readers who are interested in what you have to say. Unfortunately, comments are also used by spammers. They see a blog as their personal forum to publish links to a product they're promoting. The best way to combat spammers is to require every comment to be moderated by the blog administrator. When a comment is posted to your blog, it is not made public until you approve it. If you choose to have comments moderated, the WordPress application notifies you whenever a comment is made about one of your posts.

If you have the WordPress blogging application, another ally in your defense against spam is Akismet. This plug-in is installed automatically whenever you install a WordPress blog, and you need an API key in order to activate it. The plug-in puts comments that contain several URLs or commonly used words in a separate folder. You can review the comments at your leisure. If you decide not to review the comments Akismet flags, they are automatically deleted in 14 days. You can find the plug-in in your WordPress. com account, and you can find Akismet in the Plug-ins section of your WordPress Dashboard.

Creating meaningful categories

If you post messages about different topics — for example, new and newsworthy information about your product, company, or industry or promotions offered by your company — you can organize your posts using categories. When you write a post, you can choose from existing categories or create new ones (see Figure 2-25). Each category you create is added as a link to your blog sidebar. A visitor clicks the link to see all posts created for that category.

When you create several categories for your posts, the categories show up as menu options on your blog sidebar, as shown in Figure 2-26. Visitors can read all installments in a specific category by clicking the category name on the sidebar.

**Book III
Chapter 2**

Building Your Blog

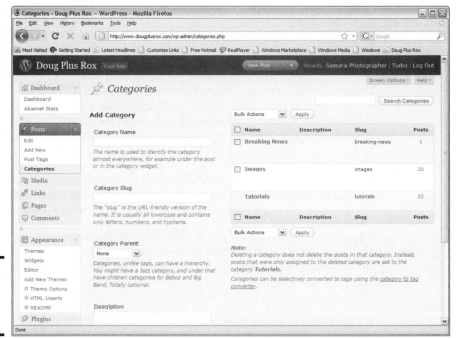

Figure 2-25:
Organizing posts with categories.

Figure 2-26:
Categories become menu options on the blog sidebar.

Sort posts into categories.

Announcing new posts

Whenever you create a new post, your subscribers are automatically notified. However, you want to add new subscribers to your blog and get your message out to more potential clients. When you create your first posts, you may have only a handful of subscribers, which means that you have to get the word out whenever you create a new blog post.

An easy way to announce new posts is by using your other social media outlets. If you're on Twitter, for example, copy the URL of the post and send it to your followers in a *tweet* (a Twitter message).

Another way to announce a post is from Facebook. In fact, you can have your blog posts (or even your Twitter messages) appear on your Facebook wall.

You can also use a Ping service to automatically announce your posts. (Pinging is discussed in detail in Book II.) Ping-o-Matic, at `www.pingomatic.com`, is a helpful service to use. Enter the URL for your podcast and click the button to ping a wide variety of services, including Google, Technorati, and Bloglines.

Using trackbacks

Trackbacks are the breadcrumbs of the Internet. Whenever another blog or Web site creates a link to one of your blog posts, the visibility of the post increases. It is seen by not only visitors to the site that created the trackback but also search engines, which gives your post a higher priority over a similar one with fewer or no trackbacks.

How do you serve up a heaping helping of these powerful trackbacks? One way is by using your other social media outlets. If you announce a new post to your Twitter followers, and one or more of them creates a link to the post, you have trackbacks. Your Facebook page can serve the same function. If you use the option to automatically show new posts on the wall of your Facebook page, your fans will notice. If they add the link on their Web sites — voilà — another trackback.

You can create trackbacks the old-fashioned way, of course, by sending a message to a Web site owner requesting a reciprocal link. However, one of the easiest and quickest ways to publicize your blog and create trackbacks is by using FeedBurner, discussed earlier in this chapter. FeedBurner makes it possible for you to publicize your feed, which in essence gets your blog out to the masses.

Moving your blog to a new domain

Moving a blog to a new domain is a big job. You might think that all you need to do is install WordPress at the new domain and you're good to go. The only problem is that after installing WordPress, you end up with a squeaky-clean MySQL database that contains zilch. Zip. Nada. You have to export the contents of the database (*not* an action to be taken by technophobes) from your old server into the squeaky-clean database from your fresh install. Contact someone at your current server and ask for a copy of all tables in your blog database. Do this right before you pull the plug on the old server. When you set up WordPress on the new server, ask a tech support rep to replace the contents of the new database with the content exported from your old Web server. Alternatively, you can ask your new service to move the entire blog for you. Many Web hosting services will move one Web site at no charge.

Chapter 3: Creating a Podcast

In This Chapter

✔ Finding a podcast host

✔ Getting podcast hardware and software

✔ Getting your podcast on the Web

✔ Recording your podcast

Suppose that you want celebrity status, not just a plain old blog. We can't say that a podcast will make you rich and famous, but doing it right bolsters your marketing efforts. People reluctant to read a lengthy blog post are more than willing to listen to an entertaining speaker talk about a subject that's near and dear to their hearts. They can even do it passively, by listening to your podcast on an iPod while they're doing something else, such as working out or cleaning the house.

Audio isn't the only option when you create a podcast. To grab the attention of potential clients, consider creating a video podcast. Now you engage two senses, as they see and hear your podcast. You may think you need a recording studio to create a podcast, but you can create a podcast in the comfort of your home or office using our tips for creating a makeshift studio. In addition, we show you the steps necessary to create a podcast, and it's up to you to supply the talent and compelling material.

For more information on podcasting, check out *Podcasting For Dummies,* by Tee Morris, Chuck Tomasi, and Evo Terra.

Getting Your Podcast Ducks in a Row

Before you even think about recording Episode 1 of your podcast, you have to set it up. You may believe that it's as simple as planting yourself in front of a camcorder and recording. But where will you record the podcast? What hardware will you use to record it? What software will you use to optimize for the Web? Where will you host it? As you can see, you have quite a bit to do before you dip your toe into the shallow end of the podcast pool. In the following sections, we show you how to prepare for a long, successful podcasting stint.

Finding a bandwidth-friendly host

It doesn't happen overnight, but eventually you attract a loyal group of subscribers who download every episode of your podcast. We strongly suggest you create at least one episode per week. The size of a podcast file can vary from a few megabytes in a simple audio podcast to 50 or more megabytes for a 20- to 30-minute video podcast. When you produce the latter, and have lots of subscribers, an incredible amount of *bandwidth* (the file size of the data being downloaded times the number of subscribers) is used.

Web hosting is cheap these days, but it's the extras that add up quickly. When you exceed the bandwidth allotted by your server, you're charged for the excess bandwidth. Therefore, find a Web server that offers unlimited bandwidth. They're out there, and many of them are quite reliable. Search for the term *unlimited bandwidth web hosting* at your favorite search engine to find a list of Web hosting companies that offer unlimited bandwidth, and reviews of those companies. Doug uses HostGator (`www.hostgator.com`) for his podcast.

Even if you're starting off with a small podcast, plan for the future. Buy unlimited bandwidth now so that you have no changes to make to your Web hosting structure when your podcast grows.

Your Web hosting company needs to have other features if you use a blog to disseminate your podcast. The server must have PHP and MySQL database capability. Check your blogging software (we recommend WordPress) for a rundown of the server-side requirements. If you're using a blog as the basis for your podcasting site, many Web hosting companies offer the option to install a blog for you. The only thing missing is the software to play the video live on the Net.

Securing hardware for your podcast

If you're creating a podcast, you need a good microphone to record it. And no, the microphone built into your computer or Webcam doesn't count. You need a microphone capable of capturing quality sound, and built-in microphones don't do the job.

Doug uses Blue microphones (`www.bluemic.com`) to record his podcast. Blue makes three models of USB mics that are perfect for podcasting: Yeti, Snowball, and Snowflake (see Figure 3-1). These professional-quality condenser microphones connect to your computer via USB cable. The Yeti and Snowball have multiple capsules, which means that you can configure the microphone for the type of recording you're creating. As of this writing, the Yeti retails for less than $150. The small, portable Snowflake microphone is the ideal solution when you're on the road. Plug the Snowflake into your laptop and launch your recording software, and you're ready to go. Audio-Technica (www.audio-technica.com), Samson (www.samsontech.com), MXL (mxlmics.com), and Nady (www.nady.com) also manufacture condenser microphones.

Figure 3-1:
Use professional-quality microphones to record your podcast.

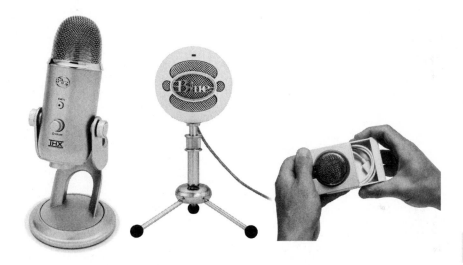

Book III Chapter 3

Creating a Podcast

Look for these features for in a microphone:

✦ **Cardioid capsule:** Captures the sound directly in front of the microphone and doesn't capture the sounds to the side or behind it — a useful option if your computer is noisy.

   If you create a podcast with an omnidirectional microphone, the microphone records — in addition to your voice — other, unwanted sounds in the room.

✦ **Bidirectional capsule:** This is a good option because it picks up sound in front of, and directly behind, the microphone — an ideal option when you're interviewing someone.

✦ **USB compatibility:** Simply plug the USB cable into your computer and you're ready to go; no need for any additional cables or mixing boxes. A good online resource for USB condenser microphones is Musician's Friend (www.musiciansfriend.com).

Many podcasters record live interviews at conventions and events. If you're in this category, you also need a good portable recording device. Doug uses the Zoom H2 Handy Recorder from Samson (www.samsontech. com), shown in Figure 3-2. Another good choice for a portable recorder is the M-Audio Microtrack II (www.m-audio.com). Both devices are capable of capturing high-quality recordings in the field. You can also use one in a pinch to create a podcast in a hotel room. The Zoom H2 uses an SD memory card; the M-Audio Microtrack II, a CF memory card.

If your goal is to create a video podcast, get the best video equipment you can afford. The Webcam attached to your computer doesn't cut the mustard. Look for a camcorder capable of capturing quality video to a flash memory card or hard drive. Camcorders capable of delivering high-quality video start at about $300.

Figure 3-2:
Use a professional-quality portable microphone to record while you're on the road.

Another option is to capture video with your digital camera. If you own a high-end digital SLR, you can shoot video of excellent quality. The only drawback is that the camera cannot change focus. If your goal is to create a video where viewers see you in a position from a fixed distance, this option is a good one.

Getting software for your podcast

To record an audio podcast, you need software that can record your voice and export the recording in a Web-friendly format. You also need an application capable of recording and mixing multiple tracks. (This part of the equation is one that doesn't require a cash outlay.) You can download Audacity (`http://audacity.sourceforge.net`), shown in Figure 3-3, a cross-platform application that even features a plug-in to convert recorded audio to an .mp3 file (an optimal format for the Web).

If you create a video podcast, you need software to mix the video file with an audio intro and exit. This process requires multiple tracks. To mix his podcast, Doug uses Sony Vegas (`http://www.sonycreativesoftware.com/moviestudiope`), which is Windows-only software), shown in Figure 3-4. Final Cut Express (`www.apple.com`) is an excellent option if you edit video on a Macintosh computer.

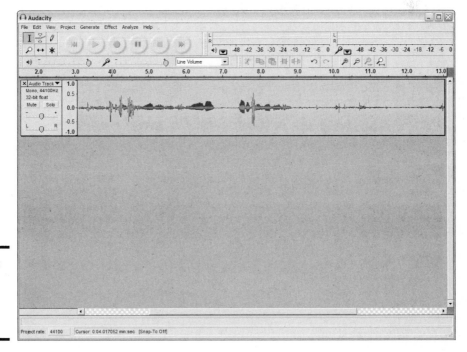

Figure 3-3:
Recording a podcast using Audacity.

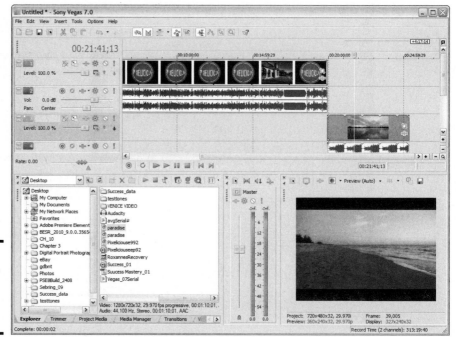

Figure 3-4:
Editing your
podcast
using Sony
Vegas.

If your podcast shows people how to use computer software, you
need a program to capture video images from your screen. Camtasia
(www.techsmith.com) lets you capture video of the screen while you
work and record commentary at the same time. The suite also features
applications to edit your screen capture and export it.

Setting up a Web site for your podcast

Using blog software is the easiest way to set up a Web site for your podcast.
We prefer WordPress because it's a flexible application with lots of plug-ins.
You make a post for each episode of your podcast and write some information
about the episode (known as *show notes*). The information can be presented
concisely with an introductory paragraph and bullet points for each major
section of your podcast. Include links to Web sites mentioned in your podcast,
and a link to the audio or video file for the episode. This gives your audience
an idea of what the podcast is all about before they invest time in viewing
or listening to it (see Figure 3-5). Show notes also help with search engine
optimization.

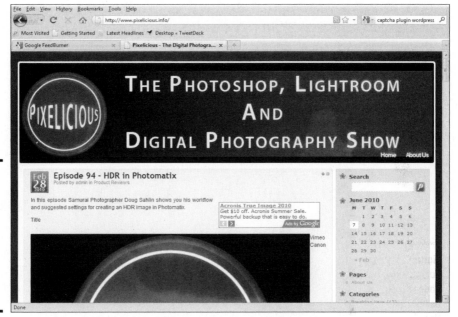

Figure 3-5:
Include show notes to give subscribers an idea of what your podcast is about.

Web sites, especially blogs, are targets for hackers. You're also at the mercy of your server's hardware. Many Web hosting companies back up your site content, but it's better to be safe than sorry. Back up your blog database and have copies of all your podcast files on external media such as an external hard drive. That way, you're prepared if disaster strikes.

Using multimedia plug-ins

Some visitors prefer not to download episodes — they prefer to view them online. To give viewers that option, install a multimedia plug-in with a player that can be used to view each episode. You can find multimedia plug-ins for WordPress at `http://wordpress.org/extend/plugins`. Try the Anarchy Media Player (`http://an-archos.com/anarchy-media-player`), shown in Figure 3-6, for this video podcast.

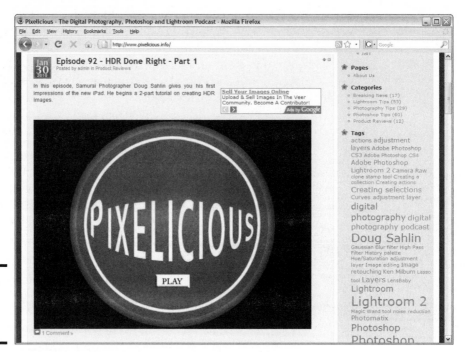

Figure 3-6:
Using a
media
player.

Recording Your Podcast

After all your ducks are in a row, it's time to record your first podcast — almost. The same wisdom that applies in first creating a blog applies also to a podcast. Create an editorial calendar with bullet points for each podcast, and map out the first four episodes (see Book I, Chapter 3 to get started on creating a Social Media Calendar). Then it's time to practice and get to know your equipment. If you've ever given presentations, this process will seem like old hat to you.

Recording tips

Recording a podcast isn't difficult. However, to put your best foot forward, you have to be as polished and professional as possible. This effect may not be easy to achieve at first, but after you have a dozen podcasts under your belt, you get the job done quicker and with fewer mistakes.

Here are some podcast recording tips for you to consider:

+ **Act as though you're telling a story to your best friend.** This strategy helps you relax and sound enthusiastic.

✦ **If you're recording a video podcast in which viewers can see you, use natural hand gestures and smile.** Your goal is to be perceived as a friendly person with important information to share.

✦ **Put a pop filter in front of your microphone.** This device prevents popping sounds when saying plosives such as the letter *p*. You can find a pop filter at your local music store.

✦ **Record your podcast in a quiet area.** If you hear an airplane or a car, stop speaking until it passes.

✦ **Do a dress rehearsal before recording begins.** The rehearsal helps you loosen up and familiarizes you with the material.

✦ **Position the microphone for optimum recording.** Place it just below your lips and about six inches from your mouth.

✦ **If you can hear your computer fan, purchase a piece of foam sound isolation material from your local music store.** It looks like a baffle and muffles the sound of the computer fan.

✦ **Drink a glass of water before you begin.** If you're not well lubricated, your voice may be a little raspy at times. Lozenges are another option if you're recording a lengthy podcast.

✦ **If you make a mistake, clap your hands in front of the microphone.** The loud noise puts a spike in the *waveform* — a graph that shows the peaks (high volume sections) and valleys (low volume sections). When you're editing your work in your video or audio editing program, the spike in the waveform is your signal that this area of the podcast needs editing.

✦ **Choose an appropriate recording location.** If you're recording a podcast that shows only your head and shoulders, for example, your desk is the ideal place to record.

✦ **Choose an appropriate background.** Remove any extraneous clutter from the desk and position the camera to include a pleasing background, such as a bookshelf or a wall displaying diplomas.

✦ **When you position the camera, consider where you'll sit as you record the podcast.** Don't position the camera so that your face is smack-dab in the middle of the frame. Position the camera so that your face is to either side of the middle of the frame. This strategy creates a more visually compelling composition.

✦ **When you record, look at the camera.** You imply eye contact with viewers and appear to be talking directly to them.

✦ **Wear a set of headphones, if you can.** Then you can monitor the sound while making a recording. You know in an instant whether your voice grows too loud or too soft. When this happens, clap your hands to signify that the sound needs editing, and then repeat the last sentence you just spoke.

**Book III
Chapter 3**

Creating a Podcast

Anatomy of a podcast

Like every good presentation, a podcast needs a beginning, a middle, and an end. The following list describes how to work with them:

✦ **An intro:** At the beginning, introduce viewers to the episode. Announce the day and date plus the episode number, to give viewers some perspective. You can play music during this brief introduction.

If a friend is a good public speaker, ask him to help you with the podcast introduction.

After the episode is announced, tell viewers what they can expect to see. This segment of the introduction shouldn't last much more than a minute. If you happen to have a sponsor, here's a good place to give her a plug.

✦ **The middle:** This part is the good stuff — the reason that viewers are watching or listening. Make sure to fill your podcast with the level of content that viewers want.

Segue between the different parts of your podcast, such as a sound effect after the intro and between each segment, to notify listeners that something different is about to happen.

✦ **An outro:** After the final section of your podcast, add a few parting words of wisdom and tell visitors what they can expect in the next episode. Thank subscribers for tuning in and sign off. You can add panache to your podcast if a jingle at the end of your podcast has the same music that began the podcast. Record a voice over the music to wrap things up.

If you plan to list your podcast in the iTunes store, add a request for positive feedback in the exit segment of every episode. A podcast with lots of positive feedback increases its rank in the iTunes store. If you can reach the coveted first page of the iTunes Store, you've done well and truly arrived.

It's a Wrap — Now What?

There's nothing like basking in the glow of another successful podcast. But after you take your headphones off and turn off the microphone, you still have quite a bit of work to do. You have to assemble the pieces of the puzzle into a complete episode. Then you have to optimize the podcast for the Web and portable devices. If you upload to iTunes, you have to add metadata so that the podcast is labeled correctly for the subscriber's device.

Putting the pieces together

If you follow our lead, you have an intro segment, the meat of the podcast, and then an exit segment. You also need a logo that's shown during the intro and exit and any other part of the podcast that has only audio. Your company logo is the ideal placeholder for audio segments and the podcast intro. Alternatively, you can create artwork for the podcast. You use your video editing software to stitch all the pieces together into a complete podcast.

Here's a guideline for you to follow when you're putting together your podcast:

1. Launch your video editing application.

For example, Sony Vegas (Windows) or Final Cut Express (Mac).

2. Import the intro and place it at the beginning of the first audio timeline.

Check your video editing software user's manual for information on how to import audio and video.

3. Import your company logo or podcast artwork and place it at the beginning of the first video timeline.

Most video editing applications have a set duration for still images — usually 5 or 6 seconds, which of course is shorter than the duration of your intro segment.

4. Increase the amount of time the podcast artwork is displayed to match the duration of the intro video.

Most applications let you drag a tab at the tail of an object on the timeline and stretch the duration for which the object is displayed. Check your video editing application manual for detailed instructions.

5. Create a new video timeline.

This step is where you add your recorded podcast.

6. Import the recorded podcast and place it on the new timeline so that it starts immediately after the intro piece.

In most applications, the object you move on the timeline snaps to adjacent media on neighboring timelines.

7. Import the exit segment of your podcast and place it on the first audio timeline so that it starts immediately after the podcast.

Add a sound effect before the exit segment, to notify viewers that the podcast is over.

8. **Add the podcast artwork or your company logo to the first video timeline so that it starts immediately after the podcast.**

9. **Increase the duration of the podcast artwork to match the duration of the exit segment.**

10. **Render the project.**

   When you render a project into a viewable video, you do so in a Web-friendly format that can be played on portable devices such as the iPod and iPhone. We suggest settings for rendering in the following section.

Optimizing your podcast for the Web and portable devices

After you render your project into a useable video, you need to optimize it into a file size that's reasonably petite and into a file format that's readable by portable devices and streams when viewed on the Web. A *streaming video* plays without interruption as soon as enough data has downloaded.

You can optimize video for the Web and portable devices when you render it or use a program specifically designed for compressing and optimizing it. Try Sorenson Squeeze (www.sorensonmedia.com) to optimize your podcast.

This list describes some suggested settings for optimizing your podcast:

✦ **File format:** Use the MPEG-4 (.mp4) file format. Almost all portable devices support it. Many video rendering applications let you specify an audio file format as well. If this is the case, choose the .aac file format.

✦ **Video dimensions:** Size videos to a width of 640 pixels and a height of 480 pixels. If a video was shot in a wide-screen format (16:9 aspect ratio), size it to 640 pixels wide by 360 pixels high.

✦ **Frames per second:** This measurement refers to the number of frames that play back per second. A higher frame rate yields a video that plays smoothly but is larger. As a rule, you can export a video with a frame rate of 15 frames per second (fps) to get acceptable results. If your podcast is a video capture of your computer screen where you show viewers how to use an application, you can squeak by with 5 fps.

✦ **Data rate:** A high data rate (the rate at which the data is processed when the video is played on a device) provides the best video quality at the expense of a large file size. For a podcast, a video rate of about 500 kbps is ideal.

✦ **Method:** The *method* refers to how data is compressed by your video application. An application uses a higher data rate for complex parts of the video, such as motion, and a lower data rate for areas of the video that are in a solid color. You can choose one of these two options:

- *Constant Bitrate (CBR):* Choose this option for a video you record from your computer screen. As implied, its data rate is constant throughout.

- *Variable Bitrate (VBR):* Choose this option to adjust the data rate as needed by the application rendering the video.

When you find the optimum settings for your podcast, save them as a preset.

Optimizing a podcast for iTunes

When your podcast is listed on iTunes, you need to do certain things — in iTunes — to make it user-friendly for the iTunes Store and for users' iPods. First, adopt a naming convention that makes sense and sorts the episodes in the order in which they were created. Then add cover art and ID3 tags (information used by audio devices to display the artist, title, and so on). The cover artwork is shown on users' devices and on iTunes.

When you name a podcast file, put the name of the podcast first, the episode next, and then the date. This strategy creates a user-friendly method of finding your podcast on a subscriber's device. For example, Episode 91 of Doug's Pixelicious podcast that was recorded January 21, 2010, has the filename p1_91_012310.mp4.

After you name the podcast, add the ID3 tags in iTunes by following these steps:

1. **Launch iTunes.**

   The iTunes application appears on your computer.

2. **Import the podcast into iTunes.**

   You can drag and drop the podcast directly into iTunes. Alternatively, choose File➪Add to Library.

3. **Select your newly created podcast and choose File➪Get Info or press Ctrl+I (Windows) or ⌘+I (Mac).**

   The file's Information dialog box appears.

4. **Click the Info tab.**

   Add information about your podcast that can be shown on portable devices such as the iPod.

5. **Enter the following information:**

   - *Name:* Enter the episode number and title of the podcast; for example, Episode 16 — Getting to Know Your New Widget.

   - *Artist:* Enter your e-mail address so that subscribers can get in touch with you.

- *Year:* Enter the current year.

- *Track:* Enter the current episode number. Do not enter a number in the Of text field.

- *Album:* Enter the name of your podcast.

- *Comments:* Enter an episode description.

- *Genre:* Enter **podcast**. This information tells iTunes the folder in which to store the file on a user's iPod and in iTunes. Figure 3-7 shows an example of information for a podcast that's online.

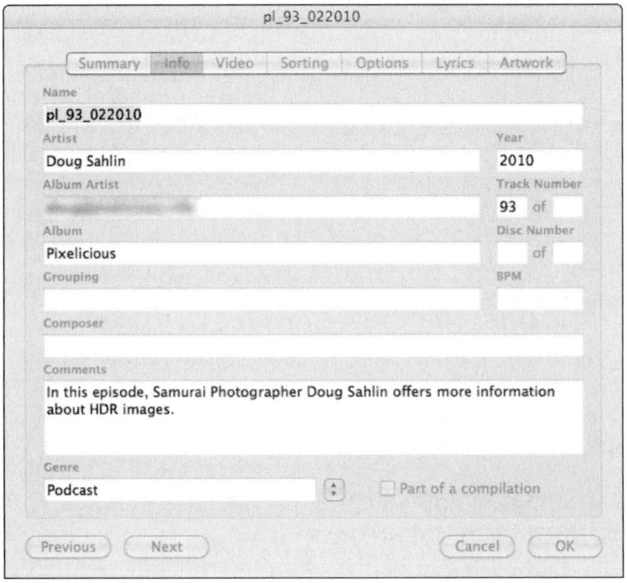

Figure 3-7: Adding podcast information.

6. **Click the Artwork tab.**

   Add album artwork measuring 640 pixels by 640 pixels with a resolution of 72 pixels per inch.

7. **Click Add.**

   The Open (Windows) or Choose a File (Macintosh) dialog box appears.

8. **Navigate to your artwork file and select it, and then click Open (Windows) or Choose (Macintosh).**

   The artwork file is added, as shown in Figure 3-8.

9. **Click OK.**

Figure 3-8:
Adding
album
artwork.

Uploading and archiving your podcast

After you have your podcast all spiffed up and ready for the world, it's time to upload it to your Web site and start receiving accolades for your work. We recommend using FileZilla (`http://filezilla-project.org`), an FTP client that's free, easy to use, and cross-platform.

After downloading and installing the software, you can upload your podcast to your Web host by following these steps:

1. **Launch FileZilla.**

   The application is fairly simple looking. The window on the left shows the files on your computer, and the window on the right shows the files on your Web site after you connect to the Web site.

2. **Enter the URL to your Web site in the Host field and then enter your username and password.**

   Check with your Web hosting company for this information. Typically, you have to set up FTP accounts in the Site Control panel.

3. **Click Quickconnect.**

   FileZilla connects to your Web site, as shown in Figure 3-9.

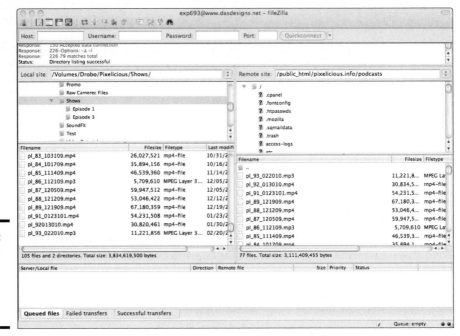

Figure 3-9:
Uploading
your
podcast
with
FileZilla.

4. **On the server side folder, navigate to the folder in which you store your podcasts.**

   Create a separate folder for podcasts, to keep the root-level directory free of unnecessary clutter. Over time, you end up with lots of podcasts on your Web site, so organization is a good idea.

5. **In the window on the left, navigate to the folder where you store your podcasts on your computer.**

6. **Drag the file from the left window to the right.**

   FileZilla uploads your file. It may take a few minutes if you have a lengthy podcast or a slow Internet connection.

After the podcast is uploaded to your site, you create a post using your blog software. At this point, you can either create a link for site visitors to download your podcast or use a multimedia plug-in in your WordPress blog.

Selecting Helpful Companion Products and Services

Your podcast won't garner a large audience of subscribers just because it's out there. You have to lend it a helping hand from your other forms of social media, such as Twitter and Facebook. You can increase the popularity of your podcast in other ways, and you can choose alternatives to a traditional podcast that allow viewers to interact with the presenter, as discussed in later sections of this chapter.

TalkShoe

www.talkshoe.com

The TalkShoe Web site lets you listen to, participate in, or host a live call. Recording a live call is an alternative to recording a podcast on your computer. As a host, you can create a public or private call. You set the date, create a call description, and invite others to participate — other people whom you're already networking with by way of social media, your blog, or your podcast. Participants can listen to your call and respond by text message or call in by way of telephone, mobile phone, or Voice Over Internet Protocol (VoIP) phone service.

Your live show is recorded and archived for future downloads. This technique is a useful way to create an original podcast and interact regularly with interested parties. You interact with them in the equivalent of an Internet chat room. Because TalkShoe is an audio program, it downloads more quickly than video. When you use a service that offers video sharing, you're limited to the number of participants in your show. Technically, the hardware used by TalkShoe can support 1,200 simultaneous online participants and chatters. Hosts use the browser-based TalkShoe application to host the show and interact with guests, as shown in Figure 3-10.

TalkShoe is similar to a podcast, but it's live and you can interact with participants. As the show host, you choose the topic and the point at which listeners can interact with the show. A private show isn't listed on the TalkShoe site (see Figure 3-11). Visitors who want to find public shows can use the site's search feature or search by category or peruse featured talkcasts. For a small fee, your talkcast can be featured on the site home page.

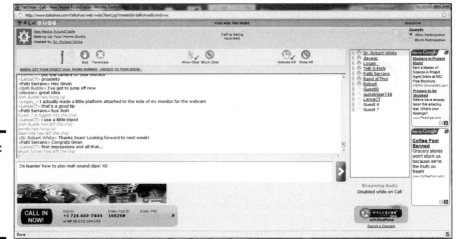

Figure 3-10:
Hosting a
show on
TalkShoe
for fun and
profit.

Figure 3-11:
As the late
television
host Ed
Sullivan
might have
said, you
can have
a really big
"shoe" on
TalkShoe.

BlogTalkRadio
www.blogtalkradio.com

If you create audio podcasts, another alternative is BlogTalkRadio (www.blogtalkradio.com). You can use this format to create a live show and talk with potential customers or other interested parties. Table 3-1 lists the flavors of services BlogTalkRadio provides.

Table 3-1		BlogTalkRadio Services		
Service	*Price*	*Number of Participants*	*Duration*	*Other Details*
Free	Free (of course)	5 in addition to you as host	One hour	Audio, video, and banner ads
Premium	$39/month	50 in addition to you as host	Two hours	Audio, video, and banner ads; host through Skype
Premium Plus	$99/month	100 in addition to you as host	Three hours	Banner advertising only; host through Skype; upload a prerecorded podcast; callers have a toll-free number

BlogTalkRadio also offers you a branded profile, which offers you the following benefits:

✦ Total control over ads that play on your broadcast and over content

✦ Sell audio, video, or banner ads and keep 100 percent of the revenue

✦ Use the advertisement placeholders as slots to hold your own content to promote your business

✦ Daisy-chain content over an RSS feed, iTunes, your other forms of social media, and mobile devices

✦ Broadcast live from an event

✦ Increased exposure throughout the BlogTalkRadio Web site

**Book III
Chapter 3**

Creating a Podcast

BlogTalkRadio has over 5 million listeners a month. Sixty percent of BlogTalkRadio listeners are male and almost 40 percent of listeners are in the 39- to 54-year-old age group. Forty-six percent of BlogTalkRadio listeners have a median household income of over $60,000 per year and 21 percent of the BlogTalkRadio audience has a median household income greater than $100,000 per year. If these demographics fit your target audience, you should give BlogTalkRadio a try.

Potential clients and fans can listen to BlogTalkRadio for free and can find your content by using the BlogTalkRadio search feature. Listeners can also peruse live shows, featured shows, popular shows, and networks by choosing the applicable navigation option from the BlogTalkRadio Web site, shown in Figure 3-12.

Figure 3-12: The BlogTalk Radio Web site.

iTunes

If you're a podcaster, iTunes is the place to be. It is without a doubt the biggest repository of podcasts. Listeners can subscribe to podcasts from their desktop version of iTunes. By default, new episodes are automatically downloaded when listeners who subscribe to a podcast sync their iPods with their computers or launch iTunes. You can change the default to download only the most recent episodes or manually download desired episodes from a show listing in iTunes.

iPod and iPhone owners find their content by using iTunes. Podcasts are listed in the iTunes Store. Users can look at the content on the first Podcast page in the iTunes store, shown in Figure 3-13, or use the Search feature to find podcasts. They're sorted by genre, which lets users easily locate specific content.

If you have an iTunes account, you can request to add your podcast to the iTunes Store. To list a podcast there, follow these steps:

1. **Launch iTunes.**

   iTunes, shown in Figure 3-14, is the way to manage content for your iPod or iPhone. If you're using a Windows computer, you find the application on the Start menu. On a Macintosh, iTunes is in the Applications folder.

2. **Click the iTunes Store icon from the Source list.**

   The iTunes Store opens for business.

3. **Click Podcasts.**

   The Podcasts section of the iTunes Store appears.

4. **Click Submit a Podcast.**

   The Submit Podcasts to the iTunes Directory dialog box appears.

Figure 3-13:
Looking for podcasts in the iTunes Store.

Figure 3-14:
iTunes
is your
portal to
the iTunes
Store.

5. **Enter the URL for your podcast feed.**

   Find out how to create a feed in Book III, Chapter 2.

6. **Click Continue.**

   iTunes verifies the feed, and you're off to the races. Now whenever you upload a new podcast episode, it automatically appears in iTunes.

Promoting Your Podcast

When your podcast is live, you want as many people as possible to see it. You can publicize your podcast by including its name and a description of it in your e-mail signature. This blurb should also be a link to the podcast. Recipients of your e-mail can click the link to view the site in their default browsers. The latest podcast is at the top of the blog for easy viewing.

Use your other social media outlets to announce new podcasts. Copy the URL of a podcast into a Twitter message, or *tweet* (be sure to use a short URL; try `bit.ly.com`). You can also mention new editions of a podcast on your Facebook wall and open it up for discussion in a LinkedIn forum.

Another way to promote a podcast is to be a guest on someone else's podcast. When you find someone willing to partner with you, record a segment for that person's show and be sure to mention the URL of your podcast. If your podcast has theme music, add it to the segment you create for your podcast partner.

When you have a special podcast or an interesting guest on your show, post a press release to let the world know. You can post them online at I-Newswire (www.i-newswire.com).

Register your podcast with podcast directories. They attract lots of visitors and are another way to get your podcast out there. Here are some podcast directories to investigate:

+ www.ilounge.com
+ www.podcastdirectory.com
+ www.podcastpickle.com
+ www.podcastcentral.com

Forums are another helpful place to promote podcasts. Find forums about the type of work you do or the products you offer. Lurk in the forums. When someone posts a question you can answer, jump on it quickly. Include the URL to your podcast in your forum signature. Don't blatantly advertise your podcast on a forum — it's considered bad taste. However, if the answer to a forum member's question resides in one of your podcasts, write the answer to the question and then post the link to your podcast as more detailed information.

Book III
Chapter 3

Creating a Podcast

Chapter 4: Producing Your Videocast

In This Chapter

✔ Getting videocast hardware

✔ Recording your videocast

✔ Optimizing video for the Web

✔ Putting your work online

*W*hen you need to deliver video to clients but not on a set schedule, a *videocast,* or *vlog* (short for *video blog*), is a helpful way to supply information. A videocast is similar to a podcast, but rather than create episodes, you create it as needed to convey information about your products and services to people who are following you on social media. You can host video at your own Web site or use an online video hosting service. When you use video hosting service, you can embed videos in your Web page or blog. The latter option has the additional benefit of not adding bandwidth charges from Web site downloads — instead, the video hosting service takes the bandwidth hit.

In this chapter, we show you how to participate in vlogging (video blogging). We cover hardware and software and show you the best online sources for hosting a videocast. We also offer recording tips and more.

Finding Hardware for Your Videocast

You may think that the cute little Webcam on top of your computer and its built-in microphone are all you need to record a videocast. The hardware that comes with your computer works fine if you're a tenth-grader who wants to post a video rant on YouTube. However, if you want to create a videocast that grabs the attention of potential consumers, you have to put your best foot forward and cough up some coin for a good camcorder and microphone. This combination enables you to create a quality videocast.

Videos you upload to a hosting service must be in an approved format. Because the hosting service also compresses your video for optimal Web delivery, you must send video in the best quality you can.

Here's a list of tasks that your new camcorder should be able to perform:

✦ **Capture video to a flash memory card or hard drive rather than to a cassette tape.** After you record a videocast, simply connect the camcorder to the computer by using a USB cable and then drag and drop the file to your computer. If you use a camcorder that records on cassette, you have to capture the video with a video capture program, which takes a long time. (Trust us: We've been there and done that.)

✦ **Capture video in the MPEG-4 format.** This format offers fairly high-quality video with a reasonably small file size that is easily viewable on computers and portable devices such as the iPod.

✦ **Capture high-definition, or HD (1080p or 720p), video.** This capability is a bonus because many sites provide HD video options for visitors.

✦ **Record stereo sound at 48 Kbps (kilobytes per second).** This gives you the highest fidelity for your videocast and compresses well for delivery on mobile devices.

✦ **Use an external microphone jack.** External microphones provide better sound quality than microphones built into your camcorder. Built-in microphones can pick up motor noise, which can be heard in the final videocast.

Camcorders with these features mentioned previously start at about $300.

 If you own a high-end digital SLR camera, you can record videos of excellent quality — the only drawback is that the camera cannot change focus. To create a video where viewers see you in a standard head-and-shoulders shot, try to use a digital camera that records high-quality video.

Here's a short list of other equipment you might need for recording videos:

✦ **An external microphone:** You must consider sound quality in your videocasts. You can use a camcorder's built-in microphone, though it often picks up mechanical noise from the camera, such as motor noise when the camcorder is zoomed in or out. An auxiliary microphone is definitely necessary if you're shooting video a fair distance from your subject. Purchase a quality lavalier microphone (which plugs into your camcorder) or a condenser microphone and stand. Contact your local retailer for more information.

✦ **A tripod for your camcorder:** A tripod steadies the camcorder if someone else is shooting the video. If you're capturing video of yourself, you simply press the record button, walk in front of the camcorder, and start your videocast without having to deal with the camcorder.

- ✦ **A mixing board and microphone for each speaker or an omni-directional microphone:** Omnidirectional microphones record all sound in the room, but if you have a relatively quiet studio, that shouldn't be a problem. Place the omnidirectional microphone equidistant from each speaker, which keeps the sound volume fairly equal across the board. Of course, you may have one speaker with a loud voice and another that speaks softly but carries a big stick. If you're recording with a single microphone in this case, experiment with different positions until you find a mix that sounds good. Alternatively, you can use a mixing board to equalize the input from each microphone to the same volume level.

If you're not sure where to purchase your equipment, check out a consumer electronics retailer such as Best Buy. If you prefer to purchase equipment online, look for reviews of the equipment you're considering. Just because a piece of gear garners a positive review doesn't mean that it's your ideal solution. Find a local retailer that handles the product you're considering. Make sure the camcorder controls are easy to reach and operate. If, after touching and feeling the product, you're sure that the camcorder is right for you, find a reputable online retailer. In addition to the excellent reputation and wide range of excellent video products at B&H (`www.bhphotovideo.com`), its helpful staff can assist you in making the right decision.

Recording a Videocast

Recording a vlog isn't difficult. However, to be able to put your best foot forward, you have to be as polished and professional as possible. Though this task may not be easy at first, after you have a dozen videocasts in the bag, you get the job done quicker and with fewer mistakes.

Here are some recording tips for you to consider:

- ✦ **Devote part of your home or office space to your recording endeavor.** This strategy is helpful if you're serious about creating videocasts to promote your business.

- ✦ **Act as though you're talking to your best friend.** Your relaxed demeanor will result in a video that looks and sounds more natural.

- ✦ **Be enthusiastic.** Use hand gestures to emphasize key points. Visuals such as charts or physical products are also beneficial.

✦ **Use a pop filter if you use an auxiliary microphone.** This small device, which looks like a small screen, is placed in front of the microphone to prevent popping sounds whenever a speaker says words with plosives such as the letter *p*. You can find a pop filter at your local music store. If you use a lavalier microphone, the pop filter looks like a little foam ball that fits over the end of the device.

✦ **Record in a quiet area.** If you hear an airplane or a car approaching, stop speaking until the vehicle passes. When you edit the file later and see an extended flat section in the waveform, you know that it has silent spots to edit out.

If ambient noise is an issue, create temporary soundproofing by draping heavy blankets over windows to muffle outside noise. If your computer is noisy and must be operating while you're recording, purchase soundproofing foam (which looks like a baffle) from your local music store and wrap the foam around your computer tower. Be careful not to block off entry and exit ducts for the cooling fan (or fans). You can also purchase soundproofing foam to muffle sounds from any nearby mechanical equipment. When you're recording, turn off any mechanical device, such as a noisy computer, that you're not using.

✦ **Leave a couple of seconds of silence at the start of the recording.** This technique gives you a "fudge factor" for adding other content, such as a video title or an audio introduction.

✦ **Complete a dress rehearsal to help you loosen up and become familiar with the material.** The rehearsal makes your recording sound more natural and inevitably helps eliminate mistakes.

✦ **Create on a chalkboard or an erasable presentation board a list of key points.** The list serves as a cue card to help keep your presentation on track.

✦ **Position the microphone just below your lips and about six inches from your mouth.** If you position the microphone too close to your mouth, your voice booms and overmodulates, resulting in distortion; if you move the mic too far away and the volume is too low, ambient noise may be heard in addition to your voice.

✦ **Drink a glass of water before recording.** It prevents your voice from sounding raspy.

✦ **If you make a mistake, clap your hands in front of the microphone.** The loud noise puts a spike in the waveform (a graph that shows the relative volume of each second of the recording). When you tweak the file later in your video editing program, the spike in the waveform is your signal that this area of the recording needs editing.

✦ **Choose an appropriate recording location.** If you're recording a videocast that only shows your head and shoulders, for example, your desk is the ideal place to record.

✦ **Create a visually appealing recording venue.** Remove extraneous clutter and position the camera to include a pleasant background, such as a bookshelf or a wall displaying a few photos or diplomas.

✦ **If you're recording team members, use a generic backdrop, such as a black sheet.** Place the backdrop several feet behind them, to avoid diverting attention. A tastefully furnished meeting room is another possibility.

✦ **When you mount your camera on a tripod, consider where you will sit during the recording.** Rather than position the camera so that your face is centered in the middle of the frame, position it so that your face is to either side of the middle of the frame. This technique creates a more visually compelling composition. When the camcorder fully zooms out, you should be able to see all podcast participants and part of the room. You can always zoom in on a participant who has the floor for an extended period.

✦ **Look directly at the camera.** This technique makes you look as though you're talking directly to your viewers.

✦ **If possible, wear a set of headphones to monitor the recording.** This way, you know in an instant if your voice grows too loud or too soft. When it happens, clap your hands to signify that the sound needs editing and then repeat your last sentence.

Finalizing a Videocast

After you record a videocast, you may think that your job is finished. In reality, you've only just begun: You need to edit the videocast to delete any mistakes and then render it in a format suitable for its intended destination and optimize the content for its intended destination. We discuss software and the editing and optimizing tasks in later sections of this chapter.

Obtaining software to edit and render a videocast

If you create a perfect take from start to finish, you're a better videographer than most people. But we're counting on your being human and making a mistake or four. In addition to having to edit mistakes, you need to add such goodies as a video title and perhaps an audio introduction. Adding still pictures is another possibility.

To edit a recording to perfection (and add the other bits), you need a good video editing application that supports multiple tracks. Adobe Premiere Elements (`http://tryit.adobe.com/us/premierelements/?sdid=EPZST`) or Sony Vegas (`http://www.sonycreativesoftware.com/movie studiope`) are both good applications for PCs. They both support multiple timelines — necessary when you need to assemble various pieces of a production. For the Macintosh, try Final Cut Express (`http://www.apple.com/finalcutexpress/`). We can't give you an in-depth tutorial on each application, but the following section shows you some guidelines for creating your masterpiece.

Putting the pieces together

When you record a videocast, you're creating the meat for a sandwich — you wrap your creation in a title or perhaps an audio introduction and display your company logo at the beginning and end of the video. This task involves using your editing software to assemble the media into a palatable video for your faithful fans. Follow these general steps:

1. **Launch your video editing application.**

2. **If you record narration to introduce the video, import the narration file and place it at the beginning of the first audio timeline.**

Check your video editing user's manual for detailed information on how to import audio and video files.

3. **Import your company logo and place it at the beginning of the first video timeline.**

Most video editing applications specify a duration for still images, usually five or six seconds — a shorter duration than for your intro segment.

You can use the features of your video editing application to create a title for your video.

4. **Increase the amount of time your logo is displayed to match the duration of the introductory video.**

Most applications let you drag the tail of an object to increase its duration on the timeline. Refer to your user's manual for additional information.

5. **Create a new video timeline.**

6. **Import the recorded videocast and place it on the new timeline so that it starts immediately after the introduction.**

In most video applications, the object you're moving snaps to adjacent media on neighboring timelines. Figure 4-1 shows a video being edited in Sony Vegas.

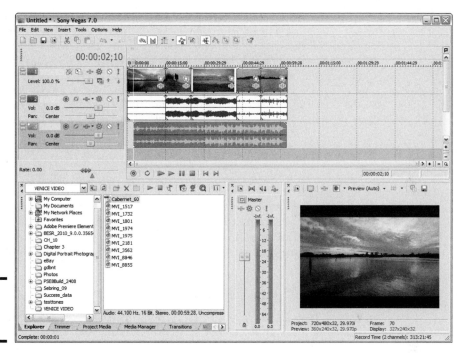

Figure 4-1:
Editing a
video.

Book III
Chapter 4

Producing
Your Videocast

7. **Add your exiting narration on the audio timeline or place your corporate logo on the video timeline.**

8. **Render the project.**

   When you render a project into a viewable movie, you do so in a Web-friendly format that matches the specifications of the service that will host your video.

   Before you render you movie, check the specification of the service you plan to host your video. You don't want to end up with a video that you can't upload later.

Optimizing your videocast for the Web

After you render a video, you optimize it into a file format matching the specifications of the service that will host the video. We discuss the most popular video hosting services in later sections of this chapter.

You can optimize the video when you render it, or you can use a program specifically designed for compressing and optimizing video. (One such program is Sorenson Squeeze at www.sorensonmedia.com.)

Here are some suggested settings for optimizing a podcast:

✦ **File format:** Use the MPEG-4 (`.mp4`) file format, supported by most video hosting services. You have to specify the audio file format: Choose `.aac`.

✦ **Video dimensions:** Size the video to 640 pixels wide and 480 pixels high. If the video was shot in a wide screen format (16:9 aspect ratio), size it to 640 pixels wide by 360 pixels high. These dimensions match the high-resolution option offered by most video hosting services, although your video hosting service may reduce the size for general playback.

✦ **Frame rate:** The *frame rate* is the number of frames per second that play back when a video is played. A higher frame rate yields a video that plays smoothly but has a larger file size. You can generally export the video with a frame rate of 15 fps (frames per second) and get acceptable results. If the file is a video capture of your computer screen that shows viewers how to use an application, you can squeak by with a frame rate of 5 fps.

✦ **Data rate:** A high *data rate* — the rate at which data is processed when a video is played back in a browser — produces the best video quality at the expense of a large file size. For a videocast, a data rate of about 800 kbps is ideal.

Finding an Online Service for Your Work

Unless your Web hosting service gives you unlimited bandwidth, you have to find a service to host your video. If you plan to create lots of videos and expect lots of people to view them, a hosting service is a blessing. You can embed the hosted video in a blog or Web page. When someone clicks the link to play your video, it's downloaded from the hosting site and plays on your site, which means that your site doesn't supply the bandwidth for the data transfer. Exceeding the allotted bandwidth from your Web hosting service adds a hefty surcharge to monthly hosting fees. In the next few sections, we explore video hosting services for you to consider.

YouTube

`www.youtube.com`

When you create an account at YouTube, you're given your own channel to which you can upload video. You also categorize your video to match the type of video you've created. Yes, you can send your faithful Twitter followers, Facebook fans, and the like to your YouTube channel. But you also have the chance to pick up some adoring fans of your own from YouTube. Creating a YouTube account is straightforward: Just go to `www.youtube.com`, click the Create Account link, and follow the instructions.

When you sign up for a YouTube account, make sure to choose the proper account type. The Standard account is for your everyday, garden-variety videos. But because you're an expert in your field, you're qualified to create a Guru account. People who are looking for instructional videos on YouTube are more likely to look for a guru, which bodes well for you.

After you're on YouTube, you can upload videos that last no longer than ten minutes or are no larger than 2GB. You can also spruce up your channel to include the URL of your Web site, and a description, as shown in Figure 4-2. You can also customize the channel. You have a wide array of options at your disposal. By using a bit of creativity, you can create a channel that looks similar to your Web site.

To customize your YouTube channel, log in to YouTube, click your username, and choose Account from the drop-down menu. Then click Customize Homepage and follow the prompts.

When you upload videos, be sure to enable comments, to give YouTube visitors a chance to comment on them. You're notified by e-mail when someone posts a comment. Figure 4-3 shows a video that has received at least one positive comment.

Figure 4-2: Creating a custom YouTube channel.

Producing Your Videocast

Figure 4-3:
Comments
are a way
for YouTube
viewers to
interact
with you.

We show you the ins and outs of uploading videos in an upcoming section.

Getting to know YouTube

When you log in to YouTube as a visitor, your first glimpse is of the home page, which shows the most popular videos. The menu choices are simple: Home, Videos, Channels, and Shows. Unless you're an entertainer, your primary focus should be on the Videos and Channels sections of YouTube.

In the Videos section, you find a long list of categories on the left side of the page, as shown in Figure 4-4. Before uploading your videos to YouTube, review the categories that seem most applicable to the type of video you're uploading and the type of business you're in. You may be surprised at what you find in certain categories. You may also find that your videos fit into several different categories. You can post videos in multiple categories.

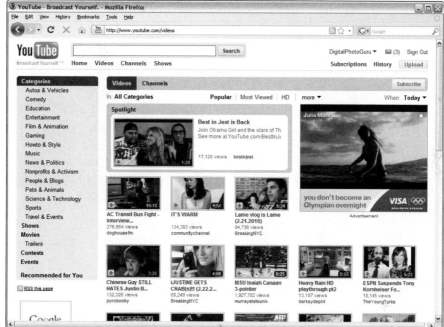

Figure 4-4:
Find the right category for your videos.

On the home page of the Channels section, you find the most-viewed channels, as shown in Figure 4-5. You can also review the most-subscribed channels. (Falling into this category is your goal.) On the left side of the page, in the channel categories, do a little exploration to find the heavy hitters in the channels related to your business. When you find a channel with lots of subscribers, view some videos by the channel creator to see what all the hubbub is about. This strategy can spark ideas for your own videos. Find some videos that you think are useful and informative, and then put on your thinking cap to see how you can create a better video. After you develop a knack for using YouTube and you understand which type of video is attracting your target market, you're ready to create your own content.

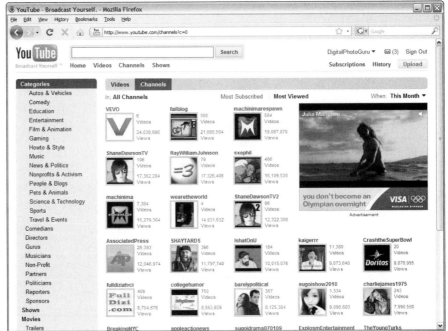

Figure 4-5:
So many
channels, so
little time.

After you upload a couple of videos to your YouTube channel, click your username and then choose Account from the drop-down menu. From the Account page, click Activity Sharing and specify how visible your actions are on YouTube. You can also share YouTube activity with your Twitter followers and Facebook fans.

Meeting YouTube video requirements

The YouTube compression algorithm is a closely guarded secret, though the site definitely compresses videos. If you upload a low-quality video, it looks awful on YouTube. If you upload a well-thought-out video, however, that's rendered to perfection and meets YouTube requirements, you'll likely be pleasantly surprised at its quality online. To ensure that you upload the highest-quality videos, YouTube recommends high-definition video that measures 1920 x 1080 pixels. It also ensures that when YouTube adds different video options, your high-resolution file yields the best possible quality for the new YouTube format. YouTube encourages you to upload video that's as close to the original as possible.

For YouTube, use a data rate of about 1200 Kbps (kilobits per second) using the MPEG-4 format. You should also use the AAC audio option and render the audio as 2-channel stereo with a sampling rate of 44.1 kHz.

Vimeo

www.vimeo.com

Another excellent video sharing service is Vimeo, shown in Figure 4-6. It offers two types of accounts:

✦ **Basic:** It's free.

✦ **Plus:** You pay $9.95 per month or $59.59 per year.

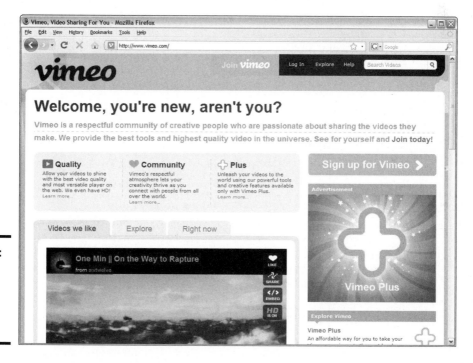

Figure 4-6:
Vimeo is
a premier
video-
sharing
service.

**Book III
Chapter 4**

**Producing
Your Videocast**

Vimeo is for noncommercial use only and will remove any videos that it deems inappropriate without warning. A soft — or nonexistent — sell is appropriate here. Check out its guidelines at www.vimeo.com/guidelines before proceeding.

If you have a free Vimeo account, you can upload 500MB of video per week. The video is compressed into the Vimeo version of high-quality video. Banner ads are displayed with your video, and your video waits in line with other videos from free accounts. In other words, if you catch Vimeo at a busy time, your video may wait a while to be converted for the site. You can upload one high-definition (HD) video per week. You can also create one group for like-minded people, one channel, and create three albums into which you organize your videos. Figure 4-7 shows how a video looks with a Basic account.

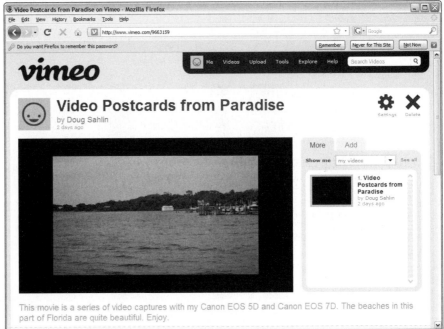

Figure 4-7:
A high-definition video uploaded from a Basic account.

A Vimeo Plus account puts you in the driver's seat. You can upload as many videos as you want and they're converted immediately to high-quality video, and you can customize the player and create an unlimited number of groups, channels, and albums. Other Plus account benefits are that you can embed videos wherever you want, hide converted videos from view on Vimeo, and download an unlimited number of converted videos per week. Plus account videos aren't subjected to banner ads.

You find lots of artists, filmmakers, producers, and photographers on Vimeo. However, the site has a place for all types of people. Whether you choose the Vimeo Basic or Vimeo Plus account, the site is a reliable place to host videos — its conversion is flawless.

blip.tv

At the blip.tv site, shown in Figure 4-8, you can find lots of video from filmmakers, producers, and actors. The cool feature at this video sharing site is that a video you upload to blip.tv is distributed to all other major players. That's right: Your video is distributed to sites such as YouTube and Vimeo.

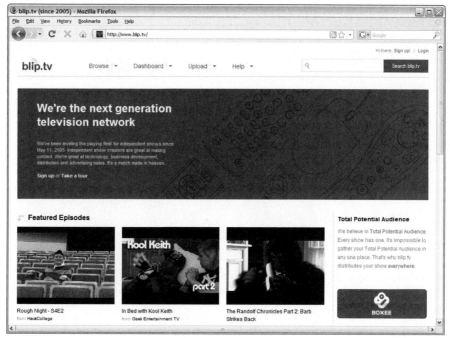

Figure 4-8:
blip.tv, your place on the Web for independent TV.

Uploading and Archiving Your Videocast

After you create a videocast, you're ready to share it with the world, if you've planted the right seeds, or at least with your target market. When you upload a video, you do other tasks, such as choose a category and add tags and descriptions.

Follow these generic steps for uploading videos to video hosting services:

1. **Log in to your account.**

2. **Click the Upload button.**

   The Upload page appears.

3. **Upload the file.**

   At Vimeo, you click the Upload a Video button. At YouTube, click Upload. This step opens a dialog box in which you choose a file.

4. **Navigate to the file you want to upload and follow the steps to upload the file.**

After uploading the file, a new dialog box appears, prompting you to enter tags and other information. On YouTube, you also have the option to specify the category in which the video will reside. Choose a category that makes sense for the type of video you're uploading.

5. **Add a title, description, and tags to your video.**

Adding this information is imperative. People who visit YouTube or Vimeo can find your videos based on the information you enter in these fields. At YouTube, you can also share your activity with your other social media contacts, such as on Twitter and Facebook, and make your file public or private. You can keep the file private and direct your social media followers and clients to your videos by sending them URLs. However, if the file remains public and you generate interest from YouTube visitors, we highly recommend that you choose the Public option for all videos you upload.

6. **Complete the uploading process.**

If you have a Vimeo Plus account, the video is processed immediately. If you have a Vimeo Basic account, your video is processed in the order in which it was received, which means that you have to wait until all videos in front of yours are processed. If you have a YouTube account, your video is processed fairly quickly, depending, of course, on the number of YouTube uploads taking place at the same time as yours.

Adding Music to Your Videocast

You can add a lot of panache to a videocast if you include music. You can use background music for the introduction and exit. If you're creative and know a little about music, you can create your own background music using software and royalty-free music samples. You can use an alternative method for adding music to a videocast, and you can license music clips. We show you both methods in later sections.

Creating royalty-free music

If you're musically inclined, you can create your own background music using software and sound loops. On the Windows platform, the excellent Acid Music Studio ($54.95; visit www.sonycreativesoftware.com/musicstudio) is quite user friendly. You can work with multiple timelines to mix and match loops to create music in just about any genre, as shown in Figure 4-9.

If you own a Macintosh computer, the GarageBand application is just what the doctor ordered. The software and lots of music loops are included with every Apple desktop and laptop. GarageBand also features multiple timelines, as shown in Figure 4-10.

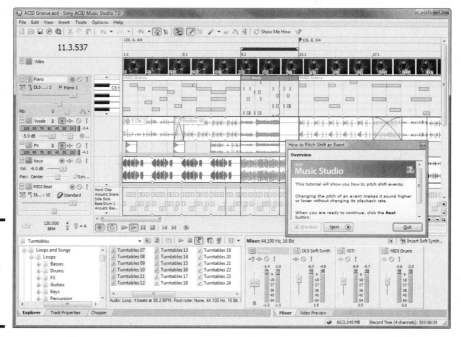

Figure 4-9:
Creating
royalty-free
music with
Acid Music
Studio.

Figure 4-10:
Creating
royalty-free
music with
GarageBand.

Finding cool royalty-free music

So you're not musically inclined, you don't have perfect pitch, and you can't tuna fish. What do you do? You purchase a license to use a product that someone has already created. To find royalty-free music for your videocast, check out these resources:

✦ www.cssmusic.com

✦ www.pond5.com

✦ www.premiumbeat.com

✦ www.royaltyfreemusic.com

✦ www.shockwave-sound.com

✦ www.uniquetracks.com

Lots of Web sites offer royalty-free music created by talented musicians. The music is covered by a Creative Commons license.

You cannot use content licensed by Creative Commons for commercial use. If you plan on charging for your videos, you must create your own music or pay for music.

Getting Your Videocast Recognized

Creating videos is a time-consuming process, especially if you do it well. Therefore, expecting some kind of return for your time investment is only reasonable. The return, of course, consists of the thousands of people and prospective clients viewing your videos who in turn become viable business prospects for you.

Here are a few tips for getting recognized:

✦ **Post in the signature of every e-mail you send a link to wherever your videos are stored online.** Most e-mail applications give you the option to create an e-mail signature and automatically insert it in every e-mail you send.

✦ **Post a line to your online video portals in every other form of social media you use.** For example, you can post a link to your videos on your Twitter and Facebook pages.

✦ **Avoid posting long videos.** If you have a lot to say about a subject, break it down into two or more episodes. Each video should be less than five minutes long.

✦ **If your videos are hosted at YouTube, be sure to upload videos to a channel that matches their content.** Getting recognized in a popular channel can be tough. If so, consider uploading your video to a different channel that matches the content but isn't as crowded.

✦ **Add multiple tags to every video you upload.** Don't overlook any possible tag. For example, if you're a published author or you're known for other work you've done on the Web, be sure to add your name as a tag. If you create instructional videos, use the tag *free tutorial*. In this day and age, people are finding that a free lunch does indeed exist and they're continually on the lookout for one.

✦ **Leave comments on other videos.** On YouTube, for example, you can leave polite video responses when you have a substantial contribution to another person's video.

✦ **Customize your YouTube channel to make a lasting impression.** When you have a large collection of videos, you can specify which one to feature, the sorting method, the page color, avatar upload instructions, and more.

✦ **Mirror the tags in your video description.** For example, if your video shows people how to do something in Photoshop, make one tag *Photoshop* and include the word *Photoshop* in the text description. The redundancy ranks your video higher than someone who hasn't repeated a tag in the video description.

✦ **If you host your videos at Vimeo, edit your profile.** You can edit your personal information to include a bio, upload a picture to display on your page, and upload a video that plays when your picture is clicked. You can also create a shortcut URL for your Vimeo page. For example, if you're a photographer, you might create the URL `vimeo.com/photoguru`, if it's available. If you create a shortcut URL, keep it as short as possible. Its purpose is to help people more easily reach your videos, not to give them carpal tunnel syndrome from typing long URLs.

✦ **Add contacts to your Vimeo profile.** A contact must be a member of Vimeo. You can add a contact to your Vimeo profile by typing that person's e-mail address in the Search box. Another way to add contacts to Vimeo is to send an e-mail invitation to colleagues or people who may be interested in viewing your videos. A person who accepts your invitation is automatically added to your contact list.

Book III
Chapter 4

**Producing
Your Videocast**

Chapter 5: Measuring Blogging, Podcasting, and Vlogging Metrics

In This Chapter

✔ **Measuring effectiveness**

✔ **Evaluating stats, comments, video, and RSS**

✔ **Measuring your return on investment**

✔ **Tracking incoming links**

Suppose that you've built a blog site or created a podcast and you've nurtured and fed it with posts and episodes. You've promoted your creative endeavor to the applicable parties, and now you want to know how many people have visited your blog or podcast. Or, if you're a vlogger, you want to know how many people have downloaded your vlog or viewed it on a video sharing site. After all, you've made a time investment and unless you're doing all the grunt work, you've dedicated some payroll funds to your effort. Therefore, in any of these areas, you must determine the return you're receiving on your investment. Video sharing sites make estimating the popularity of your vlog fairly easy, but you may need to know about your blog or podcast. In this chapter, we show you how to solve these mysteries.

Book VIII is devoted to measuring your entire marketing campaign success.

Measuring the Effectiveness of a Blog, Podcast, or Vlog

If you have a blog, podcast, or vlog, how do you know whether your message is getting out there? How do you measure your results? Sometimes you have no clue other than seeing that people are finding your media by way of your social media marketing efforts on Twitter or Facebook. How viral is your message? Is it being broadcast to people other than those who are being reached through your efforts?

If these questions are bouncing around in the three pounds of gray matter inside your head, we offer some suggestions in the following sections on how to measure the effectiveness of a blog. Your Web site stats reveal the most information, but you can also glean effective information from other areas.

Web site stats

You can find an amazing amount of information about how effective your site is using the program that tracks your Web site statistics. We give you an overview of Webalizer, one such program, later in this chapter in the "Viewing General Statistics with Webalizer" section.

You can peruse the stats to find these types of information:

✦ **The number of visitors who land on the home page of your blog:** Tells you if visitors found your site through a search engine

✦ **The number of visitors seeking specific blog posts:** Tells you that visitors found the post through an external link, or perhaps a very specific set of keywords in a search engine.

✦ **The locations where visitors are coming from:** Someone might have begun a search at a search engine, for example, or followed a direct link from another blog or Web site.

✦ **How long visitors remain on a specific post page:** If the duration of a visit is shorter than the potential length of time spent reading the post and pondering its contents, the post wasn't effective.

Capitalize on effective posts by creating similar posts. When you analyze your Web statistics, you'll know which posts are effective.

✦ **The number of unique visitors to your blog or podcast compared to the number to your Web site:** Blog posts can consist of unique information about your products or services. If you have more unique visitors to specific blog posts, or to your blog in general, it's a sign that the information is well received. If your blog attracts more unique visitors than your site does, consider creating links in your blog posts to related information on your Web site. If your site receives more hits than your blog, add some links from the specific products or services you offer to blog posts about these specific items.

✦ **The geographical location of your blog visitors:** If the majority of visitors are from a country other than your target market, change your message.

✦ **The number of people viewing your podcast:** Tells you how effective your marketing efforts are. When you have lots of visitors, you've created informative media that is in demand.

✦ **The number of unique page views in your podcast or blog:** You can figure out which episodes or posts are being received well. Use this information for planning future episodes of your podcast.

✦ **Whether blog posts with embedded videos get lots of hits:** If the blog posts with video are getting lots of hits and the video is also getting lots of views on the video hosting service, you've created an effective video. If you're seeing lots of positive comments on these posts, as well as lots of comments on the video hosting service, you've hit a home run.

✦ **Number of incoming links in your WordPress Dashboard:** Getting lots of incoming links means that you're getting noticed, and that's a good thing.

✦ **The direction of traffic:** If you have an established blog or podcast, your traffic rate and number of incoming links should be increasing. If they aren't, consider shaking things up a bit by offering different content. Look at which posts or episodes have been popular in the past. Expand on those topics or put a new spin on them, and carefully monitor the results.

If you host your blog on your own domain, you can find out a little bit more about your visitors:

✦ **How much time visitors are spending at your site and on individual posts:** You have to decipher this information. Your Web server lists the actual page name, which is not that same as the title of the blog post. For example, a post entitled "The Early Bird Gets the Photo" on `www.dougplusrox.com` is referenced by the following URL: `http://www.dougplusrox.com/?p=369`.

✦ **Which pages are most frequently used to enter or leave the site:** If visitors are entering and exiting the home page and spending only a short length of time on your site, they're skimming only one or two posts before getting out of Dodge. If you're in this situation, it's time to rethink your message. Visitors entering your site on a specific page, however, have honed in on a specific post from either a search engine result or an incoming link. If you have lots of these and visitors are spending a fair amount of time on your site and exiting from a different page, you have an effective blog.

Comments

An important way to measure your site's effectiveness is by looking for the following information in the Comments section:

✦ **Number of comments on each blog post:** This information is important if your goal is to stimulate interaction with potential customers. If certain blog posts are drawing more comments than others, this information is more relevant to your subscribers.

✦ **Comment length:** If you've written a lengthy post and you receive lengthy comments, you've struck a chord with subscribers and presented useful information. If comments are sparse, however, indicating that you haven't given your user base food for thought, consider changing the nature of your posts or the type of information you post.

✦ **The tone of comments on your posts:** If comments on the majority of your posts sound positive and you have lots of comments, you're sending the right message. You can be somewhat controversial at times and stir up provocative comments, but unless you're Rush Limbaugh or another shock jock, make it the exception and not the rule. If, on the other hand, the comments aren't flattering, you know what you need to do.

✦ **An increasing number of comments with each post:** If you're seeing more comments on posts, it means that

  • You're putting the right message out there.

  • The number of visitors to your blog is increasing.

If the number of comments for new posts is decreasing, you're losing your audience — and you must change your message.

Interesting or controversial videos garner lots of comments. If comments are positive, your message is being received well. If the majority of comments are negative, change the tone of your videos or create videos about different topics.

If you're receiving comments on individual podcast episodes, people are downloading the podcast from your Web site rather than using a subscription. Analyze which episodes reward you with the most comments — and then include that type of information in future podcasts. If a particular episode draws lots of positive comments, see whether you can create a follow-up episode or create a series based on the topic.

✦ **Number of visitors versus the number of comments:** If you have a fairly high ratio of comments to visitors, you're creating interesting material that gets visitors thinking.

Videos

When you've posted a video to a third-party site (such as YouTube or Vimeo), you can look there for some stats about these categories:

✦ **Number of subscribers:** At YouTube, you find this information on your channel. If you're creating relevant videos, you should notice a steady increase in subscribers with each new video you upload.

✦ **Growth in the number of subscribers:** You should experience steady growth as you regularly add new videos to your channel. If you notice a significant spurt after you post a video, analyze its content to determine why the video caused the growth spurt. Chances are good that you did something different or found a topic of particular interest to your subscribers. If, on the other hand, you notice a decline in new subscribers or a decrease in subscribers after posting a video, figure out what you did wrong and refrain from posting similar videos.

✦ **Number of people viewing individual videos:** You can find this information by visiting your home page. On Vimeo, you see the number of plays for each video. On your YouTube channel, view your channel to see the number of plays for each video (see Figure 5-1).

Figure 5-1:
Viewing the number of plays for your YouTube videos.

RSS

When you distribute your blog or podcast by way of Really Simple Syndication (RSS), you can find out these stats:

✦ **Access methods:** Determine how many people are getting your information from your FeedBurner feed by checking the stats at `feedburner.google.com` (see Figure 5-2). For more information on Feedburner, see Book III, Chapter 2.

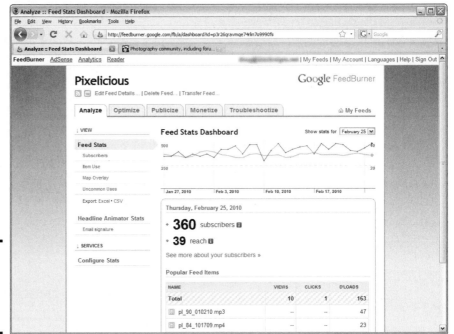

Figure 5-2:
Using
FeedBurner
to analyze
stats.

✦ **Reach:** This statistic tells you how many people are viewing or downloading specific episodes. You can find this information if your podcast feed is burned through FeedBurner.

✦ **Traffic patterns:** Does the graph show dramatic peaks and valleys? Does it show a sharp rise or a steady rise? Has the graph reached a plateau? Peaks and valleys signify the popularity of content. When you see a sharp peak in the graph, you've struck a nerve with a popular topic. Sharp valleys indicate content that went over like a lead balloon. If the graph has been relatively flat for a while, it's time to rethink your content. If the graph has been continually rising, you've found a good mix, which means it ain't broke, so don't fix it.

✦ **Appearance of your posts in social bookmarking services:** Check Delicious, reddit, or StumbleUpon.

✦ **Who's talking about you:** Find out whether your domain is garnering attention by checking out its ranking at Technorati (`http://tech norati.com/`).

✦ **Number of incoming links:** Go to Google, Yahoo!, or MSN.com and type **link:http://www.mysite.com** in the Search text field. You see a list of incoming links to your content, as shown in Figure 5-3.

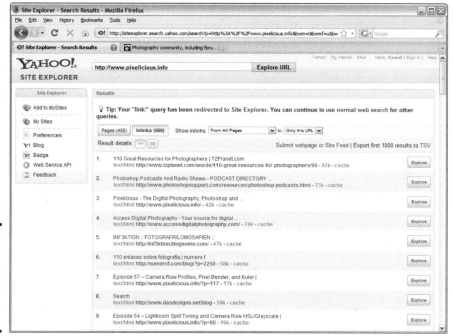

**Book III
Chapter 5**

Measuring Blogging,
Podcasting, and
Vlogging Metrics

Figure 5-3:
Tracking
incoming
links to your
podcast or
blog.

✦ **Number of people using a service to be notified of new posts or podcast episodes:** If you don't have a lot of takers, consider offering something of value, such as a free e-book, in exchange for an e-mail subscription.

Make sure that your privacy notice tells subscribers that their e-mail contact information will be kept private and used only to notify them whenever new content is posted.

Viewing General Statistics with Webalizer

As we outlined in the previous section, a way to keep tabs on the amount of traffic your blog receives is to view statistics from your Web server. To do so, you have to visit the URL associated with your site's control panel. Your Web hosting service tech-support team can lead you in the right direction.

The number of statistics you can access depends on your Web hosting company. Many of them use Webalizer; its graph shows you how many visitors stopped by your site on a specific day. The application also tallies stats by month. Figure 5-4 shows general Webalizer stats for a blog.

You can also analyze statistics by month, to see more detailed information such as the number of hits or visits per day and the referring URLs. You can also view the keywords visitors use to find you and the Web browser they use to view your site. The latter information is important if you make any major design changes; you can optimize the changes for the Web browser that's most often used to view your site (see Figure 5-5).

If you're interested in seeing which countries' residents are accessing your blog, check at the bottom of Webalizer stats page in the tastefully decorated pie chart, shown in Figure 5-6. (Mmm, pie.)

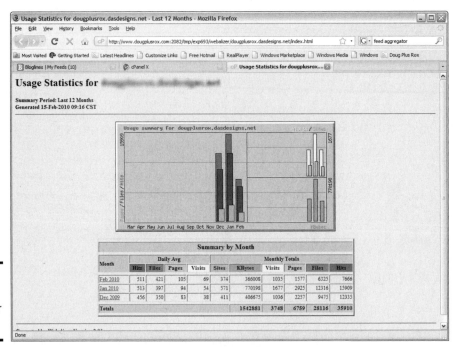

Figure 5-4:
Viewing statistics for a blog.

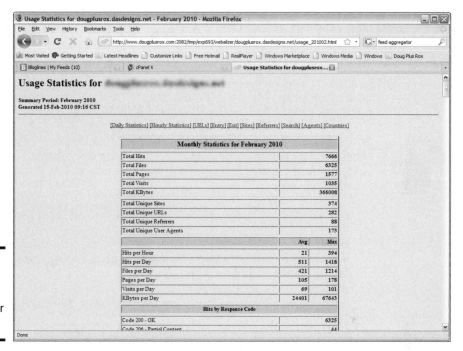

Figure 5-5:
Viewing detailed statistics for a blog.

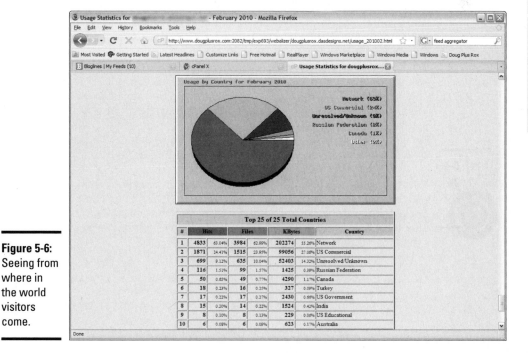

Figure 5-6:
Seeing from where in the world visitors come.

Comparing Hard and Soft Costs versus "Income"

Smart businesspeople don't spin their wheels. If something doesn't gain traction, they do something else. After analyzing the number of visitors your podcast or blog receives, or the number of views your videos receive, you have to factor in your *return on investment (ROI)*, or the amount of revenue you're receiving in return for your hard work.

As long as your media generates more interest and awareness about your product or service, as time goes on your efforts will turn into cash. If you have the right content and you've drawn lots of people to view your content, the rest will come in time.

To help calculate your return, consider these two types of costs:

+ **Hard:** The number of man-hours needed to create content for your podcast, blog, or videocast. Next would be the cost to host any media online, which would be Web hosting fees and any fees you pay to a designer to get your media online. If you're paying for premium video hosting such as Vimeo Plus, you have to factor this cost in as well.

+ **Soft:** This is the amount of time you personally spend creating content. Did that time take you away from any other profitable activities such as hobnobbing with the rich and famous, or other potential clients?

After you calculate the number of dollars you've invested in social media, you have to determine whether it has all been worthwhile. The only way you can do it is to track where your business is coming from. If you have a bricks-and-mortar presence, ask your customers: "How did you hear about us?" If you also have an online presence, include a required text field on your checkout form that asks the same question. Then you'll know exactly where your business is coming from and how much of it can be attributed to social media. If you want to fine-tune it, have your Web designer create a drop-down list that shows the different social media you're using. The purchaser can then choose which social media, if any, sent him to your online store.

You can also include a question at your online checkout that asks the user which forms of social media she's involved with. If you aren't involved with a social media network that a large number of your customers belong to, you may want to consider joining the network and seeing whether the potential exists for increasing your business.

Checking iTunes Subscribers

When you make your podcast available from the iTunes store, you're out there with the heavy hitters. You have no way, at least for now, to find out how many iTunes users are subscribed to your podcast, but you can find out how popular your podcast is, by following these steps:

1. Launch iTunes.

The lovely iTunes interface graces your computer.

2. Click Store.

The iTunes Store appears.

3. Click Podcasts.

The most popular podcasts are listed. If yours is on this page, you've made the big leagues. If it isn't, you have to do a little more work to find out how popular your podcast is.

4. Enter a keyword that's associated with your podcast.

If you're a photographer, *photography* is the key. After you enter the keyword, a list of podcasts appears, as shown in Figure 5-7.

5. Analyze the list of podcasts to see where your brainchild appears.

You can also sort podcasts by podcast name, episode name, release date, duration, popularity, or price. You're looking for popularity: When you see bars extending all the way across the Popularity column, you know that the episode is quite a popular one.

You can also use iTunes to determine which of your episodes are most popular. This information is useful in planning future episodes. To rank podcasts by popularity, follow these steps:

1. Launch iTunes.

The iTunes interface appears.

2. Click Store.

The home page of the iTunes store appears.

3. Click Podcasts.

The most popular podcasts are listed on this page.

Figure 5-7:
Determining
the
popularity
of your
podcast.

4. **Enter the name of your podcast in the Search text field.**

   Your podcast description page appears.

5. **Hover the cursor over the artwork representing the show.**

   An Information icon appears.

6. **Click the Information icon.**

   Information about your show, including its ratings, appears in another window, shown in Figure 5-8.

7. **Click the Go to This Podcast.**

   Your podcast appears against a lovely black background and displays any comments left about your podcast.

8. **Click the Popularity icon.**

   Your episodes are sorted by popularity, as shown in Figure 5-9.

Figure 5-8:
Extra,
extra —
read all
about it!

Figure 5-9:
Episodes
are
sorted by
popularity.

Book IV

Twitter

The 5th Wave   By Rich Tennant

"I'd respond to this person's comment on Twitter, but I'm a former Marine, Bernard, and a Marine never retweets."

Contents at a Glance

Chapter 1: Getting to Know Twitter

Twitter began as a simple concept: Keep friends up to date on what you're doing. Using Twitter, you can send a message from anywhere you can access the Internet — whether it's a computer or a portable device such as the iPhone or BlackBerry. From your Twitter page, or a desktop application, you can instantly post information that is received by people following you. But there's a catch: When you tell people what's on your mind, you have to say it in 140 characters or fewer — hence the term *microblogging* (a system of short text updates). Twitter users have come up with some interesting methods of saying more with less.

Twitter has evolved into a major social media hot spot. As a business, you can use the power of Twitter to attract potential clients. Think of Twitter, similar to other social media outlets, as breadcrumbs to your other content on the Internet. We introduce you to Twitter in this chapter.

For more information, check out *Twitter For Dummies,* by Laura Fitton, Michael Gruen, and Leslie Poston, or *Twitter Marketing For Dummies,* by Kyle Lacy.

Saying What's on Your Mind, 140 Characters at a Time

Twitter is an intriguing concept: Say what's on your mind, and use no more than 140 characters when you do it. People who follow your posts (known as *tweets*) can see them on their Twitter pages, as shown in Figure 1-1, or by using a desktop application such as TweetDeck, shown in Figure 1-2. Tweet Deck lets you manage your Twitter usage, do searches, and use columns to segregate searches, users, and much more. You can also use the TweetDeck on a mobile device such as a BlackBerry phone, iPhone, iPod touch, or iPad. We show you how to use TweetDeck in Book IV, Chapter 3. Your followers see your tweets, and so does anyone who searches for the specific topic you're tweeting about. So unless you send a *direct message* (the Twitter equivalent of a private message) to a follower, your messages are public.

Figure 1-1:
A user's
Twitter
page.

Figure 1-2:
The
TweetDeck
application.

You can also find Twitter messages by using a search engine. Unlike in Las Vegas, what is spoken on Twitter doesn't stay on Twitter.

In the beginning, people used Twitter to tell followers what they were having for lunch or when they were going to the gym or other mundane proclamations. Other than that Twitter user's mother or significant other, who cares? Then savvy Twitter users began to get wise. They realized that a vast network of people were using Twitter, a vast network of people who were potential clients or customers. Your mission is to tap into that vein and find gold.

Twitter demographics

Before you dip your toe into the shallow end of any swimming pool, it's nice to know who's swimming there. In other words, do the demographics of Twitter match the demographics of your ideal customer? Table 1-1 shows the Twitter demographics.

Table 1-1	Twitter Demographics
Demographic	*Percentage*
Female	55
Male	45
3–12 years old	4
13–17 years old	13
18–34 years old	45
35–49 years old	24
Over 50	14
Caucasian	69
African American	16
Asian	3
Hispanic	11
Other	1
No Kids 0–17	53
Kids 0–17	47
0–$30K	17
$30–$60K	25
$60–$100 K	27
More than $100K	30
No college	48
College	39
Graduate school	13

**Book IV
Chapter 1**

Getting to Know Twitter

What's in it for you?

WIIFM are the call letters for What's-in-it-for-me? — every businessperson's favorite radio station. There's not much in it for you if you don't work it. If you post the content that people want to read, potential clients will follow you. After you draw a few followers who hang on every word you post, they share your posts (*retweet*) with people who are following them. Chances are good that many people who receive the retweeted message aren't your followers, but would be if the retweeted message piques their curiosity or they think your post is the greatest thing since sliced bread. This is how you get followers.

Twitter followers can become customers. Think of Twitter posts and other forms of social media as breadcrumbs you sprinkle on the Internet. The breadcrumbs lead a trail to your other social media sites, your Web site, and your bricks-and-mortar business (if you have one). Therefore, you *must* plan your campaign and create quality posts that garner an ever-increasing horde of loyal followers.

You don't create a band of loyal followers overnight. Just as Rome wasn't built in a day, neither will your Twitter empire be built in a day. Tweet by tweet, follower by follower — that's how you measure your success on Twitter. The quality of your posts and your consistency and persistence are the keys to success on Twitter.

Major brands and Twitter

Many major brands are represented on Twitter. You can find major car manufacturers and computer manufacturers and many other major brands on Twitter. Why are they on Twitter? This list describes a couple of reasons, which you can apply to your business:

✦ **Twitter can facilitate excellent customer relations.** Companies post information about their products for their followers, solve problems, provide customer service, and more, which can lead to increased sales.

✦ **A presence on Twitter helps avoid bad customer relations.** Doug had a problem with a computer and was getting no resolution from the standard support team. He posted on Twitter and within half an hour received a tweet from the company's representative on Twitter. The issue was resolved, and the company avoided any further bad press. A Twitter presence can also be used to squelch false rumors.

This list describes why some major brands use Twitter:

+ **Best Buy:** Posts company information and information about new products.

+ **Dell:** Manages multiple Twitter accounts, including customer relations and customer service.

+ **Fender:** Posts information about its guitars and other interesting musical facts.

+ **Home Depot:** Offers customer service to its Twitter followers and responds to customer queries about product needs.

+ **JetBlue:** Provides online service to its Twitter followers and posts travel tips.

+ **Lowes:** Offers customer service to its Twitter followers and posts information about discounts.

+ **Starbucks Coffee:** Posts specials and answers questions from its followers.

These major companies are just a few that are keeping in touch with customers by way of Twitter.

Sometimes Twitter can be confusing. You can always click the Help link on your home page. Type your query and find an answer in the Twitter Help database.

Creating a Twitter Account

Before you can explore the wonderful world of Twitter, you need to set up an account. You can set up one for free — all you need is a valid e-mail address.

Follow these steps to set up a Twitter account:

1. **Launch your favorite Web browser and navigate to** `http://twitter.com`.

The Twitter home page appears, as shown in Figure 1-3.

2. **Click Sign Up Now.**

The page refreshes and Twitter wants to know who you are and all that good stuff, as shown in Figure 1-4.

**Book IV
Chapter 1**

**Getting to Know
Twitter**

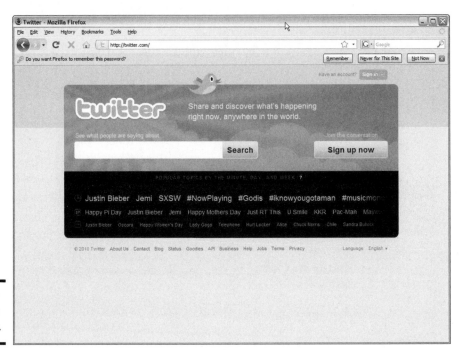

Figure 1-3:
The Twitter
home page.

Figure 1-4:
Sign up,
please.

3. **Fill out these sections:**

- *Full Name:* When you enter your full name and username, Twitter checks the availability of each one.

- *Username:* Use your own name with no spaces. If you feel compelled to add your company name, use something like JoeatCompTech. But the company name gobbles up lots of your 140 allotted characters per post. If you pique people's curiosity with your posts, they can always find out which company you work for if you include it in your bio information on your Twitter page.

   Use all lowercase letters. People on portable devices will thank you. If you choose a username with letters and numeric characters, users of portable devices have to switch screens and entering your username takes longer.

- *Password*: Even though it's unlikely that anybody would want to hack your account, you can never be too sure. Don't use an obvious password that anybody could guess. Use a combination of alphabetical characters and number, but don't use your initials and birthday. An example of an excellent password is `ymB!_375Z`.

- *Email:* You must use a functional e-mail address. Use one that's connected to your Web server. The e-mail address joe@mybusiness.com sounds much more professional than joe@aol.com.

   Accept the default option to let other people find you by using your e-mail address. Then existing contacts and customers who have your e-mail address can easily find you on Twitter.

4. **Click Create My Account.**

   A screen with captcha images appears. You have to enter the phrase to prove that you're human and not a computer robot setting up Twitter accounts.

5. **Type the weird-looking letters and then click Finish.**

   After you click Finish, the Find Sources That Interest You page appears, as shown in Figure 1-5. We talk about that topic in the next section.

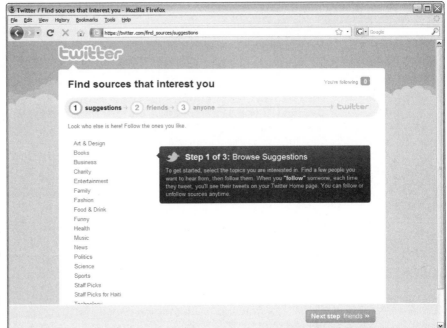

Figure 1-5:
Find
sources that
interest you.

If you wear more than one hat, or your company has more than one division, you can set up multiple presences on Twitter. Each Twitter account must have a unique e-mail address. If your corporation has a director of sales, a service manager, and a customer relations rep, each one can set up a unique account, which increases your company's presence on Twitter. If you're a one-person show, you can also create multiple accounts — you just need multiple e-mail addresses.

Finding People to Follow

You have an account on Twitter. Now it's time to find some Twitter folks who are of interest to you. Start by following people in your industry and see what they have to say.

Starting on the Find Sources That Interest You page (refer to Figure 1-5), follow these steps:

1. **Click a category name on the left side.**

   Choose a category related to your business. After you click a category of interest, the page refreshes and you see a list of Twitter account users for that category. Figure 1-6 shows Twitter users in the Art & Design category.

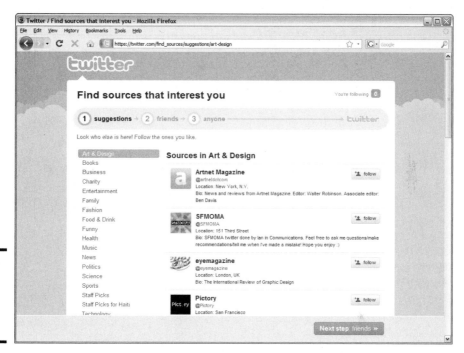

Figure 1-6:
Finding
interesting
folks to
follow.

2. **Scroll down the list. When you find a user who piques your curiosity, click the Follow button.**

   The category you choose may have lots of Twitter users. In this case, you see a More button at the bottom of the page.

   You can follow as many people as you want from this page. You may find other Twitter users from your industry, and maybe even competitors.

   Be sure to follow your competitors and other Twitter users from your industry to develop a feel for what other people in your industry are tweeting about.

3. **Continue choosing people to follow. When you're finished, click the Next Step: Friends button.**

   The page refreshes and you have options to look for friends from your e-mail address book, as shown in Figure 1-7. This trick works only if you have a Gmail, a Yahoo!, or an AOL e-mail address.

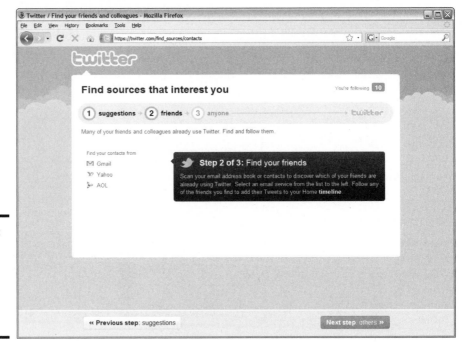

Figure 1-7:
Choosing
people
from your
address
book to
follow.

4. **If you have an e-mail account with a service listed in Step 3, click the service. If you don't, click the Next Step: Others button to skip to Step 10.**

   You're prompted for your username and password.

5. **Enter your e-mail address and password.**

   Twitter connects with your account server, scans your address book, and posts a list of your e-mail contacts who are on Twitter. You see a Send Request button next to the name of each person who is on Twitter but can't be found by e-mail address. Click the button to have a request sent to your contact indicating that you want to follow them. If an e-mail contact can be located on Twitter by using their e-mail address, a Follow button appears next to the e-mail address.

6. **Choose the contacts you want to follow.**

   You can choose as many contacts as you want from this list.

7. **After choosing contacts from your e-mail list, click the Next Step: Others button.**

   A list of e-mail contacts not on Twitter appears.

8. **Click the radio box next to the contact's e-mail address to send an invitation to join Twitter.**

   You can invite as many people as you want.

9. **After inviting contacts to join Twitter, click the Invite These Contacts button.**

   Alternatively, you can click Cancel. After you choose either option, the Search for Anyone page appears, as shown in Figure 1-8.

Figure 1-8:
Search for
anyone.

10. **Enter the name of someone you want to follow.**

    Search for businesses or people in your industry.

11. **Click Search.**

    A list of Twitter users appears. The list may or may not be the person or business you're looking for. Look at the list carefully to make sure you choose the right person.

12. **Click the Follow button next to the people you want to follow and click the Next Step: You're Done! button when you've selected everyone.**

    You're transported to your Twitter page. But you're not quite done yet — you receive an e-mail from Twitter requesting verification. You already see some tweets from people you follow, as shown in Figure 1-9, but your Twitter page is bereft of information about you and your business. (You know — plain Jane Vanilla.) We show you how to fix that problem in the next section.

**Book IV
Chapter 1**

**Getting to Know
Twitter**

Figure 1-9:
You've got
tweets.

Setting Up Your Twitter Page

You have a Twitter account, and you know what you want to tweet, but nobody on Twitter knows anything about you. You can rectify this dilemma by setting up your Twitter page. When you set it up, you add bio information or the URL to your Web site, upload a picture, or change the design.

To set up your Twitter page, follow these steps:

1. **Click Settings from your Twitter page.**

   The account settings for your Twitter page appear. In this section of the settings, you can change your e-mail address, username, enable geotagging, and more. You can also protect your tweets from the public. (Your goal, of course, is to have your tweets seen by as many people as possible.) The settings on this page are self-explanatory, as are the settings on the Password page, so in Step 2 we move on to Mobile settings.

2. **Click Mobile.**

   The Mobile settings appear, as shown in Figure 1-10. You can change settings in this section to use Twitter with text messaging from your mobile phone.

Figure 1-10:
The settings
for tweeting
from a
mobile
phone.

3. **Enter your mobile phone number.**

   You also have the option to let other people find you by using your mobile number, but unless you have an unlimited data plan, this strategy can lead to some costly phone bills.

4. **Click Start.**

   Twitter verifies your phone number.

5. **Click Notices.**

   The following options are selected by default:

   - *New Follower Emails:* Be automatically notified by e-mail whenever you have a new follower.

   - *Direct Text Emails:* Be automatically notified by e-mail whenever someone sends you a direct message.

   - *Email Newsletter:* Receive the Twitter newsletter by e-mail.

6. **Accept the default e-mail notifications or deselect the ones you don't want and then click Save.**

7. **Click Profile.**

   This page gives you the option to add information to your profile (see Figure 1-11), which is woefully blank now.

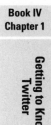

Figure 1-11:
You can
create a
compelling
profile.

8. In the picture section, click Browse.

Browse for a photo on your computer. You can upload an image in GIF, JPG, or PNG format. The file size of the image must be less than 700K. (The image looks small on your Twitter page.) Use a head-and-shoulders image of yourself or a close-up of your smiling face.

9. You should have already entered your real name. In case you didn't, do it now.

Use your real name. People on Twitter will find out who you are, anyway. If you use an alias and you become popular, someone may set up an account in your own name.

10. Enter your location.

This step is important, especially if you have a bricks-and-mortar business. Local Twitter users may follow you because you live in the area, and they may become customers.

11. Enter the URL of your Web site.

You do want Twitter users to find your Web site, don't you?

12. Enter a bio.

Twitter now becomes generous, and you can use 160 characters for your bio rather than the 140 allocated for a tweet. Put on your thinking cap and create a bio that tells as much about you and your business as possible while keeping within the character limit.

Check out the Twitter bios of other people in your industry before taking a crack at writing yours.

13. **Click the Save button and then click the Design tab.**

The Twitter Design page appears, as shown in Figure 1-12. This is your chance to trick out your Twitter page.

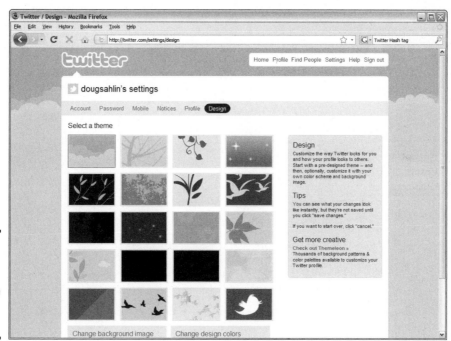

Figure 1-12: It's time to give your Twitter page the essence of cool.

14. **Choose a theme you like.**

Your choice isn't cast in stone. If you don't like a theme, you can change it later. We show you how to tweak your page in Book IV, Chapter 3.

15. **Click the Save Changes button.**

After you set up a Twitter account, you have a very basic page, as shown in Figure 1-13. With a basic Twitter page, you're ready to start communing with tweeple (see Book IV, Chapter 2).

It's important to know how to get around on your Twitter page. When you log on to Twitter, you immediately see your page. Anybody can find your

Twitter page by entering the Twitter URL followed by your username: `www.twitter.com/myusername`.

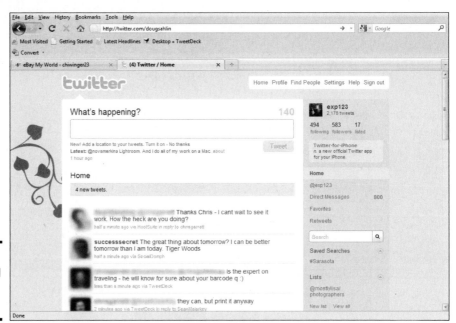

Figure 1-13:
Get your red
hot tweets
right here.

Notice the big "What's Happening?" field at the top of the page? This is where you type your words of wisdom. Tweets from the people you're following appear below the Home designation. Twitter does not update in real time, and you're not notified when someone you're following posts a tweet. You have to refresh the page to make that happen.

Getting Your Feet Wet on Twitter

Before you start creating tweets, you have to familiarize yourself with Twitter:

✦ **Take the time to watch the posts of the people or businesses you're following.** This gives you an idea of what people in your industry are saying on Twitter. When you find a businessperson who's sending tweets that pique your interest, this is the type of material you should be tweeting. When you send useful information in your Twitter posts, you get notices and garner a loyal twibe of followers.

✦ **Look at the number of Twitter users who follow the people you're following.** If a Twitter user is followed by a large number of people, chances are good that she has something good to say when she creates a post. How prolific are the people you're following? If they create only a few posts a day but are still followed by lots of people, analyze what they say. Perhaps they're sending links to useful information they've found on the Internet. If the information they're putting on Twitter is good, you've found a person you can emulate.

✦ **Look at the followers of the people you're following.** You can open a person's Twitter page by clicking the person's icon, which appears next to their tweet. If you're using an application such as TweetDeck, click the person's Twitter name to see their profile. You see their most recent tweets. If you think the person has something useful to say, follow them and learn.

✦ **Search for tweets about your information or service.** Type the information you're looking for into the Search field. For example, if you enter *photography*, you see tweets that contain the word *photography*.

Use a hashtag (#) in front of a keyword when you search. Figure 1-14 shows the search results for *#photography*. Note that the search updates tell you how many tweets have been sent since you started your search. Refresh your browser to see the newest tweets.

Figure 1-14: Searching for relevant tweets.

Chapter 2: Communing with Like-Minded People

In This Chapter

✔ **Creating a Twitter marketing strategy**

✔ **Mastering the Twitter search engine**

✔ **Communing with locals who use Twitter**

✔ **Tweeting like a pro**

You've decided that Twitter is a good fit for your social media marketing campaign and you've set up your Twitter account. Now what? Well, now would be an ideal time to find out how to use Twitter for the best possible return on your time investment. First, you create a strategy for your campaign. Then you break the ice and start searching for people to follow. After following some people, you develop an idea of what to do and what not to do on Twitter. Now comes the fun part: communing with your *tweeple* (Twitterspeak for *followers*). Then you become truly profound and send out useful information.

With a bit of luck and an equal dose of skill topped off by a heaping portion of persistence, you start picking up followers. In fact, you may soon have a *twibe* (Twitterspeak for *lots of followers*). When you reach this lofty plateau, you're well on your way to adding additional income to your bottom line. In this chapter, we show you how to get started with Twitter.

Creating a Tweet Strategy for Your Business

In Book IV, Chapter 1, we get you started on your way to Twitter success. Now it's time to roll up your sleeves and come up with a Twitter marketing strategy.

Conventional methods of marketing such as telemarketing, TV ads, e-mail promotions that you did not opt in (can you say spam?), and the like are known as methods of *interruption marketing* — you're interrupting the end user's day with your message.

When you market on Twitter, people follow you because they like what you have to say. Because you have their permission to send them tweets, it's known as *permission marketing*.

However, if you send the wrong type of message on Twitter, your followers can revoke their permission and you lose them.

When you create your campaign, the goal is to do some viable marketing to a warm audience without overstepping the bounds and making your messages sound like blatant advertisements.

Here are some ideas on how to start marketing on Twitter:

✦ **Create an account using your business name as well as your own name (see Book IV, Chapter 1).** Twitter limits you to a username of fewer than 15 characters. If your business name is longer than 15 characters, get creative. For example, the name Technical Gadgets for Less might become techstuff4less.

✦ **When creating an account for your business, use your company logo as your Twitter avatar.** When you use your logo, you're consistent with your other forms of marketing that also use your logo, such as printed materials and other online marketing endeavors.

✦ **If you have multiple accounts for your business, personalize them.** Use related names, such as socialmktgjan and socialmktgdoug.

✦ **Follow the right people.** Follow leaders in your industry, and follow competitors. When you make your first foray into Twitter, you don't know what to tweet about. Following the right people quickly educates you about the topics the heavy hitters are talking about. We provide more information on finding the right people to follow in later sections.

✦ **Don't send your first tweet until you know the lay of the land.** After following people in your industry for a couple of days, you can get the ball rolling by retweeting messages written by others that you think are useful. When you start retweeting, people notice you and you start to pick up followers. We show you the ins and outs of tweeting in the later section "Tweeting Like a Pro."

✦ **Continuously monitor your company on Twitter.** Perform a Twitter search (see the next section) for your company name to find out what people are saying about you. If you catch bad press from a Twitter user, you can respond to him quickly and nip the problem in the bud. When people say good things about your company, retweet the message.

If the person who left good vibes about your product seems to be a good writer, ask her for a testimonial, or if she's not a great writer, ask whether you can reword her tweet into a testimonial.

✦ **Monitor your competitors.** It's nice to know what type of feedback they're getting. If you run across dissatisfied customers, you may be able to convert them to your company by offering a solution to the problem that the tweet author experienced with the other company. If you can't offer a solution, follow the disgruntled user, and he may follow you in return and eventually become a customer. See the later section "Searching on Twitter" for more information.

✦ **Use industry buzzwords.** When you write a tweet, use words that people will associate with your industry. This strategy makes your Twitter posts easier to find when people use the Twitter search engine. Yes, you could say it's SEO (search engine optimization) for tweets.

✦ **Send tweets from your wireless phone at conferences.** Update followers about what your company is doing and describe any special events happening at your booth. Publicize the event on Twitter well in advance.

✦ **Dedicate part of the day to the majority of your Twitter activity.** After spending a week or so analyzing the habits of your followers, you know at which time of day your followers see your message. That's when you should be on Twitter, spreading your words of wisdom.

✦ **Give away samples of your product or e-books about your services.** If your product is expensive, offer a discount. Send a message to followers announcing your giveaway for the first ten followers who send you a direct message.

✦ **Create a contest or competition involving your industry.** For example, if your company sells camera accessories, launch a photography contest on Twitter and give away some products to the prize winners.

✦ **Promote online events such as webinars on Twitter.** Promote your local events as well. We show you how to hook up with local Twitter users in the later section "Getting in touch with local tweeple."

✦ **Announce new products.** You can also provide tips on the proper use of your product.

✦ **Allow potential customers to ask questions about your product or service before the sale.** After you establish yourself as an expert, you're bound to field questions about who you are or what you do.

✦ **Give your customers a way to get service by way of Twitter.** When you establish a relationship and turn a Twitter follower into a customer, it's only fair that the customer should have access to you or a member of your company for service after the sale.

✦ **Be a real person.** Don't come across as a zombie from your company who has been given the job of being "the Twitter person." Have fun and enjoy the interaction. If you have a chance to interject humor, by all means do so. People love to laugh, especially in a down economy. If you present yourself as a warm, likeable human being and they see your smiling face on the Twitter avatar, you're one step closer to turning a Twitter follower into a loyal customer.

✦ **Talk to people about their interests.** This strategy doesn't sell product, but it makes you seem more human. If one of your followers is interested in learning to play the guitar and you're a guitar player, send the person a direct message offering information. Your follower will be pleasantly surprised and will definitely show more interest in your tweets.

**Book IV
Chapter 2**

**Communing with
Like-Minded People**

✦ **Ask questions about your industry.** Twitter is a helpful way to get opinions. You may even learn something you can add to your product or service to get a leg up on your competition.

✦ **Spend time looking for interesting online content about your product or industry.** You can find many interesting articles about your business using social media bookmarking sites such as Digg (`www.digg.com`), StumbleUpon (`www.stumbleupon.com`), or Technorati (`www.technorati.com`). Turn the URL into a short URL (at `www.tinyurl.com` or `www.bit.ly`) and send the link with a short description to your followers. When you shorten a URL at `www.bit.ly`, you can track how many people clicked the link.

Searching on Twitter

Twitter is a vast community. And, even if it were only half as large as it is, it wouldn't be half-vast. When faced with such a large community and hundreds and hundreds of tweets per minute, finding what you want on Twitter can be like searching for a needle in the proverbial haystack. Fortunately, you don't have to sift through hundreds of tweets to find the right people or to find tweets about your product, service, or profession, thanks to Twitter Search (`http://search.twitter.com`). We show you how to use Twitter Search in the following sections.

Searching for the right tweeple (Twitter people)

Finding people to follow is one of the first steps when you begin a Twitter campaign. You found a few people to follow when you created your Twitter account (see Book IV, Chapter 1). Now it's time to do some power searching and find the right people to follow. What constitutes the right people for your business depends on the type of service or product you sell. You're sure to find leaders in your industry or product and some of your competitors on Twitter. You have Twitter Search at your disposal.

Follow these steps to use Twitter Search:

1. **Launch your favorite Web browser and navigate to `http://search.twitter.com`.**

   The Twitter search engine — looking suspiciously similar to the Google search engine — appears, as shown in Figure 2-1.

2. **Click Advanced Search.**

   Advanced options for the Twitter search engine appear, as shown in Figure 2-2. You can search by entering keywords about your product or service, or you can search for people who market your product or service.

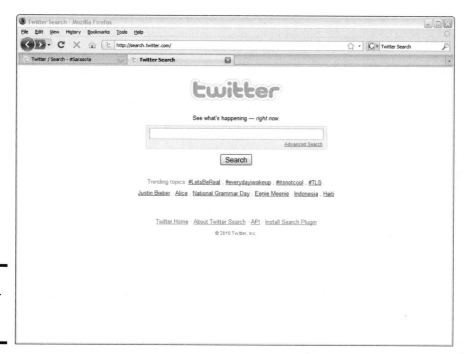

Figure 2-1:
The Twitter
search
engine.

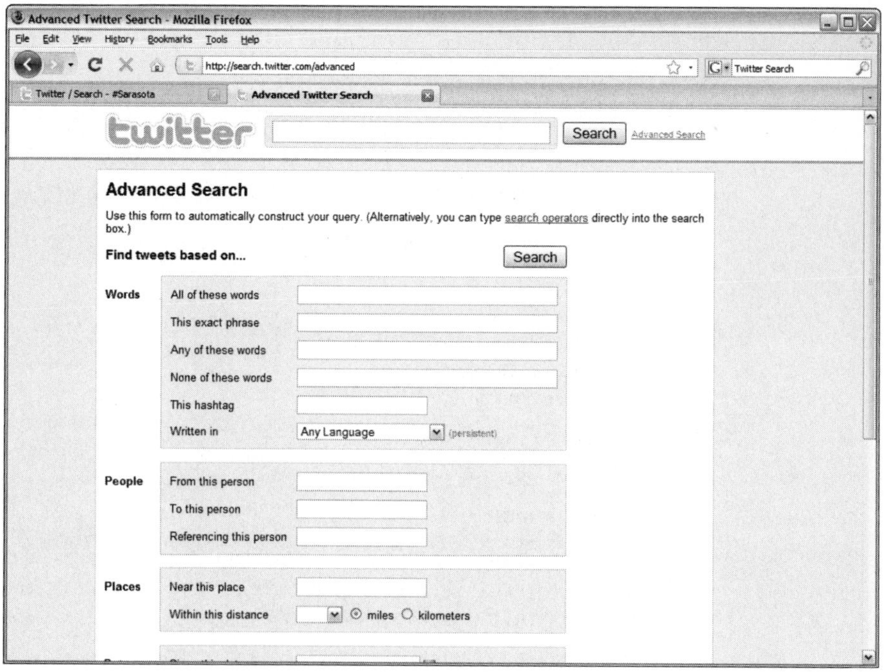

Figure 2-2:
Advanced
search
options.

Communing with
Like-Minded People

3. **In the This Exact Phrase text box, enter the name of a person or company you think may be on Twitter.**

   If the person or company is on Twitter, you see all tweets that mention the person or company. The tweets might be authored by industry professionals you want to follow.

4. **Click Search.**

   The page refreshes and shows tweets that contain the name of the person you entered in Step 3.

5. **Review the tweets and click the avatar to the left of any tweet that captures your attention.**

   The person's Twitter page appears in another window.

6. **Review the person's tweets.**

7. **If the tweets look like the right stuff, follow the person.**

8. **Review the rest of the search results.**

9. **Repeat Steps 2 through 7 using the text fields in the People section.**

   You can find tweets sent from a person, to a person, or about a person. Of course, you can do the same thing for the name of a company.

Now you should have a number of people you're following. Following people in your industry gives you a solid background to build on. If you do nothing more than read the tweets of these people, you learn proper Twitter protocol. You also see some bad examples of Twitter use. Eventually, you interact with the people you're following by sending them direct messages or responding to their tweets. You can also look at the person's Twitter home page to see whom they're following.

But Twitter isn't all about connecting with your peers. You've got to forge a connection with Twitter users who may be potential clients, which incidentally is the subject of the next section.

Searching for Twitter activity for your type of business

Searching for people associated with your trade or profession is all well and good, but you also want to find people who are looking for information about your product or service. You can do this by using the Twitter search engine:

1. **Navigate to `http://search.twitter.com` and then click Advanced Search.**

   The advanced search options appear.

2. **Enter the name of your profession in the All These Words text box.**

TIP

If your profession has a specific title, you can try the This Exact Phrase box as an option.

3. Click Search.

Twitter returns all tweets that match the phrase you entered in Step 2. Figure 2-3 shows the results of a search for the term *wedding photographer*.

Figure 2-3:
Searching for tweets about your profession.

4. Review the tweets.

Remember that you're looking for potential clients. Finding tweets from Twitter users in your profession is useful because they may be people you want to follow.

5. When someone's tweet piques your curiosity, click the author's avatar.

The user's Twitter page appears in another window, which is wonderful because you still see the results of your search in another window.

6. Browse the person's tweets.

You're looking for useful information. Imagine that you're one of your clients on Twitter, or a potential client on Twitter, and ask yourself whether this person's tweets would be of interest to you.

7. If you find the person's information useful, click Follow.

You're now following the person.

8. **Review the rest of the results from your search.**

   Follow as many people as you want. You can always unfollow someone if you find that his information isn't useful.

9. **Repeat Steps 2 through 8 with other keywords relevant to your trade or profession.**

   For example, if you're a wedding photographer, you might enter a phrase such as *bridal photography* or *wedding planner*. Repeat this process until you've found lots of potential clients.

Search for people who are in professions similar to yours. For example, if you're a wedding photographer, search for disc jockeys, event coordinators, and caterers. When you start networking with people in your industry, you can refer clients to each other.

Getting in touch with local tweeple

If you have a bricks-and-mortar business, you must communicate with local people. Although people from around the world are on Twitter, you can find local people to follow. Here's how to create a local twibe:

1. **Launch your favorite Web browser, navigate to `http://search.twitter.com`, and then type the hashtag symbol (#) followed by the name of your town. Then click Search.**

   After you click Search, you see a list of tweets that contain the hashtag and the town, as shown in Figure 2-4. You may end up with tweets about towns with the same name as yours in other parts of the world.

Use the hashtag when you perform a Twitter search. When a Twitter user puts a hashtag in front of a word, she is tweeting information regarding that word rather than it's just randomly appearing in a tweet. Find out more about hashtags in the "Using the hashtag" section of this chapter.

2. **Review the tweets.**

   Look for interesting people to follow based on the information they tweet. If the Twitter user looks like a potential candidate for your product or service, follow him. If you find tweets from companies offering similar products or services, follow them as well. You may also find companies offering companion products or services. These people are excellent people to network with as well, and their followers are probably excellent candidates for your products or services. Note that you can reply to a tweet or view the full tweet on the Twitter user's page.

3. **Click the avatar of a person whose tweet piques your curiosity.**

   The person's Twitter page opens in another browser window.

Figure 2-4:
Finding local tweeple.

4. **Review the person's tweets and follow the person if you think she's a potential candidate for your project or service or is someone with whom you want to network.**

5. **Click the Search browser window and repeat Steps 3 and 4 for other tweets that look interesting.**

6. **Repeat Steps 1 through 5 using the names of nearby towns and the county in which you live.**

   You should find lots of new people to follow, who may eventually follow you and use your product or service.

REMEMBER

You can fine-tune any Twitter search by clicking the Advanced Search button. In an advanced search, you can exclude words, search by hashtag, find tweets from one person to another, or find tweets referencing a person. You can also search for a word or phrase and then limit the search to a given distance from your hometown. For example, if you're a wedding photographer and you want to find conversations about wedding photography within 25 miles of New York City, your advanced search might look like the one show in like Figure 2-5.

Another option for you to try searching from is `http://nearbytweets. com`. You can search for tweets nearby your hometown about anything or about a specific topic. Figure 2-6 shows tweets near Sarasota, Florida, about photography. This site updates in real time.

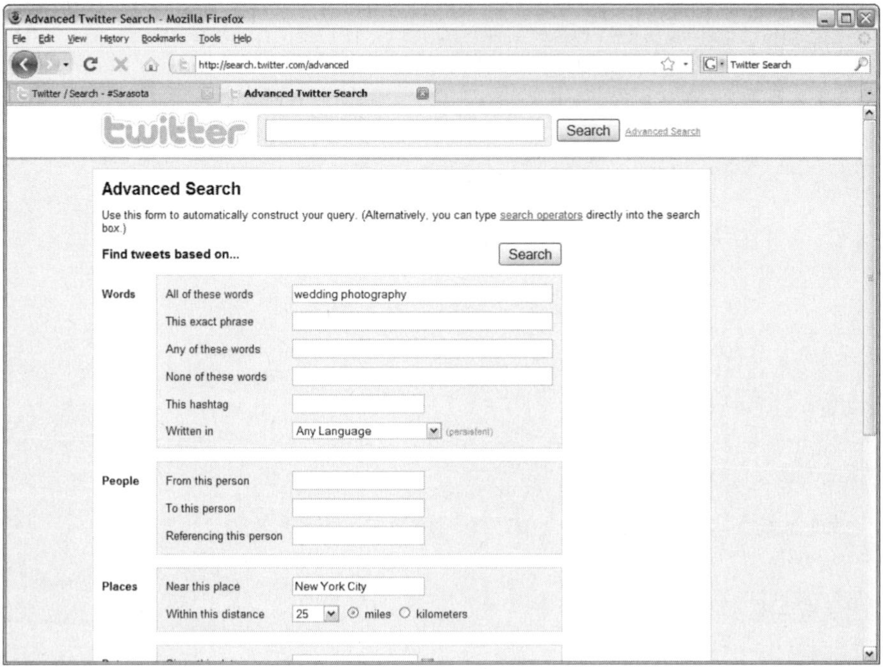

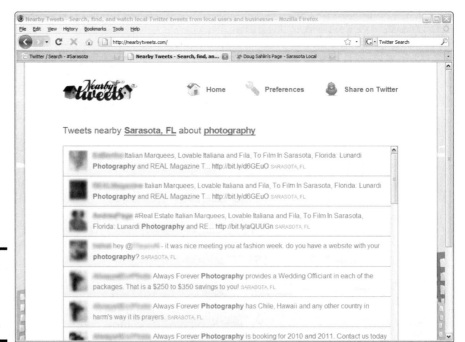

Figure 2-5:
Using the
Advanced
Search
feature.

Figure 2-6:
Finding
tweets
near your
hometown.

The last application we want to talk about is the TwitterLocal desktop application. You can download and install this free, cross-platform application from `www.twitterlocal.net`. You can then search for tweeple within a given area from your zip code, as shown in Figure 2-7.

Figure 2-7:
Using the
TwitterLocal
application.

Tweeting Like a Pro

Before you get involved in any serious tweeting, it's imperative to know what you're doing. Some conversations need to stay open to the public, and others need to be kept between yourself and one recipient. You also have ways to grab the attention of people who are interested in what you're tweeting about but are not following you. You can also hang on the coattail of someone else and regurgitate her tweet after adding your own secret sauce.

To get noticed on Twitter, you have to send some compelling tweets. Your goal is to establish yourself as an expert in your industry, by creating thoughtful informative tweets that are read by your followers. As mentioned earlier in this chapter, your followers may retweet the message, which is seen by their followers — people who may not be following you. When you start sending the right stuff, the number of people following you increases exponentially.

Ask questions on Twitter. When you ask questions, you involve users in a conversation. You can ask for information about the type of products you use or the type of information they want about your product or services. Twitter is also a great place to take an opinion poll.

You need to know lots of other information to tweet like a pro. We share this information with you in later sections of this chapter.

Catching on to Twitter lingo

When you become serious about tweeting, you have to make Twitter your second language. You can do lots of things to condense your messages. You find creative ways to condense your messages into 140 characters or fewer.

When you're creating your tweets, a space also counts as a character.

Here's an example of a message written in plain English:

I look forward to seeing your information later.

The sentence has 48 characters, including spaces.

Here's how to convert it into Twitterese:

I look 4ward 2 seeing ur info later.

This sentence has 29 characters, a net savings of 19 characters. Notice that we didn't change *later* to *L8R*. It would save two characters but would make followers think you're 12 years old.

To learn Twitterese, review the tweets of other users to see how they're condensing messages. Just remember to turn off Twitterese when you send an e-mail to someone or compose a letter.

Something else you need to condense is long URLs. At lots of different Web sites, you can condense a long URL into one that still gets the end user to the Web site without gobbling up lots of characters. Consider this URL:

`www.dougplusrox.com/?p=200`

This URL opens a blog post. It occupies a whopping 33 characters of the 140 you're allotted for a tweet.

When you need to say a lot and still have a URL in your message, launch your favorite Web browser and navigate to `www.tinyurl.com` — one of the many URL shortening services we cover in Book II, Chapter 1. After you enter your long URL in the text box and click Make TinyURL, you see the following line, for example:

```
http://tinyurl.com/yaknyeo
```

This line creates a perfectly functional URL and uses only 26 characters, a net savings of 7 characters, enough to type a short tweet and still have one character left. Here's an example of a tweet that includes a tiny URL:

> `http://tinyurl.com/yaknyeo` A blog post about being creative w/ur digital camera

This example uses 79 characters, leaving plenty of room for your followers to add a note when they retweet the information about your brilliant blog post.

Never use the entire 140 characters you're allowed. When you leave room for more characters, your followers can retweet your message and still have room for a message of their own.

Twitterspeak

Twitter has its own language. After you use Twitter for a while, you get to know its lingo. To lessen your learning curve, we've created this miniglossary:

direct message: A message sent directly to another twitter user that isn't visible to any of your other followers.

Follow Friday: A hashtag (#FF or #followfriday) used to recommend people that your followers should follow.

hashtag: A symbol (#) used to categorize tweets. For example, if you're sending a tweet for photographers, a popular hashtag is #togs or #photography. A useful resource for hashtags is `http://tagdef.com`.

retweet: A message authored by another Twitter user that you forward to your Twitter followers.

tweet: A twitter post.

tweeple, tweeps: People who use Twitter.

tweetup: A face-to-face social gathering of local tweeple.

twibe: The people who are following you.

Twitterati: Twitter celebrities or people who have a huge amount of followers.

Using the hashtag

If you want to draw attention to specific words in a post, or ensure that the post is noticed by a specific group, use the hashtag symbol (#). When people search for specific information on Twitter and want to make sure the word they're searching for is the main subject of the post and not just randomly added, they place the hashtag symbol before the word.

As an astute author of Twitter posts, you can draw attention to a specific topic. For example, if you're a photographer and you want to draw attention to your work with a wedding planner, send a tweet using `#wedding planner`. People who search for that topic will see your tweet. Come to think of it, you should send multiple tweets with the hashtag followed by the topic. Just make sure that the tweets aren't all the same. Mix it up, which is one key to success on Twitter.

Before you decide to send tweets with a hashtag, perform a search using the hashtag and your topic. This task shows you current conversations about the topic. You know whether the tweeters are your competition or potential clients. Used properly, the hashtag is quite powerful.

Replying to a Twitter user

When you see a message that's interesting, you may want to reply to the sender. When you reply to the sender, other people who are following him see it. If you send a compelling reply, his followers may end up following you. It pays to get involved in the conversation.

To reply to a message, follow these steps:

1. **Pause the cursor over a message to which you want to reply.**

   The options to reply or retweet the message appear, as shown in Figure 2-8.

2. **Click Reply.**

   A text field opens at the top of the Twitter page, shown in Figure 2-9.

3. **Enter your reply.**

   Be sure to leave the @ symbol and the username in the message. If you remove them, the message is seen by your followers and never reaches its intended user.

4. **Click Reply.**

   The reply is sent to the end user. Users can see the reply and any other messages sent to him by clicking the @ symbol and his username from his Twitter page.

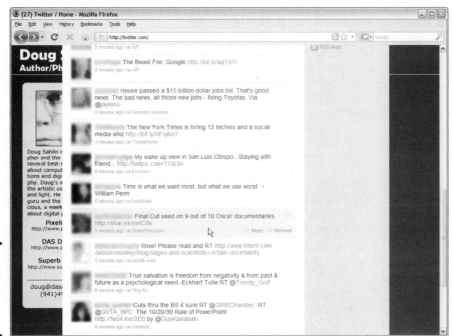

Figure 2-8:
Get involved in the conver-sation.

Figure 2-9:
Tell him what you think.

Retweeting a message

When you first set up your Twitter account, you may have no earthly idea of what you want to say. However, you can get the ball rolling by retweeting messages from other Twitter users that you're following, or from messages you found in a Twitter search. A retweet is similar to forwarding an e-mail. You may even pick up followers when people see the brilliant tweets you retweet.

As you gain more experience with Twitter, mix plenty of original information in your tweets in addition to retweet tweets.

To retweet a message you think is profound, stimulating, or interesting, follow these steps:

1. Pause the cursor over a message to which you want to reply.

The options to reply or retweet the message appear (refer to Figure 2-5).

2. Click Retweet.

A dialog box appears underneath the tweet, asking whether you want to retweet to your followers, as shown in Figure 2-10.

Figure 2-10:
Sending
a retweet
to your
followers.

3. **Click Yes.**

   The message is retweeted to your followers. Note that if the message contains close to 140 characters, the original author's username and your username may push the message over the character limit.

If the message is short enough, you can add your own words of wisdom to the retweet. You can also modify the original tweet and cut what you think is superfluous text, or you can condense the original tweet as outlined in the "Catching on to Twitter lingo" section, earlier in this chapter.

Sending direct messages

Everything you do on Twitter is public. It's seen by search engines, and every Twitter user who follows you or uses Twitter Search to look for tweets containing a word that appears in your message.

Don't send messages that contain confidential or personal information, because everything on Twitter is public.

However, sometimes you need to carry on a conversation with a Twitter user and keep it private from the rest of the world. When you need to do this, you send a *direct message* to the intended recipient.

To send a direct message, follow these steps:

1. **From your Twitter home page, click Direct Messages.**

   The page refreshes and the number of direct messages you've received and sent are displayed, as shown in Figure 2-11.

2. **Choose a user from the Send a Direct Message drop-down menu.**

   All the people who are following you and whom you are following appear on the list.

3. **Enter a message in the text field and click Send.**

   The message is sent to the recipient you selected in Step 2.

To see your direct messages, click the Direct Message link on your Twitter page. If you use TweetDeck, you can display direct messages in a separate column.

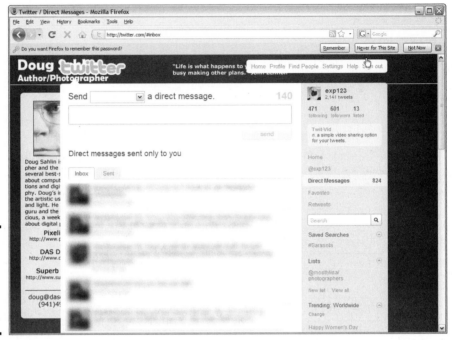

Figure 2-11:
What's written between us stays between us.

Blocking people

Twitter is all about getting your message to the right people. You do your best to follow the right people and attract the right followers. Your goal is to find a friendly twibe of Twitter folks who hang on your every syllable and eventually become clients. But sometimes in spite of your best efforts, a few bad eggs end up in the basket.

Sometimes the bad eggs latch on to you after you get a good start. They see that you're gaining headway and want to grab your coattails and tag along for the ride. Admittedly, it's flattering when you receive an e-mail from Twitter saying that you have a new follower. But before you follow her, you need to be a bit of a detective and make sure that the person's on the up-and-up. Your first clue is the message that Twitter sends you. If the person has sent only a few tweets, has only a few followers, and is following everybody, his little brother, and their next of kin, something's decidedly smelling foul in Denmark. That type of person may be trying to sell something that neither you nor any of the other thousand or more people he's following particularly want to buy.

If the e-mail from Twitter raises your suspicions, click the link to view the person's profile. Look at the tweets he has sent. Do the tweets look like pure, unadulterated spam? If so, you have the option to block the user and report him as being a spammer from the user's Twitter page. Nobody likes a spammer in the works.

Log into your Twitter account, find that person's Twitter page, and click the little icon that looks like a gear to the right of their avatar, and then click Block User.

Wait a couple of days to see what the person is up to. Waiting often tells you whether the person is legitimate or a flash in the pan. Often, you find that a person's profile has been blocked after a couple of days because that person was spamming people.

Another problem you may have with followers is that they abuse the relationship. They may pick your brain and offer nothing in return. You can unfollow the person. Log into your Twitter account, clicking the gear to the right of the person's avatar, and then click Unfollow.

Starting Your Twitter Campaign

Twitter isn't your full-time job, and it shouldn't become one. Like everything else in a normal life (except for a writer's life on a deadline), you must create a balance. Create a balance between the amount of time you spend marketing your business on Twitter with your other activities, such as selling and stopping for the occasional cup of designer decaf — which costs almost as much as a cab ride in some cities — at your favorite coffee emporium.

Make sure to schedule Twitter time into your Social Media Marketing plan (see Book I, Chapter 2).

Make no mistake about it: You have to dedicate some time to Twitter if you're going to reap benefits. Here are some suggestions for getting your Twitter campaign rolling:

✦ **Spend some time researching new and interesting things about your industry or the products you sell.** You can find this information on the Internet or from the marketing material you receive from your vendors. Keep a folder on your desktop as a tickler file of interesting material you can use for future tweets.

✦ **Find out what time your followers are active.** Schedule this time for sending tweets.

✦ **Identify some followers who retweet your messages.** If you don't have many, search as outlined previously and find people who follow the type of content you post in your tweets and follow them. Many people will follow you in return, and your retweet machine will be primed. When you have a loyal band of retweeters, you're ready to take it to the next level.

After you know what time your followers are active and you have a tickler file, you're ready to start spreading your words of wisdom.

Becoming a Resource for Your Twibe

Your goal when marketing yourself or your company on Twitter is to establish yourself as a friendly resource for the type of product or service you represent. Notice that we didn't say your product or your service. If you're a Realtor and you send useful information about searching for new homes and information about finding the best mortgage, for example, Twitter followers will recognize you as a valuable resource on real estate. Your local tweeple will take notice. If you do your job right, they'll come to you when they need a new home or they'll recommend you to a friend who's buying or selling a home or to a distant relative who's thinking of moving into the area.

How do you become a resource for your twibe? Follow these guidelines:

+ **Become a sponge.** Assimilate as much information as you can about your product or service. After you find the information, share it with your followers. They appreciate it.

+ **Initiate two-way conversations.** Put some information out there and invite people to respond to you. Or, simply ask a question. If legislation has been issued that adversely affects your industry or users of your product or service, ask fellow Twitter users what they think about it. Engaging in lively banter about topics that people are interested in and offering solutions is an excellent way to establish yourself as an expert.

+ **Mix it up.** Don't make every tweet about the business. Give followers an idea what happens behind the scenes. If you're a photographer, tell people what's involved in setting up a portrait shoot or in coordinating a makeup artist with a photo shoot.

Don't give away any trade secrets; your competitors may be following you.

+ **Be open and friendly.** After you have a few dozen tweets under your belt, your followers will know that you're an expert. At that point, tell people you're available for questions, and be sure not to limit question topics to your business. Call yourself a guru if the shoe fits; just make sure that your followers know you're open to questions and not afraid to share your expertise. Eventually, one of your solutions will be in the form of a product or a part of your service.

+ **If you hold online events, such as webinars, make sure to extend several invites to your Twitter followers.** When you tell them about the event, give a clear description of what is happening. Tell them exactly what will be discussed, and include a link to the Web page from which they can sign up for your event.

+ **Be consistent.** Send informative tweets regularly.

+ **Your Twitter followers will depend on you.** If you cannot tweet for a while, find someone else to fill your shoes and let your followers know that you have a stand-in. Lots of people are on Twitter and vying for new followers. Missing a couple of days gives your followers a reason to forget about you and bail ship.

✦ **Tweet when you're on the road.** If you're going to be out of town for a couple of days on business, use your laptop to tweet from your hotel room. You can also tweet from your mobile phone. You can use lots of apps to tweet from your mobile device, which we discuss in Book IV, Chapter 3. When you tweet from a remote location, tell your followers. They appreciate your level of commitment.

✦ **At the risk of being redundant, don't promote your business blatantly on Twitter.** Cater to the needs of potential clients and you'll make friends and be recognized as a valuable resource. You cater to the needs of your clients every day. Your Twitter followers have the same needs, which makes it easy for you to fulfill them.

✦ **Follow Twitter users in industries or professions closely related to yours.** If you don't have the answer, you can ask your Twitter colleague for it or recommend her to your follower. Take a look at their followers as well. They may be potential clients for you. People in industries related to yours can also be helpful referral sources.

Following Twitter Rules of Etiquette (Twittiquette)

Twitter is like any other form of social interaction: You can do it the right way or the wrong way. People who conform to the rules — Twitter etiquette, if you will — are accepted by the community. The community doesn't accept people who break the rules. That doesn't mean you can't add your own creativity and humor to your tweets, however — it just means that you should stay within certain guidelines to be accepted by the majority of the community.

Here are some guidelines to consider:

✦ **You don't have to follow everyone who follows you.** You may think it's rude not to return the love, but as a businessperson, you have only so many hours in the day. Follow the people who interest you and who you think will benefit your business.

✦ **Don't be offended if someone doesn't return your follow or decides to unfollow you.** If the relationship isn't reciprocal, it isn't worth it.

✦ **Don't be misleading.** Make perfectly clear that you represent a business and are there to market your company — but also make sure that followers know you will provide useful information about your product and services, not an endless stream of invites to go to your Web site or visit your online store.

✦ **Don't be a robot.** Mix it up and show your personal side. People tend to shy away from Twitter users who don't show a sense of humor.

✦ **Keep the personal stuff private.** Create a direct message when you only need to speak with one person. Twitter is crowded. Adding tweets that have no meaning to your followers clogs up their timelines.

✦ **Keep the boring tweets to yourself.** If you need to tell someone what you had for lunch, create a personal Twitter account or send the interested party a direct message. After all, only your mother and maybe your significant other care what you had for lunch.

✦ **Use the @username rather than a direct message to reply to a conversation thread.** This strategy injects your opinion into the thread.

✦ **Don't be argumentative.** Feel free to voice an opinion in response to a general conversation, but keep it polite and low key.

✦ **Don't use direct messages to ask the opinions of followers you don't know well.** Post a general message to all of your followers and ask their opinion.

✦ **Don't use all caps when you send tweets.** This style is considered shouting and is in poor taste.

✦ **Respond to important messages.** Replying to every direct message or mention can be difficult. However, responding to important messages keeps your twibe of followers intact.

✦ **When you create a tweet that you want to be retweeted, keep it to no more than 120 characters.** Followers then have a chance to retweet your message and add a comment without truncating the tweet.

✦ **If you set up a customer service Twitter account for your business, follow everyone who follows you.** If you don't follow someone who follows you, this could be taken as a sign that you're not interested in doing business with them.

✦ **Don't use foul language.** It's the equivalent of cursing loudly in a public place.

✦ **Make sure that your links work before you include them in a tweet.** We recommend cutting and pasting the URL (including any short URLs) into your browser to ensure that the right Web page appears.

✦ **Don't send tweets when you're under the influence.** One tweet while you're tipsy may be amusing, but it's not a good idea.

✦ **Make sure that your complete words are spelled correctly and use proper punctuation.** Using abbreviations and contractions is okay, but your goal is to leave a good impression with your followers.

Giving and Getting Recommendations on Follow Friday

Follow Friday is a time-honored Twitter tradition. Every Friday, Twitter users send a tweet with the hashtag `followfriday`. The tweet lists the names of the Twitter followers the sender is recommending to his followers. When a Follow Friday message is sent that recommends you, it's considered good form to add the sender to your Follow Friday list. This is a great way to get more followers and interact with the community.

If you have valuable resources on Twitter or faithful followers who you know can be knowledgeable resources for your Twitter followers, you get a chance to sing their praises once a week using a time-honored tradition known as Follow Friday. On any Friday, simply use the at-symbol (@) followed by the username you want to recognize. Separate with a space each follower you want to recommend. End the message with the hashtag symbol (#) and `followfriday`.

Here's a sample of a Follow Friday tweet:

`@curlyHoward @moeHoward @larryFine #followfriday`

Advertising on Twitter

If you decide that your writing isn't persuasive enough and you need some help to toot your horn, consider advertising on Twitter. Advertising takes the form of sponsored tweets or ads. If you decide to invest in advertising on Twitter, mix in some real tweets with the sponsored stuff. If you rely solely on ads, your followers will see it as spam and unfollow you. Here's a list of advertising sources for you to investigate:

- ✦ **adCause:** `http://adcause.com`
- ✦ **Magpie:** `http://be-a-magpie.com/en`
- ✦ **SocialSpark:** `http://socialspark.com`
- ✦ **Sponsored Tweets:** `http://sponsoredtweets.com`

Chapter 3: Twitter Applications and Other Delights

In This Chapter

✔ Tweaking your Twitter pages

✔ Tweeting from the desktop

✔ Tweeting from a mobile device

✔ Finding Twitter plug-ins and other cool add-ons

✔ Analyzing your Twitter campaign

✔ Experimenting with Twitter applications

You have a Twitter account, you've set up a Twitter strategy, and you're starting to attract a loyal band of followers. If you've been using the Twitter Web site for tweeting, you know that the page doesn't update in real time. When you navigate to the page, you see tweets from your followers up to the current moment. You have to refresh the page to see any newer tweets. Would you like to tweet from your desktop with an application that updates in real time? Or send tweets when you're on the road or at a convention? You can, thanks to some ingenious software designers.

In this chapter, we tell you about third-party Twitter applications that can do what we just described and more. We also show you how to tweak your Twitter page — say that three times, fast!

Customizing Your Twitter Page

When you set up your Twitter page, you have several options to create a unique-looking page. But the options are the same ones that everyone has at his disposal. You can take your Twitter page to the next level and create something cool, something unique that fits your personality or looks similar to your company's printed material or your Web site.

If everything associated with your company has a similar look and feel, you give a sense of continuity to clients. After all, you wouldn't want your Twitter followers to go to your Web site and think they've landed on the wrong page, would you?

In the following sections, we show you how to customize your Twitter page and your Twitter avatar.

Creating a custom Twitter background

The standard Twitter themes are quite good, but you want something unique — something that no other Twitter user has. When that's your goal, the only option is to make it yourself or hire a designer to create a custom background.

You might think that creating a background for a Twitter page is easy. However, not everybody uses browsers of the same size to surf the Net. They range from the ridiculously small desktop measuring 800 x 600 pixels to the insanely humongous desktop size of 2560 x 1440, found on 27-inch iMacs. The best thing you can do is compromise and create a background that works on a 1024 x 768 desktop.

If you don't have an image editing application that gives you the option of working with layers, check out the later sidebar "Finding a premade Twitter background."

Creating a custom background is a wonderful thing. You don't have any limit on the amount of text you can put in. In fact, if you want to, you can create a document that is very tall and put lots of text in it. However, the user will have to scroll to see all of the text.

Your Twitter background should be 1600 pixels x 1200 pixels with a resolution of 72 pixels per inch, have a file size smaller than 800KB, and in one of the following formats: JPEG, GIF, or PNG. PNG seems to be the best if you have a combination of text and images for your background.

After you create the custom background, your next step is to get it into your Twitter page. To replace the standard background with your custom background:

1. **Log in to your Twitter account.**

2. **Click Settings.**

   The Settings page appears.

3. **Click Design.**

   The Select a Theme page appears (see Figure 3-1).

4. **Click Change Background Image.**

   The Browse button appears.

5. **Click the Browse button.**

   The File Upload dialog appears.

6. **Navigate to your background image and then click Open.**

   After the image uploads, it appears in the thumbnail window.

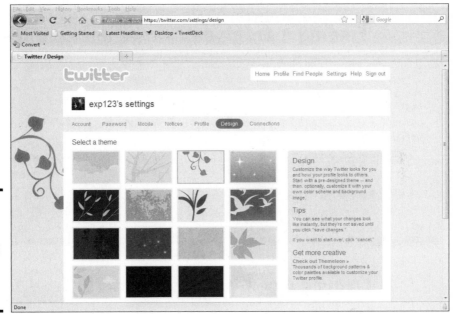

Figure 3-1:
Adding a
custom
background
to your
Twitter
page.

7. Click Save Changes.

Your cool new background appears on your Twitter page. Figure 3-2 shows a custom background. The document was optimized for a desktop that is 1280 pixels wide.

Figure 3-2:
A custom
background
displayed
on a Twitter
page.

Finding a premade Twitter background

Hmmm. You say that you have no image-editing application, and even if you did, you say that you aren't artistic. You can still include the essence of cool on your Twitter page. Check out just a few sources for custom Twitter backgrounds:

✔ **COLOURlovers:** `www.colourlovers.com/themeleon/twitter`

✔ **Limeshot Design:** `http://limeshot.com/2008/twitter-backgrounds`

✔ **TwitrBackgrounds.com:** `www.twitrbackgrounds.com`

✔ **TwitBacks:** `www.twitbacks.com`

✔ **twitrounds:** `http://twitrounds.com`

Search for the term *free Twitter backgrounds* at your favorite search engine to find a wide variety of resources. If you decide to kick it up a notch, consider having a custom background designed for your Twitter page.

Creating a custom Twitter avatar

You can upload any old photo to Twitter and use it for your page. However, you should use the best possible shot of your smiling face. Does that mean you grab your trusty point-and-shoot camera and hold it in front of you? No, not unless you like red-eye, the disease that made on-camera flash infamous.

Spend a bit of money to have a professional shoot your portrait. You can use it for not only Twitter but also your other marketing efforts.

To be used as an avatar, your photo must have

✦ A JPEG or PNG format

✦ A measurement of no more than 200 x 200 pixels

✦ A file size no larger than 700K

After the image is on your computer, follow these steps to replace the standard Twitter avatar:

1. **Log on to Twitter.**

Your lovely Twitter page appears.

2. **Click Settings and then click Profile.**

The Web page changes and displays your profile settings.

3. **Next to the current avatar, click Change Image.**

The Browse button appears.

4. **Click Browse, navigate to the image file, and follow the prompts to replace the image.**

5. **Click Save.**

   Your new avatar is on your Twitter page.

If you need a little photography assistance, check out *Digital Portrait Photography For Dummies*, by Doug Sahlin.

Tweeting from Your Desktop

The Twitter Web site is a wonderful thing. It's attractive in a Spartan kind of way and gets the job done. The site connects you to Twitter and enables you to connect with your twibe. The only problem diehard Tweeters have is that tweets don't update in real time. If you're communicating or following the tweets of your followers, you have to refresh the page to see the latest tweets. And, if it has been a while since you refreshed the page, several hundred tweets may slip offscreen when you refresh.

You have a solution for this dilemma. The powerful desktop application TweetDeck, at `www.tweetdeck.com`, updates in real time, as shown in Figure 3-3. When someone sends a tweet, it appears in TweetDeck almost instantaneously along with an alert.

Figure 3-3: Keep track of your followers with TweetDeck.

Using TweetDeck, you can

✦ **Create groups.** Monitor the tweets of your most important followers.

✦ **Create columns.** Display *mentions* (tweets containing @yourusername), direct messages, and searches.

✦ **Click a person's username.** See a person's profile. This information is the same as you find in the person's bio on her Twitter page. The links in a bio viewed in TweetDeck are fully functional, and you can also see the person's Twitter page by clicking the applicable link. In addition, you see all recent tweets in a profile viewed in TweetDeck.

✦ **Upload photos directly from TweetDeck.** After you upload a photo, you see a URL to the image in the message box, as shown in Figure 3-4. Flesh it out with information about the photo and send the tweet. Sweet.

✦ **Monitor multiple searches.** If you have more columns than you have desktop, a handy scrollbar appears at the bottom of the application.

Figure 3-4:
The multifaceted TweetDeck application.

You can use many more applications to streamline your Twitter use. The rest of the chapter is devoted to applications that enable you to send tweets from mobile devices and much more.

Tweeting from Your Phone or iPod touch

If you use the iPhone to communicate while you're on the road, you can download a version of TweetDeck that enables you to tweet on the go from `www.tweetdeck.com/iphone` or the Apple App Store. The application also works on the iPod touch, which has access to a wireless network.

Of course, the iPhone isn't the only game in town. If you use a BlackBerry, you can send tweets using the ÜberTwitter application, at `www.uber twitter.com` or BlackBerry App World. If you purchase a subscription to the application for $4.99 per year, you're entitled to unlimited upgrades and no advertisements. The alternative is to download the free version, which has advertisements.

Twitter Browser Plug-Ins, Extensions, and Interesting Web Sites

Twitter has become one of the most popular social media sites. In addition to its Web site and its desktop and mobile phone applications, it has lots of browser plug-ins to enhance your Twitter experience or tweeting skills.

The following list describes a few Twitter browser plug-ins:

✦ **Birdpie:** Store as bookmarks the URLs you tweet. This capability can come in handy as a reference. (`www.birdpie.com`)

✦ **Blip.fm:** Sync this music-sharing Web site with a Twitter account. If you need to be an Internet deejay and entertain your followers, this is the place to go. (`http://blip.fm`)

✦ **FileSocial:** At this file-sharing Web site, you can share with your Twitter followers' photos, videos, PDF files, PowerPoint presentations, and more. (`http://filesocial.com`)

✦ **FileTWT:** Share files with your Twitter twibe. (`www.filetwt.com`)

✦ **FlashTweet:** Build your twibe by acquiring targeted followers. You can try the service free for 14 days. Then you pay $6.95 per month until you cancel the service. (`http://flashtweet.com`)

✦ **Friend or Follow:** See which Twitter users you're following aren't following you and vice versa. You can also use the application to create a list of your friends — people you're following who are following you back, which is an excellent way to streamline your twibe. (`www.friendorfollow.com`)

✦ **GeoChirp:** Search for specific conversations within a given radius of the area in which you live, as shown in Figure 3-5. Enter a topic in the Search text box and the site returns a list of tweets about the subject. (www.geochirp.com)

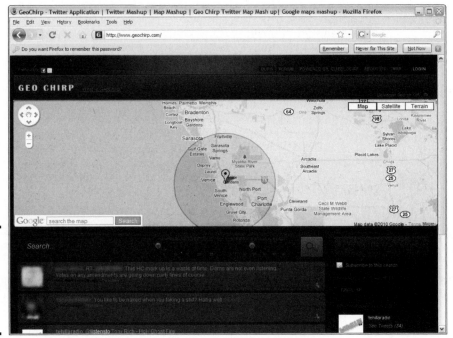

Figure 3-5:
Follow conversations near where you live.

✦ **twable:** Quickly find out who you're following that is or isn't following you and who's following you that you're not following. (http://twable.net)

✦ **Twitbin:** Manage Twitter using a browser side panel. You can use the application to send and receive tweets, send links, and more. This Mozilla Firefox plug-in works on Firefox 2.0 and newer for Mac and Windows users. (www.twitbin.com)

That's just the tip of the virtual iceberg for Twitter plug-ins and Web sites. We cover a few more in the next section, or use your favorite search engine to search for more information.

Exploring Other Twitter Applications

You've analyzed your Twitter account 27 ways to Sunday and you've experimented with all the cool stuff related to Twitter. You might think that what we've already covered would be enough for one chapter. But, wait — there's more. This list describes some other useful Twitter applications you'll find on the World Wide Web:

✦ **digsby:** Receive e-mail alerts, perform instant messaging, and manage your social media accounts. This desktop application is available as a free download for the Mac, PC, and Linux. (www.digsby.com)

✦ **hellotxt:** You can use this Web-based app to manage your social media. Sign up for a free account to read, update, and organize your presence on multiple social media networks. (http://hellotxt.com)

✦ **Tweepler:** Make managing your Twitter followers a breeze by using this free service. (The developers include a PayPal button, in case you care to make a donation to show your support.) After you enter your Twitter username and password — which aren't recorded — a list of your followers appears. You can then post followers into these three buckets:

  • *Ignore:* Followers you don't want to follow back

  • *Unprocessed:* Followers you aren't following

  • *Follow:* Followers you're following

  Your goal is to review names in the Unprocessed bin and add them to either the Follow bin (and then you're automatically following them) or the Ignore bin. (www.tweepler.com)

✦ **twhirl:** Tweet without being on the Twitter Web site. You can also use this desktop application to simultaneously post Twitter updates to Facebook and LinkedIn. If you like to experiment with different desktop apps, <ahem> give twhirl a whirl. (www.twhirl.org)

✦ **Twitdom:** Check out this database from time to time to see what's new and exciting. It has every conceivable app for desktop and mobile devices. (www.twitdom.com)

✦ **TwitPic:** Upload your images to this picture-sharing service and then add the URL to a tweet to share them with your Twitter followers. You can also upload images to the site from TweetDeck. (http://twitpic.com)

✦ **Twitterfeed:** Feed your blog posts to Twitter and Facebook. (http://twitterfeed.com)

✦ **twittervision:** When you've tweeted so much that your fingers are about to fall off and you're convinced you have carpal tunnel syndrome, check out this Mercator projection map of the world. A flag pops up from a random area of the world where someone just sent a tweet. Read the message quickly because another one pops up quickly, as shown in Figure 3-6. (www.twittervision.com)

✦ **Twitt(url)y:** Track the URLs mentioned most often in tweets. (http://twitturly.com)

✦ **twtpoll:** Find information by creating polls for your Twitter followers. You can create a Twitter-only poll for no charge. You can also create Web polls for a fee, add branding to polls, and sponsor polls. (`http://twtpoll.com`)

Figure 3-6:
When you need a break from tweeting, visit twitter-vision.

As Twitter and other forms of social media are invented, you'll see more applications popping up. Always search for new ones that are on the horizon.

Marketing on Twitter via Peashoot

You can use the Web Twitter application Peashoot, at `www.peashootapp.com`, for marketing on Twitter.

Peashoot (see Figure 3-7) offers different plans and features a 21-day free trial to see whether the application is right for you.

At Peashoot, you can

✦ **Use the audience builder to find followers.** The Peashoot audience
builder automatically finds Twitter users who are relevant to you, your
service, or your company. Having more followers helps you spread the
word about your company.

✦ **Track your Twitter return on investment (ROI).** Peashoot claims to
track exactly how much of your Web site sales can be tracked to links
you've posted on Twitter. You can then track which of your Twitter campaigns is the most successful.

✦ **Set goals and track your progress.** You can create Twitter campaigns
with specific goals. Peashoot notifies you by e-mail when you reach
them.

✦ **Track campaign activity.** Active Listening technology enables you to
track Twitter activity directly related to your campaign.

✦ **Use real-time tracking.** When you create an account with Peashoot, you
can see clicks and conversations regarding your campaign in real time.

Peashoot is totally browser based — no installation needed. You can customize your goals, create progress reports, export data to comma-separated
value (CSV) format for use in spreadsheets, and integrate data with Google
Analytics.

Chapter 4: Using Twitter with Other Social Media Marketing

*I*f you're on Twitter for more than just fun and entertainment, you have other social media. You most likely also have a Web site, a blog, and a presence on Facebook. You can use your social media outlets to feed off each other. You can use Twitter to draw attention to your Facebook fan page, your blog, and your Web site.

In this chapter, we show you how to accomplish these tasks and seamlessly dovetail Twitter into your other forms of social media.

Combining Your Blog with Twitter

You have a blog and you tweet. Ain't that tweet? (Sorry — we couldn't resist.) When you have a combination of the two, you can use your Twitter messages to feed your blog, as we show you in the next section, and you can also augment your WordPress blog with your tweets by using WordPress plug-ins.

The plug-ins we cover are up-to-date and work with the latest version of WordPress (3.0 as of this writing). A newer version of WordPress will most likely be available by the time you read this book. Make sure that any plug-in you use is still compatible with the current version of WordPress. Follow the developer's instructions to install and use the plug-in.

Here are some Twitter WordPress plug-ins you may find useful:

✦ **Elitwee MyTwitter:** Displays your recent Twitter posts in the sidebar and has its own section in the Settings area of the dashboard. After configuring the plug-in, you add it from the Widget section of the dashboard. Find it at `http://calvinf.com/projects/elitwee/mytwitter`.

✦ **Tweet This:** Adds to every post a Twitter icon that lets blog visitors retweet the post URL. You can find more information and download the plug-in at `http://richardxthripp.thripp.com/tweet-this`.

✦ **Wickett:** Displays your latest Twitter post in the sidebar of your blog. You can download the plug-in and find additional information at `http://wordpress.org/extend/plugins/wickett-twitter-widget`.

You should also have an easy way for people to connect with your Twitter account and other social media outlets. You can set up text links in your blogroll, for example, and, if you're adept at using HTML code, add a Twitter icon that's a hyperlink to your Twitter page.

Using Twitter to Draw Traffic to Your Blog

If you maintain a blog, you work hard to write useful information in a timely manner. You also tweet regularly. It's perfectly okay to combine the two, as long as your Twitter posts are informative and not thinly disguised advertisements for your business. Of course, your blog posts also need to be timely and informative with the goal of establishing yourself as an expert in your field. If you do your work well on Twitter and write good blog posts, the rest will follow.

Here are a few different ways to use Twitter in conjunction with your blog or podcast:

✦ **Announce a new blog post or podcast episode.** Tell your followers what the blog post or podcast episode is about.

Time your tweets when your followers are active. Sending the information about your new blog post a couple of times is also a good idea, as long as you don't broadcast it every hour on the hour. Your followers will quickly lose faith and perhaps unfollow you.

✦ **Solicit suggestions for your blog or podcast**. If you have loyal followers who also visit your blog site, send select followers (the ones who know you well) a direct message asking what they want to see in your next blog post.

✦ **Create a Twitter poll at `www.twtpoll.com` to find information.** You can also set up a column in TweetDeck to monitor a specific topic. In no time, you have fodder for quite a few blog posts, as shown in Figure 4-1.

Figure 4-1:
Using a
Twitter poll
to solicit
suggestions
for your next
blog post.

Using Twitter to Draw Traffic to Your Web Site

If you have no blog but maintain a Web site, you can use Twitter to draw traffic to the site. And we don't mean that you can send a tweet saying, "Check out my Web site at www.mywebsite.com."

When you post new information about your services or products on your site, you send a tweet whenever you

+ **Update your FAQ page or tips page.**

+ **Run a promotion or sale.**

Sweeten your offer for Twitter followers. Offer to all your followers or to the next ten followers who send you a direct message, for example, a discount code through Twitter. Word will get out and you'll end up with more followers, and perhaps more business.

+ **Answer questions from a follower with information from your Web site.**

If you have the answer to the follower's question in a Web page or a blog post, tell the follower that the answer can be found at a specific blog post or Web page.

**Book IV
Chapter 4**

Using Twitter with
Other Social Media
Marketing

When you send tweets about your Web site, follow these suggestions:

✦ **Make sure your initial tweet contains fewer than 120 characters.** This length gives loyal followers room to retweet your tweet with their own message to their followers. When lots of your tweets about a blog post or Web site page are retweeted, you end up with more traffic on your Web site. The more, the merrier.

✦ **Make sure your link works.** Use TinyURL (`www.tinyurl.com`) or bit. ly (`www.bit.ly`) to shrink the URL into something that fits easily into a Twitter message. If you use TweetDeck (see Book IV, Chapter 3) to send tweets, your URL is automatically shortened. Always go the extra mile, though, and copy and paste the shortened URL into a browser to ensure that it's functional and leads followers to the right page. If you use bit.ly to shorten your URL, you can track the number of click-throughs.

✦ **Tweet when your followers are online.** If you tweet about your Web site several times a day, make sure that each tweet has new and relevant information. If you don't, your followers quickly become bored and unfollow you.

Your Web site is viewed by people who may not be on Twitter. Or, perhaps they are on Twitter and aren't aware that *you're* on it. You can easily remedy this problem by including icons to all your social media outlets with direct links to your social media pages, as shown in Figure 4-2. If you aren't a Web guru or you aren't conversant with HTML, tell your Web designer what you want to do.

Figure 4-2:
Add social media icons to your Web site.

Getting Goodies from Twitter

In Book IV, Chapter 3, we mentioned cool stuff you can do with third-party applications and Web sites. But wait — there's more! Twitter has a bunch of cool goodies that you can use in conjunction with your other social media that come in two flavors: button and widget.

The buttons are something you tackle if you're conversant with Web design. Widgets give you the capability of displaying your Twitter updates on your Web site and are fairly easy to integrate on your Web site.

Adding widgets to your Web site

When you want to display your tweets on your Web site, you use a widget.

To add a Twitter widget to your Web site, follow these steps:

1. **Log in to Twitter.**

2. **Click Settings.**

The Settings page appears.

3. **Click the Connections link on the right side of the page**

The Goodies page appears, as shown in Figure 4-3.

Figure 4-3:
Get your
red-hot
goodies.

**Book IV
Chapter 4**

Using Twitter with
Other Social Media
Marketing

4. **Click the Widgets link.**

   The Select Your Widget page appears.

5. **Click the My Website link.**

   The page refreshes to show you the options available for your Web site, as shown in Figure 4-4.

Figure 4-4:
A widget
for my Web
site.

Here are your options:

- *Profile:* Lets you display your most recent tweets on your Web site
- *Search:* Lets you keep Web site visitors informed about current events by displaying Twitter search results for five events or conferences
- *Faves:* Lets you show off your favorite tweets
- *List:* Lets you put a list of your favorite tweets on your Web site

Everything except the Profile widget directs your Web site visitors to someone else's tweets, so we let you explore them at your leisure. The following steps show you how to add a Profile widget.

If you aren't familiar with cutting and pasting HTML code into a Web page, consult your favorite Web designer for help.

6. **Click Profile Widget.**

The Settings section for the Profile widget appears. If you're logged in, your username should appear.

7. **Click Preferences.**

The Preferences section for the Profile widget appears, as shown in Figure 4-5.

Figure 4-5:
Setting preferences for the Profile widget.

8. **Set these preferences:**

- *Poll for new results:* Your widget can poll for new tweets. We recommend not using this option unless you tweet 24/7.

- *Include scrollbar:* Include a scrollbar with the widget if you're displaying lots of tweets. A scrollbar on the side of the widget lets users scroll and view all displayed tweets.

- *Behavior:* Load all tweets and then choose the number to display or choose a timed *interval* — the number of tweets that occur before the display refreshes. If you choose the latter, you have the option to loop tweets and choose the interval between displayed tweets.

- *Number of tweets:* Choose the number of tweets to display from the drop-down list. This option isn't available if you choose a timed interval.

- *Display Avatars:* Choose whether to display an avatar next to each tweet.

- *Show Timestamps:* The timestamp shows when the tweet was created (the default setting). Disable this option if you tweet infrequently.

- *Show Hashtags:* Display hashtags that are in a tweet. Disable this default option if you don't want to display hashtags.

9. **Click Appearance.**

The appearance options for your Profile widget appear, as shown in Figure 4-6.

Figure 4-6:
Choose colors for your Profile widget.

10. **Choose color options.**

You can enter the hexadecimal code for the color, if you know it. If you don't know hexadecimal code, ask your Web designer to do it, or click the color swatch and mix your own color.

11. **Click Dimensions.**

The dimensions options for the widget appear, as shown in Figure 4-7.

Figure 4-7:
Setting
widget
dimensions.

12. **Accept the default measurements or enter your own.**

This task may be another one for your Web designer to handle. If you try to stick a big widget into a small space, you blow out your Web design (and your Web designer won't be happy).

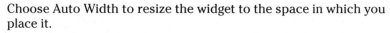

Choose Auto Width to resize the widget to the space in which you place it.

13. **Click Test Settings.**

The widget refreshes to show you what it will look like with the current settings applied. If you don't like what you see, click the applicable option to change the settings.

14. **Click Finish & Grab Code.**

The code to enable the widget in your Web site appears in a window, shown in Figure 4-8. Alternatively, you can click the Add to Blogger button if you have a blog hosted by Blogger.

15. **Copy and paste the code into a section of your Web page.**

You have a widget, as shown in Figure 4-9.

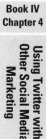

**Book IV
Chapter 4**

**Using Twitter with
Other Social Media
Marketing**

Figure 4-8:
Grab the
code, dude.

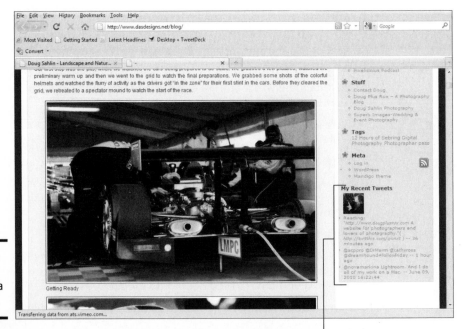

Figure 4-9:
Displaying
tweets on a
Web page.

Display your tweets on your Web site.

Linking Twitter to your Facebook page

If you have fans on Facebook who aren't Twitter users, you can post your updates on your Facebook wall for your fans to see. After you do this, every public message you send on Twitter shows up on your Facebook wall.

You can add your tweets to your Facebook wall by following these steps:

1. **Log in to Twitter.**

2. **Click Settings.**

   The Settings page appears.

3. **Click Goodies at the bottom of the page.**

   The Twitter goodies appear.

4. **Click Facebook.**

   The Facebook options appear. As of this writing, the only option is Facebook Application.

5. **Click Facebook Application.**

   The Facebook application options appear, shown in Figure 4-10. As of this writing, only one option is available.

Figure 4-10:
Adding Twitter to your Facebook page.

**Book IV
Chapter 4**

Using Twitter with Other Social Media Marketing

6. **Click Install Twitter in Facebook.**

Your tweets now appear on your wall, as shown in Figure 4-11.

Figure 4-11:
Your Twitter
tweets
appear on
Facebook.

Chapter 5: Measuring Twitter Metrics

In This Chapter

✓ Checking Web site referrals

✓ Comparing tweets to retweets

✓ Comparing mentions

✓ Measuring Twitter follower Web site visits

*A*fter your Twitter marketing campaign has been rolling for a while, it's time to check out the return on your time investment. You can do this in many ways, by looking at the information on your Twitter page or by using TweetDeck or an analytics program such as Google Analytics.

Tracking Web Site Referrals

If you use Google Analytics, you can easily track the number of referrals from Twitter to your Web site or blog. This information is quite useful if one of your marketing goals is to drive more traffic to your Web site by way of Twitter.

You must have Google Analytics enabled on the Web site you're tracking. Google Analytics is a service that enables you to track the amount of traffic your Web site is getting, where the traffic is coming from, and referring sites, for example. See Book VIII, Chapter 1 to find out where to find Google Analytics.

To see how much traffic comes to your Web site from Twitter, follow these steps:

1. **Log in to Google Analytics.**

2. **Select from the View Reports drop-down menu the Web site you want to monitor.**

3. **Click Traffic Sources.**

   The page refreshes and shows a graph of visits to your Web site.

4. **Click All Traffic Sources.**

   The page refreshes and shows a list of sources that generated visits to your Web site.

5. **Enter** Twitter **in the Filter Source/Medium text box using the default Containing parameter.**

   The page refreshes and shows you the number of visits that resulted from Twitter.

Using Twitter Analytics Applications

You can find several good analytic applications on the Web that are devoted to Twitter analytics. Enter your username to find all sorts of information such as the subjects you tweeted about, the hashtags you used, the number of tweets per day, and the extent of your reach.

Here are a few analytic programs you can try:

✦ **Twitter Analyzer,** at www.twitteranalyzer.com, dissects your activity on Twitter and offers information about these categories, shown in Figure 5-1:

   • *Tweets:* The number of tweets sent over a given period

   • *Chats:* The number of conversations you're involved in

   • *Popularity:* The number of times you're mentioned by other Twitter users

   • *Reach:* The number of Twitter users your messages reached

   • *Subjects:* The topics you talked about plus the percentage of your conversations that were about those topics

   • *Hashtags:* The topics you specified by hashtag with a legend showing the percentage that each hashtag was used compared to all hashtags

   • *Links:* The recent links you tweeted, with a legend showing the percentage of each link compared to all links

   • *Apps:* The applications you used in conjunction with your Twitter activity

   • *Other information:* Additional tabs that let you monitor friends, the number of your mentions, and the people you've mentioned, for example

✦ **TweetStats,** at http://tweetstats.com, creates graphs showing what you've been up to on Twitter. See the number of tweets sent per day, tweet density during specific times of day, and people you retweet, for example, as shown in Figure 5-2.

✦ **TwInfluence,** at www.twinfluence.com, measures your influence on Twitter. Enter your username to find out where you rank on Twitter.

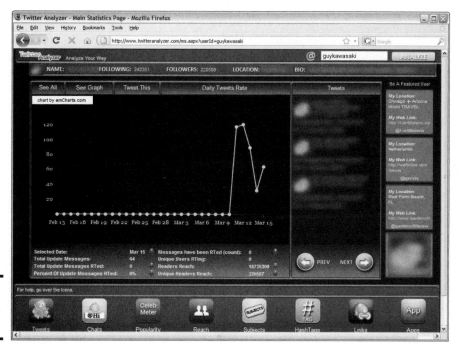

Figure 5-1:
Information,
please.

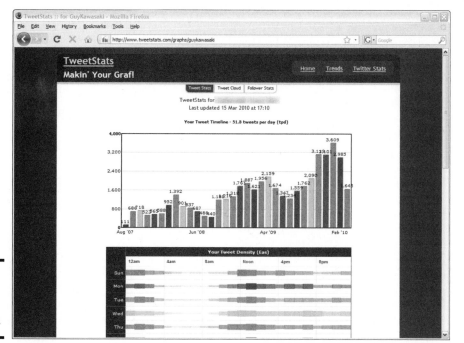

Figure 5-2:
Read all
about it at
TweetStats.

✦ **TwitterGrader.com,** at `http://twittergrader.com`, shows how you stack up against other Twitter users. After you navigate to the site, enter your Twitter username. In a few seconds — or longer, if you have lots of followers — you see your grade (100 is best), rank, and other information. You can also see your trend, which is a graph showing how you've progressed in adding followers to your ranks. You can also analyze your followers, to see a list by ranking, and analyze the people following you.

Monitoring Retweets

Another way to track your success on Twitter is to monitor the number of your messages that are retweeted compared to all the messages you've sent. No hard-and-fast rule applies to what constitutes a good ratio, but a high percentage of retweets means that you're sending the right stuff to your followers.

If you use TweetDeck, you can find out this same information through its interface.

You can easily calculate your retweets by following these steps:

1. **Visit `http://search.twitter.com`.**

   This is the all-singing, all-dancing Twitter search engine.

2. **Enter** RT@yourusername.

   The @ symbol signifies that the retweet was one of your tweets.

3. **Click Search.**

   A list of recent retweets appears on the first page. If you have lots of retweets, you see an Older link at the bottom of the first page, as shown in Figure 5-3.

4. **Analyze the retweets.**

   This step tells you two things: the topics that are hitting home with your followers and the people who are following you closely.

If you're adventurous, you can see where you rank regarding retweets in reference to all Twitter users. To see your retweet rank, follow these steps:

1. **Launch your favorite Web browser and navigate to `www.retweet rank.com`.**

   The page refreshes and you're in Retweetville.

2. **Enter your username in the Twitter Username box and click Go.**

   The page refreshes and you see your retweet rank at the top of the page, as shown in Figure 5-4. You also see a list of your recent tweets that have been retweeted by your faithful followers.

Figure 5-3:
Analyzing
your
retweets.

Figure 5-4:
Oh, my —
that's a
good rank.

3. **Analyze your recent retweets.**

This step tells you which messages are striking a chord with your followers and which followers are retweeting you most often.

Analyzing Your @replies Mentions

Whenever someone uses the @ symbol followed by your username, the message shows up on the main Twitter timeline, but directed at you. You can see which messages are getting noticed, and which Twitter followers are engaging you in conversation, by following these steps:

1. **Visit `http://search.twitter.com`.**

This is the all-singing, all-dancing Twitter search engine.

2. **Enter** @yourusername.

The @ symbol signifies that the message was directed to you or was about you.

3. **Click Search.**

A list of recent messages mentioning your username appears, as shown in Figure 5-5.

Figure 5-5:
They like me. They really like me.

4. **Analyze the messages.**

   See which users are responding to your messages and starting a conversation with you.

You also see the text *@yourusername* in Follow Friday mentions. Analyze them, too, to find who your most faithful followers are.

Checking Direct Messages

Hmmm. We know what you're thinking: Why would you want to analyze your direct messages? After all, you know to whom you send direct messages — but which of your followers sent direct messages to you, and what was their subject matter? The answer to this question tells you which followers are engaging you as a source of information and tells you the type of information they're requesting. If the same topic shows up in several direct messages, you can tweet about it and write blog posts about it.

You can analyze your direct messages by following these steps:

1. **Navigate to www.twitter.com and log on to your Twitter account.**

   Your lovely Twitter page appears, complete with your recent tweets.

2. **Click Direct Messages.**

   A list of all your direct messages appears.

3. **Analyze your messages to see who has been chatting with you and the subjects they've been chatting about.**

   Note which subjects prompted direct messages and expand on them in future tweets. Whenever you receive a direct message regarding one of your tweets, it's a good sign that the topic is worthy of further embellishment.

Using the Hashtag As a Measurement Mechanism

When people search for specific information on Twitter and want to make sure the word they're searching for is the main subject of the post and not just randomly added, they use the hashtag symbol. The use of hashtags in conjunction with your Twitter username is another way to measure your popularity on Twitter. If lots of people, including those who don't follow you, take the time to precede your username with a hashtag, you're being directly referenced in a Twitter post.

To find out whether your username is being hashtagged, follow these steps:

1. **Fire up your favorite Web browser and navigate to `http://search.twitter.com`.**

2. **Enter #yourusername in the Search field.**

   The Twitter search engine returns a list of tweets with your username preceded by the hashtage.

3. **Analyze the list.**

   You see some usernames you recognize and some you don't. You may also see some bad press. Monitoring hashtags is a wonderful way of finding out who's talking about you and what they're saying. You may also find some people you want to follow.

Calculating a Following to Follower to Updates Ratio

The number of people you follow compared to the number of people following you is important information. So is the number of updates. This information is public for any Twitter user who stops by your piece of the Twitterverse. If you're following a lot of people and not many people are following you, it appears as though you're trying to sell something, especially if you have lots of updates.

When you follow someone, the number of people you're following, the number of people you follow, and the number of updates you've sent is sent along with your Twitter avatar. If the ratio of people you follow to people who follow you is significantly greater than 50 percent of the total of the people who are following you and the people you are following and you have lots of updates, it's a red flag to potential followers. Keep track of this information regularly.

As a marketer, the percentage of people following you should be about 30 percent of the total number of followers and people you're following.

Tracking Links

You can track links from Twitter back to your Web site if you use bit.ly (at `http://bit.ly`) to shorten your URLs.

Other services that shorten URLs don't offer this capability. If you want to track your short URLs, you must use bit.ly. Turn to Book II, Chapter 1 to find out how to use bit.ly.

Paste the short URL into your favorite Web browser followed by the plus sign (+). You see exactly how many hits the short URL received, which lets you know whether the link was useful to your followers (see Figure 5-6).

Logging Visits per Follower

If your Web site or blog has statistics you can access, you can track which Twitter followers are visiting your Web site or blog. To do this, open your Web site control panel. If you're not sure how, check with the technical support team of your Web hosting service.

To track visits per follower, follow these steps:

1. **Navigate to your Web site control panel and log in.**

2. **Click the link or icon to view the site stats.**

   Many Web hosting services make the Webalizer software available for this task.

3. **Click on the month you want to analyze.**

   Most Web statistics software programs give you, at the top of the page, a graph showing visits per month.

4. **Scroll to the Referrers section of the page.**

5. **Look for any referrers that start with Twitter.**

   The Twitter Web site is followed by the username.

6. **If you're not sure who the follower is, click the link.**

   The follower's Twitter page opens in another browser window.

7. **Analyze the rest of the results to find other Twitter followers who are visiting your site.**

Book V

Facebook

The 5th Wave   By Rich Tennant

"Jim and I do a lot of business together on Facebook. By the way, Jim, did you get the sales spreadsheet and little blue pony I sent you?"

Contents at a Glance

Chapter 1: Getting to Know Facebook

In This Chapter

✔ Finding out what Facebook is

✔ Finding out who's on Facebook

✔ Creating a Facebook page

✔ Creating a page for your business

✔ Tweaking your Facebook page

✔ Adding information to your page

*F*acebook has been around for quite a while. You'll find all sorts of people on Facebook: schoolkids, adolescents, Army moms, and others. But lots of businesses are on Facebook, too, and they're reaping the rewards of participating in social media by attracting loyal fans.

Facebook made some major changes in early 2010 and did away with the concept of fans. Instead of being a fan of a business page, a person can like your page. In this chapter, we show you how to get started on Facebook.

Discovering How Facebook Can Help Your Business

The Facebook social media site appeals to all age groups. Facebook is used by rock musicians, schoolchildren, Army moms, and just about anybody else who wants an online presence to communicate with friends. Since September 2006, anyone with a valid e-mail address who's over the age of 13 can set up a Facebook page.

✦ **Personal page:** You're here to market your business, but sometimes potential customers want to know the people behind a business. Facebook gives you the arena to give your business a personal touch. The standard Facebook page is open only to friends you approve. You can post personal information and invite friends to view your profile. You can send messages privately or publicly and use a Facebook feature to chat online. You can comment on information on the walls of your friends, and your friends can comment on information posted on your wall.

People who are not your friends can view your contact information and the other information you include on your Facebook page, but they cannot view your updates, or any multimedia you upload to Facebook. If you don't want potential customers to know the intimate details of your life, you can change your account's privacy settings so that only friends can view your contact information.

✦ **Customization:** Your Facebook page doesn't have to look like everyone else's. You can customize it by adding photos and videos and applications — such as polls — to enhance your profile. Figure 1-1 shows you a customized Facebook page.

Figure 1-1:
A Facebook profile page.

✦ **News Feed:** The News Feed — which only you can see — shows recent posts by your friends or people who like your business page. It's an easy way to keep up to date with potential customers and what they need.

✦ **Wall:** Friends or people who like your business page can post messages on your wall (which is part of your page) and share them with your other friends or people who like your business page. When someone posts a comment on your wall, he is notified by e-mail whenever someone else updates the comment. Your wall is also updated whenever you add a video or photos to your profile.

You can change the manner in which you are notified by choosing Account⊅Notifications, and then choosing which events trigger an e-mail notification from Facebook.

✦ **Business Page:** The page, where you can promote your business or individual products, is a useful way to disseminate information in a highly public manner. Any Facebook user can like your business page. The downside is that you cannot see the profile of people who like your page. The upside is that there's no limit to the number of people who can like your page and you don't have to approve every person who likes your page (as you do with friends of your personal page). Figure 1-2 shows the Ford Motor Company Facebook page.

You can customize your page using applications, just like any other Facebook user. You set up the account as the official representative of your business, but you can assign administrator privileges to someone else in your company so that you can hand off Facebook responsibilities.

Figure 1-2: Henry would wonder what all this is about.

✦ **Advertising:** In addition to setting up a business page, you can promote your presence on Facebook by using ads. If you've spent any time on Facebook, you've seen the ads in the right column. You can place ads there as well.

If you're thinking about setting up a Facebook page for your business, you probably want to know who's hanging out on the site. If the people hanging out on Facebook don't fit your company's target audience, you're wasting your time and need to spend your energy more wisely. If, however, some Facebook users match at least some of your target audience, you should have a Facebook business page. Table 1-1 lists the demographics of Facebook.

Table 1-1	Facebook Demographics
Demographic	*Percentage of Users*
Female	45
Male	55
Age 3–12 years	4
Age 13–17 years	22
Age 18–34 years	42
Age 35–49 years	20
Over 50	12
Caucasian	75
African American	13
Asian	5
Hispanic	6
Other	1
Have kids 0–17	52
No kids 0–17	48
Earns as much as $30,000	14
Earns $30,000 to $60,000	24
Earns $60,000 to $100,000	30
Earns more than $100,000	32
No college	47
Some college	40
Graduate school	13

Later sections in this chapter show you how to set up a personal Facebook page and a Facebook business page.

Setting Up a Personal Facebook Account

Before you can commune with anyone on Facebook, you have to set up a Facebook account. When you set up a Facebook account, you automatically get a personal page. A Facebook friend can see all the cool information on your Facebook page, such as the wall, your photos and videos, and more.

A personal Facebook page is an easy way to share personal information with friends, relatives, and business colleagues, and you even have the option to keep your Facebook updates private if you want to keep your personal page and business page separate.

To set up a Facebook page, follow these steps:

1. **Launch your favorite Web browser and navigate to www.facebook.com.**

   The Facebook home page appears, as shown in Figure 1-3.

2. **Fill in the blanks.**

   This step is basic, so we spare you the blow-by-blow description. As long as you're over 13 years old, you're granted membership to the Facebook community. And, hey — it's free! What a bargain.

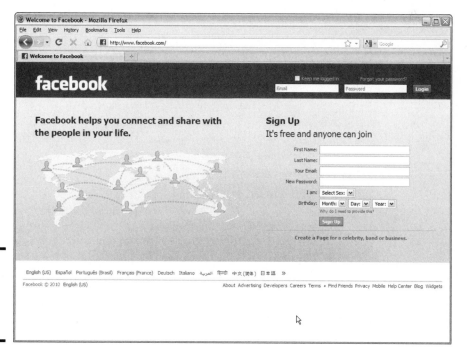

Figure 1-3:
To
Facebook
or not to
Facebook?

3. **Click Sign Up.**

   The page refreshes and one of those gnarly-looking captcha items appears.

4. **Type the captcha text and click Sign Up.**

   You have a Facebook page.

The Facebook page is for personal contact with friends and family. The information is, as you can imagine, of a personal nature; therefore, it isn't suitable for marketing your business. But a Facebook business page is eminently more useful for marketing yourself or your company. We show you how to set up a Facebook business page in the "Setting Up a Facebook Business Page" section, later in this chapter.

Setting Up Your Facebook Page

After you get a Facebook page, you need to set it up. You can add friends, set up a profile, and add your picture to the page. A-a-h, it's so much fun. After you set up the account, you see the option to add friends to your page. In fact, you see a list of people with whom Facebook thinks you may want to commune. You can add these people as friends by clicking the applicable link or just ignoring them. The next step is to search for contacts on Facebook. We show you how to do this task in the next section.

Searching for contacts on Facebook

If you have an e-mail set up with Gmail or Yahoo! or another free e-mail source, all you need to do is supply your e-mail address and password on the Find Friends page, which is Step 2 of the Facebook setup, as shown in Figure 1-4, and then click the Find Friends button. Click the Add as Friend link next to anyone you want to become friends with. After you find some friends, you can set up a profile.

Setting up your profile

Your profile is where you tell people about yourself. Initially, you add information about the schools you attended and the company you work for, as shown in Figure 1-5. Simply enter the information and click Save & Continue to navigate to the Profile Picture page. You can do much more after you have the page initially set up, which we cover in the later section "Modifying your Facebook profile."

Figure 1-4:
Finding
friends on
Facebook.

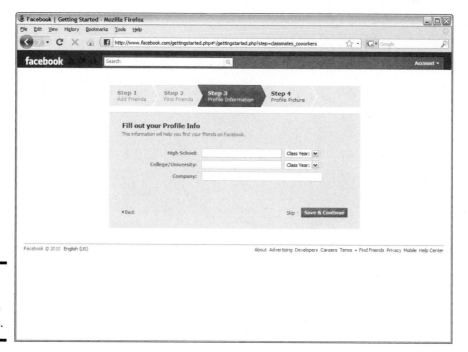

Figure 1-5:
Adding
your profile
information.

Adding a picture to your Facebook page

Whether you set up a page for business or to keep in touch with friends, you should add a picture, which is, as they say, worth a thousand words. Be sure to use a smiling head-and-shoulders shot, taken in the last decade.

Lots of people think it's cool to post a baby picture or one from high school. This photo may be cute if all you're using the page for is personal contacts, but when you use Facebook for business, you must have a recent photograph. After all, your goal is to meet customers and potential clients.

Click the Upload a Photo link, shown in Figure 1-6, and follow the prompts to add a photo to your Facebook page. You can also click the Take a Photo link and take a photo by using the webcam connected to your computer. If you choose this option, just make sure you have a good webcam.

Click Save & Continue when you're done and you'll see a very sparse page, which you can modify as we show you in the next section.

Figure 1-6: Adding a picture to your Facebook page.

Modifying your Facebook profile

After you perform the preliminary setup tasks, you have a functional Facebook page. It isn't pretty, or highly informative, but it's functional. At this point, you can flesh out the basic information about yourself, such as your interests and relationship status. Is this information important if you're a businessperson on Facebook? Perhaps. Any personal information you leave makes it easier for people to like you and eventually do business with you. Even though our society does a fair bit of business on the Internet, it's still nice to know something about the person with whom you do business. We leave it for you to decide.

After you create the page, you can edit your profile by clicking the Info tab and then clicking Edit Information. Your Info page opens in Edit mode, shown in Figure 1-7, with the Basic Information section displayed. You can make changes by entering different information in the text boxes or selecting a check box. You can also edit your personal, work, and contact information.

Figure 1-7:
Modifying
your
Facebook
profile.

In the Looking For section, choose Networking to show that you're here to network, not just play.

After making the desired changes, click Done Editing.

You can also modify your Facebook profile at any time after setting it up. To modify your Facebook profile when something changes or when you want to add some new information, follow these steps:

1. **Log in to your Facebook account.**

Your Facebook page appears.

2. **Click Profile.**

Your profile appears.

3. **Click the Edit My Profile link.**

Your profile page and all the various bells and whistles associated with your profile appear (refer to Figure 1-7).

4. **Make the changes you want and then click Save Changes.**

Your revised profile is served up.

Setting Up a Facebook Page for Your Business

A personal page is useful for finding old friends and staying in touch with friends and business associates. The best tool for businesspersons on Facebook, though, is the business page. When you set one up, you can add information about your company, a mission statement, product information, and more.

 A business page is different from an individual Facebook page. Anybody can like your Facebook page by clicking a button. When you have an individual page, each friend request must be approved, which is an arduous task if you get the response you want from your Facebook endeavor.

To set up a Facebook page for your business, follow these steps:

1. **Launch your favorite Web browser and navigate to `www.facebook.com/pages/create.php`.**

The Create a Page page opens, as shown in Figure 1-8.

2. **Choose one of the options for the type of page you want to create.**

You can create a page for a local business, brand, product, or organization or for an artist, band, or public figure.

If you're creating the page for yourself, use your own name; for your business, use your business name. Or, if you're creating a page for a product, use the product name.

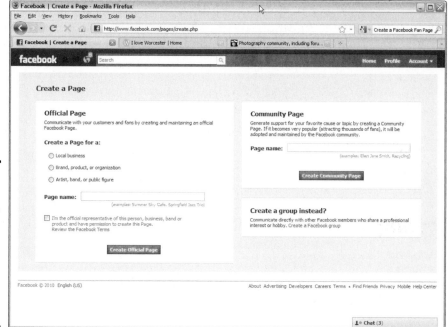

Figure 1-8:
Let's see —
using paper,
scissors,
and some
glue, you
can create
a page
for your
business.

3. **Enter a name for the page.**

   Use your own name, the name of your business, or the name of your product for the page name. Don't try to be cute with a name. Just the facts, ma'am.

4. **Select the check box to agree that you're the official representative and have the right to set up the page.**

   You may also want to click the link and read the fine print regarding the Facebook terms. Seriously, it's not *that* fine; it appears to be in 12-point Verdana type.

5. **Click the Create Official Page button.**

   You now have a bare-bones Facebook business page, as shown in Figure 1-9.

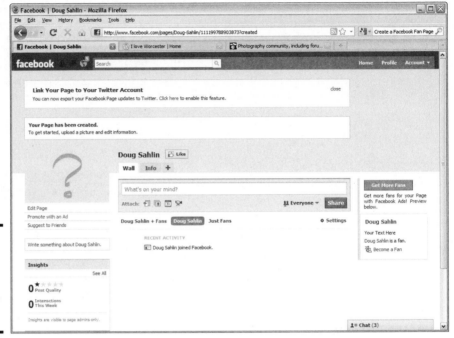

Figure 1-9:
Look, Mom
— I have a
Facebook
page for my
business!

Tweaking Your Facebook Business Page

Before your page is ready to accept adoring fans, you have to put up some window dressing. The page is bare at first, but after doing a bit of work, you can transform it into a thing of beauty that, with any luck, will attract thousands of fans and create extra revenue for your business. You can link your Facebook page to your Twitter feed, upload a picture of yourself or your company logo, and much more.

Linking your Business page to your Twitter feed

If you're on Twitter, you have followers that may or may not be on Facebook. You have more detailed information on Facebook including photos and videos than you do on Twitter. Therefore, common sense tells you that you should link your Facebook page to Twitter.

Follow these steps:

1. **From the Link Your Page to Your Twitter Account section of your page, click the Click Here link.**

The Link Your Facebook Page to Twitter page appears. You cannot do anything directly from this page, but the print and graphics look nice.

TIP

If you happen to navigate away from your new business page at any time before connecting Twitter, log into your personal page and then go to `www.facebook.com/twitter` and your business page appears.

2. **Click the Link a Page to Twitter button.**

   Another page with pretty graphics appears, as shown in Figure 1-10. (The Facebook graphical design team takes their job seriously.)

Figure 1-10:
Hmm.
Where's the
beef?

3. **Click the Link to Twitter button.**

   Hmm. Now you're in Twitter, as shown in Figure 1-11. Ain't that tweet?

4. **Enter your Twitter username and password and then click Allow.**

   This step gives Twitter permission to link your Facebook feed with your Twitter page. Twitter checks your credentials to make sure that your username and password are correct and then you're redirected to Facebook, as shown in Figure 1-12. By default, every option is linked to Twitter. Whenever you add a new friend, update your status, or add notes, for example, your followers on Twitter are notified.

Figure 1-11:
Linking to
Twitter.

Figure 1-12:
Choosing
which
types of
information
are shared
on Twitter.

5. **Accept the default options, or deselect any Facebook feature that you don't want to appear on Twitter.**

6. **Click the Save Changes button.**

   The Facebook features you select are linked to your Twitter account.

Changing your business page settings

After you add your Facebook feed to Twitter, you can do several other things to spiff up your page and add information to help you find more people to like your page.

To finish tweaking your Facebook page, follow these steps:

1. **Click the Edit Page link on the left side of your business page.**

   A plethora of options appears, as shown in Figure 1-13.

2. **In the Settings section, click Edit.**

   The Settings options you can edit appear, as shown in Figure 1-14.

Figure 1-13:
Editing your
business
page.

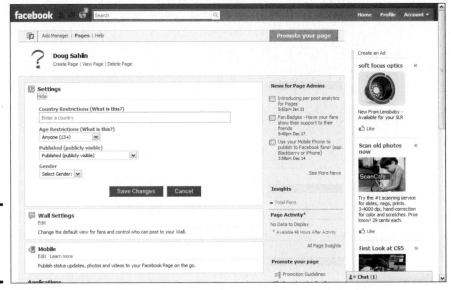

Figure 1-14:
Editing
your page
settings.

You can

- Restrict the countries from which users can like your page

- Restrict the age of the people who can become fans of your page

- Determine whether the content can be reviewed by the general public or only page administrators

- Determine whether the page is gender specific

3. **Make any changes you want.**

   You know your business, so you know which restrictions are applicable to your business page. For example, if your product is available only in the United States, you can prevent viewers from other countries from liking your page.

4. **Click the Save Changes button.**

   Your settings are saved.

Changing your wall settings

You have complete control over your business page. You can control whether people liking your page can post comments, add videos, or add photos to your page.

To edit the wall settings for your page, follow these steps:

1. **Click the Edit Page link on the left side of your fan page.**

A plethora of options appears (refer to Figure 1-13).

2. **In the Wall Settings section, click Edit.**

The settings you can edit for wall posts are displayed, as shown in Figure 1-15.

3. **In the View Settings section, choose the default view for the wall.**

This step determines whether to show only your posts or to show your fans' posts in addition to yours.

4. **In the View Settings section, choose an option from the Default Landing Tab drop-down menu.**

You can have the default landing tab be the Wall, Info, Discussions tab, or any of the other standard tabs such as Photos, Events, and so on.

5. **Choose whether to autoexpand comments on stories.**

The default option expands comments on stories by default. The other alternative is to collapse comments on stories and allow visitors to expand comments to make them all visible. The default option takes up more room on your page.

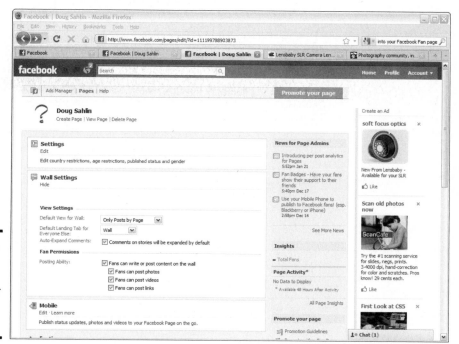

Figure 1-15:
Restrict the rights to post on your business page wall.

6. **For any permissions that you don't want your fans to have, deselect the permissions in the Fan Permissions Posting Ability section.**

   By default, fans can write or post comments, post photos, post videos, and post links to Web pages on your wall.

7. **Click your avatar.**

8. **Click the Write Something about <page name> link on your wall.**

   A window opens in which you can write a brief bio that shows up on your profile.

9. **Write a brief intro paragraph about your business.**

   You're limited to about 250 characters, so choose your words wisely. (But hey, it's more than you get on your Twitter bio.) Your bio should look like an author's bio on a book dust jacket — short, sweet, and to the point, with enough information to pique the curiosity of page visitors.

10. **Click Save Changes.**

    Your changes are saved.

Adding a photo

If you didn't add a photo when you created the page, a giant question mark (?) graces the spot where your smiling face should be. Unless you want to be a mysterious Facebook page owner, follow these steps to add a photo to your page:

1. **Click the Question Mark icon on your business page.**

   The Question Mark icon is the default avatar for a Facebook business page. You can put a much better-looking icon there, such as a picture of your smiling face or your company logo. After you click the icon, a new page appears that enables you to upload a photo, as shown in Figure 1-16.

2. **Click the Change Profile Picture link.**

   Another page opens. Again, those Facebook graphical design munchkins have done their jobs well and presented you with a less-than-compelling but oh-so-functional page from which you upload a photo, as shown in Figure 1-17. You can upload a GIF, JPEG, or PNG file that has a file size no larger than 4MB.

Figure 1-16:
Upload
a photo
to your
business
page.

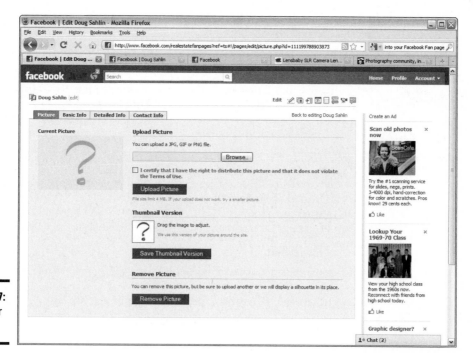

Figure 1-17:
Browse for
a photo.

3. **Click the Browse button.**

   A dialog box opens, and you can browse for a file on your computer.

4. **Follow the prompts to select the photo and then click Open.**

   The path to the image appears in the text box.

5. **Select the check box to certify that you own the rights to the image and do not violate the Facebook terms of use.**

   When you select this check box, you make the Facebook lawyers happy because the liability is on you if you upload a famous movie star's picture rather than your own. If you don't click the check mark, you can't upload an image.

6. **Click Upload Picture.**

   In a flash, you're on Facebook in the flesh. A thumbnail image also appears. This image appears on all pages except the wall. The image on the wall has a dimension of 200 x 200 pixels.

7. **Click and drag the thumbnail to adjust the image.**

   This step determines how the image will be cropped to create the thumbnail.

8. **Click the Save Thumbnail Version button.**

   Your Facebook page has come a long way, baby. But you still need to supply some information for your adoring fans.

If you travel a lot and want to update your fans when you're on the road, check out the mobile options when you edit your page. You can sign up for Facebook text messages to update your page or generate your own, unique e-mail address for your Facebook page, used to upload videos and photos to your page.

Adding Information to Your Facebook Business Page

You're almost at the point where you can start writing on your wall. We show you how to splash your wall with whatever words of wisdom you choose in the next chapter. But now it's time to add some information for your fans to see. The information you add can determine whether a visitor becomes a fan.

To add information to your Facebook business page, follow these steps:

1. **Log in to your Facebook business page and click Info.**

   You can edit the Basic Info and Detailed Info tabs.

2. **Click Basic Info.**

   The page refreshes and you can add as much or as little information in the following categories, as shown in Figure 1-18: Affiliation, Address, City/Town, Zip, Phone, and Birthday. Because you're a business, you fill in all the blanks. If you're a public figure, such as an author or artist, you probably shouldn't include your address and phone number. If you decide to add your birthday, you don't have to add the year.

3. **After modifying your basic information, click the Save Changes button.**

   Your information is saved to your page, and the Detailed Info section expands.

4. **In the Detailed Info section, add as much or as little information as you want.**

   List all Web sites associated with you and your business, including your blog and Twitter page, as shown in Figure 1-19.

   Add only the Web site URL, not the name of the site. If you try to add a name for each site, Facebook thinks it's a Web address and inserts the text *http://www* in front of it.

Figure 1-18:
Adding
your basic
information.

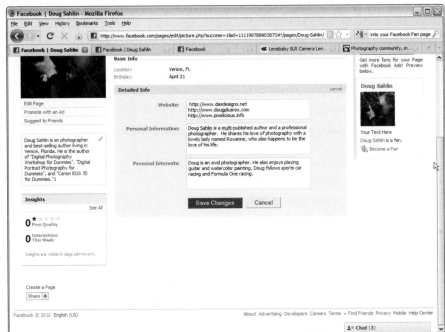

Figure 1-19:
Adding
detailed
information.

   5. **Click the Save Changes button.**

   6. **Click Done Editing.**

   Your Info page is displayed in all its glory.

Chapter 2: Getting Around on Facebook

In This Chapter

✓ Sending messages on Facebook

✓ Adding images and video to your page

✓ Posting on the wall

✓ Removing a post

✓ Replying to people who like your page and friends

✓ Chatting on Facebook

You have a Facebook page. Now what? That you're reading this book means that you're using social media as a marketing tool. The next step after creating a Facebook business page is to put some content on it. You have a few ways to interact with potential clients on Facebook:

✦ Create interesting posts and put them on your wall.

✦ Add images and videos to your Facebook page.

✦ Respond to a thread of comments from a post on your business page.

Like other social media, it's all about the conversation. Facebook is another venue for you to get your message out to potential clients and interact with them. Whether you're a multimillion-dollar business like Ford Motor Company or a wedding photographer, you can reach out to clients and potential clients using the various tools Facebook offers.

In this chapter, we show you the basic steps for putting content on your Facebook page, acquiring people who like your page, and then interacting with them. A Facebook business page without people who like it is like a bagel without a hole — it just ain't right. If you're ready to start populating your Facebook page, read on, intrepid social media marketer.

Adding Messages on Your Page

The wall on a Facebook page resembles a blog: You have to post frequently to keep friends (personal page) or people who like your page (business page) coming back and eventually turn them into paying clients.

The information you post should be useful and not a blatant advertisement. You can use a wall post to announce a new product, but don't use a Facebook post like a sledgehammer to beat your followers over the head. In fact, you should use a little bit of salesmanship in your wall posts. Pique the visitor's curiosity, but don't use a hard sell.

For example, you can tell people about a problem you solve with a new product or service. At the end of your post, leave a link to your Web site page, where people can find more information. If your message piques the curiosity of someone who likes your page, she's sure to click the link.

To add a message to your wall, follow these steps:

1. **Log in to your Facebook account.**

2. **Start entering text in the "What's on your mind" text field at the top of your wall.**

   Remember to post something useful for your people who like your page, as shown in Figure 2-1.

3. **Add information to your post.**

   Click one of the icons at the bottom of the post to add a link to a Web page, a photo, an event, or a video.

Figure 2-1:
Creating a post on your wall.

When you add a photo or video to a wall post, it's also added to the applicable tab, which enables viewers to see the content after newer posts appear at the top of your page.

4. **Click the Share button.**

    Your post is added to the wall.

Make sure your post contains no grammatical or spelling errors before you share it with the world. You cannot edit a post. If you made a mistake or created a post that ruffled someone's feathers, your only option is to remove the post entirely. Pause your cursor over the post until a Remove button appears. Click the button to permanently remove the post.

Adding Images and Video

You can add photographs and video to your Facebook page. If you're a wedding photographer, for example, you can showcase your fan page with the best pictures from your most recent gigs. If you have a video of a recent event or a demonstration of your product, add it to your Facebook page. The only limitation on content is your imagination.

Adding a Photos or Video tab

Facebook lets you conveniently organize photos and videos on tabs, which helps people who like your page to easily find this content. To add a Photos or Video tab to your Facebook fan page, follow these steps:

1. **Log in to your Facebook account and navigate to your business page.**

2. **Click the Plus Sign (+) icon to the right of the last tab on your page.**

    A drop-down menu appears with a list of tabs you can add to your page, as shown in Figure 2-2.

3. **Click Photo.**

    A Photos tab is added to your page. If you're adding photos to a business page, you probably already have the Photos tab.

4. **To add a Video tab to your page, click the Plus Sign icon again and click Video.**

    Your business page now has Photos and Video tabs, as shown in Figure 2-3.

Figure 2-2:
Adding
Photo and
Video tabs
to your
business
page.

Figure 2-3:
A place to
store your
Facebook
photos and
videos.

You can change the order in which tabs appear on your page. Click a tab and drag it to the location you want. If the tabs you want to appear on your profile are collapsed, click the right-pointing double arrow next to the last visible tab on your profile to display the hidden tabs and then drag a tab to its new position.

Uploading photos to a Facebook album

You can create a photo album for just about any purpose, such as to showcase employees, products, events, or portfolios. Whenever you need to segregate photos on a Facebook page, an album is the answer. You can upload images files in GIF, JPEG, or PNG format. File size doesn't make a difference because Facebook resamples the images to a smaller size.

To create a Facebook album, follow these steps:

1. **Organize the album images on your hard drive.**

   Store in a folder all the images you want in one album.

2. **Log in to your Facebook account.**

3. **Click the Photos tab.**

   The Photos tab expands. (If you have no Photos tab, see the earlier section "Adding a Photos or Video tab.") Initially, all you have is an album for profile pictures with one photo in it, shown in Figure 2-4.

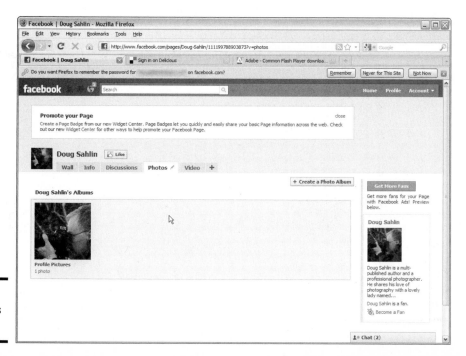

Figure 2-4:
The Photos tab.

4. **Click the Create a Photo Album button.**

The Facebook Photo Uploader dialog box appears. This Facebook plug-in lets you upload multiple images (you must have Java installed on your computer). Download it by clicking Download and following the prompts. If you prefer to upload images by using the standard Facebook photo uploader, click Cancel.

The Add New Photos page appears, as shown in Figure 2-5.

5. **Enter a name, location, and description for the album:**

- *Name:* Choose a logical name that helps people who like your page easily identify which images appear in the album.

- *Location:* This is where the photos were taken. If a location isn't applicable, leave this field blank.

- *Description:* This additional information is used to identify the type of images stored in the album.

6. **Click the Create Album button.**

The album is created and the Upload Photos page appears. Figure 2-6 shows the simplified version of the Facebook uploader, which lets you upload five images at a time.

Figure 2-5:
Creating an album into which you store images.

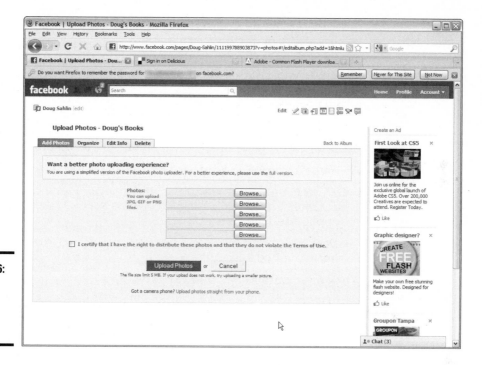

Figure 2-6:
Now it's
time to
upload
photos.

7. Click the Browse button.

The File Upload dialog box appears.

If you have a camera phone and want to upload images from it, click the Upload Photos Straight from Your Phone link, at the bottom of the Upload Photos page.

8. Navigate to a file and click Open.

The file is added to the upload queue.

9. Repeat Steps 7 and 8 for other images you want to upload.

The standard Facebook uploader limits you to five photos. If you need to upload more than five images, you have to repeat these steps to upload them. If you decide to go with the plug-in, you can upload a folder of files.

10. Select the check box that says you have the right to distribute the photos and that they don't violate the Facebook terms of use.

If you don't select the check box, you cannot upload the images. If you select the check box and you have no right to distribute the images, you run afoul of the copyright laws, which isn't a good thing.

11. **Click the Upload Photos button.**

The Uploading Photos page appears. Don't close your browser window until the upload is complete. A spiffy little series of flashing blue bars keeps you amused while the photos upload. After the photos are uploaded, the Edit Album page appears, as shown in Figure 2-7.

12. **Create a caption for each photo in the album.**

You can add a fairly lengthy description, but the best method is to create a short caption that describes what's in the photo.

13. **Click a person in the photo and enter the person's name.**

14. **Decide which photo serves as the album cover, and then click the This Is the Album Cover radio button.**

A thumbnail of this photo is displayed in the Photos tab as the album cover.

Figure 2-7:
Adding
captions to
your photos.

15. **Click the Save Changes button.**

The changes to your album are saved and the Unpublished Photos dialog box appears.

16. **Click Publish to publish the photos to your wall and profile now, or click Skip to add more photos to the album or perform other edits, such as organizing photos.**

Editing your photos and albums

After you publish an album, you still have the opportunity to fix any mistakes you made in the captions, change the album cover, organize the order in which your album images appear, and delete any photos you accidentally uploaded.

To change the order your images appear in an album, follow these steps:

1. **Click the Photos tab on your page and hover the cursor over the album you want to edit.**

A Pencil icon appears, which is your clue that you can edit the album.

2. **Click the Pencil icon.**

The Edit Album page appears, which has five tabs:

- *Edit Photos:* Change any captions, delete photos, or change the album cover.

- *Add More*: Add photos to the album.

- *Organize:* Change the order in which the photos are shown in the album.

- *Edit Info*: Change the album name, location, and description.

- *Delete:* Delete the album.

3. **Click Organize.**

Thumbnails of the images in the album appear, as shown in Figure 2-8.

4. **Click the Reverse Order button.**

This step reverses the order in which the thumbnails are displayed in the album.

Figure 2-8:
An
organized
album is
a thing of
beauty
and a joy
forever.

5. Drag a thumbnail to change its position in the album.

This step lets you arrange images in order of importance, or by the time at which a photo was taken.

6. Click the Save Changes button.

Your album is organized.

7. To delete a photo, select the Edit Photos tab, and then select the Delete This Photo check box.

You can't undo this action, so think twice before deleting a photo.

Adding video

If you own a video camera, you can post videos on your Facebook business page. You can post videos of recent events, tutorials on how to use your product, and much more. Use your imagination to think of new and interesting ways to use video in conjunction with your social media marketing efforts.

If you're already creating video Web logs, or *vlogs,* for a video hosting service such as YouTube or Vimeo, you already have a finished product for a Facebook page video.

To upload a video to your Facebook page, follow these steps:

1. **Log in to your Facebook account.**

2. **Click the Video tab on your page.**

   The Video tab appears. If you have no Video tab, check out the "Adding a Photos or Video tab" section, earlier in this chapter.

   You have two options for video: Upload a video or record a video using a webcam attached to your computer. If you have a good webcam, experiment with recording a video directly to Facebook. The remaining steps describe how to upload a video you've already created.

3. **Click Upload.**

   If you want to record a video right now, click the Record button.

   The Upload File dialog box appears, as shown in Figure 2-9.

4. **Click Browse.**

   The File Upload dialog box appears.

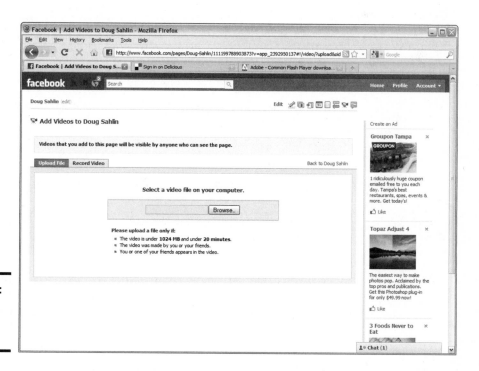

Figure 2-9:
Uploading
a video to
Facebook.

5. **Navigate to the video file you want to upload and click Open.**

   The file you upload must be smaller than 1024MB and less than 20 minutes long. After you click Open, the file starts uploading.

   Video files are large, and sometimes even humongous. Be prepared to wait a while for your video to upload. Now isn't the time for impatience.

   After the file uploads, you can enter some information, such as the title of the video, as shown in Figure 2-10.

6. **Enter information about the video.**

   You can add the names of people in the video, enter a title for the video, and enter a description of the video.

7. **After adding the information you want, click Save Info.**

   Your video is ready for viewing. It's posted on your wall (shown in Figure 2-11 and is also available from the Video tab.

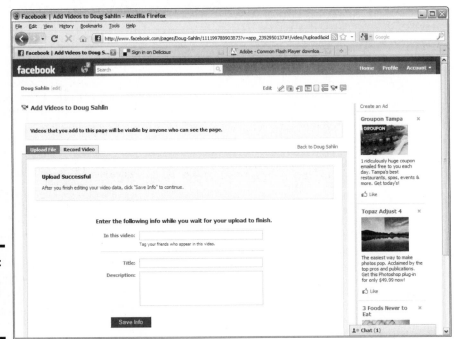

Figure 2-10: Adding information about your video.

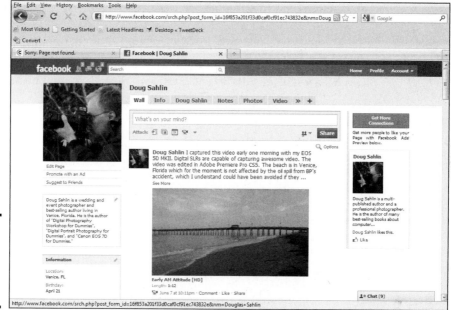

Figure 2-11:
A video
uploaded to
a Facebook
wall.

If you aren't crazy about the thumbnail image Facebook chooses for your video, click the Video tab and then click the Pencil icon to edit the video. In the Choose a Thumbnail section, use the arrow keys below the default thumbnail to navigate the thumbnails and choose one you like.

Finding People to Like Your Business Page

After you have a couple of posts under your belt, you can start getting people to like your Facebook page. The best place to start is with the people you know. Send an e-mail to everyone in your address book with a brief message and a link to your Facebook page. Not everyone is likely to be a Facebook member, but the fact that you are may entice them to join, and, of course, to like your page. Tell your friends to tell their friends about your business page. If you're on Twitter, send a tweet to your followers with the link to your Facebook page. You can also get people to like your page using Facebook resources.

If you have a personal account with Facebook in addition to your business page, you can ask your friends to like your Facebook page by following these steps:

1. Log in to Facebook.

Your personal page opens by default.

2. **Open your business page.**

   If you have created a custom URL for your page, use this to navigate to the business page. Alternatively, you can type your company name in the search field and then click the icon to open your business page.

3. **Click the Suggest to Friends text link directly beneath your avatar.**

   Your Facebook friends appear in another window.

4. **Click the friends to whom you want to send an invitation.**

   A check mark appears near the friend's avatar, as shown in Figure 2-12.

5. **Click the Send Invitations button.**

   Your invitation is sent to your friends.

After you send the invitation to your friend, be sure to ask them to recommend your business page to their friends. In addition to asking friends to like your Facebook page, you should promote it in your other online media as well. Include the URL to your fan page in your e-mail signature and any other correspondence you send. You can also send an e-mail to everyone in your address book to announce your Facebook page. Another possibility is an online press release. You can also add a badge to your Web site that, when clicked, directs your site's visitors to your Facebook business page. We show you how to add a Facebook badge to your Web site in the next section.

Figure 2-12:
Sending an invitation to friends.

That's just the tip of the iceberg for getting your Facebook page noticed. In Chapter 3 of this minibook, we show you how to use search engine optimization (SEO) to get your page noticed.

Responding to your comments

When you add a post to your wall, people who like your page can comment on your post. When your page becomes popular and you have lots of people leaving comments, you can't respond to every comment; you just won't have time. But you can add your two cents to the thread. Social media is all about being part of the conversation. When you find some interesting comments, add your own to the thread.

To add your comments to a post that has received comments, follow these steps:

1. **Log in to your Facebook account.**

2. **Review your comments.**

   You should review your comments daily, if you can. If you get some bad press, react to it immediately.

3. **When you see a comment thread you want to respond to, place the cursor in the text box at the bottom of the page and start typing, as shown in Figure 2-13.**

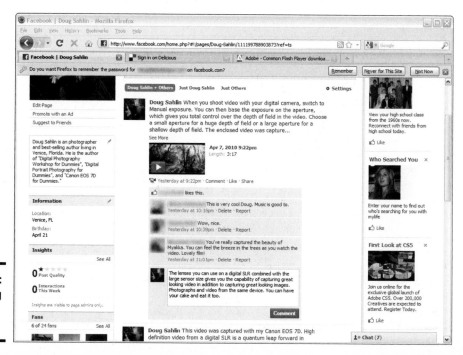

Figure 2-13: Responding to a comment.

4. **Click the Comment button.**

   Your comment is added to the thread.

Managing comments and wall posts

Most comments from people who like your page are supportive, interesting, and (possibly) amusing. But occasionally you receive a comment from a bad apple. In this case, you can manage comments. You can also manage posts on your wall.

If you disagree with a statement a user has posted, click the Delete button to remove the comment from your wall.

While moderation is a good thing to do, you don't want to develop a reputation for censoring comments. Think twice before you delete a comment from your wall or have a user banned from your page.

If the comment goes a little further than mere disagreement, you can have the user banned from your business page. To report a user for a violation of the terms of use or for making negative comments, follow these steps:

1. **Log in to Facebook and navigate to your business page.**

2. **Review comments to your posts, as shown in Figure 2-14.**

   Notice the two options below each comment: Delete and Report.

3. **When you find a comment that's negative, or spam, click Report.**

   A Report dialog box appears, showing the name of the user you're reporting. All reports are confidential.

4. **Choose an option from the Reason drop-down menu:**

   You can report a user for attacking the page owner or group or for leaving an advertisement or spam.

5. **Accept the default Banning option.**

   This option bans the user from your Facebook page and removes all content he has posted.

6. **Click Submit.**

   Note that if Facebook thinks you're reporting someone because you disagree with her statement, no action is taken.

Figure 2-14:
Reporting
a user to
Facebook.

Facebook creates a wall post by default every time something happens on
your page. You see a new post whenever someone likes your page or you
change your information, for example. If you want to remove any wall post,
including comments, follow these steps:

1. **Log in to Facebook and navigate to your business page.**

2. **Place the cursor over the post or item you want to remove from your
   wall.**

   The word *Remove* appears to the right of the post. It's a link that lets
   you remove the post.

3. **Click Remove.**

   The Delete Post dialog box appears, asking whether you're sure you
   want to delete the post.

4. **Click Delete.**

   The entry vanishes into cyberspace and beyond.

Using a Page Badge to Promote Your Business Page

If you have a Web site or a blog, you can add a Facebook badge to your site to promote visitors to your Facebook business page. This is a helpful way to cross-promote your fan page.

To add a badge to your Web site, follow these steps:

1. **Launch your favorite Web browser and navigate to `www.facebook.com/facebook-widgets/index.php`.**

The Facebook Badges page appears. You have options to create a badge with your Facebook profile and contact information, create a badge to show off your Facebook photos, create a badge to show the pages you like, or create a badge to promote your page.

2. **Click the Page Badge link.**

The Page Badges page appears (see Figure 2-15).

Figure 2-15:
Creating a
page badge.

3. **Choose the source for your badge.**

If you have an existing Blogger or TypePad account, click the applicable link and you're redirected to the applicable site. Follow the prompts to sign in and add the badge to your site. If you have your own domain, click Other that opens a window with HTML. Paste the code into your Web site. If you don't know how to edit Web pages, ask your friendly Web designer to help you.

4. **Add the badge to your Web site.**

   Your Facebook badge is visible to everyone who visits your site (see Figure 2-16).

Figure 2-16: Promoting your Facebook page from your Web site.

Facebook badge

Chatting on Facebook

If you have a personal Facebook page in addition to your business page, you can use the Facebook Chat window to chat with friends in real time. You cannot, however, chat with a person who likes your page unless he also happens to be a friend of your personal account. The Chat dialog box is available whether you're on your personal page or your business page. You can only chat with people who are your friends and not people who like your page. If a business associate in a distant market is a friend on Facebook, you can use the Chat dialog box for brainstorming.

To chat with your friends on Facebook, follow these steps:

1. **Log in to Facebook.**

   A chat window is visible in the lower right corner of your Facebook page.

2. **Click Chat.**

   The window pops up, revealing friends who are now online, as shown in Figure 2-17.

Figure 2-17:
With whom
do you want
to chat?

3. **Click the name of the person you want to chat with.**

   The window changes to reveal the name and icon of the person with whom you want to chat.

4. **Type something and then press Enter or Return.**

   Your message is sent to your friend. Your friend hears a noise that sounds like a pop to notify her that someone is tugging her chain — er, sending her a message. When your friend responds, her text appears below yours.

5. **Continue the conversation until your fingers become cramped or you see the early warning signs of carpal tunnel syndrome.**

   Chatting on Facebook can be fun. But you can also use it to get more people to like your business page. If the person with whom you're chatting is a friend of your personal account but hasn't clicked the Like button on your business page, send her the URL for your business page. If she likes your page, ask her to suggest your business page to her friends and business associates.

Chapter 3: Using Facebook Features

In This Chapter

✓ Delegating Facebook tasks

✓ Marketing with Facebook

✓ Creating a Facebook event

✓ Exploring Facebook tools and applications

✓ Exploring the Facebook blog

✓ Keeping track of the people who like your page

*I*n earlier chapters, you find out how to create a Facebook account, create a Facebook business page, and use basic Facebook features to commune with your Facebook fans. After you get the hang of using Facebook, you can use it to help market your business even more, by creating Facebook events, using Facebook applications, and much more.

In this chapter, we show you how to fine-tune your Facebook experience for your business and your marketing goals.

Adding Administrators to Your Facebook Business Page

As with any other social media outlet, using Facebook is work that takes another slice of the available hours in your workday. If you have a business partner or are part of a large organization, you can delegate your Facebook tasks by creating additional administrators. When you create them, they can log in to your Facebook business page and take some of the load off your back.

To add an administrator to your Facebook page, follow these steps:

1. Ask an associate to like your page.

Have her log in to her Facebook account, navigate to your business page, and then click the Like button.

2. **Log in to your Facebook account.**

   Your Facebook page appears in the Web browser.

3. **Scroll to the People Like This section and then click See All.**

   The people who like your page appear in a separate window, shown in Figure 3-1. Notice that the Make Admin button appears next to each name.

4. **Click the Make Admin button next to the name of the person who likes your page who you want to promote to administrator.**

   A dialog box appears, asking you to confirm that you want to promote the person's status to administrator and warning you that he will have the same control over the page as you do, as shown in Figure 3-2.

   Perhaps Facebook will someday institute options to limit the permissions level of each administrator, such as the (wonderful!) option to limit a person who likes your page to making only wall posts. For now, be absolutely certain that you want to give this person full control over your page.

5. **Click the Make Admin button.**

   Your associate now has the same control over the page as you do, except they cannot appoint new administrators or delete the page.

Figure 3-1:
Promote a friend who likes your page to an administrator.

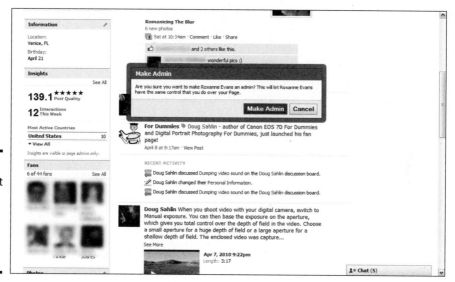

Figure 3-2:
You're about
to give your
associate
the same
powers you
have.

Using SEO to Get Your Facebook Business Page Noticed

Many businesses are using Facebook as a second home page, and that second page can be used to drive the people who like your business to their Web sites. But how do you get people to notice your Facebook business page?

Follow these tips to optimize your Facebook page for search engine optimization (SEO):

✦ **Use keywords in the information about yourself or your business.** When you write information about you or your company below your avatar, pepper it with the keywords people would use to find a company or service similar to yours on the Internet. Be as specific as possible while still creating a description that's grammatically correct and well written.

 Pull out the list of keywords you acquired for your Web sites, as described in Book II, Chapter 2.

✦ **Use the Info tab on your page to include more keywords and metadata about your business.** When you create a page for a business, you can include a company overview and a mission statement. If you create a page for a public figure, you can include personal information and interests. Add keywords to the text in the sections that people would use to find a similar business or service. Remember that each tab has a unique URL, which makes it easy for you to add your Facebook URL to an e-mail signature or create a link on one of your other Web sites.

✦ **Add URLs in your wall posts.** Whenever you write something on your wall, add a link to a page on your site where users can find more information. The additional link adds relevance to your Web site in a search and gives your business page more relevance — number of links is one criterion search engines use in ranking pages.

You can add a URL by clicking the Link icon underneath the Publisher text box. No search engine can see a URL you enter in this way. Always add URLs directly in your wall posts, for SEO purposes.

✦ **Embed hosted videos.** If you have videos at a hosting service such as YouTube or Vimeo, use the Facebook Markup Language (FBML) application to create a new tab and then embed a couple of videos in your page. A URL serves as another inbound link to your Facebook page. For more information on FBML, see the later section "Creating a custom tab for your business page."

✦ **Add keywords to photo captions and event listings.** When you add photos to an album on your Facebook page, to an album on your page, include keywords in the captions you create for your photos.

• If you're a wedding and event photographer posting a photo of a recent event, include your name in the caption as well as the town and city in which you live. You can also add keywords when you post an event on your Facebook page.

• If you're announcing a webinar, include keywords related to the subject of the event as well as any applicable URLs.

✦ **Create more inbound kinks for your business page.** Search engines rank pages according to the number of inbound links they have. Whenever you create a blog post, be sure to include a link to your Facebook business page. You can also include links to your Facebook page on your Web sites and include the link in other social media outlets you use, such as Twitter.

✦ **Draw as many people to like your page as you can.** When a Facebook user likes your page, this information is listed on the fan's page complete with a reciprocal link to your business page, which acts as another inbound link for your page.

✦ **Encourage fans to comment on your posts and like them.** When a fan posts a comment or clicks the Like icon, Facebook links the user's name with your business page, which gives the page, in essence, more relevance and popularity.

Using Facebook As a Marketing Tool

When you create a Facebook business page with the intent of marketing your business, your first goal is to find a group of people to like your page. Then you engage in a conversation with them. This strategy gives you a steady base of fans whose numbers increase as you make more relevant posts to your page.

In addition to marketing to the people who like your page, you can increase your presence on Facebook by advertising, promoting your page from your Web sites and other online media, and creating a group, as we show you in later sections of this chapter.

Advertising on Facebook

Advertising on Facebook is similar to advertising on Google: You create ads and then allocate how much money you'll spend on the campaign. It is, in essence, a bidding war — he who allocates the highest number of bucks has his ad posted most frequently. Facebook claims that your ad can reach as many as 400 million Facebook users. (That's a *lot* of people.) Any advertising guru can tell you that frequency is the name of the game. If the 400 million people see the ad once in a blue moon, you don't get good results. However, if you can increase your ad budget, your ad is shown more frequently.

When you log in to your account, Facebook teases you with a projected facsimile of your ad in the right corner of any tab except the wall, as shown in Figure 3-3. Of course, you're the only person who can see it until you create and place the ad.

Figure 3-3:
Facebook shows you what your ad can look like.

The Facebook ad process is fairly simple. Follow these steps:

1. **Log in to your Facebook account.**

   Your tricked-out Facebook page appears.

2. **Click Promote with an Ad.**

   The Design Your Ad page appears, as shown in Figure 3-4. When you create an ad for a page, people who view the ad can become fans by clicking the ad or visiting your page directly from the ad.

3. **Choose an option from the Facebook Content drop-down menu.**

   If you have more than one Facebook page in your account, it appears on this menu. The title has, by default, the same name as your Facebook content.

   You can also promote your Web site or product rather than your Facebook page. Click the I Want to Advertise a Web Page link.

4. **Accept or modify the default body text (the information that appears under your avatar).**

   You're creating an ad, and basic marketing principles tell you that an ad should satisfy a need or solve a problem. Tell potential fans how they can benefit by following you. You are limited to a maximum of 115 characters for your ad.

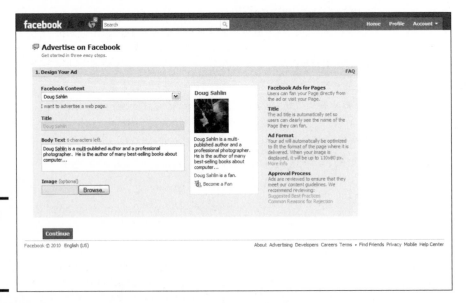

Figure 3-4:
Promote
your
Facebook
page.

Be sure to include a call to action at the end of your ad, such as asking the viewer to order online or call the number at the end of your ad.

5. **If you want an image with your ad, click Browse.**

   You can browse for an image on your hard drive and upload it. It must be 110 x 80 pixels, the maximum size for a Facebook ad image.

6. **(Optional) In the Targeting section, choose a location.**

   You can target an ad for the entire United States or limit the ad to a state or province or city. Limiting an ad to a city lets you choose to show it to users within a given radius of the city. Facebook uses IP addresses to determine user locations. (Talk about fine-tuning.)

7. **(Optional) Choose options in the Demographics section.**

   You can target an ad to a certain age group, send an ad to people on their birthdays, target the gender of ad recipients, and do much more.

8. **(Optional) Enter information in the Likes & Interests area.**

   For example, enter **photography** if your page is about photography.

9. **(Optional) Choose parameters in the Education & Work area.**

   In this area, you determine the education level of ad recipients. You can also enter information in the Workplace field to display the ad to people working for a specific company or organization.

10. **(Optional) Enter the information you want in the Connections on Facebook section.**

    You can target users who are connected by an event, page, group, or application. You can also target users who aren't connected to a page, event, group, or application. You can also target friends of connections.

11. **Click Continue.**

    The Campaigns and Pricing section appears, as shown in Figure 3-5. Notice that the estimated reach is displayed on the right side of the page.

12. **Choose an option from the Currency drop-down menu.**

    Choose the currency of the country in which you live.

13. **Enter a value for your daily budget.**

    This value represents the maximum amount you spend each day for targeted ads. The minimum bid per day is $1.00.

14. **Choose a Schedule option.**

    You can run ads daily beginning on the date you fill out the form until you cancel. You can also choose to run your ad during specified dates, which is a wise choice when you're testing the waters or advertising an event.

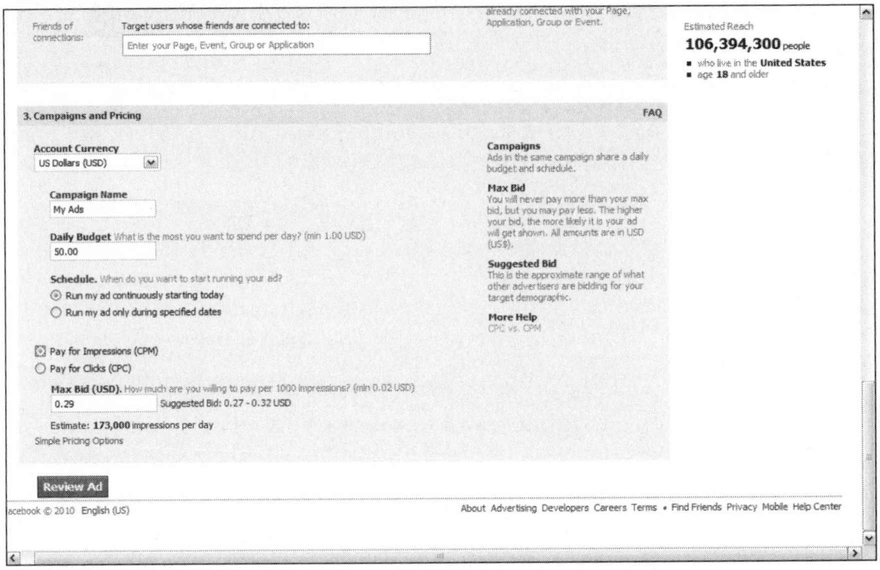

Figure 3-5:
Determining
a budget
for your
campaign.

15. **Choose whether you want to pay per impression or pay per click.**

    If you choose to pay per impression, the per-impression charge is applied to your account every time someone sees the ad. Your other option is to incur the pay-per-click charge every time someone clicks the ad.

    This amount is the maximum you're willing to pay per 1,000 impressions or per click. Facebook suggests a value based on the demographics you specify. If you enter a higher value, your ad appears more often than those from advertisers who bid lower.

16. **Click Review Ad.**

    The Review Ad page appears, as shown in Figure 3-6. At this stage, you see a preview of what your ad will look like. You also enter your credit card information.

17. **Enter your credit card information and click Place Order.**

    Your ad campaign is under way after Facebook accepts your ad. Alternatively, if you don't like the way the ad looks, click Edit Ad to change any parameter, including the budget.

    If you decide to cancel one or more of your Facebook ads, visit www. facebook.com/advertising and click the Manage My Ads link. You can select an ad and then cancel it.

Figure 3-6:
Review your
ad before
plunking
down your
hard-earned
cash.

Creating a Facebook group

Creating a Facebook group is another way for you to market your page and
your company. When you set up a Facebook group, people who are interested in the topic can join the group. Someone who hasn't clicked the Like
button on your business page, or a customer, may become one after seeing
your words of wisdom on your group page.

When you create a group, you create another Facebook entity, another way
for people to find you. Facebook users might not find your business page,
but if you find a niche about a popular subject that hasn't been filled and
you then fill that niche by creating a group, you have a powerful tool to
attract people to your business page and perhaps become paying clients.
Setting up a Facebook group is easy: All you have to do is find a niche and
create a group for that niche, and then start posting interesting material.

To create a Facebook group, follow these steps:

1. **Log in to Facebook and navigate to your Facebook page.**

2. **In the Search text field at the top of the page, enter the name of the
group you want to create and then click Search.**

A list appears, showing all results for your search query.

3. **Click Groups.**

If you see a page with no results, you can create a group with the name
you want.

4. **Click Home.**

   Your News Feed appears.

5. **Scroll down to the Groups section and click See All.**

   All groups of which you're a member are listed, as shown in Figure 3-7.

6. **Click Create Group.**

   The Create a Group page appears, as shown in Figure 3-8.

7. **Enter a name and description for the group.**

   You already researched the name — now all you need to do is enter a description of what the group is all about and give people a reason to join it.

8. **Choose an option from the Group Type drop-down menu, and then choose a subgroup from the second drop-down menu.**

   If no type fits the group you want to create, choose the closest match for the group you envision.

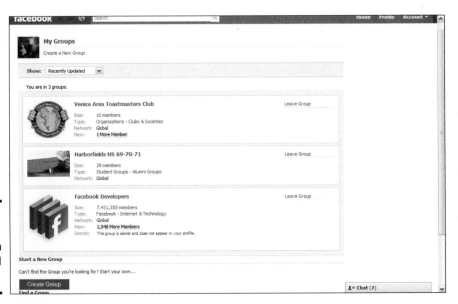

Figure 3-7:
A groupie can create a group (novel concept).

Figure 3-8:
Creating
your own
group.

9. **Enter any other information you feel is imperative.**

   This step is entirely at your discretion.

   Include a link to your Web site, rather than an e-mail address. If your group takes off, filling in an e-mail address might not be a good idea because your inbox may floweth over.

10. **Click Create Group.**

    The page labeled Step 2: Customize appears, as shown in Figure 3-9.

11. **Choose options to customize your group.**

    You have more options than the law allows — almost. You can choose whether to allow anybody to write on the wall, allow people to upload videos, allow members to post links, and much more.

12. **Click Save.**

    The Publish to Your Wall and Your Friend's Home Pages? box appears, as shown in Figure 3-10. Accept this option and the news is posted on your friends' News Feed.

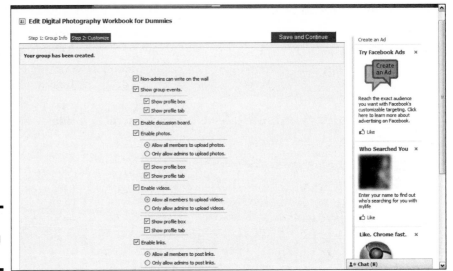

Figure 3-9:
Customizing
your group.

Figure 3-10:
Publish this
puppy.

13. **Click Publish.**

A message box indicates that your group is created. At this stage, you can invite friends to join your group, as shown in Figure 3-11.

They can, of course, invite *their* friends to join your group, and soon you have a homogeneous family of friends grooving together in the group of their choice.

14. **Click the Invite People to Join link on the left side of your group page.**

The Invite Friends dialog box opens.

15. **Choose which friends you want to invite.**

You can start exchanging information with other members when they join. At this stage, the page is sparse. You have to change your avatar picture, write something on the wall, or add a description, for example, as shown in Figure 3-12.

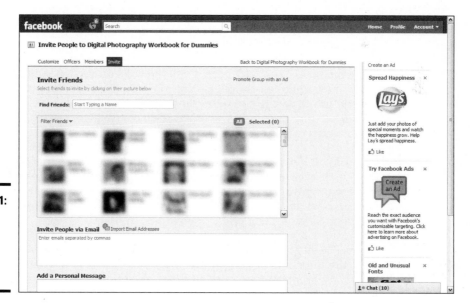

Figure 3-11:
Invite
Facebook
friends to
join your
group.

Figure 3-12:
Your group
is ready for
action.

After your page is set up, you can do pretty much everything you can do with a business Facebook page. Click the links on the left side of the page to send a message to all members. You can also promote the group with an ad, and edit group settings to determine whether members have certain rights such as posting photos to the group page or leaving messages on the page. You can also create a group event.

After you fill a popular niche by creating a Facebook group, you have to roll up your sleeves and start creating compelling content that will entice people to join your group. Update the group regularly using your Facebook tools. You can post photos and videos on your group page, ask group members questions, and create a poll, for example.

Use the Events tab to post information about an event that will be of interest to the members of your group. Your business is of interest to the group, so this is a great place to post information about an event your company is hosting.

Creating a Facebook event

If your Facebook group or company is holding an event, you can announce it on your Facebook group or business page. A group can be an Internet event such as a webinar or an event at a live location. For example, the Ford Motor Company lists car shows. If you appear at trade shows, give speeches, or demonstrate your product, creating an event on your Facebook Fan page is another way in which you can promote the event.

To create an event on your Facebook page, follow these steps:

1. **Log in to Facebook and navigate to your fan page.**

2. **Add an Events tab, if you don't already have one.**

   See Book V, Chapter 2 to find out how to add a tab to your business page.

3. **Click the Events tab.**

   Your events are listed, or you have a clean slate if you have no events, as shown in Figure 3-13.

4. **Click Create Event.**

   The Step 1 Create Event page appears, as shown in Figure 3-14.

Figure 3-13:
Adding
an event
to your
Facebook
page.

Figure 3-14:
Just the
facts,
ma'am.

5. **Enter the event information.**

The minimum required information is the event title. Add a street address or a URL if the event is online. Enter the starting and ending time as well.

6. **Click Create Event.**

The Step 2 Add Details page appears, as shown in Figure 3-15.

7. **Fill in the event details.**

You can upload a picture, choose an event category, add a description, choose event options, and more.

8. **Click Save and Continue.**

The dialog box labeled Publish to This Page's Wall and Fans' Home Pages? appears. From this dialog box, you publish the event information to your fans' wall feed.

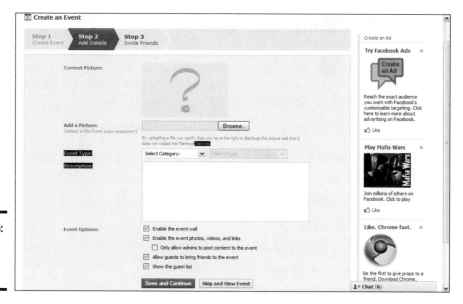

Figure 3-15:
Adding
event
details.

9. **Click Publish.**

   The Step 3 Invite Friends page appears. Choose the friends you want to invite to the event and add a personal message.

10. **Click Send Invitations.**

   Your invitations are sent, and the event is published.

Using the Facebook blog

You can post to the Facebook blog, but you may also find it a useful tool for finding information about Facebook. You can also search the blog for posts of interest. Facebook members can post comments to blog posts. If you're interested in seeing what's new on Facebook, fire up your favorite Web browser and navigate to `http://blog.facebook.com`.

Using the Discussions Tab

A discussion is another powerful way to create some lively banter on your group page. For example, if you've created a group about digital photography, you can start a discussion about which image-editing application filters are best for enhancing images.

You can create a discussion by following these steps:

1. **Log in to Facebook and navigate to your business page.**

2. **Click the Discussions tab.**

   The Discussions tab appears.

3. **Click Start New Topic.**

   The Start New Topic page appears (see Figure 3-16).

4. **Enter a topic for the discussion.**

5. **Enter text for the post.**

   An interesting question is a good way to pique the interest of your page visitors.

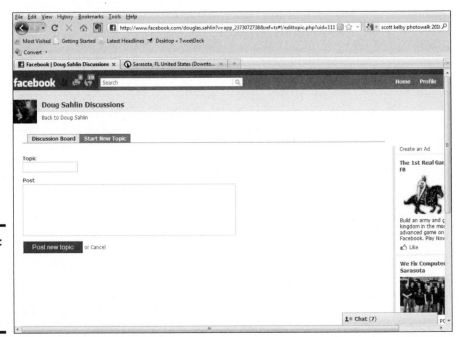

Figure 3-16: Adding a discussion to your Facebook page.

6. **Click Post New Topic.**

The topic is displayed by topic title at the top of the Discussions tab. To view a topic, visitors click the link to display the topic, display any already posted replies, and add their own (see Figure 3-17).

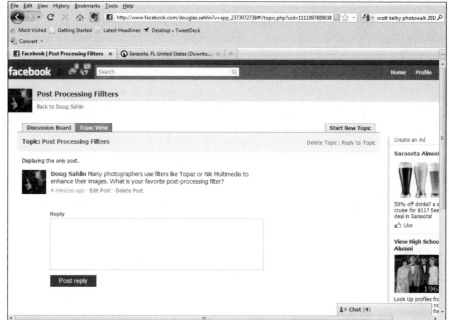

Figure 3-17:
Visitors can view and reply to your discussion topics.

If you give people who like your page the right to post to it, they can start a discussion by clicking the Discussions tab and following the steps outlined in this section. You can reply to topics posted by people by selecting the topic, reading their post, and then clicking the Reply button. You can manage topics by clicking the Edit Page links and then clicking Edit in the Discussion Boards section, which is in the Applications setting.

Using Facebook Tools and Applications

Facebook has a tool or an application for just about every need. For example, to find out what your fans think about a piece of information you can use in your marketing, you can create a Facebook poll — and you know how pointed a poll can be. You can create custom tabs on your Facebook business page, which enables you to do things like add copy from your blog to a tab, embed hosted videos in a tab, and more. In the next sections, we explore some of the most useful applications available for Facebook.

Creating a Facebook poll

You're creating new marketing material, and you have ideas about the information you should include. But you can also easily consider ideas from your Facebook fans by creating a Facebook poll.

To create a Facebook poll, follow these steps:

1. Log in to Facebook and navigate to your business page.

2. Navigate to the following URL:

   www.facebook.com/apps/application.php?id=138079047824&ref=ts

   The Poll Daddy Polls page appears, as shown in Figure 3-18. If you haven't added this application to your profile, you see an option to do so. Choose the applicable button before advancing to Step 3.

3. Click the Create a New Poll tab.

   The Create a New Poll page appears, as shown in Figure 3-19.

4. Enter a question for your poll.

   Create a question that suits your business.

5. (Optional) Select the Add Image check box.

   Selecting this option reveals a text field and a Browse button. Click the button to upload an image from your hard drive. You know the drill.

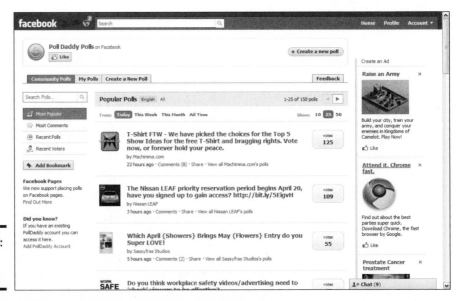

Figure 3-18:
Creating a poll.

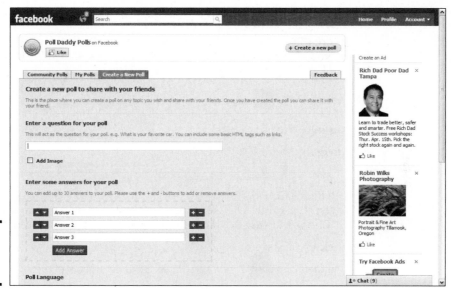

Figure 3-19:
Filling in the
blanks.

6. Enter the answers for your poll.

The default number of answers is three, but you can add additional
answers by clicking Add Answer.

**7. In the Poll Language section, choose a language from the drop-down
menu.**

**8. From the drop-down menu, choose an option in the Just for Friends or
Everyone? section.**

Accept the default answer and make your poll public.

9. Choose an option in the section Where Do You Want to Post This Poll?

You can post the poll to your wall, which is your private profile, to a
Facebook group to which you belong, or to a Facebook page you've
created. If you choose the second or third option, a drop-down menu
appears, from which you make a choice. The following steps show you
how to publish the page to your wall.

10. Click Next Step.

The Post To Wall box appears, as shown in Figure 3-20. You also have
the option to add a link on your page profile wall. The information you
enter in the text field shows up on your wall as the poll title.

Figure 3-20:
Publishing
the poll.

11. **Click Publish.**

Your poll is published.

You can follow up on your poll at any time by logging in to Facebook and navigating to the Poll Daddy Polls page. Click the My Polls link to see how people who took your poll voted.

Adding your blog to Facebook

If you write informative posts for a blog that would be useful for people who like your Facebook page, you can easily add your posts to your page. Then you don't have to write the same material for two different venues.

To import your blog into Facebook, follow these steps:

1. **Log in to Facebook and navigate to your business page.**

Your business page appears in your Web browser.

2. **Navigate to the Notes application.**

It's at www.facebook.com/apps/application. php?id=23474718568.

The Notes page opens, as shown in Figure 3-21. Your blog appears by way of the Notes application.

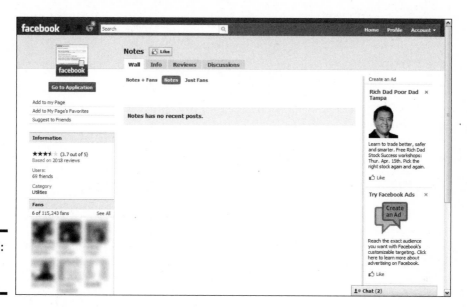

Figure 3-21:
The Notes fan page.

3. **Click the Add to My Page link.**

   A dialog box appears asking you the page to which you want to add the application to.

4. **Click Add to My Page next to the avatar for your fan page, and then click Close.**

   The application is added to your page, and the dialog box disappears into deep cyberspace.

5. **Navigate back to your fan page.**

6. **Click Edit Page and then scroll until you see the Notes app.**

7. **Click Edit.**

   The Notes settings appear (see Figure 3-22).

8. **Click the Import a Blog link.**

   The Import a Blog dialog box appears.

9. **Enter the URL to your blog's RSS feed in the Website Link field. See Figure 3-23.**

   You can find this information by clicking the orange RSS feed icon on your blog page. If you don't syndicate your blog, turn to Book II, Chapter 1 to find out how.

Figure 3-23:
Yet another
dialog box.

10. **Select the check box that tells Facebook you have the right to post the content and that the content isn't illegal or obscene.**

11. **Click the Start Importing link.**

    A preview of your latest blog post appears, as shown in Figure 3-24.

Figure 3-24:
A preview
of your blog
post.

12. **Click the Confirm Import button.**

    Your blog is imported, and the Notes application is ready to grace your page.

To display your blog directly on your page, add a Notes tab. Click the plus sign (+) next to the last tab and then choose Notes from the drop-down menu. Your blog posts appear on the Notes tab on your wall, with the newest posts appearing at the top of the page.

You can use the Networked Blogs application (apps.facebook.com/ blognetworks) to follow syndicated blogs. This app can be added as a tab on your Facebook business page. You can follow as many as five blogs. You can also add your blog to the network and follow it with the application. The application doesn't post the feeds of blogs you follow — it shows buttons for each blog you follow. Visitors to your page click the button, which opens the feed on the Networked Blogs page.

Creating a custom tab for your business page

When you use Facebook to market yourself or your business, you want to put your best foot forward. When people visit your Facebook page, the default view is the wall. People who like your page can glean information from your words of wisdom, but if you have a lot of interaction with them, the wall can be a busy place. Rather than let fans land on your wall, you can create a custom tab that tells them about you or your business, similar to the home page of your Web site. Furthermore, you can use Facebook options to have your custom tab appear whenever someone visits your page.

To create a custom tab, follow these steps:

1. **Log in to Facebook and navigate to the following URL:**

    `www.facebook.com/home.php#!/apps/application.php?id=4949752878&ref=ts`

    The Static FBML page appears, as shown in Figure 3-25. The Static FBML application lets you enter Hyper Text Markup Language (HTML) or Facebook Markup Language (FBML). If you know how to use HTML, you can write the code in the Static FBML application to insert images and text on a tab.

2. **Click the Add to My Page link.**

    A dialog box listing your Facebook pages appears.

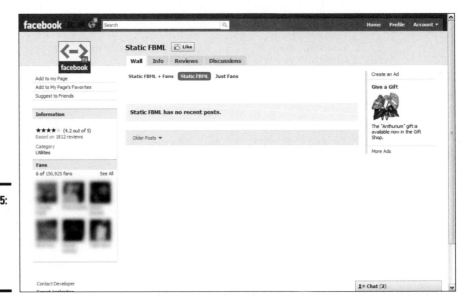

Figure 3-25:
The first step to create a custom page.

3. **Click Add to Page next to the avatar for the page for which you're creating a custom tab and then click Close.**

   The application is added to your page.

4. **Navigate to your fan page.**

5. **Click the Edit Page link.**

   The options you can edit appear.

6. **Scroll down until you see the text *Static FBML* and then click Edit.**

   The Edit FBML page appears.

7. **Enter the title of your custom tab in the Box Title field, and then enter
the page text in HTML format in the FBML field.**

   If you don't know HTML, ask your Web designer for help.

   Figure 3-26 shows the HTML to insert an image in the Static FBML
   application.

8. **Click the Save Changes button.**

   Your changes are saved.

9. **Click the link to return to your main page.**

   The link has the page name and is in the upper left corner of the
   dialog box.

Figure 3-26:
Editing the
Static FBML
application.

10. **Click the plus sign (+) icon and choose the name you gave to the Static FBML application in Step 7.**

The tab appears on your page. At this stage, you can drag the tab to a different position. However, the Wall and Info tabs always appear before any other tabs. A tad more work is required to make this tab the default option that everyone sees when they land on your Facebook wall.

11. **Click the Edit Page Link.**

The editable settings appear.

12. **Click Edit in the Wall Settings section.**

The section expands and shows the options you can modify, as shown in Figure 3-27.

13. **Choose a tab from the Default Landing Tab for Everyone Else drop-down menu.**

Visitors to your business page now see your custom tab, shown in Figure 3-28.

Figure 3-27: Editing Wall settings.

You can create other custom tabs by using the Static FBML application. Follow these steps:

Figure 3-28:
A custom
landing tab.

Doug Sahlin

Doug Sahlin has been an avid photographer since he was a child. He started his exploration into the world of shadow and light with a box camera capturing images of friends, family, and nature. As a young man, he purchased a 35mm camera and honed his craft, creating award winning photographs of landscapes and seascapes in Florida. In the past 5 years, he has written 15 books on web design, graphic, and image editing applications, co-authored 2 books on Photoshop, and co-authored 1 book on digital video. Many of his books have been best sellers at Amazon.com. While working on his books, Doug has produced commercial photographs of automobile races, fashion models, actors, authors, products, landscapes, architecture and food for his clients. His work has taken him from coast to coast, North to South, and has been seen in print and on the web.

1. **From the Wall tab of your business page, click Edit Page.**

The list of options you can edit appears.

2. **Scroll down to the custom tab you created with the Static FBML application.**

3. **Click Edit.**

The settings for the custom tab you just created appear.

4. **Click Add Another FBML box from the bottom of the dialog box.**

FBML 1 appears beneath the custom tab you just created.

5. Click Edit and follow Steps 7 through 13 in the previous step list.

The custom tabs you create with the Static FBML application appear in the Boxes tab. Click the plus sign (+) to the right of the last tab and choose Boxes. Click the Pencil icon to edit your tab. Choose Move to Wall to move the custom tab to the left column on the wall.

Finding other Facebook applications

Facebook has a plethora of applications, some created by Facebook and some created by third parties. In this chapter, we cover only the tip of the proverbial iceberg. You can explore other applications that may be suited for your business page by following these steps:

1. **Log in to your Facebook account and then navigate to your business page.**

2. **Click Edit Page.**

   A list of settings you can edit appears.

3. **Scroll to the bottom of the page and then, in the More Applications section, click Browse More.**

   A treasure trove of Facebook applications appears, as shown in Figure 3-29.

4. **Scroll the applications. When you see one you like, click the icon and then add the application to your page.**

Figure 3-29: Exploring other Facebook applications.

Creating a Custom URL for Your Business Page

You can create a custom URL for your fan page when you accumulate more than 25 fans. A custom URL is like branding, because it has the page name associated with it. You can send the custom URL as part of your e-mail signature and use it with your other social media. For example, it's much easier to use www.facebook.com/mypage rather than http://www.facebook.com/#!/profile.php?id=100000152015309.

To create a custom URL for your business page, follow these steps:

1. **Log in to Facebook and navigate to www.facebook.com/username.**

   If you've set up a personal page and you have more than 25 friends, a message box indicates that your username has been set. You also see an option to set a username for your business pages, as shown in Figure 3-30.

Figure 3-30:
Creating a custom URL for your page.

2. **Click the Set a Username link for your pages.**

   The section labeled Each Page Can Have a Username appears.

3. **Choose from the drop-down menu the page for which you want to set a custom username, as shown in Figure 3-31.**

Figure 3-31:
Creating a custom username for your page.

4. **Enter a username and then click the Check Availability button.**

   If the name is available, a message box appears and says so. Follow the prompts to specify the custom username. You can then use the custom username to direct people to your page.

Chapter 4: Analyzing Facebook Metrics

In This Chapter

✔ Analyzing your business page response

✔ Analyzing your group response

✔ Spotting trends

You've created a spiffy Facebook page and added a couple of bells and whistles to it, and you've posted religiously to your page and interacted with the people who like your page. Now it's time to see the fruits your efforts have yielded. Unless you have time on your hands, you know that your marketing efforts are paying off. You probably use Facebook as part of a much larger marketing effort. Therefore, you *must* know which form of social media is giving you the most bang for your buck. You may not think you're spending money on social media, because most of it's free. But you are spending time. And time is money.

In this chapter, we show you some ways to measure the effectiveness of your Facebook page.

Checking Referrals from Web Sites

One of your goals is probably to drive more traffic to your Web site. If your Web hosting service has a service that can track where your Web site traffic is coming from, you can use this service to see how much of it is from Facebook. Check with your Web hosting service for additional information.

If you have a Google account and you've enabled Google Analytics for the Web sites you want to track, you can use this service to see how many referrals are a result of your Facebook activity. Follow these steps:

1. **Log in to Google Analytics.**

2. **Select the Web site you want to monitor from the View Reports drop-down menu.**

3. **Click Traffic Sources.**

   When the page refreshes, you see a graph measuring visits to your Web site.

4. **Click All Traffic Sources.**

   When the page refreshes, you see a list of sources that generated visits to your Web site.

5. **Enter** Facebook **in the Filter Source/Medium text box using the default Containing parameter.**

   The page refreshes and shows you the number of visits resulting from Facebook.

We talk more about Google Analytics in Book VIII, Chapter 1.

Monitoring Post Comments

The easiest way to know how well your message is received is the number of comments left in individual posts. If you write a post that strikes a chord with the people who like your page, you receive a lot of comments. Let's face it: You can't please everybody. Some comments are good, and some are bad.

When your post receives lots of good comments, it's a sign that you're getting the right message to the people who like your page. When you receive positive comments on a post, think of similar subjects to write about or expand on the subject in future posts.

A Facebook post has a limited number of characters. To keep your fans coming back for more, break a popular subject into several small tidbits.

When you receive negative comments, analyze them carefully. See whether the fan disagrees with your point of view — or offers a spirited alternative. In the former case, refrain from creating posts about similar topics. If the latter is true, think about writing similar posts that will engage a lively conversation with the people who like your page. Sometimes it pays to spice things up a bit.

Consider also your original goals for setting up a Facebook business page: Ask yourself whether the quality of interaction from your fans is at the level you expected and whether posted comments are positive and generate visits to your Web site. See the earlier section "Checking Referrals from Web Sites" to find out how to measure Facebook traffic to your Web site.

You can also gain some insight from whatever prompts the largest amount of commenting and feedback. If you're a photographer who hears lots of "oohs" and "aahs" about your photos, for example, continue uploading them. If you're an instructor and your instructional videos receive lots more feedback than your written posts, you're doing the right thing. Analyze which types of posts are prompting comments and then consider the type of work you do or product you sell.

Measuring Link Effectiveness

When you add a link to a post, you may be tempted to type the whole URL into the message box. However, unless you dig deep into your Web site analytics, you have no way of knowing whether the Web site visit came from Facebook or another form of social media or was generated by search engine results.

The solution is a unique URL through bit.ly for your Facebook posts that you can easily track. (See Book II, Chapter 1 for more information on bit.ly and other services that create short URLs.)

After you create a shortened URL and add it to a Facebook post, you can easily track the number of hits the link receives by following these steps:

1. **Open your favorite Web browser and navigate to `http://www.bit.ly`.**

2. **Enter the shortened URL in the address window followed by the plus sign (+).**

3. **Press Enter or Return.**

   The Web site returns statistics about the shortened URL, as shown in Figure 4-1.

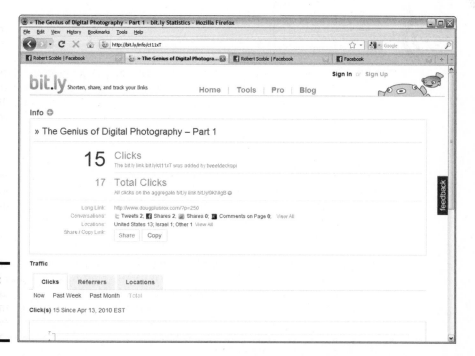

Figure 4-1:
Tracking a
shortened
URL.

Tracking Friend and Fan Requests

If you have a personal Facebook page, you acquire friends. It's almost the same as a popularity contest, and the late, great comedian George Carlin could have had a field day with the concept of Facebook friends. If you have a personal page, the trick is to turn your friends into people who like your Facebook page. To pump up your business page, increase the number of friends on your personal page and then invite them to like your business page. In return ask their friends to like your business page. The total number of friends and people who like your business page is known as your *reach*.

If people who like your page start bailing ship, figure out what you're doing wrong. Perhaps you're posting too often, or not posting enough. Another possible problem is the type of content you're posting. If lots of fans bail ship after you upload images or create a series of posts on a particular topic, it's time to cease and desist what you've been doing recently and return to the basics — the actions that you know work.

Here's another good metric to follow: If the number of people who like your page increases after uploading photos or videos, this type of material is stronger than your written posts are. You can find a lot of information from Facebook Insights, discussed in the later section "Using Facebook Insights."

Gathering Group Members

If you create a Facebook group, it goes without saying that having lots of group members can equate to having lots of people like your Facebook page. You can measure the impact a group has on your overall Facebook status by tracking how many group members end up becoming friends of your personal page and eventually liking your business page. If lots of friends of your personal page or people who like your business page become members of your group page when you create it, it indicates that you're putting out the right message and influencing people.

If you create a group about a popular subject, quite a few people will become members after searching for information about the subject. If you want these group members to eventually like your business page, follow these guidelines:

✦ Interact with group members and post frequently to the group.

✦ Encourage group members to participate, write posts on the wall, and upload photos, for example.

✦ Create a contest among group members to pump up interest.

Everything you do on Facebook — or, for that matter, in social media — dovetails. When you see a spike in group interaction, look for a corresponding spike in the number of new people who like your page. Your group can feed your business page and vice versa.

TIP

If you have a good following on Twitter, make sure your followers know about your group page. Whenever you post a new discussion there, or modify content, send a link in a tweet to your group page. Use the URL shortening service at `http://bit.ly`, and track the link as outlined in the earlier section "Measuring Link Effectiveness."

Using the Ads Manager

If you purchase ads on Facebook, you can gauge their effectiveness by the number of clicks they receive and then track this information too. Determining which of your multiple ads returns the most bang for your buck can become confusing, so Ads Manager comes to the rescue.

You can track virtually every conceivable statistic regarding your ad by following these steps:

1. **Log in to Facebook and navigate to your business page.**

2. **Click Edit.**

A list of the settings you can edit appears.

3. **Click Ads Manager.**

The Ads Manager appears, as shown in Figure 4-2.

4. **Click a link in the left column.**

You can change settings and view reports, billing information, and tracking information. The tracking information is especially helpful because it lets you see Web site activity resulting from someone clicking or seeing an ad.

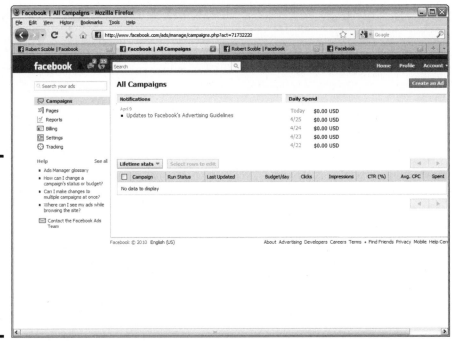

Figure 4-2:
The Ads Manager gives you pertinent information regarding your Facebook ad campaigns.

Using Facebook Insights

Facebook provides you with a method of tracking your business page activity. As the page owner, you have access to the Insights feature (located in the left column of your business page), which tells you how many people like and how much interaction they've had with your page.

To view detailed information about your business page, follow these steps:

1. **Log in to Facebook and navigate to your business page.**

2. **Scroll to the Insights box on the left side of the page and then click See All.**

    Information about your page appears, as shown in Figure 4-3, in the form of graphs.

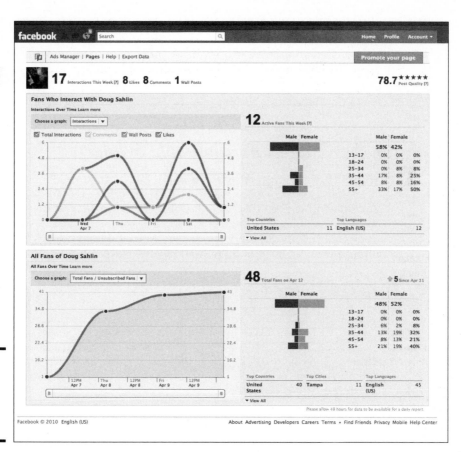

Figure 4-3:
Displaying
insights on
your fan
page.

You can find the following information in your Insight graphs:

✦ **A breakdown of activity during the previous week:** As time goes on, you see how many new subscribers you have and how many have unsubscribed. You also can see when a former subscriber decides to rejoin your ranks.

✦ **The number of interactions per post, the breakdown of active fans, and much more:** To analyze a specific metric, choose an option from the Choose a Graph drop-down menu.

✦ **A spike in the number of new fans:** When you see this type of activity, note the type of activity you posted on your fan page that day. If you posted about a new topic or uploaded a video or photo album, you know that your fans like this type of material.

Keep writing posts in this vein, or upload similar material to increase your fan base.

Making the Grade on Facebook Grader

The Web marketing company HubSpot has created Facebook Grader (`www.facebook.grader.com`), a free tool that shows you lots of information, including how you rank with other Facebook users. You simply enter the URL to your business page or enter a keyword or URL. The Web application looks for your page, analyzes certain data, and then posts a score along with other pertinent information, as shown in Figure 4-4.

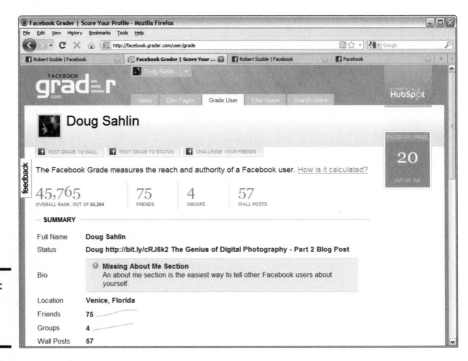

Figure 4-4: Did you make the grade?

Book VI

LinkedIn

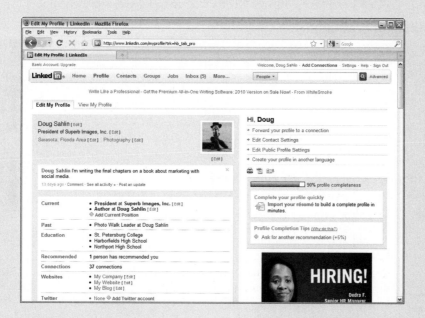

Contents at a Glance

Chapter 1: Getting Started with LinkedIn

We cover lots of different forms of social media in this book. Many social media networks are ideal for a business-to-consumer (B2C) business, but when you run a business that relies on other businesses for clients, or when you want to network with other professionals, LinkedIn is the answer.

Many business owners use LinkedIn in conjunction with other social media outlets, such as Twitter and Facebook. LinkedIn can be useful to you if you want to

✦ Network with professionals who are in your industry or supporting industries

✦ Touch base with your consumers and fuel the marketing fire

When you visit the LinkedIn site, you see a more utilitarian, albeit functional, site than Facebook or Twitter — similar to what you expect when you attend a business seminar: no frills and no bells or whistles. LinkedIn has just enough features to get the job done, and the job is to network with other business professionals to build a powerful network of professional allies who can augment, or add to, your marketing efforts.

In this chapter, we introduce you to LinkedIn and show you how to get connected.

Discovering the Benefits of LinkedIn

At the LinkedIn Web site (www.linkedin.com), you connect with other businesspeople. You can find a wide variety of professionals, from accountants to zoologists. That's what makes LinkedIn unique: You can connect with every conceivable profession and not run into a single teenager who's chatting about what she plans to do this weekend. The site is a no-nonsense, no-frills place to connect with business professionals.

If you've ever heard the theory that only six degrees of separation exist between yourself and any other person on the planet, LinkedIn proves this theory. If you need to connect with someone to further your profession or get a gig, all you have to do is look at the people you're connected to and get the word out. The people you're connected to are connected to other professionals, who are linked to other professionals, and so on. In theory, if you have connections on LinkedIn and you put out a request, eventually you can get connected to the person you need.

This list describes some LinkedIn features you can take advantage of:

+ **Create a professional profile:** When you join LinkedIn, you create a profile. Unlike on the other social media networks, your profile at LinkedIn is more similar to a résumé. Many professionals, in fact, use LinkedIn to find work or clients. You have a lot of leeway when you set up your profile on LinkedIn, as shown in Figure 1-1. You can add a picture, create a detailed bio, add links to your Web site, and much more.

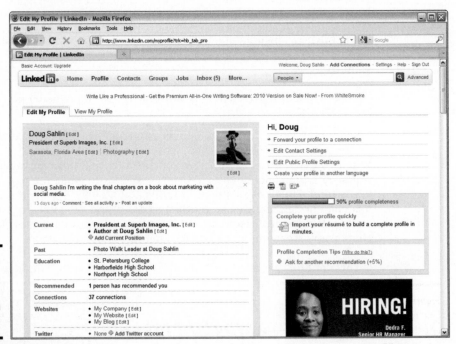

Figure 1-1: A LinkedIn profile resembles a résumé.

✦ **Expand your reach:** The theory behind LinkedIn is to create connections with people you know — *first-degree* connections. The people they're connected are *second-degree* connections, and the people connected to them are *third-degree* connections, and so on. When second- or third-degree connections are introduced to you by a first-degree connection, you can request that the person become one of your connections. That's how your LinkedIn network grows. If you pursue your LinkedIn network actively, it explodes and you have access to a wide variety of people who can help you in your quest.

✦ **Get recommended:** You can demonstrate your expertise on LinkedIn by being recommended by people who have used your services. You can also join groups and show your knowledge there. When you participate in a group, you can post a new thread in a discussion or comment on an existing thread. You can create your own discussions, too. Like other forms of social media, LinkedIn works best when you engage with the people to whom you're connected and actively seek new connections.

✦ **Keep status information up to date:** LinkedIn recently took on a Facebook-like look. An element that looks much like a Facebook news feed greets you when you visit the LinkedIn Web site, as shown in Figure 1-2. The feed is a wonderful way to see what your connections are up to. You can add your two cents by entering text in the Network Activity section and then clicking Share. Notice also the check box that lets you share the information on Twitter. In case you were wondering, LinkedIn Network Activity messages are limited to 140 characters, just as they are on Twitter.

Book VI Chapter 1

Getting Started with LinkedIn

Figure 1-2: Find out what your connections have been up to.

Determining whether LinkedIn is right for you

If you're looking for new retail customers, LinkedIn isn't the place to be. But if you're in one of the following categories, LinkedIn is the place for you:

+ Your company does business with other businesses.

+ You run a service that benefits busy professionals.

+ You network with other professionals in your industry and supporting industries.

   Be sure to join a group or follow a company that is a leader in your network to stay informed of the latest news in your industry.

LinkedIn has a wide variety of tools you can use to find other professionals. In fact, you can search for people before you even join LinkedIn, right on the home page, as shown in Figure 1-3. Notice that the entire LinkedIn member directory is available in alphabetical order. Click the link that corresponds to the first letter of the person's last name or, better, type the person's first and last names in the applicable text fields. You can also browse by country.

Figure 1-3:
Searching
for people
on LinkedIn.

At LinkedIn, you can control your online professional identity. If you're dealing with businesses in distant locales, the executive officers of potential clients or business partners can find out what they need to know by looking at your LinkedIn page. You fill the page with compelling information and links to your Web site and other online media.

The activity on LinkedIn isn't quite as frenetic as what you find on Twitter or Facebook. You set up a profile and maintain it. If you join groups, you're notified by e-mail whenever someone posts new information or adds a topic. Many businesspeople maintain identities on Facebook, LinkedIn, and Twitter and manage to be active in all groups without taking too much away from their busy days. If your goals are to network with other professionals and create business opportunities with other businesses, LinkedIn is a good place to be.

Taking a look at LinkedIn demographics

Becoming involved with any type of social media involves a commitment of time and energy. If the typical LinkedIn user doesn't fit the type of people you're trying to network with, you should expend your energy elsewhere. The demographics of LinkedIn at the time this book was written are listed in Table 1-1.

Table 1-1	LinkedIn Demographics
Demographic	*Percentage of Users*
Female	49
Male	51
Ages 13 to 17 years old	4
Ages 18 to 34 years old	27
Ages 35 to 49 years old	37
Age 50 or older	31
Caucasian	82
African American	6
Asian	7
Hispanic	4
Other	1
No kids 0 to 17	76
Kids 0 to 17	24
0 to $30,000	12
$30 to $60,000	19
$60 to $100,000	30
More than $100,000	39
No college	26
College	47
Graduate school	27

Setting Up a LinkedIn Account

If you've decided that LinkedIn is a community to which you want to belong, all you need to do is set up an account. When you set one up, you provide only basic information and then tweak your page and provide the information for your online presence.

To create a LinkedIn account, follow these steps:

1. **Launch your favorite Web browser and navigate to www.linkedin.com.**

The LinkedIn home page appears (refer to Figure 1-3).

2. **Enter your contact information.**

It's the usual Web stuff — first name, last name, e-mail address, and unique password (see Figure 1-4).

3. **Click Join Now.**

The Build Your Profile page appears. Click the link to confirm your e-mail address.

4. **Choose an option from the I Am Currently drop-down menu.**

The default option is chosen. You can also list yourself as working independently or looking for work or as a business owner or student.

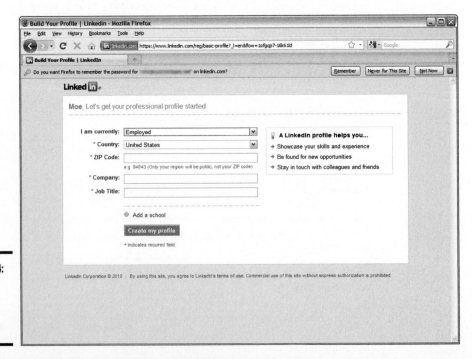

Figure 1-4:
Getting
linked
in with
LinkedIn.

5. **Choose a country from the Country drop-down menu.**

6. **Enter your zip code, company, and job title.**

   This option is the default if you indicate in Step 4 that you're employed. If you choose one of the other options, enter your zip code and the industry in which you work. If more than one industry applies, choose the one associated with your profile or in which you have the most expertise.

7. **(Optional) Click the plus sign (+) icon next to Add a School.**

   This option is available if you are a student. It displays the College/University text field. You can enter this information now or while setting up your LinkedIn profile.

8. **Click the Create My Profile button.**

   The See Who You Already Know on LinkedIn page appears.

9. **Choose an option for an e-mail server.**

   If your e-mail server is at your company's Web domain, skip this step because it applies only to e-mail servers such as Yahoo! and Gmail. After you choose an e-mail service, you click a button to log in to your e-mail service. LinkedIn compares the e-mail addresses in your address book and then notifies you when one of your correspondents is on LinkedIn.

10. **Complete the process of checking to see whether any of your recipients is a member of LinkedIn, or click Skip This Step.**

    A message appears, asking you to check your e-mail for a confirmation message from LinkedIn.

11. **Open your e-mail from LinkedIn and click the link to confirm your e-mail address.**

From your confirmation e-mail, you also have the opportunity to

✦ **Build your network by finding contacts who are already on LinkedIn:** This is similar to Step 9 in the preceding step list, but in a different dialog box, as shown in Figure 1-5.

✦ **Import a contacts file from Apple Mail or Outlook or another format:** The files must have the extension .csv (comma-separated values), .txt (text file), or .vcf (vcard file). You can find out more about importing contacts from your desktop e-mail by clicking the Learn More link.

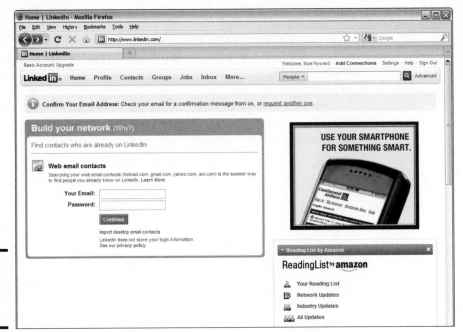

Figure 1-5:
Building
your
network.

Setting Up Your LinkedIn Profile

After you create a LinkedIn account, you have a bare-bones profile. Your success on LinkedIn depends on how well you set up your profile and how thoroughly you fill out the information. Many people set up a rigid profile that looks like it was written by a robot — no personality at all.

Set up a useful profile that tells visitors to your public profile and your contacts everything they should know about you. Write your profile in a manner similar to creating a 30-second elevator pitch. In other words, make it short, sweet, and to the point but compelling enough to show people what you're all about and what you do.

Look at the profiles of others in your industry to form an idea of what to include in your profile.

To set up your profile, follow these steps:

1. **Create a new account, as outlined in the earlier section "Setting Up a LinkedIn Account."**

When you complete the final step, you see a page with options to build your network by way of e-mail (refer to Figure 1-5). Notice the welcome message followed by your name at the top of the page.

2. **Click your name.**

   Your profile page appears, as shown in Figure 1-6. It's blank except for the titles for the information you provide.

3. **Click Add Photo.**

   The Upload a Photo page appears. Click Browse, navigate to the image, and then click Upload Photo. You can upload a GIF, JPG, or PNG file. The file size limit is 4MB. Use a professional-looking photo, preferably a head-and-shoulders portrait on a plain background.

4. **Fill in the What Are You Working On text field.**

   In this brief description of your current project, you're telling your connections, in essence, what you're doing in regard to your business. You can update this section as often as you want, and this information appears in the Network Activity section, along with other updates from people you're connected to.

5. **Add your employment information and click the Save Changes button.**

   Click the Current link to enter information about your current position or the Past link to enter information about your previous positions. You can add as many past positions as you want. However, try to limit this section to your current position and the past two previous positions.

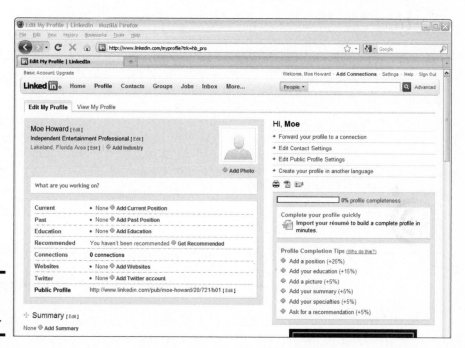

Figure 1-6:
Setting up
your profile.

6. Click Add Education.

The Add Education tab appears, as shown in Figure 1-7.

7. Enter the required information and click the Save Changes button.

If you joined any societies while in school or did something special, be sure to note them in the Activities and Societies section. If you achieved any outstanding recognition, such as making the dean's list or if you received any awards, be sure to note this information in the Additional Notes section.

At this stage, you can find some recommendations. But unless you have some contacts, it's a moot point. We show you how to get recommendations in the "Getting Recommended" section, later in this chapter.

8. Click the Add Websites link.

The Additional Information page appears, as shown in Figure 1-8.

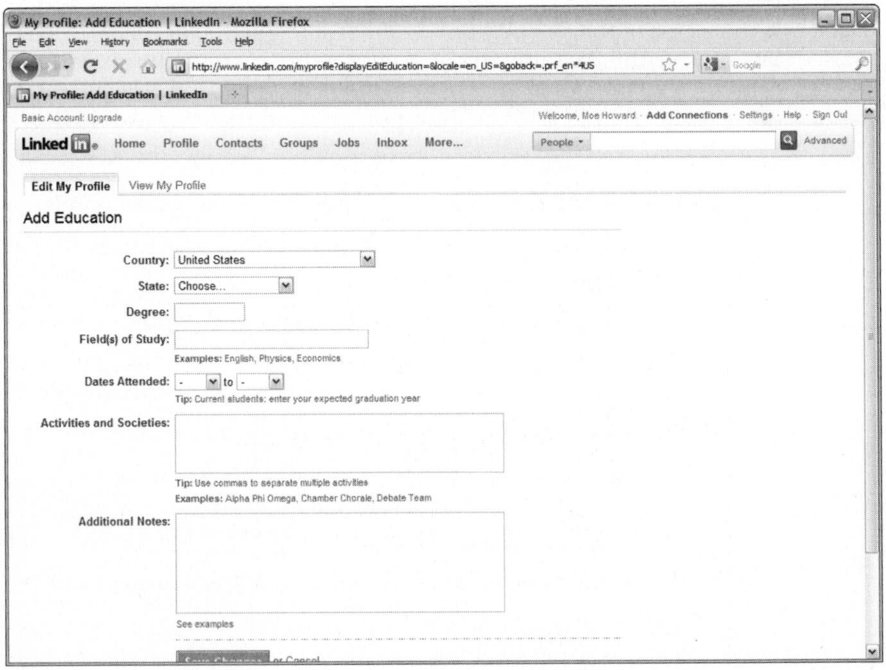

Figure 1-7:
Adding your education information.

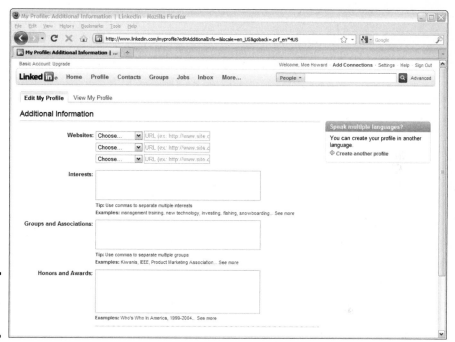

Book VI
Chapter 1

Getting Started with
LinkedIn

Figure 1-8:
Adding your
Web sites.

9. Choose an option from the Websites drop-down menu.

You can choose from My Website, My Company, My Blog, My RSS Feed, My Portfolio, or Other.

10. Enter the URL of each Web site with which you're associated.

You can add as many as three URLs on your LinkedIn profile. Choose an option for each URL from the drop-down menu, as described in Step 9.

11. Enter information in the Interests text field.

This step tells people the topics you're interested in. Choose topics related to your business or business goals. Refrain from entering any personal interests, such as snowboarding, macramé, or basket-weaving.

12. Enter information in the Groups and Associations text field.

Enter any business groups or associations to which you belong, such as local networking groups or Toastmasters. This information tells more about your business goals and the type of activities you do to support your business.

13. **Enter information in the Honors and Awards text field and click Save Changes.**

This information concerns honors and awards you've received that are related to your business. For example, if you're a sales professional and you were Salesperson of the Year, include the information here.

14. **(Optional) To connect Twitter to LinkedIn, click the Add Twitter Account button.**

You're not in LinkedIn any more, Dorothy. You're in the land of Twitter, as shown in Figure 1-9.

15. **Enter your Twitter username and password and then click Allow.**

You're redirected to LinkedIn, as shown in Figure 1-10.

16. **Choose an option.**

Choose to share all tweets with your connections or only tweets with the `in` hashtag (`#in`). If your tweets aren't all discreet, the latter option is wonderful. That way, whatever happens on Twitter stays on Twitter.

17. **Click Save.**

Your Twitter posts are now shared on your profile, as shown in Figure 1-11.

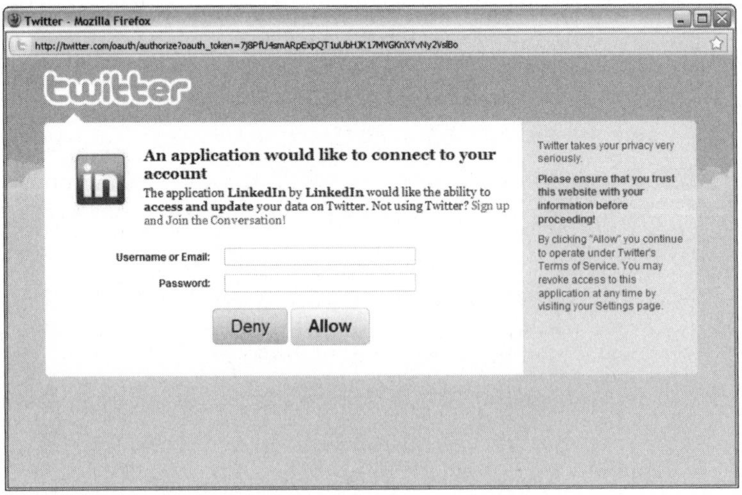

Figure 1-9: Allowing Twitter to link to your LinkedIn profile.

Figure 1-10:
Telling LinkedIn which tweets to post to your profile.

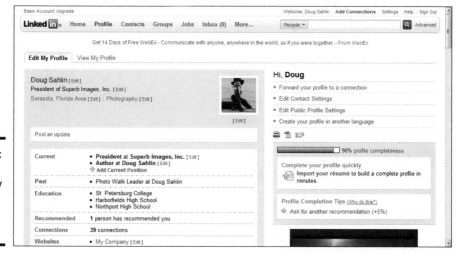

Figure 1-11:
Tweets now display on your LinkedIn profile.

These steps add lots of meat to your profile, but you can do more to beef up your profile. Click the Edit My Profile link, and scroll to the bottom of the page to add the following information to your page:

✦ **Personal Information:** If you want people to be able to get in touch with you, navigate to the Personal Information section, where you can add your phone number, address, instant messaging (IM) information, birth-date, and marital status.

✦ **Contact Settings:** Edit this section to tell people on LinkedIn how you want to be contacted, as shown in Figure 1-12. You can specify the type of messages you accept and your opportunity preferences, and leave a bit of advice to those who attempt to contact you. Completing this sec-tion alleviates a lot of contact requests from people you may not want to be in contact with.

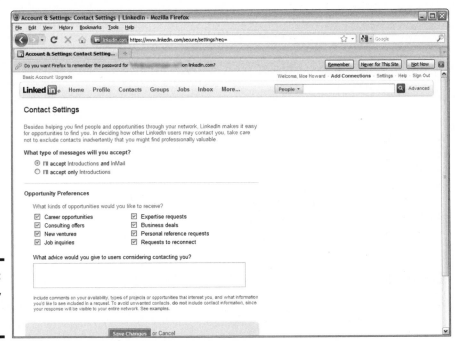

Figure 1-12:
Contact me,
but on my
terms.

✦ **Account Settings:** In this area, you have a plethora (one of Doug's favor-ite words) of options you can change. To change your account settings, click the Settings link to open your Account page, as shown in Figure 1-13. From there, you can

• Edit your profile

• Change your account picture

- Manage your recommendations
- Monitor your feed visibility

As your marketing goals and the type of people you want to be in contact with change, you can change your account settings and profiles to match your current needs. Notice also the option to upgrade your account. In essence, you pay LinkedIn for additional features. Explore this topic at your leisure.

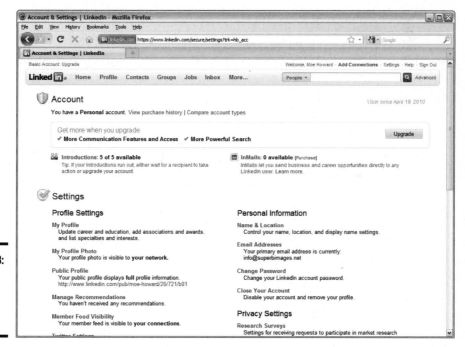

Figure 1-13:
Changing your account settings.

Getting Connected on LinkedIn

LinkedIn is all about getting connected. After you set up your profile and fine-tune it, it's time to start connecting with the type of people whom you can network with, use as mentors, and use as business partners, for example. You can find people you know who are already on LinkedIn, or send an invitation to colleagues to join LinkedIn. LinkedIn calls these people *connections.*

To get connected on LinkedIn, follow these steps:

1. **Log in to LinkedIn.**

Your profile appears.

2. **Choose Add Connections from the Contacts drop-down menu.**

   The Import Contacts and Invite page appears, as shown in Figure 1-14.

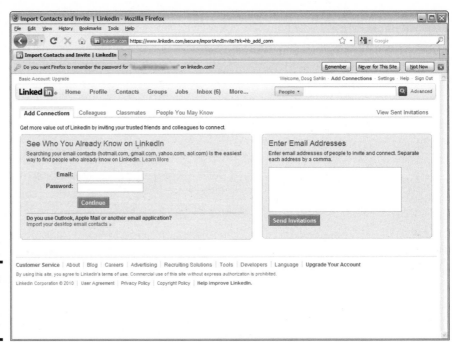

3. **Enter your e-mail address and password. Click Continue.**

   This option works if you use an e-mail service such as Yahoo! or Gmail. When you click Continue, you see a list of people from your address book who are on LinkedIn. You can pick and choose the ones with whom you want to connect.

4. **In the Enter Email Addresses text box, enter the e-mail addresses of the people with whom you want to connect.**

   Each e-mail address must be separated by a comma.

5. **Click the Send Invitations button.**

   A message appears at the top of the page, telling you that the messages have been sent. Your recipients may not be members of LinkedIn, but they receive an invite nonetheless.

6. **Click Colleagues.**

   The Colleagues page appears. If colleagues from any of the places you've worked at are on LinkedIn, you see them on this page. A button appears for each place you've listed in the Employment section of your profile as long as people from that company are on LinkedIn. Click the link and follow the prompts to connect with people with whom you've worked.

7. Click the Classmates link.

The Find Past or Present Classmates page appears, as shown in Figure 1-15, with a link from every academic institution you list on your profile.

8. Click a school link.

A list of people who are on LinkedIn and attended your school appears.

9. Click the Invite link next to the person's name to invite him to become a LinkedIn connection.

10. Continue to invite additional contacts from your schools.

11. Click the People You May Know link.

A list of people that LinkedIn thinks you may know appears, using an algorithm that only LinkedIn understands.

12. If you find a person to whom you'd like to connect, click Connect.

The Invite *Person's Name* to connect on LinkedIn dialog appears.

13. Choose an option from the How do you know <person's name>? list.

Your options are: Colleague, Classmate, We've done business together, Friend, Other, or I don't know <person's name>.

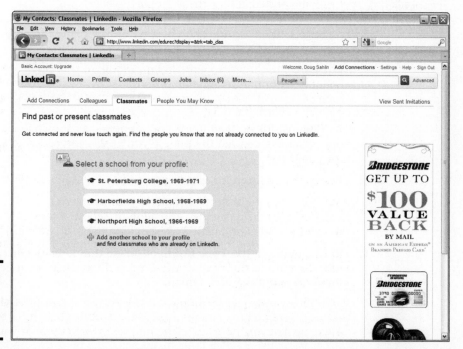

Figure 1-15:
Connecting
with former
classmates.

14. **(Optional) Fill in the personal note section.**

This can be used as a memory jogger if you haven't contacted the person in years.

15. **Click Send Invitation.**

Your invitation to connect is sent.

Getting Recommended

As you add information to your nearly completed profile, a percentage is listed on the right side of your profile, and a progress bar. As you add more information to your profile, it becomes more complete and becomes an effective business tool for networking with other professionals.

If you add recommendations to your profile, you increase the chances of connecting with like-minded businesspeople. You receive recommendations from people you know and with whom you have done business.

Getting recommendations is a two-step process: Ask for one, and then accept it.

Asking for recommendations

To get recommended, follow these steps:

1. **Log in to LinkedIn and then choose Edit My Profile from the Profile drop-down menu.**

Your LinkedIn profile appears in Edit mode. At this stage, you have some connections but no recommendations.

2. **Click Get Recommended.**

The Request Recommendations tab appears, as shown in Figure 1-16. It's your chance to contact the people you've worked with and ask them to toot your horn.

3. **Choose the position for which you want to be recommended.**

If you've listed multiple positions on your profile, you find them on a drop-down list. You can also add a job or school if they don't appear on the list. Click the applicable link and fill in the form, Norm.

4. **Fill in a name in the Your Connections text box or by clicking the LinkedIn icon to the right of the field. Add as many connections as you need and then click Finish.**

If you choose the former method, a name appears, or names appear, as you start typing the connection's name. If you choose the latter method, a list of your connections appears in the Choose Connections dialog box. Click a connection's name to add him to the list. Add as many connections as you need and then click Finish.

5. Accept the default message, or modify it.

The generic message asks for a recommendation. You can modify it if you need to remind a connection of a specific job you did for her.

6. Click Send.

Your invitation is sent to your contact.

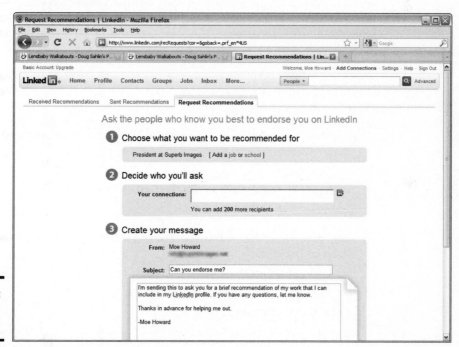

Figure 1-16:
Get recommended.

Accepting recommendations

After you ask for recommendations, you're bound to get one, if not several, recommendations. Recommendations don't automatically show up on your profile. You have to accept them, which gives you some power.

If you receive a lukewarm recommendation, you don't have to accept it. Ask your contact to send you a better one if you know her well.

When a contact sends you a recommendation, you're notified by e-mail. To accept a recommendation, follow these steps:

1. **Open the e-mail from LinkedIn that announces your recommendation.**

The message tells you which contact sent the recommendation and what it has to say.

2. **Click the button at the bottom of the message to display the recommendation.**

The recommendation is displayed on your profile.

Getting your first recommendation is exciting and does a lot to flesh out your LinkedIn profile. Get as many recommendations as you can, and make sure that the progress section of your profile shows 100 percent. Then you'll be well on your way to getting the most benefit from your time spent on LinkedIn.

Chapter 2: LinkedIn Nuts and Bolts

In This Chapter

↙ **Expanding your network**

↙ **Exploring LinkedIn features**

↙ **Sending and receiving messages**

↙ **Managing LinkedIn correspondence**

↙ **Joining a group**

↙ **Creating a group**

↙ **Becoming established as an expert**

After you set up your LinkedIn account and get connected, it's time to broaden your base and expand your network. That means getting connected to more professionals. In addition, you can join a group related to your industry. When you join a group, you're networking with more like-minded individuals who may or may not be contacts. When you join a group, it's like any other form of social media: You become part of the conversation. You can also flaunt your expertise within a group and use a group to add new connections to your profile.

When you start networking with people on LinkedIn, you receive messages and invitations to become connected with other professionals. You receive an e-mail notification whenever someone invites you to connect with them, sends you a message via LinkedIn, or posts a note on a group to which you belong.

In this chapter, we show you how to expand your network, join and create a group, and correspond with your contacts as well as manage your correspondence.

Expanding Your LinkedIn Network

After you make your initial connections, it's time to expand your network. Remember that each person to whom you're connected also has connections — connections you may not have. The easiest way to find new connections is to explore the connections you have and see whether they have any connections you should know.

Here are two ways to expand your network:

✦ **Ask for an introduction from someone you both know.** If you find an interesting person you don't know but who is connected to one of your connections, send a message to your connection asking for a virtual introduction.

✦ **Send a message directly.** Contact directly any contacts of people to whom you're connected — these people are two or three degrees from you. Send a message stating that you want to add him to your LinkedIn network; be sure to also mention the person you both have in common.

When you do the math, you can expand your network quickly by mining the gold that lies in second- and third-degree contacts. If a second- or third-degree contact doesn't accept your invitation, you've given it your best shot, which is better than no shot.

LinkedIn frowns on sending an invite to people you don't have a connection in common with. Be sure, before you send a message, that you have someone in common.

To mine the gold that lies in your second- and third-degree contacts, follow these steps:

1. **Log in to LinkedIn.**

   Your home page appears.

2. **Choose My Connections from the Contacts drop-down menu.**

   A list of your contacts appears with the person's avatar, a description, and the number of contacts he has, as shown in Figure 2-1.

3. **Examine the list and look for a contact who has lots of contacts.**

   First, choose the contacts you know well.

4. **Click the person's avatar.**

   Your contact's information appears on the right side of the browser window. You also see a link with the number of connections your contact has.

5. **Click the person's Connections link.**

   A list of your contact's contacts appears, as shown in Figure 2-2. The connections you share appear in the Shared Connections tab. The group you're interested in is All.

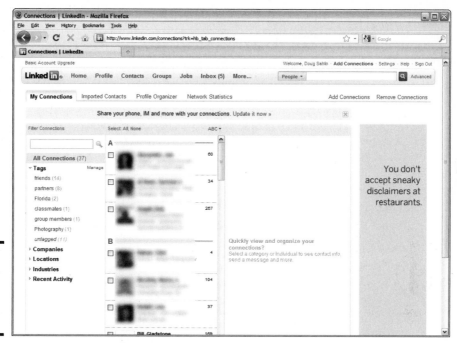

**Book VI
Chapter 2**

**LinkedIn Nuts
and Bolts**

Figure 2-1:
Mining gold
from your
contacts
list.

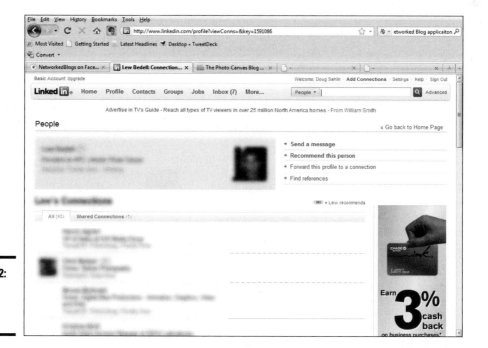

Figure 2-2:
Looking
for new
contacts.

6. Click the All tab and examine the people on this list.

Look for people you want to be connected to; perhaps people in the same or similar industries. For example, if you're a photographer and you're connected to a person who prints high-quality, fine art canvases, look for other photographers who are connected to her.

7. Click the name of a person to whom you might like to be connected.

The person's profile appears. A blue icon that says 2nd appears next to his name (see Figure 2-3). A list of options appears at the right side of his profile.

8. Choose an option.

You can

- Be introduced to the person by your contact
- Send the person a direct query
- Forward the profile to one of your connections
- Find *references,* or people in your network who have worked with the person whose profile you're perusing
- Save the person's profile

If you choose the option to connect to the person directly, a window opens with several options in it, as shown in Figure 2-4.

This icon identifies a second-degree connection.

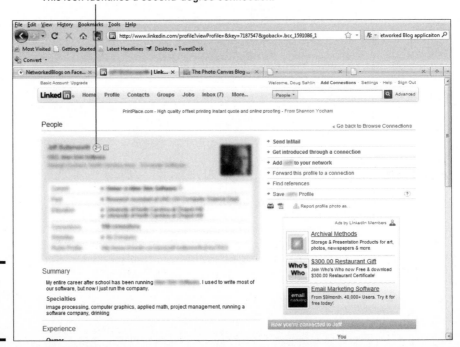

Figure 2-3:
Expanding your network.

**Book VI
Chapter 2**

**LinkedIn Nuts
and Bolts**

Figure 2-4:
Creating
a new
connection.

9. **Choose the option that best describes how you know the person.**

   If you don't know the person, choose this option and add a brief note.
   Remember to include the name of the person with whom you're connected.

10. **Click the Send Invitation button.**

   If you send the invitation to someone you don't know, a warning message appears. If you feel confident that your shared connection knows
   this person well, go ahead with the invitation. If you're at all unsure,
   however, you probably shouldn't send the connection. LinkedIn frowns
   on invading its members' privacy.

Interacting with Your LinkedIn Network

In Book VI, Chapter 1, we show you how to get connected to like-minded
people. Connections are your lifeblood on LinkedIn. As soon as you make
some connections, start communicating with them. The easiest way to start
is to post information on your profile. If you're on Facebook, this task is similar to posting on your wall. Remember that you have 140 characters to work
with if your account is connected with Twitter.

Because LinkedIn is a professional network, refrain from using too much shorthand when adding your posts. Shorthand is regarded as unprofessional. But shortening URLs is definitely a way to get the most benefit from a LinkedIn status update. Turn to Book II, Chapter 2 to find a URL-shortening service.

To update your status on LinkedIn, simply type your message in the Share an Update text field, just below your profile on your home page, as shown in Figure 2-5. You can write about your most current project or perhaps add some information about a new product or service your company is offering. You can add a link to your message.

When you add a link, using the bit.ly Web site (`http://bit.ly`) to shorten the link lets you track the number of clicks you get.

You may receive messages in return from your contacts regarding your messages. This process is similar to e-mail, but within the LinkedIn network. See the later section "Sending and receiving messages" for more information.

Figure 2-5:
Sharing information with your network.

Getting to Know LinkedIn Features

LinkedIn is a useful resource if you want to expand your network of professional contacts. All you need to do is get to know which features are available and use them to promote yourself or your business, or to make new professional contacts. The following sections highlight some of the LinkedIn features you may find useful.

Finding jobs on LinkedIn

You can look for a job on LinkedIn, and LinkedIn members can look for jobs posted by other LinkedIn members. To find a job on LinkedIn, follow these steps:

1. **Log in to LinkedIn.**

Your LinkedIn home page appears.

2. **Choose Find Jobs from the Jobs drop-down menu.**

The Jobs Home page appears, as shown in Figure 2-6.

Figure 2-6:
Looking for
a job on
LinkedIn.

3. **Enter some text in the Keywords field.**

   Enter keywords associated with the type of job you're looking for.

4. **Accept the default country name and postal code.**

   The country name and zip code are filled in by default based on your pro-file information. The default search is within 50 miles of your zip code.

5. **Click Search.**

   The page refreshes and shows results for your search, as shown in Figure 2-7. You find out more about an opportunity by clicking the link, which opens another page that gives you detailed information about the opportunity. You also have the option to apply for the job. If the person who posted the job is in your network, the second- or third-degree icon appears. If you see it, you can request a referral from the person who is your first-degree connection and who is connected to the person who posted the job opportunity.

If you didn't get the results you were after, you may have to call in the heavy artillery: Advanced Search. To perform an advanced jobs search, follow these steps:

1. **Log in to LinkedIn.**

   Your LinkedIn home page appears.

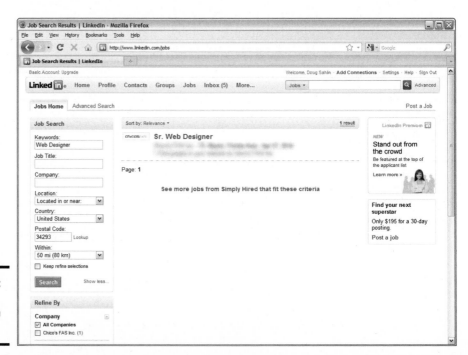

Figure 2-7:
Examining
the search
results.

2. **Choose Find Jobs from the Jobs drop-down menu.**

   The Jobs Home page appears.

3. **Click the Advanced Search tab.**

   The Advanced Search parameters appear.

4. **Enter some text in the Keywords field.**

   Describe the type of job you're looking for.

5. **Enter information in the Job Title and Company fields.**

   Fill in this optional information if you're looking for a specific position with a company. You can fill in both fields or either or none.

6. **Choose an option from the Functions list.**

   This step narrows your choices to a specific function within your field of expertise. For example, if you're a graphic artist, you can choose Art/Creative or Design.

7. **Choose an option from the Experience list.**

   Choose the option that applies to your level of expertise. If you've just finished school for a technical position, Internship may be the proper choice.

8. **Choose an option from the Industries list.**

   If your field of expertise can be used by several industries, you can limit the results to the industry in which you want to work.

9. **Choose an option from the When Posted section.**

   This option lets you choose from the most recent job postings or from older job postings.

10. **Click Search.**

    The page refreshes to show postings based on the parameters you specify.

Sending and receiving messages

LinkedIn helps you easily communicate with your contacts. You can send messages to your contacts and receive messages from them. When you send a message, your intended recipient is notified by e-mail, and you receive an e-mail whenever one of your contacts sends you a message.

To send a message on LinkedIn, follow these steps:

1. **Log in to LinkedIn and then choose My Connections from the Contacts drop-down menu.**

   A list of your connections appears in a neat little column.

2. Scroll down to the person to whom you want to send a message.

3. Click the person's icon.

The person's contact information appears in the column on the right, as shown in Figure 2-8.

Send a message to this contact.

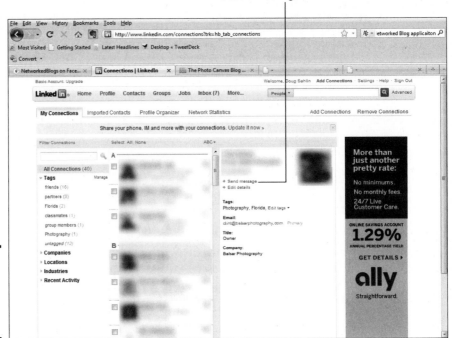

Figure 2-8:
Okay, I just gotta get a message to you.

4. Click the Send Message button.

The Compose Your Message dialog box appears, as shown in Figure 2-9. Note the icon to the right of the recipient's name. Click the icon to add recipients from your list of connections.

5. Enter a subject and write your message.

The dialog box even has spell-checking. If you misspell a word, a red, squiggly line appears beneath it.

6. Accept the default option to allow recipients to see each other's names and e-mail addresses.

If you deselect this option, you preserve the anonymity of the recipients to whom you send the message.

7. **(Optional) Select the Send Me a Copy check box.**

You guessed it — this step sends a copy to your inbox.

8. **Click Send.**

Whoosh! Your message is sent

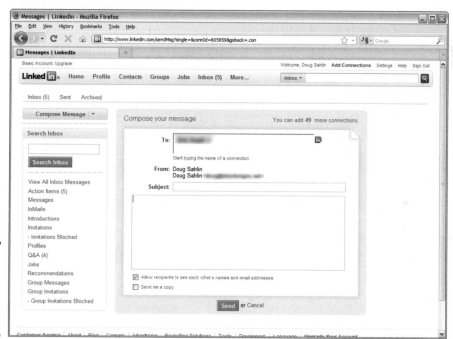

Figure 2-9:
Send me
your answer
and fill in a
form.

Managing invites and messages

LinkedIn lets you easily keep track of invites, introductions, and messages
by way of your inbox. You can react to invites and introductions, respond
to messages, and more. If you're a member of a group, or the creator of a
group, you can respond to messages in your inbox as well.

The tabs you see in your Inbox depend on your recent activity. If you have
pending invitations, you'll see a tab for that. You may also see a tab for
introductions you have been sent, Q&A if you've posted a question, Jobs, or
Group Messages, for example.

To manage your LinkedIn correspondence, follow these steps:

1. **Log in to LinkedIn.**

Your bright, shiny home page appears.

2. Click Inbox.

Your inbox opens, as shown in Figure 2-10. Notice the links on the left side of the Inbox.

3. Click a link to reveal all correspondence in that category.

4. Click a message.

The full message appears, as shown in Figure 2-11.

5. Click Reply.

If the message you received was sent to multiple recipients, you have the option to respond to the sender or to all. Either option opens the Compose Message dialog box.

6. Fill in the blanks and click Send.

You've replied to your mail.

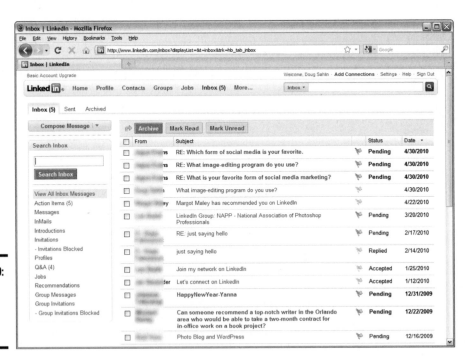

Figure 2-10:
Does your inbox floweth over?

Book VI
Chapter 2

LinkedIn Nuts
and Bolts

Figure 2-11:
Respondez,
s'il vous
plaît.

About LinkedIn Groups

LinkedIn is a diverse group of individuals spanning every possible profession. Many have created groups to discuss their professions or their companies. You also find groups of former alumni, nonprofit organizations, and more. For example, if you're a photographer who uses Canon lenses, you can join the Canon Users group to network with other photographers.

Joining a group

After you create some connections on LinkedIn, it's time to branch out and network with other professionals who have similar interests. A group is an excellent way to find other professionals who have similar interests.

When you decide to branch out and join a group, follow these steps:

1. **Log in to LinkedIn and then choose Groups Directory from the Groups drop-down menu.**

   The Groups Directory page appears, listing the featured groups, as shown in Figure 2-12.

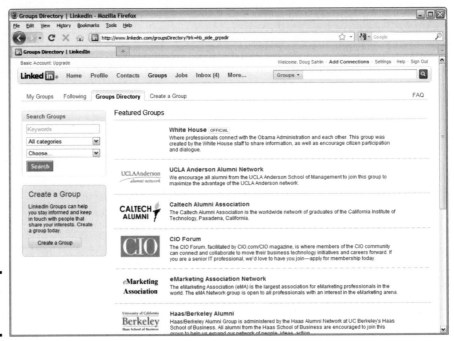

Figure 2-12:
Searching
for a group.

2. In the Search Groups directory, enter some keywords in the text field.

Enter logical keywords for the type of group you're searching for.

3. Choose an option from the Categories drop-down list.

You can choose from alumni groups, corporate groups, conference groups, or networking groups, for example.

4. Choose a language from the last drop-down list.

5. Click Search.

In a few seconds, some search results appear, as shown in Figure 2-13.

6. Scroll through the groups.

Each group has a description.

7. When you see a group you want to join, click the Join This Group link.

The Join Group page appears, as shown in Figure 2-14. This page has several options: Display the group logo on your profile, choose the e-mail address you use for contact from the group, or choose whether to receive a group digest, for example.

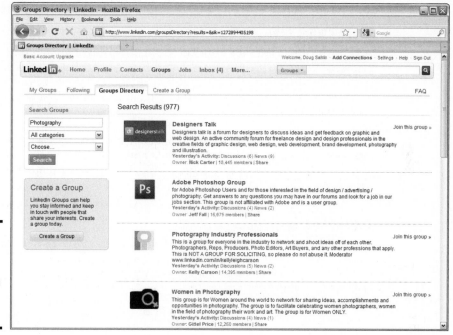

Figure 2-13:
Hmmm.
It's like
looking for a
needle in a
haystack.

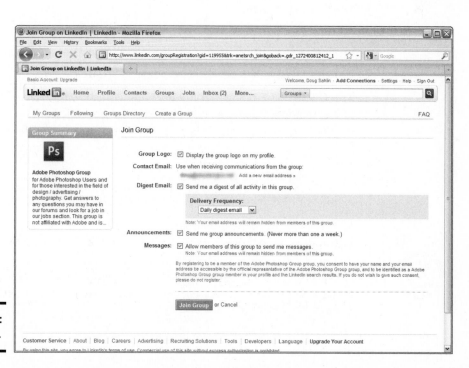

Figure 2-14:
Sign me up.

8. **Accept the default options, or change them to suit your preference.**

9. **Click the Join Group button.**

   The group is added to the My Groups section of your profile. Note that most LinkedIn groups require approval from the group owner. To send to the group owner a message explaining why you feel you would be an asset to the group, click the link that appears beneath the group in your My Groups section.

If you join more than one group, you can access all groups from the Groups tab. You can follow discussion threads and much more. Interacting with a group is a wonderful way to gain new contacts and learn more about your profession.

Creating a group

If you don't find a group you like, create one. As group owner, you have control over who joins the group, the type of group, and the logo that's displayed for the group, for example. You can also have a link to an external Web site for your group.

To create a group, follow these steps:

1. **Log in to LinkedIn.**

2. **Choose Create a Group from the Groups drop-down menu.**

   The Create a Group page appears, as shown in Figure 2-15.

3. **Click Browse.**

   The File Upload dialog box opens. Follow the prompts to upload an image from your hard drive to use as your group logo. You can upload an image with a file size of less than 100KB in the file formats GIF, JPEG, or PNG.

4. **Fill in the rest of the blanks.**

   This stuff is self-explanatory. The only thing you can't do is use LinkedIn as part of the group name. A red asterisk precedes required fields.

5. **Click the Create Group button.**

    Your group is created.

Here are some issues to consider when creating a group:

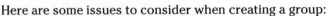

+ **The name is important.** Make sure that your group name has keywords that potential members would use to find your group.

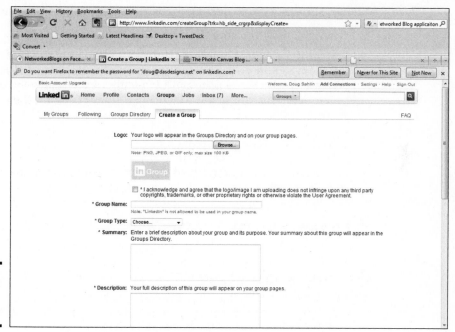

Figure 2-15:
Creating a
group.

✦ **Create a group about your industry.** People are less likely to join a group that's devoted to your company.

✦ **Create a custom logo for your group.** The area in which your logo is displayed is quite small. If your logo has too many objects, it's hard to see. If you aren't adept at using graphic design software, find someone who is and ask him to create your log.

✦ **Create a Web page devoted to your group.** Web space is cheap. You can either create a page on an existing Web site or reserve a domain name and create a site. If you create a site for the group, make sure to optimize it for search engines and include the URL to your LinkedIn group.

✦ **Display the group in the group directory and ask each member who joins to accept the option to display the group on their profile.** The added visibility helps your group stand out in the crowd.

After you create a group, it's time to find some members. Here are a few tips for promoting your group:

✦ **Spread the word by sending to all your connections a message inviting them to join your new group.** If you're a member of other groups, post a message to the other group members announcing your new group. Ask your contacts and fellow group members to spread the word as well.

✦ **Promote the group with your other social media.** Create a blog post announcing your new group and post a link on your Web site.

✦ **Invite industry experts to join your group and engage in the discussion.** If potential members see names they recognize, they're more likely to join your group.

✦ **Promote your group during any speaking engagements or webinars you participate in.**

Creating a discussion

After you join or create a group, you can peruse it to see any current discussions. If you see a discussion that piques your interest, you can add your two cents to the conversation by logging in to your group and clicking the Discussions tab. Click a discussion link to follow the discussion thread. You can choose to add your comment to the discussion and follow it.

Another alternative is to create your own discussion by following these steps:

1. **Log in to LinkedIn and choose My Groups from the Groups drop-down menu.**

A list of your groups appears.

2. **Click the icon of the group in which you want to start a discussion.**

The group's home page appears, as shown in Figure 2-16.

3. **Click the Start a Discussion link.**

The Start a Discussion page appears, as shown in Figure 2-17.

Figure 2-16:
This group
is your
group, this
group is my
group. . . .

Figure 2-17:
Starting a
discussion.

4. **Enter a topic or question in the first text box.**

   Be as concise as possible. Don't ask a general question. The more specific you can be, the livelier the discussion is.

5. **(Optional) Add details.**

   The devil is in the details, as they say. In this case, details direct the discussion and keep it on track. If you're unsure what type of information to enter here, review discussions in the group to which you want to post the discussion.

6. **Accept the default option to follow the discussion.**

   When you choose this option, you receive an e-mail notification whenever a group member adds a comment to the discussion.

7. **Click the Submit for Discussion button.**

   Your topic or question is submitted for discussion.

Establishing Yourself As an Expert

Let's face it: Social media is work. If you join a social media group and do next to nothing, you're wasting your time. Social media is all about the conversation. But you don't have to take a backseat in the conversation. Take the bull by the horns: Engage with your connections and group members.

Here's how to make the most of LinkedIn:

✦ **Start interesting conversation threads in any group you belong to.** If you own a group, make sure to post frequently and create posts that show your expertise. You can also create a discussion, as outlined in the earlier section "Creating a discussion."

✦ **Respond to questions sent directly to you.** When a connection sends a question to you, supply him with as much information as you can. If you have a blog post about the topic, send the link as part of your answer.

✦ **When you update your status on your LinkedIn home page, create compelling posts about interesting projects or new blog posts you've created.** Use the Update section of your home page similar to how you update your status on Twitter. Create a couple of compelling posts a couple of times a week. Your connections will appreciate the information and may join you in the conversation. Go out of your way to be a part of the conversation and to establish yourself as an expert.

✦ **Answer questions posted by other LinkedIn members.** If your answer is selected as the best by the person who asked the question, you gain a point of expertise in the question's category. We show you how to ask and answer questions in Book VI, Chapter 3.

Chapter 3: Maximizing LinkedIn

In This Chapter

✔ Tweaking your profile

✔ Finding customers on LinkedIn

✔ Finding staff on LinkedIn

✔ Finding information on LinkedIn

✔ Managing contacts

✔ Using applications

✔ Finding alternative business networks

I n earlier chapters in Book VI, we give you some basic information for getting set up on LinkedIn and connecting with other businesspeople. You
can use LinkedIn for a lot more than that, though. The first step is to tweak
your profile so that people can find you. When you get lots of contacts, you
can manage them. You can also find clients and employees on LinkedIn. You
can use LinkedIn to find answers to questions as well. You can use applications to enhance your LinkedIn experience and bolster your profile.

In this chapter, we show you how to maximize your presence on LinkedIn.

You can augment your LinkedIn presence with the business network Plaxo
(www.plaxo.com), Ryze (www.ryze.com), or Sologig.com (www.sologig.
com). The first two networks are similar to LinkedIn. On Sologig.com, you
post and look for jobs.

Tweaking Your Profile

Your LinkedIn *profile* is sort of an online résumé. Your profile entices other
professionals to contact you and create a connection. When people find you
on LinkedIn, the first thing they see is your profile.

Therefore, make your profile as professional as possible. It should read like
a 30-second elevator pitch, giving just enough information about you to
interest people, along with a professional-looking photo.

But no matter how effective your profile is, you need to have people see it.
Let's face it: Lots of profiles on LinkedIn were created by people in the same
line of work as you. Follow these guidelines to make your profile stand out:

✦ **Include keywords people would use to find you.** Similar to search engine optimization, you place these keywords in key positions in your profile. The most important spots to add your keywords in a LinkedIn profile are in

- Your earlier job titles

- Your summary

- Your status updates

Dig up the list of keywords you compiled for your search engine optimization efforts. Those keywords work here as well. Turn to Book II, Chapter 2 to come up with your keyword list.

✦ **Study the profiles of your contacts and other professionals in your industry.** Take the best information you see from the profiles you study and put your personal spin on it.

Your profile isn't cast in stone. You can modify it whenever your business and marketing goals change by choosing Edit Profile from the Profile drop-down menu. When you change your profile, see whether you experience a spike in requests for connections.

Managing Your LinkedIn Contacts

When you set up a LinkedIn account, your first goal is to get some contacts (*connections*, in LinkedIn-speak). However, as time goes on, you may find that a contact is no longer useful to you. You may also find that you need to add information to a contact's profile. When you have so many connections that finding a specific person becomes difficult, you can organize your contacts into groups. We show you how to manage your contacts in the following three sections.

Removing a contact

When a contact has outlived his usefulness, or has violated one of your standards, it's time for the contact to go the way of the dodo. According to LinkedIn, a contact isn't notified when you remove him.

After you remove a contact, you can't recover it (at least not at the time this book was written), so give some extra thought before you remove contacts.

You can remove any contact by following these steps:

1. **Log in to LinkedIn and then click Contacts.**

Your browser refreshes to show the Contacts page (see Figure 3-1). Notice the buttons to add and remove connections in the upper right corner of the browser window.

2. **Click the Remove Connections button.**

The Remove Connections page appears, as shown in Figure 3-2.

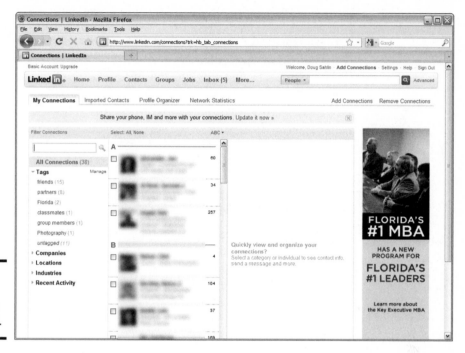

Figure 3-1:
It's time to
remove the
dead wood.

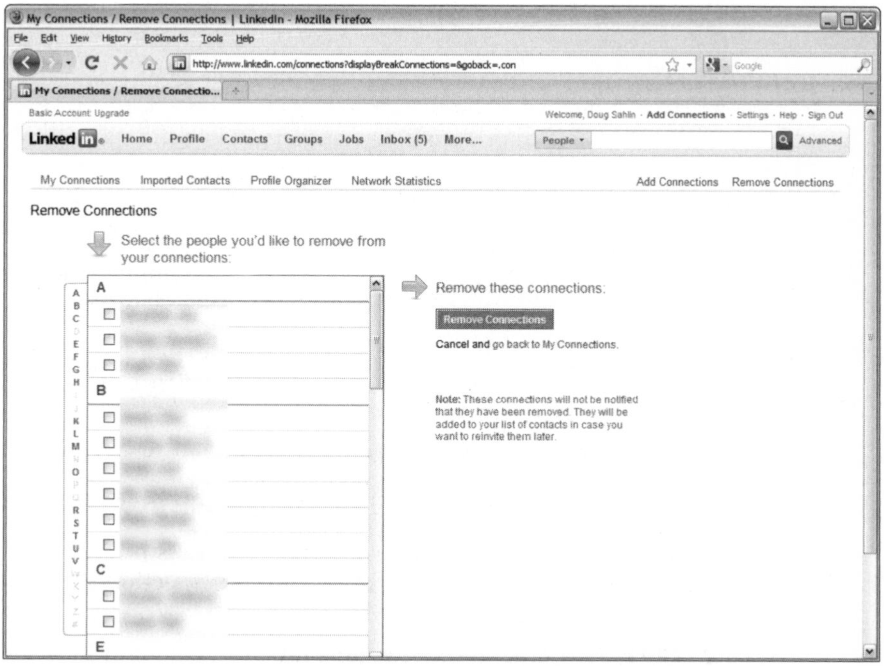

Figure 3-2:
Okay,
LinkedIn
just isn't big
enough for
all of us.

3. **Select the check box to the left of each connection you want to remove.**

   If you have lots of connections, you have to scroll through them. You can remove multiple connections by clicking multiple contacts.

4. **Click the Remove Connections button.**

   A dialog box appears, listing the connections you're about to remove, as shown in Figure 3-3. Note the warning that the action cannot be undone.

5. **Click the Yes, Remove Them button.**

   The contacts are permanently removed from your connections list.

Figure 3-3:
Oh, no!
Please don't
remove me.

Modifying a contact's information

Your contacts list certain information on their profiles. You can append this information to your own information about the contact. For example, if you know his cellphone number and you want to add it to his contact information, you can do so. The additional information is visible only to you when you select his profile from your contacts.

To modify a contact's information, follow these steps:

1. **Log in to LinkedIn and then click Contacts.**

   Your browser refreshes to show the Contacts page.

2. **Click the icon of the contact whose information you want to modify.**

   The contact's information appears on the right side of your browser window, as shown in Figure 3-4.

3. **Click the Edit Details link.**

   Your contact's information opens in another window.

4. **Add some information.**

   You can add another telephone number, addresses, or the contact's birthday, for example.

5. **Click Save Changes.**

   The changes are saved to your copy of your contact's profile.

Figure 3-4:
It's time to
edit you, my
lovely.

Tagging contacts

When you have lots of contacts, finding the one with whom you want to con-
verse can be like looking for a needle in the proverbial haystack. However,
you can organize your contacts by creating tags, and then assigning them
to certain contacts. For example, to segregate all your business contacts,
create a Business tag.

To manage your contacts with tags, follow these steps:

1. **Log in to LinkedIn and then click Contacts.**

   Your browser refreshes to show the Contacts page.

2. **Click Manage.**

   The Manage Tags window appears, as shown in Figure 3-5.

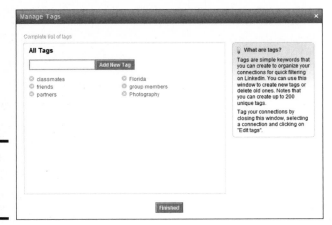

Figure 3-5:
Managing
contacts
with tags.

3. **Enter the tag in the text field.**

   Create a tag that fits several of your contacts. Your goal is to organize, not create more clutter.

4. **Click the Add New Tag button.**

   The tag is added to the list.

5. **Repeat Steps 3 and 4 to add tags as needed.**

6. **Click the Finished button.**

   Your new tags are added to the list.

To delete a tag, click the little letter *x* to the left of the tag name in the Manage Tags window and follow the prompts to remove the tag.

After you add new tags, it's time to organize your contacts. To apply a tag to a contact, follow these steps:

1. **Log in to LinkedIn and then click Contacts.**

   Your browser refreshes to show the Contacts page.

2. **Click a contact's icon.**

   The contact's information appears on the right side of the browser window.

3. **Click the Edit Tags link.**

   A dialog box opens, showing all tags you've created.

4. **Select the check box for each tag that applies to the person.**

   You can also add a tag by clicking the plus sign (+) and following the prompts.

5. **Click Save.**

   Your changes are saved.

After you edit tags for each contact, you see the number of contacts listed under each tag on the left side of your Contacts page. To see all contacts listed under that tag, click the tag.

Searching for People on LinkedIn

If your company does business with other businesses, you can use LinkedIn to find clients. If you've built up a diverse network of contacts on LinkedIn, you can ask contacts who are not your competitors to recommend you to their contacts. It's a quick way to find companies to do business with. Before you start searching for referrals, pump up your profile with recommendations from your LinkedIn contacts who have used your services. Then you're ready to start asking for referrals.

Another way to find referrals is to increase the number of contacts you have. Make it a goal to draw as many contacts as you can that are in businesses supporting, but not competing with, your industry. Your new contacts may eventually become customers or sources for referrals. Treat your new contacts like gold and nurture those relationships until you can go mining for new clients.

Posting Job Ads

Lots of people on LinkedIn are looking for jobs, including college graduates, trade school graduates, and, unfortunately, people who have lost their jobs in a down economy. You can easily find your next superstar by placing an ad on LinkedIn. According to LinkedIn, companies using its job posting service include Adobe, Expedia, Lucasfilm, Microsoft, PayPal, and Salesforce.com. At the time this book was written, a LinkedIn ad cost US$195 for a 30-day posting.

To post a job, follow these steps:

1. **Log in to LinkedIn and then click Post a Job from the Jobs drop-down menu.**

   The Post a Job section appears, as shown in Figure 3-6.

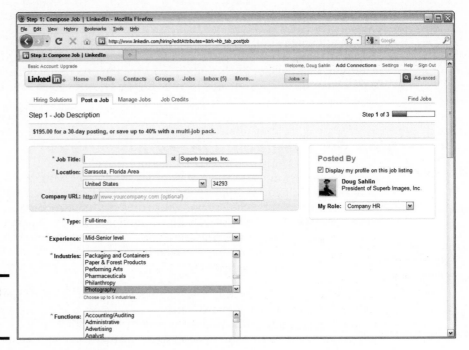

Figure 3-6:
Posting a
job.

2. **Fill in the information.**

   At the top is the standard information: job title and the name, location, and URL of your company. At the bottom, you provide information on the type of candidate you're looking for.

   As many as 4,000 characters are available to help provide an enticing job description, so don't scrimp. If your company has won awards or is listed as one of your town's or state's best places to work, be sure to include that information.

   Be as specific as possible when you fill in the Skills field.

   Allow your profile to be shown with the job posting.

3. **(Optional) Fill in the Additional Information section.**

   In this section, you can specify whether you accept only local candidates and compensate for relocation. You can also specify the option not to accept applications from third-party employment agencies.

4. **Click Continue.**

   The Options step appears, as shown in Figure 3-7.

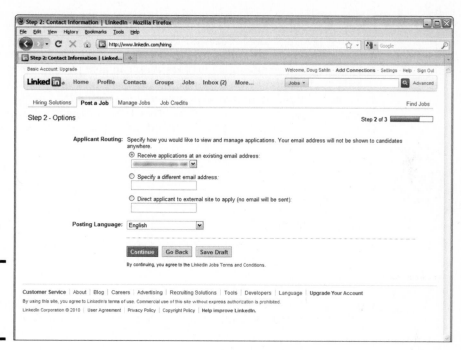

Figure 3-7:
Specifying
the post
options.

**Book VI
Chapter 3**

Maximizing
LinkedIn

Creating a job post can be an arduous task. If you need a break, or need additional information to finish writing the post, you can save your current work as a draft. Finish the draft later by choosing Manage Jobs from the Jobs drop-down menu.

5. **Specify an e-mail address for job routing.**

   You can use your own e-mail address (the default option) or specify another address to which prospective employees send their information. After this stage, it's a matter of selecting a payment method and waiting for the applications to pour in.

After you post a job, you can manage your job posts by choosing Manage Jobs from the drop-down menu.

Posting a job isn't the only way to find qualified employees. Share the information with other contacts. Use the Share an Update text field on your home page to state that you're looking for employees. You can even add a link to a job advertisement on your Web site or another Web page. Send a message to your most trusted contacts, telling them you're looking for staff. They may know qualified people who are looking for the type of jobs you're offering.

Asking and Answering Questions on LinkedIn

Lots of experts are on LinkedIn. When you need to have a question answered, you can ask those experts. You can also participate in the discussion and respond to additional comments. When you participate, you make your presence known to people on LinkedIn who may not be your contacts. Questions and answers are another way to expand your contacts on LinkedIn. We show you the Q&A ins and outs in the next couple of sections.

Explore the Closed Questions tab to find answers to previously closed questions. Even though the questions are closed, you may find some interesting information here.

Asking questions

If you have a question that has been on your mind, a question that hasn't been answered from your usual sources, consider posing the question on LinkedIn.

When you ask a question, you have complete control. You can pick the connections that you think are most likely to have the answer, or post the question to all your contacts and then wait for answers. The question is also viewed by your second- and third-degree contacts, which can possibly lead to some new contacts.

To ask a question on LinkedIn, follow these steps:

1. **Log in to LinkedIn and choose Answers from the More drop-down menu.**

The Answers Home page appears, as shown in Figure 3-8.

Someone may have already asked the same question. Before you ask, search for similar questions that have already been asked by others. Click the Advanced Answers Search tab on the Answers Home page. On this tab, enter keywords and choose a category in which to search. You can also choose to show only unanswered questions.

2. **Click the Ask a Question tab.**

The Ask a Question page appears, as shown in Figure 3-9.

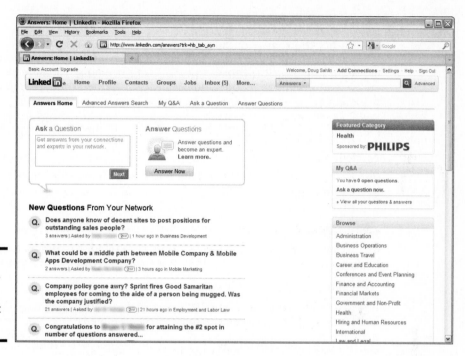

Figure 3-8:
Looking for answers in all the right places.

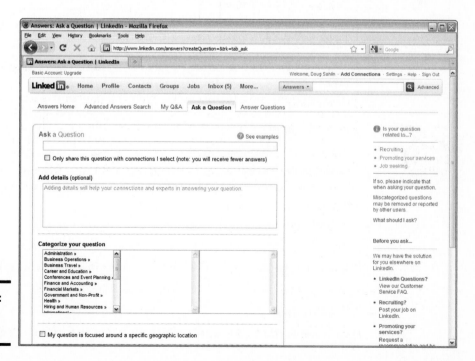

Figure 3-9:
Questions 67 and 68.

3. **Enter your question in the Ask a Question box.**

   Rather than ask a multipart or vague question, ask a specific question, such as "Which form of social media has been the most effective for your business?" If you're specific, you get detailed answers. If you're vague, people don't know how to respond to your query. Also strive to keep your question short and to the point.

4. **Accept the default option to share your question with all connections, or select the check box to choose the connections to which the question is sent.**

   If you choose the latter option, you probably receive fewer responses. Use this option if you feel that the question can be accurately answered only by some of your connections.

5. **(Optional) Add some information to the Add Details field.**

   Use this area to supply further information if your question involves a specific topic, such as choosing between two pieces of equipment.

6. **Choose a category for your question.**

   Notice the three windows. When you choose one category, you may have subcategories to consider.

7. **If applicable, select the My Question Is Focused Around a Specific Geographic Location check box.**

   If you choose this option, additional windows appear, in which you can specify a country and zip code.

8. **If applicable, choose an option from the Is Your Question Related To? section.**

   In this section, you can specify whether the question is related to recruiting, promoting your services, or seeking a job. Click the check boxes that apply.

9. **Click the Ask Question button.**

   If you specify the option to send the connection to specific contacts, the Share Your Question with Your Connections page appears, as shown in Figure 3-10.

10. **Click the blue icon to the right of Compose Your Email.**

    A dialog box opens that shows all of your connections.

11. **Choose the connections to which you want to send the question.**

    You can send the question to as many as 200 contacts.

12. **Click Finished.**

    The window refreshes to show the connections to whom the question will be sent.

13. **Click Send.**

The question is sent to your connections. After sending a question, it appears in the My Q&A section of the Answers pages on your profile.

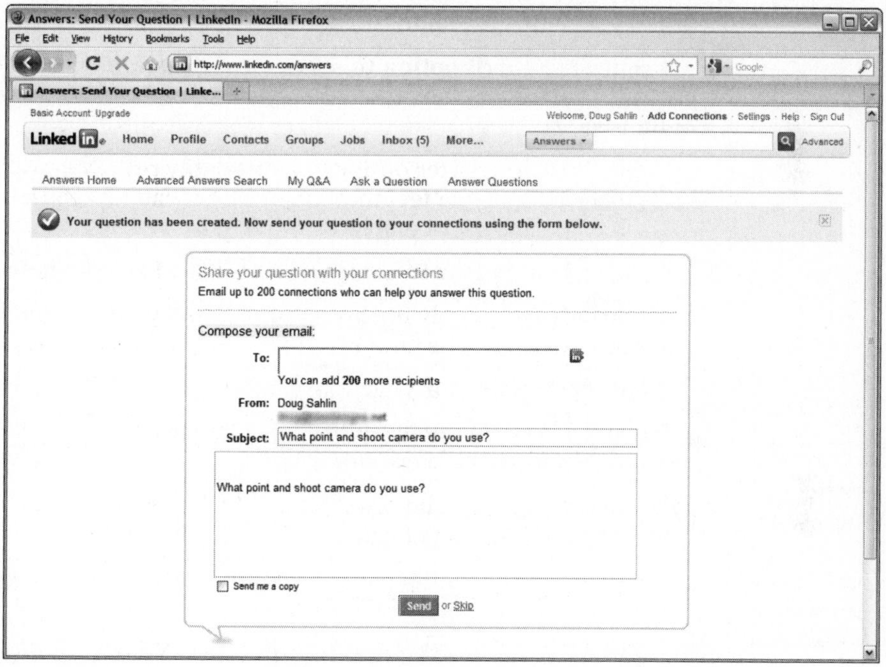

Figure 3-10:
Sending
your
question
to specific
corres-
pondents.

After your question has been answered, you can close the question by choosing Answers from the More drop-down menu and then clicking My Q&A. Select the question you want to close, and then click the Close button.

Answering questions

In addition to asking questions on LinkedIn, you can answer questions posted by contacts in your network. Your network includes first, second, and third-degree contacts as well as contacts in any group to which you belong. Questions from your first-degree contacts are sent to you directly. You should always respond to questions sent by your first-degree contacts; if you don't know the answer, thank the person for asking you the question, and offer to ask other colleagues to see if they can help.

To answer a question on LinkedIn, follow these steps:

1. **Log in to LinkedIn, choose Answers from the More drop-down menu, and then click the Answer Questions tab.**

The Browse Open Questions page appears, as shown in Figure 3-11. The answers are sorted by degree, with questions from your second-degree contacts appearing first.

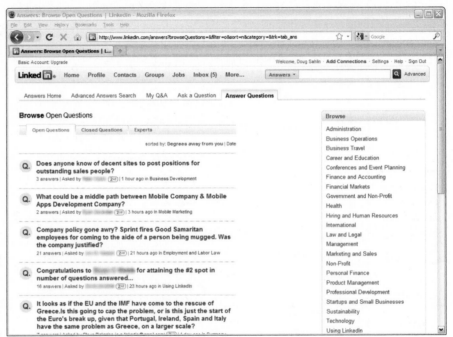

Figure 3-11:
So many
questions,
so little time.

2. **Browse the questions.**

   Lots of questions are posed on LinkedIn. Unfortunately, you have no easy way to search them, so you have to do it the old-fashioned way — question-by-question, page-by-page. Alternatively, you can narrow the focus of the questions to which you browse by clicking a link in the Browse section.

3. **When you find a question you want to answer, click it.**

   The page refreshes, showing detailed information about the question, as shown in Figure 3-12. In addition to seeing the question and detailed information, you see answers that have already been posted.

4. **Click the Answer button.**

   The page refreshes and the Your Answer field appears, as shown in Figure 3-13. You also see three fields for Web resources.

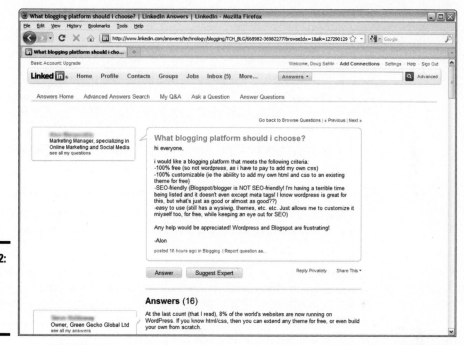

**Book VI
Chapter 3**

Maximizing
LinkedIn

Figure 3-12:
I know the
answer
to this
question.

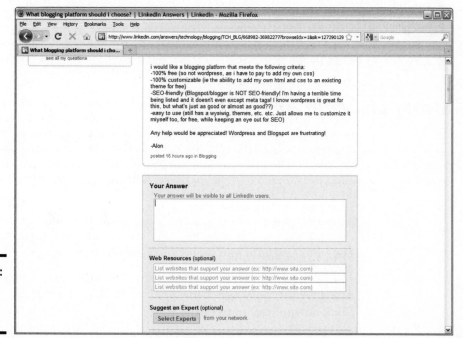

Figure 3-13:
Put your
answer
here.

5. **Answer the question and add any Web resources.**

   The Web resources can be Web pages or blog posts. If they're your Web pages or your blog posts, you've just directed more traffic to your site.

6. **(Optional) Click the Suggest Experts button.**

   The Choose Connections dialog box opens. You can choose as many as three connections that you think have expert knowledge regarding the question.

7. **Select one, two, or three experts and then click the Finished button.**

   Your experts are added to your answer.

8. **Accept the default option to write a note with your answer, or not.**

   If you accept the default option, enter a note in the text field. It's a useful way to introduce yourself to the person asking the question.

9. **Click Submit.**

   Your answer is sent to the person who made the query and is added as an answer to the original question. Your answer appears in the asker's LinkedIn inbox. LinkedIn also sends a notification to the e-mail address associated with the asker's account.

Click the Experts tab to see a list of LinkedIn experts. The experts are categorized as Experts This Week or All Time. You can find out more information about an expert by clicking her name to see all her answers. You can become an expert by having a colleague choose your answer as the best in the category. With each best answer, you gain one expertise point in that category. The more expertise points you have, the higher you rank as an expert for that category.

Using LinkedIn Applications

You can extend your LinkedIn experience by using applications. LinkedIn applications give you the option to create polls, add a reading list to your profile, create a link to your blog, and much more. Some applications require a fee and are created by third parties. (A detailed explanation of each application is beyond the scope of this book.)

Follow these steps to add a LinkedIn application to your profile:

1. **Log in to LinkedIn and then choose Application Directory from the More drop-down menu.**

   The most popular applications are listed, as shown in Figure 3-14.

2. **Click an application to install it.**

   A page appears with information about the application. Figure 3-15 shows the page that appears after installing the Reading List application by Amazon.

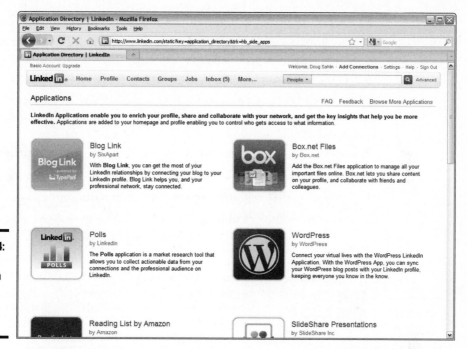

Figure 3-14:
Adding an application to your LinkedIn profile.

Figure 3-15:
Adding an application to your profile.

3. Follow the prompts to finish installing the application.

The application is added to your profile. Figure 3-16 shows the Reading List by Amazon application.

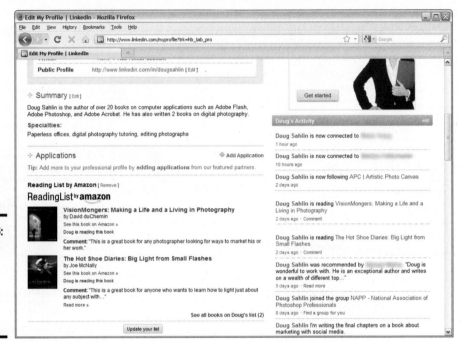

Figure 3-16: Adding the Amazon Reading List to a LinkedIn profile.

Click Browse More Applications to view other applications you can add to your LinkedIn profile.

Following a Company

In addition to finding personal profiles on LinkedIn, you can find company profiles on LinkedIn. Company profiles are similar to business pages on Facebook. You can follow a company and keep up to date on its latest developments and other news.

To follow a company on LinkedIn, follow these steps:

1. Log in to LinkedIn and choose Companies from the More drop-down menu.

The Companies Home appears, as shown in Figure 3-17.

Figure 3-17:
Finding a
company.

2. **Enter a company name or keyword in the Company Name or Keyword text field.**

3. **(Optional) Choose an option from the Location drop-down menu.**

   Your choices are Anywhere or Located In or Near. If you choose the latter option, two fields and a check box appear. You can choose the country in which the company you want to find is located, and specify a postal code. You can also select a check box to locate only the company headquarters.

4. **Click the Search Companies button.**

   LinkedIn returns a list of companies that fit the parameters you specify.

5. **Review the results and click a company name that is of interest to you.**

   The company's profile is displayed, as shown in Figure 3-18.

6. **Click the Follow Company link.**

   The company is added to the Following tab on the Companies page.

Figure 3-18:
Reviewing
a company
profile.

You can find out the latest information about a company by choosing Companies from the More drop-down menu and then click the Following tab to display the companies you're following. You see a single listing for each company. Click the company name or logo to display its profile.

When you follow a company, you're notified by e-mail whenever a noteworthy event happens. You can choose which events cause LinkedIn to send you a notification and how you receive the notification.

To change the settings for a company you follow, follow these steps:

1. **Log in to LinkedIn, choose Companies from the More menu, and then click Following.**

   The companies you follow are listed, as shown in Figure 3-19.

2. **Click the Notification Settings link.**

   The Change Following Settings dialog box appears, as shown in Figure 3-20.

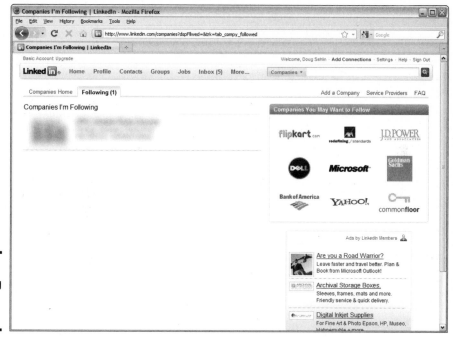

Figure 3-19:
I'm following
these
companies.

Figure 3-20:
Changing
notification
settings.

3. **Change the notification settings however you want.**

You can choose to be notified when employees join or leave or are
promoted within the company. You can choose to be notified if the
employee changes are for a person in your network or for all employees
within the company. You can also be notified whenever new job opportunities pop up or profiles are updated. You can be notified by network
update or e-mail digest. If you choose the digest, you can choose the
update frequency.

4. **Click the Save Changes button.**

Your notification changes for that company are updated.

Creating a LinkedIn Company Page

You can promote your company by adding a company page to LinkedIn. When you create the page, you add information about your company. You keep the page current by adding new activity that occurs within your company.

To create a company page on LinkedIn, follow these steps:

1. **Log in to LinkedIn; choose Companies from the More menu.**

The Companies home page appears.

2. **Click the Add a Company Link.**

The Add a Company page appears (see Figure 3-21).

3. **Enter your company name and e-mail address and then click Continue.**

A page appears telling you a confirmation e-mail has been sent to the e-mail address you provided.

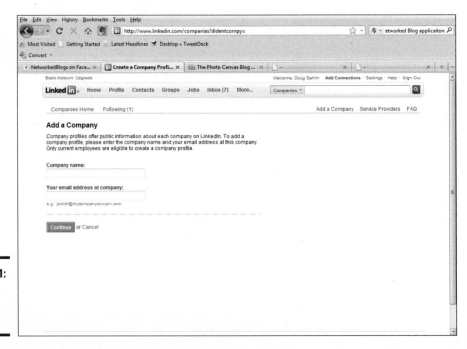

Figure 3-21:
Create a company page.

4. Check your Inbox for the confirmation e-mail and then click the link.

You're redirected to LinkedIn.

5. Click the link to confirm the e-mail.

If the e-mail address is different than your primary LinkedIn e-mail address, you're required to sign in again. Otherwise, you're directed to the Add Basic Information page (see Figure 3-22).

6. Enter the following information for your company:

- *Website URL:* The URL to your Web site.

- *Description:* A description of your company and the basic services you provide.

- *Industry:* Select the industry in which your company does business.

- *# of Employees:* Enter the number of employees in your company.

- *Type:* Choose the option that matches what type of your company.

- *Country:* Choose the country in which your business is located.

- *Postal Code:* Enter the zip code in which your company is located.

- *Your Position:* Choose the option that matches the position you hold with the company.

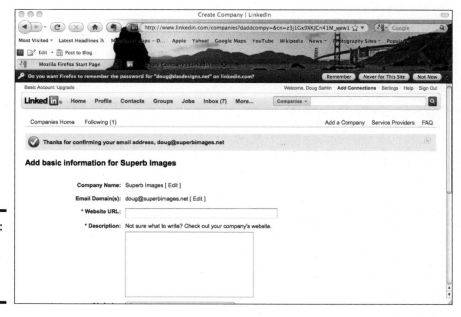

Figure 3-22:
Add basic
information
about your
company.

7. **Click Save and Continue.**

   A page appears telling you that a page has successfully been created for your company (see Figure 3-23).

8. **Click Browse beneath Company Logo to upload your company logo.**

   You can upload a GIF, JPEG, or PNG file with a file size that is 100K or less.

9. **After uploading your company logo, click Save Changes.**

   The page refreshes notifying you the logo has successfully been uploaded.

10. **(Optional) Click any or all of the following links to beef up your page:**

    - *Locations:* Lets you add detailed information about the location of your company.

    - *Financials:* Lets you add the total revenue your company earned, the year it was earned, and the currency type.

    - *Blog:* Lets you add the URL of your company blog to the profile.

11. **After adding information to a section click Save Changes.**

    Figure 3-24 shows a completed company page.

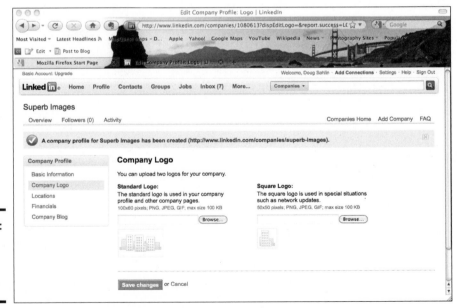

Figure 3-23: You have a company page on LinkedIn.

Figure 3-24:
A company
page on
LinkedIn.

Chapter 4: Measuring Your Results

L inkedIn is a helpful place to meet professionals and extend your network. But, as with any other marketing endeavor, it has to pay off. If you put in the time, you deserve results. However, if you aren't getting referrals or if people aren't viewing your profile or asking you to connect to their networks, you're either doing something wrong or LinkedIn is the wrong social network for you.

You have ways to measure your results. You can use analytic devices and LinkedIn options to measure your success. In this chapter, we show you how to measure your results and decide whether LinkedIn measures up.

Checking Your Web Site Referrals

One of your LinkedIn marketing goals is most likely to drive more traffic to your Web site. You can see how many people are coming to your Web site from LinkedIn by using your Web site's analytics program (such as Google Analytics, which we talk more about in Book VIII, Chapter 1).

If you have a Google account and you've enabled Google Analytics for the Web sites you want to track, you can follow these steps to see how many referrals are a result of your LinkedIn activity:

1. **Log in to Google Analytics.**

2. **Select the Web site you want to monitor and click View Report.**

   The page refreshes to show statistics for your site.

3. **Click Traffic Sources.**

   The page refreshes and shows a graph of Web site visits.

4. **Click All Traffic Sources.**

   The page refreshes and shows you a list of sources that generated visits to your Web site.

5. **Enter** LinkedIn **in the Filter Source/Medium text box using the default Containing parameter.**

   The page refreshes and shows you the number of visits that resulted from LinkedIn.

Tracking How Many People View Your Profile

When you go to the trouble of setting up a LinkedIn account and creating a compelling profile, you want to make sure that people are visiting your profile and that the visits turn into connections and recommendations. You can see the number of profile views you're getting from your home page, as shown in Figure 4-1. As you get more connections, the number of profile views will increase. The additional views will come from second- and third-degree connections. You also see profile views when you ask questions.

Figure 4-1: Checking your profile views.

If you aren't attracting a lot of profile views, take a look at your profile. You might be able to make it more compelling. See Book VI, Chapter 1 for more tips and tricks regarding your profile.

Gathering Recommendations

You gain the maximum benefit from LinkedIn when your profile is complete. A complete profile needs at least one recommendation. Get as many recommendations as possible to help your profile stand out, which means more interest, more connections, and eventually more business. When someone gives you a recommendation based on services you performed, it shows potential contacts that you are a reputable and skilled businessperson.

Here are a couple ways to get more recommendations:

+ **Ask your connections:** Your connections are busy people. Unless you do something spectacular for one of them, you have to ask for a recommendation. Put on your thinking cap and dig deep into your past. Think of gigs you've done for each of your connections, and then remind them of what a good job you did and ask for a recommendation.

+ **Ask people who aren't yet LinkedIn members:** If you've done a great job for someone, tell him about the LinkedIn network and what it has done for you. After that person becomes a member, ask him for a recommendation.

Checking Update Replies

LinkedIn isn't like Twitter — you don't update your status several times a day. But you should update your LinkedIn status a couple of times per week. Whenever you do something new or interesting that would be of interest to your connections, post an update. After you post one, monitor the response you get. If you receive comments from several of your connections every time you post an update, you're posting the right kind of update. If you post an update and receive only a few replies, you haven't piqued the curiosity of your network members. Analyze your updates to see which ones draw the largest response. Create new updates with similar information and see whether the trend of positive responses continues and you receive more replies on your updates.

Many LinkedIn users check their pages only once in a blue moon, or whenever they receive a notification that they have new messages. Make it a point to keep your LinkedIn profile current.

Share interesting articles or blog posts with your connections. Use the bit.ly Web site to condense URLs, and then you can track the number of views your article generates. See Book II, Chapter 2 to find out how to use bit.ly.

Generating Connections and Connection Requests

Your LinkedIn network is only as strong as the connections you have. Your social media net worth increases whenever you add more connections. You can't mine all the LinkedIn gold unless you have a strong network with lots of connections.

Here's how to add to the number of connections you have:

+ **Ask your current connections to introduce you to their connections.** Convert as many introductions as possible into connections. If you have 30 connections and 20 of them introduce you to 3 new connections, you have the potential to triple the number of connections.

+ **Increase the frequency with which you update your status.** If you don't update your status regularly, your connections tend to forget about you. Post interesting status updates and your connections will visit your profile more regularly.

+ **Answer questions.** Whenever you answer questions, you engage in conversation with other LinkedIn members. If you give them a good answer, they view your profile out of curiosity. Do your utmost to turn these people into connections.

+ **Join a group, take part in group discussions, and create other discussions.** If you aren't a member of a LinkedIn group, you're missing a golden opportunity to network with people with whom you share a common interest. You become established as an expert, which leads to more page visits.

+ **Create a group and promote it.** When you create a group, interested individuals view your profile and (you hope) become connections.

The number of connection requests is another measure of your LinkedIn net worth. If you're seeing a steady stream of connection requests, you're interacting in all the right places. If you aren't seeing connection requests, join a couple of groups and answer some questions.

Comparing Group Members to Connections

The group member is another piece of the puzzle. If you're a member of a couple of groups, you have great potential to grow your network. Compare the number of group members who interact with you in the group to the number that become connections.

If you aren't turning group members into connections, become more active in the group. Take part in more discussions or create intriguing discussions of your own.

Many LinkedIn members add only one comment to a discussion. Sign up for e-mail notifications whenever someone adds a thread to the discussion. Then you can easily reply to new comments more often.

You can also create a discussion to increase your presence in the group. Examine the discussions in the groups to which you belong. Notice which ones are the most active and determine when these discussions are popular. When you see a common thread, put on your thinking cap and create your own discussion.

Responding to Question and Poll Replies

When you create a question, or even use a third-party application to create a poll, you're reaching out to your connections. If you post intriguing questions or create interesting polls, you get lots of responses from your connections, plus your second- and third-degree connections. A second- or third-degree connection who answers your question creates an introduction, which is almost an invitation to become connected to you. Respond to the introduction and start a conversation with the eventual goal of turning this person into one of your connections.

If you receive a minimal response to your questions or polls, you aren't asking interesting questions. If this is the case, review the questions asked by other members of your network and notice which ones draw the most response. Chances are good that the ones with the highest level of response are created by people who have lots of connections.

Book VII

Other Social Media Marketing Sites

The 5th Wave   By Rich Tennant

"Here's an idea. Why don't you start a social network for doofuses who think they know how to set a broken leg, but don't."

Contents at a Glance

Chapter 1: Weighing the Business Benefits of Minor Social Sites

In This Chapter

✔ Reviewing goals for social media marketing

✔ Conducting social media market research

✔ Assessing audience involvement

✔ Choosing minor social communities strategically

*W*ithout a doubt, Facebook, Twitter, LinkedIn, and MySpace are the elephants in the social marketing zoo, at least in terms of the largest number of visits per month. But this is one big zoo, as shown in Figure 1-1, which displays only 50 of more than 350 social sites. Among these, you'll find lions and tigers and bears, and more than a few turtles, trout, squirrels, and seagulls.

Figure 1-1:
The zoo of social media sites is vast. Your time, however, is limited.

It's up to you to assess your business needs, research the options, and select which, if any, of these minor social marketing sites belongs in your personal petting zoo. In this chapter, we look at methods for doing just that.

With the exception of Ning (which can become your primary Web presence if you use your own domain name), these smaller sites are best used to supplement your other social marketing (rather than standalone) efforts.

Reviewing Your Goals

Book I suggests that you develop a strategic marketing plan. If you haven't done so yet, there's no time like the present. Otherwise, the task of managing your social networks can quickly spin out of control, especially as you start to add multiple smaller sites for generating or distributing content.

Marketing is marketing, whether offline or online, whether for search engine ranking or social networking. Obviously, your primary business goal is to make a profit. However, your goals for a particular marketing campaign or social media technique may vary.

As you know, social media marketing can serve multiple goals. It can help you

1. Expand your Web presence

2. Provide a free alternative or supplement to paid advertising

3. Enhance customer service

4. Disseminate news or information

5. Increase the number of inbound links

6. Improve search engine rankings

7. Improve the amount and quality of traffic to site

8. Generate qualified leads

9. Increase sales

Your challenge is to decide which of these goals applies to your business and then to quantify objectives for each one. Be sure that you can measure your achievements. You can find additional measurement information about major networks in their respective minibooks and in Book VIII. Table 1-1 suggests primary values you may have and matches several sites to the goal numbers for these major, and some minor, networks.

Table 1-1		**Matching Social Networks to Goals**	
Service	*Category*	*Primary Value*	*Fits with These Goal Numbers*
Facebook	Social networking	Strong profile rankings	1, 2, 5, 6, 8
Flickr	Photo sharing	Strong profile rankings	3, 4, 5, 6
LinkedIn	Professional networking	Strong profile rankings	1, 2, 3, 4, 6, 8
MySpace	Social networking	Strong profile rankings	1, 2, 5, 6, 8
Ning	Social networking	Strong profile rankings	1, 3, 4, 6, 7, 8, 9
Squidoo	Community	Direct link sources	2, 3, 4, 5, 9
Twitter	Community	Promote linkworthy content	2, 3, 4, 5

Source: SEOmoz.org

Researching Minor Social Networks

Doing all the necessary research to pick the right mix of social networks may seem overwhelming, but, hey, this is the Web — help is at your fingertips. Table 1-2 lists many resource Web sites with directories of social networking sites, usage statistics, demographic profiles, and valuable tips on how to use different sites. The selection process is straightforward, and the steps are quite similar to constructing a plan for paid online advertising.

Table 1-2	**Social Network Research URLs**	
Site Name	*URL*	*What It Does*
Alexa	`www.alexa.com/siteinfo`	Ranks traffic and demographic data by site
Dosh Dosh Blog	`www.doshdosh.com/list-of-social-media-news-websites`	Describes 50 social news sites
Experian Hitwise	`www.hitwise.com/us/datacenter/main/dashboard-10133.html`	Presents top 20 social sites by visits per week

(continued)

Table 1-2 *(continued)*

Site Name	URL	What It Does
GetDegrees	`www.getdegrees.com/articles/p/art-schools/top-social-networks-for-artists`	Lists top artists' social networks
Google AdPlanner	`https://www.google.com/adplanner`	Compiles traffic data by site
Google Toolbar	`www.google.com/toolbar/ff/index.html`	Installs Google Toolbar with Google PageRank
Ignite Social Media	`www.ignitesocialmedia.com/2009-social-network-analysis-report`	Compiles traffic, demographic data
Mashable	`http://mashable.com`	Presents social media news, Web tips
	`http://mashable.com/category/social-media-lists`	Lists Top 10 lists and tips
	`http://mashable.com/category/social-network-lists`	Lists Top 10 lists and tips
	`http://mashable.com/2007/10/23/social-networking-god`	Categorizes 350 social networking sites
	`http://mashable.com/2009/03/12/entrepreneur-networks`	Ranks top ten entrepreneurial social networks
	`http://mashable.com/2009/01/30/generation-y-social-networks`	Ranks top ten Gen-Y social networks
Quantcast	`www.quantcast.com`	Compiles traffic and demographic data by site
SeniorHome.net	`www.seniorhome.net/blog/2008/50-best-social-networks-for-seniors`	Ranks 50 senior social networks

Site Name	URL	What It Does
SEOmoz	`www.seomoz.org/article/social-media-marketing-tactics`	Compares 101 business social networks
Social Networking Watch	`www.socialnetworking watch.com/all_social_ networking_statistics/ index.html`	Aggregates social net news and stats
Toms Skyline Design	`www.tomsskylinedesign. com/2009/06/expand-your-social-media-vertical-markets`	Lists 17 vertical market sites
Web Strategy Blog	`www.web-strategist. com/blog/2009/01/11/a-collection-of-social-network-stats-for-2009`	Compiles statistical sources
Wikipedia	`http://en.wikipedia. org/wiki/List_of_ social_networking_ websites`	Provides directory of more than 160 social networking sites

Follow these general steps to get your research under way:

1. **Review the strategy, goals, and target markets for your social marketing campaign as described in Book I.**

   If your B2B business needs to target particular individuals during the sales cycle, such as a CFO, buyer, or project engineer, be specific in your plan.

2. **Decide how much time (yours, staff, or third parties), and possibly budget, you want to commit to minor social networking sites.**

3. **Skim the directories and lists of social media in Table 1-2 to select possibilities that fit your goals.**

   For more ideas, simply search using terms for your business area plus the words *social network* or *social media* (for example *fashion social network*).

4. **Review the demographics and traffic for each possibility by using a site such as Alexa, Google Ad Planner, or Quantcast as discussed in Book I, Chapter 2. Cull your list to keep only those that "fit."**

   Figure 1-2 displays the relative market share, according to StatCounter Global Stats (`http://gs.statcounter.com/#social_media-US-monthly-201005-201006-bar`), for the seven top-ranked social media services in the United States from May 2010 to June 2010. Market share is ranked not by traffic to the sites themselves but, rather, by "the amount of traffic they refer to other sites." This approach may be valuable for business analysis because it discounts personal users who stay on social media sites to communicate with their friends. The Other category encompasses sites such as Flickr, LinkedIn, Ning, and Squidoo.

Figure 1-2:
Relative market share, based on traffic generation capabilities, from the top social media sites from May 2010 to June 2010, according to StatCounter Global Stats.

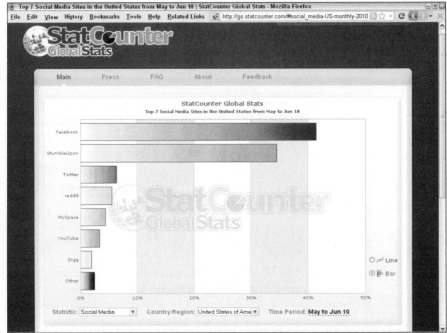

Courtesy of StatCounter Global Stats

5. **Review each network (see my suggestions in the following bullet list) to make sure you feel comfortable with its Web presence, user interaction, Google PageRank, features, ease of use, and ability to provide key reports. Prioritize your sites accordingly.**

6. **After you make your final selection, enter it in your Social Media Marketing Plan (described in Book I, Chapter 2) and set up a schedule for implementation and monitoring on your Social Media Activity Calendar (see Book I, Chapter 3.).**

7. **Implement your plan. Modify it as needed after results come in.**

   Wait at least a month before you make changes; gaining visibility within some social network sites can take time.

For leads to other social networks that appeal to your audience, look for a section named Other Sites Visited (or similar wording) on one of the statistical sites.

Keep in mind these words of caution as you review statistics in Steps 3 and 4 for various minor social networks:

✦ **Not all directories or reports on market share define the universe of social media or social networks the same way.** Some include blogs, social bookmarking sites such as delicious.com, or news aggregators. Small social networks may come and go so quickly that the universe is different even a few months later.

✦ **Confirm whether you're looking at global or U.S. data.** What you need depends on the submarkets you're trying to reach.

✦ **Determine whether the site displays data for unique visitors or visits.** A unique visitor may make multiple visits during the evaluation period. Results for market share vary significantly depending on what's being measured.

✦ **Repeat visits, pages per view, time on site, and number of visits per day or per visitor all reflect user engagement with the site.** Not all services provide this data, whose importance depends on your business goals.

✦ **Decide whether you're interested in a site's casual visitors or registered members.** Your implementation and message will vary according to the audience you're trying to reach.

✦ **Check the window of measurement (day, week, or month or longer) and the effective dates for the results.** These numbers are volatile (witness the rapid drop in MySpace usage from 2009 to 2010), so be sure you're looking at current data.

Consider online statistics, regarding social media or everything else, for relative value and trends, not for absolute numbers. Because every statistical service defines its terms and measurements differently, stick with one source to make the results comparable across all your possibilities.

Assessing the Involvement of Your Target Audience

After you finish the research process, you should have a good theoretical model of which minor social networks might be a good fit for your business. But there's nothing like being involved. Step 5 in the earlier section "Researching Minor Social Networks" includes visiting every site to assess a number of criteria, including user interaction. If you plan to engage your audience in comments, reviews, forums, or other user-generated content, you *must* understand how active participants on the network now interact.

**Book VII
Chapter 1**

**Weighing the
Business Benefits of
Minor Social Sites**

Start by signing up and creating a personal profile of some sort so that you can access all member-related activities. The actual activities, of course, depend on the particular network.

Lurking

Spend time watching and reading what transpires in every interactive venue on the site, without participating. In the "olden days" of Internet forums and chat rooms, you were *lurking*. You make a number of qualitative assessments that will help you determine whether this site is a good fit for you:

✦ **Quality of dialogue:** Do statements of any sort float in the ether, or does interaction take place? Does a moderator respond? The site owners? Other registered members? Is there one response or continual back-and-forth? If you intend to establish an ongoing business relationship with other participants on the network, you want to select a site where ongoing dialogue is already standard practice.

✦ **Quality of posts:** Are posts respectful or hostile? Do posts appear automatically, or is someone reviewing them before publication? Do they appear authentic? Since you're conducting business online, your standards may need to be higher than they would be for casual, personal interaction. Anger and profanity that might be acceptable from respondents on a political news site would be totally unacceptable on a site that engages biologists in discussion of an experiment.

✦ **Quantity of posts compared to the number of registered users:** On some sites, you may find that the same 20 people post or respond to everything, even though the site boasts 10,000 registered members. This situation signals a site that isn't successful as a social network, however successful it might be in other ways.

Responding

After you have a sense of the ethos of a site, try responding to a blog post, participating in a forum, or establishing yourself as an expert on a product review or ezine listing. Assess what happens. Do others respond on the network? E-mail you off-site? Call the office?

Use this side of the lurk-and-response routine to gain a better understanding of what you, as a member and prospective customer, would expect. Will you or your staff be able to deliver?

If a site requires more care and feeding than you have the staff to support, consider dropping it from your list.

Quantifying market presence

In addition to assessing the number of unique visitors, visits, and registered members, you may want to assess additional components of audience engagement. Sites that provide quantitative information, such as Quantcast, help you better understand your audience's behavior, learn more about their lifestyle and brand preferences, and target your message. You can learn about these concepts:

✦ **Affinity:** A statistical correlation that shows the strength of a particular user behavior, such as visiting another site, relative to that of the U.S. Internet population as a whole — for instance, whether a Flickr user is more or less likely than the general Internet population to visit YouTube.

✦ **Index:** The delivery of a specific audience segment, such as women or seniors, compared to their share of the overall Internet population

✦ **Composition:** The relative distribution of the audience for a site by audience segment, such as gender, age, or ethnicity

✦ **Addict:** The most loyal component of a site's audience, with 30 or more visits per month

✦ **Passer-by:** Casual visitor who visits a site only once per month

✦ **Regular:** A user partway between Addict and Passer-by; someone who visits more than once but fewer than 30 times per month

Choosing Social Sites Strategically

It may seem ridiculously time-consuming to select which minor social marketing sites are best for your business. Why not just throw a virtual dart at a list or choose randomly from social sites that your staff likes to visit? Ultimately, you save more time by planning and making strategic choices than by investing time in a social media site that doesn't pay off.

If you're short of time, select sites that meet your demographics requirement but on which you can easily reuse and syndicate content as described in Book II, Chapter 1. You can replicate blog postings, for instance, almost instantly on multiple sites.

If you truly have no time to select one of these sleek minor "critters," stick to one of the elephants and add others later.

Ski Dazzle, shown in Figure 1-3, is a producer of four of the world's largest ski and snowboard shows. It exemplifies a company that plans its social media marketing strategically, implements it carefully, and monitors it regularly. Working from a carefully crafted strategic marketing plan, Ski Dazzle. com built a primary social networking community on the Ning platform, with links to four Ning subnetworks that serve each of its four geographically targeted markets (on the Shows and Sales tab). You can find out more about them in the following sidebar, "Ski Dazzle's Ning Dazzle."

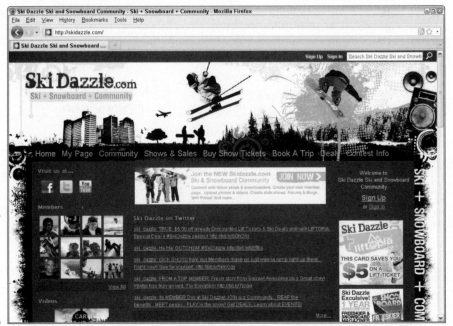

Figure 1-3:
Ski Dazzle. com has built a presence on Ning.

Ski Dazzle® is a registered U.S. Trademark owned by Ski Dazzle LLC.
All other trademark names mentioned are owned or controlled by their respective entities.

Even the smallest social network sites can be valuable if they have your target market. All the averages mean nothing. It's about *your* business and *your* audience. Niche marketing is always the effective use of your time. Fish where *your* fish are!

Ski Dazzle's Ning Dazzle

Ski Dazzle LLC (refer to Figure 1-3) owns and produces four annual consumer ski-and-snowboard shows, one apiece in Los Angeles, the San Francisco Bay Area, Sacramento, and Chicago. Ski Dazzle.com, a Ning network for a year-round community, offers links on its Shows & Sales tab to four other Ning networks, one for each geographical area. (Ning, discussed further in Book VII, Chapter 2, is an easily customizable tool for building social networks.)

Owned by Judy Gray and Jim Foster, who have promoted Ski Dazzle Ski & Snowboard shows for more than 30 years, Ski Dazzle.com acquires user-generated content through YouTube and Flickr and broadcasts its content by way of Facebook, Twitter, MySpace, Yahoo! Groups, local message boards, e-mail, and other areas where skiers and snowboarders congregate online. Discussions and feedback from these social sites help Ski Dazzle refine its content and messaging.

This intricate social media plan resulted from a strategic planning session in 2008. "The overall business model is to provide continuous value for members, in turn attracting more members, fans, followers, and friends across multiple social networks," explains marketing director Greg Hendrickson. In this model, the Ski Dazzle Web sites are the focal points for content and sales activities. "The goal is to drive/pull traffic from all other social media into the appropriate Ning community, whose value elements provide revenue opportunities for Ski Dazzle."

"The team investigated a number of social media platforms, settling on Ning for its low start-up cost and extensive do-it-yourself toolset for adding members, capturing content, and creating a flexible home page for changing annual promotions."

Ning-generated content — blogs, promotions, banners, e-mails, and events — are the primary content elements distributed to other social media. User-generated photos and videos have been supplemented with content from strategic partnerships established in 2009 with *Freeskier magazine* and *SnowBoard* magazine. "We re-purpose what we can across all our social media," Hendrickson continues. "We use Ning's share tools and home page widget capabilities for AddThis, hellotxt, Seesmic, Tweetie, twAitter, bit.ly, and SocialOomph."

All this activity requires staff. In addition to Hendrickson, Ski Dazzle has a social media content manager who handles content for Ning, Facebook, Twitter, and other social communities. During the busy show season, staff size expands to the equivalent of three or four full-time people, with outsourcing for graphic design, content development, and Web development. "While Ning provides relatively easy-to-use tools for placing and organizing content," Hendrickson notes, "graphics and content creation require development support and ongoing maintenance."

Ski Dazzle views its investment in social media as necessary based on the changes in the marketplace and the need to provide immediate and quantifiable value to both consumers and exhibitors (advertisers) all year long. For data, they rely on Google Analytics and bit.ly for Web site and campaign tracking, and on Reachmail for e-mail statistics.

Ski Dazzle cross-promotes its complex social media presence with multiple icons on the Web site and in content entries as well as in press releases, brochures, traditional advertising, online advertising, SEO, active blogging, and partnering with online ski- and snowboard-related companies.

(continued)

(continued)

The strategic plan has paid off. Web traffic increased annually by more than 150 percent in the first year of implementation, according to Hendrickson. In addition, online sales increased significantly, and Ski Dazzle was able to generate online advertising revenue, a new revenue stream for the company.

Though social media allows a business to respond more quickly than in the past, reach more people, evolve, and hone in on effective offers, campaigns, and messaging, it's a true time hog. To be effective, "you must spend time planning your social media process with two things in mind," Hendrickson cautions. You need "a specific desired outcome, and regular timeframes to review data and evolve. Without a clear objective, social media can take a huge amount of time without providing the desired benefits."

If it sounds all-absorbing, it is. Owner Judy Gray coined a phrase that aptly captures the biggest issue with social media: "Feeding the beast," she calls it. "Social media is a great tool, but be prepared to invest in it 24/7/365."

Chapter 2: Ning

In This Chapter

- ✔ Discovering about Ning
- ✔ Deciding whether Ning is the right choice for you
- ✔ Creating a Ning community
- ✔ Marketing your Ning community
- ✔ Optimizing Ning for search engines

*N*ing.com, which bills itself as "the social platform for the world's interests and passions online," is an easy-to-use platform for creating a Web presence with built-in social networking capabilities. In addition to text pages, Ning offers customizable options for member profiles, blogs, forums, photo and video uploads, and other social marketing tools.

The power of Ning rests on the idea that real communities of shared interest will hold people's attention and participation over time. In business, that idea translates into building a community that addresses the content area in which customers operate, what they do, and what they care about. In turn, that concept builds customer loyalty, which translates into word-of-mouth advertising and increased sales.

Privately held, Ning was founded in 2004 by Gina Bianchini and Marc Andreessen, a coauthor of Mosaic (the first widely used graphical Web browser) and a founder of Netscape. By May 2010, Ning had grown in flexibility, scope, and ease of use to support more than 2 million networks worldwide, register 43 million members, and absorb 5,000 new networks every day. It's strictly a paid membership, so set aside some of your social media budget if you decide to join Ning — unless you're a K–12 educator.

Ning, like all social networks, is constantly evolving. Watch for any changes it makes on the Ning blog (http://blog.ning.com) or history page (http://about.ning.com/press/history.php). Be sure to check out Table 2-2, later in this chapter, for a list of helpful resources.

Integrating Ning into Your Web Presence

You have several options for working with Ning. Because you can point a unique domain name to your individual network, a Ning site can become your primary Web presence. Alternatively, if you already have a Web site, you can link to your Ning community from the navigation tabs on your site. By pointing a subdomain to Ning (for example, http://community. YourDomainName.com), you can maintain better brand recognition and search engine ranking. A Ning community without its own domain or sub-domain name looks like YourCompany.ning.com. (Though search engines still index those pages, they're more difficult to promote online.)

The CurrySimple network on Ning (http://CurrySimple.ning.com) shown in Figure 2-1 is an example of this integrated approach. The site is a reward-based, recipe- and information-sharing community for creating Thai curries. Users can redeem reward points for products at the CurrySimple online store on its primary site at www.currysimple.com/servlet/ StoreFront. A link in the navigation of the primary site (not visible in Figure 2-1) opens the community site.

Deciding Whether Ning Is Right for You

The possibilities for Ning are limited only by your imagination. Because Ning can become the hub for your online presence, you can use it to achieve all the goals you might have for any other Web site, as well as some that are specific to its community-building features.

Engaging customers in a social community takes patience and sincerity. If you're looking for fast results, building a network may not be the right solution for you. However, if you're willing to commit to an authentic, long-term effort that results in solid customer relationships, you may find that a community network is an excellent approach.

Figure 2-1:
iLove
Curry
Simple.com
maintains
a Ning
community
(top) with
a link to its
online store
(bottom).

Courtesy CurrySimple®

Whether you have a business-to-business (B2B) or business-to-consumer (B2C) environment or a product- or service-based company, a Ning network may work well for you. Consider your budget and available time, and look at the strategic (goal-oriented) and tactical (objective-oriented) marketing issues before you decide to use Ning. This list describes some of the goals you can achieve with Ning:

✦ **Build a Web presence:** Use Ning as an inexpensive way to launch your Web presence, linking to a variety of third-party providers for services such as online shopping. After you have established traffic that contributes to your bottom line, you can afford to build a custom site or add features to your Ning site.

✦ **Enhance branding:** The more times viewers see your name, the more likely they are to remember it. By expanding opportunities for customers to interact with your company in a positive way on a name-branded site, you can increase recognition.

✦ **Network with colleagues, vendors, and prospects:** Whether the connections are between businesses, professionals, or your customers, Ning sites provide multiple ways to network by using profiles, forums, and more.

✦ **Increase customer loyalty and repeat visits:** Drawing repeat Web visitors is a key parameter for assessing the online success of your relationship-building efforts. A social networking site attracts, by its nature, repeat users. Quantcast estimates that 34 percent of Ning users are "regulars" who visit from 1 to 30 times per month, and 2 percent are "addicts" who visit more than 30 times. Together, these groups account for 83 percent of all Ning visits. Repeat visitors can be considered "self-qualifying prospects" — if they weren't interested in what you have to offer, they wouldn't return. In theory, attracting repeat visitors should increase the conversion rate on your primary site.

✦ **Improve or expand customer service:** Members of social networks like to share, by definition, common interests or experiences. Though profiles on sites such as Facebook, LinkedIn, and MySpace are listings in huge worldwide directories, Ning communities are tightly focused. Be creative. Ask yourself whether you can host a network of technical professionals, or at least an active user group, interested in addressing particular problems or helping you define a new product. Then decide whether you can attract an audience of *passionistas* — users fervently interested in politics or issues such as global warming. Determine whether you can define multiple private groups for conferences, workshops, campers, alumni members, team members, or future classmates.

Making the most of Ning

Use the independent Social Network Directory at `http://jensocial.com` or the microblogging community for Ning creators at `http://ning shouts.shoutem.com` to see how similar businesses, or even direct competitors, use Ning. A little competitor research never hurts.

To find some inspiration, review how the following businesses use their Ning communities (and don't forget to read the later sidebar "Posh Designs Scrapbook Store is a Ning community"):

✦ **AJ's Mobile in BC:** AJ's, a small, family-owned, home-and-auto detailing business in lower British Columbia, provides B2B or B2C, on-location, detailing services for autos, RVs, boats, and trucks. AJ's pairs its community site at `http://ajsmobilebc.ning.com` with its primary site at `www.ajsmobilebc.com`.

✦ **Automotive Digital Marketing:** This Ning-only, B2B community of more than 2,000 car dealers, car companies, Internet sales managers, and other automotive professionals (`www.automotivedigitalmarketing.com`) is ideal for networking, resource sharing, and strategic discussion.

✦ **Design Stories Social Network:** This 800-member B2B network (`http://mydesignstories.net`) is a Ning-only Web site that brings together interior designers, architects, and industrial designers to post profiles, upload portfolios, and find collaborators and subcontractors. The small technical forum at `www.allrealms.com` works similarly for programming professionals who want to discuss software or client-server projects.

✦ **Linkin Park:** A freestanding rock band site, the Linkin Park site (`www.linkinpark.com`) offers music videos, downloads, tour information, an active fan community, and links to purchase band merchandise, premium passes, and music from several third-party e-commerce sites.

✦ **Pickens Plan:** One of many political- and public-action-oriented sites on Ning, the PickensPlan (`www.pickensplan.com`) is T. Boone Pickens' site to promote a reduction in U.S. dependence on foreign oil. It offers multiple ways for viewers to get involved and to join a community of like-minded activists in their state.

✦ **Taste and Share:** This Ning-only community, which has more than 1,200 members, carries its own domain name at `www.tasteandshare.com`. It's also a dedicated destination for publicizing wine-tasting events and food festivals.

Posh Designs Scrapbook Store is a Ning community

Posh Designs Scrapbook Store (http://poshscrapbookstore.com), based in Montreal, Canada, opened its Web presence in 2005 with an eBay store selling prepackaged, designer scrapbooking kits. Building on that success, founder Natasha Martin opened her own online store in 2008.

With a staff of eight plus her husband, Martin has initiated a broad strategy for social network marketing, including

- ✔ **A Ning community network:** http://poshscrapbookstore.ning.com (shown in the figure)

- ✔ **A blog:** http://poshscrapbookstore.blogspot.com

- ✔ **A Facebook page:** www.facebook.com/pages/Montreal-QC/Posh-Designs-Scrapbook-Store/36013541671?ref=ts

- ✔ **A Twitter account:** http://twitter.com/PoshScrapbook

Posh Designs targets an almost all-female market segmented by craft area (for example, scrapbookers, stampers, and cardmakers), predominantly from the United States and Canada, with some additional global membership.

Getting on Ning was a bit serendipitous, explains Martin. As she struggled to integrate social features into her Web site, she received an e-mail from a friend who insisted that Ning would be like having her own Facebook page. "I decided to give it a try and loved the fact that it's a gallery [for photos], a forum, and so much more, all in one!" Martin enthused.

Martin found Ning so easy to set up that she didn't need a programmer or Web developer. Together with her design team, she created a visual theme to match her online store. Every team member now tries to spend at least a few minutes a day on Ning. Their online presence is quite important as users watch for responses to queries and for new postings.

Posh Designs relies particularly on forum, photo, and profile pages to connect with customers. The approach seems to have proved its worth, as shown in traffic statistics from Google Analytics. Martin says she has definitely seen an increase in traffic and sales, and an improved conversion rate.

To promote its Ning presence, Posh Designs uses the Broadcast Message option on Ning, a link on its Web store, and a Ning badge on its blog, with a clear statement of benefits in its call to action: "Get exclusive VIP product news, monthly contests, product giveaways, free layout projects and ideas, challenges, sketches, and more!"

Though Posh Designs uses the Ning community site primarily for active interchange with its clientele, the design store uses Facebook and Twitter to update its followers on sales, new product arrivals, and various events. Design team members use the blog to share their craft projects and ideas with readers. The suite of social marketing techniques gives users multiple ways to interact with Posh Designs while allowing the company to cast a wide net for scrapbookers. The company supplements social techniques with e-mail newsletters, print ads, and banner ads.

"If you haven't tried Ning, you really should," recommends Martin. "This platform goes beyond the usual 'threads' and 'blankness,' found in regular forums. Ning allows you to build a community for your business, which helps you add more value *and* truly connect with your customers."

Courtesy Posh Designs Scrapbook Store

Exploiting the demographics of Ning

To be successful on Ning, you have to target the correct demographic. Table 2-1 shows that U.S. visitors to Ning are predominantly female, as are many social sites that emphasize two-way communication. Teenagers 13–17 and African American audiences also significantly outpace their presence on the Internet overall, though a lower-than-average number of users are over 50 years old. If you're targeting a different demographic, Ning might not be the place for you.

Table 2-1	Ning Demographic Profile (U.S. Visitors)
Category	*Percentage of Users*
Female	545
18 or younger	25
18 to 34	34
50 or older	13
Caucasian	58
African American	26
Asian	3
Hispanic	11
Other ethnicity	1
No college	47
College	39
Graduate school	14
Income $0 to 30,000	16
Income $30 to 60,000	26
Income $60 to 100,000	28
Income $100,000 or higher	31

Source Quantcast.com www.quantcast.com/ning.com estimates through May 2010

Fish where the fish are! If you plan to build a Ning community, see whether its prospective members fall into this demographic. Determine whether they're comfortable building their own profiles, blogging, participating in forums, and uploading photos.

Getting Started with Ning

Ning is fairly straightforward to implement, at least until you try to get fancy. We review the important marketing decisions in this section to get you started.

Signing up

There are several routes to sign up as a member, which allows you to post to many public communities and to create a Ning community. While you can view public communities without becoming a member, membership allows you to see how other sites operate in greater detail and to post to others' public forums.

Follow these steps to first create an account with Ning and then to set up a basic network site.

1. **Sign up for a free Ning membership by clicking the Join Now link in the upper right corner of the Ning page.**

If you decide to fill out the boxes on the Ning.com homepage to create your own Ning network first, reverse Steps 2 and 3.

The Sign Up page appears, as shown in Figure 2-2.

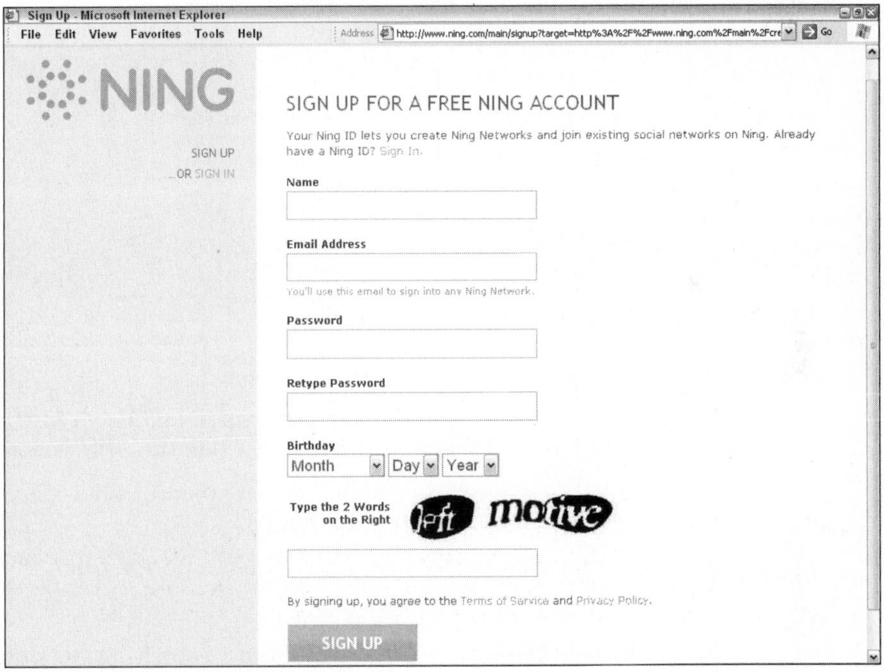

**Book VII
Chapter 2**

Ning

Figure 2-2:
Sign up
for a Ning
account.

2. **Enter your business name, business e-mail address, and password. Click the Sign Up button.**

Be sure to enter a birthday that makes you at least 21.

Ning e-mails you to verify your e-mail address.

3. **Click the link in the e-mail to go to a log-in screen. Click the Sign In button.**

The Setting Profile screen appears, as shown in Figure 2-3.

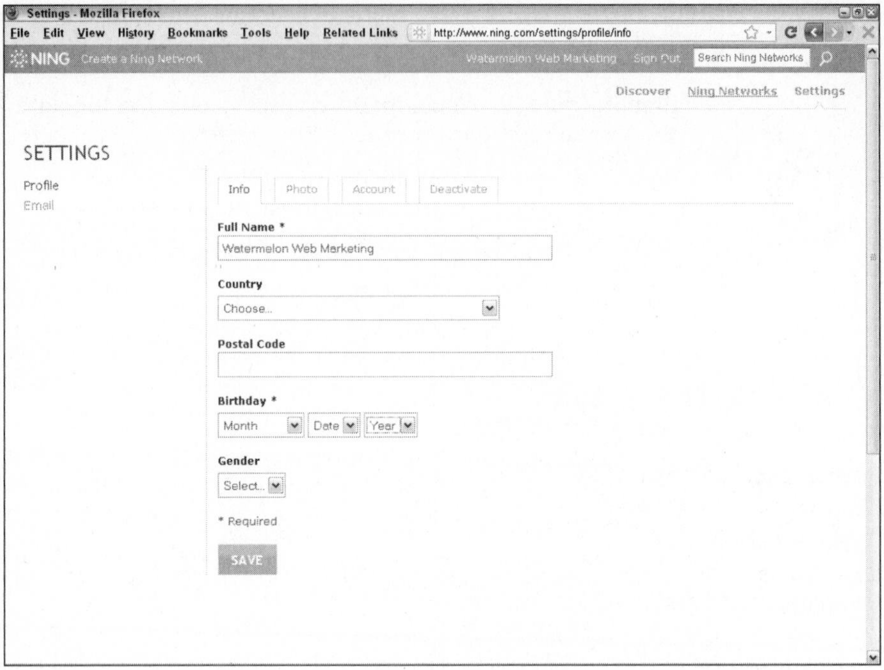

Figure 2-3:
Fill in your
profile
information.

4. **Enter your business name and address fields. Use a birthdate that make you over 21, and skip Gender. Click the Save button.**

   A dialog box appears in which you can upload a photo. If you don't see the dialog box, click the Photo tab.

5. **Upload your company logo rather than a photo. Click Done or Skip.**

   The Create a Network page opens, as shown in Figure 2-4.

6. **Enter your business name in the Name Your Ning Network box and domain name without the extension in the Pick a Web Address box. Click the Create button.**

   For now, enter the same or a related name for branding purposes in the Pick a Web Address box. (You can assign a different domain name later, as we explain in the following section.)

   The Describe Your Ning Network page appears, as shown in Figure 2-5.

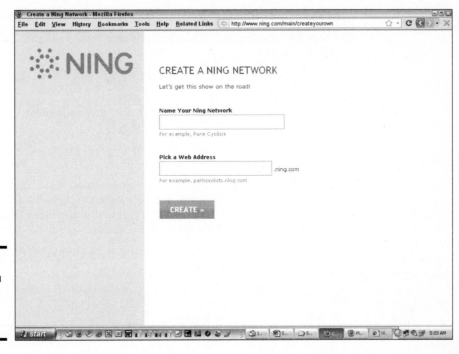

Figure 2-4:
Finally! You
can create
your Ning
network.

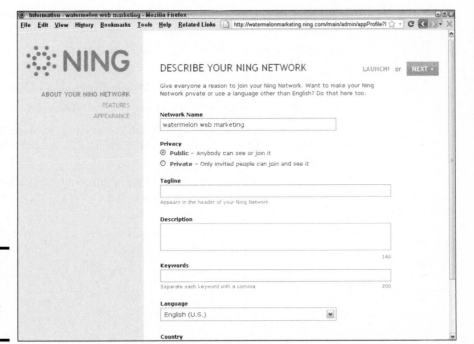

Figure 2-5:
Give Ning
details
about your
network.

7. **Fill in the following fields on the Describe Your Ning Network.**

- *Network Name:* Enter the network name you created in Step 6 (refer to Figure 2-4).

- *Public or Private:* Select the Public option for almost all business applications.

- *Tagline:* Enter your five-to-seven-word marketing tag.

- *Description:* Enter the optimized page description tag from the home page of your existing Web site (if you have one); you may need to shorten it to 140 characters.

- *Keyword:* Enter up to 10 keywords or phrases, separated by commas, to a maximum of 200 characters. Be sure to include your primary set of keywords for search engine optimization purposes. We discuss how to select keywords and write metatags in Book II, Chapter 2.

8. **When you're done, click the NEXT button in the upper right, or click the Features link to the left.**

The Add Features to Your Network page appears, as shown in Figure 2-6.

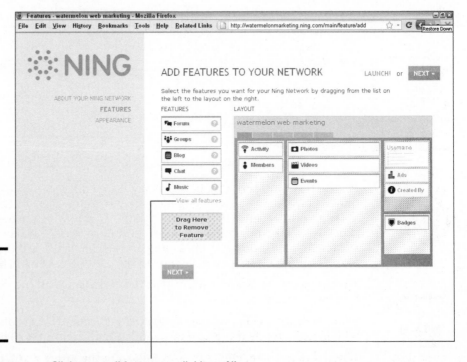

Figure 2-6:
Add features to your network.

Click to see all features available on Ning.

9. **Click the View All Features link to reveal the full list of features you can choose from. Add any features you want to include on your network.**

Drag and drop features to the location on the template where you want them to appear on the main page, as shown in Figure 2-7.

Drag features from this column   To these columns

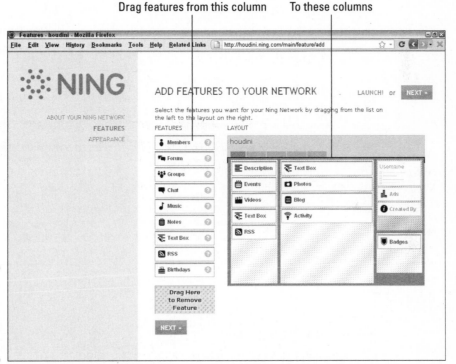

Book VII Chapter 2

Ning

Figure 2-7: Drag and drop the features you want.

Place a text or description box, which you can make fairly small and unobtrusive — just large enough for a few search terms in a title — at the top of the left or center column for search engine purposes. (Because search engines can't "read" photos or video, putting a text box at the top may improve your ranking on search engine results pages. For more information on search engine optimization, see Book II, Chapter 2.)

We discuss these features in detail in the "Choosing features and display options" section.

Remember the KISS principle (Keep It Simple, Stupid). Start off by adding just a few features and tabs; add others later as you need them.

10. **When you're done, click the Next button in the upper right, or click the Appearances link to the left.**

The Customize Appearance page appears, as shown in Figure 2-8.

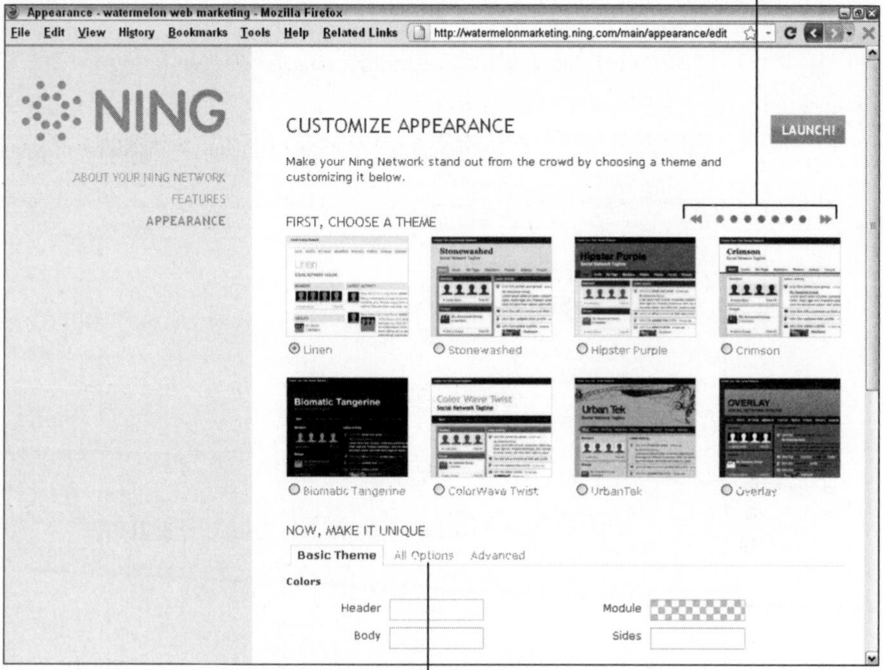

View more themes.

CUSTOMIZE APPEARANCE

Make your Ning Network stand out from the crowd by choosing a theme and customizing it below.

FIRST, CHOOSE A THEME

○ Linen   ○ Stonewashed   ○ Hipster Purple   ○ Crimson

○ Biomatic Tangerine   ○ ColorWave Twist   ○ UrbanTek   ○ Overlay

NOW, MAKE IT UNIQUE

Basic Theme   All Options   Advanced

Colors

Header ____   Module ▨▨▨
Body ____   Sides ____

Figure 2-8:
Now is your opportunity to customize your network.

Click to customize your theme.

11. **Choose a basic theme.**

Click all the buttons or arrows above the templates to see all 52 choices. Click the radio button below your selection.

12. **After you've made your selection, scroll down the page and choose the All Options tab to display all available customization choices. Scroll through the options until you finish. Click the Launch button at the top right when done.**

Choose the Advanced tab instead of the All Options tab if you want to redesign the Cascading Style Sheets (CSS) to match your primary Web site or to a custom design. Unless you feel comfortable working with CSS, hire a developer or contract for Ning support to customize your site. You may also need help with RSS feeds and widgets.

Your design appears on the next screen, as in the example shown in Figure 2-9.

**Book VII
Chapter 2**

Ning

Figure 2-9:
You almost
have a Ning
network.

13. **Click the Edit button in any block to start adding content, following
the directions on the site.**

The Manage tab, which appears only to you as the site manager, takes
you to the control panel shown in Figure 2-10. You can modify the
layout, appearance, and many other parameters as often as you want.

Your site launches with navigational tabs (refer to Figure 2-9), but you
have great flexibility.

To modify the primary and secondary navigation, choose Manage↪
Customize It↪Tab Manager. Then you can add, delete, or change tabs
and subtabs that link to internal or external pages.

After you launch your site, Ning sends you an e-mail with links to invite other
members to join your community or make changes.

Modify navigation with Tab Manager

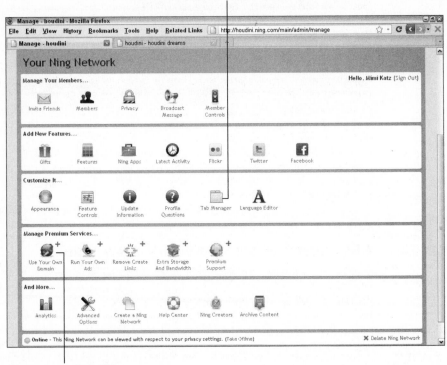

Figure 2-10:
You can
manage
your
network
from the
control
panel.

Change your site's URL.

If you plan to use Ning as your primary Web site, you might want to seek assistance from a graphic designer, copywriter, or photographer (or all three). These services are even more important when you don't have an existing site whose look and feel you can duplicate or whose content you can repurpose.

Naming your Ning community

As we mention earlier in this chapter, you have three ways to name your Ning community:

✦ Display the Ning name as the host server, as in `http://crimespace.ning.com`

✦ Buy a new domain name and point it to the Ning community, such as `www.womenssoccerunited.com`

✦ Link from your existing Web site or blog, and point a creative subdomain name to your Ning network, like `guruforum.yourcompany.com`

To change your site's URL, choose Manage⇨Add Premium Services⇨ Use Your Own Domain and follow directions.

Premium Services carry a modest fee. With Ning's new pricing structure, which we discuss in the "Selecting Your Pricing Plan" section later in this chapter, it isn't clear which premium services will be incorporated into higher-priced options and which will remain available *a la carte*. For more information about the old set of Premium Services, go to `http://help.ning.com/cgi-bin/ning.cfg/php/enduser/std_adp.php?p_faqid=2973`.

Even template-based sites have technical challenges. Though Ning offers extensive online Help and an online forum for questions, you may find that hiring a professional Web developer, or contracting with Ning for additional support, saves time, flattens the learning curve, and helps you avoid mistakes while trying to point to a domain name, for example.

Choosing features and display options

After you decide on a theme for your site, you get to choose which features to display on its main page. Ning offers so many choices that your site will end up being unique even if you choose a standard theme. Although you have more than 20 choices of features, try to limit the number of features to 12 to 15, at least at the start, to keep your Ning network from slowing down.

If you're matching a Ning network to your Web site or blog, try to maintain consistency in the navigation tabs as well as in the design.

Ning advises that the use of photos, videos, latest-activity reports, members, and events helps your Ning network grow "because they are visually pleasing, fun to use, and easy to interact with" (`http://help.ning.com/cgi-bin/ning.cfg/php/enduser/std_adp.php?p_faqid=3584`). Add two or three text boxes and one optional RSS feed, or perhaps a widget or blog, and you're done.

The following list offers some marketing considerations for the key features to include in your Ning site. My.KicksonFire.com includes many of these elements on its community page, while maintaining a consistent look-and-feel between Ning site and its blog at KicksonFire (`www.kicksonfire.com`), as shown in Figure 2-11. The two sites cross-link in their navigation bars.

Figure 2-11:
KicksonFire positions four key elements near the top of its Ning site. It maintains a consistent visual identity on its blog.

Courtesy Furqan Kahn for KicksonFire.com

✦ **Photos and videos:** Although photo and video features eventually use up your storage budget, place these features at the top of your site (before users begin to scroll), on the main page. Including these two most popular Ning features raises your probability of success.

The visual appeal of photos and videos attracts the human eye quickly and encourages user interaction. Enable members of your site to upload and share photos and videos. For even greater visibility, automatically offer them the option to embed their branded photo slide shows and videos anywhere on the Web, with a link back to your Ning network.

✦ **Latest activity:** This feature can motivate members to participate, especially as your network grows. However, you generally don't want to advertise a low activity level. You can control the display of information in the Latest Activity box, so you might want to show only a summary of What's New postings (even if they're yours) until you have more member activity to report. Ning recommends keeping this feature near the upper-left column of the screen, because it attracts and holds viewers.

✦ **Members and profiles:** Again, Ning suggests keeping the member mosaic displayed near the upper left side of the main screen. Seeing other people encourages new viewers to join. Be sure to select featured members — friendly faces with quality profile photos. Establish profile questions for incoming members by group and allow members to customize their own profiles within limits. You can even customize the advanced member search based on profile questions such as location, graduation year, or team name.

✦ **Events:** This module is an effective way to publicize happenings, sales, readings, performances, trade shows, and more. You can limit event creation to yourself or let all members post events, depending on your site. If you allow open creation, review other people's events before they post. Outdated events are automatically removed from the Events listings, keeping your site looking fresh. Figure 2-12 shows how BroadwaySpace displays its events: The two items in the left column link to detailed Events listings with links to buy tickets or make event reservations, as well as RSVP boards and a calendar.

✦ **Text boxes:** Add text boxes to your main page to use for a weekly column or special promotion or for your own changing photos, video, or graphics. Though you can have as many as ten boxes, try to keep the number to two or three. Be sure to include some search terms in your text boxes!

Figure 2-12: Broadway Space informs visitors of its upcoming events in the left column.

You can gradually add more features as your social network grows and you become more comfortable working in the Ning environment. Try the features described in this list:

✦ **Blogs:** Think carefully before enabling blogs for every member of your Ning network, because you don't have much control over the content. Consider constraining blogs to your own — at least make yours the only featured blog — and let others post comments. Even if you display only your own blog, limit posts to text, display only five to ten posts, and choose to display only titles on the main page to keep your site loading fast.

✦ **Chats:** Real-time chat, or *instant messaging,* is appropriate for only some sites. Is yours one of them? Without moderation, this feature can be "taken over" and distract from your primary business goals. If you enable chat, moderate it.

✦ **Discussion forums:** Though a forum encourages interaction between members, moderating it and nurturing it with lively discussions takes time. You can keep it simple (with a single thread that you create), or establish a multithreaded forum with topics from your members, with categories and attachments. This feature is one you might want to add later.

If you see that your blog is getting a lot of comments, with an active interchange among respondents, you might want to add a forum for ongoing conversation. All this talk takes time! You may want to ask a reliable and knowledgeable member of the forum to moderate it for you.

✦ **Groups:** You can enable groups as special interest areas or for specific regions. Each group can have its own images, comments, RSS reader, text box, discussion forum, and privacy settings. As the network creator, you can choose its features and privacy settings and control who can create groups or moderate groups before they're posted.

✦ **Moderation and privacy levels:** Ning lets you moderate just almost any of these features, from reviewing members before they join to pre-screening photos, videos, groups, events, and music. You can choose to make your Ning network public or private for members only. The settings you select for moderation and privacy depend on your goals and audience. For instance, you might want to arrange private groups by conference attendance or class membership. Or, you might want to allow people to restrict who can view their profiles, especially if they're young.

✦ **RSS feeds in and out:** For easy updating, pick your favorite RSS feed from your blog or Web site or another news source. For speed, choose to display titles only rather than use Detail view. You can turn just about any feature on a public Ning site into an outgoing RSS feed. RSS feeds, which make your social network look active and fresh, are often placed below the fold — far enough down the page that a user must scroll to see the content. For more information on RSS feeds, see `http://help.ning.com/cgi-bin/ning.cfg/php/enduser/std_adp.php?p_faqid=3000`. RSS is one of the feature blocks that you can add to your page layout (refer to Figure 2-7).

✦ **Widgets and third-party applications:** A *widget* is a small piece of code from an outside provider that's embedded on another Web page, in this case on a page of your Ning network. The widget can be a YouTube video, game, poll, survey, or Twitter feed or even another media player. You generally copy the embed code that's provided by the third party, paste the code into a text box or page on your network, and click Save. The list of Ning widgets at `http://developer.ning.com/ningapps` focuses on shopping carts, social giving, shared documents, polls, and blogs, though third-party sites offer hundreds more.

**Book VII
Chapter 2**

Ning

Pick no more than three or four embedded widgets on your main page. A page loads only as fast as its slowest widget, and you risk too much of an increase in your site's download time. Even a single Flash Player can slow your site! To keep your site fresh, you can occasionally rotate its widgets.

Posting to blogs, forums, and chat rooms — and even posting photos and media items — takes time, so be sure to budget time for this task. Moderating these functions is essential; otherwise, your Ning communities soon become filled with spam and irrelevant information.

Table 2-2 lists many helpful resource URLs.

Table 2-2	Useful Ning Resource URLs
How-To Resources	*URL*
Ad Publishing	http://help.ning.com/cgi-bin/ning.cfg/php/enduser/std_adp.php?p_faqid=3155
Application list	http://developer.ning.com/ningapps
Compare pricing plans	http://about.ning.com/announcement/plans.php
Creators' network	http://creators.ning.com
Directory	http://theningdirectory.ning.com
Domain name usage	http://help.ning.com/cgi-bin/ning.cfg/php/enduser/std_adp.php?p_faqid=3640
	http://help.ning.com/cgi-bin/ning.cfg/php/enduser/std_adp.php?p_faqid=3643
	http://help.ning.com/cgi-bin/ning.cfg/php/enduser/std_adp.php?p_faqid=2920)
Google Analytics	http://help.ning.com/cgi-bin/ning.cfg/php/enduser/std_adp.php?p_faqid=3003
Groups	http://help.ning.com/cgi-bin/ning.cfg/php/enduser/std_adp.php?p_faqid=3411
Help	http://help.ning.com
Product summary	http://about.ning.com/product.php
Selecting features	http://help.ning.com/cgi-bin/ning.cfg/php/enduser/std_adp.php?p_faqid=3605http://help.ning.com/cgi-bin/ning.cfg/php/enduser/std_adp.php?p_faqid=3000
SEO on Ning	http://help.ning.com/cgi-bin/ning.cfg/php/enduser/std_adp.php?p_faqid=3708
Workshop and tutorials	http://help.ning.com/cgi-bin/ning.cfg/php/enduser/workshop.php?

Applying the four-second rule to your Ning network

You have no more than three or four seconds to grab a viewer's attention on any Web site, including your Ning network's main page. Try to make a powerful graphical statement that hooks viewers by convincing them that "there's something in it for me." Viewers often abandon a slow-loading site before they even get to see it!

Include a disclaimer about not being responsible for the accuracy of the content that others provide, and state clearly that posters must own the copyright for any material they post or have permission to use it.

Selecting Your Pricing Plan

Ning has moved from a free base model with individually priced premium services to set pricing options. The plans have three pricing tiers:

✦ **Ning Mini:** A minimal feature set at a low price ($2.95 per month or $19.95 per year) to maintain inexpensive access for many existing small communities of 150 members or less. Ning suggests that this plan works well for "classrooms, community groups, small nonprofits, or families."

✦ **Ning Plus:** A moderately priced option ($19.95 per month or $199.95 per year) that is positioned as a branded social network (with your own domain name), a larger set of features, and customization capabilities. Ning Plus permits unlimited members; it may be an excellent, reasonably priced solution for most businesses.

✦ **Ning Pro:** The high-priced solution ($49.95 per month or $499.95 per year), enhances Ning Plus with more features, better integration with other sites and social media, premium support, and additional bandwidth for users with sophisticated needs or heavy video usage.

According to its blog, Ning has found a corporate sponsor to subsidize Ning Mini networks for K–12 educators. Teachers and students in primary through secondary school can use Ning for free in their classrooms.

For a more detailed comparison of Ning's pricing, see `http://about.ning.com/announcement/plans.php`.

Marketing Your Community

Recruiting active participation to your community may require a marketing campaign of its own. Finding and keeping community members isn't easy. To increase participation, you might aggressively combine search engine optimization (SEO) techniques, invitations, and broadcast messages on Ning with tried-and-true online techniques such as e-mail, reward programs, contests, drawings, e-newsletters, and calls to action on your Web site and on other social media pages.

You must recruit actively and continuously. Unless social communities are nurtured, they may age quickly and lose members.

Using search engine optimization techniques

Ning gets you off to a running start with SEO by following the same best practices described in Book II, Chapter 2. Ning automatically provides descriptive URLs and content page titles, for instance. Keep in mind a few other important guidelines if you want search engines to find your Ning network:

+ Your social network, except for some private forums, needs to be public, not just the main page.

+ Make sure that your social network appears in search engines by submitting it to Google, Yahoo!, and Bing, as long as it has an independent domain name (see Book II, Chapter 2).

+ Insert your keyword-loaded page description and primary search terms into the Keyword field of the Network Information section of the Manage page.

+ Tag individual pieces of content with additional content-specific keywords in the Tags field for that item. (For the Events feature, the tag field is Event Type.) You then have the opportunity to broaden the list of search terms that point to your site.

Use traffic statistics to see which search terms people use to find your community site. Then be sure to integrate those terms into at least one page of your Ning community site.

Using traffic-building techniques specific to Ning

Ning offers several ways to promote your site to new members and to keep existing members in the loop:

+ **Broadcast messages:** To send an e-mail to all members of your Ning network at one time, click the Broadcast Message link on the Manage tab. This helpful technique lets members know about new features and content.

+ **Share specific content:** Go to the page that lists the specific item. Click the Share link and then More Options. Your members receive a nicely formatted HTML message along with a thumbnail or an icon representing the content or its creator.

✦ **Send invitations through Ning:** From the Invite tab, follow the directions to enter e-mail addresses or import contacts from your address book or e-mail client. Ask your contacts to upload some photos or videos to get them involved and to get your site up and running.

✦ **Use a Ning badge:** You can post a Ning badge on your Web site, like the one shown in Figure 2-13, or on other social media pages to link viewers to your Ning community. To create a badge, go to `http://help.ning.com/cgi-bin/ning.cfg/php/enduser/std_adp.php?p_faqid=2901`.

✦ **Promote your site online:** Use Ning apps to connect to Twitter or Facebook or to embed media players on other sites. The Facebook app places Ning-branded content onto your Wall, including your logo, network name, and a link to your network. The Twitter app sends a shortened link and displays your network name whenever a member posts a tweet from within your network. Access and install both of these apps by choosing Manage➪Add New Features.

Ning badge

Book VII
Chapter 2

Ning

Figure 2-13: Zork Planet invites visitors to its main site to join its Ning network by using the linkable badge and call to action in the right column.

Courtesy Zork Ventures/ZorkPlanet.com

Marry your Ning community to a loyalty program that rewards visitors for forum participation, blog postings, or creative uploads. You can do this with widgets for prize drawings or contests or use third-party programs, such as Loyalty Lab (`http://loyaltylab.com`), to award points that can be applied to a future purchase.

Measuring your Ning results

Use Google Analytics or another statistical package, as discussed in Book VIII, Chapter 1, to measure traffic to or within your Ning community, or to monitor traffic between your Ning community and your primary Web site. Other than installing Google Analytics on your Ning community, you don't have to do anything special to generate results — Google does it for you.

Ning communities are completely compatible with Google Analytics. To install this feature, go to `http://help.ning.com/cgi-bin/ning.cfg/php/enduser/std_adp.php?p_faqid=3003`.

For more information on Google Analytics, see *Web Analytics For Dummies,* by Pedro Sostre and Jennifer LeClaire.

Chapter 3: MySpace

In This Chapter

✔ Deciding whether MySpace is right for you

✔ Recognizing the business benefits of using MySpace

✔ Understanding the basics of using MySpace

✔ Using MySpace to drive traffic to your Web site

✔ Marketing and selling with MySpace

*O*nce a pioneer in the social media cybersphere, MySpace describes itself as "a technology company connecting people through personal expression, content, and culture." MySpace was one of the first sites to offer a convenient online destination to

✦ Create a personal profile

✦ Upload photos, videos, and music

✦ Write a blog

✦ Play online games

✦ Exchange news and comments with "friends" who sign up to your account

MySpace claims to reach more than 160 million people worldwide each month, of whom about 50 million are in the United States. Though that number represents less than half as many U.S. Facebook users, 50 million users is nothing to sneeze at. If your business targets some of them, MySpace might still be an important arrow in your marketing quiver. This chapter discusses how to decide whether MySpace is right for you and how to maximize its marketing impact.

We cover here only the basic setup for a business MySpace account and best practices for business applications. For more details about using MySpace, see *MySpace For Dummies,* by Ryan Hupfer, Mitch Maxson, and Ryan Williams.

Deciding Whether MySpace Is Right for You

Leveraging the popularity of Friendster, MySpace.com launched in 2004 with the intention of offering the freewheeling cultural class in Southern

California a way to combine social networking with creative self-expression. It experienced phenomenal growth for its first few years, becoming the most visited social networking site in the United States by June 2006.

Alas, nothing lasts forever, especially dot-coms trapped in the shimmering World Wide Web. By April 2008 Facebook had eclipsed MySpace in terms of monthly unique visitors. Facebook continues to expand its market share for social media visits, much of it at the expense of MySpace, whose traffic continues to decline. Facebook had nearly twice the market share as MySpace only 18 months later, as shown in Table 3-1. Other, much smaller social marketing sites accounted for the remaining market share, but none had more than 3 percent.

Table 3-1		MySpace versus Facebook Market Share of All Social Marketing Visits				
Rank	*Site Name*	*Domain*	*Sept. 2009*	*Aug. 2009*	*Sept. 2008*	*Year-Over-Year Percentage Change*
1	Facebook	facebook. com	58.59%	55.15%	19.94%	194%
2	MySpace	myspace. com	30.26%	33.00%	66.84%	−55%

Source: Experian® Hitwise® www.hitwise.com/us/press-center/press-releases/2009/social-networking-sept-09

A site can lose market share without losing users. Some of the MySpace share loss results from Facebook attracting more new accounts during the rapid growth of the social networking base.

It's all about *your* audience. Ignore all the press reports about the decline and fall of this or that social media empire. If you can successfully reach your target market on MySpace and energize them to become prospects, qualified leads, or customers, stick with it.

Exploiting the demographics of MySpace

The number of users isn't all that matters. The degree of *engagement,* or time on site (shown in Table 3-2), is also an important measure. In terms of engagement, MySpace is still ahead, boasting the highest time on site of 155 sites measured by Hitwise (`www.hitwise.com`).

Table 3-2		MySpace versus Facebook Time on Site (Minutes:Seconds)			
Rank	*Site Name*	*Domain*	*Sept. 2009*	*Sept. 2008*	*Year-Over-Year Percentage Change*
1	Facebook	facebook. com	23:00	18:38	23%
2	MySpace	myspace. com	25:56	29:37	–12%

Source: Experian® Hitwise® www.hitwise.com/us/press-center/press-releases/2009/social-networking-sept-09

With their dark backgrounds, throbbing musical beats, and edgy — if sometimes hard to read — fonts and graphics, many MySpace pages have an urban feel that appeals to teenagers and young adults who definitely aren't upper-class, buttoned-down preppies.

The demographic profile shown in Table 3-3 shows that MySpace skews to a young adult female audience, with more than 54 percent younger than 35. By comparison, only 27 percent of the Facebook audience is under 35, but it has twice as many users 55 and over.

Table 3-3	MySpace Demographic Profile
Category	*Percentage*
Female	56
Male	44
3 to 12	5
13 to 17	27
18 to 34	44
35 to 49	16
Over 50	8
Caucasian	65
African American	13
Asian	4
Hispanic	17
Other ethnicity	1
No kids 0 to 17	43

(continued)

Table 3-3 *(continued)*

Category	Percentage
Has kids 0 to 17	57
No college	58
College	33
Grad school	8
Income $0 to $30,000	20
Income $30,000 to $60,000	26
Income $60,000 to $100,000	27
Income over $100,000	26

Source: Quantcast.com

Some analysts have discerned ethnic and class differences between MySpace and Facebook, with MySpace appearing to draw lower-income and more ethnically diverse populations, particularly Latinos and African Americans.

To reach Hispanic audiences in the United States, consider the site at http://latino.myspace.com, a primarily Spanish-language site. Latin American audiences are better reached through that section on MySpace International (http://la.myspace.com).

You can estimate MySpace demographics at https://advertise. myspace.com. Enter a test ad and then filter the audience by gender, age, education, relationship status, parental status, or geography. Education, which tiers by age, is a relatively good indicator of socioeconomic status: the more education, the higher the income. The gray bar at the bottom of the page displays the number of unique users within your filters.

If your business targets an ethnic audience, caters to a young adult market under 35, skews female, or plays to the MySpace strong suits in music, comedy, video, video games, fashion, celebrities, and other forms of entertainment, you can effectively promote your business to some of its most ardent users. Singer Gilbert Sanchez does so in Figure 3-1. Mr. G, a smooth-sounding R&B/soul singer in Albuquerque, uses his MySpace music page at myspace.com/mrgsanchez to allow visitors to listen to sample songs, buy a CD, link to his primary site at www.mrgsanchez.com, or e-mail him to book a gig.

Figure 3-1:
This singer's home page displays many standard MySpace components and references his main Web site.

The MySpace reporting system for advertising demographics isn't updated in real time. Keep this information in mind if you're planning an ad campaign or trying to decide whether you want to dedicate your social marketing efforts to MySpace.

Fitting the MySpace glove

As you plan your social media strategy, consider whether your type of business would flourish on MySpace. Though MySpace is inherently a B2C (business-to-consumer) venue, you can reach other companies, such as musicians and filmmakers, that market themselves on the site with your business-to-business (B2B) message. Think of it like marketing to exhibitors at a trade show rather than to visitors. Here are a few ideas:

✦ **Music-related businesses:** In addition to the obvious bands, singers, instrumental soloists, and deejays, think about businesses that publish or produce CDs and music videos; design CD covers; make, rent, or sell musical instruments, film equipment, or audio accessories; rent recording or rehearsal studios; act as booking agents or publicists; or teach music.

✦ **Other entertainment-related businesses:** Comedians, dancers, clowns, filmmakers, live theatres, bars, comedy clubs, sports lounges, movie theaters, and restaurants that appeal to a younger demographic can leverage their own pages with MySpace Local, a collaboration with Citysearch that allows MySpace users to review venues and share reviews with friends.

   If you don't find your business in the directory at www.citysearch.com/allstates, submit your information for a basic free listing directly to myaccount@citysearch.com or call Citysearch at 800-611-4827. An expanded paid advertising program for MySpace Local is also available:

   ```
   www.citysearch.com/aboutcitysearch/advertise_with_us/
      myspace
   ```

✦ **Educational programs, sports groups, and other institutions targeting an audience under 25:** Summer camps, especially those in drama, music, or visual arts; training programs; summer or semester-abroad programs; youth groups, private or charter middle schools and high schools recruiting students; colleges; after-school programs; and home schooling groups and organizations with volunteer programs can — and probably should — all actively recruit on MySpace. Sports training programs, SAT preparation providers, tutors, gyms, and even karate schools may find avid consumers there.

✦ **Businesses whose products or services appeal to an audience under 25:** Fashion, accessories, makeup, and hair styling for young females are no-brainers. The large group of 18-to-24-year-old cohorts on MySpace buys everything from T-shirts to tattoos, from auto decor to backpacks, from posters to running gear, and from energy drinks to lattés, not to mention CDs, DVDs, video games, and media downloads. Even younger teens who aren't legally able to use a credit card — and whose tastes are decidedly different from those even a few years older — will get their parents to purchase items for them.

Continue to watch the news about MySpace and your own traffic and sales results. At the moment, MySpace is refocusing its efforts on music, film, and entertainment, seeking to dominate the younger market rather than compete with Facebook. Whether that strategy will succeed remains an open question.

For authors such as Suzanne Crowley (see the nearby sidebar, "Teen lit author finds MySpace imperative"), whose teen lit books aim directly at this demographic, MySpace becomes a must-have service.

Teen lit author finds MySpace imperative

Suzanne Crowley, a published author of young adult books, has long since found her voice. Now she uses MySpace to find her readers. Her first novel, *The Very Ordered Existence of Merilee Marvelous*, aimed at middle-grade students, debuted in August 2007. Her second, *The Stolen One*, a young adult Elizabethan novel, came out in June 2009. She promotes it actively on MySpace, as shown in the sidebar figure.

Crowley, who's trying specifically to reach teens and young adults, initially got involved with MySpace after her publisher urged her to "join as many social networking sites as possible." Crowley questioned whether MySpace would be worth her time, but "an author friend said she had over 4,000 hits to her MySpace page and she felt it was invaluable for her sales." Crowley asked her teen daughter, Lauren, to design the page. Lauren already had experience in designing social networking sites, explains Crowley, and "she has the advantage of knowing what appeals to teenagers."

Now, with more than 2,000 hits on her MySpace page, Crowley is enthusiastic. "To me, this is invaluable free advertising. It's like a viral effect, as the more friends I have, the more the cover of my book shows up on their sites, with their friends seeing my book. I read somewhere that a person will only purchase a book after reading about it or seeing it seven times. Combine this with the data that shows teenagers are heavily influenced about book purchases after reading about it online. Being on a social network such as MySpace is imperative for a young adult author."

It wasn't all easy, however. "Initially, it was very time-consuming acquiring friends. I set a goal of having 2,000 friends. I checked out other young adult authors, and invited as many of their friends as I could, figuring that their friends were probably book-loving teenagers more likely to accept my friendship and be curious about my page, and then of course, hopefully purchase my book. I've also made friends with over 200 libraries, corresponded with their librarians, usually a teen librarian, and sent free bookmarks to their teen groups. Several of the libraries featured my book after this in their teen section."

**Book VII
Chapter 3**

MySpace

(continued)

(continued)

MySpace is only part of Crowley's social media activities, which also include Facebook, YouTube, a blog on LiveJournal, and two specialty readers' networks — Goodreads and JacketFlap. Her hub Web site links to all these social networking sites.

Crowley acknowledges that she spends "a considerable amount of time" gathering new friends, updating her social pages, and reading about other books. Still, her MySpace advice is pragmatic. "Create a simple yet vibrant page, make it interactive with links, add music that appeals to teenagers, make as many friends as possible who are your target audience, do contests, wish your friends Happy Birthday, and update as frequently as possible."

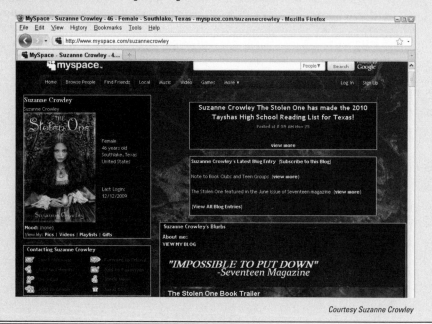

Courtesy Suzanne Crowley

Understanding How MySpace Can Benefit Your Business

The value of MySpace comes from sharing a sector of social-cyberspace with your target audience. It helps you to

✦ **Focus on branding rather than on selling.** Though you certainly can sell from MySpace, keep that task as an ancillary function. MySpace is soft-sell space, where recommendations from friends offer greater value than any pitch you make yourself.

✦ **Drive traffic to your site.** In addition to the link in your profile, place multiple links within MySpace content to other pages on your Web site.

Use *calls to action* — directions people should take — to tell people why they should visit your site. "Find out more about our next concert" is a much more appealing call to action than "Click here for more."

✦ **Communicate directly with your audience.** Comments from MySpace friends can provide important, direct feedback that you'll never hear elsewhere. Pay attention and respond. The content is more immediate than what you would get from a paid focus group, and cheaper, too.

✦ **Improve your search engine optimization (SEO) techniques.** After you optimize your site for search terms as discussed in Book II, Chapter 2, use the same essential search terms within your MySpace profile, blogs, and event listings. All those links you place to drive traffic also help improve your rank in Google results.

Update your MySpace page frequently to improve your presence in real-time search results.

Reinforcing your brand

When you pay attention to your online image and customer service, you're paying attention to your brand. The visual appearance of your MySpace page is part of your brand.

When you create your MySpace page, as described in the next section, replicate as close as possible the appearance of your Web site for consistency. On the other hand, if you're segmenting your audience — targeting a product line with a different message to a younger, hipper audience — you might need to make your MySpace presence more exciting, add music, or modify the page layout while keeping some internal image coherence.

Be sure to incorporate the following elements for branding purposes:

✦ Your logo

✦ Your marketing tag

✦ A link to your Web site, which can appear with your standard domain name but direct MySpace users to a landing page on your site designed with information and offers appropriate just for them

✦ Standard contact information addressed to a specific department or person who serves this market

You don't have a second chance to make a first impression. Users establish an immediate visual and emotional connection within three to four seconds of viewing your MySpace or Web page. Think carefully about the audience you're trying to reach and what visuals and music appeal to them.

Setting goals and objectives for MySpace

Everything goes better with a plan. Before you start developing your MySpace presence, think strategically. Whom are you trying to reach? Which goals are you trying to accomplish? Can you quantify your goals into quantifiable objectives, such as number of referrals to your site, number of sales, or number of posts? Here are some typical goals:

✦ **Friends:** *Friends,* the number of people who sign up to "pay attention" to your site, are the primary currency of MySpace. Think of your friends as prospects who might take additional action to become customers. It helps to establish a target objective and run a focused recruitment campaign to reach a targeted number of friends.

People ask to become your friend by clicking the Add to Friends link in the Contact box on your MySpace page. You decide which friend requests to accept. The friend space on your home page displays the number of friends you have as well as pictures of some of them.

A good rule is to estimate that about 5 percent of your friends might eventually click on your Web site or take another action.

Make sure to use calls to action on your Web site that remind people to become your friend and, in turn, to tell their friends about you. Just having a Follow Us icon for MySpace isn't enough! For example, the anchor text for a link to your MySpace page might read "Friend Us on MySpace." If your online store can handle promotion codes, you might even offer a discount for becoming a friend. However, you have to e-mail the promo code to each individual who befriends you, or send a bulletin with the code.

✦ **Customer service:** Using your MySpace blog or bulletins, you can respond quickly to questions or complaints about your product or service, reaching many people at a time instead of responding to one person at a time. You can also post links to product videos for training, installation, troubleshooting, or product display.

✦ **Publicity:** Following the publicity vector on social media can become overwhelming. People can refer your page to another service, add a social bookmark, or e-mail a friend quickly. In addition to watching referrals to your Web site with your traffic statistic software, use one of the alert services discussed in Book II, Chapter 1 for online mentions of your company that you didn't place.

✦ **Sales:** You can use one of the third-party shopping cart tools (see Book II, Chapter 1) to sell from MySpace, or link users to your e-commerce Web site. Use Google Analytics to trace sales back to their referring source. Be sure to measure the value of sales, not just the number, to assess whether your investment is paying off.

✦ **Connection and communication:** You can tally the quantity of comments you receive, but it's hard to measure their quality. Many friends' comments and blog posts are self-serving or self-promoting or utterly irrelevant. Your own communications, of course, are always relevant and responsive, right?

To track leads, as opposed to links, try using a MySpace-specific e-mail address (`myspace@yourcompany.com`), a person's name, or a different phone extension to identify the source of inquiries. In a pinch, you can always ask how someone heard about you.

Considering your investment of time and resources

MySpace can be time-consuming, but it isn't expensive. Unless you pay someone to develop your page or use paid advertising, you can keep your MySpace financial investment to a minimum.

However, MySpace works best when you interact with your friends. That means responding to comments, sending out birthday messages, or at least reading what others have written and moving the "conversation" along. As with any other form of social media, MySpace can rapidly morph into a time vortex that swallows you up.

You're already budgeting your social media marketing time. Allot 15 minutes every other day to monitor MySpace, respond to comments, and make updates. Make at least a small amount of content change once a week.

Beginning with MySpace

You follow the same process to sign up as a business as you would for an individual. However, you answer the questions differently. Unless you're an artist, entertainer, or author, you're generally *not* your business. Your prospective clients or customers are much more interested in what you can do for them than in your personal story.

The distinctions begin with the sign-up page, at `https://signups.myspace.com/Modules/Signup/Pages/CreateAccount.aspx??fuseaction=signup`. Musicians, comedians, and filmmakers complete slightly different forms that place their profiles into the correct category. Certain information on this page deserves your attention:

✦ **E-mail address:** Use a general business address, not your personal one — for example, `myspace@yourcompanyname.com`.

Configure your e-mail client to accept the new e-mail address.

✦ **Full name:** Enter your business name.

✦ **Date of birth:** Enter an arbitrary date, such as January 1, 1950, that makes your age 21 or over.

Do not use the age of your company, unless you have been established for more than 21 years. MySpace restricts permissible activities by age. If your age is under 13, you aren't even allowed to sign up.

✦ **Gender:** This one doesn't matter, but it's required. Flip a coin.

✦ **Photo:** After you confirm your account information, you can upload a photo. Rather than upload a picture of yourself, upload your logo or a product image.

✦ **Location:** Provide the country, city, state, and zip code for your business.

Save the form and move to the next step, creating your profile. MySpace automatically walks you through the profile process.

On the first page that appears (`http://profileedit.myspace.com/index.cfm?fuseaction=profile.username`), check the MySpace URL option in the upper-left corner to make it easier for people to find you. For branding purposes, enter a name that's as close as possible to your domain name. If it's already taken, use a variation of your company name. Don't use your personal name — it will only confuse users.

This page appears when you first create a profile, but never again. In other words, you're saddled with the URL you choose for your MySpace lifetime. Be careful.

Editing your profile

MySpace autofills some fields and outlines profile content in modules. You can fill out these fields any way you want and modify them at any time. For the MySpace audience, try to give your content a personal flair — take out the starch!

To edit your profile, choose Profile⇨Edit Profile. Work your way down the sections in the left navigation. Do what best fits your business, but here are some suggestions for each one:

✦ **About Me:** This first block is a good place to add a brief description of your business and insert your domain name. You can duplicate the Page Description metatag from the home page of your Web site, which is already optimized for certain search terms (see Book II). Be sure to include benefits and your value proposition (what sets your company apart from others). You can also include links to your Web site and to your other social media pages. In the second area (Who I'd Like to Meet), describe your target market, at least the portion of it that's likely to be on MySpace!

✦ **Interests:** Depending on the nature of your business, you might want to fill out only the General block with information about your products and services. Be sure to use some of the same search terms for which your

Web site is optimized. Fill out the blocks for Music, Movies, Television, Books, and Heroes, if they apply. However, if you're in one of those industries, consider talking about your track record and experience instead of your likes and dislikes.

✦ **Basic Info:** Modify the sign-up information you provided, change your display name, or add or substitute other images for display. With as many as four images available, you can supplement your logo with photos of your product in use or your crew at work. You can also enter a headline for your business.

Use the Headline field in the Basic Info section to insert your *marketing tag,* the five- to seven-word description of your business that appears on your business card and Web site and all your other marketing information. In the best of all possible worlds, the headline includes at least one of your preferred search terms.

✦ **Details:** You can delete this module unless you're a freelance model or actor. This section generates the demographic information, including ethnicity and marital status, that MySpace uses to target audiences for paid advertisers.

✦ **Schools:** Delete this module also, unless you're creating a profile for an educational institution or program.

✦ **Companies:** This module is designed for employment history, but if your company has multiple storefronts or divisions, you can enter that information here. Otherwise, you can delete it.

✦ **Networking:** In this valuable module, you select a field and subfield and your role from a list, and then you add a description. You can add multiple networking fields. Complete this module carefully because it categorizes your MySpace page for search purposes. If you're interested in reaching particular industry sectors with your services or products, you might want to include those fields here, too. Include search terms in the Description fields.

For instance, if you're a graphic designer who wants to create CD covers, you might select music/marketing/art design and insert a description of your creative CD covers.

If you aren't sure which fields to choose, find your competitors on MySpace by using the Search function (choose Search MySpace↪ People). Then do some basic research by looking at their MySpace pages and Web sites.

Customizing your profile

On the Profile Tab, click Customize Profile. As you hover the mouse over the various display blocks, you see options for Settings, Visibility, Edit, and Delete Module on each one.

First, you may want to delete the blocks that don't apply to your business such as the Mood module; the Details module, which provides irrelevant personal information such as marital status and height; and the Schools module. Don't worry: You can reinstall the modules later if you change your mind.

For each of the modules that you decided to keep, adjust the settings as follows:

1. **Set the visibility level.**

The Visibility setting controls which users can view a specific module. For most businesses, the settings are Everyone and Apply to All Modules. Then click to apply changes.

2. **Set the privacy levels for each module by clicking the privacy link within the Visibility dialog box or by going to** `http://profileedit.` `myspace.com/index.cfm?fuseaction=accountSettings.privacy`.

You can set different privacy levels for each module, but most businesses should select the broadest audience (Anyone) with the possible exception of preventing users under 18 from contacting you.

3. **Use the edit mode as another way to modify the content within a module.**

Once you're in Edit mode, your list of modules also appears in the left margin of the window.

4. **Click the Save Changes button after you edit each one.**

Customizing your MySpace appearance

Customize Profile also allows you to adjust the look and feel of your MySpace presence. At the top of `http://profileedit.myspace.com/` `index.cfm?fuseaction=pageeditor.profile`, you see choices for theme and layout. Here are some other options you have:

✦ **Choose a new theme:** Select the Appearances option and click Select Theme. You can choose from 157 themes organized in 16 categories. Choose the predesigned template that best matches the look and feel of your Web site, or one that you feel will appeal to your audience.

✦ **Change the layout:** Click the Change Layout option to rearrange the overall appearance of your page. Then select Modules in the left navigation in the upper left pane to if you want to add or delete additional modules from your MySpace page. Click the Preview button to see how your page will look. You can change the template at any time.

If you prefer to have your MySpace page directly mirror your Web site, you can control all settings in the Cascading Style Sheets (CSS) option or use the Advanced Edit function.

✦ **Go hybrid:** Use one of the MySpace templates for layout, but create a customized background that repeats your logo or echoes your Web site. Get technical support from your programmer if you need help with this task. In Table 3-4, you can find a summary of some handy URLs for navigating your way through the MySpace configuration process. You must be logged into your account for most of these URLs to work.

Table 3-4	Helpful URLs for MySpace	
Task You Need Help With	*URL*	*What You Can Do*
Account settings	`http://profileedit.myspace.com/index.cfm?fuseaction=accountSettings.contactInfo`	Establish administrative settings for your MySpace page.
Blog Control Center	`http://blogs.myspace.com/index.cfm?fuseaction=blog.controlcenter`	Set controls for posting and viewing blogs and obtain blog stats
Blog help	`http://faq.myspace.com/app/blogs`	Help manage your blog
Connect with MySpace	`www.myspace.com/getconnected`	Connect your MySpace page to other social media dashboards or monitoring services
Customize page appearance	`http://profileedit.myspace.com/index.cfm?fuseaction=pageeditor.profile`	Go directly to the Customize Profile page
Events and calendar	`http://events.myspace.com`	Create events to post on your calendar and view recommended events
Mail settings	`http://messaging.myspace.com/index.cfm?fuseaction=mail.settingsV3`	Establish settings for your MySpace e-mail

(continued)

Book VII Chapter 3

MySpace

Table 3-4 *(continued)*

Task You Need Help With	URL	What You Can Do
MySpace browser toolbar	`http://faq.myspace.com/ app/answers/detail/a_ id/306/kw/Blogs/ page/3/r_id/100061`	Install a MySpace toolbar in your browser
Groups Home	`http://groups. myspace.com/index. cfm?fuseaction=groups. categories`	Search, create, and manage your MySpace groups
Help	`http://faq.myspace. com/app/home`	Search for answers to common questions

Selecting other options

You can further personalize your MySpace page to maximize your marketing impact by clicking the Profile tab and selecting an option from the drop-down list:

✦ **Music:** My Playlists lets you upload an optional music clip to play when users visit your site. Match your music to the mood you're trying to establish. Be sure that you own the copyright or have the owner's permission for any music you use!

✦ **Video:** With My Videos, you can upload optional video clips that users can select to view. A still of the first one appears on the screen. Select this primary video with a specific marketing goal in mind. Again, be sure that you own the copyright or have permission.

✦ **Activity Stream:** This option displays activity on your MySpace page. It's a little like displaying a counter on your Web site. If your MySpace activity level is high, the numbers act like a testimonial. If your numbers are low, turn off this option by choosing Customize Profile⇨Modules so that you don't discourage viewers.

✦ **Applications:** Choose My Apps to choose from more than 1,000 little applications — *widgets* — to offer to your visitors. On one hand, applications such as contests, polls, quizzes, or games can keep users on your page and draw them back, reinforcing your brand. On the other hand, they can distract from your marketing message and slow the download time of your MySpace page. Choose no more than two, or ignore applications altogether.

Making the Most of MySpace

You can amplify your marketing message by taking advantage of three MySpace features: groups, blogs, and bulletins. Selecting the right groups helps you target your market, whereas blogs help you update content and interact with all viewers. Bulletins are used to communicate only with your MySpace friends, comparable to sending a bulk e-mail or e-newsletter to subscribers.

Combine your MySpace page with a MySpace Local listing, and possibly some MySpace advertising, for more marketing oomph.

Selecting groups

It might not seem obvious, but joining a MySpace group or creating a new one is a tactical marketing decision. Select groups whose membership parallels your target market.

Start by reviewing the list of group categories at `http://groups.myspace.com/index.cfm?fuseaction=groups.categories`. As you can see, often thousands of groups are within each category. Click the category name to see a brief description of each one. Look for public groups with recent activity and a reasonable number of members. Use the Search Groups function on the Groups Home page (refer to Table 3-4) to make your life a little easier. Because each of the 34 categories has tens of thousands of groups, try the Advanced Search option to filter results by keyword, category, location, and other parameters.

When you find a group you like, simply click Join Group to become a member.

By joining a group, you become more visible to MySpace members who are looking for people who share their interests — and, conversely, you have an inside track to reach your target markets.

You can join an unlimited number of groups, and you're expected to participate. Try limiting your participation to only a few groups, though you can drop out of any group at any time.

Don't judge a group by its name. Spend some time watching the interaction level in the group and be sure that it covers the interest area and draws the users you expect.

If you decide to create a group of your own, you need to spend some time promoting the group and waiting for membership to build. From a business perspective, starting with an existing group is easier. If you want to develop a group of your own, simply click the Create Group option on the Group

Home page, or go directly to `http://groups.myspace.com/index.cfm?fuseaction=groups.creategroup&lang=en`. Complete the form on that page and click the Create Group button at the bottom.

Managing your MySpace blog

As discussed in Book III, Chapter 2, blogs are one of the most useful ways to reach prospects with easily updated content. If you don't already have a blog, you can create your primary blog on MySpace and then propagate your postings elsewhere. Conversely, you can automatically update MySpace with posts from other sources by using a syndication service, such as ping.fm. (See Book II, Chapter 1 for more services.)

For most businesses, one blog is plenty. Some companies have more than one expert write a blog about their specialty.

Busting out with MySpace bulletins

Sometimes you want to communicate only with your MySpace friends and not with the general world. For instance, you might want to reward friends with a special offer or promotion code to buy something on your Web site.

Or, you may want to copy a blog posting to your friends to be sure that they see it. Your bulletin appears on all your friends' private bulletin boards, on their individual home pages. The bulletin remains visible for two weeks, and only they can see it.

You cannot "unsend" a bulletin. Be absolutely sure you want to send it.

You can find the directions to post a bulletin or to review all bulletins you've posted at `http://faq.myspace.com/app/answers/detail/a_id/310/kw/bulletins/r_id/100061`

Promoting events

The MySpace calendar is a handy way to plan and publicize your events. To generate an event posting, choose Edit Profile⇨Account Settings⇨Calendar⇨Create. Use this module to display scheduled events, from performances, gallery openings, and book signings to online or in-store sales.

Be sure to include conferences at which someone from your business will be speaking, trade shows or crafts fairs at which you're exhibiting, or other third-party events, such as trade association meetings, that you're attending. Try to use at least one of your preferred search terms within the Event Title field.

Selling through MySpace

You can't sell directly from MySpace, but you can link one of the following elements to a third-party site for e-commerce:

✦ Your own Web site.

✦ A third-party store such as Netcarnation or Sellit (see Book II, Chapter 1).

✦ Your page on a third-party site such as Amazon, eBay, or Etsy. For an example, see the Texas Tornados's MySpace page at `www.myspace.com/texastornados`, shown in Figure 3-2, which links to the Double Stereo Web site.

Book VII
Chapter 3

MySpace

Figure 3-2: To buy the latest Texas Tornados CD, viewers can click from their Purchase link.

Courtesy Texas Tornados 2010

MySpace tries to keep users on its own site. Viewers may see an interstitial message warning about phishing and requiring confirmation before they arrive at your Web site or third-party store.

Offering your MySpace friends, visitors, and blog readers something special for their loyalty makes sense. You can do it in several ways:

✦ Post a promo code in one of your blurbs and link visitors to your Web site or third-party site.

✦ Send a bulletin to your friends that includes a time-limited, special offer.

✦ Promote an offer on your home page to encourage visitors to become friends. For instance, "Become my friend this week and save 10 percent on your next purchase." Be sure to e-mail the promo code to all visitors who sign up or send them a new bulletin.

✦ Include an offer in your blog.

✦ If you're running a loyalty program on your e-commerce site, set up a special program just for MySpace users.

You cannot sell directly from MySpace. Be sure to read the terms of use carefully to see what you can and cannot do. Otherwise, your account may be suspended.

Advertising on MySpace

Consider buying pay-per-click (PPC) or pay-by-impression (CPM) banner ads on MySpace if you want to reach this demographic of users under 34 but don't want to devote time to creating and maintaining a MySpace pro-file. MySpace is part of the MyAds self-service ad program at `www.myads.com/myspace/login.html`, which serves the FOX Audience Network. The service offers a template builder for ads, statistics, and detailed targeting options.

Budgets for ad campaigns, which you can start and stop at will, can run as low as $5/month. You'll find additional information and directions for busi-nesses at `www.myads.com/businessads.html`, as well as advertising sug-gestions specifically for musicians and concert promoters, comedians, and filmmakers.

Page owners can choose not to permit most ads to display on their MySpace page by choosing Edit Profile⇨Account Settings⇨Ad Categories, and leaving all the boxes blank. To avoid distracting viewers of your MySpace page, exer-cise this "no ads" option. However, at least one leader board ad probably will still run above the MySpace header graphic.

MySpace also displays PPC text and banner ads from Google Adwords in multiple locations. If you run a Google Adwords campaign, you can select various MySpace locations and audiences as a destination for managed con-tent placements.

To set this up for your ad campaign, choose Settings⇨Networks & Devices⇨Select Content Network⇨Placements and Audiences I Manage. Save your settings. Then, from your campaign or ad group, choose Networks⇨Managed Placements⇨Add Placements⇨Try the Placement

Tool. After you enter MySpace.com into the Website box, you'll see a list of MySpace placement options (see Figure 3-3). For more information on combining social media with advertising campaigns, see Book VIII, Chapter 5.

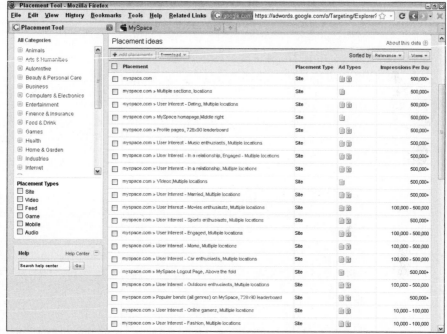

Figure 3-3: Google feeds PPC and banner ads to multiple locations on MySpace.

Buying group or bulletin access

Some MySpace sites sell advertising on their bulletins or in their groups. Be cautious. Whether those ads successfully reach your audience depends on the quality of the site that's selling the access. Those with high-quality MySpace friends and high standards may do well, but others are just people sending bulletins to each other.

It may take longer, but you'll probably find that it's more effective to promote your products and services in your own bulletins and blogs to your own carefully cultivated list of friends.

Marketing off MySpace

Cross-promoting your MySpace page on all your other social media efforts is always a good idea. Similarly, use your MySpace page to cross-promote the others.

Using the MySpace icon

Post a MySpace icon and a call to action to become your friend on your Web site, on your other social media sites, and at any other place where you have a Web presence. This icon should link directly to your own MySpace home page. You can find the icon at

```
www.myspace.com/pressroom?url=/section_display.cfm?section_
    id=18
```

Be sure to include MySpace as a Follow Us On button (as shown on mrgsanchez.com in Figure 3-4) to link people directly from your Web site to your MySpace page. Also include MySpace in your list of social sharing buttons from AddThis (`http://addthis.com`) or other sharing services (see Book II, Chapter 3). Users who select MySpace from a sharing service log in to their MySpace pages and are invited to post a link to your Web site on their own pages, bulletins, or blogs. It's a failsafe word-of-Web technique.

Figure 3-4:
The MySpace Music button on his Web site links to Gilbert Sanchez's MySpace page.

Cross-promoting on Twitter

If you also have a Twitter account, you can use Twitter Sync at www.myspace.com/twittersync to display your MySpace online status and mood automatically with Twitter. This strategy works only if you have enabled the Mood and Status module on MySpace. Conversely, you can post your tweets on MySpace.

**Book VII
Chapter 3**

MySpace

Chapter 4: Flickr

In This Chapter

✔ Deciding whether Flickr is right for you

✔ Setting up your Flickr account

✔ Uploading and organizing photos

✔ Participating in Flickr groups

✔ Using Flickr to drive traffic to your Web site

✔ Marketing with Flickr

*F*lickr is a popular, easy-to-use photo management and sharing applica-tion, and much more. Tags and other organizing tools help you easily sort your photos, which you can then post to a blog, embed on your Web site, insert in an e-newsletter, or share on other social media sites. You don't have to collect fans, friends, or followers (what a relief!), but other people can comment on your photos or designate them as their favorites (or "faves"). You can collaborate (or commiserate) with other photogra-phers by joining or creating an online group.

The Web site, blog, or Ning community that carries your domain name is still the hub for your online marketing activity. Flickr should be considered a supplemental site: In fact, Flickr's community guidelines constrain com-mercial use (www.flickr.com/guidelines.gne). If Flickr's rules are too limiting, a commercial-level or Pro account on Photobucket may offer more flexibility (http://photobucket.com).

Now owned by Yahoo!, Flickr has grown rapidly since it launched in November 2003. As of mid–October 2009, the site hosted more than 4 billion photos and received well over 20 million visitors per month from the United States alone. Amateur and professional photographers worldwide upload about 5,000 photos every minute. By some calculations, Flickr has close to 50 million members, most of which hold free accounts.

Deciding Whether Flickr Is Right for You

There are as many ways to use Flickr legitimately for business as there are creative businesses to find applications. Though Flickr is obviously useful for B2C purposes, B2B companies may also find each other through Flickr groups. If any of the following solutions would serve your marketing needs, consider expending some of your social media capital on Flickr or another photo-sharing site:

✦ **Enhance your image.** Consider documenting a special activity that you might support, such as the New York Special Olympics (`www.flickr.com/photos/nyso`), or show staff participating in community activities such as helping to refurbish the Queens Museum of Art (`www.flickr.com/photos/panoramaqueensmuseum`). Whether your staff contributes to a Habitat for Humanity house-building project, volunteers to clean wildlife, or helps serve a Thanksgiving Dinner, use Flickr to illustrate your company's involvement in issues that matter to your community.

✦ **Announce awards, exhibits, or your presence at events like trade-shows**. Brentano Fabrics does some of everything at `www.flickr.com/photos/brentanofabrics/sets`.

✦ **Draw your audience closer.** Asking members of your target audience to submit photos is a wonderful way to solidify relationships. The Nature program on the Public Broadcasting System runs contests for wildlife photography themed to its shows at `www.flickr.com/groups/pbs nature`. Consider asking your customers to upload photos of themselves assembling your products or using your services. You might even ask for photographs that might be used in future advertising. There's plenty of creative talent out there!

✦ **Cast a wider net.** Some prospects prefer looking at pictures to reading words. Use Flickr to illustrate images of your company, staff, or services, as California Fruit Company does in Figure 4-1. You can link actively to your Web site from your Flickr profile (as on `www.flickr.com/people/californiafruitcompany`), but not from photos.

✦ **Advertise to photographers.** This is a wonderful targeted site for offering goods and services to photographers, such as cameras, lenses, photo editing software, lighting equipment, workshops, studio space, or travel packages for photo safaris. Yahoo! serves ads to Flickr through its own ad network at `http://advertising.yahoo.com`.

✦ **Improve customer service.** Upload images that are limited to use by specific customers or invitees, perhaps marking them private for limited visibility. You can post pictures of work in progress, images of prospective sites or buildings, or photographs of optional product features. This feature is particularly useful when photos interest a smaller audience than the one served by your Web site.

✦ **Enhance branding and site traffic.** By using your *favicon* (a mini logo), tags, Web address, or links on your profile page, you can build name recognition and awareness of your primary site.

✦ **Improve search engine optimization.** Flickr can be helpful to your search engine optimization strategy. Tags, filenames, photo descriptions, names of sets, and profiles can all include some of your key search terms. Note, however, that comments include a `nofollow` attribute, so they don't pass "link juice" for search purposes. For more on search optimization, see Book II, Chapter 2.

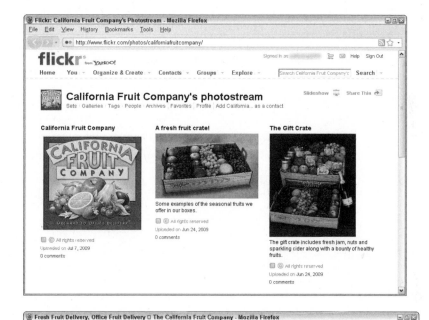

Figure 4-1: California Fruit Company uses attractive images in its Flickr photostream for informational purposes.

The California Fruit Company logos and wordmarks are the registered property of California Fruit Company.

✦ **Supplement Web site or social media pages with additional photos.** For instance, you might display thumbnails on your Web site or one image from a set or a slide sequence of photos, as long as each of the displayed images links back to its Flickr page. You can't use Flickr simply to host images for products you're selling, but you might want to maintain photos of a company event, trade show, or conference or pictures of staff or your storefront decor. Continue to pull from your Web server the images critical to your Web site and post only copies on Flickr.

According to the Flickr community guidelines (`www.flickr.com/guidelines.gne`), you cannot use Flickr for commercial purposes. Flickr doesn't want to become a collection of product catalogs so avoid shots of actual products. You can include an active link to your Web store or other selling sites in your profile, but not on individual photo pages, photo descriptions, or anywhere on your photostream page. If you aren't selling from the link (if you have a nonprofit or informational site, for example), you can include an active link in descriptions and elsewhere. Flickr may terminate violators' accounts after a warning. If you aren't sure what's allowed, contact Flickr (`www.flickr.com/help/with/other`).

Keep in mind the standard conversion rate of 2 to 4 percent for people who reach your Web site. Make a quick calculation: How many prospects need to reach your photostream to learn about your business? How many of those will reach your Web site? How many will convert to customers after that, and how much will they spend? Will you make enough to cover your cost of participation in labor and photographic services?

Use the search function for people or photos (full text) to see how many, if any, of your competitors use Flickr. The presence of many competitors is a strong hint that your business needs to be here, too. The absence of competition is ambiguous: It can give you a temporary advantage or indicate that this effort isn't worth it. Being first isn't always the best idea.

Making the Most of Flickr

Initially, you might think that Flickr would work well only for companies with tangible products that are easy to photograph. Think again! Businesses that provide services — from dog trainers and fitness centers to performing artists, tai chi clubs, and wedding planners — can show images of events, training sessions, or facilities. Though the Flickr audience is predominantly consumer, B2B companies can use it to showcase their work.

Take a look at some imaginative ways companies have found to use Flickr:

✦ **Build awareness of your portfolio.** In perhaps the most obvious application for Flickr, creative folks can display their portfolios and new work to a broad audience:

- *Visual artists:* www.flickr.com/photo/ikaminoff
- *Sculptors:* www.flickr.com/photos/stevecrowningshield
- *Public art projects:* www.flickr.com/photos/artesprit/sets/72157623548855199
- *Photographers:* www.flickr.com/photos/terretta

✦ **Display photos of completed projects or works in progress.** The Flickr organizational structure works exceedingly well for architects, builders, construction companies, and home painters as well as for interior, landscape, product, and packaging design companies and any other business with highly visual work results. The Women's Economic Self-Sufficiency Team (WESST) of New Mexico shows off its stunning new building at www.flickr.com/people/wesstnm, whereas Lux Design of Toronto shows examples of its residential and commercial interiors at www.flickr.com/photos/luxinteriordesign. Tanzania Development Support records the progress of its new dormitory under construction at www.flickr.com/photos/43749472@N07.

✦ **Entice viewers with examples.** Whether you offer pets for adoption like www.flickr.com/photos/kids4kats or bake cupcakes like Buttercream Bakery at www.flickr.com/photos/40786473@N02, you can use Flickr to lure visitors to your Web site as long as you don't post images from your online store or link to them in your photostream. Don't post your entire catalog!

✦ **Collaborate on content.** The Pharmacy School at the University of California at San Francisco (http://pharmacy.ucsf.edu) uses its Flickr account to manage its Web site photos and encourage participation from campus members. Flickr images appear on its virtual tour at http://pharmacy.ucsf.edu/tou and on other content pages. You can find a description of how UCSF uses Flickr as a collaborative activity at http://pharmacy.ucsf.edu/flickr. Note how the images link back to Flickr as required.

✦ **Build community participation and buzz.** In a novel interactive application, Marvel Comics created a Flickr group for movie lovers to post photos of themselves with statues of the Incredible Hulk that had been placed in movie theater lobbies to promote the film. Selected photos from the group at www.flickr.com/groups/hulkstatues also appeared on the Marvel site (http://marvel.com/news/movie stories.3421.Hulk_Crashes_Iron_Man~apos~s_Opening) as a way to increase its fan base and enhance word-of-mouth advertising.

TIP

Set up separate business and personal accounts on Flickr. Although you can categorize images for public versus private (friends or family) viewing, you can create confusion if other staff members are involved, not to mention cloud your statistics. You can so easily create separate Flickr accounts that you have no reason to commingle the two.

Book VII Chapter 4

Flickr

Table 4-1 shows that Flickr is one of the few social media outlets that attracts more men than women. It has a higher percentage of ethnic Asian and Hispanic users than the Internet user population overall. The income distribution on Flickr may be a consequence of the large younger-student population (19 percent of users are under 18). To reach businesses rather than consumers, you participate in groups, discussed later in this chapter.

Table 4-1	Flickr Demographic Profile
Category	*Percentage of Users*
Female	47
Male	53
Under 18	19
18 to 34	38
35 to 49	27
Over 50	17
Caucasian	73
African American	8
Asian	6
Hispanic	12
Other ethnicity	1
No college	46
College	40
Grad school	14
Income $0 to 30,000	17
Income $30,000 to 60,000	26
Income $60,000 to 100,000	28
Income over $100,000	30

Source: Quantcast.com www.quantcast.com/flickr.com for 5/10

Beginning with Flickr

Flickr (www.flickr.com) is extremely easy to use. Start by clicking the Create Your Account button on the home page. If you don't already have a Yahoo! ID, you'll be asked to create one. Because you can follow your nose from here by using onscreen directions and visiting the FAQ pages on the site, we review only the critical marketing steps.

✦ **Get oriented.** Check out the Flickr tour at `www.flickr.com/tour/share` and its list of tips for extending the value of Flickr elsewhere at `www.flickr.com/get_the_most.gne`.

✦ **Click any Get Started button.** You're asked to either log in with an existing Yahoo! ID or create one. Your Yahoo! e-mail address appears in your Flickr profile, but you can change the e-mail address in your Flickr account later.

✦ **Select your Flickr screen name.** The screen name is your first branding decision — it's attached to every photo you upload and every message you post. For branding purposes, use your business name or Web address.

✦ **Create your buddy icon (or *avatar*, in other social media venues) by uploading a small version of your logo.** Flickr helps you resize the image to 48 x 48 pixels. If you have a larger version of your favicon (the 16-x-16-pixel graphic that appears to the left of a URL in the browser address bar), use it for consistent branding.

You can make a favicon for free at `www.favicon-generator.com`.

✦ **Select a custom Flickr URL.** In the best of all possible worlds, your custom URL should be the same as your screen name, and therefore the same as your business name or Web site address.

You can't change your screen name later, so choose carefully!

✦ **Personalize your Flickr profile.** Complete the form by following the steps shown on the screen:

  • *First and Last Name:* Use your company name (preferred) or your name, or the name of your marketing person.

  • *Gender and Singleness:* Select Rather Not Say.

  • *Describe Yourself Box:* Fill out this box with a good marketing description that includes all your contact information: business address, non–Flickr and non–Yahoo! e-mail addresses, and any phone and fax numbers you have. Be sure to include your primary search terms in the text you write! You may be able to modify the already optimized text of your home page for this purpose. Because the length is unlimited, you can add some information about your featured products or services, links to your Web site and other social media pages, or information about your company. For a good example, see California Fruit Company at `www.flickr.com/people/californiafruitcompany`. Click the triangle next to "*How do I format my description?*" for directions on inserting an image or link, or using HTML to format your text.

Although you're using your profile to describe your business, avoid any sales pitches, in keeping with the Flickr atmospherics and guidelines.

Flickr may close the profile screen at this point. If so, choose the You tab at the top of the page➪Your Profile➪Edit Your Profile Information to complete the remaining details.

- *Online Bits:* Add your primary Web address and Web site name in the labeled boxes.

- *Offline Bits:* For your occupation, use your business type. Including the current city/state, country, and airport code in their appropriate boxes helps with local marketing when someone searches Flickr, as well as with geotagging, an optional flag that identifies where a photograph was created. (Ignore the Hometown box.)

- *Edit Your Profile Privacy:* After you save your profile information and return to the Your Profile page, select this option. For most businesses, highly accessible settings are preferable: Let anyone see your e-mail address, real (business) name, and current city. Set your own preference for instant messaging or constrain it to your contacts. Save again.

Before you start uploading photos, take time to establish the rest of the settings on the Your Account page (www.flickr.com/account):

1. **Click Privacy & Permissions in the breadcrumb trail at the top. Review every setting to fit with your business needs.**

Click the Edit link next to each option for more detail and choices. Although you are establishing these as global settings now, you can later customize the privacy level for specific images or sets of images. Most business owners should opt for less restrictive use, although you might want to prevent downloads of some images.

This list describes a few key fields to consider in order to control the use of your images:

Global settings

- *Who Can Download Your Stuff?:* To control dissemination, especially if you're posting creative work, select Only You as the response to the first option in the Global Settings section. If you want your imagery to have wider distribution, set the levels accordingly. You can later specify licensing levels for individual photos or sets to override these settings.

- *Who Can Share Your Photos or Video?:* Specify whether a Share This button is visible to other people on your public uploads. Display the Share This button to let people e-mail or embed a link to your photostream, much like social sharing buttons described in Book II, Chapter 3, or the tell-a-friend function, which lets users quickly e-mail others a link to your page. The setting you choose depends on your content and reason for posting photos.

- *Printing:* Select Only You to constrain the distribution of your images. If you want your material more broadly accessible, change the settings accordingly.

This advice applies also to the Who Can Blog Your Stuff option.

- *Allow Your Stuff To Be Added to a Gallery?:* Choose Yes. Allowing your photos to be added to other people's Flickr galleries may give the photos greater exposure. Being able to make photos eligible for distribution by Getty Images (at the bottom of the page) is a gift to visual artists and photographers. Most will choose Yes, unless these are personal, private, or confidential images, or images of people you don't have permission to publish.

- *Hide Your Stuff from Public Searches:* Choose No unless you're using Flickr strictly to provide access to private clients, customers, or prospects. Anything else is counterproductive, especially if you're hoping for a boost in search engine visibility. If you're a creative artist, you might want to choose Yes, though that choice may reduce your visibility in image searches on Yahoo! (http://images.search.yahoo.com) and Google (http://images.google.com).

If you're in business, choose No to the Hide Your Profile option. Your profile is the primary vehicle for conveying information about your company.

Defaults for new uploads

- For most companies, the default settings in this main section work well, but you should review them to be sure that they apply to your business. For instance, on the first option, you may want to select Anyone to let everyone see images but select Only You to ensure that you're the only one permitted to add notes, tags, and people.

- Review the options to decide which licensing level to assign to your content; this is particularly critical for visual artists and others who are uploading copyrighted material— All Rights Reserved is the most restrictive.

- Under Safety Level and Content, select the potential "offense" level and specify the type of upload — photo, video, screen shot, screencast, or illustration, art, animation, or CGI.

Content filters

- In this main section, select the appropriate settings for your level of comfort with potentially offensive imagery provided by others and specify the content types to include when you search.

- You can change these options later for individual photos or sets of photos, and you can modify your global and default settings at any time.

2. **Click the Emails & Notifications link in the breadcrumb trail at the top. Add or change the e-mail address that serves as your primary notification address for messages from Flickr.**

This setting doesn't change your Yahoo! login. After you confirm the new address, you can specify it as your primary contact (the one that viewers see). Set the notification level you're comfortable with. Note the e-mail address you can use to e-mail uploads directly to Flickr or configure settings to update your blog with Flickr postings.

3. **Click the Sharing & Extending link in the breadcrumb trail at the top.**

   Depending on your marketing strategy and the progress of your implementation plan for social marketing, you can link your Flickr account to your blog, Facebook, Twitter, or Yahoo! Updates, and to other third-party applications.

Uploading Photos

Flickr gives you multiple options for uploading photos and videos. Start by returning to the You tab at the top of the page and select Upload Photos and Videos at `www.flickr.com/photos/upload`.

✦ **Individually:** Click on Choose Photos and Videos to select an image from your hard drive or other storage location. As you add each image, you can set its individual privacy level. Select the Add More link or Upload Photo button when you are ready.

✦ **In bulk:** Use the Basic Uploader at `www.flickr.com/photos/upload/basic` or one of the newer, fancier uploading tools at `www.flickr.com/tools`. Images uploaded through these methods will share the same tags and privacy settings, unless you modify them later in the Organizr described later in this chapter.

✦ **By e-mail:** Go to `www.flickr.com/account/uploadbyemail` to obtain a dedicated e-mail address for uploading your pictures. When you e-mail your photo, enter the title in the Subject line and the description in the body of the message.

✦ **By cellphone:** Visit `www.flickr.com/tools/mobile` to see the available mobile tools for using Flickr. As of August 2009, the iPhone is the most frequently used camera on Flickr!

Before you upload images, rename image files so that they're descriptive, or include search terms to increase their visibility within Flickr search results and on external image search engines. You have much better luck when you use `bathing-black-labrador-dog.jpg` than with `picture1234567.jpg`.

Determining what to upload

Obviously, the content of your photos or videos depends on your business, your target market, and your goals and objectives for establishing a Flickr presence.

You can use pictures of installed products in use, service deliveries, facilities, studio and store tours, events, trade shows, or whatever else seems appropriate. If you're an individual service provider or artist, you might want to include a picture of yourself to personalize your Flickr page. The series of images you upload is called your *photostream*. Images appear in reverse chronological order, with most recent first.

Upload only good images! Because you're using Flickr to create an impression, photo quality matters. If your photos aren't well lit, well cropped, and well composed, hire a professional photographer. You may be able to find one by searching Flickr member pages for photographers in your city.

You must have a signed waiver giving you permission to use another person's likeness if your photos include recognizable faces. Just search for *photo waiver form* or *photo release form* at `www.google.com` or another search engine to find a model release form. Parents or legal guardians must sign for their underage children.

The dimensions and file size of individual files and the total monthly upload limit depend on whether you have a free account or upgrade to the Pro version for $24.95 per year. Table 4-2 compares the two types of accounts.

Table 4-2	Flickr Pro Version versus Flickr for Free
Pro	*Free*
Unlimited display	Photostream limited to the 200 most recent images
Unlimited photo uploads (20MB per photo)	100MB monthly photo upload limit (10MB per photo)
Full count and referrer stats available	Limited availability of activity stats
Photo or video posting limit in group pools: 60	Photo posting limit in group pools: 10
Unlimited sets and collections	Sets only, no collections
Unlimited video uploads (90-second maximum and 500MB per video)	Two monthly video uploads (90-second maximum and 150MB per video)
High-definition (HD) video	Not available
Six layout choices	Four layout choices
Access and archive your original high-resolution image	Access to only smaller, resized images
Ad-free browsing and sharing	Not available
Photo replacement	Not available

Under no circumstances should you upload anyone else's work without permission. You must own or have the right to use whatever images you upload.

Hey, big spender. Unless you plan to have only a minimal Flickr presence, upgrade to a Pro account for $24.95 per year. You can then access important statistics, display an unlimited number of images, and upload larger files.

Flickr has calls to action to upgrade to the Pro version on almost every public page, or you can go directly to www.flickr.com/upgrade and click the big Buy Now button.

Adding titles, tags, and descriptions

After you upload photos on Flickr, you have a chance to create a title, add as many as 75 tags (similar to keywords), and write a descriptive paragraph for each image, either individually or by set.

Flickr prompts you to add these tags, titles, and descriptions every time you upload an individual image or a batch of images. You can get to this screen, www.flickr.com/photos/upload, only as part of the upload process, but you can always add this information later in several ways:

✦ Use the Organizr at www.flickr.com/photos/organize (see Figure 4-2, in the following section); you can find more information on the Organizr in the next section, "Setting Up Sets and Collections."

✦ Log into Flickr and click the individual photo in your photostream. This takes you to the individual detail page for that photo. On the right side are several links, including one near the bottom of the page to Edit the Title, Description, and Tags.

Be sure that the Title, Tag, and Description fields include at least one of your primary search terms apiece. The Description and Tag fields can also include your company name and location.

Because of constraints on commercial use of Flickr, be discrete in the Description field. Though you can talk about benefits and features, be careful with calls to action (what you tell the viewer to do). In particular, don't include a Buy Now link, though you may be able to write "Get more information about Day-Glo coloredwhozee-whatz at MyWebSite.com," as long as the URL is not an active link.

Finally, use geotags to put your photos on the map. This indication of where a photo was taken can be quite helpful, especially if you own a tourism-related or hospitality business, or want to let local customers know where they can buy items or obtain business services. To add a geotag, click the individual photo in your photostream to go to its detail page. Click the Add to Map link in the lower-right corner and follow the directions. Batch options are available for geotagging in the Organizr, too.

Though you can use Flickr-stored images on your site, don't use Flickr to host your Web site's logos, banners, icons, avatars, or other *nonphotographic* images. Violating this Flickr no-no (www.flickr.com/guide lines.gne) can terminate your account.

Setting Up Sets and Collections: A Tactical Choice

Flickr is a dream site for compulsive organizers. Even if you like a cluttered desk, take advantage of the easy sorting features on Flickr. Unlike a traditional directory structure in which an image "lives" in one folder, the Flickr Organizr lets you assign each image to no sets, one set, or many sets of photos.

If you have a Pro account, you can group sets into collections and even gather collections into metacollections. Your tactical choice is defining which images belong in each set or collection. Grouping photos from each product line into their own set is tempting but isn't always the most effective marketing solution. Consider whether you should create sets, segmented by target market, that cut across product lines.

You can set the privacy level for each set or collection separately as you create them or in the Organizr.

Suppose that you sell laboratory equipment to high schools and colleges and several different industries. Though you can group photos of all balance scales into one set, you might want to also create sets that include scales, flasks, beakers, and burners appropriate to each market segment. These items can vary by price, quality, use, or size.

An artist or artisan might organize a portfolio into sets and collections by medium (oil, acrylic, or watercolor, for example), by content (portrait, landscape, abstract), or chronologically — or in all three ways. The Pharmacy School at the University of California at San Francisco (www.flickr.com/photos/ucsf/sets) uses sets to categorize locations, activities, and other types of items, as shown in Figure 4-2. Most sets contain multiple photos.

After you upload some photos, simply click the Organize & Create tab at the top of any page. Across the bottom of the page, you see a gray bar named the Findr. It contains a timeline of all your photo uploads in chronological order, with the newest on the left and the oldest on the right.

Click the Set tab. Then it's just a matter of dragging and dropping the images you want into each set. Name and save a set and off you go. Use descriptive names for sets, including a tag or search term, if possible. For more information, view the Organizr FAQ at www.flickr.com/help/organizr. This resource URL and others we mention in this chapter are compiled in the table in the nearby sidebar, "Useful Flickr resource URLs."

Book VII Chapter 4

Flickr

Courtesy UCSF School of Pharmacy

Figure 4-2:
The UCSF School of Pharmacy uses Flickr sets to arrange dozens of photos by location and activity.

Useful Flickr resource URLs

Resource You're Looking For	URL	What You Can Do
The App Garden	www.flickr.com/services	Find free third-party applications to attract attention
Badge	www.flickr.com/badge.gne	Create a Flickr badge for your Web site
Collections	www.flickr.com/help/collections	Read collection FAQs
Creative Commons	www.flickr.com/creativecommons	Post photos allowed for public use under license
Community guidelines	www.flickr.com/guidelines.gne	Read what you can and can't do on Flickr
Explore	www.flickr.com/explore	View featured photos
Explore	bighugelabs.com/faq.php?section=scout	Explore FAQs

Resource You're Looking For	URL	What You Can Do
FAQs	www.flickr.com/ help/faq	See the site map for commonly asked questions
Advice for getting the most from Flickr	www.flickr.com/get_ the_most.gne	Maximize your use of Flickr
Groups	www.flickr.com/help/ groups	Read group FAQs
Interestingness	www.flickr.com/ explore/interesting	Find out how interesting you are to Flickr visitors
Making stuff	www.flickr.com/tour/ makestuff	Turn your photos into promotional items, corporate gifts, and branding tools
Organizr	www.Flickr.com/help/ organizr	Read Organizr FAQs
Photos	www.flickr.com/help/ photos/#34	Check out photo uploading guidelines
Pro version	www.flickr.com/ upgrade	Sign up for the Pro version for $24.95 per year
Scout	bighugelabs.com/ scout.php	Determine whether your photos are on Explore
Search	www.flickr.com/ search	Search for photos, groups, or people
Site map	www.flickr.com/ sitemap.gne	Find a topic in the page index
Terms of use	www.flickr.com/ terms.gne	Read the Yahoo! terms of service
Tour	www.flickr.com/tour	Get introduced to Flickr
Uploading tools	www.flickr.com/tools	Select options for uploading images
Uploader Basic	www.flickr.com/ photos/upload/basic	Use the simplest uploading tool

To speed the process of building sets and collections, plan them on paper first, either in outline form or as a tree diagram.

Take advantage of the many shortcuts built into the Organizr interface — for instance:

✦ Double-click the image for the set to gain the option to arrange the sequence of images within a set or to batch-edit titles, tags, permissions, and other parameters, as shown in Figure 4-3.

✦ Double-click any individual image in the Findr to open a window and edit parameters for that image.

✦ Select the Batch Organize tab at the top of the screen to edit parameters for multiple sets or photos at the same time.

To get to the Organizr for your images, simply click the Organize & Create tab at the top of any page with photographs.

For simplicity, start by duplicating the organization of your Web site or online store or other social media pages with Flickr sets and collections. If you have designed your site with separate pages or store categories based on market segments, rather than by service or product line, so much the better.

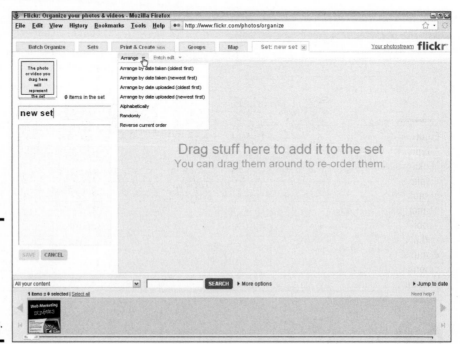

Figure 4-3:
Use the Organizr feature in Flickr to manage your photos.

Participating in the Flickr Community

As with other social networking sites supported by a large user base, gaining traction on Flickr is difficult. The only solution is to target distinct niche markets. As with Facebook and MySpace, groups are the easiest way to do it.

Flickr groups, which are organized by a volunteer administrator, can be

✦ Public

✦ Public by invitation only

✦ Private

The groups themselves are fairly similar. Every group has a discussion board and a place to share photos in a group pool, as seen in Figure 4-4. Membership can vary from several to several thousand. For more information on group how-tos, see www.flickr.com/help/groups.

Book VII Chapter 4

Flickr

Figure 4-4: A typical Flickr group displays photos from its members "pool" and allows discussion among members.

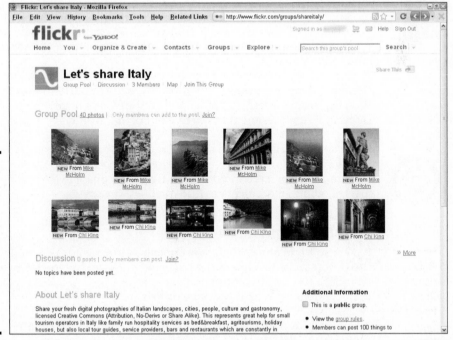

Top row photographs courtesy of Mike McHolm. Bottom row photographs courtesy of Chi King

Getting into groups

Start searching groups by tag or interest area or another search term. After you have a list, you can sort by relevance, activity, size, or age (how long the group has existed). It pays to sort the same list several different ways because you also want to find groups that

+ Have been around for at least six months

+ Continue to attract new members

+ Display a high level of activity, with frequent postings from many participants

+ Have more than one or two people dominating the conversation and postings

+ Demonstrate a clear need or want for the type of products or services you offer

Participating in a small group can take as much work as in a large one. To ensure that your time investment pays off, look for groups with at least 200 members, if not more. This number, of course, is somewhat dependent on your business. For instance, a relatively small group of film directors might be happy to share production tips and shooting angles with each other.

Click the More link to view samples of the group photo pool and to monitor the tone of the discussion. When you're ready to participate, click Join and then confirm your entry. You might want to join a dozen or so groups initially and then winnow them to five or six that produce the best leads.

If you sell or service only a specific region, use a search term that includes your location (for example, *Albuquerque balloon*) to find groups that draw from or are interested in your area. By geographically narrowing your target market, you're more likely to find qualified prospects.

Creating your own group

If you can't find any groups, you can easily start your own. Simply select the Group tab at the top of the page and click the Create Your Own Group link. Click the Create button under the level of group accessibility you want: Public, Public by Invitation Only, or Private.

If you create a public group, you might have to make a serious commitment of time and effort to reach a critical mass of members, and you may find yourself conducting a membership campaign.

Posting properly

The etiquette for participating in a Flickr group is standard for groups everywhere:

 ✦ Comply with the group's posting rules.

 ✦ Lurk and listen before you participate.

 ✦ Participate often in the discussion board, but avoid hard-sell techniques or blatant advertising. You can leave your screen name or Web address as a branding tool.

 ✦ Share your photos with the group pool.

 ✦ Don't try to stuff search terms into text on the group discussion board.

 ✦ Comment on or "fave" the photos produced by others in the group; they're more likely than random viewers to return the favor.

Because Flickr generally doesn't permit the commercial use of groups, you can't set up a company-based group. The only way around this restriction is to become an official sponsored group.

Casting bread upon the Flickr waters

In addition to groups, all participation options described in this section provide an opportunity for you to become known to others within the Flickr community. Think of it like you're networking a party: Decide whom you want to meet — your prospects or vendors, presumably — and then do one of these favors for them.

A vendor or prospect who receives a notification of your favor may be intrigued enough to visit your photostream out of curiosity, if nothing else. At least the person then finds out about your company and perhaps returns the favor. Who knows? You might even gain a customer.

Groups and favors can become time-consuming retail marketing methods. Be sure to schedule time to nourish your Flickr presence.

Follow these guidelines to begin putting together a community on Flickr:

 ✦ **Faves:** Mark someone else's photos as one of your favorites (faves) by clicking the Add to Faves button in the upper-left corner above the image on an individual photo page. You can fave an unlimited number of photos by other people, but you can't fave your own photos — not even one.

 ✦ **Galleries:** A gallery is a "curated" set of as many as 18 photos that you recommend to others. Click the Add to Gallery button in the upper-right corner of the set of options above the image on an individual photo page. You can't include your own images in your galleries. But you can create as many galleries as you'd like with other people's photos.

 ✦ **Comments:** Comments are made on your own or other contributors' individual photo pages or set pages. If you receive a positive comment, pay it back or pay it forward. Making comments encourages other people to visit your site and say something positive in turn. This strategy adds to your interestingness, a Flickr characteristic we discuss in the later section

"Extending Your Market Reach with Flickr." When it comes to comments, remember what Thumper said in *Bambi:* "If you can't say something nice, don't say nothing at all." You can refer to your Web presence in your own comments, but don't do it on other contributors' photos. Your screen name is enough branding.

✦ **Contacts:** Add people whose work you want to follow as contacts by clicking the Add As a Contact link in the list of options above someone's photostream. You might add specific group members, collaborating companies, or prospects to your contacts list. You can include current clients who need ongoing access to private sets of images and mark them as a friend. Because the latest uploads from your contacts appear on *your* contacts list and home page, you may not want to include competitors or anyone else whose work would distract from your own company's presence. For more information, see www.flickr.com/photos/friends.

✦ **Testimonials:** Testimonials written by others appear at the bottom of your profile page. You can ask mutual friends or contacts to write them for you, or you can write them for others. To create a testimonial for someone (call her Pixtaker), you and Pixtaker must first select each other as a contact, and you must each have at least one photo or video in your photostream. Then scroll down to the bottom of Pixtaker's Profile until you see the Testimonials section. Click the Write a Testimonial about Pixtaker link. Pixtaker has to approve your testimonial before it appears on her Profile page. To manage your testimonials, choose You➪Your Profile and then click the Write and Review Testimonials link in the options list on the right or go directly to www.flickr.com/testimonials_manage.gne.

Use calls to action in the Description or Comment fields to ask people to fave your photo, add it to their galleries, write a testimonial, or leave their own comment. Remind people how to do it.

Extending Your Market Reach with Flickr

In addition to building viewership through community participation, you can attract people to your Flickr pages by conducting audience-building activities, promoting your Flickr presence on your own Web site and other people's Web sites, and using search engine optimization techniques to drive traffic to your Flickr images.

Building an audience on Flickr

Flickr provides several ways to attract new people to your site:

✦ **Invitations:** When you sign up (or at any other time), Flickr offers to e-mail customized invitations to join Flickr and view your photos at www.flickr.com/invite. It also offers to help you find contacts already on Flickr by searching your Gmail, Hotmail, or Yahoo! Mail address books.

✦ **Guest passes and sharing:** A guest pass (www.flickr.com/help/guestpass) is a way to offer clients, customers, and prospects a chance to view one set of images or your entire photostream without their having to become Flickr members themselves. Simply click the Share This button in the upper right corner of your photostream or set page and e-mail a link. Track your history of offers and acceptance for invitations and guest passes at www.flickr.com/invite/history.

✦ **Explore:** Flickr features about 500 diverse images each day in its Explore space. Flickr uses its own proprietary "interestingness" algorithm to select these images, which are meant to intrigue and involve viewers, not to showcase photographers. Interestingness is based on such uncontrollable factors as the number of visits to a photo, where visitors come from, who comments, who marks a photo as a favorite, the presence of tags and geotags, the number of groups that include the image, and how often and when these actions occur. (The more frequently within a fixed period, the better.) You can't do anything to list your images on Explore, other than to be active in the Flickr community, follow best practices, and try to build buzz for a particular photo by using invitations, passes, and offsite exposure.

Use the Scout tool (bighugelabs.com/scout.php), shown in the table in the sidebar "Useful Flickr resource URLs," to see whether one of your photos has been "Explored."

Using Flickr to build an audience offsite

You can easily expose to a larger audience all your hard work on Flickr by embedding images elsewhere online, posting a Flickr badge, linking Flickr with your other social media sites, or distributing your images on items or as stock photos. Remember to use calls to action to tell viewers what you want them to do or the benefits they'll receive by visiting your Flickr site.

Embedding photos or photostreams offsite

Posting photos, sets, slide shows, or photostreams on your Web site or blog or other social media pages or including them in e-mail messages or newsletters is simple. Just click the Share This link in the upper-right corner of any page. Click to select Grab the Link to obtain the URL for the image to copy and paste elsewhere. For more information, see www.flickr.com/help/faq/search/?q=embedding+photos.

Flickr guidelines require that you link back any Flickr images posted on an external Web site to their respective Flickr pages.

These HTML links "break" easily. Whenever you rotate, resize, or reset the privacy level of an image, its filename changes. If you delete a photo from your photostream, the image filenames of other photos change, too. Viewers then see a blank box with an X in it rather than the image that once appeared.

To avoid broken links, create permalink URLs for the images you post elsewhere. On an individual photo page, click the All Sizes button and select the size image you want to use. Copy and paste into your Web page the HTML code that appears in the first box beneath the photo. This code also includes the required link back to Flickr.

Adding a Flickr badge

A Flickr badge on your Web site or other social media pages acts like a banner ad. The badge links to one of your Flickr pages. Flickr has an easy widget to create badges at `www.flickr.com/badge.gne`, or you can use a third-party badge builder. Select a static HTML graphic or a Flash-driven badge, with your choice of photos and layouts. The badge acts as a teaser to your Flickr site, particularly because it can present multiple images at a time.

Figure 4-5 shows the Flickr badge for the Just Add Worms site (`www.justaddworms.com`). This Flash-driven version of a badge, in which rotating images are randomly enlarged, links to the Just Add Worms photostream page on Flickr (`www.flickr.com/photos/justaddworms`).

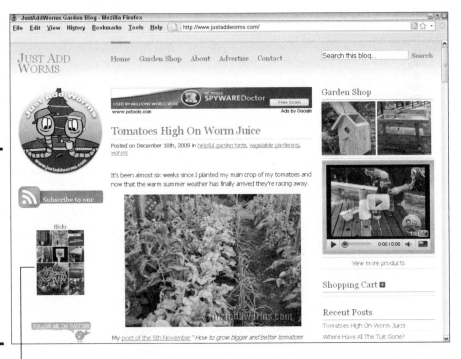

Figure 4-5:
Just Add Worms posts a Flickr badge on its Web site to entice viewers to see more images on Flickr.

Flickr badge

Linking to other social media marketing sites

Flickr makes it easy to coordinate your social media marketing efforts, saving you time and helping you build your audience.

Flickr has prebuilt options for updating your blog (or blogs), including Twitter and Facebook. Choose You⇨Your Account and then click the Sharing & Extending link in the breadcrumb trail. Follow the wizards in the Your Blogs or Your Facebook Account options to configure these connections. Contemporaneous updates keep your other sites active, without requiring extra effort on your part.

You can upload directly to Flickr and sites such as Twitter simultaneously, or you can tweet a photo that's already on Flickr.

Flickr also provides RSS feeds for your photostream, sets, group discussions, favorites, and other elements. When viewers subscribe to a feed, they receive automatic notifications whenever new content appears on that page. Any Flickr page with an RSS feed displays at the bottom of the page the standard orange RSS icon. Users with an RSS reader simply click the appropriate link next to the icon (most people use the Latest link) and follow the directions to add it to their favorite RSS readers. For more information about RSS, see Book II, Chapter 1, or go to `www.flickr.com/help/faq/search/?q=rss`.

Use the Description field or Comment field to remind people to activate the RSS feed and tell them how to do it.

Disseminating your images and name on products

Flickr lets you easily send photos to third-party applications to create cards, business gifts, promotional items, awards, loyalty rewards, or event commemoratives. All these branding opportunities are ways to keep your name (and Web address!) in front of customers even when they're offline.

From the Organize & Create tab, select Prints & Photo Products and then Create Photo Products. You have your choice of photo books, calendars, cards, collages, canvas prints, and other items from the Flickr partner Snapfish. For a broader range of options and providers, visit the App Garden at `www.flickr.com/services`, where creative third-party developers offer additional photo ideas, such as screen savers, wallpaper, magnets, mugs, puzzles, or ID badges. You can also find alternative sources for photo products, such as Qoop at `www.qoop.com`.

Of course, you can always send your Flickr images to sites such as CafePress (`www.cafepress.com`) for a broader range of branding and company-identification products.

Disseminating your work as stock photography

If you're an artist or a photographer, Flickr offers an opportunity to receive payment for professional work by using the well-known stock photo site Getty Images (www.gettyimages.com) and a way to introduce your name and work into the public eye by using Creative Commons. Consider both options as marketing avenues for your work.

To be considered for Getty Images, choose You⇨Your Account and then click the Privacy & Permissions link in the breadcrumb trail at the top. Choose Yes to the option to make photos eligible for invitation by Getty Images. If you don't want to wait for Getty to find you, you can submit your work for consideration to Getty's call for artists at www.flickr.com/groups/callforartists. For more information, see www.flickr.com/help/gettyimages.

As an unpaid alternative, consider offering *some* of your work under a license from Creative Commons (www.creativecommons.org), a nonprofit organization that supports ways to retain your copyright while still distributing your work, under certain conditions, as a branding and publicity opportunity.

Create a set containing the work you're willing to share under a Creative Commons license. For instance, you might create a set that offers only thumbnails, only older work, or only work on certain topics or in specific genres. You can indicate in the Description field that other sizes, views, or uses are available for a fee on your Web site.

At Flickr, you can start with a preferred licensing level at a global level by choosing You⇨Your Account and clicking the Privacy & Permissions link in the breadcrumb trail at the top. In the Defaults for New Uploads section, click Edit next to the question "What license will your content have?" (You should be on www.flickr.com/account/prefs/license/?from=privacy.) If you aren't sure what to do, select the most restrictive option, All Rights Reserved, as your global setting and decide whether to liberalize your policy later for certain images.

Creative Commons licenses are irrevocable. As a professional, you may depend on copyright protection for your livelihood. Though you can change your mind about distribution going forward, you can't withdraw a license from someone who has already exercised it.

The next most restrictive choice is the third button, Attribution NonCommercial NoDerivs. Creative Commons calls it the "free advertising" license because "it allows others to download your works and share them with others as long as they mention you and link back to you, but they can't change them in any way or use them commercially." For more information about protecting your photos online, see www.flickr.com/creativecommons.

Treat Creative Commons as an important resource. Read the list of issues to think about first at `http://wiki.creativecommons.org/Before_Licensing`. A wizard at the site can help you select the right licensing level: It's at `http://creativecommons.org/choose`.

Using Flickr to improve search engine rankings

Because Google, Yahoo!, and Bing all crawl Flickr, it pays to use good SEO practices, as outlined in Book II, Chapter 2. By aligning your Flickr content with your overall SEO strategy, you can help improve the appearance of your business in relevant search results and indirectly increase traffic.

Try to incorporate some of your preferred search terms in appropriate fields for Flickr. These fields, described in the following list, automatically become available after uploading an image, or go to the individual photo page and scroll to the end of the options in the right column to edit the title, description, and tags. (It's the last option under Additional Information.)

✦ **Filename:** If necessary, rename your files before uploading them. Be descriptive and include a search term such as "snowshoe-siamese-cat-plays-piano.jpg" instead of "image12345.jpg."

✦ **Title field:** Like the filename, the title should be descriptive and include a search term.

✦ **Description field:** In addition to incorporating the search terms that appear in the title and filename, you might want to include your business name and address and your Web address (without an active link), if appropriate. Don't use blatant calls to action or hard-sell language. From the point of view of an external search engine, the description is "surrounding content" and essential to assessing the relevance of search terms.

✦ **Tag list:** Tags, which work like keywords, help users search for images on Flickr as well as externally. You can use as many as 75 tags per image, so all your preferred search terms plus tags specific to the image might comprise your tag list. You can include your business name, address, city, and unlinked Web address in your tags. Separate individual tags with spaces; put a tag with multiple words between double quote marks. For a good example, see how Brentano fabrics handles its tags at `www.flickr.com/photos/brentanofabrics/tags` and `www.flickr.com/photos/brentanofabrics/alltags`.

**Book VII
Chapter 4**

Flickr

Save time by using the bulk editing feature in the Organizr to add shared tags and descriptive content to sets or already uploaded images. Choose Organize & Create. Then drag the photos you want to modify from the Findr bar at the bottom into the large box in the center of the page. Click the Batch Organize tab, choose Edit Photos⇨Titles, Tags, and Descriptions. Enter and save the shared tags and description. For after-the-fact editing of all tags, choose You⇨Your Tags and select the All Your Tags option.

Measuring Your Flickr Results

Basic statistical information about usage of your Flickr account is available in the free version; the Pro version offers additional detail. For more general information, see `www.flickr.com/help/stats`.

To gain the most value from your statistics, review them in the context of the overall statistics on your primary Web site, as discussed in Book VIII. In particular, look at referrers to your primary Web site to see how much traffic to your site comes from Flickr, as compared to other Web sites, other social media efforts, advertising, or search engines.

Reviewing free stats

You can see either a quick snapshot of your Flickr activity for all time or somewhat more information for a specific timeframe. For the snapshot, go to your photostream. Then click Popular, an option that only you — and not other viewers — can see. In addition to showing which of your photos is the most popular (viewed most often), these four options summarize your site's all-time activity:

✦ **Interesting:** Provides the relative "interestingness" ranking of images within your photostream (and varies continually)

✦ **Views:** Measures every view of your photostream, except for the times you viewed it yourself

✦ **Favorites:** Tells you how many times other people have labeled one of your photos as a Favorite

✦ **Comments:** Totals how many comments others have left

For more data, choose You⇨Recent Activity⇨Custom View. This generates a column of choices on the right. In the drop-down menu, choose a timeframe, which ranges from as recently as "the last hour" to as far back as "since the beginning" of your account. Then check all options that matter to you in terms of activities on your photos, replies you've made, or other people's actions related to you. Your home page then displays aggregate numbers for your photostream activity during the timeframe you specified.

Set a schedule for checking your stats. Unless you're tracking the impact of a specific marketing initiative or managing a huge online marketing budget, checking stats monthly is generally enough for Flickr and all your other online marketing activities.

Reviewing Pro stats

For more detail by image or by sets for marketing purposes, purchase the Pro version of Flickr for $24.95 per year. If Flickr is a major component of your social media strategy, the detailed information may be worth it. For a peek at the extended information and graphic displays in the Pro version, see `www.flickr.com/photos/me/stats`. This list describes its advantages:

✦ **Referrers:** List of where your Flickr visitors have come from

✦ **Statistics:** Page views broken down by individual image, sets, or collections

✦ **Traffic:** Charts of visits over time

✦ **Popularity:** Rankings for individual photos and videos by number of views

Statistics offer valuable insight and feedback. Use your results to help guide future uploads, to listen to your target audience, and to modify your Flickr behavior. There's no point in looking at numbers for numbers' sake.

Protecting Your Photos on Flickr

No matter what you try, you always risk losing control of your pictures. This concern matters particularly to professional artists, artisans, photographers, and designers whose business is imagery. A delicate balance exists between getting your name out and getting ripped off.

In addition to selecting the most restrictive options discussed in this chapter (no downloads, no blogging, and no printing by others, selecting All Rights Reserved as the licensing level), you have a few other options to reduce your risk. Follow these guidelines:

✦ Rotate visible stock. Either delete images or remove them regularly from public view.

✦ Post only a small sample of your work to whet users' appetites without presenting a significant loss if the images are misused.

✦ Display only thumbnails or low-resolution images of limited usefulness.

✦ File a copyright claim with the U.S. Copyright Office at `www.copyright.gov`. Prices start at $35 per image.

✦ Watermark images with your copyright notice, domain name, and business name. You can find free versions for watermarking a small number of photos online at `http://picmarkr.com`, `www.watermarktool.com`, and `www.webwatermarks.com`. The first two sites also offer paid, full-featured versions to batch-watermark many photos or integrate watermarking with your photostream.

If you have serious concerns, consult with an intellectual property attorney about your exposure on Flickr, licensing agreements, photo waivers, copyright infringement, or other legal matters.

Chapter 5: Maximizing Stratified Social Communities

In This Chapter

✓ Valuing stratified social communities

✓ Making business connections online

✓ Searching for options by industry

✓ Searching for options by target market

✓ Searching for options by type of activity

Social networking communities, like other marketing outlets, can be sliced and diced many ways. They can be sorted vertically by industry or horizontally by demographics, such as age, gender, ethnicity, education, or income. By doing a little research, you can *stratify* (classify) them according to other commonly used marketing segmentation parameters such as geographical location, life stage (student, young married, family with kids, empty nester, retired), or psychographics (beliefs or behaviors).

In this chapter, we discuss how you can find these smaller, niche sites and how you can get value out of them.

Becoming a Big Fish in a Small Pond

These stratified sites may have much smaller audiences than sites such as Facebook and MySpace. However, if you choose correctly, the users of these sites will closely resemble the profile of your typical client or customer, making them better prospects. Consider the difference between advertising at the Super Bowl versus distributing a flyer at a local high school football game. It all depends where your audience is.

Your business can also make a much bigger splash on smaller sites. Frankly, it's so difficult to gain visibility and traction on a large social networking site that you almost need a marketing campaign just for that purpose (for instance, to acquire 2,000 friends on MySpace).

On a smaller site, your business becomes a big fish in a small pond, quickly establishing itself as an expert resource or a source of great products or services.

The use of social media by business — blogs, social networks, social bookmarks, and news aggregators — is already in transition from trial stage to strategic implementation.

This statement is confirmed by spending patterns: A 2009 CMO Survey found that businesses already spend 3.5 percent of their marketing budgets on social media marketing, with that figure predicted to grow to 6.1 percent by 2010 and to 13.7 percent by 2014. To maintain your market share, you need to decide how you will communicate just as effectively across numerous platforms. Fortunately, all it takes is time.

Taking Networking to the Next Level

From your own experience, you know the importance of offline networking to find vendors, employees, and customers. From tip networks to trade associations, networking is a mantra for business owners. Social media marketing is, first and foremost, a method of networking online.

Business connection sites have proliferated in the past several years. These sites are generally appropriate for soft selling, not for hard-core marketing. Though referrals are used primarily for making business-to-business (B2B) connections, especially when targeting those with a specific job title, you never know when a referral will bring you a customer.

Make a habit of including a link to your primary Web site on every profile and using some of your preferred search terms within your profile title and text. These techniques increase your inbound links and may help with search engine ranking.

Table 5-1 lists cross-industry directories. Visit the ones that seem appropriate, using the tactics described in Book VII, Chapter 1 to make your selections:

Table 5-1	Business Networks	
Web Site	*URL*	*What It Is*
Biznik	`http://biznik.com`	Community of entrepreneurs and small businesses
Chief Financial Officer Network	`www.linkedin.com/groups?home=&gid=51826`	Network of high-level CFOs, financial executives, and accounting leaders (requires LinkedIn membership)
Doostang	`www.doostang.com`	Career community for professionals seeking new jobs

Web Site	URL	What It Is
E.Factor	`www.efactor.com`	Global network and virtual marketplace for entrepreneurs and investors
Entrepreneur Connect	`http://econnect.entrepreneur.com`	Community for entrepreneurial networking
Fast Company	`www.fastcompany.com/company-of-friends`	One of the first business social networks, organized by groups
Fast Pitch	`http://fastpitchnetworking.com`	One-stop network for professionals and business marketing
Jigsaw	`www.jigsaw.com`	Business card networking directory
MeettheBoss	`www.meettheboss.com`	Invitation-based network for executives and senior management, across industries
Naymz	`www.naymz.com`	Networking platform for professionals
PartnerUp	`www.partnerup.com`	Network for small-business owners
Plaxo Pulse	`www.plaxo.com`	Business address book for staying up-to-date with colleagues; LinkedIn alternative
Ryze	`http://ryze.com`	Business connections for jobs, careers, and sales
Spoke	`www.spoke.com`	Worldwide professional business directory
StartupNation	`www.startupnation.com`	Entrepreneurial business advice and networking
Talkbiznow	`www.talkbiznow.com`	Business services and collaboration network
The Funded	`http://thefunded.com`	Community of entrepreneurs who rate and compare investors and funding sources
Xing	`www.xing.com`	Global networking for professionals
Women about Biz	`www.womenaboutbiz.com`	Businesswomen's online resource center
Yammer	`www.yammer.com`	Free networking tool for networking within a company

**Book VII
Chapter 5**

**Maximizing
Stratified Social
Communities**

It's too time-consuming to participate in multiple sites productively. Keep clear records of all sites that have your business profile. If your situation changes, you probably have to update your profiles individually. Figure 5-1 shows a networking profile for Suzanne the Magician, a magician and corporate entertainer in Minneapolis, on the Plaxo network. Suzanne participates in half a dozen other social networks, including Facebook, LinkedIn, MySpace, YouTube, and Twitter, and on several magic forums as well. Since leads may come from any of them, she must update profiles on many services. While you can syndicate content postings, you usually cannot syndicate profile entries.

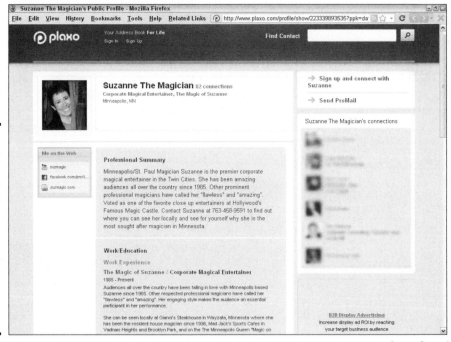

Figure 5-1: Suzanne the Magician uses her Plaxo profile to provide a testimonial to the quality of her work and a link to her Web site.

Courtesy Suzanne!

Submit your profile to several likely sites on a one-time basis, but commit to only one in terms of community participation.

Selecting Social Networks by Vertical Industry Sector

Whether you're marketing B2B or B2C, you find dozens of industry- or interest-specific social networks. Search online for communities in your industry, using the strategies described in Book VII, Chapter 1. As long as the social network is large enough to support your time investment, and continues to attract new users, you should enjoy enough of a payback to make your effort worthwhile.

Vertical industry sites, other than shopping, are particularly appealing for B2B marketers. If you use some adroit maneuvering, you can intersect with the sales cycle, reaching the appropriate decision-maker with the right message.

For the retail community, the growth of social shopping sites is a new avenue to reach consumers who want to spend after they see what everyone else is buying. Users flock to these sites for the latest product reviews, real-time deals, and news about the hottest items.

Track results so that you can decide which sites work best for you. If a site doesn't produce leads or sales after a few months, find another.

If you want to promote your products or services to more than one online community, customize your profiles and messages accordingly. For instance, a sporting goods store might promote camping gear on a social network for backpackers and running gear on one for joggers.

The list of vertical market social networks seems endless and ever changing. Table 5-2 provides a sample of some of these networks just to give you an idea of the range. This list includes no blog-only, bookmarking, or news aggregator sites.

Table 5-2	Vertical Market Social Networks	
Web Site	*URL*	*Description*
	Art	
ArtSlant	`www.artslant.com`	Contemporary art network with profiles for artists, art professionals, art organizations, and art lovers
deviantART	`www.deviantart.com`	Post and share international art
Humble Voice	`www.humblevoice.com`	Virtual artistic space for "artists and those who appreciate them"
Imagekind	`www.imagekind.com`	CafePress-owned community for buying, selling, and creating art
Independent Collectors	`www.independent-collectors.com`	Online tool targeted at modern art collectors
Myartinfo	`www.myartinfo.com`	Facebook-like site for the art community with profiles, portfolios, and votes on art
quarterlife	`www.quarterlife.com`	Sharing site for artists, thinkers, and doers

(continued)

Table 5-2 *(continued)*

Web Site	URL	Description
Auto		
AutoSpies	`http://autospies.com`	Blogs about car care reviews; auto news aggregator
CarGurus	`www.cargurus.com`	Automobile community with reviews, photos, and share opinions
Motortopia	`www.motortopia.com`	Community for lovers of cars, motor bikes, planes, and boats
Books		
Goodreads	`www.goodreads.com`	Book recommendations to share
LibraryThing	`www.librarything.com`	Book recommendations and online catalog
The Mystery Reader	`http://themysteryreader.com`	Mystery book reviews
Design		
Design Float	`www.designfloat.com`	Design-related content sharing, advertising, digital art, and branding
Decorati	`http://decorati.com`	Interior designer community enabling users to post items for sale and exchange
Environment		
BeGreen	`www.begreennow.com`	Carbon offsets for sale
TreeHugger	`www.treehugger.com`	Environmental topics at interactive community
Entertainment, film, and music		
CreateSpace	`www.createspace.com`	Creation, collaboration, and distribution for writers, musicians, and filmmakers
Fanpop	`www.fanpop.com`	Network of fan clubs for fans of television, movies, music, and more
Flixster	`www.flixster.com`	Movie lovers community
Last.fm	`www.last.fm`	Music community
mediabistro.com	`www.mediabistro.com`	Careers and community for media professionals

Web Site	URL	Description
	Medical	
PatientsLikeMe	www.patientslikeme.com	Patients, healthcare professionals, and industry organizations making connections
Sermo	www.sermo.com	Largest online physician community in the U.S.
	Legal	
Lawyers.com	www.lawyers.com	International social networking community for lawyers and law students
	Philanthropy and nonprofits	
Care2	www.care2.com	Online community for people passionate about making a difference
Changing ThePresent	www.changingthepresent.org	Nonprofit fundraising community with membership of more than 400 nonprofits
	Pets	
MyCatSpace	www.mycatspace.com	Community for cat lovers
MyDogSpace	www.mydogspace.com	Community for dog lovers
Uniteddogs	http://en.uniteddogs.com	Social networking for dogs and their owners
	Shopping, fashion, and collecting	
Curiobot	www.curiobot.net	Collection of the most interesting items for sale on the Internet
iliketotallyloveit.com	www.iliketotallyloveit.com	Product recommendations with public link to online shops
Kaboodle	www.kaboodle.com	Product discovery, recommendations, and sharing
lolligift	http://lolligift.com	Group gift buying service
Polyvore	www.polyvore.com	Product mixing and matching from any online store
Stylehive	www.stylehive.com	Stylish people connecting
ThisNext	www.thisnext.com	Product recommendation swaps

**Book VII
Chapter 5**

Maximizing
Stratified Social
Communities

(continued)

Table 5-2 *(continued)*

Web Site	URL	Description
UsTrendy	`www.ustrendy.com`	Vote on and shop for new items from indie designers
Wists	`http://wists.com`	Create and share wishlists with products from any Web site
Sports		
BallHype	`http://ballhype.com`	Aggregated sports news, blogs, and fan forums
beRecruited.com	`www.berecruited.com`	Connecting high school athletes and college coaches
Science and technology		
ScienceStage.com	`http://sciencestage.com`	Hub for research scientists
Sphinn	`http://sphinn.com`	Internet marketing news and forums

As always, include a link to your primary Web site and use some of your preferred search terms within your postings and profiles. If these sites have blogs or accept photos, video, or music, remember that you can syndicate that type of content to many sites simultaneously. For example, Blue Hill Hydraulics, a B2B company, uses the vertical social media site ScienceStage. com to reach prospective customers and employees at `sciencestage.com/blue-hill-hydraulics`. Its profile, under the About My Work section links to its Web site and is loaded with keywords.

Selecting Social Networks by Demographics

No one ever has enough staff and time to do everything. You already know that the more tightly you focus your marketing efforts, the better the payoff from your investment. If you created a strategic plan in Book I, Chapter 1, return to it to analyze and segment your markets demographically into smaller, niche markets that you can reach with a coordinated campaign.

Think online guerrilla marketing. Go after one niche market online at a time. After you conquer one, go after the next. If you scatter your efforts across too many target markets at one time, your business won't have enough visibility in any of them to drive meaningful traffic your way.

Table 5-3 describes some sites that are primarily demographically and geographically stratified. You can find many, many more. As usual, qualify the sites for your business by following the concepts described in Book VII, Chapter 1.

Table 5-3   Demographically and Geographically Stratified Sites

Web Site	URL	Description
Ethnic		
Black Business Woman Online	`http://mybbwo.com`	A social network for black business women and women entrepreneurs
AsianTown.net	`http://my.asiantown.net/index.html`	Asian social community and news
BlackPlanet.com	`www.blackplanet.com`	African American professional network that includes job section by way of Monster.com
MiGente.com	`www.migente.com`	Largest Latin American community; includes job section by way of Monster.com
MyTribalSpace.com	`www.mytribalspace.com/tribal`	Native American social network
High school and college		
Classmates.com	`www.classmates.com`	Networking with members of your graduating class at all levels
myYearbook	`www.myYearbook.com`	Networking site for high school and college students and grads
reunion.com	`www.reunion.com`	Networking with members of your high school graduating class
The Quad	`http://thequad.com`	College networking site with an emphasis on Greek life
Generational		
20 Something Bloggers	`www.20sb.net`	Ning community for 20-somethings
Brazen Careerist	`www.brazencareerist.com`	Career-building community for GenY and millennials (born 1982 to 2000)
Club Penguin	`http://clubpenguin.com`	Disney site for children under 12
Eons	`www.eons.com`	Online community for boomers (born 1946 to 1964)
iMantri	`www.imantri.com`	Peer-to-peer mentoring for GenY and millennials

(continued)

Book VII Chapter 5

Maximizing Stratified Social Communities

Table 5-3 *(continued)*

Web Site	URL	Description
Make Me Sustainable	http://makeme sustainable.com	Environmental community with GenY appeal
More	www.more.com	Community for women over 40
Geographical		
foursquare	http://four square.com	Mobile application to find friends and local businesses
MerchantCircle	www.merchant circle.com	Find, review, and comment on local businesses
tribe.net	www.tribe.net	Local-resident connections for advice and sharing about local resources
Yelp	www.yelp.com	Local-business reviews and comments
International		
Badoo	http://badoo.com	Popular European social networking site
Nexopia	www.nexopia.com	Canada's largest social networking site for young people
Orkut	www.orkut.com/ Main#Home	Google-owned alternative to MySpace and Facebook, now popular in Brazil
Sonico	www.sonico.com	Global Spanish language site with large U.S. membership
Zorpia	http://en.zorpia. com	International friendship network
Moms		
CafeMom	www.cafemom.com	Largest social networking and community site for moms and parenting
MomJunction	www.momjunction. com	Advice-sharing community for moms
Mommysavers	http://mommy savers.com	Money-saving community and tips for moms
MothersClick	www.mothersclick. com	First social network and parenting resource for moms
Seniors		
Grandparents. com	www.grandparents. com	Photo sharing and news site for grandparents

Web Site	URL	Description
ReZoom.com	www.rezoom.com	Social network and information for seniors
Senior Enquirer	www.senior enquirer.com	Senior social network for people over 60
Tweens and young teens		
GirlSense	www.girlsense.com	Online dress-up games for girls
UGAME	www.ugame.net	Social network for video gamers
Wealthy		
ASMALLWORLD	www.asmallworld.net	Private international community of culturally influential people

As usual, customize your message and profile for the audience you're trying to reach. Be sure to include a link to your primary Web site and some of your key search terms in any profile or posting. Figure 5-2 shows how businesses took advantage of the photo uploading feature at `http://mybbwo.com`, a social network for black business women online.

Figure 5-2:
Multiple businesses post photos of their products on myBBWO, a social network for African American businesswomen.

Courtesy LaShanda Henry, creator of Black Business Women Online

Selecting Social Networks by Activity Type

We can imagine what you're thinking. Why in the world would you want more than one service of a particular type, such as video sharing or blogging? The answer is simple: to improve search engine rankings and inbound links from high-ranking sites. When your content appears on multiple sites, such as those listed by activity in Table 5-4, you're simply casting a wider net and hoping to catch more fish.

Table 5-4	Social Networks by Activity Type	
Web Site	**URL**	**Description**
Networking and profiles		
Bebo	`www.bebo.com/c/site/index`	Facebook-style site with global reach
eHow	`www.ehow.com`	Squidoo-like site with content submissions on how to do things
FriendFeed	`http://friendfeed.com`	Create personal networks to share with friends, family, and co-workers
Friendster	`www.friendster.com`	Older global online social network; popular in southeast Asia
Gather	`www.gather.com`	Facebook-style social network
hi5	`http://hi5.com`	Social entertainment for the youth market worldwide with MySpace-style profiles
HubPages	`http://hubpages.com`	Like Squidoo, allows users to publish expert content
MocoSpace	`www.mocospace.com`	Online community that's cell-phone compatible
Tagged	`www.tagged.com`	Large, teen-oriented social network with a history of spamming and scamming; has recently reformed its privacy and security practices as a result of lawsuits
Photo sharing (Flickr alternatives)		
HoverSpot.com	`http://hoverspot.com`	Free social network with good photo sharing capabilities
Photobucket	`http://photobucket.com`	Free image hosting and photo and video sharing

Web Site	URL	Description
Video sharing (YouTube alternatives)		
Dailymotion	`www.dailymotion.com`	Post videos, music, and movies
Jing	`http://jingproject.com`	Video-sharing over Web, IM, and e-mail
LiveVideo	`www.livevideo.com`	Social networking and video hosting site
Motionbox	`www.motionbox.com`	Easy video sharing site
Multiply	`http://multiply.com`	Share photos and videos with friends and family
Revver	`http://revver.com`	Online media network with shared ad revenue
Ustream	`www.ustream.tvi`	Platform for live, interactive, broadcast video
Vimeo	`http://vimeo.com`	Created by filmmakers and videographers to share creative work
Microblogging (Twitter alternatives)		
Plurk	`www.plurk.com`	A Twitter alternative for events with calendar display
Seesmic	`http://seesmic.com`	Twitter client that permits photo and video sharing
ShoutEm	`www.shoutem.com`	Mobile, location-based, micro-blogging network
Unique services		
Maholo.com	`www.mahalo.com`	Users with questions connecting with volunteers who write answers
Meetup	`www.meetup.com`	Local-group organizing for face-to-face meetings
QOOP	`http://www.qoop.com`	Build creative mash-ups to share or sell
wetpaint.com	`www.wetpaint.com`	Site for creating wikis (shared content)

The secret to keeping this situation manageable is syndication, via RSS or Ping.fm or a similar service as discussed in Book II, Chapter 1. You post a photo, video, or blog entry to your primary site and automatically update other services with the same content.

Even with syndication, use some common sense. It doesn't help to drive the "wrong" fish to your Web site and dilute your conversion rate. Of course, if you've monetized your site by showing ads by the impressions, then the more eyeballs, the merrier.

Because setting up multiple accounts can be time consuming, you may want to stagger the process. Of course, by now you automatically include in any profile or posting a link to your primary Web site and some of your key search terms.

Figure 5-3 shows how PC Solutions of Illinois, Inc., cleverly used a Gather (www.gather.com) blog post titled "How to Find a Quality Computer Repair Company" to direct readers to its Web site (www.pcsolutionstech.com) using the search term *Click here for information on Chicago computer repairs.*

Figure 5-3:
Sammie Moon of PC Solutions uses a Gather blog post to direct users to his company Web site.

Courtesy PC Solutions of Illinois, Inc.

Book VIII

Measuring Your Results; Building on Your Success

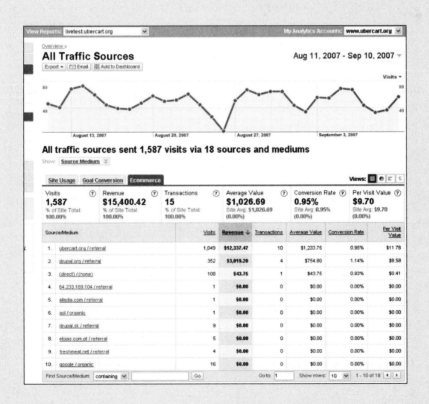

Contents at a Glance

Chapter 1: Delving into Data

In This Chapter

✔ Understanding the difference between monitoring and measuring

✔ Setting up your measurement plan

✔ Selecting tools that meet your marketing objectives

✔ Learning to use Google Analytics

*W*eb analytics is the practice of analyzing performance and business statistics for a Web site, social media marketing, and other online marketing efforts to better understand user behavior and improve results. Some might call Web analytics more art than science; to others, it's black magic.

The amount of data that can be acquired from online marketing efforts vastly exceeds the amount available using traditional offline methods. That statement alone makes online marketing, including social media, an attractive form of public relations and advertising.

In the best of all possible worlds, the results of your marketing efforts should appear as increased profits — in other words, as an improved bottom line with a nice return on investment (ROI). You're more likely to achieve this goal if you make your analytics program part of a process of continuous quality improvement.

For more information on measuring the performance of Web sites and online marketing campaigns, see *Web Analytics For Dummies,* by Pedro Sostre and Jennifer LeClaire.

 Before getting mired in the swamp of online marketing data, assess the performance of your central Web hub. If you aren't making a profit from that core investment, it doesn't matter whether you fill the funnel with fantastic traffic from social media, exhibit a soaring click-through rate, or tally revenues through the roof. If you aren't sure how your hub site is performing, use the tools in this chapter and ask your Web developer and bookkeeper for help.

Planning a Measurement Strategy

The basic principle "You can't manage what you don't measure" applies doubly to the online universe. Do you know whether Facebook or LinkedIn drives more traffic to your site? Whether more people buy after reading a blog posting about pets than from a blog posting about plants? If not, you're simply guessing at how to expend your precious marketing dollars and time.

To make the most of your effort, return to the goals and objectives you established on your Social Media Marketing Goals form (see Book I, Chapter 1). Ask yourself what you need to measure to determine your accomplishments. Would interim measurements help you decide whether a particular aspect of a social media campaign is working?

For instance, if one of your goals is to substitute social media marketing for paid advertising, compare performance between the two. If you initiated social media activities to improve a ranking on search engine results pages, you must measure your standing by keywords at different times. In either case, of course, you might want to track visitors to the site who arrive from either a social media or natural search to see whether they continue to a purchase.

Fortunately, computers do one thing extremely well: Count. Chances are good that if you have a question, you can find an answer.

Because computers count just about everything, you can quickly drown in so much data that you find it impossible to gather meaningful information, let alone make a decision. The last thing you need is a dozen reports that you don't have time to read.

Unless you have a very large site, monitoring statistics monthly or quarterly is usually sufficient. You might check more often when you first initiate a specific social media or another online marketing activity, if you invest significant amounts of money or effort into a new campaign, or if you support your site by way of advertising (in which case, monitoring traffic is the *sine qua non* of your existence).

Add to your Social Media Marketing Plan (from Book I, Chapter 2) your choice of measurement parameters and analytical tools and the names of the people who will be responsible for creating reports. Schedule the frequency of analytical review on your Social Media Activity Calendar (see Book I, Chapter 3).

Monitoring versus measuring

For the purposes of this book, we discuss only quantitative data as part of the measurement process. Use monitoring tools to review such qualitative data from social media as

✦ The degree of customer engagement

✦ The nature of customer dialogue, sometimes called *sentiment*

✦ Your brand reputation on a social network

✦ The quality of relationships with your target market

✦ The extent of participation in online conversations

✦ Positioning in your industry versus your competitors

If you have no monitoring tools in place yet, turn to Book II, Chapter 1.

"Real people" usually review subjective monitoring data to assess such ineffable qualities as the positive or negative characteristics of consumer posts, conversational tone, and brand acknowledgment. Notwithstanding Hal in the movie *2001: A Space Odyssey,* we don't yet have analytical software with the supple linguistic sophistication of the human brain.

Setting aside the "squishy" qualitative data, you still have two types of quantitative data to measure:

✦ **Internal performance measurements:** Measure the effectiveness of your social media, other marketing efforts, and Web site in achieving your objectives. Performance measurements include such parameters as traffic to your social pages or Web site, the number of people who clickthrough to your hub presence, which products sell best, and *conversion rate,* or the percentage of visitors who buy or become qualified leads.

✦ **Business measurements:** Primarily dollar-based parameters — costs, revenues, profits — that go directly to your business operations. Such financial items as the cost of customer or lead acquisition, average dollar value per sale, the value assigned to leads, break-even point, and ROI fall into this category.

Deciding what to measure

Most of the key performance indicators (KPI) and business criteria you measure fall into one of these categories:

✦ **Traffic:** You must know the number and nature of visitors to any of the sites that are part of your Web presence.

✦ **Leads:** Business-to-business (B2B) companies, service professionals, and companies that sell expensive, complex products often close their sales offline. Online efforts yield prospects, many of whom — you hope — will become qualified leads as they move down the conversion funnel.

✦ **Financials:** Costs, sales, revenue, and profits are the essential components of business success. Analytics let you track which sales arrive from which sources, and how much revenue they generate.

✦ **Search marketing:** As discussed in Book II, Chapter 2, optimizing social media can improve visibility in natural search. Not only do many social media sites appear in search results but your hub site also gains valuable inbound links from direct and indirect referrals.

✦ **Other business objectives:** You may need customized analytics to track goals and objectives that don't fall into the other categories.

Book VIII, Chapter 2 discusses KPIs in depth.

Don't plan on flying to the moon based on the accuracy of any statistical Web data. For one thing, definitions of parameters differ by tool. Does a new visitor session start after someone has logged off for 24 minutes or 24 hours? For another, results in real-time tools sometimes oscillate unpredictably.

If a value seems "off," try running your analytics again later, or run them over a longer period to smooth out irregularities.

Relative numbers are more meaningful than absolute ones. Is your traffic growing or shrinking? Is your conversion rate increasing or decreasing? Focus on ratios or percentages to make the data more meaningful. Suppose that 10 percent of a small number of viewers to your site converted to buyers before you started a blog, compared to only 5 percent of a larger number of viewers afterward. What does that tell you?

Figure 1-1 shows what most businesses are measuring online. You can find lots of research about typical performance on different statistical parameters. Though it's nice to know industry averages for benchmarking purposes, the only statistics that matter are your own.

Figure 1-1: This chart shows what most other businesses are measuring and monitoring. Note that two of the criteria (sentiment and engagement) are qualitative.

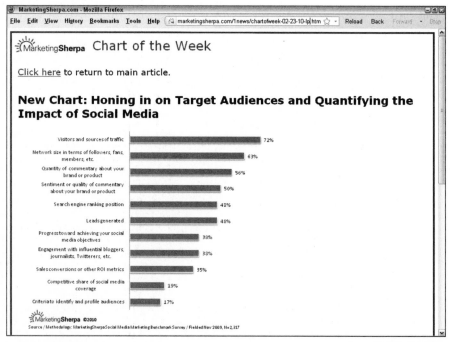

Source: MarketingSherpa.com

Regardless of how you go about the measurement process, you must define success before you begin. Without some sort of target value, you cannot know whether you've succeeded. Keep your handy, dandy Social Media Marketing Goals (see Book I, Chapter 1) accessible as you review this chapter.

A good measurement strategy determines how much data to leave out as well as how much to measure. Unless you have a huge site or quite a complex marketing campaign, you can focus on just a few parameters.

Establishing responsibility for analytics

Chances are good that your business isn't large enough to field an entire team whose sole responsibility is statistical analysis. Even if you aren't running an employment agency for statisticians, you can still take a few concrete steps to ensure that the right data is collected, analyzed, and acted on:

1. Ask your marketing person (is that you?) to take responsibility for defining what needs to be measured based on business objectives.

   Consult with your financial advisor, if necessary.

2. Have your programmer, Web developer, or go-to IT person select and install the analytics tools that will provide the data you need.

   Make ease of use, flexibility, and customizability important factors in the decision.

3. If it isn't part of the analytical package, ask your IT person to set up a one-page *dashboard* (a graphical "executive summary" of key data).

   Try the Google Analytics dashboard, shown in Figure 1-2, or the Hub Spot dashboard for multiple social media, shown in Figure 1-3. A dashboard displays essential results quickly, preferably over easy-to-change time frames of your choice.

4. Let your marketing, IT, and content management folks work together to finalize the highest-priority pages (usually landing pages and pages within your conversion funnels). When possible, set up tracking codes for links coming from social marketing pages. IT should test to ensure that the data collection system works and adjust as needed.

5. Your marketing person can be responsible for regularly monitoring the results, adjusting marketing campaigns, and reporting to you and other stakeholders. Have your IT person validate the data and audit tracking tags at least twice a year — they can easily get out of sync.

6. Be sure to integrate the results of your social media and online marketing efforts with offline marketing and financial results for a complete picture of what's happening with your business. Compare against your business goals and objectives and modify as needed.

**Book VIII
Chapter 1**

Delving into Data

Figure 1-2: A typical Google analytics dashboard displays key Web statistics.

Figure 1-3: A HubSpot dashboard page provides a high-level summary showing the flow from visitors to leads to sales distinguished by source type for a B2B company.

Aggregate all analytics into one place. You're unlikely to find a premade dashboard that includes everything you need to measure for your specific campaigns. Your programmer may have to export data into Excel, PDF, or e-mail format and save it all in one place. Then build a custom spreadsheet to generate combined reports for your review.

Selecting a Statistical Package

Ask your developer or Web host which statistical packages are available for your site. Unless you have a fairly large site or need real-time data, one of the free packages in Table 1-1 should work well. Review your choices to select the best fit for your needs. In many cases, Google Analytics is the best answer.

Table 1-1	Free Statistical Packages	
Name	*URL*	*Notes*
AddFreeStats	`www.addfreestats.com`	Graphical display; real-time, adjustable time frame
Analog and Report Magic	`www.analog.cx`	Displayed by `www.reportmagic.org`
AWStats	`http://awstats.org`	Log analysis tool
FeedBurner	`www.google.com/support/feedburner/bin/answer.py?hl=en&answer=78948`	Analytics for RSS and other forms of social media
Clicky	`http://getclicky.com`	All the basics for small, single sites; data storage limited to 30 days. offers paid options
GoingUp!	`www.goingup.com/features`	Customizable dashboard with graphs and charts
Google Analytics	`www.google.com/analytics`	Can include social media
Piwik	`http://piwik.org`	Open source analytics, including RSS
SociafyQ	`www.sociafyq.com`	Social network analytics
StatCounter	`www.statcounter.com`	Accepts and analyzes WordPress traffic
Webalizer	`www.mrunix.net/webalizer`	Simple graphical display that works well with small sites

(continued)

Table 1-1 *(continued)*

Name	URL	Notes
Woopra	www.woopra.com	Basic version, designed for blog analytics and social media
XinuReturns. com	http://xinureturns. com	Used for quick estimates on social media
Yahoo! Web Analytics	http://web. analytics.yahoo.com	Can include social media (formerly IndexTools)

If your developer or Web host tells you that you don't need statistics, find another provider. It's nearly impossible to measure success without easy access to statistics.

Depending on what you're trying to measure, you may also need data from some of the specific social media analytical tools described in Table 1-2, or statistics from social bookmarking sites such as AddThis (www.AddThis. com) or URL shorteners such as bit.ly. Gathering analytics for Facebook (Book V) and WordPress (Book III) is particularly challenging. See specific books about each major social media network for additional tools.

Table 1-2   Social Media Specific Analytics

Name	URL	Description
Facebook	http://www.facebook. com/help/?page=914	Information about using Facebook Insights for data gathering (must be logged in)
Facebook Grader	http://facebook. grader.com	Assess power and reach of Facebook pages
Flickr	www.flickr.com/ help/stats/?search= statistics#1863	Statistics available only with Pro account
Kontagent	www.kontagent.com	Free Facebook analytics
LinkedIn	http://linkedin.com/ network?trk=hb_tab_net	Network statistics
MySpace	http://faq.myspace. com/app/answers/list/ kw/statistics/r_ id/100061/search/1	Dashboard statistics
TweetStats	http://tweetstats.com	Free Twitter metrics

Name	URL	Description
Twitalyzer	`http://twitalyzer.com`	Free and paid Twitter analytics packages
Twitter Grader	`http://twitter.grader.com`	Assess power and reach of Twitter profile
WordPress	`http://en.support.wordpress.com/stats`	Free internal stats

Register for optional statistics whenever you can. Take advantage of bit.ly and AddThis and other sites that provide data not available anywhere else. The availability of stats may influence your choice of tools. (See Book II, Chapters 2 and 3 for more information.)

Unfortunately, you can't count on getting comparable results when you mix and match different tools. Each one defines parameters differently (for example, what constitutes a repeat visitor). Consequently, you need to watch trends, not absolute numbers.

If you have a large site with heavy traffic or extensive reporting requirements, free packages — even Google Analytics — might not be enough. You can find dozens of paid statistical programs in an online search; Table 1-3 lists a few. Several are fairly inexpensive, but the ones marked "Enterprise-level solution" in Column 3 can escalate into real money.

Table 1-3	Paid Statistical Packages	
Name	**URL**	**Cost**
Chartbeat	`http://chartbeat.com`	$10 to $150 per month based on pages views, including blogs
Coremetrics	`www.coremetrics.com`	Enterprise-level solution; includes social media
eXTReME Tracking	`http://extremetracking.com/?npt`	$4.50 per month
Log Rover	`www.logrover.com`	$99 to $499
Lyris HQ	`www.lyris.com/solutions/lyris-hq/web-analytics`	$200 per month; enterprise-level solution; includes social media
ObjectiveMarketer	`http://objectivemarketer.com`	Varies by number of users; targets medium-size businesses

(continued)

Table 1-3 *(continued)*

Name	URL	Cost
Omniture Site Catalyst	`www.omniture.com`	Enterprise-level solution; includes social media
PostRank	`https://analytics.postrank.com`	$9 per month; good for social media analytics and blogs; integrates with Google Analytics
Sawmill LITE	`www.sawmill.net/lite.html`	$99
Site Stats Lite	`www.sitestats.com/home/home.php`	Cost varies by traffic; starts at $15 per month
Site Meter	`http://sitemeter.com`	Premium starts at $6.95 per month
uberVU	`www.ubervu.com`	$30 per month
Unica NetInsight	`www.unica.com/products/enterprise-web-analytics.htm`	Enterprise-level solution
VisitorVille	`www.visitorville.com`	Real-time 3D statistics; $6.95 per month
Webtrends Social Measurement	`www.webtrends.com/Products/Social Measurement.aspx`	Enterprise-level solution; includes social media

Not all marketing channels use the same yardstick, nor should they. Your business objectives drive your choice of channels and therefore your choice of yardsticks.

Some paid statistical packages are hosted on a third-party server. Others are designed for installation on your own server. Generally, these solutions offer these benefits:

✦ Real-time analytics (no waiting for results)

✦ Sophisticated reporting tools by domain or across multiple domains, departments, or enterprises

✦ Customizable data-mining filters

✦ Path-through-site analysis, tracking an individual user from entry to exit

+ Integrated traffic and store statistics

+ Integrated qualitative and quantitative analytics for multiple social media services

+ Analysis of downloaded PDF, video, audio, or another file type

+ Mapping host addresses to company names and details

+ Clickstream analysis to show which sites visitors arrive from and go to

Don't collect information for information's sake. Stop when you have enough data to make essential business decisions.

Getting Started with Google Analytics

Google Analytics is so popular that it justifies some additional discussion. It's popular because this free, high-quality analytics tool works well for most Web site owners. It now incorporates many social media services as part of its analysis and scales well from tiny sites to extremely large ones.

Start with the free Google Analytics and switch to an enterprise-level solution when and if your Web effort demands it.

Among its many advantages, Google Analytics offers

+ More in-depth analysis than most other free statistical packages

+ Plenty of support, as shown in Table 1-4

+ Easy-to-set specific timeframes to compare results to other years

+ Many of the more sophisticated features of expensive software, such as path-through-site

+ Customization of the dashboard display

+ Conversion funnel visualization, shown in Figure 1-4

+ Analysis by *referrer* (where traffic to your site has linked from) or search term

+ Tracking of such key performance indicators as returning visitors and *bounce rate* (percentage of visitors who leave without visiting a second page)

+ Customizable reports to meet your needs and be e-mailed automatically

+ Seamless integration with AdWords, the Google pay-per-click program, though you don't need a paid AdWords campaign to take advantage of it

**Book VIII
Chapter 1**

Delving into Data

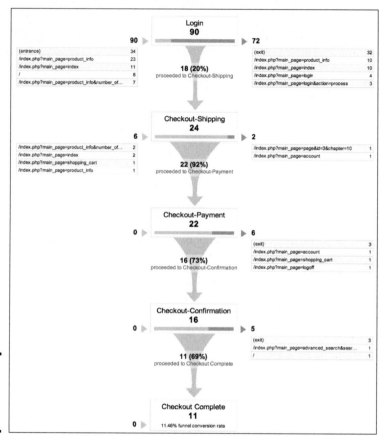

Figure 1-4:
A sample conversion funnel.

WebReach Ireland Ltd. (www.webreach.ie)

Table 1-4	**Helpful Google Analytics Resource URLs**	
Name	*URL*	*Description*
Analytics Blog	`http://analytics.blogspot.com`	Google blog for all things analytic
Conversion University	`www.google.com/support/conversionuniversity/bin/static.py?hl=en&page=iq_learning_center.cs`	Online Google Analytics training
Analytics Goal-Setting	`http://analytics.blogspot.com/2009/05/how-to-setup-goals-in-google-analytics.html`	Setting up interim and final goals needed to track path to conversions

Name	URL	Description
Analytics Guide	www.smashingmagazine.com/2009/07/16/a-guide-to-google-analytics-and-useful-tools	All-in-one guide for using Google Analytics
Analytics Support	www.google.com/support/analytics/?hl=en	Google Analytics help center
Analytics for Video	http://youtube-global.blogspot.com/2008/03/youtube-reveals-video-analytics-tool.html	Analytics for YouTube channel
Garmahis.com Blog	http://garmahis.com/tips/google-analytics	Useful Google Analytics tips and tricks

You must tag each page of your Web site with a short piece of JavaScript. The tagging task isn't difficult. If your site uses a template or a common server-side include (for example, for a footer), you place the Analytics code once and it appears on all pages. You should start seeing results within 24 hours.

Web analytics, from Google or anywhere else, are valuable only if you use them to improve users' experience on your site and your bottom line.

Google offers plenty of directions for setting up Analytics for your Web site. Two elements, however, are worth special attention: how to integrate statistical results from other social media services into your reports and how to set up conversion funnels for social media.

Installing Google Analytics

Google provides steps for installing Analytics at www.google.com/analytics/sign_up.html.

Some of these steps involved in setting up Analytics are geeky. This task definitely isn't for anyone who is faint-of-programming-heart.

Get help from your developer. For detailed information on installing Google Analytics, refer to the help sites listed in Table 1-4 or go to www.google.com/support/analytics/bin/answer.py?hl=en&answer=66983.

Book VIII Chapter 1

Delving into Data

Integrating social media analytics

You have four ways to integrate social media analytics into Google:

✦ Some social media services, such as Ning (`http://help.ning.com/cgi-bin/ning.cfg/php/enduser/std_adp.php?p_faqid=3003`) and Twitter (Twitalyzer at `www.twitalyzer.com/dashboard.asp`) already have their own statistics or are compatible with third-party statistics that you can integrate with Google Analytics. Of course, the Google-owned Blogger and FeedBurner are already compatible with Analytics.

✦ Install tags on links (see Book II, Chapter 2) or use filters and events within Google Analytics to track visitors who arrive from various social media sources. After you set them up, your referrer reports include social media data. Figure 1-5 shows a referrer report with social media sources.

✦ For geeks only! Implement workarounds that integrate social media data with Google Analytics. First, export the results from third-party analytics programs (refer to Tables 1-1 and 1-2), such as data from Facebook Insights (see Figure 1-6) or from Woopra (see Figure 1-7). Then integrate those data in a spreadsheet with similar data downloaded from Analytics. This is a near-geek solution.

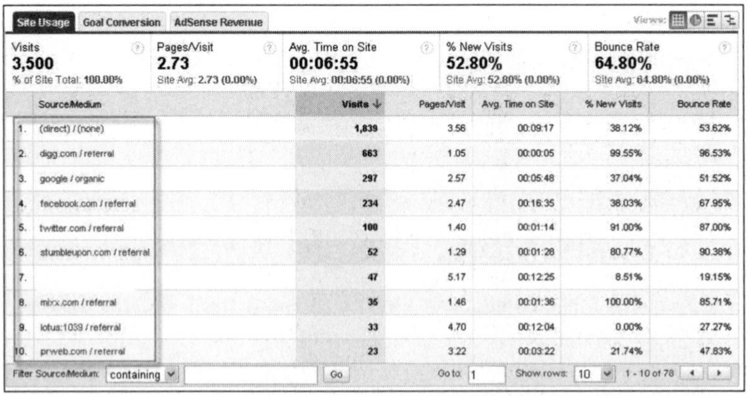

Figure 1-5:
The referrer report in Google Analytics can include multiple social media sites. You can group all social media sites into one category by using a filter.

Site Usage	Goal Conversion	AdSense Revenue				Views:
Visits **3,500** % of Site Total: 100.00%	Pages/Visit **2.73** Site Avg: 2.73 (0.00%)	Avg. Time on Site **00:06:55** Site Avg: 00:06:55 (0.00%)	% New Visits **52.80%** Site Avg: 52.80% (0.00%)	Bounce Rate **64.80%** Site Avg: 64.80% (0.00%)		

	Source/Medium	Visits ↓	Pages/Visit	Avg. Time on Site	% New Visits	Bounce Rate
1.	(direct) / (none)	1,839	3.58	00:09:17	38.12%	53.62%
2.	digg.com / referral	663	1.05	00:00:05	99.55%	96.53%
3.	google / organic	297	2.57	00:05:48	37.04%	51.52%
4.	facebook.com / referral	234	2.47	00:16:35	38.03%	67.95%
5.	twitter.com / referral	100	1.40	00:01:14	91.00%	87.00%
6.	stumbleupon.com / referral	52	1.29	00:01:28	80.77%	90.38%
7.		47	5.17	00:12:25	8.51%	19.15%
8.	mixx.com / referral	35	1.46	00:01:36	100.00%	85.71%
9.	lotus:1039 / referral	33	4.70	00:12:04	0.00%	27.27%
10.	prweb.com / referral	23	3.22	00:03:22	21.74%	47.83%

Filter Source/Medium: containing ⌄ [ ] Go   Go to: 1   Show rows: 10 ⌄   1 - 10 of 78 ◄ ►

Screenshot © Google Inc. Used with permission.

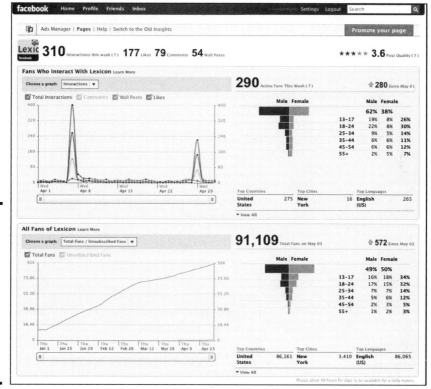

Figure 1-6:
The
Facebook
Insights
dashboard
provides
basic
information
about a
Facebook
fan page.

Figure 1-7:
A Woopra
dashboard
compares
data from
multiple
social media
sources in
real-time by
clicking on
each one.

Courtesy iFusion Labs, LLC

**Book VIII
Chapter 1**

Delving into Data

For a good example of how to track social media campaigns with Google Analytics, read the story about the 2009 Lollapalooza Music Festival at `http://analytics.blogspot.com/2009/05/lollapalooza-tracks-social-media.html`. Lollapalooza, whose social media strategy appears in Figure 1-8, incorporated Facebook, MySpace, Twitter, e-mail sharing, and AddThis social bookmarking. The results of campaign analytics for 2009 helped in the formation of 2010 marketing plans.

Figure 1-8:
The Lollapalooza Music Festival used Google Analytics to track the results of its social media campaign.

Courtesy Lollapalooza.com

You can find a shareware or freeware version of Social Media Metrics Plugin for Google Analytics at `http://userscripts.org/scripts/show/35080`. It pulls social media metrics from Digg, Sphinn, Mixx, reddit, StumbleUpon, Delicious, and Yahoo! Site Explorer Inlink Data service.

Installing filters to track social media sites in Analytics

Google Analytics automatically tracks referrals from Facebook, LinkedIn, and other networking services in the Traffic Sources section. However, each social media service appears individually; minor social sites such as Plaxo or reddit may be buried in a long list of referring sites. For the purpose of measuring your social media activities, you may want to group together the referrals from all social media sites.

By default, Google groups traffic into three categories (or *mediums,* in Google-speak), in its Traffic Medium report:

✦ **Organic traffic** for nonpaid visits from search engines

✦ **None** for direct traffic when a visitor types your URL or uses a bookmark

✦ **Referral** for everything else, including social media

By using a filter, you can move social media sites from the Referral category to a new category or medium.

Always create a duplicate profile before playing with any changes to your Analytics settings. (See `www.google.com/support/googleanalytics/bin/answer.py?hl=en&answer=55493`.) Make changes to the new, duplicate profile. Then no mistakes mess up your historical data.

After you duplicate your profile, follow the steps listed at `www.zencart optimization.com/2010/02/11/how-to-track-your-social-media-roi-in-google-analytics` (check that site for additional information and other solutions). During the process, you should see an entry such as `stumbleupon|facebook|twitter|linkedin`, that includes each of the social media referrers you want, separated by a vertical bar. At the very end, choose Traffic Sources⇨Medium to find a report that displays a category title that you have specified (for example, "All Social"). When you click it, you see aggregated visits from all the social media referrers you selected, separated from your other referrals.

Creating a workaround for Facebook fan page analytics

If you search, you find a number of free workarounds to bring third-party social media analytics into Google.

For instance, the Facebook Insights statistics program offers access to limited demographic and usage information for your Fan page but nowhere near as much information as Google Analytics. To view the Insights page (refer to Figure 1-6), click the Insights button in the left margin of your Facebook page. You can also use the Export Data command to run an external analysis on your Corporate page. For more information on Facebook Insights, go to `www.facebook.com/help/?search=insights`.

Unfortunately, you can't put Google JavaScript code on Facebook fan and profile pages to track usage, though you can place it on self-created tab pages that accept HTML code, as discussed in Book II, Chapter 2. Social Media Examiner published a solution for moving statistics for Facebook fan pages into Google Analytics on its blog at `www.socialmediaexaminer.com/how-to-add-google-analytics-to-your-facebook-fan-page`.

Alternatively, you can implement a workaround, by using Google Analytics code as an image rather than as JavaScript, on custom Facebook (FBML or HTML) pages you create (see `www.webdigi.co.uk/blog/2010/creating-a-custom-facebook-page` for directions on creating these pages). First, in Analytics, set up a new Web site profile for Facebook, with its own name, and generate Analytics tracking code. Second, create a custom HTML `<img>` tag for *each* Facebook page you want to track. (Use the Webdigi tool at `http://ga.webdigi.co.uk` to generate the tag code.) Third, paste the custom HTML `<img>` tag at the bottom of the code for each of your Facebook FBML fan pages (for example, above the closing `</body></html>` tag). In about a day, you start to see results in Analytics. For more information, see `www.webdigi. co.uk/blog/2010/google-analytics-for-facebook-fan-pages`.

Creating goals and funnels for social media

The process of establishing conversion goals and funnels for social media, such as a blog or Ning community, is the same as though you were doing it for your Web site in general. You may be able to do it yourself. If it's too confusing, ask your Web developer for help.

To create a goal, follow these steps:

1. **Identify your business objectives and associated visitor action.**

   You might create a post, join a group, sign up for a newsletter, upload user-generated content, register for a white paper, or buy a product.

2. **Identify the steps users must take to complete an action.**

   Write down the URLs for the specific pages they need to pass through (for example, open shopping cart or enter billing information). These steps become your conversion funnel.

   Usually, a specific page (for example, `thankyou.html`, `registration_comfirmed.html`) "counts" as the completed action.

3. **Configure the Goal Setting information for each profile that shares this goal, whether it's for your Web site, Ning community, blog, or other social media service.**

If you haven't already established separate profiles for each subdomain or domain name, you may need to create them first. Follow these steps:

1. **Go to the Google Analytics Account Overview page.**

2. **Click Edit next to the profile account you want to change. (It's under the Actions column on the right.)**

3. **Click Add Goal on the right end of the row labeled Goals (Set 1).**

   A new screen opens, labeled Enter Goal Information.

4. **For the goal name, enter the phrase that will appear in your conversion reports.**

5. **Set Active Goal to On. The Goal Position drop-down list indicates only where it will appear in the list on the Reports page.**

If this is your first goal, you can leave it as is. Otherwise, adjust as needed.

6. **Select the Goal Type — usually, URL Destination.**

   This step opens another dialog box for Goal Details on the same page.

7. **Complete the Goal Details box. Under Match Type, choose Exact Match if you don't have any parameters in the URL (usually there's an =); choose Head Match if the content is generated dynamically.**

   For help with this, ask your developer or go to `https://www.google.com/support/googleanalytics/bin/answer.py?answer=72285&hl=en_US`.

8. **For Goal URL, enter the concluding URL without the domain name (just use the part that appears after the "/").**

   Do not check the box for *Case Sensitive* unless it's necessary. If your goal has a dollar value, enter it next to *Goal Value* (optional).

9. **Under Goal Funnel, click Yes, Create a Funnel or This Goal.**

10. **Enter the URL and a name for each step in your funnel.**

11. **Save your goal.**

12. **Wait a few days for results. From the Goals section in your Analytics results, open the Funnel Visualization Report.**

    Figure 1-4, earlier in this chapter, shows a funnel example: 90 users logged in; 18 proceeded to Checkout-Shipping (plus 6 who arrived from a different route), 22 continued to Checkout-Payment, and 16 successfully completed their purchase.

13. **See which percentage of people who start the process complete it.**

    Find out whether they're getting "stuck" somewhere.

14. **Use the funnel information to guide design or wording changes that might improve the conversion rate, if necessary.**

    For ideas, try using the Google Website Optimizer at `www.google.com/websiteoptimizer`.

The URLs for funnel and goal pages don't need to have identical domain names, as long as the correct tracking code appears on the pages. The thank-you page for a purchase is sometimes on a third-party storefront, for instance. Or, perhaps you want to track how many people go from a particular page on your main Web site to post a comment on one of your social network sites or blog.

Pink Cake Box ices social marketing

Pink Cake Box, at `PinkCakeBox.com`, seen in the nearly figure, bakes spectacular cakes, cupcakes, and cookies for special occasions such as weddings, bar and bat mitzvahs, birthdays, baby showers, and bridal showers. Its cakes have been featured in *Modern Bride, People, Elegant Bride, The Knot,* a Martha Stewart TV special, and two of TLC's Ultimate Cake-Off competitions. It recently won one of them with their Legoland Birthday cake. Pink Cake Box typically delivers within 100 miles of its Denville, New Jersey, storefront, but ships cookies nationally.

Founded by pastry chef Anne Heap in 2005, the company has ten employees plus interns, with revenues of more than $700,000. (That's a lot of cake!) Though primarily a B2C company, it has B2B clients such as wedding halls, caterers, and party and wedding planners.

Chief information officer Jesse Heap says that Pink Cake Box debuted socially immediately after it opened, starting its blog, at `http://blog.pinkcakebox.com`, in 2005. "At the time, many competitors had relatively static sites that lacked the interaction and connection that social mediums like a blog could provide," he explains. He wanted "to encourage our users to interact with and share our content through their own, personal channels."

Plus, Heap notes, a blog can support syndication, using an RSS feed to repurpose content across multiple sites with minimal effort. "A single post on the blog will be repurposed into different sections on the Web site depending on its category and shared externally with other social media sites . . .to build brand recognition and drive traffic."

The blog, which remains the centerpiece of the Pink Cake Box social media strategy, now has more than 350,000 unique visitors a month; Internet-originated inquiries constitute the majority of orders.

Pink Cake Box has a vibrant social presence, as the list at the end of this sidebar shows. It also participates in other specialty social media sites such as Project Wedding (`www.projectwedding.com`), CookEatShare (`http://cookeatshare.com`), Foodbuzz (`www.foodbuzz.com`), BakeSpace (`http://bakespace.com`), and WeddingWire (`www.weddingwire.com`). "It does sound like a lot," but Heap insists that updating all these sites is easy with RSS syndication.

Given its limited resources as a small business, Pink Cake Box "participates actively in the top three external social media sites that generate the most qualified traffic, while we participate passively in others that allow us to republish our RSS feed. These 'other' social media sites typically fall into the food category, which complements our company's products. Currently, our top three sites are Facebook, YouTube, and WeddingWire. So, for these sites, we try to stay engaged and responsive to customers' questions and inquiries."

The marketing strategy is more sophisticated than sheer numbers, however. Heap focuses on sites such as WeddingWire, which targets brides, for lead generation, and others, such as YouTube, with its broader audience, for brand identity.

Heap uses social media strategically to help position Pink Cake Box in search engine rankings, which now include video, images, and social media. By developing a strong following on YouTube (as of April 2010, the branded Pink Cake Box channel had more than 1,350 subscribers and nearly 700,000 views), it has generated additional organic search engine rankings. "Ultimately," says Heap, "our goal is to channel traffic back to PinkCakeBox.com." For him, all these external sites are filling the funnel.

Pink Cake Box uses Google Analytics to track the number of visitors who submit online inquiries, but doesn't yet track how many inquiries turn into orders. Although this approach doesn't track Web visitors who phone, it's close enough for tracking purposes. However, Heap notes, this approach doesn't always work. Because links cannot be displayed on individual YouTube pages, he uses YouTube Insight tool to confirm that the videos generate interest.

SEO is a major component of the Pink Cake Box marketing strategy. Heap actively monitors traffic and certain high-value keywords to maintain traffic growth on the terms that contribute most to revenue. "There is an interesting relationship between SEO, social media, and content," he observes.

As the company grew, it shifted from an initial approach of "The more traffic, the better." "We began focusing our content on products that lead to better order conversions," Heap explains. Rather than measure aggregate traffic, they studied traffic from their strategic focus areas. "Put simply, we examined which products generate most of our revenue and made sure our marketing strategy focused on those products." That meant featuring varieties of their best-selling products on the blog, ensuring that they targeted social media sites catering to people who like those products, and using Analytics to monitor keyword traffic. Heap is justifiably proud of the results. "We've successfully grown our total Web properties to nearly 500,000 unique visitors a month, and have experienced double-digit revenue growth since our start in 2005. We attribute a lot of this success to our digital marketing strategy."

Though Pink Cake Box staff members handle most social media tasks in-house, the blog and Web site receive an outside technical boost. The Web site, which runs off the WordPress.org blogging platform, is customized with unique features, such as the "most popular cakes of the day" based on user views (`http://blog.pinkcakebox.com/todays-popular-cakes`). Features such as those require more

programming and design knowledge than they have on staff. Heap estimates that the staff spends, on average, 10 to 15 hours a week on online marketing. Though it's hard to delineate how much effort qualifies as social media, the majority of their time is spent creating content for the blog. "Admittedly, our product lends itself well to social media. Our cakes are unique and inspire much conversation and excitement." Obviously, small businesses with less photogenic products may need a different strategy.

Pink Cake Box also uses pay-per-click ads and attends bridal shows and cake competitions, but hasn't needed standard press releases. "Our strategy of saturating the Internet with photos and videos of our products helped spark initial interest from CNN, Martha Stewart, and the Food Network. Since then, we've continued to build relationships with media contacts to open additional doors," Heap notes. They also send personalized e-mail newsletters to an "influencer" customer list when big news occurs.

Finally, the site does a lot of on-site cross-promotion to connect users to multiple social marketing experiences. In addition to standard calls to action for social sharing, the Share Pink Cake Box page shown in the nearby figure (`http://blog.pinkcakebox.com/share-pink-cake-box`) has two widgets that allow users to syndicate photos and videos of their cakes on their own blogs. The same page includes SweetTweet, a Twitter application that allows users to tweet virtual birthday cakes, and a cake delivery map displaying where Pink Cake Box has delivered.

Heap has found only one problem with sharing content so openly, but he's philosophical about it. "There are individuals who exploit that trust either by taking our photos — or copying our cakes and passing them off as their own without proper credit. We've come to accept this as the cost of the strategy we've taken for digital marketing. We could have taken the approach

(continued)

(continued)

of strictly controlling our content and not allowing users to share it. But that goes against the democratization of the Internet and the Web 2.0 movement. As the saying goes, a few bad apples do not (and should not) spoil the entire batch." (Watermarking photos with the company logo may be an unobtrusive means of discouraging this problem.)

"The biggest piece of advice I can give," says Heap, "is to focus on content. The best social media strategy in the world won't generate much interest if the content isn't compelling and worthwhile to the end user. Our company produces outrageous and unique cakes every week. That's the foundation. [It] drives our entire digital marketing strategy."

Pink Cake Box URLS

www.pinkcakebox.com

http://blog.pinkcakebox.com

www.blogcatalog.com/
blogs/pink-cake-box.html

www.flickr.com/photos/pinkcakebox

www.youtube.com

twitter.com/pinkcakebox

www.facebook.com/pink
cakebox

www.weddingwire.com/biz/pink-cake-
box-denville/1be8dde9d853b1d0.html

http://m.pinkcakebox.com
(mobile blog version)

http://es.pinkcakebox.com
(Spanish blog version)

Courtesy Pink Cake Box www.pinkcakebox.com

Chapter 2: Comparing Metrics from Different Marketing Techniques

In This Chapter

✔ Comparing metrics among social media

✔ Integrating social media metrics with Web metrics

✔ Analyzing social media with advertising metrics

✔ Juxtaposing social media with other online marketing

✔ Contrasting online with offline metrics

*B*y now, you may be asking yourself whether Web *metrics* (the science of measurement) are worth the trouble. They certainly matter if you have a business with a finite amount of time, money, or staff — which covers just about every business.

Metrics aren't about determining whether your company is the "best" in any particular marketing or advertising channel. They're about deciding which channels offer your company the best value for achieving your business objectives. Not to denigrate your instinct, but metrics are simply the most objective way to optimize your marketing effort.

Marketing isn't rocket science. If your metrics show that a particular tactic is working, keep doing it. If they show it isn't working, try something else.

Establishing Key Performance Indicators

The most important items to measure — the ones that reflect your business goals and objectives — are *key performance indicators* (KPIs). They may vary by type of business, but after they're established, should remain consistent over time.

An e-retailer, for instance, may be more interested in sales by product category or at different price points, though a business-to-business (B2B) service company might want to look at which sources produce the most qualified prospects. The trick is to select five to ten relevant metrics for your business.

If something isn't measured, it cannot be evaluated. If it cannot be evaluated, it isn't considered important.

As you read this chapter, you can establish your own KPIs. Then in Book VIII, Chapter 3, you can turn your attention to how your various marketing efforts contribute to sales and leads, to your bottom line, and to the return on your investment (ROI). Armed with this information, you'll be in a position to make strategic business decisions about your marketing mix, no matter what size your company.

Enter at least one key performance indicator for each business goal on your Social Media Marketing Plan (Book I, Chapter 2). Some business goals share the same KPI. Schedule a review of the comparative metrics on your Social Media Activity Calendar (Book I, Chapter 3) at least once per month, or more often if you're starting a new endeavor or running a brief, time-constrained effort or you handle a large volume of traffic.

Overcoming measurement challenges

Measuring success among forms of social media, let alone between social media and any other forms of marketing, is a challenge. You're likely to find yourself comparing apples to not only oranges but also mangoes, pineapples, kiwis, pears, and bananas. In the end, you have to settle for a fruit salad or smoothie.

Install the same statistical software, whether it's Google Analytics or another package, on all your sites. Not all sites may have identical goals (for instance, users may not be able to purchase from your LinkedIn profile or request a quote from your wiki), but starting with the same software helps. In fact, the availability of compatible analytics packages may influence your selection of a host, development platform, or even Web developer.

Using A/B testing

You may want to apply *A/B testing* (comparing a control sample against other samples in which only one element has changed) to your forays into social media. Just as you might use A/B testing to evaluate landing pages or e-mails (see Book VIII, Chapter 1), you can compare results between two versions of a blog posting or a headline within one social media venue and keep all other content identical.

If you're comparing performance (click-throughs to your site) of content placed in different locations — for example, on several different social bookmarks or social news services — be sure to use identical content for greater accuracy.

Don't rely on "absolute" measurements from any online source. Take marketing metrics with a shaker full of salt; look more at the trends than at the exact numbers. Be forewarned, though, that the temptation to treat "numbers" as sacrosanct is hard to resist.

To no one's surprise, an entire business has grown up around Web metrics. If you have a statistical bent, join or follow the discussions on the resource sites listed in Table 2-1.

Table 2-1	Online Metrics Resources	
Site Name	*URL*	*What It Offers*
ABtests.com	www.abtests.com	Help setting up A/B tests
BrianCray AB testing	http://briancray.com/2009/08/04/ultimate-ab-testing-resources	A/B testing resources
eMetrics	www.emetrics.org	Events and conferences on marketing optimization
MarketingExperiments	www.marketingexperiments.com/improving-website-conversion/ab-split-testing.html	Information on A/B split testing
Mashable	http://mashable.com/2009/04/19/social-media-analytics	Helpful analytics overview and links
Omniture	http://www.omniture.com/en/resources/guides	Best practice guides and white papers on analytics
Social Media Measurement Using Google Analytics	www.slideshare.net/ArtWilbur/social-media-measurement-using-google-analytics	Helpful slide show about implementing social media analytics
Web Analytics Association	www.webanalyticsassociation.org	Professional association for analytics practitioners

(continued)

Table 2-1 *(continued)*

Site Name	URL	What It Offers
Web Analytics Demystified Blog	`http://blog.web analytics demystified.com`	Digital measurement techniques
Web Analytics World Blog	`www.webanalytics world.net`	Current news on the Web analytics front
webanalytics Forum	`http://tech.groups. yahoo.com/group/ webanalytics`	Discussion forum hosted by the Web Analytics Association
WebProNews	`www.webpronews.com`	Breaking news blog for Web profession-als, including analytics topics
Webtrends	`www.webtrends.com/ education.aspx`	White papers and Webcasts on analytics

Comparing Metrics across Social Media

We talk throughout this book about various genres of social media services. Each genre has its own, arcane measurements from hash tags to comments, from posts to ratings, from membership numbers to sentiment.

Use medium-specific metrics to gauge the efficacy of different campaigns within that medium or to compare results from one site within a genre to another.

However, to assess the overall effectiveness of social media efforts and your total marketing mix, you find common metrics that cross boundaries. Surprise! These common metrics look a lot like the statistics discussed in Book VIII, Chapter 1. By using the right tools, or by downloading analytics to a spreadsheet and creating your own graphs, you can compare data for various social media.

Online traffic patterns may vary for all sorts of reasons and for different businesses. Watch for cyclical patterns across a week or by comparing the same timeframes a year apart. Merchants often do this for same-store sales to compare how a store is performing compared to past years.

Carefully aggregate measurements over exactly the same timeframe and dates. You obviously don't compare weekly data from a blog to monthly data for a Web site. But neither should you compare Tuesday traffic on one source to Saturday traffic on another, or compare November–December clicks for an e-commerce site selling gift items (which is probably quite high) to January–February clicks (which are probably low). Compare, instead, to the same timeframes from the preceding year.

In most cases, these metrics become some of the KPIs on your list:

✦ **Traffic (visits):** The overall measure of the number of visits (not visitors) made to your site or to a particular social media presence over a set period. Twitter analytics from `http://getclicky.com` display this type of data; see Figure 2-1. Facebook Insights offers page administrators a limited set of similar data in its free analytics at `www.facebook.com/help/?search=insights`.

✦ **Unique users:** The number of different users (or, more specifically, IP addresses) who visited. Depending on your business model, you may want to know whether you have ten visits apiece from 100 ardent fans (multiple repeat users) or 1,000 users, each of whom drops in once. This type of detail is available for some, but not all, social media services.

✦ **Keywords:** The list of search terms or tags used to find a particular Web posting. Phrases are often more useful than individual words.

Figure 2-1: Twitter analytics from the Clicky Web Analytics site include both Twitter-specific metrics and general traffic metrics.

Book VIII Chapter 2

Comparing Metrics from Different Marketing Techniques

✦ **Referrers:** A list of traffic sources that tells you how many visitors arrive at your Web entities from such sources as search engines, other Web sites, paid searches, and many, but not all, other social media services. Some even identify referrers from Web-enabled cell phones. You can find this section in your analytics program. Track sources that include an identifying code in the link from the Entry Pages section. They can be aggregated and displayed graphically for easy review, as shown in Figure 2-2, in the traffic display from HubSpot.

Keeping track of users' paths among many components of a complicated Web presence isn't easy, but it's worth it. You may find that your marketing strategy takes B2B prospects from LinkedIn to your blog and then to a microsite. Or, you may watch B2C clients follow your offers from a social news service to a store widget on Facebook before they conclude with a purchase on your site. We talk more about tracking your links in the following section.

✦ **Click-through rate (CTR):** The number of click-throughs to your site from a particular source divided by the number of visitors (traffic) that arrived at that source. If 40 people view your Facebook stream in one day, for instance, and 4 of them click-through to your primary site, the CTR is 10 percent. You may need to derive this data by combining traffic measurements from particular social media services with information from the Referrers or Entry Pages sections of your analytics program. In some cases, the CTR becomes the conversion measure for a particular social media service.

Figure 2-2:
The HubSpot reporting system for inbound marketing provides a graphical display of traffic aggregated by source category.

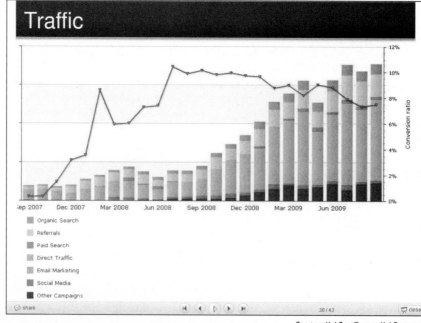

Courtesy HubSpot® www.HubSpot.com

Table 2-2 lists the key performance indicators you can track by genre and social media platform.

Table 2-2	Social Media by Genre and KPI	
Social Genre	*Site Examples*	*Useful KPIs to Check*
Bookmarking	Delicious, StumbleUpon	traffic, keywords, CTR
Community	Forums, Ning, Google Groups, Yahoo! Groups	traffic, users, time, keywords, CTR
Information	Blogs, webinars, wikis	traffic, users, time, keywords, referrers, CTR
Media sharing	Flickr, podcasts, YouTube	traffic, users, time, keywords, CTR
Network	Facebook, LinkedIn, MySpace, Twitter	traffic, users, time, keywords, CTR
News	Digg, reddit	traffic, keywords, CTR
Review	Angie's List, Epinions, TripAdvisor	traffic, CTR
Shopping	Kaboodle, ThisNext	traffic, keywords, CTR

Tagging links

Tagging your links with identifying code is especially helpful for tracking clicks that arrive from e-newsletters, e-mail, widgets, banner ads, and links from a phone because they otherwise aren't distinguishable in the referrer list. An unidentified referrer is usually displayed on a row with only a / (slash) in its name. This unspecified / category includes people who type your URL on the address bar of their browsers because they remembered it or were told about it or who have bookmarked your site.

To tag your links for tracking purposes, use the URL builder at `www.google.com/support/googleanalytics/bin/answer.py?hl=en&answer=55578`. Enter the referrer name, medium, keywords, content, and campaign name. You end up with a link that looks something like `http://www.yoursite.com/landingpage.html?utm_source=050110Ycoupon&utm_medium=mobile&utm_campaign=mothersday`. For more information, see `www.labnol.org/internet/design/google-analytics-track-clicks-emails-rss-feeds-web-pages/2476`.

If you have only a few such unspecified sources, simply adjust the inbound link to look like `www.yoursite.com/landingpage?src=tweet041510`, where the information after the question mark gives the source site and date or enough other content identification to distinguish the incoming link.

As far as the user is concerned, the link automatically redirects to the correct landing page, but you can count each distinctive URL in the Entry Pages section or, in the case of Google Analytics, by choosing Traffic Sources⇨Campaign. The process of tagging links may be time-consuming, but being able to monitor a particular campaign more accurately is worth your trouble.

Generate a separate, unique shortened link for microblogging and mobile sites, if needed. *Always* test to ensure that the modified link works correctly.

Analyzing the clickstream

Clickstream analysis is a fancy name for tracking users' successive mouse clicks (the clickstream) to see how they surf the Web. Clickstream analytics are usually monitored on an aggregate basis.

Server-based clickstream analysis provides valuable insight into visitor behavior. For instance, by learning which paths users most frequently take on a site and which routes lead to sales, you can make changes in content and calls to action, as well identifying ways to simplify navigation and paths to checkout.

On a broader level, clickstream analysis gives you a good idea where your visitors were before they arrived at your Web site or social media service and where they went afterward.

Aggregated data about user behavior or industry usage is useful as you design your social media marketing strategy. This analysis may also help explain why a campaign is or isn't working.

In the end, however, the only data that truly matters is the data that shows what's happening with your business, your Web presence, your customers, and your bottom line.

Figure 2-3 displays a clickstream analysis of where visitors went after checking tweets on Twitter in February 2010. (This data reflects only those who viewed tweets on www.twitter.com, not those who read them on their cellphones or who used a desktop client such as TweetDeck.) Interestingly, about 60 percent of tweet-readers clicked through to other social network and entertainment sites, but only about 12 percent visited shopping, business and finance, or lifestyle pages. The implication is that Twitter may not be the best place to generate new customers for certain types of businesses.

Clickstream data vary over time as users run hot and cold about a particular service, as the user population changes, or as a social media technique evolves. You can find a free open source tool for clickstream analysis of your Web site at www.opensymphony.com/clickstream. You can also set up a clickstream analysis for sites by using the "reverse funnel" on Google Analytics.

Figure 2-3:
Clickstream data from Experian Hitwise shows where visitors go after using Twitter.

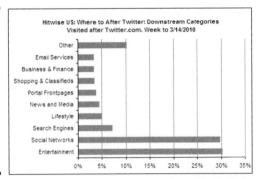

Courtesy Experian Hitwise

Google Analytics lets you track outbound, downstream clicks from your own pages. Your programmer must tag all outbound links you want to track, which involves some JavaScript customization. Send your programmer to www.google.com/support/googleanalytics/bin/answer. py?answer=55527 and http://code.google.com/apis/analytics/ docs/tracking/eventTrackerGuide.html for more information. For additional help, take a look at www.labnol.org/internet/design/ google-analytics-track-clicks-emails-rss-feeds-web-pages/ 2476. If you need to tag many external links, try the automated tagging solution at www.iqcontent.com/blog/files/taglinks.js. To see the number of clicks to each external link in Google Analytics, choose Content⇨Top Content Report and look under whatever category name your programmer set up to track these external links.

Integrating Social Media with Web Metrics

In addition to creating your hub Web site, you may have developed sites either as subdomains within your primary domain name or with auxiliary domain names. These sites may take several forms:

✦ **Microsites:** These small, dedicated sites that have their own domain names are usually developed for a specific event, product or product line, service, or another promotion, or as specialized landing pages for an advertising campaign. Whether the microsite is permanent or temporary, you must make a strategic choice to create one, judging cost, branding needs, SEO, and other marketing efforts against potential benefits.

✦ **Blogs:** All blogs and other information sharing sites, such as webinars and wikis, can be fully tracked with analytical software. Some sites, such as Ning and Blogger, offer full Google Analytics integration, but not all hosted solutions do so. Though you can obtain statistics from certain hosted communities or blogs (for example, http://wordpress.org/ extend/plugins/stats), you may not be able to customize them or integrate them with your other statistics.

**Book VIII
Chapter 2**

Comparing Metrics from Different Marketing Techniques

✦ **Communities:** All Ning communities, forums, chat rooms, and message boards fall into this category. Though they may have their own, internal statistics, also investigate whether you can customize those statistics to meet your needs before you select software or a hosted platform. For instance, Yahoo! (`http://groups.yahoo.com`) and Google Groups (`http://groups.google.com`) are inexpensive, user opt-in alternatives, but provide only limited statistics.

For statistical purposes as well as search engine optimization, you should own the domain names of these sites rather than host them on another server (`http://myblog.wordpress.com`). Sites can almost always be tracked with your preferred analytics package if they are separately registered domains (`www.mymicrosite.com`), were created as subdirectories (`http://blog.yourdomain.com`), or live within a directory (`www.yourdomain.com/blog/blog-title`).

The use of KPIs at these additional sites makes it easier to integrate what happens with social media with what happens after users arrive at your primary Web site. To complete the analysis, add a few more comparative indicators, each of which you can analyze independently:

✦ **Conversion rate:** You're already computing the percentage of visitors who complete tangible goals on your primary Web site, whether they purchase a product or complete a request form. Now compare the conversion rate (for the same available goal) by traffic source to the average conversion rate across all sources for that goal. Obviously, you can't compare goals, such as newsletter sign-ups, that may not be available on all social media channels or all your various Web entities. A Web development and IT integration company named non-linear creations shared its traffic and conversion data on its blog at `www.nonlinearcreations.com/blog/index.php/2008/04/08/case-study-comparing-marketing-effectiveness-of-linkedin-facebook-myspace-stumbleupon-and-twitter`, as shown at the top of Figure 2-4. You might want to have your programmer implement a similar graphic method of reporting. Of course, your results may be very different.

✦ **Sales and lead generation:** These numbers may come from your storefront package or be based on measurements tracked offline. We discuss them in greater depth in Book VIII, Chapter 3.

✦ **Downloads:** Track the number of times users download video or audio files, slide show PDF files, white papers, or application forms from your sites.

To track downloads, see `www.labnol.org/internet/design/google-analytics-track-clicks-emails-rss-feeds-web-pages/2476` or `www.google.com/support/googleanalytics/bin/answer.py?answer=55529&topic=11006`. If you have a lot of downloads, try the automated solution at `www.goodwebpractices.com/roi/track-downloads-in-google-analytics-automatically.html`.

Figure 2-4:
The non~linear creations site analyzed its inbound traffic from all types of referrals (upper left). Then it compared conversion rate (upper right), pages per visit (lower left), and time on site (lower right) for individual social media sources against site visitors overall.

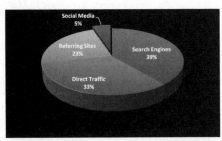

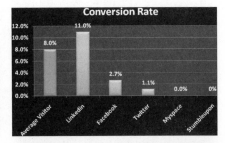

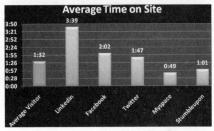

Courtesy non~linear creations inc.

✦ **Pages per view, pages viewed:** Microsites, communities, and blogs usually offer enough content to make these parameters reasonable to measure. Tracking this information by social media source, however, as shown in the lower left area of Figure 2-4, can be valuable. Page views are available for most blogs and Ning sites, but not necessarily for all other services.

✦ **Time per visit:** The average length of time spent viewing material (refer to the lower right area of Figure 2-4), is a good, but not exact, proxy for the number of pages per view. Naturally, users spend less time reading a single tweet than they might spend on your blog or Web site, but fractions of a second are indications of trouble everywhere.

✦ **Bounce rate:** For another indication of interest in your content, determine the percentage of visitors who leave without visiting a second page (related to time per visit). As with pages per view or time per visit, the bounce rate may be a bit misleading. If many people have bookmarked a page so that they can immediately find the information they want, your

**Book VIII
Chapter 2**

Comparing Metrics
from Different
Marketing Techniques

bounce rate may be higher than expected, though pages per view or time per visit may be low. You may want to sort bounces by upstream source.

Using Advertising Metrics to Compare Social Media with Other Types of Marketing

Because you generally don't pay social media services, social media marketing is incredibly appealing as a cost-effective substitute for paid ads. You can convert the advertising metrics in the following sections to compare the cost effectiveness of your various social media efforts or to analyze social media outlets versus other forms of promotion, online and off.

Obtaining metrics for paid advertising

With the exception of pay-per-click advertising, which exists only online, the metrics used for paid advertising are the same whether you advertise online or offline. Most publishers offer advertisers a *media kit* that includes demographics, ad requirements, and ad rates based on one or more pricing models.

Advertising costs vary over time based on demand and availability and the overall economy. Ad prices are generally based on "what the market will bear." New, real-time bidding schemes for online advertising may make prices even more volatile. Life is negotiable in many advertising marketplaces, except for those that operate as self-service networks. It never hurts to ask for what you want. For more information, see *AdWords For Dummies,* by Howie Jacobson, PhD, or *Advertising For Dummies,* 2nd Edition, by Gary Dahl.

Many social media sites don't charge for posting content because their true goal is to sell either premium services or advertising. Your content generates what they sell: an audience. The more user "eyeballs" a social media service can deliver to its advertisers, the greater its own advertising revenue. In essence, you manufacture their product in exchange for getting some of that traffic for yourself.

CPM

Cost per thousand (CPM) impressions, one of the most consistently used metrics in advertising, work across all forms of media. CPM is based on the number of times an ad is viewed whether it's calculated for ads on TV, billboards, or in print magazines, received as dedicated e-mails, or viewed on Web pages.

CPM is simple to calculate: Divide the cost by $\frac{1}{1000}$ (.001) of the number of impressions (views). The more narrowly defined the audience, the higher the CPM. You can find a handy CPM calculator at `www.clickz.com/cpm_calculator`.

For instance, the CPM for a 30-second Super Bowl ad in 2010 averaged about $2.60, but the true cost of an ad was high because the worldwide audience was huge. By contrast, CPM for a small, highly targeted audience of CEOs in high-tech companies may run $100 or more.

Computing other factors given the CPM is easy. For example, for the total cost of the Super Bowl ad, multiply the CPM ($2.60) by the number of viewers divided by 1,000 (1 billion worldwide viewers divided by 1,000 = 1 million) for an average cost of $2.6M. That's roughly ¼-cent per impression (divide CPM by 1,000 = 0.26 cents), but you still need deep pockets for a Super Bowl buy.

Because you may have difficulty tracking from impression to action in some channels, CPM models are often used to measure branding campaigns. Figure 2-5 shows the average CPM for a variety of media. CPM rates for online media are all over the place; eMarketer put them at $2.46 in 2008 in their analysis at `www.emarketer.com/Article.aspx?R=1007053`.

Figure 2-5: The average CPM for digital media in 2008 puts its cost between outdoor (billboard) advertising and radio.

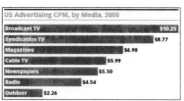

Courtesy eMarketer

CPA and CPC

Compare CPM with a *cost-per-action* (CPA) advertising model and its subset, *cost-per-click* (CPC) ads. CPA advertising triggers payment only when a user takes a specific action, such as downloads a white paper, signs up for a newsletter, registers for a conference, or becomes a fan, friend, or follower. At the far end of the CPA spectrum, when CPA is based on a user purchase, it approaches a sales commission model.

In the classic definition of CPA, CPC, and CPM, rates don't include the cost of producing an ad, the commission paid to an agency, or your own labor to research and review ad options. From a budget point of view, you need to include all these factors in your cost estimates.

A Web-only metric, CPC (or sometimes *PPC,* for pay-per-click), falls within the CPA model because advertisers are charged only when a viewer clicks a link to a specified landing page. The CPC model is often used for not only ads in the rightmost columns of search engines but also clicks obtained from banner, video, and online classified ads and from shopping comparison sites and paid directory listings. For additional resources for paid online advertising, consult Table 2-3.

Table 2-3	Online Advertising Resources	
Name	*URL*	*What You Can Find*
Adotas	`http://research.adotas.com`	Online advertising research and news
AdRatesOnline	`www.adratesonline.com`	Sample rates for online advertising of various types and sizes
Advertising.com	`https://publisher.advertising.com/affiliate/glossary.jsp`	Glossary of interactive marketing terms
DoubleClick	`www.doubleclick.com/insight/research/index.aspxa`	Research reports
iMedia Connection	`www.imediaconnection.com/adnetworks/index.asp`	Resources for online advertising
Internet Advertising Bureau	`www.iab.net/iab_products_and_industry_services/1421/1443/1452`	List of standard online ad sizes
Internet Advertising Competition	`www.advertisingcompetition.org/iac`	Annual Internet ad competition sponsored by The Web Marketing Association
The Webby Awards	`www.webbyawards.com/webbys/categories.php#interactive_advertising`	Online ad competition
WebsiteTips.com	`http://websitetips.com/articles/marketing/#banner-ads-tutorials`	Banner ad tutorials
Word of Mouth Marketing Association	`http://womma.org`	Membership group, resources, events

Always ask which statistics a publisher provides to verify the results of your ads. Some confirm impressions as well as clicks or other actions (check against your own analytics program); some provide only impressions; and some publishers cannot — or will not — provide either one.

Even if you pay a flat fee, such as for an annual directory listing, you can compute CPC and CPM after the fact, as long as the publisher provides you with the number of impressions and you can identify click-throughs.

Reach

Reach is the estimated number of potential customers (qualified prospects) you can target in a specific advertising medium or campaign. You can apply the concept of reach, by extension, to specific social media channels, anticipated traffic on your Web site, or other populations, such as the addresses on your e-mail list. Reach is sometimes expressed as a fraction of the total audience for an advertising campaign, for example, potential customers divided by total audience.

The number of potential customers may be the total number of viewers in a highly targeted campaign, or only a segment of them. In the case of the Super Bowl example in the earlier section on "CPM," for instance, a beer ad may be targeted at males ages 25 to 64; only that demographic percentage of the audience is calculated in reach. (For the Super Bowl, 64 percent of viewers were male, 75 percent of whom were in the target age group, making the worldwide reach 480 million.)

For the best results, identify advertising venues where the number of potential customers (reach) represents a large share of potential viewers (impressions). Return to your early market research for viewer demographics from Quantcast or Alexa.com, or review media kits to estimate the reach of each publication or social media site you're considering.

Applying advertising metrics to social media

Because publishers receive no payments for most social media appearances, comparing "free" social media marketing to paid advertising requires a little adjustment. How can you compare the CPM or CPC for something that's free versus something you pay for? Though you can acquire information about page views *(impressions),* clicks, and other actions (conversion goals) from your analytics program, cost requires a little thought.

One possibility is to modify the cost of advertising to include labor and hard costs for production, management, and commission and any fees for services, such as press release distribution. Then estimate the hard costs and the amount of work in labor dollars required to create and maintain various elements of your social media presence. If you outsource the creation of ads or social media content to contractors such as copywriters, videographers, photographers, or graphic designers, include those expenses.

Don't go crazy trying to calculate exact dollar amounts. You simply estimate the relative costs of each medium or campaign to compare the cost-effectiveness of one form of promotion to another. Social media marketing may be relatively inexpensive, but if you see only one action or impression after 20 hours of labor, you need to decide whether it's worth it.

Juxtaposing Social Media Metrics with Other Online Marketing

Regardless of any other online techniques you use, you can combine links with source tags, analytics program results, and advertising metrics to compare social media results to results from other online techniques.

Refine your list of KPIs for these elements:

✦ **E-mail newsletters:** Whether you use your own mailing list or rent one, you measure

- *Bounces:* Bad e-mail addresses

- *Open rate:* The percentage of good addressees that open your newsletter, roughly equivalent to reach as a percentage of impressions

- *Click-through rate, or CTR:* The percentage of people who click through to a Web page after opening a newsletter

- *Landing pages:* Where newsletter recipients "went"

Well-segmented, targeted lists result in better reach. If you rent lists, be sure to include the acquisition cost per thousand names, as well as the transmission cost, in your total cost for CPM comparison. Most newsletter services and list-rental houses provide all these metrics.

✦ **Coupons, promotion codes:** Online coupons can be tracked similarly to regular banner ads. However, for both promotion codes and coupons, track which offers produce the best results, which are almost always sales or registrations.

✦ **Press releases:** Sometimes press releases are hard to track online because many free press distribution services don't provide information on page views or click-throughs. By contrast, most paid distribution services tell you the click-through rate and the number of impressions (or number of times someone viewed your release) on their servers. Though these services can tell you where the release was distributed, they don't know what happened afterward. A press release is a good place to include an identifier in the links as described earlier in the "Tagging Links" section. The tag enables you to track entry pages. You may also see a spike in daily or hourly traffic to your site shortly after the distribution time.

✦ **Product placement in games and other programs:** Advertisers can now place the equivalent of banner ads or product images within online video games. If the ads are linkable, you can find the CTR and impressions to calculate CPM and CPC. Offline games with product placement must be treated as offline marketing elements.

✦ **Online events:** Track live concerts, chats, speeches, and webinars with KPIs for registration — request an e-mail address, at minimum — even if the event is free. Though not everyone who registers attends, this approach also provides a helpful set of leads and a built-in audience to notify of future events. Of course, you can also check referrers and entry pages.

✦ **Disaggregated components, such as third-party blogs, chat rooms, Gmail ads, RSS feeds, regular e-mail, or instant messaging:** Tagged links that pass through from these forms of communication probably comprise your best bet, though Google lets you track other elements of Gmail (`www.labnol.org/internet/email/track-gmail-with-google-analytics/8082`). Incorporate a special tag for links forwarded by others, though you might not be able to tell how they completed the forwarding (for example, from a Tell-a-Friend feature versus retweeting). It all depends on what you're trying to measure.

Be sure to register for optional analytics when you install a Share function from sites such as AddThis or ShareThis, which integrate with Google Analytics. Then you can see where and how often users forward your link through these services.

Contrasting Word-of-Web with Word-of-Mouth

Word-of-mouth is, without a doubt, the most cost-effective form of advertising. Ultimately, that force powers all social media, with its peer-to-peer recommendations and referrals.

Seminal research on word-of-mouth done in the 1990s by TARP Research — long before the advent of social media — offers several sobering statistics:

✦ People will tell twice as many friends about a bad experience as about a good one.

✦ On average, an unhappy customer tells ten people about his experience.

✦ Each of those ten people tells another five, so a total of 60 people hear about someone's bad experience.

✦ Thirteen percent of unhappy customers tell at least 20 other people.

Now, multiply those numbers by the power of the Web, for good or ill. These days, a happy customer may tell five friends, but a posting by an unhappy customer may inform thousands. The moral of the story: Keep your customers happy!

You can monitor mentions of your company online and the tone of those responses, as discussed in Book II.

Your analytical task here is to compare the efficacy of "word-of-Web" by way of social media to its more traditional forms. Tracking visitors who arrive from offline is the trickiest part. These visitors type your URL in the address bar of their browsers either because they've heard of your company from someone else (word-of-mouth) or as a result of offline marketing.

Offline marketing may involve print, billboards, radio, television, loyalty-program keychain tags, promotional items, packaging, events, or any other great ideas you dream up.

By borrowing the following techniques from direct marketing, you can find ways, albeit imperfect, to identify referrals from offline sources or other individuals:

- ✦ **Use a slightly different URL to identify the offline source.** Make the URL simple and easy to remember, such as `yourdomain.com/tv`, `yourdomain.com/wrapper`, `yourdomain.com/nyt`, or `yourdomain.com/radio4`. These short URLs can show viewers a special landing page — perhaps one that details an offer or a contest encouraged by an offline teaser — or redirect them to an existing page on your site. Neither those long, tagged URLs that are terrific for online sourcing nor those hard-to-remember shortened URLs are helpful offline.

- ✦ **Identify referrals from various offline sources.** Use different response e-mail addresses, telephone numbers, extensions, or people's names.

- ✦ **Provide an incentive to the referring party.** "Tell a friend about us. Both of you will receive $10 off your next visit." This technique can be as simple as a business card for someone to bring in with the referring friend's name on the back. Of course, the card carries its own unique referral URL for tracking purposes.

- ✦ **Stick to the tried-and-true method.** Always ask, "May I ask how you heard about us?" and tally the results.

You can then plug these numbers into a spreadsheet with your online referral statistics to compare offline methods with online social media.

HubSpot (`www.hubspot.com`) compared the subjective importance of various sources of B2B leads by marketing channel, including some offline activities, in its survey *The State of Inbound Marketing 2010*. The results, shown in Figure 2-6, show that marketing professionals view online activities as more important sources of leads than traditional offline marketing venues, with social media and natural search seen as the most important, followed closely by blogs and e-mail. Think about where you're spending your marketing dollars.

Figure 2-6: Rating the importance of various marketing channels for generating B2B leads in 2009 versus 2010, including some, but not all, offline marketing channels.

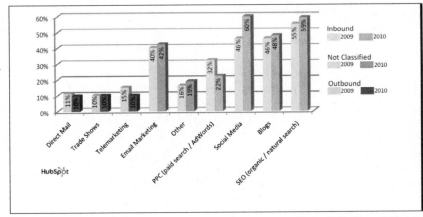

Courtesy HubSpot® www.HubSpot.com

Chapter 3: Tallying the Bottom Line

In This Chapter

✔ **Estimating the cost of customer acquisition**

✔ **Figuring sales metrics and revenue**

✔ **Managing and converting leads**

✔ **Breaking even**

✔ **Calculating return on investment (ROI)**

*B*ook VIII, Chapter 2 deals with performance metrics as parameters of success; in this chapter, we deal with business metrics to determine whether you see a return on investment (ROI) in your social media marketing channels. In other words, let's get to the bottom line!

By definition, the business metric ROI involves revenues. Alas, becoming famous online isn't a traditional part of ROI; it might have a public relations value and affect business results, but in and of itself, fame doesn't make you rich. This chapter starts by examining the cost of acquiring new customers, tracking sales, and managing leads. After you reach the break-even point on your investment, you can (in the best of all worlds) start toting up the profits and then calculate your ROI.

To get the most from this chapter, review your business plan and financial projections. You may find that you need to adjust some of your data collection efforts to ensure that you have the information for these analyses.

If numbers make your head spin, ask your bookkeeper or accountant for assistance in tracking important business metrics from your financial statements. That person can ensure that you acquire the right data, set up spreadsheets to calculate key metrics, and provide regular reports — and then teach you how to interpret them.

Don't participate in social media marketing for its own sake, or just because everyone else is doing it. Make the business case for yourself.

Preparing to Calculate Return on Investment

To calculate ROI, you have to recognize both costs and revenue related to your social media activities; neither is transparent, even without distinguishing marketing channels.

Surprisingly, the key determinant in tracking cost of sales, and therefore ROI, is most likely to be your sales process, which matters more than whether you sell to other businesses (B2B) or consumers (B2C) or whether you offer products or services.

The sales cycle (length of time from prospect identification to customer sale) affects the timeline for calculating ROI. If a B2B sale for an expensive long-term contract or product takes two years, expecting a return on your investment within a month is pointless.

For a pure-play (e-commerce only) enterprise selling products from an online store, the ROI calculation detailed in this chapter is fairly standard. However, ROI becomes more complicated if your Web site generates leads that you must follow up offline, if you must pull customers from a Web presence into a brick-and-mortar storefront (or sometimes "bricks-and-clicks"), or if you sell different products or services in different channels. You can find resource sites that relate to these issues and other business metrics in the nearby table.

Include the business metrics you intend to monitor in the Business Goals section of your Social Media Marketing Plan, found in Book I, Chapter 2, and the frequency of review on your Social Media Activity Calendar discussed in Book I, Chapter 3.

Resources for business metrics

Site Name	URL	What You Can Do
ClickZ	www.clickz.com/ _imgs/calculator/ Optimization_ Calculator_WEB.swf	Use the ROI tool online to calculate ROI for Web and social media sites
Frogloop.com	www.frogloop.com/ social-network- calculator	Download or calculate online your social media ROI
Harvard Business School Toolkit	http://hbswk.hbs.edu/ archive/1262.html	Use the break-even analysis tool

Site Name	*URL*	*What You Can Do*
Harvard Business School Toolkit	http://hbswk.hbs.edu/archive/1436.html	Calculate lifetime customer value
Interactive Insight Group	http://www.interactiveinsightsgroup.com/blog1/social-media-metrics-superlist-measurement-roi-key-statistics-resources/	Scan annotated super-list of dozens of articles on social media ROI and measurement
MarketingProfs	www.marketingprofs.com/charts/2010/3620/social-mobile-video-marketing-roi-tough-to-measure	Review surveys from marketers about social media ROI; must log in
Olivier Blanchard Basics Of Social Media ROI	www.slideshare.net/thebrandbuilder/olivier-blanchard-basics-of-social-media-roi	View an entertaining slideshow introduction to ROI
Online Marketing for Local Businesses	http://onlinemarketinglocal.com/calculator/customer-acquisition-costs.php	Calculate the cost of customer acquisition
Panalysis	www.panalysis.com/sales_target_calculator/index.php	Forecast online sales
Shop.org	www.shop.org/web/guest/researchandindustryinfo	Peruse reports about research, consumer data, and the state of retailing online (SORO)
SearchCRM.com	http://searchcrm.techtarget.com	Find information about customer relationship management (CRM)
Whatis.com	http://whatis.techtarget.com	Search a dictionary and an encyclopedia of business terms
ZenCart	www.zencartoptimization.com/2010/02/11/how-to-track-your-social-media-roi-in-google-analytics	Find directions for implementing ROI in Google Analytics

Accounting for Customers Acquired Online

The *cost of customer acquisition (CCA)* refers to the marketing, advertising, support and other types of expenses, required to convert a prospect into a customer. CCA usually excludes the cost of a sales force (salary, commissions) or payments to affiliates. Some companies carefully segregate promotional expenses, such as loyalty programs, that relate to branding or customer retention. As long as you apply your definition consistently, you're okay.

If your goal in social media marketing is branding or improving relationships with existing customers, CCA may be a bit misleading, but it's still worth tracking for comparison purposes.

The definition of your customers and the cost of acquiring them depends on the nature of your business. For instance, if you have a purely advertising-supported, Web-only business, visitors to your site may not even purchase anything. They simply show up, or perhaps register to download some information online. Your real customers are advertisers. However, a similar business that's only partially supported by advertising may need to treat those same registrants as leads who might later purchase services or pay for subscriptions.

The easiest way to define your customers is to figure out who pays you money.

Comparing the costs of customer acquisition

You may want to delineate CCA for several different revenue streams or marketing channels: consumers versus businesses; products versus services (for example, software and support contracts); online sales versus offline sales; consumers versus advertisers. Compare each one against the average CCA for your company overall. The formula is simple:

```
cost of customer acquisition = marketing cost ÷ number of
    leads
```

Be careful! This formula can be misleading if you calculate it over too short a timeframe. The CCA may be too high during quarters that you undertake a new activity or special promotion (such as early Christmas sales or the introduction of a new product or service) and too low during quarters when actual spending is down but you reap benefits from an earlier investment in social media.

Calculate your CCA over six months to a year to smooth out unique events. Alternatively, compute rolling averages to create a better picture of what's going on.

In Figure 3-1, Rapport Online ranks the return on investment, defined as cost-effectiveness in generating leads, for a variety of online marketing tactics. The lowest ROI appears at the bottom of the cube and the highest at the top.

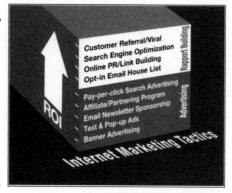

Figure 3-1:
The social media would fit near the top of the ROI scale for Internet marketing tactics.

Courtesy Rapport Online Inc., ROI-web.com

Social media marketing runs the gamut of "rapport building" options, because it involves some or all of these techniques. On this scale, most social media channels would probably fall between customer referral and SEO or between SEO and PR/link building, depending on the type and aggressiveness of your effort in a particular marketing channel. Traditional offline media, by contrast, would have a lower ROI than banner advertising.

As with performance metrics, business metrics such as CCA and ROI aren't perfect. If you track everything consistently, however, you can at least compare results by marketing channel to help you make informed business decisions.

If you garner leads online but close your sales and collect payments offline, you can frame CCA as the cost of lead acquisition, recognizing that you may need to add costs for staff, collateral, demos, travel, and other items to convert a lead.

For a rough idea of your cost of customer acquisition, complete the spreadsheet shown in Figure 3-2, which is adapted from the spreadsheet at www. forentrepreneurs.com. For start-up costs, include the labor expense, contractors for content development, and any other hard costs related to your social media activities. Or, try the CCA calculator at http://online marketinglocal.com/calculator/customer-acquisition-costs. php, substituting social media costs for Web expenses.

To put things in perspective, remember that the traditional business school model for offline marketing teaches that the CCA is roughly equivalent to the profit on the amount a customer spends during the first year.

Because you generally see most of your profits from future sales to that customer, you must also understand the *lifetime customer value* (how much and how often a customer will buy), not just the revenue from an initial sale. The better the customers, the more it's worth spending to acquire them. Harvard Business School offers an online calculator for determining lifetime customer value at http://hbswk.hbs.edu/archive/1436.html.

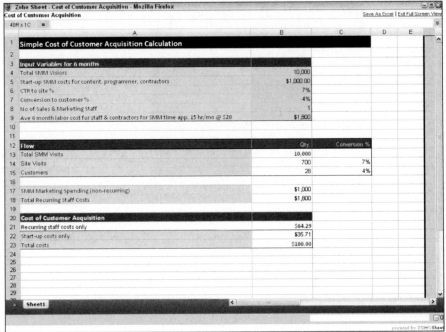

Figure 3-2: Compare CCA for social media marketing with the average CCA across your entire business.

Courtesy www.forentrepreneurs.com

WARNING!

Don't make the mistake that CDNOW Online made during the dot-com bubble. It spent about $40 to acquire each new customer but saw only $25 in lifetime customer value. The more customers CDNOW acquired, the more money it lost. Obviously, that business model isn't a helpful one to emulate.

In its *State of Retailing Online 2009* report for Shop.org, Forrester Research estimated that the cost of acquiring an online customer is now about half the cost of acquiring an offline customer. However, as shown from the earlier calculations in Figure 3-2, *half* doesn't mean *cheap*.

TIP

Try to keep the total cost of marketing by any method to 6 to 11 percent of your revenues. Remember, customer acquisition is only part of your total marketing budget; allow for customer retention and branding expenses as well. Small businesses (under 100 employees), new companies, and new products usually need to spend toward the high end of the scale on marketing initially — perhaps even more. By comparison, mature, well-branded product lines and companies with a large revenue stream can spend a lower percentage on marketing.

Obviously, anything that can reduce marketing costs offers a benefit. See whether your calculation bears out that cost level for your investment in social media. CCA may go down over time as brand recognition and word of mouth kick in.

One is silver and the other gold

You might remember the words to that old Girl Scout song: "Make new friends but keep the old; one is silver and the other gold"? To retain customers, apply that philosophy to your policy of customer satisfaction. That may mean anything from sending holiday greetings to establishing a loyalty program with discounts for repeat buyers; from entering repeat customers into a special sweepstakes to offering a coupon on their next purchase when they sign up for a newsletter.

The Chief Marketing Officer Council has estimated that "acquiring new customers can cost five times more than satisfying and retaining current customers." In case you needed it, the CMO Council's statement gives you a significant financial reason to listen to customers' concerns, complaints, product ideas, and desires.

While you lavish time and attention on social marketing to fill the top of your funnel with new prospects, don't forget its value for improving relationships with current customers and nurturing their engagement with your brand.

Selling a product to an existing customer is almost always less expensive to attend to than to acquire a new one.

Establishing Key Performance Indicators for Sales

If you track ROI, at some point you must track revenue and profits as business metrics. Otherwise, there's no ROI to compute.

If you sell online, your storefront should provide ways for you to slice and dice sales to obtain crucial data. However, if your sales come from services, from a brick-and-mortar store, or from large contractual purchases, you probably need to obtain revenue statistics from financial or other external records to plug into your ROI calculation.

If you manage a bricks-and-clicks operation, you may want to integrate your online and offline operations by selecting e-commerce software from the vendor who provides the *point-of-sales (POS)* package for your cash registers. That software may already be integrated with your inventory control and accounting packages.

Just as with performance metrics, you should be able to acquire certain key performance indicators (KPI) for sales by using storefront statistics:

- ✦ Determine how often customers buy (number of transactions per month); how many new customers you acquire (reach); and how much they spend per transaction (yield).

- ✦ Look for sales reports by average dollar amount as well as by number of sales. Plugging average numbers into an ROI calculation is easier, and the results are close enough as long as the inputs are consistent.

✦ You should be able to request order totals for any specified timeframe so that you can track sales tied to promotions, marketing activities, and sale announcements.

✦ Look for the capability to sort sales by new and repeat customers, to allow for future, personalized offers and to distinguish numbers for CCA.

✦ Your sales statistics should include a conversion funnel. Try to trace the path upstream so that you can identify sales initiated from social media.

✦ Check that data can be exported to a spreadsheet.

✦ Make sure that you can collect statistics on the use of promotion codes by number and dollar value so that you can decide which promotions are the most successful.

✦ Having store reports that break down sales by product is helpful. Sometimes called a *product tree,* this report shows which products are selling by SKU and category.

Table 3-1 lists some storefront options that integrate with social media and offer sales analytics. Unfortunately, not all third-party storefront solutions offer ideal tracking. Many storefront solutions use Google Analytics, shown in Figure 3-3, to track transactions.

Table 3-1 Social Media Store Solutions Offering Sales Statistics

Name	URL	Type of Sales Stats Available
Google E-Commerce Tracking	`http://code.google.com/apis/analytics/docs/tracking/gaTrackingEcommerce.html`	Google Analytics or e-commerce used
ProductCart	`www.earlyimpact.com`	Google Analytics integration; can track social media widgets as affiliates
Mercantec	`www.mercantec.com`	Google Analytics e-commerce tracking and statistics
Wishpot	`www.wishpot.com/social-commerce`	View and click tracking on profile pages and synced social networks; can identify user demographics

If you created alternative SKUs for products sold by way of social media for tracking purposes, be sure to merge them into the same category of your product tree. Using multiple SKUs isn't recommended if your storefront solution includes inventory control.

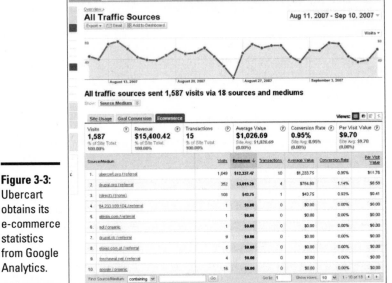

Figure 3-3: Ubercart obtains its e-commerce statistics from Google Analytics.

You can input the numbers from your sales metrics into a sales calculator to forecast unit sales needed to meet your goals. Figure 3-4 shows a calculator from Panalysis at `www.panalysis.com/sales_target_calculator/index.php`.

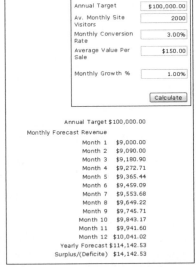

Figure 3-4: Sales forecasting calculator from Panalysis.

Tracking leads

Often, your social media or Web presence generates leads instead of, or in addition to, sales. If your sales process dictates that some or all sales are closed offline, you need a way to track leads from initiation to conversion. Marketing Sherpa, a marketing research firm, tracks the process of tracking leads from the initial acquisition of customers' names or e-mail addresses from sales. Percentages given are for each step compared to the original number of visitors. See Figure 3-5.

Customer Relationship Management (CRM) software helps you track prospects, qualified leads, and customers in an organized way. A simple database might allow different managers, salespeople, and support personnel to share a client's concerns or track its steps within the selling cycle.

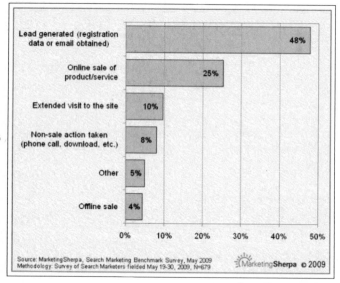

Figure 3-5:
A typical progression from tracking leads to converting a buyer.

Source: MarketingSherpa.com

The process of CRM and lead management may also include qualifying and nurturing leads, managing marketing campaigns, building relationships, and providing service, all while helping to maximize profits. You can find a list of some lead monitoring and CRM software options in Table 3-2.

Though often thought of as the province of B2B companies offering high-ticket items with a long sales cycle, lead-tracking tools can help you segment existing and prospective customers, improve the percentage of leads that turn into clients, and build brand loyalty.

Table 3-2	**Lead Monitoring and CRM Software**		
Name	*URL*	*What You Can Do*	*Cost*
BatchBook	`www.batchblue.com`	Integrate social media with CRM	Free 30-day trial or as many as 200 contacts; starts at $9.95 per month
HubSpot	`www.hubspot.com`	Manage inbound leads	Free 7-day trial, starts at $250 per month
LEADS Explorer	`www.leadsexplorer.com`	See who's visiting your Web site	Free 30-day trial; starts at $34 per month
Splendid CRM	`www.splendidcrm.com/Products/SplendidCRM Community/tabid/71/Default.aspx`	Install open source CRM software	Free core version; fee starts at $10 per user per month
Zoho CRM	`www.zoho.com/crm/index.html`	Implement customer relationship management software	Free for 3 users; starts at $12 per user per month

Figure 3-6 shows the distribution of leads and sales respectively with analytical tools provided by HubSpot. Note how the distribution of leads by marketing channels differs from the ultimate distribution of sales.

You can export your Google Analytics results to a spreadsheet and create a similar graphical display.

Understanding Other Common Business Metrics

Your bookkeeper or accountant can help you compute and track other business measurements to ensure that your business turns a profit. You may want to pay particular attention to estimating your break-even point and your profit margin.

Break-even point

Computing the *break-even point* (the number of sales needed for revenues received to equal total costs) helps determine when a product or product line will become profitable. After a product reaches break-even, sales start to contribute to profits.

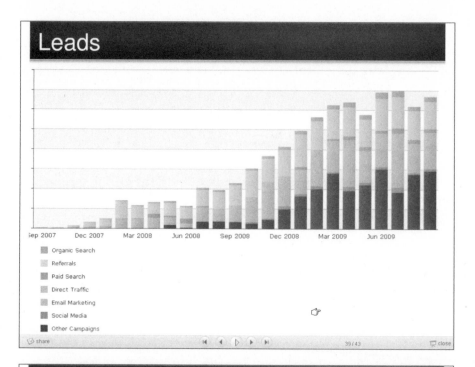

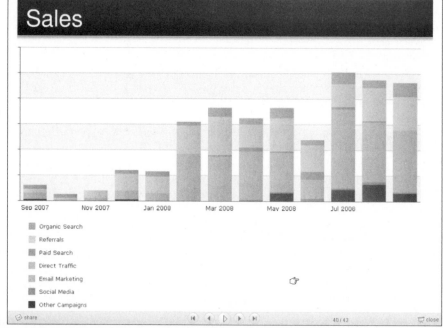

Figure 3-6:
HubSpot
offers lead
monitoring
software
that
displays the
distribution
of leads and
sales by
originating
marketing
channel.

Courtesy HubSpot® www.HubSpot.com

To calculate the break-even point, first you need to figure out the *cost of goods* or *average variable costs* (costs such as materials, shipping, or commission that vary with the number of units sold) and your *fixed costs* (charges such as rent or insurance that are the same each month regardless of how much business you do). Then plug the amounts into these two formulas:

```
revenues - cost of goods (variable) = gross margin
fixed costs ÷ gross margin = break-even point (in unit sales)
```

Figure 3-7 shows this relationship. This graph of the break-even point shows fixed costs (the flat horizontal line) to variable costs (the diagonal line) to plot total costs. After revenues surpass the break-even point, each sale contributes to profits (the shaded area on the right).

The break-even analysis tool from the Harvard Business School Toolkit (`http://hbswk.hbs.edu/archive/1262.html`) can also help calculate your break-even point.

Figure 3-7:
The break-even point to plot total costs. Each sale contributes to profits (the shaded area on the right).

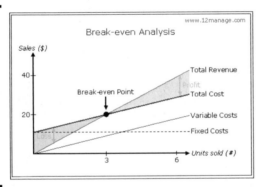

Profit margin

Net profit margin is defined as earnings (profits) divided by revenues. If you have $10,000 in revenues and $1,500 in profits, your profit margin is 15 percent. Don't confuse your net profit margin with the gross margin (refer to Figure 3-7).

Revenue versus profit

One of the most common errors in marketing is to stop analyzing results when you count the cash in the drawer. If you don't believe this statement, check out the CDNOW example from the earlier section "Comparing the costs of customer acquisition."

You can easily be seduced by growing revenues, but it's profit that matters. Profit determines your return on investment, replenishes your resources for growth, and rewards you for taking risks.

Determining Return on Investment

Return on investment (ROI) is a commonly used business metric that evaluates the profitability of an investment or effort compared to its original cost. This versatile metric is usually presented as a ratio or percentage (multiply the following equation by 100). The formula itself is deceptively simple:

```
ROI = (Gain from Investment - Cost of Investment)÷
    Cost of Investment
```

The devil is, as usual, in the details. The cost of an investment means more than cold, hard cash. Depending on the type of effort for which you're computing ROI, you may need to include the cost of labor (including your own!), subcontractors, fees, and advertising for an accurate picture. When calculating ROI for your entire business, be sure to include overhead, cost of goods, and cost of sales.

You can affect ROI positively by either increasing the return (revenues) or reducing costs. That's business in a nutshell.

Because the formula is flexible, be sure that you know what others mean when they talk about ROI.

You can calculate ROI for a particular marketing campaign or product or an entire year's worth of marketing expenses. Or, compare ROI among channels, comparing the net revenue returned from an investment in social media or SEO to paid advertising.

Run ROI calculations monthly, quarterly, or yearly, depending on the parameter you're trying to measure.

Try the interactive ROI calculator at www.clickz.com/_imgs/ calculator/Optimization_Calculator_WEB.swf, also shown in Figure 3-8. You can modify this model for social media by treating Monthly Site Visits as social media visits; Success Events as click-throughs to your main site, and Value of Success Events as the value of a sale.

ROI may be expressed as a *rate of return* (how long it takes to earn back an investment). An annual ROI of 25 percent means that it takes four years to recover what you put in. Obviously, if an investment takes too long to earn out, your product — or your business — is at risk of failing in the meantime.

If your analysis predicts a negative ROI, or even a very low rate of return over an extended period, stop and think! Unless you have a specific tactical plan (such as using a product as a loss leader to draw traffic), look for an alternative effort with a better likelihood of success.

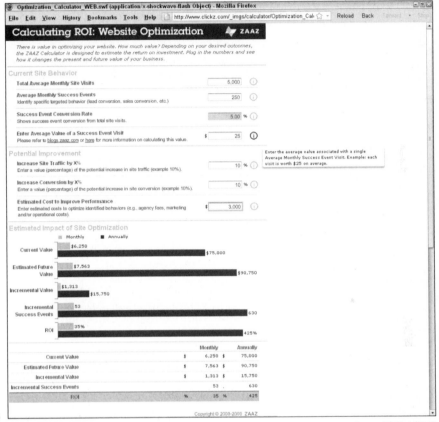

Figure 3-8:
See what happens when you improve the business metric (the value of a sale) instead of, or in addition to, improving performance (site traffic or conversion rate).

Courtesy ZAAZ and ClickZ

Technically speaking, ROI is a business metric, involving the achievement of business goals, such as more clicks from social media that become sales, higher average value per sale, more repeat sales from existing customers, or reduced cost of customer acquisition.

Many people try to calculate ROI for social media based on performance metrics such as increases in

✦ The amount of traffic to Web site or social media pages

✦ The number of online conversations that include a positive mention of your company

✦ References to your company versus references to your competitors

✦ The number of people who join your social networks or bookmark your sites

✦ The number of people who post to your blog, comment on your Facebook wall, or retweet your comments

**Book VIII
Chapter 3**

**Tallying the
Bottom Line**

These measurements may be worth monitoring, but they're only intermediate steps in the ROI process, as shown in Figure 3-9.

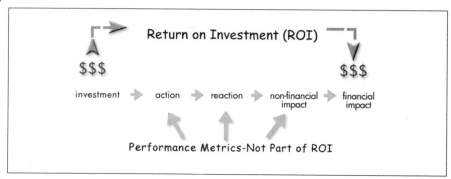

Source: BrandBuilder, "Olivier Blanchard Basics Of Social Media Roi" www.slideshare.net/thebrand
builder/olivier-blanchard-basics-of-social-media-roi (#35)

Here's how to calculate your return on investment:

1. **Establish baselines for what you want to measure before and after your effort.**

   For example, you may want to measure year-over-year growth.

2. **Create activity timelines that display when specific social media marketing activities take place.**

   For example, when you start a blog or Twitter campaign.

3. **Plot business metrics over time, particularly sales revenues, number of transactions, and net new customers.**

4. **Measure transactional precursors, such as positive versus negative mentions online, retail store traffic, or performance metrics.**

   For example, blog posts or site visits.

5. **Line up the timelines for the various relevant activities and transactional (business) results.**

6. **Look for patterns in the data that suggest a relationship between business metrics and transactional precursors.**

7. **Prove those relationships.**

Improvement in performance metrics doesn't necessarily produce better business results. The only two metrics that count toward ROI are whether your techniques reduce costs or improve revenue.

Crafty Chica does it all

Crafty Chica is an excellent example of a business that integrates multiple types of social media into an online identity strategy, with a really high return on investment.

The lifestyle Web site CraftyChica.com provides creative inspiration through crafts and writing and living a more artful life. Kathy Cano-Murillo, an artist, an author, and a newspaper columnist — and the owner and sole employee of Crafty Chica — posts hundreds of projects on her Web site so that other people can make them, too.

What started as hobby in May 2001 became a full-time enterprise in 2007 when iLoveToCreate.com, a Duncan Enterprises company, hired Murillo to turn Crafty Chica into a national brand and launch a retail product line. Murillo has since demonstrated her crafts on national TV shows, appeared in such high-profile publications as *USA Today* and *The New York Times* and on NPR on *Weekend Edition Sunday,* and authored seven craft books under the Crafty Chica label.

Crafty Chica targets creative women who incorporate art into their lives, with submarkets of crafters, do-it-yourselfers, Latinos, and teachers. That demographic, which closely matches that of social media users, is ideal for the multifaceted Web presence Murillo has embraced.

In addition to the CraftyChica.com Web site (shown in the nearby figure) and three others, you can find Murillo on multiple social media outlets: her blogs (http://thecrafty chica.blogspot.com and www. chicawriter.com), Twitter (www. Twitter.com/craftychica), Facebook (www.Facebook.com/thecrafty chica), MySpace (www.Myspace.com/ craftychica), YouTube (www.Youtube. com/craftychica), Flickr (www. flickr.com/craftychica), LinkedIn (www.linkedin.com/in/crafty chica), Goodreads, and Amazon. "Each one is different," Murillo notes. "I fine-tune my activity to fit them. Even though [I may] duplicate info, I often reword it or give it a different presentation to fit that certain crowd."

An early adopter of social media, Murillo says, "I look at each of these social networking sites as a happening party that I have to go to and be seen [at]! The party doesn't come to you — you have to go to the party!"

All these services "expose my work and my brand to new people," she explains. "My business is about art, and art is about seeing," Murillo points out. "Many people don't want to read all the details; they just want to see the picture. I upload pictures of everything I make, as well as events I attend." She promotes her social media presence with links on her home page and in her blogs, which she also uses to describe other projects, such as her crafts cruise or new books.

"I often trade button ads with other sites [and] do a lot of cross-blogging." Ever aware of marketing, Murillo always takes a stack of postcards to all her events and crafts fairs. "I do contests, photo contests — anything to keep the content exciting!"

Murillo has some pointed advice to business users of social media. "Take it seriously, learn to improve your photo skills, and get involved in the community — so many new people to meet. Let your pictures tell your story and sell your brand!"

(continued)

(continued)

Craft Chica Web Sites

`CraftyChica.com` (primary site)

`ChicaWriter.com` (for her books)

`ChicanoPopArt.com` (her online store for original fine art)

`iLoveToCreate.com/craftychica.aspx` (online store for the Crafty Chica product line)

Courtesy `www.craftychica.com`

Chapter 4: Making Decisions by the Numbers

In This Chapter

✔ **Using metrics to make decisions**

✔ **Diagnosing problem campaigns**

✔ **Returning to basics**

✔ **Reenergizing your creativity**

A 2009 eMarketer survey showed that only 16 percent of professionals whose companies use social media said that they measure their return on investment (ROI). By using the tools for assessing qualitative and quantitative results, including ROI, you can certainly count yourself among those happy few who do!

However, there's no point in collecting metrics just to save them in a virtual curio cabinet. The challenge is to figure out how to use the numbers to adjust your online marketing campaigns, whether they need fine-tuning or a major overhaul.

In spite of the hype, social media is, at its core, a form of strategic marketing communications. As a business owner, you must balance the subjective aspects of branding, sentiment, good will, and quality of leads with the objective performance metrics of traffic and click-through rate (CTR) and the business metrics of customer acquisition costs, conversion rate, sales value, and ROI. The balance point is unique to each business at a specific time. Alas, no fixed rules exist.

As part of your balancing act, you'll undoubtedly also tap your instincts, incorporating casual feedback from customers, the ever-changing evolution of your market, your budget, and your assessment of your own and your staff's available time and skills.

Even after you feel confident about your marketing program, keep watching your metrics as a reality check. Data has a funny way of surprising you.

Don't become complacent. Continue to check your performance and business metrics at least monthly. How do they compare to what your instinct is telling you?

Knowing When to Hold and When to Fold

There are a few things you'll watch for in your metrics. As always, you evaluate comparative results, not absolute numbers. Keep an eye on these characteristics:

✦ Negative and positive trends that last for several months

✦ Abrupt or unexpected changes

✦ "No change" in Key Performance Indicators in spite of social media marketing activities

✦ Correlations between a peak in traffic or sales with a specific social marketing activity

Layering activity timelines with metrics, as shown in Figure 4-1, is a simple, graphical way to spot this type of correlation. Establishing baseline metrics for your hub presence first truly helps in this process. It also helps if you add social media techniques one at a time — preferably with tracking codes.

Figure 4-1: Correlating an activity timeline with key performance indicators provides useful information.

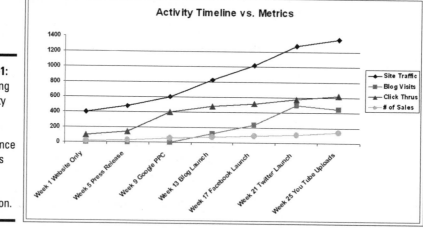

Copyright 2010 Watermelon Mountain Web Marketing www.watermelonweb.com.

Don't make *irreversible* decisions based on one event or from an analytical timeframe that's too short for the marketing channel you're trying to implement. There are no rules for a timeframe that is too short or too long. Your overall campaign may take 6 to 12 months to bear fruit. Be patient. Monitor your social media campaigns and rely on your business instincts.

You may find a time delay between the initiation of an effort and its impact on metrics, for these reasons:

✦ Viewers may wait to see a history of posts before engaging, let alone clicking through to your main hub.

✦ By definition, establishing a relationship with viewers or prospects takes time, just as it does in real life.

✦ Our brains haven't changed in spite of the Internet: As every brand marketer knows, most people still need to see something seven times to remember it.

✦ Many types of social media display a greater cumulative effect over time as viral marketing takes hold.

✦ Your mastery of a new medium usually improves as you climb the learning curve.

With positive results, the answer is simple: Keep doing what you're doing, and even more so. After you identify the elements responsible for your success, repeat them, amplify them, multiply them, and repurpose them.

Neutral or negative results force you to evaluate whether you should drop the activity or invest the effort needed to identify the problem and try to fix it. Ultimately, only you can decide whether you want to continue sinking time and effort into a social marketing method that doesn't produce results you want.

Make a chart for yourself like the one produced by the Robert H. Smith School of Business at the University of Maryland, shown in Figure 4-2. It shows how small businesses rate the effectiveness of social media against their expectations. How does your program match up to what you expected?

Figure 4-2:
Small businesses are generally realistic in their analysis of how social media can help their companies, but the number of new customers falls short of expectations.

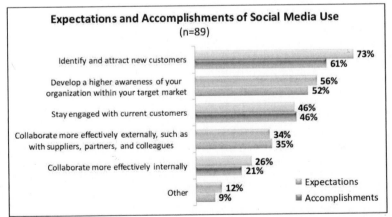

Expectations and Accomplishments of Social Media Use (n=89)

2009 Small Business Success Index commissioned by Network Solutions in partnership with the Robert H. Smith School Business, University of Maryland (temporary)

Behind the Burner, an online culinary branding experience, assesses its results weekly to adjust its marketing activity, as described in the nearby sidebar "Behind the Burner is cooking!" As an advertising-supported program, Behind the Burner must deliver qualified viewers to its advertisers, making it exquisitely sensitive to the results of its social media campaigns.

Behind the Burner is cooking!

For CEO Divya Gugnani, founding the site at www.behindtheburner.com is an opportunity to harness her skills and training in venture capital with her passion for everything culinary. A culinary media brand with both B2B and B2C components, Behind the Burner, shown in the nearby figure, launched in November 2008. Its cluster of Web properties already generates nearly a million dollars in revenues from advertising, advertorials, product placement, and branded content.

The site distributes expert-generated content (videos, blogs, and articles) about food, wine, mixology, and nutrition through a syndication network to a younger generation of food and drink enthusiasts. Gugnani has nurtured strong syndication relationships with offline partners like NBC and leveraged social media services such as Dailymotion, MySpace, and YouTube and online outlets such as Bravotv.com and Yahoo! Shine.

The company's marketing goals are to build its brand and awareness, and at times drive traffic. "Like most startups," Gugnani acknowledges, "I quickly realized that a marketing budget of $0 did not [have to] mean ZERO results for marketing. . . . Social media truly allows companies to reach millions of people and spread viral messages without spending any money at all."

Unlike most start-up CEOs, Gugnani already had experience writing for other blogs and maintaining a personal social media presence on Facebook and Twitter. She uses her personal sites to boost her corporate visibility, and encourages her staff to do the same. For her, the diverse opinions, perspectives, and personalities of her staff add interest to their blog.

"The one thing I insist upon is for our team to be genuine and real. We act like ourselves in our social media profiles and activities. We don't take a strong stance of having a company account that just spits out content for traffic. For me, social media is a conversation. You need to be a part of conversation: Talk, but also listen. People often ask me why [I] follow so many people on Twitter. I want to listen to what they have to say!"

Behind the Burner added all its many channels at launch. The blog page tempts engagement through all forms of social media, with call-to-action buttons for following on Twitter, becoming a fan on Facebook, and viewing Flickr photos.

The Behind the Burner team continually experiments with new social media platforms and tools (for example, ÜberTwitter, Ping.fm, TwitVid) to manage its presence and assess the results. Most recently, Gugnani says, the company has found ads on Su.pr (StumbleUpon) to be highly effective. "It's advertising with a viral marketing multiplier."

The team has also experimented with pay-per-click, Facebook, and Yahoo! ads, but generally found only modest success. "Banner swaps and newsletter ad swaps can be moderately effective for people, but we haven't gone that route yet," Gugnani adds.

The company relies on Google Alerts to monitor its keywords and company name. "It is always interesting to see who links to our site, features us on their blog, or embeds one of our videos. By using alerts, we can see how people are connecting with our brand and what pieces of content they find most relevant and interesting," explains Gugnani. The feedback provides guidance for what to do next.

In addition, the team runs Google Analytics weekly with reports on Q&As, recipes, articles, videos, blogs, and deals. It looks at overall traffic statistics and patterns, keywords that drive traffic, and which pages are viewed most often. The team analyzes sources of traffic by type and site to assess results of their social media efforts and syndication deals.

When Gugnani observes experiential differences among social media channels, she adjusts her tactics accordingly. For instance, she says, "We get most of our traffic through organic Google search. We have found that Facebook and Twitter are very powerful tools for engaging people with our culinary content. The Su.pr ads are good for driving traffic, but not as good in terms of engagement and repeat visits."

Ever alert to trends unearthed in Google Analytics, Gugnani has found that broadcast TV segments drive the largest swings in traffic and also subscribers for the Burner newsletter. Press mentions of Behind the Burner, particularly online ones such as DailyCandy, help build awareness with new audiences and inspire them to return as part of the online community. By integrating observations such as these into Behind the Burner's social media tactics, the overall marketing plan becomes more effective.

Behind the Burner staff handles all social media tasks except the ones that require adding radio buttons to the Web site. In addition to help from Web-savvy interns, Gugnani estimates that they spend a few hours a week managing their corporate Twitter account. The bulk of media management time is spent creating written and multimedia content provided by a network of freelance contributors.

In addition, staff members spend time managing their own personal accounts and sharing Behind the Burner videos, articles, blogs, and recipes with friends and family in their personal networks.

"I think it is important to have your whole team involved," Gugnani advises. "Our networks are all different, and we are able to reach many different niche audiences, by collectively sharing our favorite Behind the Burner media assets with our networks. Creating strong content is the most important activity. At the end of the day, if your content is good, it will be viral."

Behind the Burner Sites

www.behindtheburner.com	www.behindtheburner.com/blog/index
www.facebook.com/behindtheburner	www.flickr.com/photos/32016191@N07
www.youtube.com/user/BehindtheBurner	http://twitter.com/behindtheburner
http://twitter.com/dgugnani	www.linkedin.com/pub/divya-gugnani/0/98/6ba
www.naymz.com/divya_gugnani_1541092	www.myspace.com/behindtheburner_fans

Book VIII
Chapter 4

Making Decisions by the Numbers

(continued)

(continued)

Courtesy Behind the Burner

Diagnosing Problems with Social Media Campaigns

Put on your business hat when you detect a problem. Some techniques may be worth modifying and trying again, while others should be dropped. Ultimately, it's a business decision, not a technological one.

Be patient when assessing cost of customer acquisition and ROI, though a few trend lines in your metrics might give you pause:

+ Traffic to a social media service never picks up, or falls and remains low after an initial burst.

+ Traffic to the social media site holds steady, but the CTR to your master hub or other sites is low.

+ Follow-through on intermediate calls-to-action is low in performance metrics.

+ Traffic and click-throughs increase but the leads aren't well qualified.

+ Traffic and engagement, which had been increasing for quite a while, fall and continue to fall; small dips and rises are natural.

+ A conversion rate tracked back to a social media service is unintentionally lower than from other sources, and average sales value is lower. (Good strategic reasons for these results might exist, of course. You might deliberately target the younger student audience on MySpace or foursquare with less expensive options than those offered to an older, more affluent audience on Facebook.)

+ The cost of customer or lead acquisition is much higher than for other channels, making the return on investment unattractive. For example, a high-maintenance blog might generate a few leads but be relatively expensive compared to prescheduled tweets that drive more traffic successfully.

Fixing Problems

Underlying problems with low traffic on social media usually can be slotted into a few categories:

+ Problems locating your social media presence

+ Mismatch between channel and audience

+ Poor content

+ No audience engagement

+ Problems with the 4Ps — product, price, placement or position (distribution), and promotion — of marketing

After these problems are diagnosed, they can be handled in roughly the same way regardless of the social media venue used.

Before you panic, make sure that you have set reasonable expectations for performance and business metrics. Research the range of responses for similar companies, or view your competitors' social media sites to see how many responses, comments, and followers they have. Though you cannot divine their ROI, you can assess their traffic and inbound links. Your results from social media may be just fine!

Use the social monitoring tools described in Book II, Chapter 3 to compare how your competitors are doing on social media compared to your business. Many of these tools allow you to check any domain name.

Be careful with interpretation, however; if your competitors began working on their social media campaigns long before you did, they are likely to have very different results.

Remember that the social media audience is quite fickle. A constant demand exists for changes in content, approach, tools, and tone to keep up.

Your social presence can't be found

Driving traffic to your social media presence is as challenging as driving people to your site. If traffic is still low after about four weeks, ensure that all your social media sites are optimized for external search engines such as Google and internal (on-site) search tools used by different social media services. Turn to Book II, Chapter 2 for optimization techniques.

The source of the problem may be poorly selected search terms or tags, a headline or description that contains no keywords, or content that hasn't been optimized. Unless your hub presence, whether it's a blog or Web site, is well optimized itself, your social media presence may suffer also.

Be sure that posts occur often enough for your social media page to appear in real-time search results.

Inappropriate match between channel and audience

The symptoms for a mismatch usually show up quickly: People take little or no interest in your social media postings, you suffer from low CTR, and your bounce rate is high whenever visitors click-through.

To start with, you may have chosen an inappropriate social media service or the "wrong" group within a network. For example, young tech males like Digg, but if you want a social site about cooking and gardening, try `kirtsy.com` instead.

The solution: Return to your Social Media Marketing Plan (found in Book I, Chapter 2). Review the demographics and behavioral characteristics for the social media service you're using. They may have changed over time; for example, Facebook, which started as a site for college students, is now heavily favored by the over-55 demographic. Find a social venue that's a better fit, revise your plan, and try again.

Use Quantcast or Alexa to check demographics on sites.

Poor content

Content problems are a little harder to diagnose than visibility problems, especially if the problem appears with your first posts. In that case, the problem may also look like a channel mismatch, with content that simply doesn't appeal to your target market or is inappropriate for the channel.

However, if you experience a persistent dip in traffic, comments, or CTR from your blog, Facebook stream, Flickr, podcast, or YouTube account, you have other difficulties. Perhaps the content has "aged," isn't updated frequently enough, or has degraded in quality and interest.

Content creators are commonly enthusiastic at the beginning of a project, or to start with a backlog of media that can be repurposed and posted initially. Later content may not be as valuable to your market, lack appropriate production values, or simply become boring.

Watch for burnout. After the backlog of media is used up, the insistent demands for new content can easily become a burden. It isn't surprising to have creators lose interest or focus on quantity rather than on quality.

Compare the individual posts that produced an increase in traffic, responses, or CTR to ones that are failing. Tally posts by the names of their creators and what they were about. Start by asking previously successful creators to develop new material along the lines of older, successful content. If that doesn't work, watch the "most popular" tags to see what interests visitors and try to tie new content into those topics, if appropriate.

Finally, try assigning fresh staff members, recruiting guest writers and producers, or hiring professionals for a while. If this change produces better results, you have indicators for a long-term solution.

Lack of audience engagement

If you see traffic to the social media service holding steady but lack follow-throughs from calls to action or you have an unusually low click-through rate to your hub site, you may not be engaging your audience. Watch especially for engagement parameters that never take off or that dip persistently.

Review user comments, retweets, and other interactions on each service. You can use the internal performance metrics for Twitter, Facebook, and your blog to assess numerical results of engagement. Then review the chain for interaction between social media visitors and your staff. (See Books III, IV, and V for information on blogs, Twitter, and Facebook.)

Are visitor responses being acknowledged? Is there follow-up? One of the biggest challenges in social media is establishing a relationship with your visitors and maintaining a back-and-forth conversation. A lack of engagement may presage a lack of brand recognition, loss of customer loyalty, and reduced referrals from visitors to their friends or colleagues.

Use the behavioral calculator from Forrester Research (http://forrester.com/Groundswell/profile_tool.html), shown in Figure 4-3, to assess the level of engagement to expect from your market demographics. You can find the definitions for these consumer groups at www.forrester.com/Groundswell/ladder.html.

Figure 4-3:
The Forrester consumer profile tool offers a yardstick to predict degrees of engagement based on the demographics of your target market.

The four Ps of marketing

Perhaps you're getting traffic and click-throughs to your hub site and generating plenty of leads but still not closing or converting to sales. It might be time to go back to basics.

Review a Web analytics report generated before you started your social media marketing efforts. Make sure your Web site is well optimized for search, your online store (if you have one) is working well, and your conversion rate is solid. Fix any problems with your Web site before you try to adjust your social media campaign.

Product, price, placement or position (distribution), and promotion — the four Ps — are considered the basic elements of traditional marketing. These terms apply to social media and other forms of online marketing as well.

Product

Your *product* is whatever good or service you sell, regardless of whether the transaction takes place online or off. Product also includes such elements as performance, warranties, support, variety, and size. Review your competition to see which features, benefits, or services they offer, and which products they're featuring in social media. If you have an online store, look at your entire product mix and merchandising, not just at individual products. Ask yourself these questions:

✦ Are you selling products that the people you're targeting with social media want to buy?

✦ Do you have enough products or services to compete successfully in this environment?

✦ Are you updating your offerings regularly and promoting new items often?

Price

Price comparison sites such as Shopping.com and discount stores online already put price pressure on small businesses. Now social media shopping sites, with the rapid viral spread of news about special offers and price breaks, have put cost-conscious shoppers firmly in the driver's seat.

No longer can you check only competitors' Web sites and comparison-shopping sites for prices. Now you must check to see what they offer their Facebook, Twitter, LinkedIn, blog, e-newsletter, and social shopping visitors to gain new customers and hold onto them as loyal, repeat buyers. Any single product or service may now have multiple prices depending on who's buying.

Use social shopping and other sites to assess your prices against your online competition. Are yours significantly higher or lower or price competitive?

Your small business can have difficulty competing in the market for standard manufactured goods such as baby clothes or DVDs unless you have excellent wholesale deals from manufacturers or distributors. But you can compete on price on customized goods or services or by offering unique benefits for buying from your company.

If you must charge higher prices than your social media competitors, review your value proposition so that people perceive an extra benefit. It might be a $5 promotional code for a discount on another purchase, a no-questions-asked return policy, exclusivity, or very accessible tech support.

Be careful not to trap yourself into matching prices against large companies with deep pockets. Make tactical financial decisions about loss leaders and discounts for users of particular social media. Consider a less-than-full-featured product or service package for social media users if needed (sometimes called the *freemium* business model).

Placement or position

Placement or position refers to how products and services are delivered to consumers (distribution channels). Where and how are your products and services available? Your Web site needs to serve as a 24/7 hub for customer research, support, and sales online, but social media offers brand-new opportunities to serve your clients. Best Buy, for example, has already became famous for its twelpforce, in which employees use Twitter to field customer support questions and make product recommendations.

With multiple social marketing outlets, watch for the effects of *channel cannibalization* (the use of multiple distribution channels that pull sales from each other). Products or services sold directly from social media outlets may depress the sales numbers on your Web site.

Promotion

Your online and social media marketing plans fall into the *promotion* category, which includes all the different ways you communicate with customers and prospects, both online and offline. This also includes making people aware of your multiple points of visibility online, almost as though you're marketing another product. Careful cross-promotion among all your online venues is now as critical as integrating online and offline advertising. Are people aware of all your social media pages? Are you using the right calls to action on those pages to get people to buy?

Don't continue investing in a social media technique just because "everyone else is doing it."

Adjusting to Reality

Many times, expectations determine whether a marketing technique is seen as a success or a waste of time or something in between. It isn't possible for a particular social media channel to produce extraordinary changes in traffic or conversions. In most cases, though, your victories will be hard-won, as you cobble together traffic from multiple social media sources to build enough of a critical mass to gain measurable sales.

Achieving that goal usually involves many people, each of whom may become a committed champion of the method she has been using. When you decide to pull the plug on one of your social media techniques — or just decide to leave it in a static state — try to keep your employees engaged as well.

Unless social media participants have proved themselves to be nonperformers, try to shift them into another channel so that they can retain a direct relationship with customers.

Avoid the temptation to recentralize your social media marketing in one place, whether it's PR, marketing communications, management, or customer support. Instead, try to maintain the involvement of someone from each of those functional areas, as well as subject area experts from such diverse departments as manufacturing, sales, and R&D.

Marketing is only part of a company, but all of a company is marketing.

As wild a ride as social media may seem, it's more of a marathon than a sprint. Given that it may take 6 to 12 months to see the return on your marketing efforts, you need to nourish your social media sites for quite a while.

Feeding the hungry maw of the content monster week in and week out isn't easy. You need to not only keep your staff engaged and positive but also keep your content fresh. Take advantage of brainstorming techniques that involve your entire team to generate some new ideas each month. Here are a few suggestions to get you started:

✦ Create unique, themed campaigns that last one to three months. Find an interesting hook to recruit guest posts or writers, perhaps letting a few people try your product or service and write about it.

✦ Distribute short-term "deals" using some of the up-and-coming social media techniques described in Book VIII, Chapter 6, such as location-based coupons on cellphones or to meet-up attendees or "group" coupons from Groupon.

✦ Write a Wikipedia entry about your product or business from a consumer's point of view.

✦ Make friends with Twitter by incorporating an interactive application, such as a poll or sweepstakes entry.

✦ Reach one or more of your discrete niche markets by using some of the smaller alternative social media services listed in Book VII, Chapter 6 or in Book II, Chapter 3.

✦ If you aren't gaining traction with groups on Twitter or Facebook, post on an old-fashioned forum, message board, or chat room on a relevant topic.

✦ Tell a story about your product or service in pictures (not video — too easy!) and upload them to Flickr or another photo service.

Any marketing problem has an infinite number of solutions. You have to find only one of them. Taos Sacred Places, a tourism mini-site for a yearlong promotion of Taos, New Mexico, as a vacation destination, decided to use Twitter to engage local poets and writers, as well as tourists, in a haiku contest, shown in Figure 4-4.

**Book VIII
Chapter 4**

**Making Decisions
by the Numbers**

Figure 4-4:
This haiku contest on Twitter is part of a creative tourism promotion for the town of Taos, New Mexico.

Courtesy Webb Design, Inc. for TaosSacredPlaces.com

Chapter 5: Multiplying Your Impact

In This Chapter

✓ **Integrating social media with e-mail campaigns**

✓ **Incorporating social media, publicity, and public relations**

✓ **Combining social media with paid advertising**

✓ **Leveraging social media with Web site features**

S ocial media has become such an essential way of "getting the word out" that it now also has become a powerful tool for leveraging other forms of online marketing. All your marketing goes viral when you take advantage of social media channels. Integration with social media can help you

✦ Increase newsletter subscriptions

✦ Broaden the audience for event announcements

✦ Maximize the distribution of press releases and other news

✦ Find additional paid online advertising opportunities

✦ Drive traffic to your hub Web site to encourage users to take advantage of special features

We discuss simple integration techniques in earlier chapters, such as displaying chiclets to invite people to follow your company on social media outlets and implementing Social Share buttons to encourage viewers to share your pages with others. In this chapter, we discuss more advanced methods for integrating social media into your overall marketing plans.

Though integration is generally easy and effective, it still calls for a little strategic planning beforehand and some tactical execution. Eventually, though, these tactics become a matter of habit.

Include your integrated marketing tactics on your Social Media Marketing Plan in Book I, Chapter 2 and schedule activities on your Social Media Activity Calendar in Book 1, Chapter 3.

Thinking Strategically

For many businesses, social media marketing adds to the richness of the company's marketing mix, but others see it as a low-cost substitute for paid advertising, pay-per-click (PPC) campaigns, standard press release distribution, loyalty programs, or other forms of marketing.

If you're planning to swap tactics, proceed with caution because a social media campaign may take six months to a year to reach maturity. Don't stop using other tactics that now reach your target markets successfully. Wait for results from metrics showing that social media perform at least as well.

Whether you're planning a substitution or an addition, take advantage of the measurement tools we discuss in earlier chapters to establish baselines for traffic, click-through rate (CTR), conversion rates, and return on investment (ROI) for existing marketing methods so that you can detect any lift (or drop) that integration brings.

You don't know what to measure unless you first set goals for your integration efforts, which we discussed in Book I, Chapter 1. Sometimes you're after sales, sometimes leads, sometimes brand recognition, or sometimes just your 15 minutes of fame.

In its *2010 Social Media Marketing Benchmark Survey*, Marketing Sherpa asked businesses to assess the effectiveness of social media integration with other marketing tactics they used. Businesses reported that some forms of integration worked better than others, as shown in Figure 5-1. You might want to consider their experiences as you move forward with your own plans for integration.

As always, be sure to define the specific form your integration methods will take, who will execute them and when, and how you will measure the results. Create a block diagram showing how content will flow as part of your integration plans (see Book I, Chapter 2).

Integrating with E-Mail

It may seem counterintuitive, given all the hype about social media, but recent studies show that people who use social media are *more* avid e-mail users than others. A December 2009 analysis by www.sharethis.com reveals that most users still prefer to share content via e-mail and that e-mail retains the highest level of engagement per click-through, as shown in Table 5-1.

Figure 5-1:
Businesses
like the
ease of
social media
integration
and how
well they
can track
from initial
engagement
to
conversion.

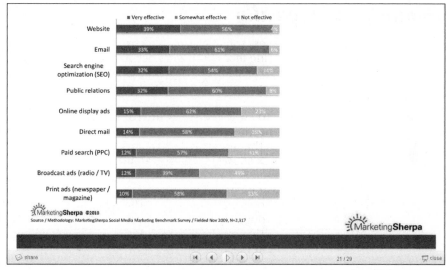

Source: MarketingSherpa.com

Table 5-1	Preferred Methods of Sharing Content	
Method	*Preferred Sharing Method*	*Engagement per Click*
E-mail	46%	2.95 page views
Facebook	33.32%	2.76 page views
Twitter	5.82%	1.66 page views
Other	14.17%	N/A

Source: http://sharethis.com/news/press-releases/sharethis-releases-the-
social-engagement-of-sharing

Confirming these observations, *View from the Social Inbox 2010*, a study published by the marketing agency Merkle (www.merkleinc.com/viewfrom socialinbox2010), indicates that

✦ Forty-two percent of social networkers check their e-mail four or more times a day, compared to just 27 percent of those who don't use the current top social networking sites.

✦ Sixty-three percent of social networkers use the same e-mail account for their social networking messages and the majority of their permission, or *opt-in,* e-mail.

**Book VIII
Chapter 5**

**Multiplying
Your Impact**

✦ Twenty percent of Facebook, MySpace, and Twitter users have posted or shared something from permission e-mail to their social accounts by using a Share option.

With numbers like these, you have every reason to integrate e-mail with social media to attract new subscribers, promote your newsletter, obtain content ideas, and identify issues to address in your e-mail newsletters. For more information on e-mail marketing, see *E-Mail Marketing For Dummies*, by John Arnold.

Gaining more subscribers

Wherever and whenever prospects discover your presence on social media, try to provide them with other opportunities to find out how you might be able to solve their problems. Your newsletter is certainly one of those opportunities. Follow these guidelines:

✦ **Include a link for newsletter subscription on your blog, all your other social media pages, and your e-mail signature block.** Constant Contact (`http://apps.facebook.com/ctctjmml`) and MailChimp (`www.mailchimp.com/campaign/getsocial`), among others, have apps you can add to your Facebook page to allow your fans to sign up for your newsletter directly from your Facebook page (see Figure 5-2). You never know — you might reach dozens, hundreds, maybe thousands of new prospects.

✦ **Treat your newsletter as an event on social media networks.** Add a preview of topics or tweet an announcement of your newsletter a day or so in advance. Include a linkable call-to-action to subscribe in both cases.

✦ **Post a teaser line in your social media outlets with a linkable call to action.** You might say, for example, "If you need to learn more about healthcare reform for small businesses, sign up for our newsletter."

✦ **Post newsworthy findings.** Use material from your newsletter on social news services to attract more readers.

✦ **Link to a sample newsletter or newsletter archive on your blog, Web site, or Static FBML (Facebook Markup Language) page so that prospective subscribers can see its usefulness.** Of course, you indicate the frequency with which you e-mail newsletters.

Figure 5-2:
Facebook newsletter sign-up on Nicolette Tallmadge Designs. Both the Info and Wall pages display a smaller e-mail sign-up block in the right margin.

Finding more followers and connections

E-mail integration with social media works both ways: You can drive people from your newsletter to social media, or use these techniques to gain subscribers:

✦ Use your newsletter to drive traffic to social media outlets as does poet-philosopher and inspirational speaker Noah benShea, shown in Figure 5-3.

✦ Include Social Share and Follow Us On buttons in every issue of your newsletter.

✦ Add options for signing up for social media on the e-mail registration page on your Web site (if possible).

✦ Use your e-newsletter to make an offer or run a contest for social media participants as Bluefly.com, a retailer of discount designer apparel for women. This innovative contest spurs interaction by having participants "vote" on entries using the Like feature on Facebook.

Courtesy Noah benShea.com/SkyViewProjects.com

Figure 5-3:
This
newsletter
drives traffic
to multiple
social media
outlets,
as well as
to Noah
benShea's
primary
Web site.

Cross-promote your e-mail newsletter on all your social media channels. Remember to post all your social venues, not just your hub Web site, in your e-mail signature block.

Finding and sharing content

Writing content continuously for newsletters and social media is always a challenge. However, you can exploit the easy interaction between the two to lighten your writing burden.

- ✦ **Take advantage of social marketing capabilities available by way of your e-mail service provider.** Many companies now let you easily send your e-mail directly to Facebook and other social networking pages.

- ✦ **Mine social media for content.** Read related information on social news sites, listen to hot topics that come up in LinkedIn and Facebook groups, and watch for trending topics. Pay attention to comments on your own and other people's forums, message boards, and social communities. They may clue you in to concerns, trends, or industry news.

✦ **Use Google Alerts, Social Mention, Twitter Search, and other search functions for mentions of your company.** You can turn positive comments into testimonial content on your newsletter, social media outlet, or Web site (with permission) or respond to many people at a time who may have read a negative comment.

✦ **Create a Q&A section in your regular newsletter.** Respond to questions that are common across social media venues.

✦ **Use keywords and tags to identify social news and content related to your industry.** In turn, be sure to include keywords in any newsletters or newsletter announcements that may be reposted on the Web.

✦ **Pursue market intelligence even further by using the advanced Twitter search features.** Sort tweets geographically by search term. Then segment your mailing list accordingly, if appropriate. Visit `http://search.twitter.com/advanced`.

Use Google Insights (`www.google.com/insights/search/#`) to figure out the time of day, day of week, and time of year that users are most likely to use specific search terms. Use that information to schedule your topical e-mail blasts. There's nothing like having information show up in someone's inbox just when they're looking for it! You'll be way beyond "top of mind."

Integrating with Public Relations and Press Releases

The reasons for dealing with public relations and press release distribution haven't changed since the explosion of social media — just the methodology. Where once you worried only about the care and feeding of a small covey of journalists, now you must nourish a veritable horde of bloggers, individual influencers, authors of ezine articles, editors of online publications, and individuals who will recommend your article on a social news service.

In companies that view social media primarily as a public relations vehicle, the public or community relations person may be the one who coordinates the social media marketing strategy.

All these venues, not just standard media, now open a door to public attention. Take advantage of all of them as a cost-effective way to achieve these goals:

✦ **Broadcast announcements of products, appearances, and events:** Alerting target markets to new possibilities is one of the most traditional uses of publicity.

✦ **Build brand recognition:** Whether it's acknowledgment of your participation in community events, awareness of your position within your industry, or simply the frequent repetition of your name in front of your audience, press coverage brings you publicity at a relatively low cost.

✦ **Ask journalists, authors, or bloggers to write about your company:** Stories about your firm — at least the positive ones — boost your credibility, extend your reach, and provide you with "bragging" destinations for links from your site. The trade press is especially critical to business-to-business (B2B) companies.

✦ **Drive traffic to your Web site:** Online press releases almost always have at least one link to your central Web presence, and often more. Social media offers a mechanism for distributing linkable press content around the Web that others may embed. The accumulation of long-lasting inbound links obviously has a greater impact than a one-time release alone.

✦ **Improve search engine ranking:** You can gain many inbound links to your site when your release posts on multiple press outlets. Press sites generally transfer high "link juice," and Google in particular weighs press mentions highly. Your visibility on preferred search terms may also rise, especially if you have optimized your press releases and headlines for keywords.

Setting up an online newsroom

If you haven't already done so, set up an online newsroom (media page) for the press on your primary Web site. Use this newsroom to present any press releases you create, provide writers with downloadable logos and images, link to articles and posts written about your company, and let writers sign up for RSS feeds for future release.

You might want to set up this newsroom as a separate section in blog format (another way to integrate social media!) to aggregate queries, moderated posts, and trackbacks from individual releases. Give each release a unique URL and place your headline on the page title.

Cultivating influencers

Identifying influencers is one key way to get into a conversation. Influencers are people whose blogs, tweets, or Facebook pages drive much of the conversation in a particular topic area. They often have a loyal following of readers who engage in dialog, repeat, and amplify discussions the influencer began. In the olden days, press folks would cultivate public relations and press contacts the same way you now cultivate influencers.

Here's a quick checklist for finding these key figures to approach with a request for coverage:

✦ **Find conversations on blogs, Twitter, Facebook, forums, message boards, communities, and industry-specific social media by using keywords relevant to your company, brand, product, industry, and competitors.** This task is easier now that Google includes social media in its search results. To see only results from social media, be sure to choose Show Options⇨Updates⇨Your Timeframe in the left side of a search results page. Join appropriate groups when you find them.

✦ **Use search tools on particular networks and aggregator searches such as Social Mention, too.** Those who post most often, or who have a lot of connections or followers, may be the experts or influencers you seek. Monitor the conversations for a while to be sure you've identified the right folks.

✦ **Use standard search techniques to locate trade publications or related newsletters.** Publication sites may include links to their own social media sites. Or, identify specific writers and editors whose interests sync with yours and search for their individual blogs and social networking accounts.

✦ **Become a contributor who answers questions on related subjects.** You can (and should) identify yourself, without promoting your company or products in your comments. Before you ask for anything, engage in the conversation and offer links to related posts and articles. Because links are the currency of social media, link from your site to influencers' sites, blogs, and tweets, and become a connection or follower.

To track your contacts, bookmark the conversations you find, organizing them in subfolders by the name of influencer.

Distributing your news

Frankly, the more sites the merrier. Though you pay a penalty for duplicate content in search engines, press releases don't seem to suffer.

Be sure to place identifying tags on links in different press releases so that you can tell which releases generate click-throughs to your site. If you create only one release a month, this isn't essential; however, if you have an active campaign with numerous press mentions, or other types of postings on the same source sites, it's absolutely critical.

Table 5-2 shows a partial list of press and PR online resources.

Table 5-2	Publicity and PR Resources	
Name	*URL*	*Description*
BuzzStream	`www.buzzstream.com/social-media`	Fee-based social CRM and monitoring service
ClickPress	`www.clickpress.com`	Free press release posting on site
Free Press Release	`www.free-press-release.com`	Free press release distribution; includes social media
Help a Reporter Out	`http://helpareporter.com`	Matching reporters to sources
HubSpot	`ww.slideshare.net/HubSpot/new-research-on-news-release-best-practices`	Tips for optimizing press releases and PR for SEO
Mashable Social Media Guide	`http://mashable.com/2007/10/20/press-releases`	List of 20+ free press release distribution sites
Muck Rack	`http://muckrack.com/beats`	Journalists on Twitter by beats
Muck Rack	`http://muckrack.com/press_releases/submit`	Fee-based Twitter pitch to journalists, $50 minimum
PitchEngine	`www.pitchengine.com`	Social PR platform, social media release creation and distribution; free and paid versions
Press About	`www.pressabout.com`	Free press release distribution in form of blog
PressDoc	`www.pressdoc.com`	Write, edit , publish and share social media releases online; €10 per release
Press Release Grader	`http://pressrelease.grader.com`	Free assessment of press releases for links and SEO
reddit	`www.reddit.com`	Social news site that accepts links to releases
Shift Communications	`http://www.shiftcomm.com/downloads/SMR_v1.5.pdf`	Social media press release format
The Open Press	`www.theopenpress.com`	Free press release posting onsite

Posting on your own sites

Post your release, at minimum, on your own Web site and blog. You can, however, easily add releases to your other social networking profiles, if it's appropriate. For instance, an author might post a release for each book she writes, but wouldn't necessarily post a press release for everyone hired at her company.

To simplify your life, use syndication techniques such as Ping.fm or RSS (see Book II, Chapter 1) to post both press release and newsletter content on your blog, Facebook pages, and elsewhere. Of course, then the content will be identical.

Using standard press distribution sources

Many, many paid online press release distribution sources exist. Among the most well known are BusinessWire, PR Newswire PR Web, and marketwire.com.

Sometimes, distribution services offer levels of service at different prices depending on the quantity and type of distribution, geographical distribution, and whether distribution includes social media, multimedia, offline publications, or other criteria.

Table 5-2, a little earlier in this chapter, includes several options for free distribution. Many free services don't distribute your releases — except perhaps to search engines — but, rather, simply post them on their sites for finite periods. Whether they're free or paid, be sure to read carefully what you're getting.

Perhaps the most straightforward example of integrating press releases with social media is the distribution of a release announcing your new social media presence, as Taipan Publishing Group did, shown in Figure 5-4. It distributed its press release through `24-7pressrelease.com`, one of many paid press release distribution services.

Post linkable event announcements on calendars all over the Web, as well as on event pages on Facebook, MySpace, and other social media. Calendars may be an "old-fashioned," presocial technique, but many high-ranking calendar pages feed "link juice" until your event occurs and the listing expires.

Using bloggers as a distribution channel

You've laid the groundwork by identifying appropriate bloggers and other influencers and participated on their publications. The next step is to get them to post your news. The most discrete way is to e-mail it (or a link to it) with a cover note to see whether the recipient wants to share the article with readers or comment on its content.

Figure 5-4:
Taipan
Publishing
Group
issued
a press
release
announcing
its social
media
campaign.

Courtesy Taipan Publishing Group

Because you're "pitching" the bloggers, include in your cover note the reason that you think readers of the blog would be interested and a descriptive paragraph about your company. It's considered bad form to submit your press release as a post on most blogs — bad enough that a moderator probably would exclude it.

If you include a product sample with your release, implicitly asking for an independent review, the blogger now has to disclose that fact. In October 2009, the Federal Trade Commission published final guidelines for endorsement and testimonials. For more information, see www.ftc.gov/opa/2009/10/endortest.shtm.

Using social news services and other social networks

You can send similar e-mails to individuals and influencers you have identified as participating in key discussions about related products or issues, including a short notice about the press release on Twitter and a mention to groups and professionals on sites like Facebook and LinkedIn.

You can submit your release to the few social news services, such as reddit, that permit you to submit your own link to your press release. Figure 5-5 shows a link on reddit to a release from http://huladancehq.com. In other cases, you may need to submit to social news and bookmark services from another identity, or wait until the story appears on a blog and submit the blog post instead.

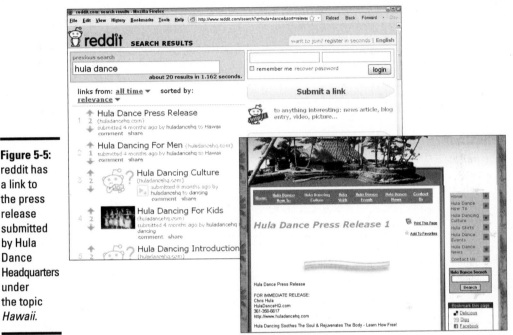

Courtesy HulaDanceHQ.com

Figure 5-5: reddit has a link to the press release submitted by Hula Dance Headquarters under the topic *Hawaii.*

If your press release includes multimedia or you've created a video or audio release, be sure to submit it to relevant directories such as `www.blog talkradio.com`, `www.digitalpodcast.com`, or `www.bloguniverse.com/video-blogs`.

Emphasizing content

As always, content, tone, and interest level are the keys. Keep your release to about 400 words or fewer if you're including multimedia. Keep your headline to about 80 characters and use an `<h1>` HTML header tag.

Combine anchor text with the URL in parentheses right next to it (to cover all bases), but don't use the same anchor text twice. On some press distribution services, and of course on social media, you have a chance to submit keywords or tags, an essential process for leveraging your press release for search engine optimization (SEO) purposes. Be sure that some or all of these keywords are also included in the headline or first paragraph of the release. Try to use at least some of your primary set of search terms, as described in Book II, Chapter 2.

**Book VIII
Chapter 5**

Multiplying Your Impact

Rethinking the press release for social media

Over the past several years, users have debated the value of a new format for social media press releases. The biggest differences are that the social media release

✦ Usually has three or four embedded links with anchor text for search engines, rather than URLs only (although you can mix the two)

✦ May include embedded video and other multimedia options

✦ Allows reports to "rip" content electronically and re-purpose it

✦ May include tags and sharing options

In its *2009-10 B2B Marketing Benchmark Report*, Marketing Sherpa found the social media release roughly comparable to traditional releases in terms of the resulting quantity and quality of leads. The biggest difference they saw was that businesses use the new format only about half as often as the traditional one. HubSpot, on the other hand, found that traditional releases were republished in full about 20 percent more often.

In others words, "You pays your money and you takes your choice." The social media release is a convenient way to ensure that your master release format has all the elements you might need for various social media submissions.

You can find templates for your press releases; Figure 5-6 shows one. You can pick and choose the bits and pieces to submit as appropriate to different services. If you're using a standard press release distribution service, you can easily extract the pure text version and adjust the URLs.

The template is only a suggested one, so feel free to modify it. A sample of a prepared social media release is shown in Figure 5-7.

For more information, watch the HubSpot presentation at `http://bit.ly/3DnjW`.

Measuring results

The same social monitoring tools that you use to find influencers can be applied to track key performance indicators for your press efforts, such as Google Alerts, Social Mention, and `search.twitter.com`. This is a good place to use all that "qualitative" data, as well as advertising measurements for online brand awareness and equity. (See, for example, `www.questionpro.com/brand-awareness.html` or `www.businessknowhow.com/internet/socialmedia.htm`.)

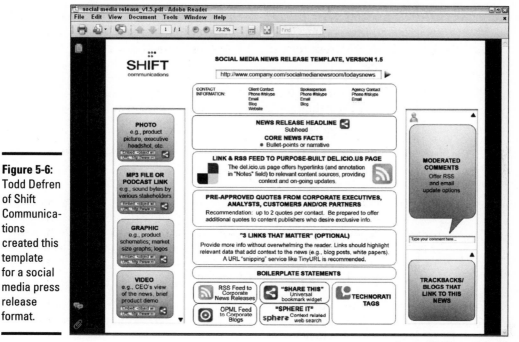

Figure 5-6:
Todd Defren
of Shift
Communica-
tions
created this
template
for a social
media press
release
format.

Figure 5-7:
A press
release in
social media
format
produced
by way of
PitchEngine.

**Book VIII
Chapter 5**

Multiplying
Your Impact

Measure baselines before you begin your press campaigns! Be sure that before-and-after results are for comparable timeframes. Here are a few of the key performance indicators you might find relevant:

✦ Number of online mentions of company, brand, product or service line, and/or individual products or services anywhere online, including social media, during a specific time frame.

✦ Number and location of media placements — where and when mentions occurred, a press release was published, or an article about your company or product appeared on a recognized media outlet, whether online or offline.

✦ Site traffic generated from press releases and other linkable press-related mentions (see referrer logs in your Web stats software for number of inbound links from each source); include comparative click-through rates, and conversion rates, if available. To make this process easier, tag links with the identifiers related to the topic or date of the press release.

✦ Social media campaign participation and sentiment using monitoring tools; see Book II, Chapter 1.

✦ Average frequency of the product, company, or brand conversations related to the release compared to the frequency of conversations before the release.

✦ Estimated costs (hard dollars and labor) that were spent. Be sure to include costs for paid distribution, if used. To compare ROI for publicity to other methods, you compare costs to the value of sales that can be traced back to the release (if any). If you can't trace back sales, you might be able to compare brand engagement.

Integrating with Paid Advertising

Social media has the advertising world in ferment. As applications from social media companies mature, audiences grow, and technology improves, the companies expand their advertising opportunities to make money for their investors — everyone is just trying to make a buck. Within weeks in 2010, major advertising announcements had the virtual world aflutter.

First, Facebook decided to end the display of traditional banner ads in favor of ads that feature social actions (called *engagement ads*), ending a long agreement with Microsoft. Then Twitter announced that it would start placing "promoted tweets" (paid advertising) at the top of Twitter search results.

Both announcements indicate ways in which social media may affect your online marketing plans: First, they become destination opportunities for your own paid advertising; second, social media technology is fueling the growth of the new engagement ad.

Advertising on social media sites

Many social media sites have long accepted advertising that you can incorporate into your plans for paid advertising (if any). Some, like Ning and Squidoo and many smaller social media venues display standard PPC, banner, and/or multimedia ads from Google Adsense. Flickr ads are served by Yahoo! Ad Solutions (`http://advertising.yahoo.com/advertisers`). Until recently, Bing served display ads to Facebook, but not any longer; Facebook now handles all its graphical ads.

A recent eye-tracking study by Oneupweb showed that users really do look at paid ads appearing on the search results pages of social media services.

For more information on online advertising, see *Advertising For Dummies,* by Gary Dahl.

Self-service ads

Larger sites, such as MySpace and Facebook, have long sold display ads using their on-site, self-service tools for ad creation and targeting. Table 5-3 lists popular social media sites offering paid advertising options.

Table 5-3	Social Media Sites That Offer Paid Advertising	
Name	*URL for Media Kit and Advertising Information*	*Notes*
Facebook	`www.facebook.com/advertising`	Demographics information at `www.facebook.com/help/?page=863`
LinkedIn	`http://advertising.linkedin.com`	Demographics at `http://advertising.linkedin.com/audience`
MySpace	`https://advertise.myspace.com`	Demographics at `https://advertise.myspace.com/targetedadvertising.html`
reddit	`www.reddit.com/ad_inq`	Demographics at `quantcast.com/reddit`
Twitter	`http://blog.twitter.com/2010/04/hello-world.html`	Promoted tweets starting with selected advertisers

To be sure, some of these user-generated ads are plug-ugly, much like newsletters in the early days of desktop publishing. In the future, social networks may add prepackaged, preformatted ads to which you need to add only your text.

You can and should take advantage of targeting your audience as closely as the tools allow, selecting by geography, demographics, education, and interest area whenever possible. Some people have objected to the targeting: Older women seem to receive a disproportionate number of ads for skin creams and diets; those who change their status to Engaged are quickly deluged with ads for wedding service providers.

You can evaluate advertising placements on these sites just as you would evaluate advertising placed anywhere else. Using the advertising metrics discussed in Book VIII, Chapter 2, consider cost per click (CPC), cost per 1000 impressions (CPM), click-through rate, and resulting conversions to decide whether any of these ads pay off for you.

Results so far indicate that ads appearing on social media pages generally perform slightly worse than banner ads on other publications. The average click-through rate (CTR) on banners in 2009 was only 0.1 — 0.3 percent; on PPC ads it was closer to 1 to 3 percent. However, so many variables affect CTR — ad size, placement, quality of the ad, match to audience, and value of the offer — that it's hard to generalize. Anecdotal evidence indicates that the CTR on Facebook display ads ran about half the average.

Averages are averages. The range at both ends may be extreme. Like so much material on the Web, the only metrics that matter are your own. Test the same ad in several places at the same time to see which publishers yield the most bang for your advertising buck.

In addition to self-serve ads, many social media sites offer other alternatives for advertising. For instance, you can use a static FBML page to insert an entire page (or pages) of HTML advertising content, as BMW did with its BMW Inside page at `www.facebook.com/BMW#!/BMW?v=app_7146470109`.

Targeting your market is primary. Spiceworks, a provider of free network management software, is so successful at delivering a target audience of highly coveted IT professionals on its forum pages (`http://community.spiceworks.com`) that paid advertising supports the company. With click-through rates of 2 to 20 percent, it can charge a premium for its ads. Don't overlook small social sites that can deliver your audience directly to your site. They're worth it!

Promoted tweets

The industry has long anticipated the Twitter rollout of some form of advertising to monetize its site. The only question was when and what form it would take. Twitter is starting with a few large company pioneers and will eventually extend it to others.

Twitter claims it will measure whether the promoted tweets "resonate" with users to decide whether the promotions should be continued. Resonance involves a proprietary algorithm that involves multiple factors. Charges initially are based on a CPM model, but that's expected to change as Twitter obtains more data on other ways to measure ad value.

Though labeled as "promoted," the tweets are sent to those who follow a brand. Because users can perform standard actions — such as reply, retweet, and "favorite" — on these promoted tweets, the tweets are expected to have a longer shelf-life and larger audience than if they were simply published only once or limited just to a brand's enrolled followers.

As an advertiser, you need to maintain your communication effort with Twitter users; promoted tweets don't replace that. Put on your imagination thinking cap: You may need to revise your advertising creatives and offers to fit better with what the Twitter user expects and what promotion is most likely to be replied, retweeted, and otherwise spread around.

Some expect that promoted tweets will eventually infiltrate users' individual Twitter streams and end up redisplayed on other sites. Eventually, third-party sites will probably be able to negotiate to show ads and share revenue. One thing is certain: Lots of change is coming to the online advertising world. Stay up-to-date on promoted tweets at `http://blog.twitter.com`.

Engagement ads

Users have obviously started to tune out banner ads, even when the ads spill all over content and refuse to close, irritate eyeballs with annoying animation, or interrupt concentration with surprising bursts of unwanted sound.

The fuse was lit for innovation and social media technologies ignited it, for good or ill. The marriage of advertising message with individual user information — with the potential of turning every viewer into a shill — has serious implications for privacy. Although the Interactive Advertising Bureau (IAB) has published best practices for user opt-in and privacy protection (`www.iab.net/socialads` and `www.iab.net/sm_buyers_guide`), it isn't clear how well they will be followed.

The IAB defines these engagement ads, sometimes called *social banners,* as "a type of banner that incorporates social or conversational functionality within it. . . . The key to success is for social banner ads to enable consumers to have a real interactive experience within the unit, as opposed to just passively viewing the content within the ad."

Comment-style ads seem to work well for entertainment, new products, cars, and clothes, though virtual gift ads seem to attract consumer product and entertainment advertisers. Clicking the Like button on an ad now turns viewers into connections for that brand. This call-to-action ad works well for any established brand, luxury products, and products or entertainers with a passionate following.

More complex engagement ads draw content from a social network: the photo image and name from a profile (presuming an emotionally effective brand endorsement) or user-generated phrases from tweets, blogs, or RSS feeds. Users review the modified ads; if they agree to allow it, the ads are then distributed to their personal networks. For these complex ads to operate, the user must already be connected to her social network. (One could imagine using these ads to play an interesting game of rumor.)

Anyone can create a self-service display ad, though having the assistance of an experienced graphic designer helps. However, these interactive engagement ads probably require involvement from tech support or your Web developer.

Like the promoted tweets, engagement ads have an enhanced value based on how often others share them. If the sharing results in a cascading effect of recommended impressions to presumably qualified prospects, who just so happen to be friends, all the better for you. However, you need to watch for changes in pricing and business models as engagement ads take hold.

Integrating with Your Web Site

Any Web site can incorporate a myriad of features that integrate with social media, going well beyond the obvious and oft-repeated reminders to include Follow Us On and Share buttons everywhere, including product pages within stores. You can get clever: Include links to your Help forum or YouTube video tutorials as part of the automated purchase confirmation e-mail you send to buyers.

In some cases, "old-fashioned" versions of social media, such as onsite forums, chat rooms, product reviews, and wikis effectively draw repeat visitors to the hub site, avoiding any integration with third-party social media sites.

More advanced sites have already implemented Web 2.0 techniques onsite, including blogs and communities and other calls for user-generated content, including photos and videos of people using your product or suggesting creative new designs and applications.

Several strategic factors may affect your decision whether to implement such techniques onsite or off:

✦ The cost of development, storage, and support and ongoing maintenance versus costs offsite

✦ SEO and link strategies

✦ Plus-and-minus points of managing a more centralized and simplified Web presence

A few onsite techniques, like loyalty programs, don't seem to integrate particularly well with social media, but three other popular methods practically cry out for integration: coupons, discounts, and freebies; games and contests; and microsites. For more information about onsite and other forms of online marketing, see Jan's book *Web Marketing For Dummies,* 2nd Edition.

Coupons, discounts, and freebies

It doesn't take much monitoring of Facebook and Twitter and social news, bookmarking, and shopping streams to see how frequently they're used to offer time-limited deals, coupons, special promotions, discounts, and free samples.

Certainly, longer-term offers can be made to LinkedIn and Plaxo members, to groups on Facebook or Flickr, or to members of a forum on any topic. However, the sense of urgency in certain social media environments catches viewers' interest. Just like the competitive energy of an auction may cause bidders to offer more than they intend, the ephemeral nature of real-time offers may inspire viewers to grab for a coupon they might otherwise have passed up. Though some of the interest in savings and discounts may be encouraged by the recent recessionary mood, which makes people hyperattentive to opportunities to save money; interest in getting "a deal" may also simply be human nature.

The upside and downside of real-time social media is precisely the immediacy of these offers and how quickly a chain of other posts extinguishes them from awareness. On one hand, you have a chance to move overstock quickly, bring in business on a slow day, or gain new prospects from a group you might not otherwise reach without making a long-term, and perhaps too-expensive commitment. On the other hand, you have to preplan and schedule your posts, repeating them frequently enough throughout the day to appear in real-time search results and near the top of chronologically organized posts on any social media site.

Always link back to your primary Web site or blog, not only to explain the details of the offer, but also to enjoy the inbound link value, offer additional goods and services, and capture prospect information. Be sure to use a unique promotion code for each offer, and tag your links with identifiers to track the source of click-throughs and conversions.

Most of the hundreds of online coupon sites already have a presence on Twitter, Facebook, Digg, and elsewhere. You can use their services or simply create a coupon of your own. Figure 5-8 shows a Twitter coupon generator application (twtQpon), along with the tweet that goes with it. The tweet links to a coupon on twtQpon, which in turn offers a discount at the UrbanLatinoRadio store. This app may be surpassed by the new promoted tweets, or it may remain popular if it proves to be more cost-effective. Wouldn't it be nice to have a crystal ball?

**Book VIII
Chapter 5**

**Multiplying
Your Impact**

Courtesy Sofrito Media Group and Urban Latino Radio

Figure 5-8: A Twitter message links to a coupon on the third-party site.

Whether you offer a discount through your Web site, social media, or any other form of advertising, be sure to include the impact of the discount in your cost analysis. Giving away a free soda may cost a business only 10 cents (mostly for the cup!), but if it gives away 1,000 drinks, the discount costs $100.

In the next chapter, we discuss a new model for coupons that is dependent on volume use reaching a critical mass.

Contests and games

Your imagination is the only limit to contests and games that you can post on your site and cross-promote via social media. As usual, make sure that viewers link back and forth among your sites, ensuring that an inbound link to your primary Web presence exists. The goals of your contest may vary:

✦ Branding and name recognition

✦ Building relationships through entertainment

✦ Obtaining feedback and building community through customer-generated content

✦ Locating hard-to-find resources, clients, or vendors

✦ Cross-promoting

✦ Acquiring testimonials

✦ Getting input into your own brainstorming process about where your product or service should go

TIP

As with special offers, be sure to include the cost of prizes and the labor involved in running the contest in your analysis of ROI. Depending on the goal of the contest, you may be looking for new visitors, repeat visitors, leads, or sales.

For a good example, review the SmartyPig contest shown in Figure 5-9. The goal of the monthly trivia contest, which runs on both Twitter (@SmartyPig) and Facebook (`www.facebook.com/SmartyPig`), is to create recognition for the company and its services, incentivize current customers, and incidentally to draw new visitors to its Web site, which, through its partnership with an FDIC insured bank, offers online savings accounts.

Answers to the trivia question are at SmartyPig.com. Winners, chosen randomly from those who respond correctly, receive a $100 gift card. SmartyPig announces the winners on its blog with a humorous video of the selection process. Rules are also posted on the blog `http://blog.smartypig.com/read/smartypig-march-madness-twitter-and-facebook-contests`.

You can find many more game ideas at the Mashable posting at `http://mashable.com/2009/08/11/social-media-contests`. The ideas range from simple to complex, but they will start your wheels turning.

Figure 5-9: SmartyPig teases and then announces its contest in a series of timed tweets. Winners appear on the blog.

Book VIII Chapter 5

Multiplying Your Impact

Microsites

Microsites, which the Interactive Advertising Bureau also calls "brand conversation hubs," are branded environments specific to a particular product, line, or brand. Often used in conjunction with a new product introduction or special promotion, microsites may facilitate social-media-style activities specific to that project. Often, user conversations or user-generated content contributions are incorporated into the site.

Figure 5-10 shows an interactive microsite that was incorporated into an integrated campaign for a benefits administration company. The company wanted commuters to ask their employers to set up commuter benefits programs. The overall marketing plan also included a contest to win free commuting passes, social media integration, and teams of people who handed out literature at bus and subway stations.

Figure 5-10: This microsite was part of an integrated campaign to encourage employers to set up benefit programs for employees who commute.

Commuter Nation and Commuter Check are registered trademarks of Edenred Corporation.
Campaign created and implemented by One Pica.

When commuters visited the Web site, they learned about benefits available and could enter the contest by filling out a form. In addition, they were invited to e-mail a link to their employers and send links to their friends via e-mail, Facebook, or Twitter. The results were phenomenal.

Many microsites incorporate highly focused video presentations to launch a new product, turn a sale into an event, provide "how-to" instruction, or target specific demographic groups.

TIP

Brainstorm ways that an integrated media campaign might succeed for you. Diagram it and figure out what you'll measure to assess your accomplishments.

Masi Bikes rolls along with social media

A small bicycle manufacturer in California, Masi Bicycles became a division of Haro Bicycles in 2004. It designs and produces road bicycles as well as city, commuting, and lifestyle bikes, and parts. Masi sells primarily to bike shops (go to `www.masibikes.com` for bikes or `www.brevM.com` for parts) but also some clothing and accessories to consumers at `www.masibikes.com/store`.

Brand manager Tim Jackson is one of two people assigned to Masi, of 30 total at Haro. Although the Masi brand had been in Italy for 70 years and in the United States since the 1970s, it had little market recognition at the time Haro purchased the brand. Jackson's task was to bring the brand back. In 2005, when Jackson realized his "marketing budget was too anemic to support the kinds of growth I was hoping for," he knew he had to find another way to get the Masi name out and find people to build a Masi community. "Ultimately, social media provided an opportunity to level the playing field with our competitors, allowing us to look larger than we are."

Jackson started by creating an accessible persona at his personal blog, Masiguy.com. It was so successful that the company now has its own blog at each Web site (a blog posting for Masi Bikes at `www.masibikes.com/2009/12/masi-shirts-are-in-stock` appears in the nearby figure) plus matching Facebook, Twitter, and RSS accounts, and a video channel for Masi. "The best form of targeting I've found is to participate in conversations where consumers are hanging out. I want to drive consumers into shops for the products, and I want to develop relationships of trust with the retailers and consumers both." Jackson writes less formal conversations on Facebook and Twitter, and

more detailed information on the blogs. He's also used the blogs for surveys and to invite participants to shape the future of the brand.

"I have numerous comments from people who say they bought a bike because of something they saw on a blog, or elsewhere in social media areas. I have shops tell me they bought a bike for a consumer because they came in the shop and said they 'heard it from the Masiguy.' Those things are like gold to me and I cherish each one." The results come in sales. "In the first two years I was with the company, sales doubled. Within four years, they quadrupled. To me, those stats are the ones that matter most."

Jackson spends a few hours a day on social media, much of it after hours: "I live in the space." It pays off, he insists. "Consumers have so many choices now that the winner is often the one they like better, rather than the one with the best price."

Masi also runs a few print ads in magazines, does some limited banner advertising, and sends a few press releases, along with many trade shows and events. "But mostly, I just talk a lot!" laughs Jackson. "The community of Masi fans has taken on a large role in making noise for the brand. People tend to eat up the minutiae that we take for granted, so exposing them to the details feeds their curiosity much better than I ever dreamed."

"I wish I had known it was going to be this easy and this fun," he adds. "In the beginning I was so scared of getting it wrong, but I have learned that the community is actually very forgiving and is willing to help you learn and grow.... Engaging people in conversations and treating them with respect will get you a lot further than you might think, even though it is common sense."

Book VIII Chapter 5

Multiplying Your Impact

(continued)

(continued)

"Conversations are going on about your brand/product/service whether you're a part of it or not. So why not be involved and have a role in shaping the outcome? You can bet that if you don't [participate] in this social media environment, your competition will. Why give them the chance to take your customers away? Another important piece of advice is to just have fun with it. I know it sounds like a cliché, but it really shows when you are having a good time or are passionate — that's always a good thing."

URLs for Masi Bikes

www.masibikes.com

http://masiguy.blogspot.com

www.facebook.com/pages/Masi-Bicycles/162818742818

http://twitter.com/MasiBicycles

http://themasiguypodcast.wordpress.com

http://feeds.feedburner.com/MasiBikes

www.brevM.com

www.masiguy.com

www.facebook.com/pages/Brev-M/196260872441

http://twitter.com/BrevM

http://vimeo.com/user1984344

http://feeds.feedburner.com/Brevm

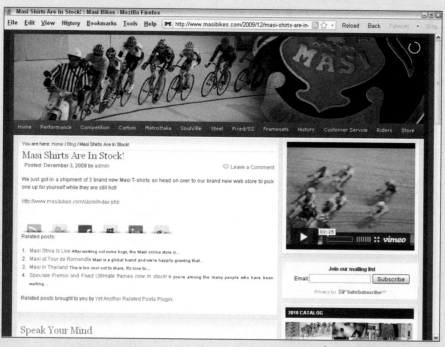

Courtesy Masi Bicycles/Brev M Parts

Chapter 6: Staying Ahead of the Curve

In This Chapter

✔ Shopping collectively

✔ Gaming the system

✔ Living virtually

✔ Making it mobile

✔ Locating customers in real space

✔ Buzzing around with Google

The variations of social media marketing are infinite. Particular services always wax and wane; add-on applications are always too numerous to track. However, the underlying concept of social media — using the Internet to connect real people to each other — is here to stay.

As a business owner, you already have your hands full with existing marketing techniques. Who has time to keep an eye open for new opportunities?

If you take a breather every once in a while, just for the fun of it, experiment with one of the latest trends in social media described in this chapter — or one that no one has heard of yet. If it works, you might discover a new route to success; if it doesn't, you'll still have learned something and kept your creative juices flowing.

Gaining Customers, Sharing Savings

A group of friends hitting the mall is an offline version of social shopping. Online, the term means something quite different: An entire group of strangers saves money by volume buying while they become new customers for your business. The group coupon has emerged as a new way to aggregate (collect as a whole) buyers in specific cities by offering a one-day promotion online or by e-mail.

Services such as Groupon (www.groupon.com), shown in Figures 6-1 and 6-2, and LivingSocial (www.livingsocial.com) offer discounts of 50 percent or more on products or services. The catch: A deal goes through only if a minimum number of buyers sign up for it. As the merchant, you define the deal and set the minimum number of sales high enough to mitigate your risk. You can also set a maximum number of deals to limit your exposure.

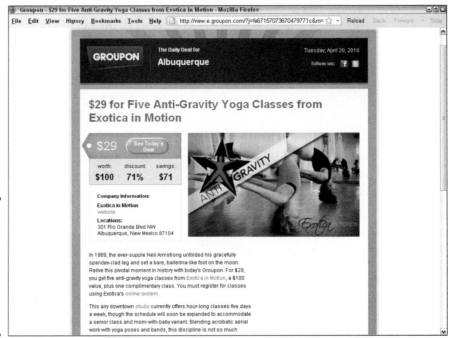

Figure 6-1:
Groupon writes clever copy in a unique style for all the ads it features.

Groupon is a registered trademark of Groupon Inc.

Figure 6-2:
A detail page for another offer shows the minimum number of purchases required and other conditions set by the company.

Groupon is a registered trademark of Groupon Inc.

You set the timeframe over which buyers can exercise a deal, usually several months to a year. You don't end up with all the buyers on your doorstep in one day — unless the offer is for a scheduled event, or if you set a short period for redemption. Unlike other forms of advertising with upfront payments, you pay a fee (a percentage of revenue) only if the minimum number of sales occurs. Your business benefits from this approach by obtaining a stream of new customers in a relatively short length of time, compared to how long it takes other forms of advertising to produce new business.

This obvious business-to-consumer (B2C) technique works well for both service and product companies, including bars and restaurants, tourist destinations, health and beauty salons, events, recreation, personal services, and more.

You can make this approach work for business-to-business (B2B) offers, though it's a little more complicated. A B2B offer would depend on the quality of the e-mail list, a product that applies to both individuals and companies (bookkeeping or office supplies, perhaps), or on recommendations from employees to employers.

Even if you're offering a loss leader on one of these collective coupon sites, try not to sell too far below cost. You may not always be able to specify a maximum number of deals. Giving away hundreds of $4 ice cream cones for half-price is one thing; giving away hundreds of $40 haircuts at half-price may leave you short on the rent.

Groupon

Like Don Vito Corleone in *The Godfather*, Groupon makes "an offer [they] can't refuse" to daily e-mail subscribers and casual site visitors in more than 50 cities.

Often, after an offer brings prospects in the door, satisfied customers proceed to spend more money through these avenues:

✦ **Impulse buys and add-ons:** Buyers get 50 percent off on a specialty burrito and proceed to spend their "savings" on drinks and sides.

✦ **Take-home purchases:** "This slice of cake from the offer was so good that I'm buying a whole cake to take home."

✦ **Ongoing services:** One good massage and that client may be yours every two weeks for years.

✦ **Word-of-mouth:** Buyers bring their friends to share the experience.

Groupon was first out of the box with this approach to advertising, based on the concept of the tipping point used to build a critical mass for social action or contributions. (See The Point at www.thepoint.com.)

From its inception in November 2008 through June 2010, Groupon claims to have sold more than 6.3 million coupons to more than 6.3 million e-mail subscribers, and contends that more than 97 percent of featured merchants want to make an offer again.

For financial reasons, craft carefully your offer, discount, minimum sales requirement, and sold-out maximum amount, recognizing that Groupon takes 50 percent of sales revenue. (Groupon helps you with this task.) Factor estimated add-on purchases as well as lifetime customer value into your calculation. Obviously, new customers who make multiple, repeat purchases are more valuable than customers who buy only once. Try to make your offer something worth a repeat buy!

Groupon selects which businesses participate and determines the schedule for featuring them. In preparation, you may want to create a separate landing page on your Web site for the Groupon offer; a link to it appears in the offer.

After the offer appears, you can promote the deal in your own newsletter and social media outlets and elsewhere, although you may not have much notice. The "share-this-deal" functionality encourages people who receive your daily Groupon e-mail, or those who visit your site, to tell their friends about the deal on Facebook and Twitter and by e-mail.

Groupon may be an excellent way to bring in new customers, especially if your target audience matches their demographic profile of educated, young, single women who work and have discretionary income. (See it at www.grouponworks.com/demographics.)

If a deal goes through, Groupon charges the credit cards of successful buyers. After deducting its 50 percent fee, Groupon sends you a check. It also sells advertising and side deals that appear in its e-mails and on its site. For more information, go to www.grouponworks.com.

Speak with your accountant about how to handle revenue from Groupon and similar deals. Prepaid income is usually treated as a liability on your balance sheet until you fulfill the obligation, or until the time expires to exercise the offer. (Think gift cards.) You may also encounter state-by-state issues regarding sales tax.

Imitation is the sincerest form of flattery. Watch for more competitors to the Groupon model. For example, Gilt (www.gilt.com), the luxury discount site, has launched a weekly local deal in New York City with plans to expand. Similar programs, sometimes with a little twist, are opening internationally.

LivingSocial

One of many recent competitors to Groupon, LivingSocial (http:// livingsocial.com) offers enticing coupon deals along with peer-recommended local activities and events. Launched in August 2009, it reached 14 cities within the first nine months and is rolling out across the country. It works much like Groupon, except that buyers receive a unique link they can share with others while the deal is on.

The benefits are the same as with Groupon: brand awareness, direct appeal to locally targeted markets, word-of-mouth advertising, high visibility to a new customer stream, no charge unless your minimum number is sold, and an easy way to track results.

Like Groupon, LivingSocial is predominantly a location-based advertisement, although Groupon now accepts offers in specific markets for a deal redeemed online, as opposed to an offer redeemed locally.

Neither of these is the best way to reach a national audience all at once, unless you're willing to target multiple individual cities within your national audience with separate offers. This approach might work for franchises or branches in several cities.

Because LivingSocial promises to save visitors 50 to 70 percent, be sure to set the minimum number of buyers high enough to make up for losses and the percentage that goes to LivingSocial. Include in your calculations an allowance for the LivingSocial share-for-free deal. (If three or more people purchase the deal using the link sent to the original buyer, the original buyer receives a freebie.) This strategy can get expensive if groups organize to purchase a deal — 25 percent of your traffic on the deal might pay nothing!

Most businesses don't set an upper limit on the number of sales, but a cap makes sense in certain situations, especially for event organizers or service providers. For example, your equity waiver theater may have a fixed number of seats, you may have room for only a certain number of people in a dance class, or you may have enough stylists to handle only a certain number of haircuts per day. You can protect yourself from unhappy customers by requiring appointments and allowing adequate time to redeem the offer.

LivingSocial allows users to enter comments below its Things to Do feature. It integrates with Facebook, Twitter, e-mail, and the iPhone to share deals. Claiming more than a million subscribers, LivingSocial also offers an affiliate option for internal Deal Bucks (not cash). For more information on signing up, go to http://livingsocial.com/merchants.

Gaming the System

Social gaming refers to the transfer of video, online, and cellphone games to social network platforms. According to www.insidesocialgames.com, at least 16 games on Facebook already boast more than 10 million monthly players apiece; the Zynga FarmVille game alone has more than 82 million monthly players.

The platform shift alters the interaction between users, making it possible for people to play games with their friends rather than with strangers. It may portend a change in the entire sociology of gaming; it has already changed the demographics. And that's where your business opportunity arrives.

PlayFish and Zynga now offer the greatest number of social games on Facebook and MySpace, but that's expected to change as other companies transfer their popular programs to social networking platforms. Table 6-1 lists some of the many social games and their creators. If you're interested in advertising, product placement, or sponsorship, investigate each one individually and contact the company. Life is negotiable in the gaming world, social or otherwise.

Table 6-1	Companies That Create Social Games	
Company Name	*URL*	*Game Name*
Booyah	http://booyah.com	MyTown
Heatwave Interactive	www.platinumlife.com	Platinum Life
PlayFirst	www.playfirst.com	Diner Dash
Playfish	www.playfish.com	Hotel City, Gangster City, Restaurant City, Country Story, Pet Society, Crazy Planets, more
PopCap Games	www.popcap.com	Bejeweled Blitz
Take-Two Interactive Software	www.take2games.com www.facebook.com/civnetwork?v=info	Sid Meieir's Civilization Network
Zynga	www.zynga.com	Cafe World, FarmVille, Fashion Wars, FishVille, Mafia Wars, PetVille, ,Poker Blitz, Treasure Isle, YoVille, Zynga Poker, and more

Before you decide to advertise, observe and play a game for a while. Remember to check the user demographics, which may vary by game. If you plan to make a serious investment in social gaming, confirm that your target audience is actively participating.

Tracking who's playing

A 2010 survey of social gaming in the United States and United Kingdom released by game-maker PopCap and Information Solutions Group offers some fascinating insights. More than 24 percent of respondents said they play social games on networks such as Facebook and MySpace, indicating a user base of 100 million in the U.S. alone.

Analysts expect the social gaming industry to generate revenues of more than $1 billion in 2010. PopCap Games (`http://popcap.mediaroom.com/index.php?s=43&item=149 www.infosolutionsgroup.com/2010_PopCap_Social_Gaming_Research_Results.pdf`) offers these intriguing demographics (numbers shown are for U.S. only):

✦ The average age of U.S. gamers is 48, with 46 percent age 50 or older.

✦ Women make up the majority of U.S. social gamers: 54 percent versus 46 percent male, which is quite different from the profile of young males who dominate action-packed video games.

✦ Gamers' income profile is across the board: 34 percent below $35,000, 38 percent from $35,000 to $74,000; 23 percent over $75,000.

✦ Women are more likely to play with people they know (68 percent versus 56 percent for men), whereas men are more likely to play with strangers (41 percent versus 33 percent);

✦ Eighty-three percent of respondents have played social games on Facebook versus 24 percent on MySpace, and single digits on other social networks.

✦ Friends' recommendations are the number-one factor influencing social game selection.

✦ Sixty-one percent of social gamers play for more than half an hour; 95 percent play multiple times per week; 68 percent of U.S. gamers play daily.

✦ Thirty-two percent have purchased a virtual gift while playing a social game; 28 percent have purchased in-game currency with real money.

✦ Among the specific games studied, *Bejeweled Blitz* and *FarmVille* were more popular with women; *Mafia Wars* and *Texas Hold'em Poker* were more popular with men.

Book VIII Chapter 6

Staying Ahead of the Curve

Changing the game for marketers

Another report released by the Social Media World Forum in 2009 claimed that 80 percent of the women who play social media games clicked ads or signed up for promotional features in return for points and virtual currencies.

From a marketing point of view, you have several ways to take advantage of social gaming to reach these rather astonishingly large and devoted audiences, generally limited only by your ingenuity and your budget.

Many in-game advertising solutions are so expensive that only the largest companies can afford them.

Try these ideas:

✦ Advertise on games so that your ads appear where characters would see them in reality: on billboards, signs, subway posters, street flags, or store signage.

✦ Let players "buy" your products with virtual currency, give them as virtual gifts, or win them as prizes.

✦ Give away points or virtual goods for clicking through to your online or video ads instead of ignoring them. The ads might appear as interstitials (between screens), as pop-ups or pop-unders, or between rounds of play.

✦ Place your product so that it appears as a prop or part of the "stage set" for a game, just as it would in a movie, TV show, or video game. It can be a cereal box on a table, a book on a shelf, or branded running shoes worn by a character.

✦ Sponsor branded items within the game that players can acquire, such as jobs or T-shirts. Think big. Elite Taami Nutz, an Israeli candy manufacturer, sponsors a peanut crop on FarmVille on Facebook, the first advertiser to do so, at `http://apps.facebook.com/elitenutz/?toolID=8QQL83`. The large sign in the center welcomes users to the first-ever sponsorship on FarmVille. The text on the crates tells players they can buy the peanuts for 20 and sell them at 78. The top tabs are navigation, and the new Nutz candy bar appears in the lower right corner.

Living Virtually

When reality becomes too much to handle, beating a hasty retreat to a virtual world sounds tempting. These 3D worlds combine animation, video, and audio to provide an all-encompassing experience for users. Though virtual worlds have been around for almost a decade, their technological sophistication continues to increase. The format is appealing not only as a game environment but also for virtual meetings, training, teaching, modeling, conferences, and more.

Users, or *residents,* interact with each other by using avatars, which can socialize, participate in activities, travel, or create and trade virtual property. Indeed, an active virtual economy crosses over into the real world, to the tune of more than $560 million in 2009.

The best-known virtual world, *Second Life* (`http://secondlife.com`), has about 1 million users, of whom about three-quarters log in more than once a month. You might also want to take a look at OpenSim, an open source virtual world application (`http://opensimulator.org/wiki/Main_Page`). Table 6-2 contains some useful *Second Life* advertising resources. For more information on virtual worlds, see *Second Life For Dummies,* by Sarah Robbins and Mark Bell.

Table 6-2	*Second Life* **Advertising Resources**
Description	*URL*
Blog describing do's and don'ts of advertising in *Second Life*	`http://secondthoughts.typepad.com/second_thoughts/2006/10/dos_and_donts_f.html#more`
Free, categorized *Second Life* business directory	`www.slbiz2life.com`
Inventory of online advertising opportunities	`http://world.secondlife.com/place/f43e2972-b091-50c5-c413-dc3fc65671a0`
Linkable resource list for *Second Life* marketing	`http://wiki.secondlife.com/wiki/Advertising_in_Second_Life#Advertising_networks_in_Second_Life_2`
Second Life blogs	`http://blogs.secondlife.com/index.jspa`

Advertising in *Second Life* is much like advertising within games: You can post your advertising in different *Second Life* environments, including signs and billboards, some of which are controlled by residents. Or, you can trade your goods virtually or in reality; some folks sell rain, snow, barking dogs, and fancy outfits, though most sell real estate.

The unique exception is that you can create your own environment within *Second Life*. Users can interact with the environment while learning about your products and services and building relationships. Saint Leo University, whose real-world address is Saint Leo, Florida, does this well with its virtual campus in *Second Life*.

The university uses its presence in *Second Life,* shown in Figure 6-3, as not only a dynamic opportunity for online meetings and education but also a marketing tool to attract students from around the world to enroll in online classes. Prospective and current students, staff, faculty, parents, and friends can all gather in *Second Life* to get a "taste" of the college. For more information on Saint Leo University's virtual presence, see `http://info.saintleo.edu/col/SL.cfm`.

Figure 6-3: The campus of Saint Leo University in *Second Life.*

Courtesy Saint Leo University, Inc.

Making Social Mobile

Social media is no longer confined to a "standard" computer of any size. The integration of social media with mobile devices, from cellphones to iPads, creates both opportunities and challenges for your marketing campaigns. The proliferation of smartphones and apps, 3G networks, more affordable data plans, built-in Web browsers, and mobile-ready Web sites have all contributed to the growth of mobile social activities, though the human factor is a major component, too.

A February 2010 study from Ruder Finn, a large public relations agency, looked at how people use their mobile phones. Americans spend nearly three hours per day on their phones — 91 percent of them use it to socialize, compared to 79 percent of PC users. Aha! Table 6-3 details what those 91 percent are up to.

Table 6-3	How Mobile Users Socialize
Task	*Percentage Who Use This Method*
Send instant messages	62
Forward e-mails	58
Post comments on social networking sites	45
Connect to people on social networking sites	43
Share content with others	40
Share photos	38

www.prnewswire.com/news-releases/new-study-shows-intent-behind-mobile-internet-use-84016487.html

Not too surprisingly, usage also differs by gender and age. According to the same study:

✦ **Men look at prices but women buy:** Men are more likely than women to compare prices (47 percent versus 30 percent), but women are more likely to purchase (40 percent versus 30 percent).

✦ **Women express themselves while men do business:** Women are more likely than men to personally express themselves (49 percent versus 35 percent), but men are more likely to conduct business (62 percent versus 57 percent).

✦ **Youth are the target for retailers:** Youth (44 percent) are more likely to shop over their mobile phones than the average mobile user (35 percent).

You'll find additional resources on mobile phones in Table 6-4.

Table 6-4	Mobile Social Media Resources	
Name	*URL*	*Description*
Broadtexter	www.broadtexter.com	Free mobile club to text marketing messages
Facebook Mobile	http://m.facebook.com	Mobile Facebook
LinkedIn Mobile	http://m.linkedin.com/session/new	Mobile LinkedIn
MobGold	www.mobgold.com	Mobile advertising network
MySpace Mobile	http://m.myspace.com/login.wap	Mobile MySpace
Ruder Finn	www.prnewswire.com/news-releases/new-study-shows-intent-behind-mobile-internet-use-84016487.html	Study of mobile phone use
SocialMediaTrader.com	http://socialmediatrader.com/38-social-networking-sites-for-your-mobile	List of mobile social networking services
Twitter Mobile	http://mobile.twitter.com	Mobile Twitter
Wadja	www.wadja.com	Mobile social networking service
Zannel	www.zannel.com	Social media syndication including mobile applications for text, images, and video
Zinadoo	www.zinadoo.com	Free mobile Web site creation tool

Source: http://socialmediatrader.com/38-social-networking-sites-for-your-mobile

If you haven't already created a mobile Web site as part of your suite of Web pages, do it now. Zinadoo offers a free starter tool at www.webdesignfor mobiledevices.com/wordpress-mobile-templates.php.

It's hard to say which is the chicken and which is the egg: smartphones or social media? It doesn't matter. What matters now is that Facebook and Twitter and other social networking services have become do-it-now, do-it-anywhere-on-the-phone activities. Social media is convenient, easy, and cool, and it can be done in bits and snips.

Mobile social marketing offers far more opportunities to "reach out and touch someone" with your message. The challenge, of course, is that everyone else is trying to do that, too. Your efforts have to cut through an increasing amount of clutter.

Locating Yourself with Social Mapping

Location. Location. Location. It works in real estate. Now, apparently, it's another key to successful social media marketing. Several applications of location-based services, including social mapping (identifying where people are), and location-based games, now exist. They are evolving as a loyalty-program offering rewards to consumers for patronizing particular retailers.

The convergence of GPS, mobile phones, and social media offers the holy grail of opportunity for marketers. Theoretically, you can inform potential customers that you offer exactly what they're looking for, when they're looking for it, and within just a few miles of their locations. In March, foursquare added a tool that lets businesses monitor foursquare visitors who check in by number, gender, day of week, and time of day. You won't see a better service until cyberpsychics start offering their services.

Going geo or staying put

Whether you should use these social mapping services depends on the nature of your business, whether your customer base is using them, and which location-based activities consume your prospective customers' time. Consider these issues:

✦ **Many cellphone apps already offer a service (for example, a weather report, road conditions, a list of gas prices at various stations around town) and then add a sponsor.** If all you're trying to do is reach the consumer-on-the-go who is ready to buy, do you need more than that? Maybe a pay-per-click (PPC) ad on a mobile search engine solves your needs.

✦ **Enough people have to be using a particular application to make it worth the effort.** The chart shown in Figure 6-4 might give you pause. As of spring 2010, the number of local users of two of the most hyped location games (foursquare and Gowalla) was relatively small. You need to determine how many people you need to reach to have enough of them become customers, and you have to know whether privacy is an issue for them.

Local's Long Tail Challenge

	U.S. Total Population	City/U.S.	foursquare 500,000	Gowalla 100,000
New York	8,363,717	2.71%	13,539	2,708
Los Angeles	3,833,998	1.24%	6,206	1,241
Chicago	2,853,116	0.92%	4,618	924
Houston	2,242,195	0.73%	3,629	726
Phoenix	1,567,925	0.51%	2,538	508
Philadelphia	1,447,396	0.47%	2,343	469
Dallas	1,279,911	0.41%	2,072	414
Detroit	912,063	0.30%	1,476	295
San Francisco	808,977	0.26%	1,310	262
Minneapolis	662,196	0.21%	1,072	214

(U.S. Total Population 308,885,867)

Figure 6-4: The rate of adoption for foursquare and Gowalla seems surprisingly low compared with their hype.

Chart created by Ryan Kazda & Kevin Nakao for WhitePages, Inc

Estimate the number of users available in your location before you commit. Of course, a high-tech conference that draws a huge number of users may be a one-time opportunity worth taking advantage of.

✦ **Prospective customers must be participating.** For example, the demographics of foursquare users are a bit surprising. According to Quantcast (www.quantcast.com), users are two-thirds female, and the majority are over 35. Like politics, all marketing is local. You may draw a large audience of foursquare users if you happen to own the pizza place across the street from the computer science department at the local college.

Miracles do happen. Joe Sorge of Milwaukee attracted 161 foursquare users to a "swarm" at his burger place, AJ Bombers. The 161 users, of fewer than 400 in the area, boosted his Sunday afternoon sales by 110 percent in sales. All he offered was the virtual swarm badge and a contribution to a cause. He promoted the event via Twitter, Facebook, video, Flickr, and viral mentions on other people's social networks.

✦ **Hardware is still a problem.** The usefulness of mobile apps depends on battery life. Continuous location tracking eats energy faster than the old *Pac-Man* games. Is the application you're considering practical? Other technical issues remain, too. Devices must know "where they are," which is sometimes more than where a satellite thinks they are. Second, satellite-positioning data must be translated into data that a user can understand, such as an address. Neither is trivial.

✦ **The temptation is great to "go geo."** Current estimates show that locally targeted ads may produce results ten times better than untargeted advertising. Of course, you can expect soon to pay ten times as much, too. At the same time, geotargeted inventory is limited. Some manufacturers don't let GPS be used for advertising alone; they require some customer benefit and functionality.

Applying social mapping to B2B

Most users of social mapping have been business-to-consumer (B2C) businesses in hospitality, tourism, and recreation. HubSpot Internet Marketing, however, identified four implications of social marketing for business-to-business (B2B) companies (`http://blog.hubspot.com/blog/tabid/6307/bid/5815/Forget-Retail-The-B2B-Applications-of-Foursquare.aspx`):

✦ Location is likely to become part of search engine optimization in the future, so you may need to reoptimize content.

✦ Trade show marketing, which is about connecting and building relationships, may be affected because location apps do something similar. They may even change how to sponsor events — for example, the standard hospitality suite at the Consumer Electronics Show may be replaced with a foursquare swarm.

✦ Location apps may affect customer relationship management tools and databases, making it easier to schedule visits by salespeople to hot leads.

✦ Location data may affect the process of identifying prospects and facilitating lead generation. After you know where your target market "hangs out," you can easily connect with them.

If your analysis — or your curiosity — impels you forward with social mapping, check site user numbers in your area with both the service provider and a third-party source such as Quantcast. The numbers can fluctuate widely. Then select from one of the applications we talk about in the following section or many others that are blooming on the geolocation tree. Your best bet: Ask your customers what they are using.

foursquare

Foursquare, at www.foursquare.com is riding high at the moment, having reached 500,000 active users in barely a year of operation. This location-based game awards virtual "badges" to users who check in at targeted locations using their cellphones. It's now compatible with the iPhone, Android, and BlackBerry.

You'll have difficulty determining whether playing foursquare and similar games is a temporary geek-craze or will turn out to have long-term appeal to folks who simply needed a nudge (as in "discount") to try something new.

Early adopters, mostly local restaurants and bars, have lined up in certain locations to offer discounts to new or repeat customers. For some of these businesses, foursquare acts like a loyalty program. And, it's a useful way to fill a place during a slow time.

Foursquare offers self-service tools for business owners to create, manage, and track how their offers perform, at http://foursquare.com/businesses. You can choose from a variety of specials:

+ **Mayor:** Can be used only by the "Mayor," the user who has checked in most often in the past 60 days, as shown in Figure 6-5.

+ **Count-based:** Available after a user checks in a certain number of times.

+ **Frequency-based**: Available multiple times after a certain number of check-ins per users.

+ **Wildcard:** Always available, but the user has to meet certain conditions before receiving the special. A swarm badge, shown in Figure 6-5, is an example of a badge awarded for participating in an event with 50 others.

Businesses promote their foursquare participation in many ways: on their own social media feeds, on signs at cash registers, and on sandwich boards in the streets. Foursquare notifies players by text message whenever an offer is available nearby.

Users can analyze their foursquare usage compared to others at http://square.grader.com. You can view foursquare badges at http://square.grader.com/badge/summary.

Gowalla

Gowalla is a location-based application in which players check in at places of interest. Using a GPS-enabled smartphone, iPad, or the Web, they can share their locations with friends and write comments about where they are via Facebook, Twitter, or Gowalla (www.gowalla.com). Figure 6-6 shows how for each location displayed on the screen, viewers can see how many other Gowalla Passport holders have visited and how many times they have checked in.

Figure 6-5:
Standing Sushi Bar of Singapore offers two free pieces of sushi to the daily Mayor of the Moment (top). A swarm badge is awarded to each of 50 or more participants checked in at a foursquare flash mob event (bottom).

Standing Sushi Bar, Singapore (www.standingsushibar.com) Courtesy foursquare

Figure 6-6:
Gowalla
searches
for nearby
locations by
category.

Courtesy Gowalla (temporary) Map in screenshot © Google Inc. Used with permission. (temporary)

A reward system of "stamps" marks users' achievement based on the number and location of places where they check in. As a location game, Gowalla involves searching for virtual objects in the physical world (a twist on geocaching). It makes a nice application for tracking scavenger hunts, visiting national parks, compiling bucket lists, or making sequential stops on a tour that awards a prize for completion at the end. (Imagine *Around the World in 80 Days* using Gowalla.)

Local businesses can advertise with branded spots or directly target customers through specials, promotions, and loyalty programs. Branding campaigns may involve virtual goods, sponsorships, or custom "stamps."

Loopt

Loopt is another location-based social mapping service. It enables users to connect where they are with whom they know. Using their mobile phones, users can share location information, comments, photos, and personal recommendations with friends in real time. ("I found the car in row XX space 12 on the green level.") It claims to have more than 3 million registered users, partnerships with every major U.S. mobile phone carrier, and availability on more than 100 phone models and the iPad.

Its recommendation function, called Pulse!, provides reviews from multiple sources, and allows its users to rate places and leave tips.

The local review site Yelp, at `www.yelp.com`, has accomplished a similar result by adding a location-based, check-in feature to its cellphone version.

Loopt offers its own reward program to compete with foursquare and Gowalla. Called LooptStar, the program lets consumers compete with friends and win rewards from retailers by checking in to locations and meeting certain requirements. Rewards may be real-world coupons, branded items from participating organizations, or virtual achievements. Loopt has structured its new program as a "cost-per-visit" model.

Location apps on Facebook and Twitter

The importance of integrating social media with location hasn't been lost on Facebook, Twitter, or many other applications.

Twitter has already installed @anywhere, which lets users add geolocation information to regular Twitter feeds, whereas developers can add Twitter functionality to other location-based apps. Twitter plans to expand location information in other ways, including its own tool for organizing tweets by geolocation in real time. Both users and developers are expected to have more control over how their geolocations are used and to whom they are available.

Third-party developers already offer some location-based Twitter apps based on the locations listed in user profiles. Twellowhood (`www.twellow.com/twellowhood`) locates a list of tweeters in a specified area; TwitterLocal. net, an Adobe AIR client, filters tweets by profile location; and NearbyTweets (`www.nearbytweets.com`) sorts tweets by topic within a specified region.

Facebook plans to add its new Places feature to incorporate location information on Facebook pages. Though details are still vague, one aspect allows users to decide whether to share location information with friends; another provides software tools to third parties to develop location-based applications.

Meet-ups and tweet-ups

Meet-ups and tweet-ups bridge the gap between the cyberworld and the one we live in. They both make it easy for people with similar interests to organize meetings for fun, advocacy, or learning or simply to meet one another.

Meetup (`www.meetup.com`), which has been around since 2002, bills itself as "the world's largest network of local groups," claiming that more than 6 million monthly site visitors attend some 180,000 meetings located in 45,000 cities. The site reached great popularity as an organizing tool during the 2008 presidential election. Meetup charges organizers a fee starting at $12 per month for using its platform.

Meetup technology lets people find or start a group located near them. The system includes an easy-to-use interface to identify meetings within a certain distance and to reply by RSVP, find directions, and check out the history of a Meetup group. Meetup integrates nicely with Facebook events and RSVPs; it has an application for integrating Meetup with other applications. Figure 6-7 shows a Meetup search page.

In an inevitable mashup, Meetup now allows Groupon fans to hook up at "official" and self-organized events through `www.meetup.com/Groupon`.

What an easy way to find your target market in a location close to you!

The term *tweetup* has been part of the Twitter lexicon for a long time to describe a live meeting of Twitter users or, more generally, any face-to-face event organized by way of social media.

While there is not yet a nationwide site that facilitates connections the way Meetup.com does, local sites exist. For example, in addition to its feed at Twitter.com/BostonTweetUp (shown in Figure 6-8), Boston Tweetup maintains a calendar and reviews technology-oriented events at its Web site `http://bostontweetup.com`.

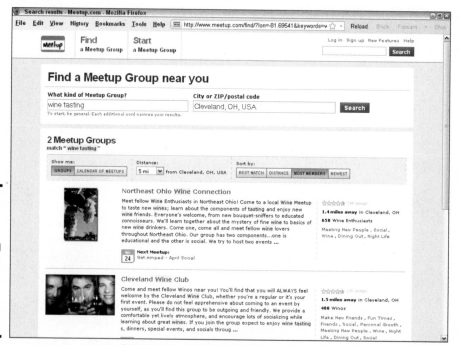

Figure 6-7: A Meetup search for wine-tasting groups near Cleveland produces several results.

Figure 6-8:
Boston is serious about its tweet-ups.

Twitter is already influencing traditional gatherings such as large conferences and seminars. Small groups with a particular interest or agenda can now more easily meet with each other socially or in a rump session. And many attendees have started tweeting questions and commentary during presentations, using the hashtag (#) to mark tweets related to a particular session. This technique can either unnerve or energize presenters. Some tech-savvy people read the tweet stream as the session goes on, and respond to questions on the fly.

In either case, a tweet-up is definitely another way to take networking to the next level.

Marketing with meet-ups and tweet-ups

Meet-ups and tweet-ups offer you an exquisite opportunity to reach out to new customers. Contact meeting organizers to see whether you can

✦ Host an event at your restaurant or another event location

✦ Offer a discount to members or for the event

✦ Give a presentation or teach a class at a future meeting

✦ Provide information to members

**Book VIII
Chapter 6**

**Staying Ahead of
the Curve**

Attending a meeting first is helpful (but not required) to make sure that the make-up of the group fits your target audience and to meet the leaders.

Organizing a meet-up or tweet-up

Nothing keeps you from organizing your own meet-up or tweet-up — just don't make it overtly self-serving. Creating a successful event can bring you recognition as a leader, enhance your credibility, attract media attention, and quickly bring new followers to your social media sites.

To ensure a successful event, promote it from your blog and e-mail newsletter and all your own social media channels, as well as by way of Meetup, Facebook events, Twitter, online calendars, and ordinary press releases. The more promotional channels, the better. You can find a set of helpful tools at www.twitip.com/planning-an-tweetup.

As with other location-dependent activities, make sure that a critical mass of local folks are interested in the event you're planning. In some cases, they may already need to be following you on the social networks you've identified as your promotion channels.

You can gauge interest by using Meetup to estimate the number of members in similar groups in your locations. Or take advantage of the following Twitter tools to help your planning:

✦ Geogtagging makes it easier for people to find you. Log in to your Twitter account and open your settings. Select the Add a Location to Your Tweets check box. For each tweet, you can now choose to enter a specific location, a general area, or no location. For more information see http://twitter.zendesk.com/forums/26810/entries/78525.

✦ The search function can help you estimate the number of local Twitter users within a city or radius. Go to http://search.twitter.com/advanced. In the Places section, enter your city; then select the radius in miles or kilometers (for example, Near: Albuquerque within 25 miles). It isn't a perfect system, but it's helpful.

At the event itself, do the basics:

✦ Check out the location ahead of time for size, lighting, quality, and service.

✦ Provide name tags and pens.

✦ Stay active, by facilitating discussions, resolving problems, making introductions, and generally acting as host.

You may want to take advantage of other event planning tools, such as Eventbrite (www.eventbrite.com), Cvent (www.cvent.com), or Amiando (www.amiando.com) if you're expecting a large group. If you use ConstantContact for your e-mail newsletters, look at its Event Marketing tool at www.constantcontact.com/event-marketing/index.jsp.

Buzzing Around

As traffic skyrocketed on Facebook, Google launched its own competing social networking site, Buzz (www.google.com/buzz), in February 2010. Users can easily share text, links, photos, and videos. Buzz leverages the Gmail platform, tying together an entire suite of Google applications such as Picasa, YouTube, and Reader, as well as integrating with Flickr, Twitter, and more.

With its instant Gmail user base of more than 100 million global users (compared to more than 400 million for Facebook and 75 million for Twitter), Google Buzz quickly climbed to more than 160,000 posts and comments per hour, more than 9 million posts in fewer than three days, and nearly 300,000 mobile check-ins daily. Convenient, familiar, and easy to use, Buzz was primed for success.

The Google Buzz button appears directly below the Inbox link for Gmail users, making it simple for people who have never explored social networking to stumble into it. Buzz is already compatible with Android and the iPhone and several other phone models, and it incorporates Google Latitude for social mapping. Google also plans a paid Enterprise-level version of Buzz oriented toward internal collaboration. Eventually, Google will probably add advertising to Buzz pages.

Adding one significant advantage, Google Buzz (see Figure 6-9) organizes message streams by threads, not chronologically, making it much easier to follow conversations. Clicking the link to expand a post produces not only the original post but also related comments.

Using Buzz for business

If you have already implemented other social networking accounts, you may legitimately question the benefits of adding Buzz. Consider some of these as you make your business and marketing decision:

✦ **SEO:** Because Google indexes Buzz profiles and content, sharing your content and obtaining inbound links may help boost your standings in search engine results. Remember that Google includes social media in real-time search. Because Google always loves its own solutions best, your profile and Buzz postings may rank high in search results.

Figure 6-9: The Google Buzz page shows threaded discussions to the left. Its related links appear on the right side, along with a My Places map displaying its location.

✦ **Customer relationships:** You can take advantage of customers' and prospects' existing Gmail addresses to invite them to follow you and to start following them. Because of the threaded nature of the discussions, you may find that managing interactions requiring several back-and-forth messages on Buzz is easier than on other social networks. Threads make it easier to obtain highly focused feedback and to solicit answers to specific questions from a selected group of users.

✦ **Geolocation features:** The Google mobile version of Buzz points to the location you choose (MyPlaces on your profile). Another feature, the Nearby stream, identifies posts from people near that location even if they aren't following you. You may be able to generate a message to nearby users to draw them into your business.

✦ **Your customers use it:** This logic trumps everything. If your customers use Buzz, so must you.

Absolutely include Google Buzz within your sets of Follow Us and Social Share buttons. Most of the social share services, such as ShareThis and AddThis, already include Buzz as a choice.

Unless your customers are already on Buzz, don't rush headlong into it. In the meantime, Buzz is an easy-to-use platform for interacting with prospective customers, distributing keyword-loaded content, and gaining inbound links.

The initial launch of Google Buzz is oriented toward individuals, so you may need to tweak it a bit to meet your needs. Be sure to add Buzz to your Social Media Marketing Plan, discussed in Book I, Chapter 2, if you decide to use it.

Copy-and-paste buttons for Buzz are available at `http://buzz.google.com/stuff`. Follow the directions at the links for Post or Follow widgets. Select the button style you want and paste in the supplied code.

Opening a Gmail account

Buzz is intimately tied to Gmail. If you already have a Gmail account, you may want to establish a brand-new one that's strictly for Buzz business. Otherwise, you may find yourself automatically following your frequent Gmail contacts and having to unfollow them. It isn't difficult, but it's time-consuming.

However, without making much of a commitment, you can establish a Gmail account, build a profile for search benefits, and prepare a Buzz account for the future.

The steps are simple:

1. **Set up a new Gmail account at `www.gmail.com`.**

   If possible, use the same handle, or nickname, that you use at your other social media accounts; that name appears on your Buzz account. Verify your e-mail address via the e-mail confirmation message that Google sends you.

2. **Import business-related e-mail addresses that you might want to follow or invite to follow you.**

   Unless you have already segregated business e-mail addresses from personal ones, this process can be time-consuming. You can further segment your business addresses into groups to direct different posts to different groups in the future. Or, start over with a blank address book that grows organically from your new Buzz activities.

3. **Click Buzz in the left menu to get to your blank Buzz home page.**

4. **Click the Edit link next to your name at the top of the page.**

   You go to a Profiles page where you create or edit your business-oriented Google profile. If you need help with this step, we discuss profiles in the next section.

In any case, set up separate Google profiles for your personal use and for your business.

Setting up a Google business profile

After you have enabled a Gmail account, you need to create or update your profile. Because people may use this profile to determine whether they want to follow you, treat it as a marketing opportunity. For more information on profiles, visit www.google.com/support/accounts/bin/answer. py?answer=97703&hl=en.

At the moment, Buzz has no good search function; just wait a while. In the meantime, you can find mentions of your company on Buzz by going to www.google.com. In the Search box, enter **site:google.com YourCompanyName**. To limit results to relatively current mentions, choose Show Options⇨Updates in the upper left corner of the results page.

Go to www.google.com/profiles and follow these steps to edit your existing public profile:

1. **Click the Edit link and change the following information:**

- Select the Display My Full Name and Allow People to Follow Me options. As a business, you generally want people to find you and to follow you.

- Deselect the Display the List of People I'm Following and People Following Me option. In most cases, there is no reason to make that information public; the number of followers is still visible.

2. **Click the Photo link and do the following:**

- Upload the logo or avatar graphic you use for your other social media.

- Using the Photos tab at the top, you can upload additional photos from Flickr or Picasa or other services, or even your hard drive. These photos comprise a horizontal slide show at the top of your page.

Be cautious about using identifiable photos of people unless you have a permission waiver. Photos of employees or photos taken on public streets are generally acceptable.

3. **Click the About Me tab, and fill in the boxes with business information, wherever possible, just as you did for business profiles on other social networks.**

For instance, use your business name for First Name and Last Name and your business address for Where I Live Now. Other Names should be the handle you use for other social marketing purposes. Enter your marketing tag under What I Do and your company name as Current Company. Ignore boxes for schools and other irrelevant personal information.

4. **If it isn't already verified, click to verify your e-mail address at the displayed domain name.**

5. **Incorporate your preferred search terms in the Short Bio box, which should include a brief summary of your products or services and a benefits statement. Enter preferred search terms or tags in the Interests box.**

   This step is important because Google scans public profiles for search engine ranking.

6. **Click the Contact Info tab. Add all your current contact information and make it publicly available.**

   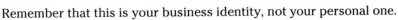 Remember that this is your business identity, not your personal one.

   Add names to identify who can view your profile. If you wish, create Groups on this screen. (Click the View link and follow the prompts.)

7. **Click the About Me tab. In the Add Links area, enter your business Web site URL and all your other social media pages.**

   Make the anchor text a call to action, such as "Follow us on Twitter."

8. **Customize your profile URL, using your nickname, handle, or Gmail username.**

9. **Click Save to save your changes.**

   Your Profile page goes live. If you see a message at the top saying that your profile isn't eligible to be featured in Google search, reedit it to include more information until you get a positive result. You can easily edit your profile at any time by clicking the Edit Profile link.

To find Buzz, follow these steps:

1. **Click the Gmail link in the upper left corner.**

2. **If this account is new, click the Check Out Buzz box. Then click the Buzz link in the left navigation, directly below Inbox.**

3. **Click the Connected Sites link at the top of the inset box to incorporate feeds from other sites.**

   A dialog box with the names of services appears.

4. **Click the Add button for the accounts that you want to associate with Buzz, and click Save.**

   Your current location (from the Where I Live Now option in the About Me section) should automatically appear on the My Places map. If it doesn't, set your location at www.google.com/latitude/intro. html or use Buzz Mobile (www.google.com/intl/en/mobile/buzz) or enter **buzz.google.com** on your phone's browser.

Cross-promote your Buzz account just as you do your Facebook, Twitter, and other social media accounts. Be sure to include Buzz as a destination for syndicating content from your blog, Twitter, and other social media accounts.

Now you're ready to start posting. You can easily use Buzz whenever (and only when) you use Gmail. As soon as you click in the box to post text, you see links to insert photos or links and to set the distribution for the post.

To see statistics for your Google Buzz account, go to your Google dashboard at www.google.com/dashboard. Sign in and navigate to the Buzz section for some basic data.

Index

• M •